Skoda Fabia
Owners Workshop Manual

A K Legg AAE MIMI

Models covered

(4376 - 368)

Hatchback, Saloon and Estate, including vRS and special/limited editions

Petrol engines: 1.2 litre (1198cc) 3-cylinder and 1.4 litre (1397cc & 1390cc) 4-cylinder

Diesel engines: 1.4 litre (1422cc) 3-cylinder and 1.9 litre (1896cc) 4-cylinder, including turbo

Does not cover 1.0 litre OHV engine or 2.0 litre 16-valve petrol engines

© Haynes Publishing 2006

A book in the **Haynes Service and Repair Manual Series**

ISBN-10: **1 84425 376 7**
ISBN-13: **978 1 84425 376 0**

British Library Cataloguing in Publication Data
A catalogue record for this book is available from the British Library.

ABCDE
FGHIJ
KLMNO

Printed in the USA

Haynes Publishing
Sparkford, Yeovil, Somerset BA22 7JJ, England

Haynes North America, Inc
861 Lawrence Drive, Newbury Park, California 91320, USA

Editions Haynes
4, Rue de l'Abreuvoir
92415 COURBEVOIE CEDEX, France

Haynes Publishing Nordiska AB
Box 1504, 751 45 UPPSALA, Sverige

Contents

LIVING WITH YOUR SKODA FABIA

Safety first!   Page   0•5
Introduction to the Skoda Fabia   Page   0•6

Roadside repairs

If your car won't start   Page   0•7
Jump starting   Page   0•8
Wheel changing   Page   0•9
Identifying leaks   Page   0•10
Towing   Page   0•10

Weekly checks

Introduction   Page   0•11
Underbonnet check points   Page   0•11
Engine oil level   Page   0•13
Coolant level   Page   0•14
Brake (and clutch) fluid level   Page   0•14
Washer fluid level   Page   0•15
Battery   Page   0•15
Tyre condition and pressure   Page   0•16
Electrical systems   Page   0•17
Wiper blades   Page   0•17

Lubricants and fluids   Page   0•18

Tyre pressures   Page   0•18

MAINTENANCE

Routine maintenance and servicing

Petrol models   Page   1A•1
   Servicing specifications   Page   1A•2
   Maintenance schedule   Page   1A•3
   Maintenance procedures   Page   1A•8
Diesel models   Page   1B•1
   Servicing specifications   Page   1B•2
   Maintenance schedule   Page   1B•2
   Maintenance procedures   Page   1B•6

Contents

REPAIRS AND OVERHAUL

Engine and associated systems

1.2 litre petrol engine in-car repair procedures	Page	2A•1
1.4 litre OHV petrol engine in-car repair procedures	Page	2B•1
1.4 litre DOHC engine in-car repair procedures	Page	2C•1
Diesel engine in-car repair procedures	Page	2D•1
Engine removal and overhaul procedures	Page	2E•1
Cooling, heating and air conditioning systems	Page	3•1
Petrol engine fuel systems	Page	4A•1
Diesel engine fuel system	Page	4B•1
Emission control and exhaust systems	Page	4C•1
Starting and charging systems	Page	5A•1
Ignition system – petrol engines	Page	5B•1
Preheating system – diesel engines	Page	5C•1

Transmission

Clutch	Page	6•1
Manual transmission	Page	7A•1
Automatic transmission	Page	7B•1
Driveshafts	Page	8•1

Brakes and Suspension

Braking system	Page	9•1
Suspension and steering systems	Page	10•1

Body equipment

Bodywork and fittings	Page	11•1
Body electrical systems	Page	12•1
Wiring diagrams	Page	12•21

REFERENCE

Dimensions and weights	Page	REF•1
Conversion factors	Page	REF•2
Buying spare parts	Page	REF•3
Vehicle identification numbers	Page	REF•3
General repair procedures	Page	REF•4
Jacking and vehicle support	Page	REF•5
Disconnecting the battery	Page	REF•5
Tools and working facilities	Page	REF•6
MOT test checks	Page	REF•8
Fault finding	Page	REF•12
Glossary of technical terms	Page	REF•22

Index

	Page	REF•30

Advanced driving

Many people see the words 'advanced driving' and believe that it won't interest them or that it is a style of driving beyond their own abilities. Nothing could be further from the truth. Advanced driving is straightforward safe, sensible driving - the sort of driving we should all do every time we get behind the wheel.

An average of 10 people are killed every day on UK roads and 870 more are injured, some seriously. Lives are ruined daily, usually because somebody did something stupid. Something like 95% of all accidents are due to human error, mostly driver failure. Sometimes we make genuine mistakes - everyone does. Sometimes we have lapses of concentration. Sometimes we deliberately take risks.

For many people, the process of 'learning to drive' doesn't go much further than learning how to pass the driving test because of a common belief that good drivers are made by 'experience'.

Learning to drive by 'experience' teaches three driving skills:

☐ Quick reactions. (Whoops, that was close!)
☐ Good handling skills. (Horn, swerve, brake, horn).
☐ Reliance on vehicle technology. (Great stuff this ABS, stop in no distance even in the wet...)

Drivers whose skills are 'experience based' generally have a lot of near misses and the odd accident. The results can be seen every day in our courts and our hospital casualty departments.

Advanced drivers have learnt to control the risks by controlling the position and speed of their vehicle. They avoid accidents and near misses, even if the drivers around them make mistakes.

The key skills of advanced driving are **concentration,** effective all-round **observation, anticipation** and **planning.** When **good vehicle handling** is added to these skills, all driving situations can be approached and negotiated in a safe, methodical way, leaving nothing to chance.

Concentration means applying your mind to safe driving, completely excluding anything that's not relevant. Driving is usually the most dangerous activity that most of us undertake in our daily routines. It deserves our full attention.

Observation means not just looking, but seeing and seeking out the information found in the driving environment.

Anticipation means asking yourself what is happening, what you can reasonably expect to happen and what could happen unexpectedly. (One of the commonest words used in compiling accident reports is 'suddenly'.)

Planning is the link between seeing something and taking the appropriate action. For many drivers, planning is the missing link.

If you want to become a safer and more skilful driver and you want to enjoy your driving more, contact the Institute of Advanced Motorists at www.iam.org.uk, phone 0208 996 9600, or write to IAM House, 510 Chiswick High Road, London W4 5RG for an information pack.

Working on your car can be dangerous. This page shows just some of the potential risks and hazards, with the aim of creating a safety-conscious attitude.

General hazards

Scalding

• Don't remove the radiator or expansion tank cap while the engine is hot.
• Engine oil, automatic transmission fluid or power steering fluid may also be dangerously hot if the engine has recently been running.

Burning

• Beware of burns from the exhaust system and from any part of the engine. Brake discs and drums can also be extremely hot immediately after use.

Crushing

• When working under or near a raised vehicle, always supplement the jack with axle stands, or use drive-on ramps. *Never venture under a car which is only supported by a jack.*
• Take care if loosening or tightening high-torque nuts when the vehicle is on stands. Initial loosening and final tightening should be done with the wheels on the ground.

Fire

• Fuel is highly flammable; fuel vapour is explosive.
• Don't let fuel spill onto a hot engine.
• Do not smoke or allow naked lights (including pilot lights) anywhere near a vehicle being worked on. Also beware of creating sparks (electrically or by use of tools).
• Fuel vapour is heavier than air, so don't work on the fuel system with the vehicle over an inspection pit.
• Another cause of fire is an electrical overload or short-circuit. Take care when repairing or modifying the vehicle wiring.
• Keep a fire extinguisher handy, of a type suitable for use on fuel and electrical fires.

Electric shock

• Ignition HT voltage can be dangerous, especially to people with heart problems or a pacemaker. Don't work on or near the ignition system with the engine running or the ignition switched on.

• Mains voltage is also dangerous. Make sure that any mains-operated equipment is correctly earthed. Mains power points should be protected by a residual current device (RCD) circuit breaker.

Fume or gas intoxication

• Exhaust fumes are poisonous; they often contain carbon monoxide, which is rapidly fatal if inhaled. Never run the engine in a confined space such as a garage with the doors shut.
• Fuel vapour is also poisonous, as are the vapours from some cleaning solvents and paint thinners.

Poisonous or irritant substances

• Avoid skin contact with battery acid and with any fuel, fluid or lubricant, especially antifreeze, brake hydraulic fluid and Diesel fuel. Don't syphon them by mouth. If such a substance is swallowed or gets into the eyes, seek medical advice.
• Prolonged contact with used engine oil can cause skin cancer. Wear gloves or use a barrier cream if necessary. Change out of oil-soaked clothes and do not keep oily rags in your pocket.
• Air conditioning refrigerant forms a poisonous gas if exposed to a naked flame (including a cigarette). It can also cause skin burns on contact.

Asbestos

• Asbestos dust can cause cancer if inhaled or swallowed. Asbestos may be found in gaskets and in brake and clutch linings. When dealing with such components it is safest to assume that they contain asbestos.

Special hazards

Hydrofluoric acid

• This extremely corrosive acid is formed when certain types of synthetic rubber, found in some O-rings, oil seals, fuel hoses etc, are exposed to temperatures above 400ºC. The rubber changes into a charred or sticky substance containing the acid. *Once formed, the acid remains dangerous for years. If it gets onto the skin, it may be necessary to amputate the limb concerned.*
• When dealing with a vehicle which has suffered a fire, or with components salvaged from such a vehicle, wear protective gloves and discard them after use.

The battery

• Batteries contain sulphuric acid, which attacks clothing, eyes and skin. Take care when topping-up or carrying the battery.
• The hydrogen gas given off by the battery is highly explosive. Never cause a spark or allow a naked light nearby. Be careful when connecting and disconnecting battery chargers or jump leads.

Air bags

• Air bags can cause injury if they go off accidentally. Take care when removing the steering wheel and/or facia. Special storage instructions may apply.

Diesel injection equipment

• Diesel injection pumps supply fuel at very high pressure. Take care when working on the fuel injectors and fuel pipes.

Warning: Never expose the hands, face or any other part of the body to injector spray; the fuel can penetrate the skin with potentially fatal results.

Remember...

DO

• Do use eye protection when using power tools, and when working under the vehicle.

• Do wear gloves or use barrier cream to protect your hands when necessary.

• Do get someone to check periodically that all is well when working alone on the vehicle.

• Do keep loose clothing and long hair well out of the way of moving mechanical parts.

• Do remove rings, wristwatch etc, before working on the vehicle – especially the electrical system.

• Do ensure that any lifting or jacking equipment has a safe working load rating adequate for the job.

DON'T

• Don't attempt to lift a heavy component which may be beyond your capability – get assistance.

• Don't rush to finish a job, or take unverified short cuts.

• Don't use ill-fitting tools which may slip and cause injury.

• Don't leave tools or parts lying around where someone can trip over them. Mop up oil and fuel spills at once.

• Don't allow children or pets to play in or near a vehicle being worked on.

The Skoda Fabia models covered by this manual were manufactured between March 2000 and December 2005.

Models included in this Manual are available with 1.2 litre 3-cylinder SOHC 6-valve, 1.2 litre 3-cylinder DOHC 12-valve, 1.4 litre 4-cylinder 8-valve, and 1.4 litre 4-cylinder 16-valve petrol engines. The diesel engines available are 1.4 litre 3-cylinder (6-valve) and 1.9 litre 4-cylinder (8-valve). 1.0 litre OHV and 2.0 litre

16-valve petrol engines are not covered in this Manual. 1.9 litre diesel engines are available in normally-aspirated and turbocharged versions. All petrol engines use multi-point fuel injection, and are fitted with a wide range of emission control systems. All the engines are of a well-proven design and, provided regular maintenance is carried out, are unlikely to give trouble.

Skoda Fabia models are available in 5-door

Hatchback, 4-door Saloon and 5-door Estate bodystyles.

Fully-independent front suspension is fitted, with the components attached to a subframe assembly; the rear suspension is semi-independent, with a torsion beam and trailing arms.

A five-speed manual gearbox is fitted, with a four-speed automatic gearbox available as an option for 1.4 litre 16-valve petrol engine models. **Note:** *At the time of writing, no information was available for the 6-speed gearbox (code 0A8) fitted to vRS models.*

A wide range of standard and optional equipment is available within the model range to suit most tastes, including anti-lock braking, traction control and air conditioning.

For the home mechanic, Skoda Fabia models are straightforward vehicles to maintain, and most of the items requiring frequent attention are easily accessible.

Your Skoda Fabia Manual

The aim of this manual is to help you get the best value from your vehicle. It can do so in several ways. It can help you decide what work must be done (even should you choose to get it done by a garage). It will also provide information on routine maintenance and servicing, and give a logical course of action and diagnosis when random faults occur. However, it is hoped that you will use the manual by tackling the work yourself. On simpler jobs it may even be quicker than booking the car into a garage and going there twice, to leave and collect it. Perhaps most important, a lot of money can be saved by avoiding the costs a garage must charge to cover its labour and overheads.

The manual has drawings and descriptions to show the function of the various components so that their layout can be understood. Tasks are described and photographed in a clear step-by-step sequence.

References to the 'left' and 'right' of the vehicle are in the sense of a person in the driver's seat facing forward.

Acknowledgements

Thanks are due to Draper Tools Limited, who provided some of the workshop tools, and to all those people at Sparkford who helped in the production of this manual.

This manual is not a direct reproduction of the vehicle manufacturer's data, and its publication should not be taken as implying any technical approval by the vehicle manufacturers or importers.

We take great pride in the accuracy of information given in this manual, but vehicle manufacturers make alterations and design changes during the production run of a particular vehicle of which they do not inform us. No liability can be accepted by the authors or publishers for loss, damage or injury caused by any errors in, or omissions from, the information given.

The following pages are intended to help in dealing with common roadside emergencies and breakdowns. You will find more detailed fault finding information at the back of the manual, and repair information in the main chapters.

If your car won't start and the starter motor doesn't turn

☐ If it's a model with automatic transmission, make sure the selector is in P or N.
☐ Open the bonnet and make sure that the battery terminals are clean and tight.
☐ Switch on the headlights and try to start the engine. If the headlights go very dim when you're trying to start, the battery is probably flat. Get out of trouble by jump starting (see next page) using a friend's car.

If your car won't start even though the starter motor turns as normal

☐ Is there fuel in the tank?
☐ Is there moisture on electrical components under the bonnet? Switch off the ignition, then wipe off any obvious dampness with a dry cloth. Spray a water-repellent aerosol product (WD-40 or equivalent) on ignition and fuel system electrical connectors like those shown in the photos. (Note that diesel engines don't usually suffer from damp).

A Check the condition and security of the battery connections (remove the cover first)

B Check the fuses and fusible links in the fusebox located on top of the battery

C Check the wiring to the ignition coils beneath the engine top cover (petrol models only)

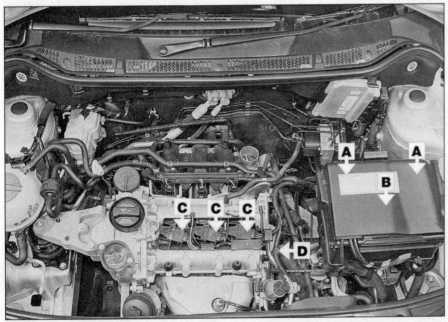

Check that electrical connections are secure (with the ignition switched off) and spray them with a water-dispersant spray like WD-40 if you suspect a problem due to damp

D Check that all engine wiring is secure

Jump starting

When jump-starting a car using a booster battery, observe the following precautions:

✔ Before connecting the booster battery, make sure that the ignition is switched off.

✔ Ensure that all electrical equipment (lights, heater, wipers, etc) is switched off.

✔ Take note of any special precautions printed on the battery case.

✔ Make sure that the booster battery is the same voltage as the discharged one in the vehicle.

✔ If the battery is being jump-started from the battery in another vehicle, the two vehicles MUST NOT TOUCH each other.

✔ Make sure that the transmission is in neutral (or PARK, in the case of automatic transmission).

 Jump starting will get you out of trouble, but you must correct whatever made the battery go flat in the first place. There are three possibilities:

1 *The battery has been drained by repeated attempts to start, or by leaving the lights on.*

2 *The charging system is not working properly (alternator drivebelt slack or broken, alternator wiring fault or alternator itself faulty).*

3 *The battery itself is at fault (electrolyte low, or battery worn out).*

1 Connect one end of the red jump lead to the positive (+) terminal of the flat battery

2 Connect the other end of the red lead to the positive (+) terminal of the booster battery.

3 Connect one end of the black jump lead to the negative (-) terminal of the booster battery

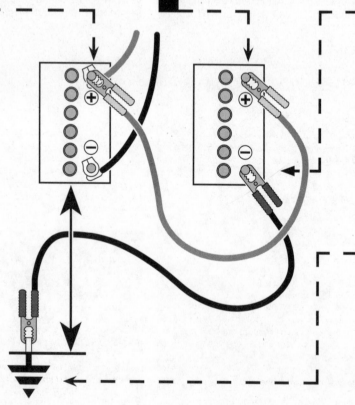

4 Connect the other end of the black jump lead to a suitable metal part of the engine on the vehicle to be started

5 Make sure that the jump leads will not come into contact with the fan, drive-belts or other moving parts of the engine.

6 Start the engine using the booster battery and run it at idle speed. Switch on the lights, rear window demister and heater blower motor, then disconnect the jump leads in the reverse order of connection. Turn off the lights etc.

Wheel changing

Caution: Some of the details shown here will vary according to model.

 Warning: Do not change a wheel in a situation where you risk being hit by other traffic. On busy roads, try to stop in a lay-by or a gateway. Be wary of passing traffic while changing the wheel – it is easy to become distracted by the job in hand.

Preparation

- [ ] When a puncture occurs, stop as soon as it is safe to do so.
- [ ] Park on firm level ground, if possible, and well out of the way of other traffic.
- [ ] Use hazard warning lights if necessary.

- [ ] If you have one, use a warning triangle to alert other drivers of your presence.
- [ ] Apply the handbrake and engage first or reverse gear (or P on models with automatic transmission).

- [ ] Chock the wheel diagonally opposite the one being removed – a couple of large stones will do for this.
- [ ] If the ground is soft, use a flat piece of wood to spread the load under the jack.

Changing the wheel

1 The spare wheel and tools are stored in the luggage compartment. Lift out the jack and wheel changing tools from the centre of the spare wheel.

2 Unscrew the retainer and lift out the wheel.

3 Use the wire hook to remove the wheel trim. Where applicable, use the plastic puller from the tool kit to remove the cover from the anti-theft wheel bolt.

4 Slacken each wheel bolt by half a turn (using the special splined adapter for the anti-theft bolt).

5 Locate the jack below the reinforced point on the sill (don't jack the vehicle at any other point of the sill) and on firm ground, then turn the jack handle clockwise until the wheel is raised clear of the ground.

6 Unscrew the wheel bolts (using the special splined adapter for the anti-theft bolt) and remove the wheel. Fit the spare wheel, and screw in the bolts. Lightly tighten the bolts with the wheelbrace then lower the vehicle to the ground.

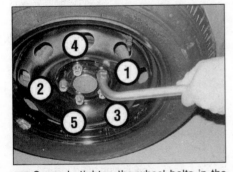

7 Securely tighten the wheel bolts in the sequence shown then refit the wheel trim/hub cap. Stow the punctured wheel back in the spare wheel well. Note that the wheel bolts should be tightened to the specified torque at the earliest possible opportunity.

Finally . . .

- [ ] Remove the wheel chocks.
- [ ] Stow the jack and tools in the spare wheel.
- [ ] Check the tyre pressure on the wheel just fitted. If it is low, or if you don't have a pressure gauge with you, drive slowly to the nearest garage and inflate the tyre to the correct pressure.

Note: *If a temporary 'space-saver' spare wheel has been fitted, special conditions apply to its use. This type of spare wheel is only intended for use in an emergency, and should not remain fitted any longer than it takes to get the punctured wheel repaired. While the temporary wheel is in use, ensure it is inflated to the correct pressure, do not exceed 50 mph (80 kph), and avoid harsh acceleration, braking or cornering.*

Identifying leaks

Puddles on the garage floor or drive, or obvious wetness under the bonnet or underneath the car, suggest a leak that needs investigating. It can sometimes be difficult to decide where the leak is coming from, especially if the engine bay is very dirty already. Leaking oil or fluid can also be blown rearwards by the passage of air under the car, giving a false impression of where the problem lies.

Warning: Most automotive oils and fluids are poisonous. Wash them off skin, and change out of contaminated clothing, without delay.

HAYNES HiNT *The smell of a fluid leaking from the car may provide a clue to what's leaking. Some fluids are distinctively coloured.*
It may help to clean the car carefully and to park it over some clean paper overnight as an aid to locating the source of the leak.
Remember that some leaks may only occur while the engine is running.

Sump oil

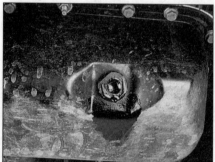

Engine oil may leak from the drain plug...

Oil from filter

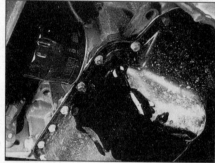

...or from the base of the oil filter.

Gearbox oil

Gearbox oil can leak from the seals at the inboard ends of the driveshafts.

Antifreeze

Leaking antifreeze often leaves a crystalline deposit like this.

Brake fluid

A leak occurring at a wheel is almost certainly brake fluid.

Power steering fluid

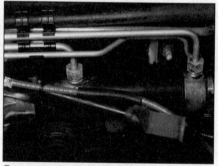

Power steering fluid may leak from the pipe connectors on the steering rack.

Towing

When all else fails, you may find yourself having to get a tow home – or of course you may be helping somebody else. Long-distance recovery should only be done by a garage or breakdown service. For shorter distances, DIY towing using another car is easy enough, but observe the following points:
☐ Use a proper tow-rope – they are not expensive. The vehicle being towed must display an ON TOW sign in its rear window.
☐ Always turn the ignition key to the 'On' position when the vehicle is being towed, so that the steering lock is released, and the direction indicator and brake lights work.
☐ Only attach the tow-rope to the towing eyes provided.

☐ Before being towed, release the handbrake and select neutral on the transmission. On models with automatic transmission, do not exceed 30 mph (50 kph) and do not tow for more than 30 miles (50 km). If in doubt, do not tow, or transmission damage may result.
☐ Note that greater-than-usual pedal pressure will be required to operate the brakes, since the vacuum servo unit is only operational with the engine running.
☐ Because the power steering will not be operational, greater-than-usual steering effort will be required.
☐ The driver of the car being towed must keep the tow-rope taut at all times to avoid snatching.

☐ Make sure that both drivers know the route before setting off.
☐ Only drive at moderate speeds and keep the distance towed to a minimum. Drive smoothly and allow plenty of time for slowing down at junctions.
☐ The front towing eye is located in the tool kit, and is screwed into position behind the vent/cover on the right-hand side of the front bumper. The eye has a left-hand thread.
☐ The rear towing eye is located beneath the right-hand side of the rear bumper.

Introduction

There are some very simple checks which need only take a few minutes to carry out, but which could save you a lot of inconvenience and expense.

These *Weekly checks* require no great skill or special tools, and the small amount of time they take to perform could prove to be very well spent, for example:

☐ Keeping an eye on tyre condition and pressures, will not only help to stop them wearing out prematurely, but could also save your life.

☐ Many breakdowns are caused by electrical problems. Battery-related faults are particularly common, and a quick check on a regular basis will often prevent the majority of these.

☐ If your car develops a brake fluid leak, the first time you might know about it is when your brakes don't work properly. Checking the level regularly will give advance warning of this kind of problem.

☐ If the oil or coolant levels run low, the cost of repairing any engine damage will be far greater than fixing the leak, for example.

Underbonnet check points

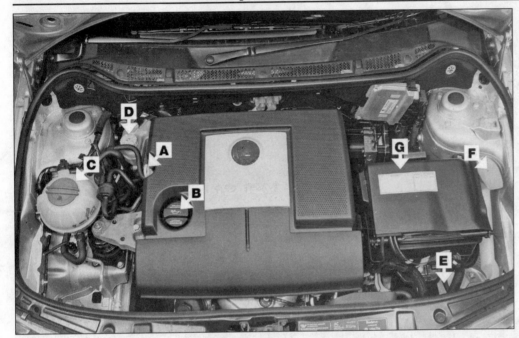

◀ 1.2 litre petrol DOHC

A *Engine oil level dipstick*

B *Engine oil filler cap*

C *Coolant expansion tank*

D *Brake fluid reservoir*

E *Power steering fluid reservoir*

F *Screen washer fluid reservoir*

G *Battery*

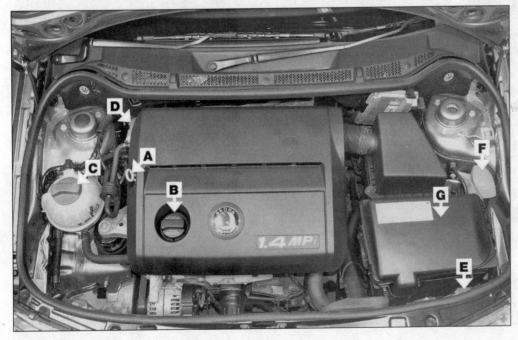

◀ 1.4 litre petrol OHV

A *Engine oil level dipstick*

B *Engine oil filler cap*

C *Coolant expansion tank*

D *Brake fluid reservoir*

E *Power steering fluid reservoir*

F *Screen washer fluid reservoir*

G *Battery*

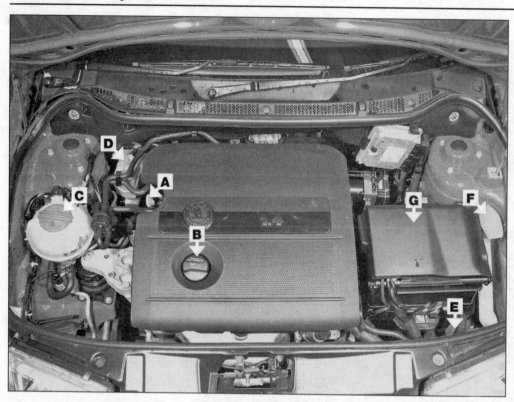

◀ **1.4 litre petrol DOHC**

A *Engine oil level dipstick*
B *Engine oil filler cap*
C *Coolant expansion tank*
D *Brake fluid reservoir*
E *Power steering fluid reservoir*
F *Screen washer fluid reservoir*
G *Battery*

◀ **1.4 litre diesel**

A *Engine oil level dipstick*
B *Engine oil filler cap*
C *Coolant expansion tank*
D *Brake fluid reservoir*
E *Power steering fluid reservoir*
F *Screen washer fluid reservoir*
G *Battery*

◀ **1.9 litre diesel**

A *Engine oil level dipstick*

B *Engine oil filler cap*

C *Coolant expansion tank*

D *Brake fluid reservoir*

E *Power steering fluid reservoir*

F *Screen washer fluid reservoir*

G *Battery*

Engine oil level

Before you start

✔ Make sure that the car is on level ground.
✔ Check the oil level before the car is driven, or at least 5 minutes after the engine has been switched off.

 HAYNES HiNT *If the oil is checked immediately after driving the vehicle, some of the oil will remain in the upper engine components, resulting in an inaccurate reading on the dipstick.*

The correct oil

Modern engines place great demands on their oil. It is very important that the correct oil for your car is used (see *Lubricants and fluids*).

Car care

● If you have to add oil frequently, you should check whether you have any oil leaks. Place some clean paper under the car overnight, and check for stains in the morning. If there are no leaks, then the engine may be burning oil.

● Always maintain the level between the upper and lower dipstick marks. If the level is too low, severe engine damage may occur. Oil seal failure may result if the engine is overfilled by adding too much oil.

1 The dipstick is often brightly coloured for easy identification (see *Underbonnet check points* for exact location). Withdraw the dipstick, then use a clean rag or paper towel to wipe the oil from it. Insert the clean dipstick into the tube as far as it will go, then withdraw it again.

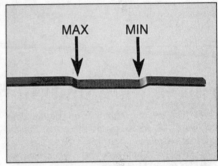

2 Note the level on the end of the dipstick, which should be between the upper (MAX) and lower (MIN) mark.

3 Oil is added through the filler cap aperture. Unscrew the cap.

4 Place some cloth rags around the filler cap aperture, if necessary, then top-up the level. A funnel may help to reduce spillage. Add the oil slowly, checking the level on the dipstick frequently. Avoid overfilling (see *Car care*).

Coolant level

⚠️ **Warning: Do not attempt to remove the expansion tank pressure cap when the engine is hot, as there is a very great risk of scalding. Do not leave open containers of coolant about, as it is poisonous.**

Car Care

● With a sealed-type cooling system, adding coolant should not be necessary on a regular basis. If frequent topping-up is required, it is likely there is a leak. Check the radiator, all hoses and joint faces for signs of staining or wetness, and rectify as necessary.

● It is important that antifreeze is used in the cooling system all year round, not just during the winter months. Don't top up with water alone, as the antifreeze will become diluted.

1 The coolant level varies with the temperature of the engine. When the engine is cold, the coolant level should be between the MIN and MAX marks.

2 If topping-up is necessary, wait until the engine is cold. Slowly unscrew the cap to release any pressure present in the cooling system, and remove the cap.

3 Add a mixture of water and the specified antifreeze (see *Lubricants and fluids*) to the expansion tank until the coolant level is halfway between the level marks. Refit the cap and tighten it securely.

Brake (and clutch) fluid level

Note: *On manual transmission models, the fluid reservoir also supplies the clutch master cylinder with fluid*

Before you start

✔ Make sure that the car is on level ground.
✔ Cleanliness is of great importance when dealing with the braking system, so take care to clean around the reservoir cap before topping-up. Use only clean brake fluid.

Safety first!

● If the reservoir requires repeated topping-up, this is an indication of a fluid leak somewhere in the system, which should be investigated immediately.

● If a leak is suspected, the car should not be driven until the braking system has been checked. Never take any risks where brakes are concerned.

⚠️ **Warning: Brake fluid can harm your eyes and damage painted surfaces, so use extreme caution when handling and pouring it. Do not use fluid which has been standing open for some time, as it absorbs moisture from the air, which can cause a dangerous loss of braking effectiveness.**

1 The MIN and MAX marks are indicated on the reservoir. The fluid level must be kept between the marks at all times. Note that the level will drop naturally as the brake pad linings wear, but must never be allowed to fall below the MIN mark.

2 If topping-up is necessary, first wipe clean the area around the filler cap to prevent dirt entering the hydraulic system. Unscrew and remove the reservoir cap.

3 Carefully add fluid, taking care not to spill it onto the surrounding components. Use only the specified fluid (see *Lubricants and fluids*); mixing different types can cause damage to the system. On completion, securely refit the cap and wipe away any spilt fluid.

Washer fluid level

● Screenwash additives not only keep the windscreen clean during bad weather, they also prevent the washer system freezing in cold weather – which is when you are likely to need it most. Don't top-up using plain water, as the screenwash will become diluted, and will freeze in cold weather.

 Warning: On no account use engine coolant antifreeze in the screen washer system – this may damage the paintwork.

1 The screenwash fluid reservoir is located on the left-hand side of the engine compartment, behind the headlight. Pull up the filler cap to release it from the reservoir.

2 When topping-up the reservoir, a screenwash additive should be added in the quantities recommended on the bottle.

Battery

Caution: Before carrying out any work on the vehicle battery, read the precautions given in 'Safety first!' at the start of this manual.

✔ Make sure that the battery tray is in good condition, and that the clamp is tight. Corrosion on the tray, retaining clamp and the battery itself can be removed with a solution of water and baking soda. Thoroughly rinse all cleaned areas with water. Any metal parts damaged by corrosion should be covered with a zinc-based primer, then painted.

✔ Periodically (approximately every three months), check the charge condition of the battery as described in Chapter 5A.

✔ If the battery is flat, and you need to jump start your vehicle, see *Roadside Repairs*.

1 The battery is located in the front left-hand corner of the engine compartment. Remove the heat protective cover by pressing the side buttons to gain access to the battery terminals. The exterior of the battery should be inspected periodically for damage such as a cracked case or cover.

2 Check the security and condition of all the battery and fuse connections. The exterior of the battery should be inspected periodically for damage such as a cracked case or cover.

3 If corrosion (white, fluffy deposits) is evident, remove the cables from the battery terminals (refer to *Disconnecting the battery* in the Reference chapter at the end of this manual), clean them with a small wire brush, then refit them. Automotive stores sell a tool for cleaning the battery post . . .

4 . . . as well as the battery cable clamps. **Note:** *Skoda specifically prohibit the use of grease on the battery terminals.*

Tyre condition and pressure

It is very important that tyres are in good condition, and at the correct pressure - having a tyre failure at any speed is highly dangerous. Tyre wear is influenced by driving style - harsh braking and acceleration, or fast cornering, will all produce more rapid tyre wear. As a general rule, the front tyres wear out faster than the rears. Interchanging the tyres from front to rear ("rotating" the tyres) may result in more even wear. However, if this is completely effective, you may have the expense of replacing all four tyres at once!

Remove any nails or stones embedded in the tread before they penetrate the tyre to cause deflation. If removal of a nail does reveal that the tyre has been punctured, refit the nail so that its point of penetration is marked. Then immediately change the wheel, and have the tyre repaired by a tyre dealer.

Regularly check the tyres for damage in the form of cuts or bulges, especially in the sidewalls. Periodically remove the wheels, and clean any dirt or mud from the inside and outside surfaces. Examine the wheel rims for signs of rusting, corrosion or other damage. Light alloy wheels are easily damaged by "kerbing" whilst parking; steel wheels may also become dented or buckled. A new wheel is very often the only way to overcome severe damage.

New tyres should be balanced when they are fitted, but it may become necessary to re-balance them as they wear, or if the balance weights fitted to the wheel rim should fall off. Unbalanced tyres will wear more quickly, as will the steering and suspension components. Wheel imbalance is normally signified by vibration, particularly at a certain speed (typically around 50 mph). If this vibration is felt only through the steering, then it is likely that just the front wheels need balancing. If, however, the vibration is felt through the whole car, the rear wheels could be out of balance. Wheel balancing should be carried out by a tyre dealer or garage.

1 Tread Depth - visual check
The original tyres have tread wear safety bands (B), which will appear when the tread depth reaches approximately 1.6 mm. The band positions are indicated by a triangular mark on the tyre sidewall (A).

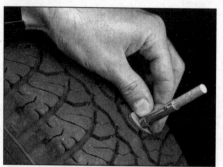

2 Tread Depth - manual check
Alternatively, tread wear can be monitored with a simple, inexpensive device known as a tread depth indicator gauge.

3 Tyre Pressure Check
Check the tyre pressures regularly with the tyres cold. Do not adjust the tyre pressures immediately after the vehicle has been used, or an inaccurate setting will result.

Tyre tread wear patterns

Shoulder Wear

Underinflation (wear on both sides)
Under-inflation will cause overheating of the tyre, because the tyre will flex too much, and the tread will not sit correctly on the road surface. This will cause a loss of grip and excessive wear, not to mention the danger of sudden tyre failure due to heat build-up.
Check and adjust pressures
Incorrect wheel camber (wear on one side)
Repair or renew suspension parts
Hard cornering
Reduce speed!

Centre Wear

Overinflation
Over-inflation will cause rapid wear of the centre part of the tyre tread, coupled with reduced grip, harsher ride, and the danger of shock damage occurring in the tyre casing.
Check and adjust pressures

If you sometimes have to inflate your car's tyres to the higher pressures specified for maximum load or sustained high speed, don't forget to reduce the pressures to normal afterwards.

Uneven Wear

Front tyres may wear unevenly as a result of wheel misalignment. Most tyre dealers and garages can check and adjust the wheel alignment (or "tracking") for a modest charge.
Incorrect camber or castor
Repair or renew suspension parts
Malfunctioning suspension
Repair or renew suspension parts
Unbalanced wheel
Balance tyres
Incorrect toe setting
Adjust front wheel alignment
Note: *The feathered edge of the tread which typifies toe wear is best checked by feel.*

Electrical systems

✔ Check all external lights and the horn. Refer to the appropriate Sections of Chapter 12 for details if any of the circuits are found to be inoperative.

✔ Visually check all accessible wiring connectors, harnesses and retaining clips for security, and for signs of chafing or damage.

HAYNES HiNT *If you need to check your brake lights and indicators unaided, back up to a wall or garage door and operate the lights. The reflected light should show if they are working properly.*

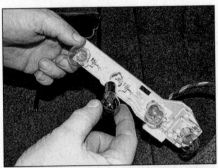

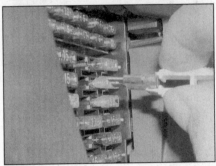

1 If a single indicator light, brake light or headlight has failed, it is likely that a bulb has blown and will need to be renewed. Refer to Chapter 12 for details. If both brake lights have failed, it is possible that the brake light switch operated by the brake pedal has failed. Refer to Chapter 9 for details.

2 If more than one indicator light or headlight has failed, it is likely that either a fuse has blown or that there is a fault in the circuit (see *Electrical fault finding* in Chapter 12). The main fuses are in the fusebox beneath a cover on the right-hand end of the facia panel. Use a small screwdriver to prise off the cover. The circuits protected by the fuses are shown on the inside of the cover. Additional heavy duty fuses and fusible links are in the fusebox located on top of the battery.

3 To renew a blown fuse, pull it from its location in the fusebox, using the plastic pliers provided. Fit a new fuse of the same rating, available from car accessory shops. It is important that you find the reason that the fuse blew (see *Electrical fault finding* in Chapter 12).

Wiper blades

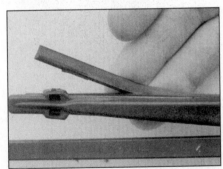

1 Check the condition of the wiper blades; if they are cracked or show any signs of deterioration, or if the glass swept area is smeared, renew them. For maximum clarity of vision, wiper blades should be renewed annually, as a matter of course.

2 To remove a windscreen wiper blade, pull the arm fully away from the screen until it locks. Swivel the blade through 90°, press the locking tab with your fingers, and slide the blade out of the hooked end of the arm.

3 Where applicable, don't forget to check the tailgate wiper blade as well. To remove the blade, depress the retaining tab and slide the blade out of the hooked end of the arm.

Lubricants and fluids

Engine (petrol)

Standard (distance/time) service interval . . . .   Multigrade engine oil, viscosity SAE 5W/40 to 20W/50, to API SG/CD

LongLife (variable) service interval . . . .   Skoda LongLife engine oil (Skoda 503 00 or better)*

Engine (diesel)

Standard (distance/time) service interval . . . .   Multigrade engine oil, viscosity SAE 5W/40 to 20W/50, to API SG/CD

LongLife (variable) service interval . . . .   Skoda LongLife engine oil (Skoda 506 00 or better)‡

Cooling system . . . .   Skoda additive G12 only (antifreeze and corrosion protection)

Manual transmission . . . .   Skoda G50 synthetic gear oil, viscosity SAE 75W/90†

Automatic transmission

Main transmission . . . .   Skoda ATF

Final drive . . . .   Skoda G50 synthetic gear oil, viscosity SAE 75W/90

Braking system . . . .   Hydraulic fluid to SAE J1703F or DOT 4

Power steering reservoir . . . .   Skoda hydraulic oil G 002 000

* A maximum of 0.5 litres of standard Skoda 502 00 oil may be used for topping-up when LongLife oil is unobtainable
‡ A maximum of 0.5 litres of standard Skoda 505 00 oil may be used for topping-up when LongLife oil is unobtainable
† At the time of writing, no information was available for the 6-speed transmission fitted to vRS models

Tyre pressures

Note: *The recommended tyre pressures for each vehicle are given on a sticker attached to the rear of the fuel filler flap. The pressures given are for the original equipment tyres – the recommended pressures may vary if any other make or type of tyre is fitted; check with the tyre manufacturer or supplier for latest recommendations. The following pressures are typical.*

	Front	Rear
Normal load	2.0 bars (29 psi)	2.2 bars (32 psi)
Full load	2.2 bars (32 psi)	2.8 bars (41 psi)

Note: *Where a space-saver spare tyre is fitted, its pressure must be 4.2 bars (61 psi).*

Chapter 1 Part A:
Routine maintenance and servicing – petrol models

Contents

	Section number
Air filter element renewal	24
Airbag unit check	19
Antifreeze check	9
Automatic transmission fluid level check	28
Auxiliary drivebelt check and renewal	26
Auxiliary drivebelt check	8
Battery check	17
Brake (and clutch) fluid renewal	30
Brake hydraulic circuit check	10
Brake pad/lining check	4
Coolant renewal	31
Driveshaft check	15
Engine management self-diagnosis memory fault check	21
Engine oil and filter renewal	3
Exhaust system check	6
Headlight beam adjustment	11

	Section number
Hinge and lock lubrication	18
Hose and fluid leak check	7
Introduction	1
Manual transmission oil level check	13
Pollen filter element renewal	12
Power steering hydraulic fluid level check	27
Regular maintenance	2
Resetting the service interval display	5
Road test and exhaust emissions check	23
Spark plug renewal	25
Steering and suspension check	16
Sunroof check and lubrication	22
Timing belt renewal	29
Underbody protection check	14
Windscreen/tailgate/headlight washer system check	20

Degrees of difficulty

Easy, suitable for novice with little experience	Fairly easy, suitable for beginner with some experience	Fairly difficult, suitable for competent DIY mechanic	Difficult, suitable for experienced DIY mechanic	Very difficult, suitable for expert DIY or professional

Lubricants and fluids . . . .   Refer to end of *Weekly checks* on page 0•18

Engine codes
1.2 litre:
  SOHC . . . .   AWY
  DOHC . . . .   AZQ, BME
1.4 litre OHV:
  44 kW . . . .   AZE and AZF
  50 kW . . . .   AME, ATZ and AQW
1.4 litre DOHC:
  55 kW . . . .   AUA and BBY
  74 kW . . . .   AUB and BBZ

Capacities

Engine oil – including filter
1.2 litre:
  Engine code AWY . . . .   2.4 litres
  Engine codes AZQ and BME . . . .   2.8 litres
1.4 litre:
  Engine codes AME, AQW, ATZ, AZE and AZF . . . .   4.0 litres
  Engine codes AUA, BBY, AUB and BBZ . . . .   3.2 litres

Cooling system
1.2 litre engine . . . .   5.1 litres
1.4 litre:
  Engine codes AME, AQW, ATZ, AZE and AZF . . . .   6.0 litres
  Engine codes AUA, BBY, AUB and BBZ . . . .   5.5 litres

Transmission
Manual transmission:
  Type 02T . . . .   1.9 litres
  Type 002 . . . .   2.0 litres
Automatic transmission . . . .   5.7 litres

Fuel tank (approximate) . . . .   45 litres

Cooling system
Antifreeze mixture:
  40% antifreeze . . . .   Protection down to -25°C
  50% antifreeze . . . .   Protection down to -35°C
Note: *Refer to antifreeze manufacturer for latest recommendations.*

Ignition system

Spark plugs:	Type	Electrode gap
1.2 litre:		
Engine code AWY	NGK PZFR5J-11	1.0 mm
	NGK ZFR 5P-G	0.9 mm
	Bosch F7 HER2	0.9 mm
Engine codes AZQ and BME	Bosch F7 HER2	0.9 mm
	NGK ZFR5P-G	0.8 mm
1.4 litre:		
Engine codes AME, AQW, ATZ, AZE and AZF	Champion RC-89 PYC	0.8 mm
Engine codes AUA, BBY, AUB and BBZ	NGK BKUR 6ET-10	1.0 mm

Brakes
Brake pad minimum thickness:
  Including backing plate:
    Front . . . .   7.0 mm
    Rear . . . .   7.6 mm
  Friction lining only:
    Front and rear . . . .   2.0 mm
Rear brake shoe friction material minimum thickness . . . .   1.5 mm

Torque wrench settings

	Nm	lbf ft
Alternator mounting bolt	20	15
Automatic transmission level plug	15	11
Manual gearbox filler/level plug	25	18
Oil filter housing cap (1.2 litre engines)	25	18
Roadwheel bolts	120	89
Spark plugs	30	22
Sump drain plug	30	22

Maintenance schedule

The maintenance intervals (shown overleaf) in this manual are provided with the assumption that you, not the dealer, will be carrying out the work. These are the minimum intervals recommended by us for vehicles driven daily. If you wish to keep your vehicle in peak condition at all times, you may wish to perform some of these procedures more often. We encourage frequent maintenance, since it enhances the efficiency, performance and resale value of your vehicle.

When the vehicle is new, it should be serviced by a dealer service department, in order to preserve the factory warranty.

All Skoda models are equipped with a service interval display indicator in the instrument panel. Every time the engine is started the panel will illuminate for approximately 20 seconds with service information. With the standard fixed interval display, the service intervals are in accordance with specific distances and time periods. With the LongLife display, the service interval is variable. Once the service interval has been reached, the display will flash 'OIL service' for an oil change service or 'INSP service' for an inspection service.

For models using the LongLife schedule, the occurrence of either service reminder on the display unit will depend on how the vehicle is being used (number of starts, length of journeys, vehicle speeds, brake pad wear, bonnet opening frequency, fuel consumption, oil level and oil temperature). For example, if a vehicle is being used under extreme driving conditions, the service may occur at 10 000 miles, whereas, if the vehicle is being used under moderate driving conditions, it may occur at 20 000 miles, although the maximum length of time between INSP services is 2 years. It is important to realise that this system is completely variable according to how the vehicle is being used, and therefore the service should be carried out when indicated on the display. **Note:** *Models with the variable service interval system are equipped with an engine oil level sensor, brake pad wear indicator, battery with a 'magic eye' charge indicator, and a variable service indicator.*

The LongLife variable service intervals are only applicable to models with a PR number of QG1 or QG2 (shown in the vehicle Service Schedule booklet, on a service interval plate inside the luggage compartment or on the Next Service sticker located on the driver's door pillar). For QG1 vehicles, the engine oil change and all other maintenance procedures are at variable intervals, however, for QG2 vehicles, the engine oil change and brake pad check is carried out at fixed intervals but all other maintenance procedures are at variable intervals.

With the variable (LongLife) service interval on models with a PR number of QG1, the engine must **only** be filled with the recommended **LongLife** engine oil (see *Recommended lubricants and fluids*); on models with a PR number of QG2, standard engine oil can be used.

After completing a service, Skoda technicians use a special instrument to reset the service display to the next service interval, and a print-out is put in the vehicle service record. The display can be reset by the owner as described in Section 5, but note that for models using the LongLife interval QG1, the procedure will automatically reset the schedule to an amended LongLife interval (QG2) in which oil renewal and brake pad checks are based on distance/time while every other system remains LongLife. To have the display reset to the full LongLife schedule (QG1), it is necessary to take the vehicle to a Skoda dealer who will use a special instrument to encode the on-board computer.

Every 250 miles or weekly

☐ Refer to *Weekly checks*

'OIL service' on display

☐ Renew the engine oil and filter (Section 3)

Note: *Frequent oil and filter changes are good for the engine. We recommend changing the oil at least once a year.*

☐ Check the front and rear brake pad thickness (Section 4)
☐ Reset the service interval display (Section 5)

'INSP service' on display

Note: *In addition to the items given above.*

☐ Check the condition of the exhaust system and its mountings (Section 6)
☐ Check all underbonnet components and hoses for fluid and oil leaks (Section 7)
☐ Check the condition of the auxiliary drivebelt (Section 8)
☐ Check the coolant antifreeze concentration (Section 9)
☐ Check the brake hydraulic circuit for leaks and damage (Section 10)
☐ Check the headlight beam adjustment (Section 11)
☐ Renew the pollen filter element (Section 12)
☐ Check the manual transmission oil level (Section 13)
☐ Check the underbody protection for damage (Section 14)
☐ Check the condition of the driveshafts (Section 15)
☐ Check the steering and suspension components for condition and security (Section 16)
☐ Check the battery condition, security and electrolyte level (Section 17)
☐ Lubricate all hinges and locks (Section 18)
☐ Check the condition of the airbag unit(s) (Section 19)
☐ Check the operation of the windscreen/tailgate/headlight washer system(s) (as applicable) (Section 20)
☐ Check the engine management self-diagnosis memory for faults (Section 21)
☐ Check the operation of the sunroof and lubricate the guide rails (Section 22)
☐ Carry out a road test and check exhaust emissions (Section 23)

Every 40 000 miles or 4 years, whichever comes first

Note: *Many dealers perform these tasks with every second INSP service.*

☐ Renew the air filter element (Section 24)
☐ Renew the spark plugs (Section 25)
☐ Check the condition of the auxiliary drivebelt (Section 26)
☐ Check the power steering hydraulic fluid level (Section 27)
☐ Check the automatic transmission fluid level (Section 28)

Every 60 000 miles

☐ Renew the timing belt (Section 29)

Note: *Skoda specify timing belt inspection after the first 60 000 miles and then every 20 000 miles until the renewal interval of 120 000 miles, however, if the vehicle is used mainly for short journeys, we recommend that this shorter renewal interval is adhered to. The belt renewal interval is very much up to the individual owner but, bearing in mind that severe engine damage will result if the belt breaks in use, we recommend the shorter interval.*

Every 2 years

☐ Renew the brake (and clutch) fluid (Section 30)
☐ Renew the coolant (Section 31)*

* Note: *This work is not included in the Skoda schedule and should not be required if the recommended Skoda G12 LongLife coolant antifreeze/inhibitor is used.*

Underbonnet view of a 1.2 litre model

1 Engine oil filler cap
2 Engine oil dipstick
3 Coolant expansion tank
4 Windscreen/headlight washer fluid reservoir
5 Power steering fluid reservoir
6 Ignition coils and spark plugs
7 Fuel injectors
8 Front suspension strut upper mountings
9 Brake master cylinder fluid reservoir
10 Inlet manifold
11 Air conditioning hoses
12 Brake ABS unit
13 Engine management ECU
14 Battery
15 EGR valve
16 Oxygen (lambda) sensor
17 Oil filter
18 Auxiliary drivebelt
19 Right-hand engine mounting

Front underbody view of a 1.2 litre model

1 Sump drain plug
2 Manual transmission
3 Rear engine mounting/link
4 Driveshaft
5 Anti-roll bar link
6 Front brake caliper
7 Steering track rod
8 Front suspension lower arm
9 Front suspension subframe
10 Exhaust front pipe
11 Auxiliary drivebelt
12 Air conditioning compressor
13 Radiator electric cooling fan
14 Cooling system drain plug
15 Oxygen sensor

Rear underbody view of a 1.2 litre model

1 Rear axle assembly
2 Fuel tank
3 Rear brake flexible hose
4 Rear suspension coil springs
5 Handbrake cables
6 Rear suspension shock absorbers
7 Exhaust rear silencer and tailpipe
8 Fuel tank filler pipe
9 Rear brake hydraulic lines
10 Fuel filter

Underbonnet view of a 1.4 litre OHV model

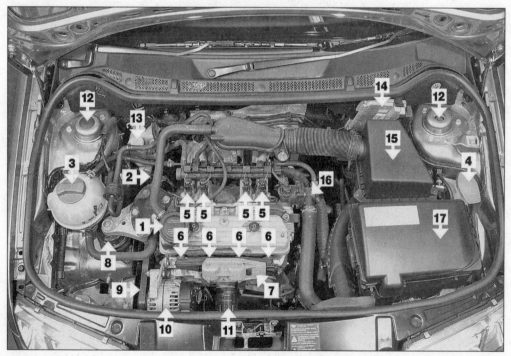

1 Engine oil filler cap
2 Engine oil dipstick
3 Coolant expansion tank
4 Windscreen/headlight washer fluid reservoir
5 Fuel injectors
6 Spark plugs
7 Ignition coil module
8 Right-hand engine mounting
9 Auxiliary drivebelt
10 Alternator
11 Oil filter
12 Front suspension strut upper mountings
13 Brake master cylinder fluid reservoir
14 Engine management ECU
15 Air filter housing
16 Coolant distribution housing
17 Battery

Front underbody view of a 1.4 litre OHV model

1 Sump drain plug
2 Manual transmission
3 Rear engine mounting/link
4 Driveshaft
5 Anti-roll bar link
6 Front brake caliper
7 Steering track rod
8 Front suspension lower arm
9 Front suspension subframe
10 Alternator
11 Oil filter
12 Radiator electric cooling fan
13 Radiator bottom hose
14 Radiator drain plug
15 Exhaust front pipe
16 Coolant pipe leading from radiator to coolant pump

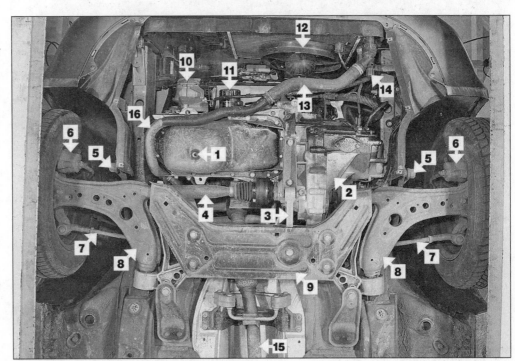

Underbonnet view of a 1.4 litre DOHC model

1 Engine oil filler cap
2 Engine oil dipstick
3 Coolant expansion tank
4 Windscreen/headlight washer fluid reservoir
5 Battery
6 Spark plugs and HT coils
7 Fuel injectors
8 Right-hand engine mounting
9 Front suspension strut upper mountings
10 Brake master cylinder fluid reservoir
11 Air conditioning lines
12 Brake ABS hydraulic unit
13 Engine management ECU
14 EGR unit

Front underbody view of a 1.4 litre OHV model

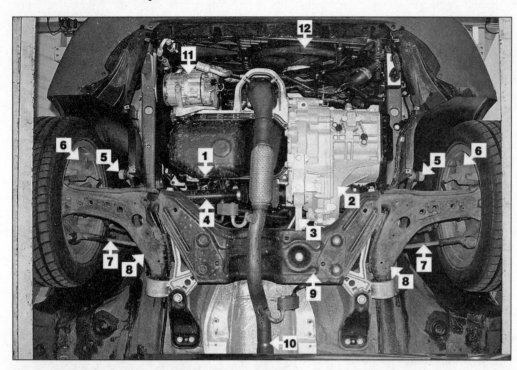

1   Sump drain plug
2   Manual transmission
3   Rear engine mounting/link
4   Driveshaft
5   Anti-roll bar link
6   Front brake caliper
7   Steering track rod
8   Front suspension lower arm
9   Front suspension subframe
10 Exhaust front pipe
11 Air conditioning compressor
12 Radiator electric cooling fan

Maintenance procedures

1 Introduction

This Chapter is designed to help the home mechanic maintain his/her vehicle for safety, economy, long life and peak performance.

The Chapter contains a master maintenance schedule, followed by Sections dealing specifically with each task in the schedule. Visual checks, adjustments, component renewal and other helpful items are included. Refer to the accompanying illustrations of the engine compartment and the underside of the vehicle for the locations of the various components.

Servicing your vehicle will provide a planned maintenance programme, which should result in a long and reliable service life. This is a comprehensive plan, so maintaining some items but not others will not produce the same results.

As you service your vehicle, you will discover that many of the procedures can – and should – be grouped together, because of the particular procedure being performed, or because of the proximity of two otherwise unrelated components to one another. For example, if the vehicle is raised for any reason, the exhaust can be inspected at the same time as the suspension and steering components.

The first step in this maintenance programme is to prepare yourself before the actual work begins. Read through all the Sections relevant to the work to be carried out, then make a list and gather all the parts and tools required. If a problem is encountered, seek advice from a parts specialist, or a dealer service department.

2 Regular maintenance

1 If, from the time the vehicle is new, the routine maintenance schedule is followed closely, and frequent checks are made of fluid levels and high-wear items, as suggested throughout this manual, the engine will be kept in relatively good running condition, and the need for additional work will be minimised.
2 It is possible that there will be times when the engine is running poorly due to the lack of regular maintenance. This is even more likely if a used vehicle, which has not received regular and frequent maintenance checks, is purchased. In such cases, additional work may need to be carried out, outside of the regular maintenance intervals.
3 If engine wear is suspected, a compression test (refer to Chapter 2A, 2B or 2C) will provide valuable information regarding the overall performance of the main internal components. Such a test can be used as a basis to decide on the extent of the work to be carried out. If, for example, a compression test indicates serious internal engine wear, conventional maintenance as described in this Chapter will not greatly improve the performance of the engine, and may prove a waste of time and money, unless extensive overhaul work is carried out first.
4 The following series of operations are those most often required to improve the performance of a generally poor-running engine:

Primary operations

a) Clean, inspect and test the battery (See 'Weekly checks').
b) Check all the engine-related fluids (See 'Weekly checks').
c) Check the condition and tension of the auxiliary drivebelt (Section 8).
d) Renew the spark plugs (Section 25).
e) Check the condition of the air filter, and renew if necessary (Section 24).
f) Check the condition of all hoses, and check for fluid leaks (Section 7).

5 If the above operations do not prove fully effective, carry out the following secondary operations:

Secondary operations

All items listed under Primary operations, plus the following:
a) Check the charging system (see Chapter 5A).
b) Check the ignition system (see Chapter 5B).
c) Check the fuel system (see Chapter 4A).
d) Renew the ignition HT leads (where applicable).

'OIL service' on display

3 Engine oil and filter renewal

1 Frequent oil and filter changes are the most important maintenance procedures which can be undertaken by the DIY owner. As engine oil ages, it becomes diluted and contaminated, which leads to premature engine wear.

2 Before starting this procedure, gather all the necessary tools and materials. Also make sure that you have plenty of clean rags and newspapers handy, to mop-up any spills. Ideally, the engine oil should be warm, as it will drain better, and more built-up sludge will be removed with it. Take care, however, not to touch the exhaust or any other hot parts of the engine when working under the vehicle. To avoid any possibility of scalding, and to protect yourself from possible skin irritants and other harmful contaminants in used engine oils, it is advisable to wear gloves when carrying out this work. Access to the underside of the vehicle will be greatly improved if it can be raised on a lift, driven onto ramps, or jacked up and supported on axle stands (see *Jacking and vehicle support*). Whichever method is chosen, make sure that the vehicle remains level, or if it is at an angle, that the drain plug is at the lowest point. Where necessary, undo the retaining screws and remove the engine undershield(s), then also remove the engine top cover where applicable.

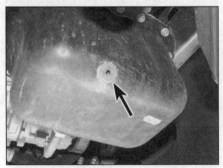

3.3 The engine oil drain plug location on the sump

3 Using a socket and wrench or a ring spanner, slacken the drain plug about half a turn (see illustration). Position the draining container under the drain plug, then remove the plug completely (see Haynes Hint). Recover the sealing ring from the drain plug.

4 Allow some time for the old oil to drain, noting that it may be necessary to reposition the container as the oil flow slows to a trickle.

5 After all the oil has drained, wipe off the drain plug with a clean rag, and fit a new sealing washer. Clean the area around the drain plug opening, and refit the plug. Tighten the plug to the specified torque.

6 If the filter is also to be renewed, move the container into position under the oil filter. On 1.2 litre engines, the filter is located beneath a cap on the front right-hand end of the engine. On 1.4 litre engines, the canister-type filter is located on the front of the engine (see illustration).

7 On 1.2 litre engines, unscrew the cap several turns from the oil filter housing until its sealing face is level with the side peg. Leave the cap in this position for at least one minute, to allow the oil to drain from the filter and housing. Cover the alternator with cloth rags, to prevent entry of oil. Completely unscrew the cap and withdraw it together with the

HAYNES HiNT

Keep the drain plug pressed into the sump while unscrewing it by hand the last couple of turns. As the plug releases, move it away sharply so the stream of oil issuing from the sump runs into the container, not up your sleeve.

filter. If the filter comes out together with the cap, tap the cap bottom extension lightly on a wooden base to release the filter. Using a screwdriver, remove the O-ring seal from the cap and discard it – a new one must be used when refitting (see illustrations).

8 On 1.4 litre engines, using an oil filter removal tool if necessary, slacken the filter initially, then unscrew it by hand the rest of the way. Empty the oil in the filter into the container. Check the old filter to make sure that the rubber sealing ring has not stuck to the engine. If it has, carefully remove it.

9 Use a clean rag to remove all oil, dirt and sludge from the filter housing and cap, or filter sealing area (as applicable).

10 On 1.2 litre engines, fit a new O-ring seal to the cap, then insert the new filter in the housing and screw on the cap. Tighten the cap to the specified torque. Wipe away any excess oil.

11 On 1.4 litre engines, apply a light coating of clean engine oil to the sealing ring on the new filter, then screw it into position on the engine. Tighten the filter firmly by hand only – **do not** use any tools. Wipe away any excess oil.

12 Remove the old oil and all tools from under the car. Refit the engine undershield(s), tighten the retaining screws securely, then lower the car to the ground. Also refit the engine top cover where applicable.

13 Remove the dipstick, then unscrew the oil filler cap from the cylinder head cover. Fill the engine, using the correct grade and type of oil (see *Lubricants and fluids*). An oil can spout or funnel may help to reduce spillage. Pour in half the specified quantity of oil first, then wait a few minutes for the oil to run to the sump. Continue adding oil a small quantity at a time until the level is up to the maximum mark on the dipstick. Refit the filler cap.

14 Start the engine and run it for a few minutes; check for leaks around the oil filter seal and the sump drain plug. Note that there may be a few seconds delay before the oil pressure warning light goes out when the engine is started, as the oil circulates through the engine oil galleries and the new oil filter (where fitted) before the pressure builds-up.

3.6 On 1.4 litre engines, the oil filter is located on the front of the engine

3.7a Unscrew the cap and remove the oil filter

3.7b Tap the bottom extension of the cap to release the filter

4.1 The outer brake pads can be observed through the holes in the wheels

15 Switch off the engine, and wait a few minutes for the oil to settle in the sump once more. With the new oil circulated and the filter completely full, recheck the level on the dipstick, and add more oil as necessary.

16 Dispose of the used engine oil safely, with reference to *General repair procedures* in the *Reference* section of this manual.

4   Brake pad/lining check

Front and rear disc brakes

1 The outer brake pads can be checked without removing the wheels, by observing the brake pads through the holes in the wheels **(see illustration)**. If necessary, remove the wheel trim. The thickness of the pad lining must not be less than the dimension given in the Specifications.

2 If the outer pads are worn near their limits, it is worthwhile checking the inner pads as well. Jack up vehicle and support it on axle stands (see *Jacking and vehicle support*). Remove the roadwheels.

3 Use a steel rule to check the thickness of the brake pads, and compare with the minimum thickness given in the Specifications **(see illustration)**.

4 For a comprehensive check, the brake pads should be removed and cleaned. The operation of the caliper can then also be checked, and the condition of the brake disc itself can be fully examined on both sides. Refer to Chapter 9.

5 If any pad's friction material is worn to the specified minimum thickness or less, all four pads at the front or rear, as applicable, must be renewed as a set.

6 On completion of the check, refit the road-wheels and lower the vehicle to the ground.

Rear drum brakes

7 Chock the front wheels, then jack up the rear of the vehicle and support it on axle stands (see *Jacking and vehicle support*).

8 For a quick check, the thickness of friction material remaining on one of the brake shoes can be observed through the hole in the brake backplate which is exposed by prising out the rubber sealing grommet. If a rod of the same diameter as the specified minimum friction material thickness is placed against the shoe friction material, the amount of wear can be assessed. A torch or inspection light will probably be required. If the friction material on any shoe is worn down to the specified minimum thickness or less, all four shoes must be renewed as a set.

9 For a comprehensive check, the brake drum should be removed and cleaned. This will allow the wheel cylinders to be checked, and the condition of the brake drum itself to be fully examined (see Chapter 9).

10 On completion of the check, refit the roadwheels where removed, and lower the vehicle to the ground.

5   Resetting the service interval display

1 After all necessary maintenance work has been completed, the service interval display must be reset. Skoda technicians use a special dedicated instrument to do this, and a print-out is then put in the vehicle service record. It is possible for the owner to reset the display as described in the following paragraphs, but note that on models with 'LongLife' service intervals, there is no distinction between the PR codes QG1 and QG2. If there is any doubt, have the display reset by a Skoda dealership using the special dedicated instrument.

4.3 The thickness (a) of the brake pads must not be less than the specified amount

2 To reset the standard display manually, switch off the ignition, then press and hold down the trip reset button beneath the speedometer. Switch on the ignition and observe the service interval, then hold the button down for 10 seconds until '- - -' appears followed by the trip readout. If the 'Oil' and 'Insp' intervals were reached at the same time, depress the button again for 10 seconds to reset the remaining interval.

3 To reset the LongLife display manually, switch off the ignition, then press and hold down the trip reset button beneath the speedometer. Switch on the ignition and release the reset button, and note that the relevant service will appear in the display. Turn the reset button clockwise, and the display will now return to normal. Switch off the ignition to complete the resetting procedure. Do not zero the display otherwise incorrect readings will be shown.

4 Note that for models using the LongLife interval QG1, the procedure will automatically reset the schedule to an amended LongLife interval (QG2) in which oil renewal and brake pad checks are based on distance/time while every other system remains LongLife. To have the display reset to the full LongLife schedule (QG1), it is necessary to take the vehicle to a Skoda dealer who will use a special instrument to encode the on-board computer.

'INSP service' on display

6   Exhaust system check

1 With the engine cold (at least an hour after the vehicle has been driven), check the complete exhaust system from the engine to the end of the tailpipe. The exhaust system is most easily checked with the vehicle raised on a hoist, or supported on axle stands, so that the exhaust components are readily visible and accessible (see *Jacking and vehicle support*).

2 Check the exhaust pipes and connections for evidence of leaks, severe corrosion and damage. Make sure that all brackets and mountings are in good condition, and that all relevant nuts and bolts are tight. Leakage at any of the joints or in other parts of the system will usually show up as a black sooty stain in the vicinity of the leak.

3 Rattles and other noises can often be traced to the exhaust system, especially the brackets and mountings. Try to move the pipes and silencers. If the components are able to come into contact with the body or suspension parts, secure the system with new mountings. Otherwise separate the joints (if possible) and twist the pipes as necessary to provide additional clearance.

7   Hose and fluid leak check

1 Visually inspect the engine joint faces, gaskets and seals for any signs of water or oil leaks. Pay particular attention to the areas around the camshaft cover, cylinder head, oil

filter and sump joint faces. Bear in mind that, over a period of time, some very slight seepage from these areas is to be expected – what you are really looking for is any indication of a serious leak. Should a leak be found, renew the offending gasket or oil seal by referring to the appropriate Chapters in this manual.

2 Also check the security and condition of all the engine-related pipes and hoses. Ensure that all cable-ties or securing clips are in place and in good condition. Clips which are broken or missing can lead to chafing of the hoses, pipes or wiring, which could cause more serious problems in the future.

3 Carefully check the radiator hoses and heater hoses along their entire length. Renew any hose which is cracked, swollen or deteriorated. Cracks will show up better if the hose is squeezed. Pay close attention to the hose clips that secure the hoses to the cooling system components. Hose clips can pinch and puncture hoses, resulting in cooling system leaks.

4 Inspect all the cooling system components (hoses, joint faces, etc) for leaks (see Haynes Hint). Where any problems of this nature are found on system components, renew the component or gasket with reference to Chapter 3.

5 Where applicable, inspect the automatic transmission fluid cooler hoses for leaks or deterioration.

6 With the vehicle raised, inspect the petrol tank and filler neck for punctures, cracks and other damage. The connection between the filler neck and tank is especially critical. Sometimes a rubber filler neck or connecting hose will leak due to loose retaining clamps or deteriorated rubber.

7 Carefully check all rubber hoses and metal fuel lines leading away from the petrol tank. Check for loose connections, deteriorated hoses, crimped lines, and other damage. Pay particular attention to the vent pipes and hoses, which often loop up around the filler neck and can become blocked or crimped. Follow the lines to the front of the vehicle, carefully inspecting them all the way. Renew damaged sections as necessary.

8 From within the engine compartment, check the security of all fuel hose attachments and pipe unions, and inspect the fuel hoses and vacuum hoses for kinks, chafing and deterioration.

9 Where applicable, check the condition of the power steering fluid hoses and pipes.

8 Auxiliary drivebelt check

1 Apply the handbrake, then jack up the front of the vehicle and support it on axle stands (see Jacking and vehicle support).

2 Using a socket on the crankshaft pulley bolt, turn the engine slowly clockwise so that the full length of the auxiliary drivebelt can be examined. Look for cracks, splitting and fraying on the surface of the belt; check

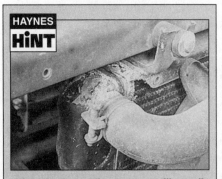

HAYNES HiNT

A leak in the cooling system will usually show up as white- or rust-coloured deposits on the area adjoining the leak.

also for signs of glazing (shiny patches) and separation of the belt plies. Use a mirror to check the underside of the drivebelt (see illustration). If damage or wear is visible, or if there are traces of oil or grease on it, the belt should be renewed (see Section 26).

9 Antifreeze check

1 The cooling system should be filled with the recommended G12 antifreeze and corrosion protection fluid – do not mix this antifreeze with any other type. Over a period of time, the concentration of fluid may be reduced due to topping-up (this can be avoided by topping-up with the correct antifreeze mixture – see Specifications) or fluid loss. If loss of coolant has been evident, it is important to make the necessary repair before adding fresh fluid.

2 With the engine cold, carefully remove the cap from the expansion tank. If the engine is not completely cold, place a cloth rag over the cap before removing it, and remove it slowly to allow any pressure to escape.

3 Antifreeze checkers are available from car accessory shops. Draw some coolant from the expansion tank and observe how many plastic balls are floating in the checker. Usually, 2 or 3 balls must be floating for the correct concentration of antifreeze, but follow the manufacturer's instructions.

4 If the concentration is incorrect, it will be

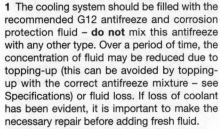

8.2 Checking the underside of the auxiliary drivebelt with a mirror

necessary to either withdraw some coolant and add antifreeze, or alternatively drain the old coolant and add fresh coolant of the correct concentration (see Section 31).

10 Brake hydraulic circuit check

1 Check the entire brake hydraulic circuit for leaks and damage. Start by checking the master cylinder in the engine compartment. At the same time, check the vacuum servo unit and ABS units for signs of fluid leakage.

2 Raise the front and rear of the vehicle and support it on axle stands (see Jacking and vehicle support). Check the rigid hydraulic brake lines for corrosion and damage.

3 At the front of the vehicle, check that the flexible hydraulic hoses to the calipers are not twisted or chafing on any of the surrounding suspension components. Turn the steering on full lock to make this check. Also check that the hoses are not brittle or cracked.

4 Lower the vehicle to the ground after making the checks.

11 Headlight beam adjustment

1 Accurate adjustment of the headlight beam is only possible using optical beam-setting equipment, and this work should therefore be carried out by a Skoda dealer or service station with the necessary facilities.

2 Basic adjustments can be carried out in an emergency, and further details are given in Chapter 12.

12 Pollen filter element renewal

1 The pollen filter is located on the heater assembly, and is removed into the passenger footwell – on RHD models it is on the left-hand side, and on LHD models it is on the right-hand side.

2 Reach under the glovebox, and press back the retaining catches of the pollen filter.

3 Withdraw the filter downwards from the heater assembly, and remove from inside the car.

4 Separate the filter from the frame.

5 Fit the new filter to the frame, then insert it into the heater assembly until the catches lock the frame.

13 Manual transmission oil level check

1 Park the car on a level surface. For improved access to the filler/level plug, apply the handbrake, then jack up the front of the

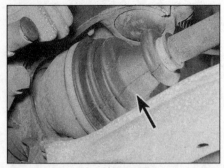

15.1 Check the condition of the driveshaft gaiters (arrowed)

vehicle and support it on axle stands (see *Jacking and vehicle support*), but note that the rear of the vehicle should also be raised to ensure an accurate level check. The oil level must be checked before the car is driven, or at least 5 minutes after the engine has been switched off. If the oil is checked immediately after driving the car, some of the oil will remain distributed around the transmission components, resulting in an inaccurate level reading.

2 As applicable, undo the retaining screws and remove the engine undershield(s). Wipe clean the area around the transmission filler/level plug which is situated in the following location:

a) *1.2 litre engines and 1.4 litre DOHC engines (02T transmission) – the filler/level plug is situated on the rear, inner face of the transmission, above the engine rear mounting/torque link.*

b) *1.4 litre OHV engines (002 transmission) – the filler/level plug is situated on the front, left-hand end of the transmission.*

3 The oil level should reach the lower edge of the filler/level hole. A certain amount of oil will have gathered behind the filler/level plug, and will trickle out when it is removed; this does **not** necessarily indicate that the level is correct. To ensure that a true level is established, wait until the initial trickle has stopped, then add oil as necessary until a trickle of new oil can be seen emerging. The level will be correct when the flow ceases; use only good-quality oil of the specified type.

4 If the transmission has been overfilled so that oil flows out when the filler/level plug is

16.4 Check for wear in the hub bearings by grasping the wheel and trying to rock it

removed, check that the car is completely level (front-to-rear and side-to-side), and allow the surplus to drain off into a suitable container.

5 When the oil level is correct, refit the filler/level plug and tighten it to the specified torque. Wipe off any spilt oil then refit the engine undershield(s), tighten the retaining screws securely, and lower the car to the ground.

14 Underbody protection check

Raise and support the vehicle on axle stands (see *Jacking and vehicle support*). Using an electric torch or lead light, inspect the entire underside of the vehicle, paying particular attention to the wheel arches. Look for any damage to the flexible underbody coating, which may crack or flake off with age, leading to corrosion. Also check that the wheel arch liners are securely attached with any clips provided – if they come loose, dirt may get in behind the liners and defeat their purpose. If there is any damage to the underseal, or any corrosion, it should be repaired before the damage gets too serious.

15 Driveshaft check

1 With the vehicle raised and securely supported on stands, slowly rotate the roadwheel. Inspect the condition of the outer constant velocity (CV) joint rubber gaiters, squeezing the gaiters to open out the folds. Check for signs of cracking, splits or deterioration of the rubber, which may allow the grease to escape, and lead to water and grit entry into the joint. Also check the security and condition of the retaining clips. Repeat these checks on the inner joints **(see illustration)**. If any damage or deterioration is found, the gaiters should be renewed (see Chapter 8).

2 At the same time, check the general condition of the CV joints themselves by first holding the driveshaft and attempting to rotate the wheel. Repeat this check by holding the inner joint and attempting to rotate the driveshaft. Any appreciable movement indicates wear in the joints, wear in the driveshaft splines, or a loose driveshaft retaining nut.

16 Steering and suspension check

1 Raise the front and rear of the vehicle, and securely support it on axle stands (see *Jacking and vehicle support*).

2 Visually inspect the track rod end balljoint dust cover, the lower front suspension balljoint dust cover, and the steering rack-and-pinion

gaiters for splits, chafing or deterioration. Any wear of these components will cause loss of lubricant, together with dirt and water entry, resulting in rapid deterioration of the balljoints or steering gear.

3 Check the power steering fluid hoses for chafing or deterioration, and the pipe and hose unions for fluid leaks. Also check for signs of fluid leakage under pressure from the steering gear rubber gaiters, which would indicate failed fluid seals within the steering gear.

4 Grasp the roadwheel at the 12 o'clock and 6 o'clock positions, and try to rock it **(see illustration)**. Very slight free play may be felt, but if the movement is appreciable, further investigation is necessary to determine the source. Continue rocking the wheel while an assistant depresses the footbrake. If the movement is now eliminated or significantly reduced, it is likely that the hub bearings are at fault. If the free play is still evident with the footbrake depressed, then there is wear in the suspension joints or mountings.

5 Now grasp the wheel at the 9 o'clock and 3 o'clock positions, and try to rock it as before. Any movement felt now may again be caused by wear in the hub bearings or the steering track rod balljoints. If the inner or outer balljoint is worn, the visual movement will be obvious.

6 Using a large screwdriver or flat bar, check for wear in the suspension mounting bushes by levering between the relevant suspension component and its attachment point. Some movement is to be expected as the mountings are made of rubber, but excessive wear should be obvious. Also check the condition of any visible rubber bushes, looking for splits, cracks or contamination of the rubber.

7 With the car standing on its wheels, have an assistant turn the steering wheel back-and-forth about an eighth of a turn each way. There should be very little, if any, lost movement between the steering wheel and roadwheels. If this is not the case, closely observe the joints and mountings previously described, but in addition check the steering column universal joints for wear, and the rack-and-pinion steering gear itself.

8 Check for any signs of fluid leakage around the front suspension struts and rear shock absorber. Should any fluid be noticed, the suspension strut or shock absorber is defective internally, and should be renewed. **Note:** *Suspension struts/shock absorbers should always be renewed in pairs on the same axle to ensure correct vehicle handling.*

9 The efficiency of the suspension strut/shock absorber may be checked by bouncing the vehicle at each corner. Generally speaking, the body will return to its normal position and stop after being depressed. If it rises and returns on a rebound, the suspension strut/shock absorber is probably suspect. Examine also the suspension strut/shock absorber upper and lower mountings for any signs of wear.

17 Battery check

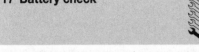

1 The battery is located in the front, left-hand corner of the engine compartment. Where a heat protective jacket is fitted, unclip the cover and remove the jacket to gain access to the battery **(see illustration)**.

2 Where necessary, open the fuse holder plastic cover (squeeze together the locking lugs to release the cover) to gain access to the battery positive (+) terminal and fuse holder connections.

3 Check that both battery terminals and all the fuse holder connections are securely attached and are free from corrosion. **Note:** *Before disconnecting the terminals from the battery, refer to 'Disconnecting the battery' in the Reference Chapter at the end of this manual.*

4 Check the battery casing for signs of damage or cracking and check the battery retaining clamp bolt is securely tightened. If the battery casing is damaged in any way the battery must be renewed (see Chapter 5A).

5 If the vehicle is not fitted with a sealed-for-life maintenance-free battery, check the electrolyte level is between the MAX and MIN level markings on the battery casing. If topping-up is necessary, remove the battery (see Chapter 5A) from the vehicle then remove the cell caps/cover (as applicable). Using distilled water, top the electrolyte level of each cell up to the MAX level mark then securely refit the cell caps/cover. Ensure the battery has not been overfilled then refit the battery to the vehicle (see Chapter 5A).

6 Some models are fitted with a battery with a 'magic eye' which shows the state of the battery and level of electrolyte. The 'magic eye' is located on the top of the battery, near the negative terminal. If the eye is green, the battery is in good condition and charged up. If the eye is black, the battery is flat and should be charged. If the eye is colourless or yellow, the electrolyte is low and in a critical condition, and should be topped-up with distilled water. If charging the battery does not return the eye to green, the battery should be scrapped.

7 On completion of the check, clip the cover securely back onto the fuse holder and close up the insulator cover (where fitted).

18 Hinge and lock lubrication

1 Lubricate the hinges of the bonnet, doors and tailgate with a light general-purpose oil. Similarly, lubricate all latches, locks and lock strikers. At the same time, check the security and operation of all the locks, adjusting them if necessary (see Chapter 11).

2 Lightly lubricate the bonnet release mechanism and cable with a suitable grease.

19 Airbag unit check

Inspect the exterior condition of the airbag(s) for signs of damage or deterioration. If an airbag shows signs of damage, it must be renewed (see Chapter 12). Note that it is not permissible to attach any stickers to the surface of the airbag, as this may affect the deployment of the unit.

20 Windscreen/tailgate/headlight washer system check

1 Check that each of the washer jet nozzles are clear and that each nozzle provides a strong jet of washer fluid.

2 The tailgate jet should be aimed to spray at the centre of the screen, using a pin.

3 The windscreen washer jet nozzles are preset by the manufacturer and cannot be adjusted.

4 The headlight inner jet should be aimed slightly above the horizontal centreline of the headlight, and the outer jet should be aimed slightly below the centreline.

5 Especially during the winter months, make sure that the washer fluid frost concentration is sufficient.

21 Engine management self-diagnosis memory fault check

This work should be carried out by a Skoda dealer or diagnostic specialist using special equipment. The diagnostic socket is located behind a hinged cover beneath the driver's side of the facia.

22 Sunroof check and lubrication

1 Check the operation of the sunroof, and leave it in the fully open position.

2 Wipe clean the guide rails on each side of the sunroof opening, then apply lubricant to them. Skoda recommend using lubricant spray G 052 778.

23 Road test and exhaust emissions check

Instruments and electrical equipment

1 Check the operation of all instruments and electrical equipment including the air conditioning system.

2 Make sure that all instruments read correctly,

17.1 Removing the battery cover

and switch on all electrical equipment in turn, to check that it functions properly.

Steering and suspension

3 Check for any abnormalities in the steering, suspension, handling or road 'feel'.

4 Drive the vehicle, and check that there are no unusual vibrations or noises which may indicate wear in the driveshafts, wheel bearings, etc.

5 Check that the steering feels positive, with no excessive 'sloppiness', or roughness, and check for any suspension noises when cornering and driving over bumps.

Drivetrain

6 Check the performance of the engine, clutch (where applicable), gearbox/transmission and driveshafts.

7 Listen for any unusual noises from the engine, clutch and gearbox/transmission.

8 Make sure the engine runs smoothly at idle, and there is no hesitation on accelerating.

9 Check that, where applicable, the clutch action is smooth and progressive, that the drive is taken up smoothly, and that the pedal travel is not excessive. Also listen for any noises when the clutch pedal is depressed.

10 On manual gearbox models, check that all gears can be engaged smoothly without noise, and that the gear lever action is smooth and not abnormally vague or 'notchy'.

11 On automatic transmission models, make sure that all gearchanges occur smoothly, without snatching, and without an increase in engine speed between changes. Check that all the gear positions can be selected with the vehicle at rest. If any problems are found, they should be referred to a Skoda dealer.

12 Listen for a metallic clicking sound from the front of the vehicle, as the vehicle is driven slowly in a circle with the steering on full-lock. Carry out this check in both directions. If a clicking noise is heard, this indicates wear in a driveshaft joint, in which case renew the joint if necessary.

Braking system

13 Make sure that the vehicle does not pull to one side when braking, and that the wheels do not lock when braking hard.

14 Check that there is no vibration through the steering when braking.

15 Check that the handbrake operates correctly without excessive movement of the lever, and that it holds the vehicle stationary on a slope.

16 Test the operation of the brake servo unit as follows. With the engine off, depress the footbrake four or five times to exhaust the vacuum. Hold the brake pedal depressed, then start the engine. As the engine starts, there should be a noticeable 'give' in the brake pedal as vacuum builds-up. Allow the engine to run for at least two minutes, and then switch it off. If the brake pedal is depressed now, it should be possible to detect a hiss from the servo as the pedal is depressed. After about four or five applications, no further hissing should be heard, and the pedal should feel considerably harder.

17 Under controlled emergency braking, the pulsing of the ABS unit must be felt at the footbrake pedal.

Exhaust emissions check

18 Although not part of the manufacturer's maintenance schedule, this check will normally be carried out on a regular basis according to the country the vehicle is operated in. Currently in the UK, exhaust emissions testing is included as part of the annual MOT test after the vehicle is 3 years old. In Germany the test is made when the vehicle is 3 years old, then repeated every 2 years.

Every 40 000 miles or 4 years

24 Air filter element renewal

1.2 litre engines

1 The air filter element is incorporated into the engine top cover.

2 On engine code AWY, disconnect the inlet hose from the lock carrier on the front of the engine compartment, then lift the engine top cover from the rubber grommets and disconnect the vacuum and crankcase ventilation hoses **(see illustrations)**.

3 On engine codes AZQ and BME, lift the engine top cover from the rubber grommets, disconnect the crankcase ventilation hose by compressing the adapter, then disconnect the vacuum hose.

4 With the top cover upside down on the bench, undo the screws and remove the cover, then withdraw the air filter element **(see illustrations)**.

5 Fit the new air filter element, ensuring that the edges are securely seated.

6 Refit the cover and tighten the screws.

7 Reconnect the hoses then press the top cover into the rubber grommets. Reconnect the inlet hose on engine code AWY.

1.4 litre

OHV engines

8 Undo the screws and lift the cover from the air filter housing located on the left-hand rear corner of the engine compartment **(see illustration)**.

9 Note how the element is fitted, then remove it **(see illustration)**.

10 Remove any debris and wipe clean the interior of the housing.

11 Fit the new air filter element in position, ensuring that the edges are securely seated.

12 Refit the cover and secure with the screws.

24.2a Disconnecting the vacuum hose . . .

24.2b . . . and crankcase ventilation hose

24.4a Undo the screws . . .

24.4b . . . and release the clips to remove the air filter housing . . .

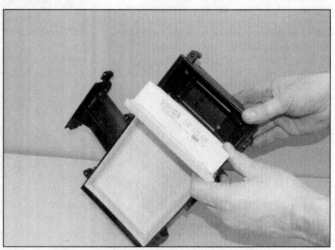

24.4c . . . then remove the air filter element –
1.2 litre engines

24.8a Undo the screws . . .

24.8b . . . and remove the cover . . .

24.9 . . . then remove the air filter element

DOHC engines

13 The air filter element is incorporated into the engine top cover.

14 Lift the engine top cover from the rubber grommets and disconnect the hoses as necessary.

15 With the top cover upside down on the bench, undo the screws and remove the cover, then withdraw the air filter element and gasket. Check the gasket for condition and renew if necessary.

16 Fit the gasket and the new air filter element, ensuring that the edges are securely seated.

17 Refit the cover and tighten the screws.

18 Reconnect the hoses then press the top cover into the rubber grommets.

25 Spark plug renewal

1 The correct functioning of the spark plugs is vital for the correct running and efficiency of the engine. It is essential that the plugs fitted are appropriate for the engine (a suitable type is specified at the beginning of this Chapter). If this type is used and the engine is in good condition, the spark plugs should not need attention between scheduled renewal intervals. Spark plug cleaning is rarely necessary, and should not be attempted unless specialised equipment is available, as damage can easily be caused to the firing ends.

1.2 litre engine

2 Remove the engine top cover.

3 The HT coils must now be pulled from the tops of the spark plugs. Skoda technicians use a special tool to do this as the coils are very tight in their holders, however, a length of strong welding rod or similar, bent at right-angles at one end, will do the task. Hook the rod under the wiring connector/HT coil then pull directly upwards **(see illustrations)**.

1.4 litre engine

OHV engines

4 Remove the engine top cover.

5 Disconnect the wiring from the HT coil module located on the front of the engine.

6 Undo the screws and carefully pull the module from the tops of the spark plugs.

Engine codes BBY and BBZ

7 Remove the engine top cover. The HT coils must now be pulled from the tops of the spark plugs. Skoda technicians use a special tool to do this as the coils are very tight in their holders, however, a length of strong welding rod or similar, bent at right-angles at one end, will do the task. Hook the rod under the wiring connector/HT coil then pull directly upwards **(see illustrations 25.3a and 25.3b)**.

Engine codes AUA and AUB

8 Remove the engine top cover. Disconnect the HT leads from the spark plugs, taking care to pull on the connectors and not the leads.

All engines

9 It is advisable to remove the dirt from the spark plug recesses using a clean brush, vacuum cleaner or compressed air before removing the plugs, to prevent dirt dropping into the cylinders.

10 Unscrew the plugs using a spark plug spanner, suitable box spanner or a deep socket and extension bar **(see illustration)**. Keep the socket aligned with the spark plug – if it is forcibly moved to one side, the ceramic insulator may be broken off. The use of a universal joint socket will be helpful. As each plug is removed, examine it as follows.

11 Examination of the spark plugs will give a good indication of the condition of the engine. If the insulator nose of the spark plug is clean and white, with no deposits, this is indicative of a weak mixture or too hot a plug (a hot plug transfers heat away from the electrode slowly, a cold plug transfers heat away quickly).

12 If the tip and insulator nose are covered with hard black-looking deposits, then this is indicative that the mixture is too rich. Should the plug be black and oily, then it is likely that the engine is fairly worn, as well as the mixture being too rich.

13 If the insulator nose is covered with light tan to greyish-brown deposits, then the mixture is correct and it is likely that the engine is in good condition.

14 The spark plug electrode gap is of considerable importance as, if it is too large or too small, the size of the spark and its efficiency will be seriously impaired. On

25.3a Use a bent rod to release the HT coils . . .

25.3b . . . then remove them from the cylinder head

25.10 Removing the spark plugs – 1.2 litre engines

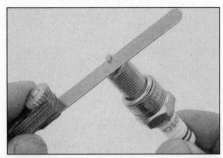

25.15a If single electrode plugs are being fitted, check the electrode gap using a feeler gauge . . .

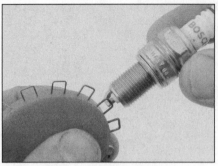

25.15b . . . or a wire gauge . . .

25.16 . . . and if necessary adjust the gap by bending the electrode

HAYNES HiNT

It is very often difficult to insert spark plugs into their holes without cross-threading them. To avoid this possibility, fit a short length of rubber hose over the end of the spark plug. The flexible hose acts as a universal joint to help align the plug with the plug thread, the hose will slip on the spark plug, preventing thread damage to the aluminium cylinder head.

engines fitted with multi-electrode spark plugs, it is recommended that the plugs are renewed rather than attempting to adjust the gaps. On other spark plugs, the gap should be set to the value given by the manufacturer.

15 To set the gap on single electrode plugs, measure it with a feeler blade and then bend open, or closed, the outer plug electrode until the correct gap is achieved. The centre electrode should never be bent, as this may crack the insulator and cause plug failure, if

nothing worse. If using feeler blades, the gap is correct when the appropriate-size blade is a firm sliding fit **(see illustrations)**.

16 Special spark plug electrode gap adjusting tools are available from most motor accessory shops, or from some spark plug manufacturers **(see illustration)**.

17 Before fitting the spark plugs, check that the threaded connector sleeves are tight, and that the plug exterior surfaces and threads are clean. It's often difficult to screw in new spark plugs without cross-threading them – this can be avoided using a piece of rubber hose **(see Haynes Hint)**.

18 Remove the rubber hose (if used), and tighten the plug to the specified torque using the spark plug socket and a torque wrench. Refit the remaining spark plugs in the same manner.

19 Reconnect the HT leads/ignition coils using a reversal of the removal procedure, then refit the engine top cover.

26 Auxiliary drivebelt check and renewal

Checking

1 See Section 8.

Renewal

2 For improved access, apply the handbrake, then jack up the front of the vehicle and support it on axle stands (see *Jacking and*

vehicle support). Remove the right-hand front roadwheel and wheelarch liner.

3 On 1.2 litre engines, lever off the cover (where fitted) from the tensioner pulley, then use a Torx key or spanner (as applicable) to turn the pulley anti-clockwise against the tension spring **(see illustration)**. If necessary, the tensioner may be retained with a drill bit inserted through the hole in the pulley arm and body.

4 On 1.4 litre OHV engines *with* air conditioning, an automatic tensioner is fitted to the alternator/compressor bracket on the right-hand front of the engine. The tensioner is released by inserting a tool (T30022) through the rear of the tensioner spring housing. If this tool is not available, use an adjustable spanner to turn the tensioner arm.

5 On 1.4 litre OHV engines *without* air conditioning, the auxiliary drivebelt is tensioned by moving the alternator on its mounting. Loosen the alternator pivot bolt, link bolt and link pivot bolt, then swivel the alternator in towards the engine **(see illustration)**.

6 On 1.4 litre DOHC engines *with* air conditioning, use a spanner to turn the tensioner central bolt clockwise to release the tension on the drivebelt **(see illustration)**.

7 On 1.4 litre DOHC engines *without* air conditioning, a tensioner spring is fitted between the alternator and bracket to tension the drivebelt. Loosen the upper pivot bolt and lower tension bolt, then swivel the alternator towards the engine to release the tension on the drivebelt.

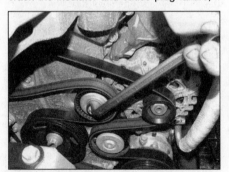

26.3 Use a spanner to turn the tensioner anti-clockwise in order to release the auxiliary drivebelt – 1.2 litre engines

26.5 Loosen the alternator pivot and adjustment bolts to remove the auxiliary drivebelt – 1.4 litre OHV engine without air conditioning

26.6 Auxiliary drivebelt removal – 1.4 litre DOHC engine with air conditioning

8 Note how the drivebelt is routed, then remove it from the crankshaft pulley, alternator pulley, power steering pump pulley, and air conditioning compressor pulley (where applicable).

9 On all engines except 1.4 litre engines *without* air conditioning, locate the new drivebelt on the pulleys, and release the tensioner. Check that the belt is located correctly in the multi-grooves in the pulleys.

10 On 1.4 litre OHV engines *without* air conditioning, locate the drivebelt around all the pulleys, ensuring that the belt ribs are engaged properly with the pulley grooves. Tighten the adjustment link nut and bolt hand-tight, so that the alternator can still be moved, then pull the alternator towards the front of the car to tension the drivebelt. Use a lever between the alternator and the cylinder block if necessary, but take care not to lever against any part of the engine which may be damaged. The drivebelt tension is correct when the belt can be deflected by 10 to 15 mm when depressed in the middle of its top run – between the alternator and coolant pump pulleys. When the drivebelt tension is correct, tighten the adjustment link nut and bolt, followed by the alternator mounting bolt.

11 On 1.4 litre DOHC engines *without* air conditioning, push the alternator towards the engine to locate the drivebelt on the pulley, then release it so that the spring tensions the drivebelt. Before tightening the mounting bolts, Skoda state that the engine must be cranked with the starter approximately 10 turns. To do this without starting the engine, disable the ignition system by disconnecting the wiring plug from the DIS ignition module (engine codes AUA and AUB) or ignition coils (engine codes BBY and BBZ). The drivebelt is now correctly tensioned. Tighten the lower mounting bolt followed by the upper mounting bolt to the specified torque.

12 Refit the wheelarch liner and roadwheel, and lower the vehicle to the ground.

27 Power steering hydraulic fluid level check

1 Turn the front roadwheels to the straight-ahead position without starting the engine. If the vehicle has been left standing for an hour or more, the power steering fluid will be cold (below 50°C), and the 'cold' level markings must be used. If, however, the engine is at normal temperature (above 50°C), the fluid will be hot, and the 'hot' level markings must be used.

2 The reservoir for the Electrically Powered Hydraulic Steering (EPHS) is located on the front left-hand corner of the engine compartment. **Note:** *On some models with a high capacity battery, the battery and tray must be removed in order to access the reservoir filler cap.* The fluid level is checked

27.2 Unscrew the cap from the hydraulic fluid reservoir

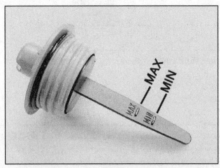

27.3b Alternative power steering cap markings

with the dipstick attached to the reservoir filler cap. Unscrew the cap from the hydraulic fluid reservoir, and wipe clean the integral dipstick with a clean cloth **(see illustration)**.

3 Screw on the cap hand-tight then unscrew it again and check the fluid level on the dipstick. The fluid level must be between the MIN (or lower) and MAX (or upper) marks **(see illustrations)**. If the fluid is cold (below 50°C), it must be at least above the lower level mark or MIN. If the fluid is hot (above 50°C), it must not be above the upper level mark or MAX.

4 If the level is above the maximum level mark, syphon off the excess amount. If it is below the minimum level mark, add the specified fluid as necessary *(see Lubricants and fluids)*, but in this case also check the system for leaks **(see illustration)**. On completion, screw on the cap and tighten. Refit the battery and tray where removed.

28 Automatic transmission fluid level check

Note: *An accurate fluid level check can only be made with the transmission fluid at a temperature of between 35°C and 45°C, and if it is not possible to ascertain this temperature, it is strongly recommended that the check be made by a Skoda dealer who will have the instrumentation to check the temperature and to check the transmission electronics for fault codes. Overfilling or underfilling adversely affects the function of the transmission.*

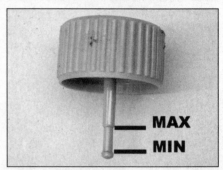

27.3a The power steering fluid level must be between the upper and lower marks

27.4 Topping-up the fluid level

1 Take the vehicle on a short journey to warm the transmission slightly (see Note at the start of this Section), then park the vehicle on level ground and engage P with the selector lever. Raise the front and rear of the vehicle and support it on axle stands (see *Jacking and vehicle support*), ensuring the vehicle is kept level. Undo the retaining screws and remove the engine undershield(s) to gain access to the base of the transmission unit.

2 Start the engine and run it at idle speed until the transmission fluid temperature reaches 35°C.

3 Unscrew the fluid level plug from the bottom of the transmission sump **(see illustration overleaf)**.

4 If fluid **continually** drips from the level tube as the fluid temperature increases, the fluid level is correct and does not need to be topped-up. Note that there will be some fluid already present in the level tube, and it will be necessary to observe when this amount has drained before making the level check. Make sure that the check is made before the fluid temperature reaches 45°C. Check the condition of the seal on the level plug and renew it if necessary. Refit the plug and tighten to the specified torque.

5 If no fluid drips from the level tube, even when the fluid temperature has reached 45°C, it will be necessary to add fluid as follows while the engine is still running.

6 Using a screwdriver, lever off the cap from the filler tube on the front of the transmission. **Note:** *The locking device will be permanently damaged and a new cap must be obtained.*

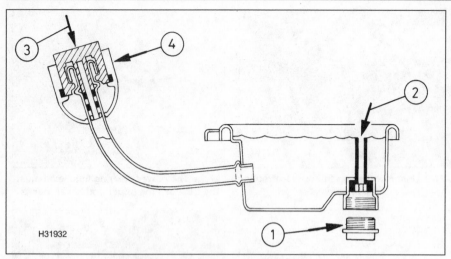

28.3 Automatic transmission fluid level check

1 Level plug   2 Level tube   3 Filler cap   4 Retaining clip

7 With the cap removed, pull out the filler tube plug then add the specified fluid until it drips out of the level tube. Check the condition of the seal on the level plug and renew it if necessary. Refit the plug and tighten to the specified torque.

8 Refit the filler tube plug and the new cap.

9 Switch off the ignition then refit the engine undershield(s), tighten the retaining screws securely, and lower the vehicle to the ground.

10 Frequent need for topping-up indicates that there is a leak, which should be found and corrected before it becomes serious.

Every 60 000 miles

29 Timing belt renewal

Note: This procedure only applies to 1.4 litre DOHC engines.

1 Refer to Chapter 2C.

Every 2 years

30 Brake (and clutch) fluid renewal

⚠️ **Warning: Brake hydraulic fluid can harm your eyes and damage painted surfaces, so use extreme caution when handling and pouring it. Do not use fluid that has been standing open for some time, as it absorbs moisture from the air. Excess moisture can cause a dangerous loss of braking effectiveness.**

1 The procedure is similar to that for the bleeding of the hydraulic system as described in Chapter 9, except that the brake fluid reservoir should be emptied by syphoning, using a clean poultry baster or similar before starting, and allowance should be made for the old fluid to be expelled when bleeding a section of the circuit. Since the clutch hydraulic system also uses fluid from the brake system reservoir, it should also be bled at the same time by referring to Chapter 6, Section 2.

2 Working as described in Chapter 9, open the first bleed screw in the sequence, and pump the brake pedal gently until nearly all the old fluid has been emptied from the master cylinder reservoir.

 HAYNES HiNT *Old hydraulic fluid is often much darker in colour than the new, making it easy to distinguish the two.*

3 Top-up to the MAX level with new fluid, and continue pumping until only the new fluid remains in the reservoir, and new fluid can be seen emerging from the bleed screw. Tighten the screw, and top the reservoir level up to the MAX level line.

4 Work through all the remaining bleed screws in the sequence until new fluid can be seen at all of them. Be careful to keep the master cylinder reservoir topped-up to above the MIN level at all times, or air may enter the system and greatly increase the length of the task.

5 When the operation is complete, check that all bleed screws are securely tightened, and that their dust caps are refitted. Wash off all traces of spilt fluid, and recheck the master cylinder reservoir fluid level.

6 On models with a manual transmission unit, once the brake fluid has been changed the clutch fluid should also be renewed. Referring to Chapter 6, bleed the clutch until new fluid is seen to be emerging from the slave cylinder bleed screw, keeping the master cylinder fluid level above the MIN level line at all times to prevent air entering the system. Once the new fluid emerges, securely tighten the bleed screw then disconnect and remove the bleeding equipment. Securely refit the dust cap then wash off all traces of spilt fluid.

7 On all models, ensure the master cylinder fluid level is correct (see *Weekly checks*) and thoroughly check the operation of the brakes and (where necessary) clutch before taking the car on the road.

31 Coolant renewal

Note: This work is not included in the Skoda schedule and should not be required if the recommended Skoda G12 LongLife coolant antifreeze/inhibitor is used. However, if standard antifreeze/inhibitor is used, the work should be carried out at the recommended interval.

⚠️ **Warning: Wait until the engine is cold before starting this procedure. Do not allow antifreeze to come in contact with your skin, or with the painted surfaces of the vehicle. Rinse off spills immediately with plenty of water. Never leave antifreeze lying around in an open container, or in a puddle in the driveway or on the garage floor. Children and pets are attracted by its sweet smell, but antifreeze can be fatal if ingested.**

Cooling system draining

1 With the engine completely cold, unscrew the expansion tank cap.

2 Firmly apply the handbrake then jack up the front of the vehicle and support it on axle stands (see *Jacking and vehicle support*). Undo the retaining screws and remove the engine undershield(s) to gain access to the base of the radiator.

3 Position a suitable container beneath the

coolant drain plug which is located in the bottom hose fitting to the left-hand bottom end of the radiator. Unscrew the drain plug and pull it out slightly (there is no need to remove it completely) and allow the coolant to drain into the container **(see illustration)**. If desired, a length of tubing can be fitted to the drain outlet to direct the flow of coolant during draining. Where no drain outlet is fitted to the hose end fitting, remove the retaining clip and disconnect the bottom hose from the radiator to drain the coolant (see Chapter 3).

4 On engines with an oil cooler, to fully drain the system, also disconnect one of the coolant hoses from the oil cooler which is located at the front of the cylinder block.

5 If the coolant has been drained for a reason other than renewal then, provided it is clean, it can be re-used.

6 Once all the coolant has drained, securely tighten the radiator drain plug or reconnect the bottom hose to the radiator (as applicable). Where necessary, also reconnect the coolant hose to the oil cooler and secure it in position with the retaining clip. Refit the undershield(s), tighten the retaining screws securely.

Cooling system flushing

7 If the recommended Skoda coolant has not been used and coolant renewal has been neglected, or if the antifreeze mixture has become diluted, the cooling system may gradually lose efficiency, as the coolant passages become restricted due to rust, scale deposits, and other sediment. The cooling system efficiency can be restored by flushing the system clean.

8 The radiator should be flushed separately from the engine, to avoid excess contamination.

Radiator flushing

9 To flush the radiator, first tighten the radiator drain plug.

10 Disconnect the top and bottom hoses and any other relevant hoses from the radiator (see Chapter 3).

11 Insert a garden hose into the radiator top inlet. Direct a flow of clean water through the radiator, and continue flushing until clean water emerges from the radiator bottom outlet.

12 If after a reasonable period the water still does not run clear, the radiator can be flushed with a good proprietary cleaning agent. It is

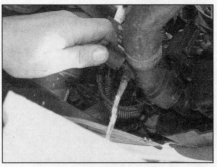

31.3 Unscrew the drain plug and allow the coolant to drain into the container

important that the manufacturer's instructions are followed carefully. If the contamination is particularly bad, insert the hose in the radiator bottom outlet, and reverse-flush the radiator.

Engine flushing

13 To flush the engine, remove the thermostat (see Chapter 3).

14 With the bottom hose disconnected from the radiator, insert a garden hose into the thermostat housing. Direct a clean flow of water through the engine, and continue flushing until clean water emerges from the radiator bottom hose.

15 When flushing is complete, refit the thermostat and reconnect the hoses (see Chapter 3).

Cooling system filling

16 Before attempting to fill the cooling system, ensure the drain plug is securely closed and make sure that all hoses are securely connected and their retaining clips are in good condition. If the recommended Skoda coolant is not being used, ensure that a suitable antifreeze mixture is used all year round, to prevent corrosion of the engine components (see following sub-Section).

17 Remove the coolant temperature sensor from the coolant distribution housing on the left-hand end of the cylinder head with reference to Chapter 3.

18 Remove the expansion tank filler cap and slowly fill the system with coolant **(see illustration)**, until bubble-free coolant runs from the temperature sensor hole, then refit the sensor immediately with reference to Chapter 3. Continue to fill the system until the level is up to the MAX level mark on the expansion tank. Help to bleed the air from the

31.18 Filling the cooling system

system by repeatedly squeezing the radiator bottom hose.

19 Refit the cap to the expansion tank, then run the engine at a fast idle speed until the cooling fan cuts in. Wait for the fan to stop then switch the engine off and allow the engine to cool.

20 When the engine has cooled, check the coolant level with reference to *Weekly checks*. Top-up the level if necessary, and refit the expansion tank cap.

Antifreeze mixture

21 If the recommended Skoda coolant is not being used, the antifreeze should always be renewed at the specified intervals. This is necessary not only to maintain the antifreeze properties, but also to prevent corrosion which would otherwise occur as the corrosion inhibitors become progressively less effective.

22 Always use an ethylene-glycol based antifreeze which is suitable for use in mixed-metal cooling systems. The quantity of antifreeze and levels of protection are indicated in the Specifications.

23 Before adding antifreeze, the cooling system should be completely drained, preferably flushed, and all hoses checked for condition and security.

24 After filling with antifreeze, a label should be attached to the expansion tank, stating the type and concentration of antifreeze used, and the date installed. Any subsequent topping-up should be made with the same type and concentration of antifreeze.

25 Do not use engine antifreeze in the windscreen/tailgate washer system, as it will damage the vehicle paintwork. A screenwash additive should be added to the washer system in the quantities stated on the bottle.

Notes

Chapter 1 Part B:
Routine maintenance and servicing – diesel models

Contents

Air filter element renewal 27
Airbag unit check 22
Antifreeze check 12
Auxiliary drivebelt check and renewal 29
Auxiliary drivebelt check 11
Battery check 20
Brake (and clutch) fluid renewal 33
Brake hydraulic circuit check 13
Brake pad/lining check 5
Coolant renewal 34
Driveshaft check 18
Engine management self-diagnosis memory fault check 24
Engine oil and filter renewal 3
Exhaust system check 7
Fuel filter renewal (vehicles using high sulphur diesel fuel) 10
Fuel filter renewal (vehicles using standard diesel fuel) 28
Fuel filter water draining (vehicles using high sulphur fuel) 4
Fuel filter water draining (vehicles using standard fuel) 9
Headlight beam adjustment 14
Hinge and lock lubrication 21
Hose and fluid leak check 8
Introduction 1
Manual transmission oil level check 16
Pollen filter element renewal 15
Power steering hydraulic fluid level check 30
Regular maintenance 2
Resetting the service interval display 6
Road test and exhaust emissions check 26
Steering and suspension check 19
Sunroof check and lubrication 25
Timing belt and tensioning roller renewal (engines with 'unit' injectors) 31
Timing belt and tensioning roller renewal (engines with injection pump) 32
Underbody protection check 17
Windscreen/tailgate/headlight washer system check 23

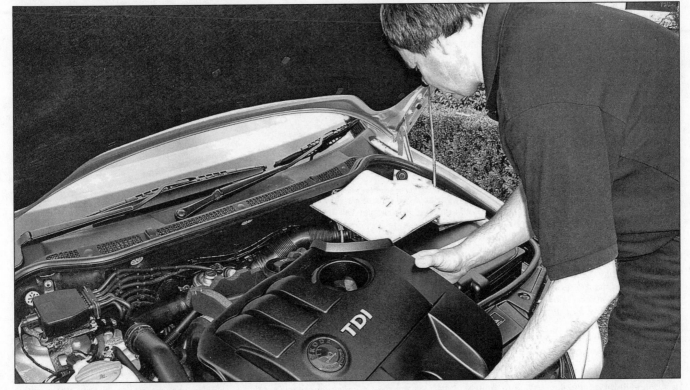

Degrees of difficulty

| Easy, suitable for novice with little experience | Fairly easy, suitable for beginner with some experience | Fairly difficult, suitable for competent DIY mechanic | Difficult, suitable for experienced DIY mechanic | Very difficult, suitable for expert DIY or professional |

Lubricants and fluids

Refer to the end of *Weekly checks* on page 0•18

Capacities

Engine oil (including filter)
1.4 litre engines . . . .   4.2 litres
1.9 litre engines . . . .   4.3 litres

Cooling system
1.4 litre engines . . . .   6.2 litres
1.9 litre:
    Engine code ASY . . . .   6.6 litres
    Engine codes ASZ and ATD . . . .   6.8 litres

Transmission
Manual transmission:
    Type 02T . . . .   1.9 litres
    Type 02R . . . .   2.0 litres

Fuel tank (approximate) . . . .   45 litres

Cooling system

Antifreeze mixture:
    40% antifreeze . . . .   Protection down to -25°C
    50% antifreeze . . . .   Protection down to -35°C
Note: *Refer to antifreeze manufacturer for latest recommendations.*

Brakes

Brake pad minimum thickness:
    Including backing plate:
        Front . . . .   7.0 mm
        Rear . . . .   7.6 mm
    Friction lining only:
        Front and rear . . . .   2.0 mm
Rear brake shoe friction material minimum thickness . . . .   1.5 mm

Torque wrench settings

	Nm	lbf ft
Alternator mounting bolt.	20	15
Manual gearbox filler/level plug	25	18
Roadwheel bolts.	120	89
Sump drain plug.	30	22

Maintenance schedule

The maintenance intervals in this manual are provided with the assumption that you, not the dealer, will be carrying out the work. These are the minimum intervals recommended by us for vehicles driven daily. If you wish to keep your vehicle in peak condition at all times, you may wish to perform some of these procedures more often. We encourage frequent maintenance, since it enhances the efficiency, performance and resale value of your vehicle.

When the vehicle is new, it should be serviced by a dealer service department, in order to preserve the factory warranty.

All Skoda models are equipped with a service interval display indicator in the instrument panel. Every time the engine is started the panel will illuminate for approximately 20 seconds with service information. With the standard fixed interval display, the service intervals are in accordance with specific distances and time periods. With the LongLife display, the service interval is variable. Once the service interval has been reached, the display will flash 'OIL service' for an oil change service or 'INSP service' for an inspection service.

For models using the LongLife schedule, the occurrence of either service reminder on the display unit will depend on how the vehicle is being used (number of starts, length of journeys, vehicle speeds, brake pad wear, bonnet opening frequency, fuel consumption, oil level and oil temperature). For example, if a vehicle is being used under extreme driving conditions, the service may occur at 10 000 miles, whereas, if the vehicle is being used under moderate driving conditions, it may occur at 20 000 miles, although the maximum length of time between INSP services is 2 years. It is important to realise that this system is completely variable according to how the vehicle is being used, and therefore the service should be carried out when indicated on the display. **Note:** *Models with the variable service interval system are equipped with an engine oil level sensor, brake pad wear indicator,* *battery with a 'magic eye' charge indicator, and a variable service indicator.*

The LongLife variable service intervals are only applicable to models with a PR number of QG1 or QG2 (shown in the vehicle Service Schedule booklet, on a service interval plate inside the luggage compartment or on the Next Service sticker located on the driver's door pillar). For QG1 vehicles, the engine oil change and all other maintenance procedures are at variable intervals, however, for QG2 vehicles, the engine oil change and brake pad check is carried out at fixed intervals but all other maintenance procedures are at variable intervals.

With the variable (LongLife) service interval on models with a PR number of QG1, the engine must **only** be filled with the recommended **LongLife** engine oil (see *Recommended lubricants and fluids*); on models with a PR number of QG2, standard engine oil can be used.

After completing a service, Skoda

technicians use a special instrument to reset the service display to the next service interval, and a print-out is put in the vehicle service record. The display can be reset by the owner as described in Section 6, but note that for models using the LongLife interval QG1, the procedure will automatically reset the schedule to an amended LongLife interval (QG2) in which oil renewal and brake pad checks are based on distance/time while every other system remains LongLife. To have the display reset to the full LongLife schedule (QG1), it is necessary to take the vehicle to a Skoda dealer who will use a special instrument to encode the on-board computer.

Every 250 miles or weekly

☐ Refer to *Weekly checks*

'OIL service' on display

☐ Renew the engine oil and filter (Section 3)

Note: *Frequent oil and filter changes are good for the engine. We recommend changing the oil at least once a year.*

☐ Fuel filter water draining* (Section 4)
☐ Check the front and rear brake pad thickness (Section 5)
☐ Reset the service interval display (Section 6)

* Only when using high sulphur diesel fuel not conforming to DIN EN 590 or when using RME fuel (diester)

'INSP service' on display

In addition to the items listed above, carry out the following:

☐ Check the condition of the exhaust system and its mountings (Section 7)
☐ Check all underbonnet components and hoses for fluid and oil leaks (Section 8)
☐ Fuel filter water draining* (Section 9)
☐ Renew the fuel filter** (Section 10)
☐ Check the condition of the auxiliary drivebelt (Section 11)
☐ Check the coolant antifreeze concentration (Section 12)
☐ Check the brake hydraulic circuit for leaks and damage (Section 13)
☐ Check the headlight beam adjustment (Section 14)
☐ Renew the pollen filter element (Section 15)
☐ Check the manual transmission oil level (Section 16)
☐ Check the underbody protection for damage (Section 17)
☐ Check the condition of the driveshafts (Section 18)
☐ Check the steering and suspension components for condition and security (Section 19)
☐ Check the battery condition, security and electrolyte level (Section 20)
☐ Lubricate all hinges and locks (Section 21)
☐ Check the condition of the airbag unit(s) (Section 22)
☐ Check the operation of the windscreen/tailgate/headlight washer system(s) (as applicable) (Section 23)

'INSP service' on display (continued)

☐ Check the engine management self-diagnosis memory for faults (Section 24)
☐ Check the operation of the sunroof and lubricate the guide rails (Section 25)
☐ Carry out a road test and check exhaust emissions (Section 26)

* Only when using diesel fuel conforming to DIN EN 590
** Only when using high sulphur diesel fuel not conforming to DIN EN 590 or when using RME fuel (diester)

Every 40 000 miles or 4 years, whichever comes first

Note: *Many dealers perform these tasks with every second INSP service.*

☐ Renew the air filter element (Section 27)
☐ Renew the fuel filter* (Section 28)
☐ Check the condition of the auxiliary drivebelt (Section 29)
☐ Check the power steering hydraulic fluid level (Section 30)

* Only when using diesel fuel conforming to DIN EN 590

Every 60 000 miles

☐ Renew the timing belt and tensioner roller on engines with 'unit' injectors, ie, without an injection pump (Section 31)

Every 80 000 miles

☐ Renew the timing belt and tensioner roller on engines with an injection pump, ie, without 'unit' injectors (Section 32)

Every 2 years

☐ Renew the brake (and clutch) fluid (Section 33)
☐ Renew the coolant* (Section 34)

** **Note:** This work is not included in the Skoda schedule and should not be required if the recommended Skoda G12 LongLife coolant antifreeze/inhibitor is used.*

Underbonnet view of a 1.4 litre model

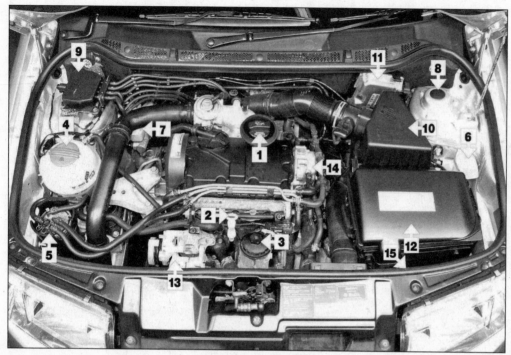

1 Engine oil filler cap
2 Engine oil dipstick
3 Oil filter
4 Coolant expansion tank
5 Fuel filter
6 Windscreen/headlight washer fluid reservoir
7 Master cylinder brake fluid reservoir
8 Front suspension strut upper mounting
9 Valve block
10 Air cleaner housing
11 Engine management ECU
12 Battery
13 Alternator
14 Brake vacuum pump
15 Power steering fluid reservoir

Front underbody view of a 1.4 litre model

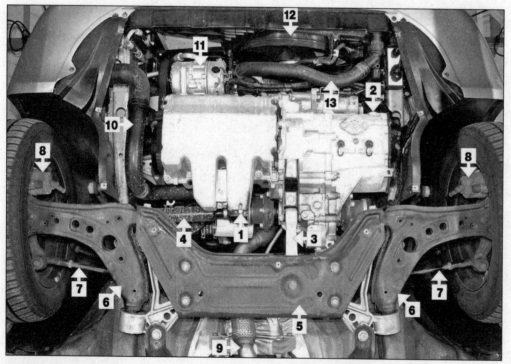

1 Sump drain plug
2 Manual transmission drain plug
3 Engine rear mounting/link
4 Driveshaft
5 Front suspension subframe
6 Front suspension lower arm
7 Steering track rod
8 Front brake caliper
9 Front exhaust pipe
10 Intercooler hose to turbocharger
11 Air conditioning compressor
12 Radiator electric cooling fan
13 Radiator bottom hose

Rear underbody view of a 1.4 litre model

1 Fuel tank
2 Rear axle assembly
3 Rear suspension coil spring
4 Rear shock absorber
5 Exhaust rear silencer
6 Rear axle assembly front mountings
7 Handbrake cables
8 Hydraulic brake line
9 Spare wheel well

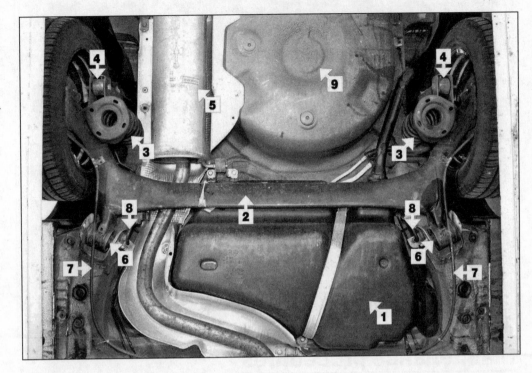

Underbonnet view of a 1.9 litre model

1 Engine oil filler cap
2 Engine oil dipstick
3 Oil filter
4 Coolant expansion tank
5 Fuel filter
6 Windscreen/headlight washer fluid reservoir
7 Master cylinder brake fluid reservoir
8 Alternator
9 Auxiliary drivebelt
10 Vacuum reservoir for inlet manifold flap valve
11 Brake vacuum pump
12 Air hose from intercooler to inlet manifold
13 Valve block
14 EGR valve
15 Air mass meter
16 Engine management ECU
17 Front suspension strut upper mounting
18 Air cleaner housing
19 Battery
20 Power steering fluid reservoir

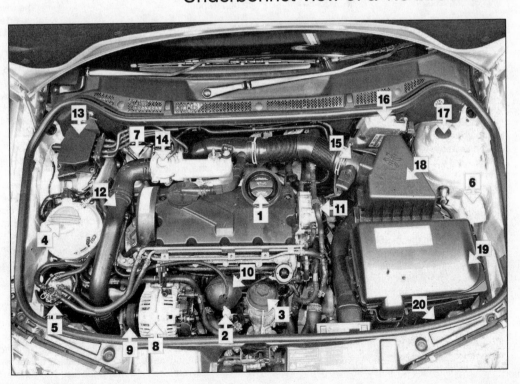

Front underbody view of a 1.9 litre model

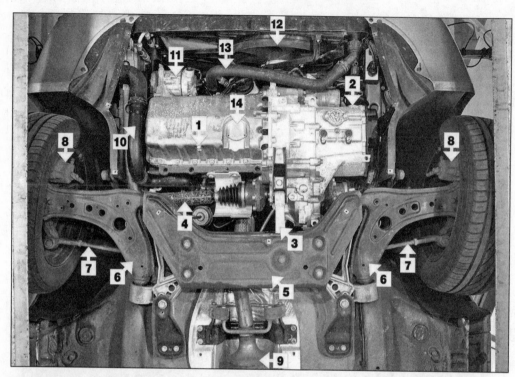

1 Sump drain plug
2 Manual transmission drain plug
3 Engine rear mounting/link
4 Driveshaft
5 Front suspension subframe
6 Front suspension lower arm
7 Steering track rod
8 Front brake caliper
9 Front exhaust pipe
10 Intercooler hose to turbocharger
11 Air conditioning compressor
12 Radiator electric cooling fan
13 Radiator bottom hose
14 Oil level/oil temperature sensor

Maintenance procedures

1 Introduction

This Chapter is designed to help the home mechanic maintain his/her vehicle for safety, economy, long life and peak performance.

The Chapter contains a master maintenance schedule, followed by Sections dealing specifically with each task in the schedule. Visual checks, adjustments, component renewal and other helpful items are included. Refer to the accompanying illustrations of the engine compartment and the underside of the vehicle for the locations of the various components.

Servicing your vehicle will provide a planned maintenance programme, which should result in a long and reliable service life. This is a comprehensive plan, so maintaining some items but not others will not produce the same results.

As you service your vehicle, you will discover that many of the procedures can – and should – be grouped together, because of the particular procedure being performed, or because of the proximity of two otherwise unrelated components to one another. For example, if the vehicle is raised for any reason, the exhaust can be inspected at the same time as the suspension and steering components.

The first step in this maintenance programme is to prepare yourself before the actual work begins. Read through all the Sections relevant to the work to be carried out, then make a list and gather all the parts and tools required. If a problem is encountered, seek advice from a parts specialist, or a dealer service department.

2 Regular maintenance

1 If, from the time the vehicle is new, the routine maintenance schedule is followed closely, and frequent checks are made of fluid levels and high-wear items, as suggested throughout this manual, the engine will be kept in relatively good running condition, and the need for additional work will be minimised.

2 It is possible that there will be times when the engine is running poorly due to the lack of regular maintenance. This is even more likely if a used vehicle, which has not received regular and frequent maintenance checks, is purchased. In such cases, additional work may need to be carried out, outside of the regular maintenance intervals.

3 If engine wear is suspected, a compression test (refer to Chapter 2D) will provide valuable information regarding the overall performance of the main internal components. Such a test can be used as a basis to decide on the extent of the work to be carried out. If, for example, a compression test indicates serious internal engine wear, conventional maintenance as described in this Chapter will not greatly improve the performance of the engine, and may prove a waste of time and money, unless extensive overhaul work is carried out first.

4 The following series of operations are those most often required to improve the performance of a generally poor-running engine:

Primary operations

a) Clean, inspect and test the battery (See 'Weekly checks').
b) Check all the engine-related fluids (See 'Weekly checks').
c) Drain the water from the fuel filter (Section 4).
d) Check the condition and tension of the auxiliary drivebelt (Section 11).
e) Check the condition of the air filter, and renew if necessary (Section 27).
f) Check the condition of all hoses, and check for fluid leaks (Section 8).

5 If the above operations do not prove fully effective, carry out the following secondary operations:

Secondary operations

All items listed under *Primary operations*, plus the following:
a) Check the charging system (see Chapter 5A).
b) Check the preheating system (see Chapter 5C).
c) Renew the fuel filter (Section 10) and check the fuel system (see Chapter 4B).

'OIL service' on display

3 Engine oil and filter renewal

1 Frequent oil and filter changes are the most important preventative maintenance procedures which can be undertaken by the DIY owner. As engine oil ages, it becomes diluted and contaminated, which leads to premature engine wear.
2 Before starting this procedure, gather all the necessary tools and materials. Also make

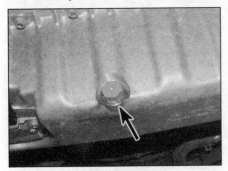

3.3 Sump drain plug

Keep the drain plug pressed into the sump while unscrewing it by hand the last couple of turns. As the plug releases, move it away sharply so the stream of oil issuing from the sump runs into the container, not up your sleeve.

sure that you have plenty of clean rags and newspapers handy, to mop-up any spills. Ideally, the engine oil should be warm, as it will drain better, and more built-up sludge will be removed with it. Take care, however, not to touch the exhaust or any other hot parts of the engine when working under the vehicle. To avoid any possibility of scalding, and to protect yourself from possible skin irritants and other harmful contaminants in used engine oils, it is advisable to wear gloves when carrying out this work. Access to the underside of the vehicle will be greatly improved if it can be raised on a lift, driven onto ramps, or jacked up and supported on axle stands (see *Jacking and vehicle support*). Whichever method is chosen, make sure that the vehicle remains level, or if it is at an angle, that the drain plug is at the lowest point. Undo the retaining screws and remove the engine undershield(s), then also remove the engine top cover where applicable.
3 Slacken the sump drain plug about half a turn. Position the draining container under the drain plug, then remove the plug completely **(see illustration and Haynes Hint)**. Recover the sealing ring from the drain plug.
4 Allow some time for the old oil to drain, noting that it may be necessary to reposition the container as the oil flow slows to a trickle.
5 After all the oil has drained, wipe off the drain plug with a clean rag, and fit a new sealing washer. Clean the area around the

drain plug opening, and refit the plug. Tighten the plug securely.
6 Remove the engine top cover and packing to gain access to the oil filter housing. Place absorbent cloths around the filter housing to catch any spilt oil.
7 Unscrew and remove the cap from the top of the oil filter housing using an oil filter strap or suitable spanner. Recover the large sealing ring from the cap, and the small sealing ring from the centre rod. Lift out the filter element **(see illustrations)**. Dispose of the element.
8 Using a clean rag, wipe all oil and sludge from the inside of the filter housing and cap(s).
9 Fit new sealing rings to the cap, then insert the new element and cap, and tighten securely **(see illustration)**. Wipe up any spilt oil before refitting the engine top cover(s).
10 Remove the old oil and all tools from under the car then refit the undershield(s) and lower the car to the ground. Also refit the engine top cover.
11 Remove the dipstick, then unscrew the oil filler cap from the cylinder head cover. Fill the engine, using the correct grade and type of oil (see *Lubricants and fluids*). An oil can spout or funnel may help to reduce spillage. Pour in half the specified quantity of oil first **(see illustration)**, then wait a few minutes for the oil to run to the sump (see *Weekly checks*). Continue adding oil a small quantity at a time until the level is up to the maximum mark on the dipstick. Refit the filler cap.

3.7a Unscrew the cap . . .

3.7b . . . and remove the filter element

3.7c Remove the sealing ring from the cap

3.9a Lubricate the O-ring seal with engine oil

3.9b Insert the filter element together with the cap

3.11 Pour in half the specified quantity of oil first, wait, then add the rest

12 Start the engine and run it for a few minutes; check for leaks around the oil filter cap and the sump drain plug. Note that there may be a few seconds delay before the oil pressure warning light goes out when the engine is started, as the oil circulates through the engine oil galleries and the new oil filter (where fitted) before the pressure builds-up.

⚠️ **Warning: Do not increase the engine speed above idling while the oil pressure light is illuminated, as considerable damage can be caused to the turbocharger.**

13 Switch off the engine, and wait a few minutes for the oil to settle in the sump once more. With the new oil circulated and the filter completely full, recheck the level on the dipstick, and add more oil as necessary.

14 Dispose of the used engine oil safely, with reference to *General repair procedures* in the *Reference* section of this manual.

4 Fuel filter water draining (vehicles using high sulphur fuel) 🔧

Note: *Carry out this procedure at this interval only when using high sulphur diesel fuel not conforming to DIN EN 590 or when using RME fuel (diester). This fuel is not available in the UK.*

1 Periodically, the water collected from the fuel by the filter unit must be drained out.

2 The fuel filter is mounted on the inner wing, above the right-hand wheel arch **(see illustration)**. At the top of the filter unit, release the clip and lift out the control valve, leaving the fuel hoses attached.

4.2 The fuel filter is mounted on the inner wing, above the right-hand wheel arch

3 Slacken the screw and raise the filter in its retaining bracket

4 Position a container below the filter unit and pad the surrounding area with rags to absorb any fuel that may be spilt.

5 Unscrew the drain valve at the base of the filter unit, until fuel starts to run out into the container. Keep the valve open until about 100 cc of fuel has been collected.

6 Refit the control valve to the top of the filter and insert the retaining clip. Close the drain valve and wipe off any surplus fuel from the nozzle.

7 Remove the collecting container and rags, then push the filter unit back into the retaining bracket and tighten the bracket securing screw.

8 Run the engine at idle and check around the fuel filter for fuel leaks.

9 Raise the engine speed to about 2000 rpm several times, then allow the engine to idle again. Observe the fuel flow through the transparent hose leading to the fuel injection pump and check that it is free of air bubbles.

5 Brake pad/lining check 🔧

Front and rear disc brakes

1 The outer brake pads can be checked without removing the wheels, by observing the brake pads through the holes in the wheels **(see illustration)**. If necessary, remove the wheel trim. The thickness of the pad lining must not be less than the dimension given in the Specifications.

2 If the outer pads are worn near their limits, it is worthwhile checking the inner pads as well. Jack up vehicle and support it on axle stands (see *Jacking and vehicle support*). Remove the roadwheels.

3 Use a steel rule to check the thickness of the brake pads, and compare with the minimum thickness given in the Specifications **(see illustration)**.

4 For a comprehensive check, the brake pads should be removed and cleaned. The operation of the caliper can then also be checked, and the condition of the brake disc itself can be fully examined on both sides. Refer to Chapter 9.

5.1 The outer brake pads can be observed through the holes in the wheels

5 If any pad's friction material is worn to the specified minimum thickness or less, all four pads at the front or rear, as applicable, must be renewed as a set.

6 On completion of the check, refit the road-wheels and lower the vehicle to the ground.

Rear drum brakes

7 Chock the front wheels, then jack up the rear of the vehicle and support it on axle stands (see *Jacking and vehicle support*).

8 For a quick check, the thickness of friction material remaining on one of the brake shoes can be observed through the hole in the brake backplate which is exposed by prising out the rubber sealing grommet. If a rod of the same diameter as the specified minimum friction material thickness is placed against the shoe friction material, the amount of wear can be assessed. A torch or inspection light will probably be required. If the friction material on any shoe is worn down to the specified minimum thickness or less, all four shoes must be renewed as a set.

9 For a comprehensive check, the brake drum should be removed and cleaned. This will allow the wheel cylinders to be checked, and the condition of the brake drum itself to be fully examined (see Chapter 9).

10 On completion of the check, refit the roadwheels where removed, and lower the vehicle to the ground.

6 Resetting the service interval display 🔧

1 After all necessary maintenance work has been completed, the service interval display must be reset. Skoda technicians use a special dedicated instrument to do this, and a print-out is then put in the vehicle service record. It is possible for the owner to reset the display as described in the following paragraphs, but note that on models with 'LongLife' service intervals, there is no distinction between the PR codes QG1 and QG2. If there is any doubt,

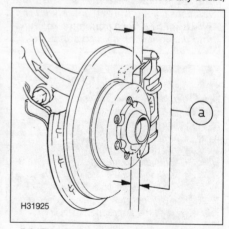

H31925

5.3 The thickness (a) of the brake pads must not be less than the specified amount

have the display reset by a Skoda dealership using the special dedicated instrument.

2 To reset the standard display manually, switch off the ignition, then press and hold down the trip reset button beneath the speedometer. Switch on the ignition and observe the service interval, then hold the button down for 10 seconds until '- - -' appears followed by the trip readout. If the 'OIL' and 'INSP' intervals were reached at the same time, depress the button again for 10 seconds to reset the remaining interval.

3 To reset the LongLife display manually, switch off the ignition, then press and hold down the trip reset button beneath the speedometer. Switch on the ignition and release the reset button, and note that the relevant service will appear in the display. Turn the reset button clockwise, and the display will now return to normal. Switch off the ignition to complete the resetting procedure. Do not zero the display otherwise incorrect readings will be shown.

4 Note that for models using the LongLife interval QG1, the procedure will automatically reset the schedule to an amended LongLife interval (QG2) in which oil renewal, fuel filter draining on certain models and brake pad checks are based on distance/time while every other system remains LongLife. To have the display reset to the full LongLife schedule (QG1), it is necessary to take the vehicle to a Skoda dealer who will use a special instrument to encode the on-board computer.

'INSP service' on display

7 Exhaust system check

1 With the engine cold (at least an hour after the vehicle has been driven), check the complete exhaust system from the engine to the end of the tailpipe. The exhaust system is most easily checked with the vehicle raised on a hoist, or supported on axle stands, so that the exhaust components are readily visible and accessible (see *Jacking and vehicle support*).

2 Check the exhaust pipes and connections for evidence of leaks, severe corrosion and damage. Make sure that all brackets and mountings are in good condition, and that all relevant nuts and bolts are tight. Leakage at any of the joints or in other parts of the system will usually show up as a black sooty stain in the vicinity of the leak.

3 Rattles and other noises can often be traced to the exhaust system, especially the brackets and mountings. Try to move the pipes and silencers. If the components are able to come into contact with the body or suspension parts, secure the system with new mountings. Otherwise separate the joints (if possible) and twist the pipes as necessary to provide additional clearance.

8 Hose and fluid leak check

1 Visually inspect the engine joint faces, gaskets and seals for any signs of water or oil leaks. Pay particular attention to the areas around the camshaft cover, cylinder head, oil filter and sump joint faces. Bear in mind that, over a period of time, some very slight seepage from these areas is to be expected – what you are really looking for is any indication of a serious leak. Should a leak be found, renew the offending gasket or oil seal by referring to the appropriate Chapters in this manual.

2 Also check the security and condition of all the engine-related pipes and hoses. Ensure that all cable-ties or securing clips are in place and in good condition. Clips which are broken or missing can lead to chafing of the hoses, pipes or wiring, which could cause more serious problems in the future.

3 Carefully check the radiator hoses and heater hoses along their entire length. Renew any hose which is cracked, swollen or deteriorated. Cracks will show up better if the hose is squeezed. Pay close attention to the hose clips that secure the hoses to the cooling system components. Hose clips can pinch and puncture hoses, resulting in cooling system leaks.

4 Inspect all the cooling system components (hoses, joint faces, etc) for leaks **(see Haynes Hint)**. Where any problems of this nature are found on system components, renew the component or gasket with reference to Chapter 3.

5 With the vehicle raised, inspect the petrol tank and filler neck for punctures, cracks and other damage. The connection between the filler neck and tank is especially critical. Sometimes a rubber filler neck or connecting hose will leak due to loose retaining clamps or deteriorated rubber.

6 Carefully check all rubber hoses and metal fuel lines leading away from the petrol tank. Check for loose connections, deteriorated hoses, crimped lines, and other damage. Pay particular attention to the vent pipes and hoses, which often loop up around the filler neck and can become blocked or crimped.

HAYNES HINT

A leak in the cooling system will usually show up as white- or rust-coloured deposits on the area adjoining the leak.

Follow the lines to the front of the vehicle, carefully inspecting them all the way. Renew damaged sections as necessary.

7 From within the engine compartment, check the security of all fuel hose attachments and pipe unions, and inspect the fuel hoses and vacuum hoses for kinks, chafing and deterioration.

8 Check the condition of the power steering fluid hoses and pipes.

9 Fuel filter water draining (vehicles using standard fuel)

Note: *Carry out this procedure at this interval only when using diesel fuel conforming to DIN EN 590 (standard fuel in the UK).*

Refer to Section 4.

10 Fuel filter renewal (vehicles using high sulphur diesel fuel)

Note: *Carry out this procedure at this interval only when using high sulphur diesel fuel not conforming to DIN EN 590 or when using RME fuel (diester). This fuel is not available in the UK.*

1 The fuel filter is mounted on the inner wing, above the right-hand wheel arch **(see illustration)**. Position a container underneath the filter unit and pad the surrounding area with rags to absorb any fuel that may be spilt.

10.1 The fuel filter is mounted on the inner wing, above the right-hand wheel arch

10.2a Release the clip . . .

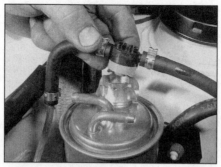

10.2b . . . and lift out the control valve, leaving the fuel hoses attached to it

10.4a Loosen the securing screw . . .

10.4b . . . and raise the filter out of its retaining bracket

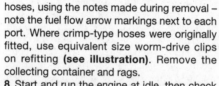

10.7 Reconnect the fuel supply and delivery hoses

2 At the top of the filter unit, release the clip and lift out the control valve, leaving the fuel hoses attached to it **(see illustrations)**.

3 Slacken the hose clips and pull the fuel supply and delivery hoses from the ports on the of the filter unit. If crimp-type clips are fitted, cut them off using snips, and use equivalent size worm-drive clips on refitting. Note the fitted position of each hose, to aid correct refitting later.

Caution: Be prepared for an amount of fuel loss.

4 Slacken the securing screw and raise the filter out of its retaining bracket **(see illustrations)**.

5 Fit a new fuel filter into the retaining bracket and tighten the securing screw.

6 Refit the control valve to the top of the filter and insert the retaining clip.

7 Reconnect the fuel supply and delivery

11.2 Checking the underside of the auxiliary drivebelt with a mirror

hoses, using the notes made during removal – note the fuel flow arrow markings next to each port. Where crimp-type hoses were originally fitted, use equivalent size worm-drive clips on refitting **(see illustration)**. Remove the collecting container and rags.

8 Start and run the engine at idle, then check around the fuel filter for fuel leaks. **Note:** *It may take a few seconds of cranking before the engine starts.*

9 Raise the engine speed to about 2000 rpm several times, then allow the engine to idle again. Observe the fuel flow through the transparent hose leading to the fuel injection pump and check that it is free of air bubbles.

11 Auxiliary drivebelt check

1 Apply the handbrake, then jack up the front of the vehicle and support it on axle stands (see *Jacking and vehicle support*).

2 Using a socket on the crankshaft pulley bolt, turn the engine slowly clockwise so that the full length of the auxiliary drivebelt can be examined. Look for cracks, splitting and fraying on the surface of the belt; check also for signs of glazing (shiny patches) and separation of the belt plies. Use a mirror to check the underside of the drivebelt (see illustration). If damage or wear is visible, or if there are traces of oil or grease on it, the belt should be renewed (see Section 29).

12 Antifreeze check

1 The cooling system should be filled with the recommended G12 antifreeze and corrosion protection fluid – **do not** mix this antifreeze with any other type. Over a period of time, the concentration of fluid may be reduced due to topping-up (this can be avoided by topping-up with the correct antifreeze mixture – see Specifications) or fluid loss. If loss of coolant has been evident, it is important to make the necessary repair before adding fresh fluid.

2 With the engine **cold**, carefully remove the cap from the expansion tank. If the engine is not completely cold, place a cloth rag over the cap before removing it, and remove it slowly to allow any pressure to escape.

3 Antifreeze checkers are available from car accessory shops. Draw some coolant from the expansion tank and observe how many plastic balls are floating in the checker. Usually, 2 or 3 balls must be floating for the correct concentration of antifreeze, but follow the manufacturer's instructions.

4 If the concentration is incorrect, it will be necessary to either withdraw some coolant and add antifreeze, or alternatively drain the old coolant and add fresh coolant of the correct concentration (see Section 34).

13 Brake hydraulic circuit check

1 Check the entire brake hydraulic circuit for leaks and damage. Start by checking the master cylinder in the engine compartment. At the same time, check the vacuum servo unit and ABS units for signs of fluid leakage.

2 Raise the front and rear of the vehicle and support it on axle stands (see *Jacking and vehicle support*). Check the rigid hydraulic brake lines for corrosion and damage.

3 At the front of the vehicle, check that the flexible hydraulic hoses to the calipers are not twisted or chafing on any of the surrounding suspension components. Turn the steering on full lock to make this check. Also check that the hoses are not brittle or cracked.

4 Lower the vehicle to the ground after making the checks.

14 Headlight beam adjustment

1 Accurate adjustment of the headlight beam is only possible using optical beam-setting equipment, and this work should therefore be carried out by a Skoda dealer or service station with the necessary facilities.

2 Basic adjustments can be carried out in an emergency, and further details are given in Chapter 12.

15 Pollen filter element renewal

1 The pollen filter is located on the heater assembly, and is removed into the passenger footwell – on RHD models it is on the left-hand side, and on LHD models it is on the right-hand side.

2 Reach under the glovebox, and press back the retaining catches of the pollen filter.

3 Withdraw the filter downwards from the heater assembly, and remove from inside the car.

4 Separate the filter from the frame.

5 Fit the new filter to the frame, then insert it into the heater assembly until the catches lock the frame.

16 Manual transmission oil level check

1 Park the car on a level surface. For improved access to the filler/level plug, apply the handbrake, then jack up the front of the vehicle and support it on axle stands (see *Jacking and vehicle support*), but note that the rear of the vehicle should also be raised to ensure an accurate level check. The oil level must be checked before the car is driven, or at least 5 minutes after the engine has been switched off. If the oil is checked immediately after driving the car, some of the oil will remain distributed around the transmission components, resulting in an inaccurate level reading.

2 As applicable, undo the retaining screws and remove the engine undershield(s). Wipe clean the area around the transmission filler/level plug which is situated in the following location:

a) *On the 02T transmission (see Chapter 7A for engine codes), the filler/level plug is situated on the rear, inner face of the transmission, above the engine rear mounting/torque link.*

b) *On the 02R transmission (see Chapter 7A for engine codes), the filler/level plug is situated on the front, left-hand end of the transmission.*

3 The oil level should reach the lower edge of the filler/level hole. A certain amount of oil will have gathered behind the filler/level plug, and will trickle out when it is removed; this does **not** necessarily indicate that the level is correct. To ensure that a true level is established, wait until the initial trickle has stopped, then add oil as necessary until a trickle of new oil can be seen emerging. The level will be correct when the flow ceases; use only good-quality oil of the specified type.

4 If the transmission has been overfilled so that oil flows out when the filler/level plug is removed, check that the car is completely level (front-to-rear and side-to-side), and allow the surplus to drain off into a suitable container.

5 When the oil level is correct, refit the filler/level plug and tighten it to the specified torque. Wipe off any spilt oil then refit the engine undershield(s), tighten the retaining screws securely, and lower the car to the ground.

17 Underbody protection check

Raise and support the vehicle on axle stands (see *Jacking and vehicle support*). Using an electric torch or lead light, inspect the entire underside of the vehicle, paying particular attention to the wheel arches. Look for any damage to the flexible underbody coating, which may crack or flake off with age, leading to corrosion. Also check that the wheel arch liners are securely attached with any clips provided – if they come loose, dirt may get in behind the liners and defeat their purpose. If there is any damage to the underseal, or any corrosion, it should be repaired before the damage gets too serious.

18 Driveshaft check

1 With the vehicle raised and securely supported on stands, slowly rotate the roadwheel. Inspect the condition of the outer constant velocity (CV) joint rubber gaiters, squeezing the gaiters to open out the folds. Check for signs of cracking, splits or deterioration of the rubber, which may allow the grease to escape, and lead to water and grit entry into the joint. Also check the security and condition of the retaining clips. Repeat these checks on the inner joints **(see illustration)**. If any damage or deterioration is found, the gaiters should be renewed (see Chapter 8).

18.1 Check the condition of the driveshaft gaiters (arrowed)

2 At the same time, check the general condition of the CV joints themselves by first holding the driveshaft and attempting to rotate the wheel. Repeat this check by holding the inner joint and attempting to rotate the driveshaft. Any appreciable movement indicates wear in the joints, wear in the driveshaft splines, or a loose driveshaft retaining nut.

19 Steering and suspension check

1 Raise the front and rear of the vehicle, and securely support it on axle stands (see *Jacking and vehicle support*).

2 Visually inspect the track rod end balljoint dust cover, the lower front suspension balljoint dust cover, and the steering rack-and-pinion gaiters for splits, chafing or deterioration. Any wear of these components will cause loss of lubricant, together with dirt and water entry, resulting in rapid deterioration of the balljoints or steering gear.

3 Check the power steering fluid hoses for chafing or deterioration, and the pipe and hose unions for fluid leaks. Also check for signs of fluid leakage under pressure from the steering gear rubber gaiters, which would indicate failed fluid seals within the steering gear.

4 Grasp the roadwheel at the 12 o'clock and 6 o'clock positions, and try to rock it **(see illustration)**. Very slight free play may be felt, but if the movement is appreciable, further

19.4 Check for wear in the hub bearings by grasping the wheel and trying to rock it

20.1 Removing the battery cover

investigation is necessary to determine the source. Continue rocking the wheel while an assistant depresses the footbrake. If the movement is now eliminated or significantly reduced, it is likely that the hub bearings are at fault. If the free play is still evident with the footbrake depressed, then there is wear in the suspension joints or mountings.

5 Now grasp the wheel at the 9 o'clock and 3 o'clock positions, and try to rock it as before. Any movement felt now may again be caused by wear in the hub bearings or the steering track rod balljoints. If the inner or outer balljoint is worn, the visual movement will be obvious.

6 Using a large screwdriver or flat bar, check for wear in the suspension mounting bushes by levering between the relevant suspension component and its attachment point. Some movement is to be expected as the mountings are made of rubber, but excessive wear should be obvious. Also check the condition of any visible rubber bushes, looking for splits, cracks or contamination of the rubber.

7 With the car standing on its wheels, have an assistant turn the steering wheel back-and-forth about an eighth of a turn each way. There should be very little, if any, lost movement between the steering wheel and roadwheels. If this is not the case, closely observe the joints and mountings previously described, but in addition check the steering column universal joints for wear, and the rack-and-pinion steering gear itself.

8 Check for any signs of fluid leakage around the front suspension struts and rear shock absorber. Should any fluid be noticed, the suspension strut or shock absorber is defective internally, and should be renewed. **Note:** *Suspension struts/shock absorbers should always be renewed in pairs on the same axle to ensure correct vehicle handling.*

9 The efficiency of the suspension strut/shock absorber may be checked by bouncing the vehicle at each corner. Generally speaking, the body will return to its normal position and stop after being depressed. If it rises and returns on a rebound, the suspension strut/shock absorber is probably suspect. Examine also the suspension strut/shock absorber upper and lower mountings for any signs of wear.

20 Battery check

1 The battery is located in the front, left-hand corner of the engine compartment. Where a heat protective jacket is fitted, unclip the cover and remove the jacket to gain access to the battery **(see illustration)**.

2 Where necessary, open the fuse holder plastic cover (squeeze together the locking lugs to release the cover) to gain access to the battery positive (+) terminal and fuse holder connections.

3 Check that both battery terminals and all the fuse holder connections are securely attached and are free from corrosion. **Note:** *Before disconnecting the terminals from the battery, refer to 'Disconnecting the battery' in the Reference Chapter at the end of this manual.*

4 Check the battery casing for signs of damage or cracking and check the battery retaining clamp bolt is securely tightened. If the battery casing is damaged in any way the battery must be renewed (see Chapter 5A).

5 If the vehicle is not fitted with a sealed-for-life maintenance-free battery, check the electrolyte level is between the MAX and MIN level markings on the battery casing. If topping-up is necessary, remove the battery (see Chapter 5A) from the vehicle then remove the cell caps/cover (as applicable). Using distilled water, top the electrolyte level of each cell up to the MAX level mark then securely refit the cell caps/cover. Ensure the battery has not been overfilled then refit the battery to the vehicle (see Chapter 5A).

6 Some models are fitted with a battery with a 'magic eye' which shows the state of the battery and level of electrolyte. The 'magic eye' is located on the top of the battery, near the negative terminal. If the eye is green, the battery is in good condition and charged up. If the eye is black, the battery is flat and should be charged. If the eye is colourless or yellow, the electrolyte is low and in a critical condition, and should be topped-up with distilled water. If charging the battery does not return the eye to green, the battery should be scrapped.

7 On completion of the check, clip the cover securely back onto the fuse holder and close up the insulator cover (where fitted).

21 Hinge and lock lubrication

1 Lubricate the hinges of the bonnet, doors and tailgate with a light general-purpose oil. Similarly, lubricate all latches, locks and lock strikers. At the same time, check the security and operation of all the locks, adjusting them if necessary (see Chapter 11).

2 Lightly lubricate the bonnet release mechanism and cable with a suitable grease.

22 Airbag unit check

Inspect the exterior condition of the airbag(s) for signs of damage or deterioration. If an airbag shows signs of damage, it must be renewed (see Chapter 12). Note that it is not permissible to attach any stickers to the surface of the airbag, as this may affect the deployment of the unit.

23 Windscreen/tailgate/headlight washer system check

1 Check that each of the washer jet nozzles is clear and that each nozzle provides a strong jet of washer fluid.

2 The tailgate jet should be aimed to spray at the centre of the screen, using a pin.

3 The windscreen washer jet nozzles are preset by the manufacturer and cannot be adjusted.

4 The headlight inner jet should be aimed slightly above the horizontal centreline of the headlight, and the outer jet should be aimed slightly below the centreline.

5 Especially during the winter months, make sure that the washer fluid frost concentration is sufficient.

24 Engine management self-diagnosis memory fault check

This work should be carried out by a Skoda dealer or diagnostic specialist using special equipment. The diagnostic socket is located behind a hinged cover beneath the driver's side of the facia.

25 Sunroof check and lubrication

1 Check the operation of the sunroof, and leave it in the fully open position.

2 Wipe clean the guide rails on each side of the sunroof opening, then apply lubricant to them. Skoda recommend using lubricant spray G 052 778.

26 Road test and exhaust emissions check

Instruments and electrical equipment

1 Check the operation of all instruments and electrical equipment including the air conditioning system.

2 Make sure that all instruments read correctly, and switch on all electrical equipment in turn, to check that it functions properly.

Steering and suspension

3 Check for any abnormalities in the steering, suspension, handling or road 'feel'.

4 Drive the vehicle, and check that there are no unusual vibrations or noises which may indicate wear in the driveshafts, wheel bearings, etc.

5 Check that the steering feels positive, with no excessive 'sloppiness', or roughness, and check for any suspension noises when cornering and driving over bumps.

Drivetrain

6 Check the performance of the engine, clutch, gearbox and driveshafts.

7 Listen for any unusual noises from the engine, clutch and gearbox.

8 Make sure the engine runs smoothly at idle, and there is no hesitation on accelerating.

9 Check that the clutch action is smooth and progressive, that the drive is taken up smoothly, and that the pedal travel is not excessive. Also listen for any noises when the clutch pedal is depressed.

10 Check that all gears can be engaged smoothly without noise, and that the gear lever action is smooth and not abnormally vague or 'notchy'.

11 Listen for a metallic clicking sound from the front of the vehicle, as the vehicle is driven slowly in a circle with the steering on full-lock. Carry out this check in both directions. If a clicking noise is heard, this indicates wear in a driveshaft joint, in which case renew the joint if necessary.

Braking system

12 Make sure that the vehicle does not pull to one side when braking, and that the wheels do not lock when braking hard.

13 Check that there is no vibration through the steering when braking.

14 Check that the handbrake operates correctly without excessive movement of the lever, and that it holds the vehicle stationary on a slope.

15 Test the operation of the brake servo unit as follows. With the engine off, depress the footbrake four or five times to exhaust the vacuum. Hold the brake pedal depressed, then start the engine. As the engine starts, there should be a noticeable 'give' in the brake pedal as vacuum builds-up. Allow the engine to run for at least two minutes, and then switch it off. If the brake pedal is depressed now, it should be possible to detect a hiss from the servo as the pedal is depressed. After about four or five applications, no further hissing should be heard, and the pedal should feel considerably harder.

16 Under controlled emergency braking, the pulsing of the ABS unit must be felt at the footbrake pedal.

Exhaust emissions check

17 Although not part of the manufacturer's maintenance schedule, this check will normally be carried out on a regular basis according to the country the vehicle is operated in. Currently in the UK, exhaust emissions testing is included as part of the annual MOT test after the vehicle is 3 years old. In Germany the test is made when the vehicle is 3 years old, then repeated every 2 years.

Every 40 000 miles or 4 years

27 Air filter element renewal

1 The air filter is housed in the air cleaner, which is situated on the left-hand side of the inner wing, behind the battery.

2 Undo the screws and lift the cover from the top of the air cleaner body **(see illustration)**.

3 Lift out the air filter element **(see illustration)**.

4 Remove any debris that may have collected inside the air cleaner.

5 Fit a new air filter element in position, ensuring that the edges are securely seated.

6 Refit the air cleaner top cover and secure with the screws.

28 Fuel filter renewal (vehicles using standard diesel fuel)

Note: *Carry out this procedure at this interval only when using diesel fuel conforming to DIN EN 590 (standard fuel in the UK).*

Refer to Section 10.

29 Auxiliary drivebelt check and renewal

Check

1 See Section 11.

Renewal

2 For improved access, apply the handbrake, then jack up the front of the vehicle and support it on axle stands (see *Jacking and vehicle support*). Where applicable, remove the engine undertray.

3 Remove the right-hand front roadwheel, then remove the wheel arch liner.

4 The tensioner must now be turned clockwise to release the tension on the drivebelt. To do this, either use a spanner to turn the tensioner central bolt clockwise (models with air conditioning) **(see illustration)**, or use a spanner on the square-shaped lug on the top of the tensioner (models without air conditioning). On the latter type, it is possible to retain the tensioner with a pin inserted through the holes provided.

27.2 Remove the cover . . .

27.3 . . . and lift out the air filter element

29.4 On models with air conditioning, turn the tensioner clockwise . . .

29.5 . . . and remove the auxiliary drivebelt

30.2 Unscrew the cap from the hydraulic fluid reservoir

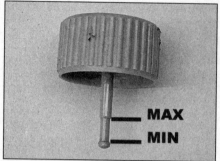

30.3a The power steering fluid level must be between the upper and lower marks

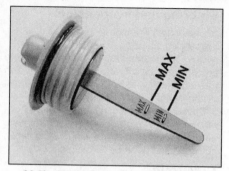

30.3b Alternative power steering cap markings

30.4 Topping-up the fluid level

5 Note how the drivebelt is routed, then remove it from the crankshaft pulley, alternator pulley, power steering pump pulley, and air conditioning compressor pulley (where applicable) **(see illustration)**.
6 Locate the new drivebelt on the pulleys, then release the tensioner. Check that the belt

is located correctly in the multi-grooves in the pulleys.
7 Refit the access panel and roadwheel, and lower the vehicle to the ground.

30 Power steering hydraulic fluid level check

1 Turn the front roadwheels to the straight-ahead position without starting the engine. If the vehicle has been left standing for an hour or more, the power steering fluid will be cold (below 50ºC), and the 'cold' level markings must be used. If, however, the engine is at normal temperature (above 50ºC), the fluid will be hot, and the 'hot' level markings must be used.
2 The reservoir for the Electrically Powered Hydraulic Steering (EPHS) is located on the front left-hand corner of the engine compartment. **Note:** *On some models with*

a high capacity battery, the battery and tray must be removed in order to access the reservoir filler cap. The fluid level is checked with the dipstick attached to the reservoir filler cap. Unscrew the cap from the hydraulic fluid reservoir, and wipe clean the integral dipstick with a clean cloth **(see illustration)**.
3 Screw on the cap hand tight then unscrew it again and check the fluid level on the dipstick. The fluid level must be between the MIN (or lower) and MAX (or upper) marks **(see illustrations)**. If the fluid is cold (below 50ºC), it must be at least above the lower level mark or MIN. If the fluid is hot (above 50ºC), it must not be above the upper level mark or MAX.
4 If the level is above the maximum level mark, syphon off the excess. If it is below the minimum level mark, add the specified fluid as necessary *(see Lubricants and fluids)*, but in this case also check the system for leaks **(see illustration)**. On completion, screw on the cap and tighten. Refit the battery and tray where removed.

Every 60 000 miles

31 Timing belt and tensioning roller renewal (engines with 'unit' injectors)

1 Refer to Chapter 2D for details of renewing the timing belt and tensioning roller.

Every 80 000 miles

32 Timing belt and tensioning roller renewal (engines with injection pump)

Note: *This work at this interval only applies to engines with an injection pump (see Chapter 4B).*
1 Refer to Chapter 2D for details of renewing the timing belt and tensioning roller.

Every 2 years

33 Brake (and clutch) fluid renewal

⚠ *Warning: Brake hydraulic fluid can harm your eyes and damage painted surfaces, so use extreme caution when handling and pouring it. Do*

not use fluid that has been standing open for some time, as it absorbs moisture from the air. Excess moisture can cause a dangerous loss of braking effectiveness.
1 The procedure is similar to that for the bleeding of the hydraulic system as described in Chapter 9, except that the brake fluid reservoir should be emptied by syphoning, using a clean poultry baster or similar before starting, and allowance should be made for

the old fluid to be expelled when bleeding a section of the circuit. Since the clutch hydraulic system also uses fluid from the brake system reservoir, it should also be bled at the same time by referring to Chapter 6, Section 2.
2 Working as described in Chapter 9, open the first bleed screw in the sequence, and pump the brake pedal gently until nearly all the old fluid has been emptied from the master cylinder reservoir.

3 Top-up to the MAX level with new fluid, and continue pumping until only the new fluid remains in the reservoir, and new fluid can be seen emerging from the bleed screw. Tighten the screw, and top the reservoir level up to the MAX level line.

4 Work through all the remaining bleed screws in the sequence until new fluid can be seen at all of them. Be careful to keep the master cylinder reservoir topped-up to above the MIN level at all times, or air may enter the system and greatly increase the length of the task.

5 When the operation is complete, check that all bleed screws are securely tightened, and that their dust caps are refitted. Wash off all traces of spilt fluid, and recheck the master cylinder reservoir fluid level.

6 Once the brake fluid has been changed the clutch fluid should also be renewed. Referring to Chapter 6, bleed the clutch until new fluid is seen to be emerging from the slave cylinder bleed screw, keeping the master cylinder fluid level above the MIN level line at all times to prevent air entering the system. Once the new fluid emerges, securely tighten the bleed screw then disconnect and remove the bleeding equipment. Securely refit the dust cap then wash off all traces of spilt fluid.

7 Ensure the master cylinder fluid level is correct (see *Weekly checks*) and thoroughly check the operation of the brakes and clutch before taking the car on the road.

34 Coolant renewal

Note: *This work is not included in the Skoda schedule and should not be required if the recommended Skoda G12 LongLife coolant antifreeze/inhibitor is used. However, if standard antifreeze/inhibitor is used, the work should be carried out at the recommended interval.*

⚠ *Warning: Wait until the engine is cold before starting this procedure. Do not allow antifreeze to come in contact with your skin, or with the painted surfaces of the vehicle. Rinse off spills immediately with plenty of water. Never leave antifreeze lying around in an open container, or in a puddle in the driveway or on the garage floor. Children and pets are attracted by its sweet smell, but antifreeze can be fatal if ingested.*

Cooling system draining

1 With the engine completely cold, unscrew the expansion tank cap.

2 Firmly apply the handbrake then jack up the front of the vehicle and support it on axle stands (see *Jacking and vehicle support*).

Undo the retaining screws and remove the engine undershield(s) to gain access to the base of the radiator.

3 Position a suitable container beneath the coolant drain plug which is located in the bottom hose fitting to the left-hand bottom end of the radiator. Unscrew the drain plug and pull it out slightly (there is no need to remove it completely) and allow the coolant to drain into the container **(see illustration)**. If desired, a length of tubing can be fitted to the drain outlet to direct the flow of coolant during draining. Where no drain outlet is fitted to the hose end fitting, remove the retaining clip and disconnect the bottom hose from the radiator to drain the coolant (see Chapter 3).

4 On engines with an oil cooler, to fully drain the system, also disconnect one of the coolant hoses from the oil cooler which is located at the front of the cylinder block.

5 If the coolant has been drained for a reason other than renewal, then provided it is clean, it can be re-used.

6 Once all the coolant has drained, securely tighten the drain plug or reconnect the bottom hose to the radiator (as applicable). Where necessary, also reconnect the coolant hose to the oil cooler and secure it in position with the retaining clip. Refit the undershield(s), tighten the retaining screws securely.

Cooling system flushing

7 If the recommended Skoda coolant has not been used and coolant renewal has been neglected, or if the antifreeze mixture has become diluted, the cooling system may gradually lose efficiency, as the coolant passages become restricted due to rust, scale deposits, and other sediment. The cooling system efficiency can be restored by flushing the system clean.

8 The radiator should be flushed separately from the engine, to avoid excess contamination.

Radiator flushing

9 To flush the radiator, first tighten the radiator drain plug.

10 Disconnect the top and bottom hoses and any other relevant hoses from the radiator (see Chapter 3).

11 Insert a garden hose into the radiator top inlet. Direct a flow of clean water through the radiator, and continue flushing until clean water emerges from the radiator bottom outlet.

12 If after a reasonable period, the water still does not run clear, the radiator can be flushed with a good proprietary cleaning agent. It is important that the manufacturer's instructions are followed carefully. If the contamination is particularly bad, insert the hose in the radiator bottom outlet, and reverse-flush the radiator.

Engine flushing

13 To flush the engine, remove the thermostat (see Chapter 3).

14 With the bottom hose disconnected from the radiator, insert a garden hose into

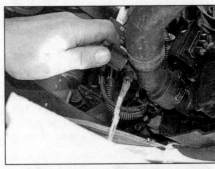

34.3 Unscrew the radiator drain plug and allow the coolant to drain into the container

the thermostat housing. Direct a clean flow of water through the engine, and continue flushing until clean water emerges from the radiator bottom hose.

15 When flushing is complete, refit the thermostat and reconnect the hoses (see Chapter 3).

Cooling system filling

16 Before attempting to fill the cooling system, ensure the drain plug is securely closed and make sure that all hoses are securely connected and their retaining clips are in good condition. If the recommended Skoda coolant is not being used, ensure that a suitable antifreeze mixture is used all year round, to prevent corrosion of the engine components (see following sub-Section).

17 Remove the coolant temperature sensor from the coolant distribution housing on the left-hand end of the cylinder head with reference to Chapter 3.

18 Remove the expansion tank filler cap and slowly fill the system with coolant **(see illustration)**, until bubble-free coolant runs from the temperature sensor hole, then refit the sensor immediately with reference to Chapter 3. Continue to fill the system until the level is up to the MAX level mark on the expansion tank. Help to bleed the air from the system by repeatedly squeezing the radiator bottom hose.

19 Refit the cap to the expansion tank, then run the engine at a fast idle speed until the cooling fan cuts in. Wait for the fan to stop then switch the engine off and allow the engine to cool.

34.18 Filling the cooling system

20 When the engine has cooled, check the coolant level with reference to *Weekly checks*. Top-up the level if necessary, and refit the expansion tank cap.

Antifreeze mixture

21 If the recommended Skoda coolant is not being used, the antifreeze should always be renewed at the specified intervals. This is necessary not only to maintain the antifreeze properties, but also to prevent corrosion which would otherwise occur as the corrosion inhibitors become progressively less effective.

22 Always use an ethylene-glycol based antifreeze which is suitable for use in mixed-metal cooling systems. The quantity of antifreeze and levels of protection are indicated in the Specifications.

23 Before adding antifreeze, the cooling system should be completely drained, preferably flushed, and all hoses checked for condition and security.

24 After filling with antifreeze, a label should be attached to the expansion tank, stating the type and concentration of antifreeze used, and the date installed. Any subsequent topping-up should be made with the same type and concentration of antifreeze.

25 Do not use engine antifreeze in the windscreen/tailgate washer system, as it will damage the vehicle paintwork. A screenwash additive should be added to the washer system in the quantities stated on the bottle.

Chapter 2 Part A:
1.2 litre petrol engine in-car repair procedures

Contents

Section number

Camshaft(s) and hydraulic tappets – removal, inspection and
  refitting 7
Compression test – description and interpretation 2
Crankshaft oil seals – renewal 12
Crankshaft pulley – removal and refitting 4
Cylinder head – removal, inspection and refitting 8
Engine assembly and valve timing marks – general information and
  usage 3
Engine oil and filter renewal . . . . See Chapter 1A
Engine oil level check . . . . See *Weekly checks*

Section number

Engine/transmission mountings – inspection and renewal 14
Flywheel – removal, inspection and refitting 13
General information 1
Oil pressure warning light switch – removal and refitting. 11
Oil pump, drive chain and sprockets – removal, inspection and
  refitting 10
Sump – removal and refitting 9
Timing chain, tensioner and sprockets – removal, inspection and
  refitting 6
Timing cover – removal and refitting 5

Degrees of difficulty

Easy, suitable for novice with little experience	Fairly easy, suitable for beginner with some experience	Fairly difficult, suitable for competent DIY mechanic	Difficult, suitable for experienced DIY mechanic	Very difficult, suitable for expert DIY or professional

Specifications

General

Type	Three-cylinder in-line, chain-driven single (SOHC) or double (DOHC) overhead camshaft, four stroke, liquid-cooled
Manufacturer's engine codes*:	
1198 cc SOHC	AWY
1198 cc DOHC	AZQ, BME
Maximum power output:	
AWY	40 kW at 4750 rpm
AZQ, BME.	47 kW at 5400 rpm
Maximum torque output:	
AWY	106 Nm at 3000 rpm
AZQ, BME.	112 Nm at 3000 rpm
Bore	76.5 mm
Stroke.	86.9 mm
Compression ratio:	
AWY	10.3 : 1
AZQ, BME.	10.5 : 1
Compression pressures:	
Minimum compression pressure	Approximately 11.0 bars
Maximum difference between cylinders.	Approximately 3.0 bars
Firing order	1 – 2 – 3
No 1 cylinder location.	Crankshaft pulley end
Direction of crankshaft rotation	Clockwise (when viewed from right-hand side of vehicle)

* **Note:** *See 'Vehicle identification' at the end of this manual for the location of engine code markings.*

Lubrication system

Oil pump type.	Chain-driven from crankshaft
Minimum oil pressure (oil temperature 80°C) at 2000 rpm.	2.0 bar

Camshaft

Camshaft endfloat (maximum)	0.20 mm

Torque wrench settings

	Nm	lbf ft
Air conditioning compressor	23	17
Auxiliary drivebelt tensioner and guide pulley	40	30
Camshaft bearing caps (AZQ and BME engines):		
Stage 1	10	7
Stage 2	Angle-tighten a further 90°	
Camshaft cover (AWY engine):		
Stage 1	6	4
Stage 2	Angle-tighten a further 90°	
Camshaft position sensor	8	6
Camshaft sprocket:		
Stage 1	20	15
Stage 2	Angle-tighten by 90°	
Coolant pump pulley	22	16
Crankshaft pulley:		
Stage 1	90	66
Stage 2	Angle-tighten a further 90°	
Cylinder head bolts:		
Stage 1	30	22
Stage 2	Angle-tighten a further 90°	
Stage 3	Angle-tighten a further 90°	
Cylinder head cover/housing:		
AWY engine:		
Stage 1	6	4
Stage 2	Angle-tighten a further 90°	
AZQ and BME engines:		
Stage 1	10	7
Stage 2	Angle-tighten a further 90°	
Engine lifting eye	20	15
Flywheel bolts (new)*:		
Stage 1	60	44
Stage 2	Angle-tighten a further 90°	
Left-hand engine mounting:		
Mounting to body:		
Stage 1	50	37
Stage 2	Angle-tighten a further 90°	
Mounting to transmission:		
Stage 1	40	30
Stage 2	Angle-tighten a further 90°	
Oil filter cap	25	18
Oil filter housing	24	18
Oil level and temperature sender	8	6
Oil pressure switch	25	18
Oil pump	24	18
Oil pump chain tensioner	15	11
Oil pump sprocket:		
Stage 1	20	15
Stage 2	Angle-tighten a further 90°	
Rear mounting link:		
To transmission:		
Stage 1	30	22
Stage 2	Angle-tighten a further 90°	
To subframe:		
Stage 1	40	30
Stage 2	Angle-tighten a further 90°	
Right-hand engine mounting:		
Pedestal to engine	45	33
Mounting to body:		
Stage 1	20	15
Stage 2	Angle-tighten a further 90°	
Intermediate bracket to pedestal:		
Stage 1	30	22
Stage 2	Angle-tighten a further 90°	
Sump bolts	9	7
Sump oil drain plug	30	22
Timing chain guide (AZQ and BME engines)	15	11
Timing chain hydraulic tensioner	15	11

Torque wrench settings (continued)

	Nm	lbf ft
Timing cover:		
Engine code AWY (see illustration 5.19a):		
Bolt 3	45	33
Bolts 1 and 2	45	33
Bolts 22 and 23	25	18
All other bolts	10	7
Engine codes AZQ and BME (see illustration 5.19b):		
Bolts 1, 2 and 3	50	37
Bolts 4 and 5	25	18
Bolts 6, 7, 8, 11 and 14, and all other bolts:		
Stage 1	8	6
Stage 2	Angle-tighten a further 90°	
Timing chain tensioner guide pivot	18	13

Use thread-locking compound.

1 General information

How to use this Chapter

This Part of Chapter 2 describes those repair procedures that can reasonably be carried out on the engine while it remains in the vehicle. If the engine has been removed from the vehicle and is being dismantled, as described in Part E, any preliminary dismantling procedures can be ignored.

Note that while it may be possible physically to overhaul certain items while the engine is in the vehicle, such tasks are not usually carried out as separate operations, and usually require the execution of several additional procedures (not to mention the cleaning of components and of oilways); for this reason, all such tasks are classed as major overhaul procedures, and are described in Part E of this Chapter.

Caution: The pistons, connecting rods and crankshaft must not be removed on these engines. If these components are excessively worn or damaged, the complete cylinder block and pistons must be renewed as an assembly.

Part E describes the removal of the engine/transmission from the vehicle and the full overhaul procedures that can then be carried out.

Engine description

The engine is an overhead camshaft (OHC), in-line three-cylinder unit, which is mounted transversely at the front of the vehicle, with the manual transmission bolted to the left-hand end of the engine. **Note:** *This engine is not fitted with automatic transmission.*

The engine is available with a single camshaft (SOHC) as engine code AWY or with double camshafts (DOHC) as engine codes AZQ and BME. The cylinder block is identical on both engines, and incorporates a gear-driven balancer shaft.

Caution: It is not permitted to dismantle the balancer shaft and gears.

The cylinder block, cylinder head and valve cover are all cast in aluminium alloy. The cylinder bores are machined in the cylinder block. The crankshaft has four main bearings, and thrustwashers are fitted to number 3 main bearing to control crankshaft endfloat. A balancer shaft is located in a housing beneath the cylinder block, and is driven by a gear located on the end of the crankshaft.

Camshaft drive is by chain from the crankshaft, and the chain is tensioned by a hydraulic tensioner. The valves are closed by coil springs and the camshafts actuate the valves by roller rockers and hydraulic tappets. On the SOHC engine there are 2 valves per cylinder, and on the DOHC engine there are 4 valves per cylinder. The flywheel is located on a flange at the left-hand end of the crankshaft. The main bearings and the big-end bearings are of shell type, whilst the connecting rod small-end bearings are of the bronze bush type, being pressed into the connecting rod and reamed to suit.

The oil pump is chain-driven from the end of the crankshaft. Oil is drawn from the sump through a strainer and circulated through an externally-mounted filter to the various engine components.

Operations with engine in car

The following work can be carried out with the engine in the vehicle:

a) *Compression pressure – testing.*
b) *Crankshaft pulley – removal and refitting.*
c) *Timing cover – removal and refitting.*
d) *Timing chain – renewal.*
e) *Timing chain tensioner and sprockets – removal and refitting.*
f) *Camshaft(s) and hydraulic tappets – removal and refitting.*
g) *Cylinder head – removal and refitting*.*
h) *Cylinder head – decarbonising.*
i) *Sump – removal and refitting.*
j) *Oil pump – removal, overhaul and refitting.*
k) *Crankshaft oil seals – renewal.*
l) *Engine/transmission mountings – inspection and renewal.*
m) *Flywheel – removal, inspection and refitting.*

* *Cylinder head dismantling procedures are detailed in Chapter 2E.*

2 Compression test – description and interpretation

1 When engine performance is down, or if misfiring occurs which cannot be attributed to the ignition or fuel systems, a compression test can provide diagnostic clues as to the engine's condition. If the test is performed regularly, it can give warning of trouble before any other symptoms become apparent.

2 The engine must be fully warmed-up to normal operating temperature, the battery must be fully-charged, and the spark plugs must be removed (Chapter 1A). The aid of an assistant will also be required.

3 Disable the ignition system by unplugging the wiring plug from the ignition coil module or HT coils. Also, disconnect the wiring from the fuel injectors. **Note:** *This will generate a fault code in the engine management memory, and it will be necessary to have this code erased by a Skoda dealer on completion of the test.*

4 Fit a compression tester to the No 1 cylinder spark plug hole – the type of tester which screws into the plug thread is to be preferred.

5 Have the assistant hold the throttle wide open and crank the engine on the starter motor; after one or two revolutions, the compression pressure should build-up to a maximum figure and then stabilise. Record the highest reading obtained.

6 Repeat the test on the remaining cylinders, recording the pressure in each.

7 All cylinders should produce very similar pressures, of the order of 11 to 15 bars. Any one cylinder reading below 11 bars, or a difference of more than 3 bars between cylinders, suggests a fault.

8 Note that the compression should build-up quickly in a healthy engine; low compression on the first stroke, followed by gradually increasing pressure on successive strokes, indicates worn piston rings.

9 A low compression reading on the first stroke, which does not build-up during successive strokes, indicates leaking valves or a blown head gasket (a cracked head could also be the cause).

10 If the pressure in any cylinder is reduced

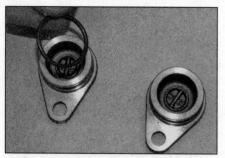

3.7 Fit new O-rings before refitting the caps

to 11 bars or less, carry out the following test to isolate the cause. Introduce a teaspoonful of clean oil into that cylinder through its spark plug hole and repeat the test.

11 If the addition of oil temporarily improves the compression pressure, this indicates that bore or piston wear is responsible for the pressure loss. No improvement suggests that leaking or burnt valves, or a blown head gasket, may be to blame.

12 A low reading from two adjacent cylinders is almost certainly due to the head gasket having blown between them; the presence of coolant in the engine oil will confirm this.

13 If one cylinder is about 20 percent lower than the others and the engine has a slightly rough idle, a worn camshaft lobe could be the cause.

14 On completion of the test, refit the spark plugs and reconnect the ignition system. Refit the fuel injector wiring. Have the fault code (see paragraph 3) erased by a Skoda dealer.

3.9a Fit the camshaft TDC tools . . .

3.9c Crankshaft TDC tool

3 Engine assembly and valve timing marks – general information and usage

1 Top dead centre (TDC) is the highest point in its travel up-and-down its cylinder bore that each piston reaches as the crankshaft rotates. While each piston reaches TDC both at the top of the compression stroke and again at the top of the exhaust stroke, for the purpose of timing the engine, TDC refers to the No 1 piston position at the top of its compression stroke.

2 No 1 piston and cylinder are at the right-hand end of the engine. Note that the crankshaft rotates clockwise when viewed from the right-hand side of the vehicle.

3 Disconnect the battery negative lead (refer to *Disconnecting the battery* in the *Reference* Chapter at the end of this manual). Remove all the spark plugs as described in Chapter 1A.

Engine code AWY

Note: *Skoda TDC setting tools T10120 and T10121 will be required for this procedure. Alternatively, pattern setting tools may be obtained from a car accessory shop.*

4 Unbolt the camshaft position sensor from the cylinder head cover.

5 Unbolt the crankshaft position/speed sender from the cylinder block rear flange.

6 Insert the camshaft TDC tool in the cylinder head cover hole, then turn the engine with a socket on the crankshaft pulley bolt until the TDC tool fully enters the hole in the camshaft.

3.9b . . . and tighten the bolts

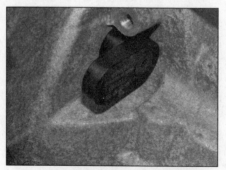

3.9d Crankshaft TDC tool fitted through the cylinder block rear flange

The engine is now at TDC compression for No 1 cylinder and the remaining TDC tool can be inserted through the cylinder block rear flange into the hole in the flywheel.

Engine codes AZQ and BME

Note: *Skoda TDC setting tools T10123 and T10121 will be required for this procedure. Alternatively, pattern setting tools may be obtained from a car accessory shop.*

7 At the left-hand end of the cylinder head, unbolt the caps from the ends of the inlet and exhaust camshafts. **Note:** *New O-rings must be fitted before refitting the caps* (see **illustration**).

8 Unbolt the crankshaft position/speed sender from the cylinder block rear flange.

9 Turn the engine with a socket on the crankshaft pulley bolt until the grooves at the left-hand ends of the camshafts are both horizontal. Now insert the tools T10123 into the camshafts and secure with the bolts. The engine is now at TDC compression for No 1 cylinder and the remaining TDC tool can be inserted through the cylinder block rear flange into the hole in the flywheel (see **illustrations**).

All engines

10 If necessary, as a further check that No 1 cylinder is on its compression stroke, remove the TDC tools and turn the engine back a little from the position described in paragraph 6 or 9. Now turn the engine forwards again to TDC with a finger placed over No 1 spark plug hole. If No 1 piston is rising on a compression stroke, pressure will be felt building-up as the engine is turned forwards to TDC.

11 Once No 1 cylinder has been positioned at TDC on the compression stroke, TDC for any of the other cylinders can then be located by rotating the crankshaft clockwise 240° at a time and following the firing order (see Specifications).

4 Crankshaft pulley – removal and refitting

Removal

1 Remove the engine top cover and air filter as applicable.

2 Mark the auxiliary drivebelt for normal rotation to ensure correct refitting. Note the routing of the drivebelt for ease of refitting.

3 Lever off the cover from the centre of the drivebelt tensioner roller, then use a 50 mm Torx key to turn the tensioner anti-clockwise to the stop. Hold the tensioner in this position and remove the drivebelt from the pulleys. Release the tensioner or, if preferred, retain the tensioner in this position by inserting a suitable pin/drill bit through the hole provided.

4 Have an assistant engage 4th gear and apply firm pressure to the footbrake pedal, then loosen the crankshaft pulley bolt and

4.4a Unscrew the crankshaft pulley bolt . . .

4.4b . . . and remove the crankshaft pulley

4.5 Angle-tightening the crankshaft pulley bolt

remove it together with the pulley (see illustrations). Skoda state that the bolt must be renewed whenever removed.

Refitting

5 Locate the pulley and new bolt on the end of the crankshaft, then tighten it to the specified torque and angle while holding it stationary using the method for removal (see illustration).

6 Locate the auxiliary drivebelt on the pulleys while holding the tensioner against the spring pressure, then release the tensioner making sure that the ribs of the drivebelt locate correctly in the pulley grooves. Refit the cover to the centre of the tensioner roller.

7 Refit the engine top cover and air filter as applicable.

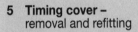

5 Timing cover – removal and refitting

Removal

1 Remove the engine top cover and air filter as applicable.

2 Apply the handbrake, then jack up the front of the vehicle and support it on axle stands (see Jacking and vehicle support). Remove the right-hand front roadwheel. For improved access, also remove the right-hand front wheel arch liner.

3 Mark the auxiliary drivebelt for direction of rotation to ensure correct refitting. Lever off the cover from the centre of the drivebelt

tensioner roller, then use a 50 mm Torx key to turn the tensioner anti-clockwise to the stop. Hold the tensioner in this position and remove the drivebelt from the pulleys. Release the tensioner or, if preferred, retain the tensioner in this position by inserting a suitable pin/drill bit through the hole provided (see illustration).

4 Hold the coolant pump pulley stationary using an oil filter strap or similar tool, then unscrew the retaining bolts and remove the pulley from the drive flange.

5 On models with air conditioning, unbolt the auxiliary drivebelt guide pulley from the cylinder block.

6 Unbolt the auxiliary drivebelt tensioner and pulley from the cylinder block (see illustration).

7 Remove the alternator as described in Chapter 5A.

8 Unclip the coolant expansion tank purge hose, and place it to one side

5.3 Insert a suitable pin/drill bit to retain the auxiliary drivebelt tensioner

9 Have an assistant engage 4th gear and apply firm pressure to the footbrake pedal, then use a multi-splined key to loosen the crankshaft pulley bolt and remove it together with the pulley. Alternatively, use a home-made tool to retain the pulley (see illustrations). Skoda state that the bolt must be renewed whenever removed.

10 Remove the sump as described in Section 9. If necessary, remove the exhaust front pipe as described in Chapter 4C to provide additional working room (see illustrations).

11 Unbolt and remove the oil level dipstick tube (see illustration) and, where applicable, remove the oil level/temperature sender from the cylinder block.

12 The right-hand end of the engine must now be supported while the engine mounting is removed, and the engine then held in a safe position in order to carry out the remaining work. To do this, use a hoist or support bar

5.6 Auxiliary drivebelt tensioner and pulley

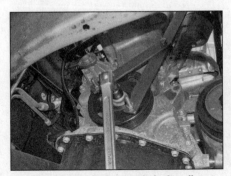

5.9a Unscrew the crankshaft pulley bolt . . .

5.9b . . . and remove it together with the pulley

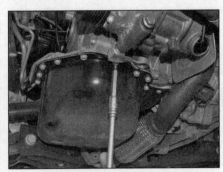

5.10a Undo the screws . . .

5.10b . . . and remove the sump

5.11 Removing the oil level dipstick tube mounting bolt

Refitting

17 Before refitting, carefully clean away all residues of sealant from the cover and engine. Also, check that the cover M6 retaining bolts still have thread sealant on their threads, and if not, renew them.

18 Apply a 3.0 mm diameter bead of sealant to the inside of the cover, making sure that the bead is on the inside of the bolt holes **(see illustrations opposite)**. Do not forget the upper and lower centre holes. **Note:** *The timing cover must be refitted within 15 minutes of applying the sealant to the cylinder head.* Apply a little sealant to the joint between the cylinder head and block on the engine, at the front and rear points where the cover makes contact.

19 Carefully locate the timing cover on the engine, insert the bolts, and progressively tighten them to the specified torque in sequence **(see illustrations)**. Note that there are different torques according to the position of the bolts, and on engine codes AZQ and BME some bolts require a torque plus angle-tightening.

20 Refit the sleeve to the end of the crankshaft together with a new O-ring. Skoda state that the cover oil seal must not be lubricated with either oil or grease.

21 Refit the PCV valve together with a new O-ring and tighten the retaining bolt.

attached to the engine lifting eyes – this is preferable to using a trolley jack beneath the engine **(see illustration)**. With the engine supported, remove the right-hand engine mounting with reference to Section 14.

13 Unbolt the PCV valve (crankcase ventilation) from the timing cover and recover the O-ring **(see illustration)**.

14 Progressively unscrew and remove all of the retaining bolts, then remove the timing cover from the engine. If necessary, tap the cover lightly to release the sealant, then withdraw the cover from the location dowels **(see illustrations)**.

15 With the cover removed, slide the sleeve

and O-ring from the end of the crankshaft. **Note:** *This is necessary as the sleeve must be assembled onto the crankshaft **after** refitting the timing cover.*

16 If the timing cover has been removed in order to carry out other work (ie, timing chain or cylinder head removal), the pistons must be positioned away from their TDC positions as a precaution against them touching the valves. To do this, temporarily refit the crankshaft pulley, then insert and tighten the crankshaft pulley bolt, using the TDC locking tool to hold the crankshaft stationary. Now, remove the locking tool and turn the crankshaft 45° anti-clockwise.

5.12 Engine support bar attached to the right-hand end of the engine

5.13 Removing the PCV valve (crankcase ventilation) from the timing cover

5.14a Removing the timing cover

5.14b Unscrew the bolts . . .

5.14c . . . and remove the insert from the timing cover

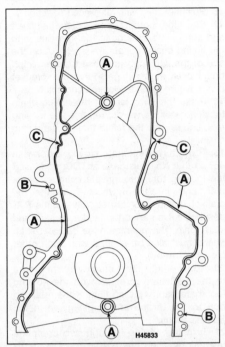

5.18a Apply a bead of sealant as shown – engine code AWY

A 3.0 mm bead
B Location dowels
C Joint between cylinder block and head

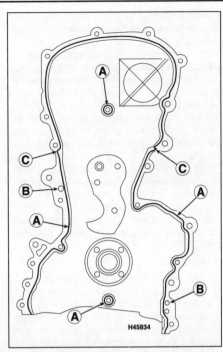

5.18b Apply a bead of sealant as shown – engine codes AZQ and BME

A 3.0 mm bead
B Location dowels
C Joint between cylinder block and head

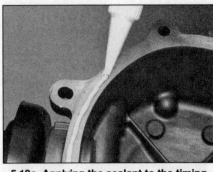

5.18c Applying the sealant to the timing cover

22 Refit the right-hand engine mounting with reference to Section 14 and remove the hoist/support bar.

23 Refit the oil level/temperature sender and the oil level dipstick tube.

24 Refit the sump with reference to Section 9.

25 Refit the crankshaft pulley and bolt, then tighten the bolt to the specified torque and angle. Hold the crankshaft stationary using the method described in paragraph 9.

26 Refit the cooling system ventilation pipe.

27 Refit the alternator with reference to Chapter 5A.

28 Refit the auxiliary drivebelt tensioner and pulley and, where applicable, the drivebelt guide pulley. Tighten the retaining bolts to the specified torque.

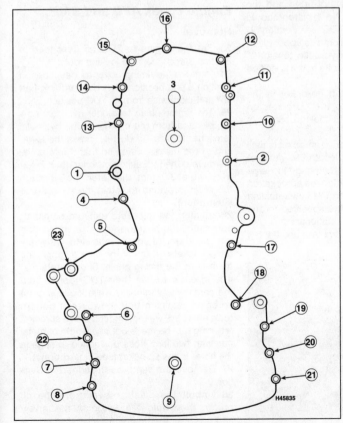

5.19a Timing chain cover bolt tightening sequence – engine code AWY

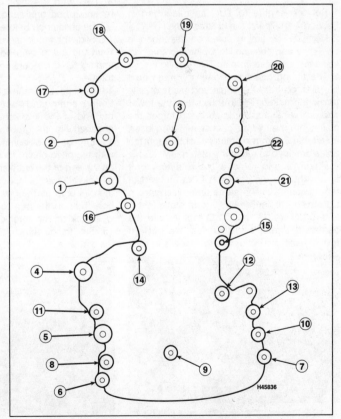

5.19b Timing chain cover bolt tightening sequence – engine codes AZQ and BME

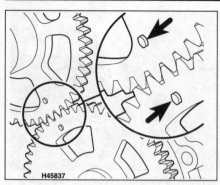

6.19 Balance shaft gear alignment indents

29 Refit the coolant pump pulley and tighten the retaining bolts.
30 Refit the auxiliary drivebelt with the rotational marking pointing the correct way.
31 Refit the wheel arch liner and roadwheel, and lower the vehicle to the ground.
32 Refit the engine top cover and air filter as applicable.

> **6 Timing chain, tensioner and sprockets** – removal, inspection and refitting

Engine code AWY

Removal

1 Set the engine to TDC as described in Section 3 and insert the locking tools.
2 Remove the timing cover as described in Section 5 and position No 1 piston/crankshaft 45° anti-clockwise from its TDC position.
3 The timing chain tensioner rail must now be released from the chain and the hydraulic tensioner locked. To do this, press the lower end of the rail rearwards so that it forces the piston into the hydraulic tensioner, then insert a suitable 3.0 mm diameter tool through the holes provided to retain the piston.
4 Unscrew and remove the retaining bolt and withdraw the sprocket from the end of the camshaft, at the same time disengaging it from the timing chain. Skoda state that it is in order to use their TDC tool to hold the camshaft stationary, however, if a pattern tool is used, we recommend that a sprocket

6.25 Insert a 3.0 mm diameter drill bit in the hole to retain the timing chain tensioner piston

retaining tool be made out of a length of metal bar, with two long bolts positioned to engage the holes in the sprocket.
5 Remove the sump as described in Section 9.
6 Unbolt the plastic cover from the oil pump, then hold the sprocket stationary and unscrew the retaining bolt – discard the bolt as a new one must be used on refitting. Slide the small sprocket from the end of the crankshaft and place the chain and sprockets to one side. **Note:** *The sprocket is not keyed to the crankshaft.*
7 Slide the crankshaft sprocket together with the timing chain from the crankshaft. **Note:** *The sprocket is keyed to the crankshaft.*
8 Slide the tensioner rail from its upper pivot. If necessary, unbolt the remaining guide rail and hydraulic tensioner from the cylinder block.

Inspection

9 Thoroughly clean all components, then examine the timing chain and oil pump drive chain for excessive wear. Also check the sprocket teeth for wear. If the engine has covered a high mileage, the chain and sprockets should be renewed as a matter of course.
10 The crankshaft pulley bolt must be renewed whenever removed.

Refitting

11 Check that the camshaft is still positioned at TDC with the locking tool fitted and the retaining bolt tightened. No 1 piston should still be positioned before TDC (see Section 5).
12 Slide the tensioner rail onto its upper pivot. Refit the guide rail and hydraulic tensioner, and tighten the mounting bolts to the specified torque.
13 Engage the crankshaft sprocket in the timing chain and locate the sprocket on the end of the crankshaft, making sure it is engaged with the groove.
14 Engage the oil pump drive sprocket (small) with the drive chain, then locate the sprocket on the end of the crankshaft. Engage the large sprocket in the chain, position the sprocket on the oil pump and screw on the new retaining bolt. Tighten the bolt to the specified torque while holding the sprocket stationary.
15 Refit the oil pump plastic cover and tighten the screws.

6.26a Hold the sprocket while loosening the bolt . . .

16 Refit the sump with reference to Section 9.
17 Clean the contact surfaces of the camshaft and sprocket and engage the sprocket with the timing chain. Locate the sprocket on the end of the camshaft and insert the retaining bolt, loosely at this stage so that the sprocket can move freely on the locked camshaft.
18 Press the lower end of the timing chain tensioner rail rearwards, remove the locking tool, and release the rail to tension the timing chain.
19 Turn the crankshaft slowly clockwise 45° so that No 1 piston is at TDC, and insert the locking tool through the cylinder block rear flange into the flywheel – note that the crankshaft should be turned *slowly* to the TDC position; if it is turned too far, turn it back and start again. The indents on the balancer shaft gears must also be aligned with each other **(see illustration)**.
20 Apply slight anti-clockwise pressure to the camshaft sprocket with the holding tool (paragraph 4), then tighten the retaining bolt to the torque and angle given in the Specifications.
21 Turn the engine through two complete revolutions, then check that the TDC tools can be fitted to the camshaft and flywheel. Remove the tools.
22 Unbolt and remove the crankshaft pulley from the end of the crankshaft, then refit timing cover with reference to Section 5.

Engine codes AZQ and BME

Removal

23 Set the engine to TDC as described in Section 3 and insert the locking tools.
24 Remove the timing cover as described in Section 5 and position No 1 piston/crankshaft 45° anti-clockwise from its TDC position.
25 The timing chain tensioner rail must now be released from the chain and the hydraulic tensioner locked. To do this, press the lower end of the rail rearwards so that it forces the piston into the hydraulic tensioner, then insert a suitable 3.0 mm diameter tool through the holes provided to retain the piston **(see illustration)**.
26 Identify the inlet and exhaust camshaft sprockets for position, then unscrew and remove their retaining bolts and withdraw the sprockets, at the same time disengaging them from the timing chain. Skoda state that it is in order to use their TDC tool to hold the camshafts stationary while loosening the sprocket retaining bolt, however, if pattern tools are used, we recommend that a sprocket retaining tool be made out of a length of metal bar, with two long bolts positioned to engage the holes in the sprocket **(see illustrations)**.
27 Remove the sump as described in Section 9.
28 Unbolt the plastic cover from the oil pump, then hold the sprocket stationary and unscrew the retaining bolt – discard the bolt as a new one must be used on refitting. Slide the small sprocket from the end of the

6.26b . . . then remove the bolt and sprocket

6.29 Removing the timing chain sprocket from the crankshaft

6.30a Slide the tensioner rail from its upper pivot . . .

6.30b . . . then unbolt the remaining guide rail

6.30c Removing the timing chain tensioner

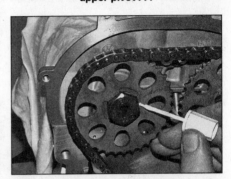

6.42 Mark the bolt and sprocket to apply the tightening angle

crankshaft and place the chain and sprockets to one side. **Note:** *The sprocket is not keyed to the crankshaft.*

29 Slide the crankshaft sprocket together with the timing chain from the crankshaft **(see illustration)**. **Note:** *The sprocket is keyed to the crankshaft.*

30 Slide the tensioner rail from its upper pivot. If necessary, unbolt the remaining guide rail and hydraulic tensioner from the cylinder block **(see illustrations)**.

Inspection

31 Thoroughly clean all components, then examine the timing chain and oil pump drive chain for excessive wear. Also check the sprocket teeth for wear. If the engine has covered a high mileage, the chain and sprockets should be renewed as a matter of course.

32 The crankshaft pulley bolt must be renewed whenever removed.

Refitting

33 Check that the camshafts are still positioned at TDC with the locking tools fitted and the retaining bolts tightened. No 1 piston should still be positioned before TDC (see Section 5).

34 Slide the tensioner rail onto its upper pivot. Refit the guide rail and hydraulic tensioner, and tighten the mounting bolts to the specified torque.

35 Engage the crankshaft sprocket in the timing chain and locate the sprocket on the end of the crankshaft, making sure it is engaged with the groove.

36 Engage the oil pump drive sprocket

(small) with the drive chain, then locate the sprocket on the end of the crankshaft. Engage the large sprocket in the chain, position the sprocket on the oil pump and screw on the new retaining bolt. Tighten the bolt to the specified torque while holding the sprocket stationary.

37 Refit the oil pump plastic cover and tighten the screws.

38 Refit the sump with reference to Section 9.

39 Clean the contact surfaces of the camshafts and sprockets and engage the sprockets with the timing chain. Locate the sprockets on the end of the camshafts and insert the retaining bolts, loosely at this stage so that the sprockets can move freely on the locked camshafts.

40 Press the lower end of the timing chain tensioner rail rearwards, remove the locking tool, and release the rail to tension the timing chain.

41 Turn the crankshaft slowly clockwise 45° so that No 1 piston is at TDC, and insert the locking tool through the cylinder block rear flange into the flywheel – note that the crankshaft should be turned *slowly* to the TDC position; if it is turned too far, turn it back and start again. The indents on the balancer shaft gears must also be aligned with each other **(see illustration 6.19)**.

42 Apply slight anti-clockwise pressure to the camshaft sprocket with the holding tool (paragraph 4), then tighten the retaining bolt to the torque and angle given in the Specifications. The angle-tightening can be made by marking the bolt and sprocket with dabs of paint **(see illustration)**.

43 Turn the engine through two complete revolutions, then check that the TDC tools can be fitted to the camshaft and flywheel. Remove the tools.

44 Unbolt and remove the crankshaft pulley from the end of the crankshaft, then refit the timing cover with reference to Section 5.

7 Camshaft(s) and hydraulic tappets – removal, inspection and refitting

Engine code AWY

Removal

1 Remove the timing cover as described in Section 5.

2 Remove the camshaft sprocket as described in Section 6.

3 Progressively unscrew the retaining bolts from the cylinder head cover/housing. Lift the cover/housing from the cylinder head. If it is tight, tap it with a wooden or hide mallet. Discard the bolts as new ones must be used during refitting.

4 Lift the camshaft from the cylinder head.

5 Obtain a suitable box with compartments for each of the roller/rocker arms and hydraulic tappets, so that they can be identified for their correct position to ensure correct refitting. Remove the rocker arms and hydraulic tappets and place them in the box.

6 Clean away the sealant from the cylinder head and cover, and also clean the camshaft bearings.

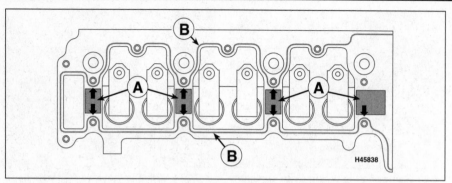

7.15 Grease the shaded areas (A) and apply a 2.0 to 3.0 mm wide bead (B) of sealant as shown

Arrows indicate areas to keep clear

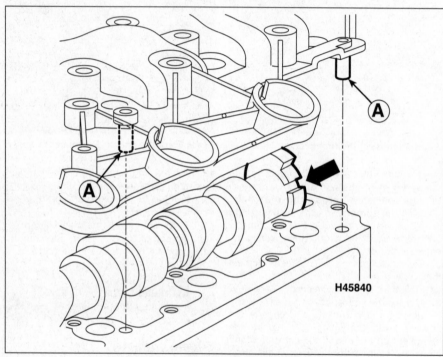

7.16 Position the camshaft TDC cut-out as shown

A Location dowels

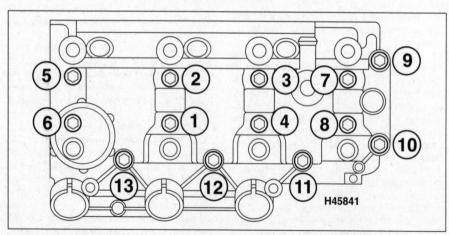

7.18 Cylinder head cover/housing bolt tightening sequence

Inspection

7 Visually inspect the camshaft for evidence of wear on the surfaces of the lobes and journals. Normally their surfaces should be smooth and have a dull shine; look for scoring, erosion or pitting, and areas that appear highly polished, indicating excessive wear. Accelerated wear will occur once the hardened exterior of the camshaft has been damaged, so always renew worn items.

8 If the machined surfaces of the camshaft appear discoloured or blued, it is likely that it has been overheated at some point, probably due to inadequate lubrication.

9 To measure the camshaft endfloat, temporarily locate it on the cylinder head without the rockers and hydraulic tappets. Anchor a DTI gauge to the end of the cylinder head and align the gauge probe with the camshaft axis. Push the camshaft to one end of the cylinder head as far as it will travel, then rest the DTI gauge probe on the end of the camshaft, and zero the gauge display. Push the camshaft as far as it will go to the other end of the cylinder head, and record the gauge reading. Verify the reading by pushing the camshaft back to its original position and checking that the gauge indicates zero again. Repeat the checking procedure for the remaining camshaft.

10 Check that the camshaft endfloat measurement is within the limit given in the Specifications. Wear outside of this limit is unlikely to be confined to any one component, so renewal of the camshaft and cover must be considered.

11 Inspect the hydraulic tappets for obvious signs of wear or damage, and renew if necessary. Check that the oil holes in the tappets are free from obstructions.

Refitting

12 Remove the crankshaft TDC locking tool, then turn the engine anti-clockwise by 45° so that none of the pistons are at their TDC position.

13 Lubricate the roller/rocker arms and hydraulic tappets with engine oil and refit them to their correct positions on the cylinder head. Check that the arms are located correctly on the valve stems and hydraulic tappets.

14 Apply a film of grease to the camshaft bearing surfaces in the cylinder head and cover/housing.

15 Apply a 2.0 to 3.0 mm wide bead of sealant as shown **(see illustration)** to the cylinder head. Make sure that the sealant is not allowed onto the camshaft bearing surfaces, and make sure that the bead runs around the inside of the bolt holes. **Note:** *The cylinder head cover must be refitted within 15 minutes of applying the sealant to the cylinder head.*

16 Carefully lay the camshaft on the cylinder head with the TDC cut-out just above the upper face of the head, and pointing forwards towards the exhaust manifold position. Refit the cylinder head cover/housing, making sure that the location dowels enter the holes in the head **(see illustration)**.

17 Insert *new* retaining bolts and initially hand-tighten all of them.

18 Tighten the retaining bolts to the specified torque and angle given in the Specifications, and in sequence **(see illustration opposite)**.

19 Refit the camshaft sprocket with reference to Section 6.

20 Refit the timing cover as described in Section 5.

Engine codes AZQ and BME

Removal

21 Remove the timing cover as described in Section 5.

22 Remove the camshaft sprockets as described in Section 6.

23 Remove the ignition coils with the power output stage. Note that Skoda technicians use a special tool (T10094) to remove the coils, however, a length of bent welding rod or similar hooked under the wiring plugs, may be used to extract the coils.

24 Unscrew the cylinder head cover bolts in the **reverse** order to that shown for tightening in paragraph 41, and remove them **(see illustration)**.

25 Remove the cylinder head cover complete with camshafts from the cylinder head **(see illustration)**. If it is tight, use a mallet or rubber hammer to tap the top of the cover in several places in order to release it from the locating dowels.

26 Clean away the sealant from the cylinder head and cover.

27 With the cylinder head cover on the bench, loosen the camshaft bearing cap/housing bolts in the **reverse** order to that shown for tightening in paragraph 36. Lift the caps/housings from the cover **(see illustration)**. Identify the caps/housings for location to ensure correct refitting.

28 Identify each camshaft for location and position, then lift them out from the cylinder head cover **(see illustration)**. Note: *The inlet camshaft has a lug which is positioned over the hole for the Hall sender.*

29 Obtain a suitable box with compartments for each of the roller/rocker arms and hydraulic tappets, so that they can be identified for their correct position. Remove the rocker arms and hydraulic tappets from the cylinder head and place them in the box **(see illustrations)**.

30 Clean the camshaft bearing surfaces in the cover and caps/housings.

Inspection

31 Refer to paragraphs 7 to 11, but note that the camshafts and caps/housings will have to be temporarily refitted to the cover to measure the endfloat.

Refitting

32 Remove the crankshaft TDC locking tool, then turn the engine anti-clockwise by 45° so that none of the pistons are at their TDC position.

33 Lubricate the roller/rocker arms and hydraulic tappets with engine oil and refit

7.24 Progressively unscrew the bolts . . .

7.25 . . . and remove the cylinder head cover complete with camshafts

7.27 Removing camshaft bearing caps

7.28 Removing the camshafts from the cylinder head cover

them to their correct positions on the cylinder head **(see illustration)**.

34 Apply a film of grease to the camshaft bearing surfaces in the caps/housings and cover.

35 Carefully locate the camshafts in their

7.29a Roller/rocker arms

7.29b Remove the roller/rocker arms and hydraulic tappets from the cylinder head . . .

correct positions in the cover, noting that the lug on the inlet camshaft must be positioned over the hole for the Hall sender.

36 Refit the bearing caps/housings and initially hand-tighten the retaining bolts. It is important that the caps are not tilted as

7.29c . . . and place them in the box

7.33 Fitting the roller/rocker arms and hydraulic tappets

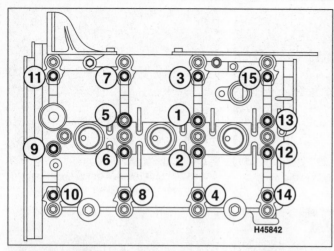

7.36 Camshaft bearing cap/housing bolt tightening sequence

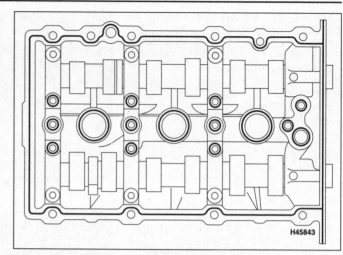

7.37a Apply a bead of sealant as shown –
engine codes AZQ and BME

7.37b Apply the sealant carefully to the
cylinder head cover

7.39 Refitting the cylinder head cover

the bolts are tightened. Tighten the bolts in sequence (see illustration) to the torque and angle given in the specifications.

37 Apply a 2.0 to 3.0 mm wide bead of sealant as shown (see illustrations) to the cylinder head cover. Make sure that the sealant is not allowed onto the camshaft bearing surfaces, and make sure that the

bead runs around the inside of the bolt holes. Note: *The cylinder head cover must be refitted within 15 minutes of applying the sealant to the cylinder head.*

38 Check that the roller/rocker arms are correctly located on the valve stems and hydraulic tappets.

39 Lower the cover onto the cylinder head

making sure that the location dowels enter their holes correctly (see illustration).

40 Insert *new* retaining bolts and initially hand-tighten all of them.

41 Tighten the retaining bolts to the specified torque and angle given in the Specifications, and in sequence (see illustration).

42 Refit the ignition coils and power output stage, followed by the pipe sections.

43 Refit the camshaft sprockets (Section 6) and timing cover (Section 5).

8 Cylinder head –
removal, inspection
and refitting

Removal

1 Remove the timing cover as described in Section 5. Also, if required, remove the inlet and exhaust manifolds.

2 Remove the camshaft sprocket(s) as described in Section 6.

3 On engine code AWY (SOHC) remove the camshaft and hydraulic tappets as described in Section 7.

4 On engine codes AZQ and BME (DOHC) remove the cylinder head cover complete with camshafts, then remove the hydraulic tappets as described in Section 7. It is not necessary to remove the camshafts from the cover unless it is specifically required to work on them.

5 Progressively slacken the cylinder head bolts in the **reverse** order to that given for tightening in paragraph 20. Remove the cylinder head bolts. Note: *The bolts must not be re-used – obtain new ones.*

6 With all the bolts removed, lift the cylinder head from the block (together with the inlet and exhaust manifolds, if not removed) (see illustration). If the cylinder head is stuck, tap it with a soft-faced mallet to break the joint. **Do not** insert a lever into the gasket joint.

7 Lift the cylinder head gasket from the block (see illustration).

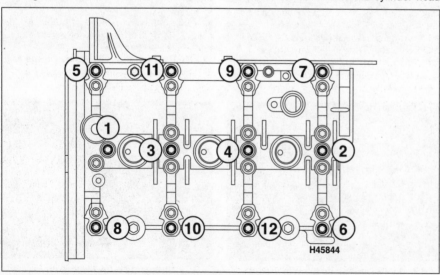

7.41 Cylinder head cover bolt tightening sequence

8.6 Removing the cylinder head from the block

8.7 Cylinder block with head removed

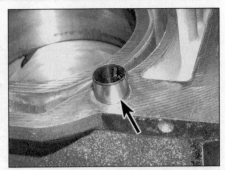

8.17a Cylinder head locating dowel on the block

8.17b Fitting a new cylinder head gasket

8.17c Typical cylinder head gasket markings

8.18 Lowering the cylinder head onto the gasket

8 If desired, the inlet and exhaust manifolds can be removed from the cylinder head with reference to the relevant part of Chapter 4.

Inspection

9 Dismantling and inspection of the cylinder head is covered in Part E of this Chapter.
10 The mating faces of the cylinder head and block must be perfectly clean before refitting the head.
11 Use a scraper to remove all traces of gasket and carbon, also clean the tops of the pistons. Take particular care with the aluminium surfaces, as the soft metal is easily damaged.
12 Make sure that debris is not allowed to enter the oil and water passages – this is particularly important for the oil circuit, as carbon could block the oil supply to the camshaft and crankshaft bearings. Using adhesive tape and paper, seal the water, oil and bolt holes in the cylinder block. To prevent carbon entering the gap between the pistons and bores, smear a little grease in the gap. After cleaning a piston, rotate the crankshaft to that the piston moves down the bore, then wipe out the grease and carbon with a cloth rag. Clean the other piston crowns in the same way.
13 Check the head and block for nicks, deep scratches and other damage. If slight, they may be removed carefully with a file. More serious damage may be repaired by machining, but this is a specialist job. If warpage of the cylinder head is suspected, use a straight-edge to check it for distortion, as described in Part D of this Chapter.

Refitting

14 Ensure that the cylinder head bolt holes in the cylinder block are clean and free of oil. Syringe or soak up any oil left in the bolt holes. This is most important in order that the correct bolt tightening torque can be applied, and to prevent the possibility of the block being cracked by hydraulic pressure when the bolts are tightened.
15 Ensure that the crankshaft has been turned to position No 1 piston slightly down its bore from the TDC position (refer to timing chain refitting in Section 6). This will eliminate any risk of piston-to-valve contact as the cylinder head is refitted.
16 Where applicable, refit the inlet and exhaust manifolds to the cylinder head.
17 Ensure that the cylinder head locating dowels are in place in the cylinder block (see illustration), then fit a new cylinder head

8.19a Lightly oil the threads and heads of the bolts . . .

gasket over the dowels, ensuring that the part number is uppermost. Where applicable, the OBEN/TOP marking should also be uppermost (see illustrations). Note that Skoda recommend that the gasket is only removed from its packaging immediately prior to fitting.
18 Lower the cylinder head into position on the gasket, ensuring that it engages correctly over the dowels (see illustration).
19 Lightly oil the threads and heads of the new cylinder head bolts, then insert them and screw in as far as possible by hand (see illustrations).
20 Working in sequence, tighten all the cylinder head bolts to the specified Stage 1 torque (see illustrations).
21 Again working in sequence, tighten all the cylinder head bolts through the specified Stage 2 angle (see illustration).

8.19b . . . and screw them in as far as possible by hand

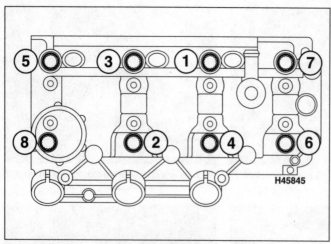

**8.20a Cylinder head bolt tightening sequence –
engine code AWY**

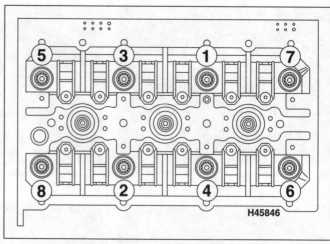

**8.20b Cylinder head bolt tightening sequence –
engine codes AZQ and BME**

**8.20c Tightening the bolts to the torque
setting**

**8.21 Tightening the bolts through the
specified angle**

22 Finally, tighten all the cylinder head bolts, in sequence, through the specified Stage 3 angle.
23 Refit the hydraulic tappets, camshaft(s) and cylinder head cover with reference to Section 7.
24 Refit the camshaft sprocket(s) as described in Section 6.
25 Refit the timing cover as described in Section 5.

9 Sump –
removed and refitting

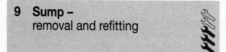

Removal

1 Apply the handbrake, then jack up the front of the vehicle and support securely on axle stands (see *Jacking and vehicle support*).
2 Remove the securing screws and withdraw the engine undershield(s).
3 Drain the engine oil as described in Chapter 1A.
4 Where fitted, disconnect the wiring connector from the oil level/temperature sender on the sump.
5 Unscrew and remove the bolts securing the sump to the cylinder block, then withdraw

the sump **(see illustrations)**. If necessary, release the sump by tapping with a soft-faced mallet.

Refitting

6 Commence refitting by thoroughly cleaning the mating faces of the sump and cylinder block. Ensure that all traces of old sealant are removed.
7 Ensure that the cylinder block mating face of the sump is free from all traces of old sealant, oil and grease, and then apply a 2.0 to 4.0 mm thick bead of silicone sealant (D 176404 A2 or equivalent) to the sump. Note that the sealant should be run around the inside of the bolt holes in the sump **(see illustration)**. The sump must be fitted within 5 minutes of applying the sealant.
8 Offer the sump up to the cylinder block, then refit the retaining bolts, and progressively tighten them in diagonal sequence to the specified torque.
9 Reconnect the wiring to the oil level/ temperature sender on the sump.
10 Refit the engine undershield(s) and lower the vehicle to the ground.
11 Allow at least 30 minutes from the time of refitting the sump for the sealant to dry, then refill the engine with oil, with reference to Chapter 1A.

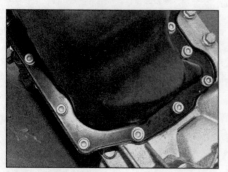

9.5a Unscrew the bolts . . .

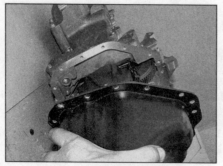

9.5b . . . and withdraw the sump

9.7 Applying a bead of sealant to the sump

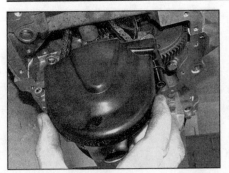

10.2a Unbolt the plastic cover from the oil pump . . .

10.2b . . . then use a tool to hold the sprocket while the retaining bolt is loosened . . .

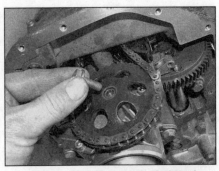

10.2c . . . then remove the bolt and sprocket

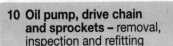

10 Oil pump, drive chain and sprockets – removal, inspection and refitting

Removal

1 Remove the sump as described in Section 9. It is not necessary to remove the timing cover unless renewing the timing chain.

2 Unbolt the plastic cover from the oil pump, then hold the sprocket stationary and unscrew the retaining bolt **(see illustrations)**. Discard the bolt as a new one must be used on refitting.

3 Swivel the chain tensioner outwards and release the sprocket from the oil pump. Leave the sprocket hanging in the chain.

4 Unscrew the mounting bolts and withdraw the oil pump from the dowels in the cylinder block **(see illustrations)**.

5 If it is required to remove the oil pump chain and tensioner, first remove the timing cover as described in Section 6. Mark the chain and sprockets to ensure they are refitted the original way around. Slide the small sprocket from the end of the crankshaft, then remove both sprockets from the chain. **Note:** *The sprocket is not keyed to the crankshaft.* Unbolt and remove the tensioner **(see illustrations)**.

Inspection

6 Thoroughly clean all components, then examine the oil pump drive chain for excessive wear. Also check the sprocket teeth for wear. If the engine has covered a high mileage, the

10.4a Unscrew the mounting bolts . . .

chain and sprockets should be renewed as a matter of course.

7 The crankshaft pulley bolt must be renewed whenever removed.

Refitting

8 If removed, refit the oil pump drive chain as follows. Refit the tensioner, then engage the small sprocket with the drive chain, then locate the sprocket on the end of the crankshaft making sure that it is the correct way around.

9 Locate the oil pump on the cylinder block dowels, insert the mounting bolts and tighten them to the specified torque.

10 Where removed, engage the oil pump sprocket in the chain. Swivel the chain tensioner outwards, then position the sprocket on the oil pump and screw on the new retaining bolt. Tighten the bolt to the specified torque and angle while holding the sprocket stationary.

10.4b . . . and remove the oil pump

11 Refit the oil pump plastic cover and tighten the screws.

12 Refit the sump with reference to Section 9.

11 Oil pressure warning light switch – removal and refitting

Removal

1 The oil pressure warning light switch is located on the left-hand end of the cylinder head.

2 Disconnect the wiring connector and wipe clean the area around the switch.

3 Unscrew the switch from the cylinder head and remove it, along with its sealing washer. If the switch is to be left removed from the engine for any length of time, plug the cylinder head aperture.

10.5a Removing the oil pump sprocket from the crankshaft

10.5b Remove the oil pump chain and sprocket . . .

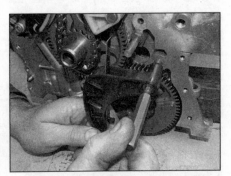

10.5c . . . then unbolt and remove the tensioner

12.3 Removing the old oil seal

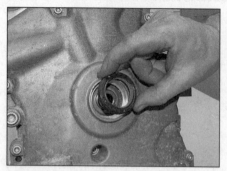

12.5a Locate the new oil seal in the timing cover . . .

12.5b . . . and use a suitable socket to tap it into position

12.6a Refit the O-ring seal . . .

12.6b . . . and insert the sleeve

12.8 Note the fitted depth of the oil seal before removing it

Refitting

4 Examine the sealing washer for signs of damage or deterioration and if necessary renew.

5 Refit the switch, complete with washer, and tighten it to the specified torque.

6 Securely reconnect the wiring connector then check and, if necessary, top-up the engine oil as described in *Weekly checks*.

12 Crankshaft oil seals
– renewal

Right-hand oil seal

1 Remove the crankshaft pulley as described in Section 4, then note the fitted depth of the oil seal in the timing cover.

2 Slide the sleeve from the end of the crankshaft. **Note:** *This is necessary as the sleeve must be assembled onto the crankshaft through the oil seal.* If necessary, remove the sleeve-sealing O-ring from the crankshaft.

3 Carefully lever the old seal out of the timing cover using a suitable flat-bladed screwdriver **(see illustration)**, taking great care not to damage the cover or crankshaft. Alternatively, punch or drill two small holes opposite each other in the seal, then screw a self-tapping screw into each and pull on the screws with pliers to extract the seal.

4 Clean the seal housing, and polish off any burrs or raised edges on the crankshaft which may have caused the seal to fail in the first place.

5 Note that the new oil seal **must not** be oiled or greased, and the contact surfaces of the timing cover must be completely dry. New oil seals are provided with a fitting adapter. Locate the adapter and new seal over the

crankshaft and onto the timing cover, and press it into position until it is at the fitted depth previously noted. If necessary, the seal can be tapped into position using a suitable tubular drift, such as a socket, which bears only on the hard outer edge of the seal **(see illustrations)**. Note that the sealing lips must face inwards.

6 If necessary, locate a new O-ring seal on the crankshaft, then carefully insert the sleeve through the new oil seal onto the crankshaft **(see illustrations)**.

7 Refit the crankshaft pulley as described in Section 4.

Left-hand oil seal

8 Remove the flywheel as described in Section 13, then note the fitted depth of the oil seal in the timing cover **(see illustration)**.

9 Carefully punch or drill two small holes opposite each other in the seal. Screw a self-tapping screw into each hole, and pull on the screws with pliers to extract the seal **(see illustration)**.

10 Clean the cylinder block/crankcase, and polish off any burrs or raised edges on the crankshaft which may have caused the seal to fail in the first place.

11 Note that the new oil seal **must not** be oiled or greased, and the contact surfaces of the housing and crankshaft must be completely dry. New oil seals are provided with a fitting adapter. Locate the adapter and new seal over the crankshaft and into the housing, and press it into position until it is at the fitted depth previously noted **(see illustrations)**. If necessary, the seal can be

12.9 Removing the crankshaft left-hand (flywheel end) oil seal

12.11a Locate the adapter and new oil seal over the crankshaft . . .

12.11b . . . and tap it into position

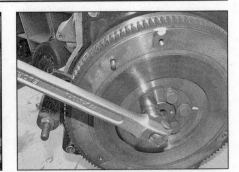

13.2 Home-made tool used to hold the flywheel stationary

13.3 Unscrewing the flywheel retaining bolts

tapped into position using a suitable tubular drift, such as a socket, which bears only on the hard outer edge of the seal. Note that the sealing lips must face inwards.

12 Refit the flywheel as described in Section 13.

13 Flywheel – removal, inspection and refitting

Removal

1 Remove the transmission as described in Chapter 7A, then remove the clutch assembly as described in Chapter 6.

2 Prevent the flywheel from turning by locking the ring gear teeth **(see illustration)**, or by bolting a strap between the flywheel and the cylinder block/crankcase.

3 Unscrew and remove the flywheel retaining bolts **(see illustration)**; discard the bolts, as they must be renewed whenever they are disturbed.

4 Remove the flywheel, and if necessary remove the engine rear plate **(see illustration)**. Do not drop it, as it is very heavy. **Note:** *The bolt holes are offset, so it is only possible to fit the flywheel in one position.*

Inspection

5 If the clutch mating surface of the flywheel is deeply scored, cracked or otherwise damaged, the flywheel must be renewed, unless it is possible to have it surface-ground. Seek the advice of a Skoda dealer or engine reconditioning specialist.

6 If the ring gear teeth are badly worn, it must be renewed, but this job is best left to a Skoda dealer or engine reconditioning specialist. The temperature to which the new ring gear must be heated for installation (150°C minimum) is critical and, if not done accurately, the hardness of the teeth will be destroyed.

7 If it is felt necessary, use the correct-size tap to clean the threads in the crankshaft of any old thread-locking fluid.

Refitting

8 Clean the mating surfaces of the flywheel and crankshaft, then refit the rear plate and locate the flywheel on the crankshaft.

13.4 Removing the engine rear plate

9 If the new flywheel retaining bolts are not supplied with their threads already pre-coated **(see illustration)**, apply a suitable thread-locking compound to the threads of each bolt. Fit the bolts, tightening them by hand only at this stage.

10 Lock the flywheel using the method employed on dismantling, and tighten the retaining bolts to the specified torque wrench and angle settings **(see illustrations)**.

11 Refit the clutch as described in Chapter 6, then remove the locking tool and refit the transmission as described in Chapter 7A.

14 Engine/transmission mountings – inspection and renewal

Inspection

1 If improved access is required, jack up the

13.10a Tighten the bolts to the specified torque . . .

13.9 Fitting the new flywheel retaining bolts

front of the vehicle, and support it securely on axle stands (see *Jacking and vehicle support*). Remove the securing screws and remove the engine undershield(s).

2 Check the mounting rubbers to see if they are cracked, hardened or separated from the metal at any point; renew the mounting if any such damage or deterioration is evident.

3 Check that all the mountings are securely tightened; use a torque wrench to check if possible.

4 Using a large screwdriver or a crowbar, check for wear in the mounting by carefully levering against it to check for free play. Where this is not possible, enlist the aid of an assistant to move the engine/transmission back-and-forth, or from side-to-side, whilst you observe the mounting. While some free play is to be expected, even from new components, excessive wear should be obvious. If excessive free play is found, check first

13.10b . . . and angle

14.9 Removing the right-hand engine mounting bracket

that the fasteners are correctly secured, then renew any worn components as described in the following paragraphs.

Renewal

Right-hand mounting

Note: *New mounting securing bolts will be required on refitting.*

5 Attach a hoist and lifting tackle to the engine lifting brackets on the cylinder head, and raise the hoist to just take the weight of the engine. Alternatively the engine can be supported on a trolley jack under the engine. Use a block of wood between the sump and the head of the jack, to prevent any damage to the sump.

6 Where necessary, unbolt the coolant reservoir and move it to one side, leaving the coolant hoses connected.

7 Where applicable, move any wiring harnesses, pipes or hoses to one side to enable removal of the engine mounting.

8 Unscrew the mounting centre nut securing the bracket to the flexible mounting.

9 Unscrew the three bolts securing the mounting bracket to the engine and remove the bracket **(see illustration)**.

10 Unbolt and remove the flexible mounting from the body.

11 Refitting is a reversal of removal, bearing in mind the following points.

   a) Use new securing bolts.

   b) Tighten all fixings to the specified torque.

Left-hand mounting

Note: *New mounting bolts will be required on refitting (there is no need to renew the smaller mounting-to-body bolts).*

12 Remove the engine top cover which also incorporates the air filter.

13 Attach a hoist and lifting tackle to the engine lifting brackets on the cylinder head, and raise the hoist to just take the weight of the engine and transmission. Alternatively the engine can be supported on a trolley jack under the transmission. Use a block of wood between the transmission and the head of the jack, to prevent any damage to the transmission.

14 Remove the battery, as described in Chapter 5A, then disconnect the main starter motor feed cable from the positive battery terminal box.

15 Release any relevant wiring or hoses from the clips on the battery tray, then unscrew the four securing bolts and remove the battery tray.

16 Unscrew the bolts securing the mounting to the transmission, and the remaining bolts securing the mounting to the body, then lift the mounting from the engine compartment.

17 Refitting is a reversal of removal, bearing in mind the following points:

   a) Use new mounting bolts.

   b) Tighten all fixings to the specified torque.

Rear mounting (torque arm)

Note: *New mounting bolts will be required on refitting.*

18 Apply the handbrake, then jack up the front of the vehicle and support securely on axle stands (see *Jacking and vehicle support*). Remove the engine undershield(s) for access to the rear mounting (torque arm).

19 Support the rear of the transmission beneath the final drive housing. To do this, use a trolley jack and block of wood, or alternatively wedge a block of wood between the transmission and the subframe.

20 Working under the vehicle, unscrew and remove the bolt securing the mounting to the subframe.

21 Unscrew the two bolts securing the mounting to the transmission, then withdraw the mounting from under the vehicle.

22 Refitting is a reversal of removal, but use new mounting securing bolts, and tighten all fixings to the specified torque.

Chapter 2 Part B:
1.4 litre OHV petrol engine in-car repair procedures

Contents

Section number

Camshaft and hydraulic tappets – removal and
  refitting . . . . .See Chapter 2E
Compression test – description and interpretation 2
Crankshaft oil seals – renewal 10
Cylinder head and manifolds – removal, separation and refitting . . . 6
Engine oil and filter renewal . . . . .See Chapter 1A
Engine oil level check. . . . . .See Weekly checks
Engine/transmission mounting rubbers – inspection and renewal. . . 12
Flywheel – removal, inspection and refitting 11

Section number

General information 1
Oil pump – removal, inspection and refitting 8
Rocker cover – removal and refitting 4
Rocker gear assembly – removal, inspection and refitting 5
Sump – removal and refitting 9
Timing cover, chain and sprockets – removal, inspection and
  refitting 7
Top Dead Centre (TDC) for No 1 piston – locating. 3

Degrees of difficulty

Easy, suitable for novice with little experience	Fairly easy, suitable for beginner with some experience	Fairly difficult, suitable for competent DIY mechanic	Difficult, suitable for experienced DIY mechanic	Very difficult, suitable for expert DIY or professional

Specifications

General

Type	Four-cylinder in-line, overhead valve (OHV), four stroke, 8-valve, liquid-cooled
Manufacturer's engine codes*:	
1397 cc 44 kW	AZE and AZF
1397 cc 50 kW	AME, AQW and ATZ
Maximum power output:	
AZE and AZF	44 kW at 5000 rpm
AME, AQW and ATZ.	50 kW at 5000 rpm
Maximum torque output:	
AZE and AZF	118 Nm at 2600 rpm
AME, AQW and ATZ.	120 Nm at 2500 rpm
Bore	75.5 mm
Stroke.	78.0 mm
Compression ratio	10.1 : 1
Compression pressures:	
Minimum compression pressure	Approximately 7.5 bars
Maximum difference between cylinders.	Approximately 3.0 bars
Firing order.	1 – 3 – 4 – 2
No 1 cylinder location.	Crankshaft pulley end
Direction of crankshaft rotation	Clockwise (when viewed from right-hand side of vehicle)

* Note: *See 'Vehicle identification' at the end of this manual for the location of engine code markings.*

Lubrication system

Oil pump type.	Gear-driven from camshaft, force-feed
Oil pump clearances:	
Drivegear shaft-to-cover:	
Standard.	0.02 to 0.10 mm
Wear limit	0.13 mm
Pin-to-driven gear:	
Standard.	0.014 to 0.050 mm
Wear limit	0.1 mm
Gear-to-pump cover (endfloat) – maximum	0.13 mm
Minimum oil pressure (oil temperature 80°C) at 2000 rpm.	2.0 bar

Torque wrench settings

	Nm	lbf ft
Air conditioner compressor:		
Single rear mounting bolt	45	33
Pulley end mounting bolts	25	18
Alternator:		
Air conditioned models	25	18
Non-air conditioned models:		
Top link	25	18
Bottom mounting	30	22
Lower bracket-to-block:		
Top	45	33
Lower	25	19
Upper bracket-to-head	20	15
Auxiliary drivebelt:		
Roller with left-hand thread (non-air conditioned models)	20	15
Tensioner lever (air conditioned models)	10	7
Tensioner idler (air conditioned models)	35	26
Tensioner spring housing (air conditioned models)	20	15
Big-end (connecting rod) bearing cap nut	40	30
Camshaft position sensor	8	6
Camshaft sprocket bolt:		
With tab washer	35	26
Without tab washer*	25	18
Camshaft thrustplate bolts	5	4
Crankshaft pulley	100	74
Cylinder head bolts:		
Stage 1	20	15
Stage 2	Angle-tighten a further 90°	
Stage 3	Angle-tighten a further 90°	
Cylinder head nuts	20	15
Engine/transmission left-hand mounting to transmission:		
Stage 1	40	30
Stage 2	Angle-tighten a further 90°	
Engine/transmission left-hand mounting to body:		
Stage 1	50	37
Stage 2	Angle-tighten a further 90°	
Engine/transmission rear mounting bracket to transmission:		
Stage 1	30	22
Stage 2	Angle-tighten a further 90°	
Engine/transmission rear mounting link to subframe:		
Stage 1	40	30
Stage 2	Angle-tighten a further 90°	
Engine/transmission right-hand mounting to engine:		
Stage 1	20	15
Stage 2	Angle-tighten a further 90°	
Engine/transmission right-hand mounting to body:		
Stage 1	30	22
Stage 2	Angle-tighten a further 90°	
Flywheel bolts (new)*:		
Stage 1	30	22
Stage 2	Angle-tighten a further 90°	
Knock sensor	20	15
Main bearing cap bolt	75	55
Oil pump pick-up/strainer	8	6
Oil pump	8	6
Oil seal housing bolts	8	6
Timing cover*	7	5
Rocker gear retaining bolts	25	18
Sump bolts*	10	7
Sump support bracket to transmission	45	33
Sump drain plug	30	22
Rocker cover nuts	3	2

* Use thread-locking compound.

1 General information

How to use this Chapter

This Part of Chapter 2 describes those repair procedures that can reasonably be carried out on the engine while it remains in the vehicle. If the engine has been removed from the vehicle and is being dismantled as described in Part E, any preliminary dismantling procedures can be ignored.

Note that while it may be possible physically to overhaul items such as the piston/connecting rod assemblies while the engine is in the vehicle, such tasks are not usually carried out as separate operations, and usually require the execution of several additional procedures (not to mention the cleaning of components and of oilways); for this reason, all such tasks are classed as major overhaul procedures, and are described in Part E of this Chapter.

Part E describes the removal of the engine/transmission from the vehicle and the full overhaul procedures that can then be carried out.

Engine description

The engine is an overhead valve (OHV), in-line four-cylinder unit, which is mounted transversely at the front of the vehicle; the clutch and transmission are situated on the left-hand end of the engine.

The cylinder block, cylinder head and rocker cover are all cast in aluminium alloy. The cylinder bores are formed by removable cast-iron cylinder liners that are located in the cylinder block at their lower ends; sealing gaskets are fitted at the base of each liner to prevent the escape of coolant into the sump. The camshaft is supported by three bearings in the cylinder block. The valves are opened and closed by hydraulic tappets in contact with the camshaft, and pushrods operating rocker arms on the top of the cylinder head.

The crankshaft has three main bearings. The clutch and flywheel are located on a flange at the left-hand end. A double sprocket fitted onto the right-hand end serves to drive the camshaft by a double-row timing chain. The main bearings and the big-end bearings are of the shell type, whilst the connecting rod small-end bearings are of the bronze bush type, being pressed into the connecting rod and reamed to suit.

The camshaft has a helical gear bolted to its right-hand end which drives the oil pump through a vertical shaft.

The force-feed lubrication system consists of a gear-driven pump, which draws oil from the sump through a strainer and circulates the lubricant to the various engine components, through a filter mounted externally on the front of the cylinder block.

Operations with engine in car

The following work can be carried out with the engine in the vehicle:
a) *Auxiliary drivebelt – removal and refitting.*
b) *Rocker cover – removal and refitting.*
c) *Rocker gear – removal and refitting.*
d) *Cylinder head – removal and refitting.**
e) *Timing cover – removal and refitting.*
f) *Timing chain and sprockets – removal and refitting.*
g) *Oil pump – removal, inspection and refitting.*
h) *Sump – removal and refitting.*
i) *Cylinder head and pistons – decarbonising.*
j) *Crankshaft oil seals – renewal.*
k) *Flywheel – removal, inspection and refitting.*
l) *Engine/transmission mountings – inspection and renewal.*
Cylinder head dismantling procedures are detailed in Chapter 2E.
Note: *It is possible to remove the pistons and connecting rods (after removing the cylinder head and sump) without removing the engine. However, this is not recommended. Work of this nature is more easily and thoroughly completed with the engine on the bench, as described in Chapter 2E.*

2 Compression test – description and interpretation

Note: *Turning the engine with the ignition module and fuel injection system disabled may generate fault codes in the engine management ECU. On completion of the test the vehicle should be taken to a Skoda dealer for these codes to be erased.*

1 When engine performance is down, or if misfiring occurs which cannot be attributed to the ignition or fuel systems, a compression test can provide diagnostic clues as to the engine's condition. If the test is performed regularly, it can give warning of trouble before any other symptoms become apparent.

2 The engine must be fully warmed-up to normal operating temperature, and the battery must be fully-charged. Remove the engine top cover, then remove the spark plugs as described in Chapter 1A. This involves removing the ignition module first. The aid of an assistant will also be required for the compression test.

3 Remove fuse 35 with reference to Chapter 12 in order to disable the fuel injectors. This will prevent any damage to the catalytic converter.

4 Fit a compression tester to the No 1 cylinder spark plug hole – the type of tester which screws into the plug thread is to be preferred.

5 Have the assistant hold the throttle wide open and crank the engine on the starter motor; after one or two revolutions, the compression pressure should build-up to a maximum figure and then stabilise. Record the highest reading obtained.

6 Repeat the test on the remaining cylinders, recording the pressure in each.

7 All cylinders should produce very similar pressures of at least 7.5 bars. Any one cylinder reading less than this, or a difference of more than 3.0 bars between cylinders, suggests a fault.

8 Note that the compression should build-up quickly in a healthy engine; low compression on the first stroke, followed by gradually increasing pressure on successive strokes, indicates worn piston rings.

9 A low compression reading on the first stroke, which does not build-up during successive strokes, indicates leaking valves or a blown head gasket (a cracked head could also be the cause).

10 If the pressure in any cylinder is reduced to less than 7.5 bars, carry out the following test to isolate the cause. Introduce a teaspoonful of clean oil into that cylinder through its spark plug hole and repeat the test.

11 If the addition of oil temporarily improves the compression pressure, this indicates that bore or piston wear is responsible for the pressure loss. No improvement suggests that leaking or burnt valves, or a blown head gasket, may be to blame.

12 A low reading from two adjacent cylinders is almost certainly due to the head gasket having blown between them; the presence of coolant in the engine oil will confirm this.

13 If one cylinder is about 20 percent lower than the others and the engine has a slightly rough idle, a worn camshaft lobe could be the cause.

14 On completion of the test, refit the spark plugs and ignition module, then refit the fuel injector fuse.

3 Top Dead Centre (TDC) for No 1 piston – locating

1 Top dead centre (TDC) is the highest point in its travel up-and-down its cylinder bore that each piston reaches as the crankshaft rotates. While each piston reaches TDC both at the top of the compression stroke and again at the top of the exhaust stroke, for the purpose of timing the engine, TDC refers to the piston position (No 1) at the top of its compression stroke.

2 No 1 piston and cylinder are at the right-hand end of the engine (timing chain end). Note that the crankshaft rotates clockwise when viewed from the right-hand side of the vehicle.

3 Disconnect the battery negative terminal, and remove all the spark plugs as described in Chapter 1A. This involves removing the ignition module first.

4 The engine must now be turned using a socket on the crankshaft pulley bolt, located at the right-hand end of the engine. If necessary, remove the engine undertray for access to the bolt. Alternatively, jack up the right-hand

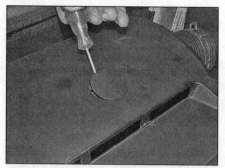

4.2a Lever off the plastic cover . . .

4.2b . . . and the central logo

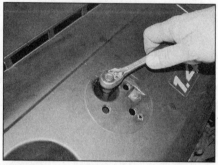

4.2c . . . and unscrew the nuts . . .

4.2d . . . then remove the dipstick, and lift off the engine top cover together with the oil filler cap

front of the car, then engage 4th gear and turn the roadwheel clockwise which will rotate the engine.

5 There are no markings on the crankshaft pulley, and the camshaft/crankshaft sprockets

are only visible after removing the timing cover, so there are only two methods of finding top dead centre (TDC). The first (and easiest) is to turn the crankshaft clockwise while holding a finger over the No 1 cylinder spark plug hole.

When compression is felt, insert a suitable thin rod through the No 1 spark plug hole onto the top of the piston, then slowly turn the engine until the piston reaches TDC. It will be necessary to turn the engine back-and-forth to determine the exact position.

6 The alternative method involves removing the rocker cover and observing the movement of the valves. Rotate the engine until the inlet and exhaust valves of cylinder No 1 are fully closed, and the valves of cylinder No 4 are 'rocking' (ie, exhaust closing and inlet opening). The TDC position of the No 1 piston can be determined by inserting a suitable thin rod through the No 1 spark plug hole onto the top of the piston. It will be necessary to turn the engine back-and-forth to determine the exact position.

7 With the crankshaft in this position, No 1 cylinder is now at TDC compression, and No 4 cylinder is at TDC exhaust.

8 Once No 1 cylinder has been positioned at TDC on the compression stroke, TDC for any of the other cylinders can then be located by rotating the crankshaft clockwise 180° at a time and following the firing order (see Specifications).

4 Rocker cover – removal and refitting

Removal

1 Disconnect the battery negative lead (refer to *Disconnecting the battery* in the *Reference* Chapter at the end of this manual).

2 Remove the engine top cover as follows. Lever off the central logo and the plastic cover from the rear retaining nut, then unscrew the two nuts. Pull the engine oil level dipstick from its tube, then lift off the top cover. There is no need to remove the oil filler cap. Remove the cap attached to the bottom of the top cover, and place it over the oil filler inlet on the rocker cover **(see illustrations)**.

3 Loosen the clips and disconnect the hoses from the crankcase ventilation outlets on the rocker cover **(see illustrations)**.

4 Unscrew the two nuts and lift the rocker cover from the cylinder head. If it is stuck, tap it lightly with a mallet to release it from

4.2e Remove the cap from the bottom of the top cover . . .

4.2f . . . and fit it to the oil filler inlet

4.3a Using a screwdriver, release the securing clips . . .

4.3b . . . and disconnect the breather hoses from the rocker cover oil filler neck

4.4a Remove the retaining nuts (arrowed) . . .

the gasket. Recover the gasket and the two seals from the retaining nut holes (**see illustrations**).

Refitting

5 Carefully clean the cylinder head and rocker cover, removing all traces of old gasket and oil. Locate the gasket in the rocker cover groove (**see illustration**).

6 Refit the rocker cover to the cylinder head and locate it over the studs, ensuring that the gasket is correctly seated beneath it. Refit the two seals then progressively tighten the retaining nuts. **Do not** over-tighten the nuts as this may distort the rocker cover.

7 Reconnect the crankcase ventilation hoses and tighten the clips. If the original Skoda clips are still fitted, use screw-type clips when refitting (**see illustration**).

8 Refit the engine top cover and reconnect the battery negative lead. Check for oil leaks when the engine is next run.

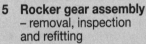

5 Rocker gear assembly
– removal, inspection and refitting

Caution: The rocker gear assembly is retained by two cylinder head bolts, and there is a very small chance that the cylinder head gasket may be disturbed and subsequently not seal correctly onto the wet liners when the bolts are retightened. The following procedure describes removing the two bolts; the alternative method is to remove the cylinder head completely.

Removal

1 Remove the rocker cover as described in Section 4.

2 Using a 10 mm Allen key, slacken and remove the two cylinder head bolts which secure the left- and right-hand rocker pedestals to the cylinder head.

3 Evenly and progressively slacken the four rocker gear retaining bolts by half a turn at a time, until all valve spring pressure has been relieved from the rocker arms. Remove the bolts and washers, noting the correct fitted position of the oil splash plate which is fitted

4.4b ... lift off the rubber spacers ...

4.5 Ensure that the rocker cover seal is correctly seated in its groove

4.4c ... and lift the rocker cover away from the engine

4.7 Replace the original Skoda clips with screw-type clips when refitting

to the top of the right-hand pedestal, and lift the rocker gear assembly off the cylinder head (**see illustration**).

4 If necessary, the rocker gear assembly can be dismantled by removing the circlip from one end of the rocker shaft and sliding the various components off the end of the shaft (**see illustrations**). Keeping all components in their correct fitted order, make a note of each component's correct fitted position as it is removed, to ensure it is positioned correctly on reassembly.

5 If necessary, remove the pushrods from their location on the hydraulic tappets, but keep them identified for position so that they can be refitted in their original locations.

Inspection

6 With the rocker gear dismantled, examine the rocker arm and shaft bearing surfaces for

wear ridges and scoring. If there are obvious signs of wear the affected rocker arm(s) and/or shaft must be renewed.

Refitting

7 If the rocker gear was dismantled, reassemble it by reversing the dismantling sequence, and secure all components in position with the circlip. Ensure that the circlip is correctly located in its groove, and check that all rocker arms are free to rotate smoothly around the shaft.

8 If removed, refit the pushrods to their correct locations on the hydraulic tappets.

9 Lower the rocker gear assembly into position on the cylinder head, ensuring that all the rocker arm adjusting screws correctly engage with their respective pushrod ends (**see illustration**).

10 Refit the four rocker gear retaining bolts

5.3 Slacken the retaining bolts and lift the rocker gear away from the cylinder head

5.4a To dismantle the rocker gear, remove the circlip ...

5.4b ... and slide off the various components, keeping them in their correct fitted order

5.9 On refitting, ensure all rocker arm adjusting screws are correctly located in the pushrod ends

5.10a Don't forget to refit the oil splash plate to the right-hand pedestal

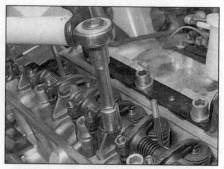

5.10b Tighten the rocker gear retaining bolts to the specified torque setting as described in text

and, ensuring that the oil splash plate is correctly positioned on the right-hand pedestal, tighten them evenly and progressively to the specified torque setting **(see illustrations)**.

11 Refit the two cylinder head bolts securing the left- and right-hand pedestals in position and tighten them first to the specified Stage 1 torque setting, and then through the angles specified for their Stage 2 and 3 tightening. Refer to Section 6 for further information.

12 If the rocker gear assembly components have been renewed, it is necessary to carry out the following basic setting adjustment of the hydraulic tappets. If the original components are being refitted, there is no need to make the adjustment.

13 Turn the engine until the valves of cylinder No 4 are 'rocking' (inlet valve opening and exhaust valve closing). Using a ring spanner and screwdriver, loosen the adjustment locknuts of No 1 cylinder rocker arms. Back off the adjusters until there is some clearance between them and the valve stem, then turn the adjusters clockwise until they just contact the valve stems. From this point, turn the adjusters clockwise a further two turns each, then tighten the locknuts.

14 The basic setting adjustment must now be carried out for the remaining cylinders. Turn the engine through 180° so that the valves of cylinder No 2 are 'rocking', then adjust the basic setting on the valves of cylinder No 3. Turn the engine through a further 180° so that the valves of cylinder No 1 are 'rocking', and adjust the basic setting on the valves of cylinder No 4. Finally, turn the engine through a further 180° so that

the valves of cylinder No 3 are 'rocking', and adjust the valves of cylinder No 2.
Caution: If the hydraulic tappets have been renewed, leave the engine stationary for 30 minutes and check the adjustment again.
15 Refit the rocker cover as described in Section 4.

6 Cylinder head and manifolds – removal, separation and refitting

Removal

1 Disconnect the battery negative lead (refer to *Disconnecting the battery* in the *Reference* Chapter at the end of this manual).

2 Set the engine to TDC as described in Section 3, then turn the crankshaft back by a few degrees, away from the TDC position. If preferred, for maximum safety, the pistons can be positioned halfway down their bores, with No 1 piston on its upstroke – ie 90° before TDC. It is important that the engine is **not** at TDC, to avoid the possibility of piston/valve contact when the head is refitted.

3 Drain the cooling system and remove the spark plugs as described in Chapter 1A.

4 Remove the air cleaner and air inlet components as described in the relevant part of Chapter 4. Pull off the warm-air duct from the air cleaner inlet and the stub on the exhaust manifold collector plate.

5 Remove the rocker gear as described in Section 5, however, progressively unscrew

and remove *all* of the cylinder head bolts and nuts in the **reverse** order to that shown in illustration 6.40. Note the location of the engine lifting eye brackets, and note that the relevant bolts are also fitted with washers. There are three lengths of cylinder head bolt – note where they are fitted **(see illustration)**.

6 Lift out each pushrod in turn and store it in its correct fitted order by pushing it through a clearly-marked cardboard template **(see illustration)**. This will ensure that the pushrods are refitted in their original positions on reassembly. Note that the inlet valve pushrods are made of aluminium, while the exhaust valve pushrods are steel.

7 Note that the following text assumes that the cylinder head will be removed with both inlet and exhaust manifolds attached; this is easier, but makes it a bulky and heavy assembly to handle. If it is wished first to remove the manifolds, proceed as described in the Chapter 4C.

8 Remove the exhaust front pipe together with the catalytic converter as described in the relevant part of Chapter 4.

9 Disconnect the following wiring:
a) *Throttle valve control unit.*
b) *Inlet manifold pressure and temperature senders.*
c) *Coolant temperature sender (see illustration).*
d) *Fuel injectors.*

10 Release the clips and open the wiring loom conduit located behind the fuel injectors, then remove the wiring loom and place it to one side.

6.5 Removing the cylinder head bolts

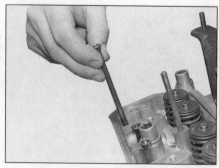

6.6 Lift out the pushrods from the engine and store them in a cardboard template

6.9 Disconnecting the wiring plug from the coolant temperature sender

11 Disconnect the crankcase ventilation hoses from the rocker cover.

12 Disconnect the coolant hoses from the thermostat housing.

13 Disconnect the vacuum hose from the brake servo unit.

14 Unbolt and remove the inlet manifold support brackets.

15 Unbolt the dipstick tube from the exhaust manifold.

16 Disconnect the wiring from the ignition coil module on the front of the engine.

17 Place cloth rags around the fuel supply and return hoses at the fuel rail, then disconnect them **(see illustration)**. Alternatively, disconnect the quick-release connectors at the fuel supply and return pipes located on the right-hand side of the engine compartment. The fuel system is under pressure, so expect some leakage.

18 Disconnect the hose from the coolant expansion tank.

19 Disconnect the ventilation hose from the solenoid valve.

20 On models with air conditioning, remove the auxiliary drivebelt with reference to Chapter 1A.

21 Unbolt and remove the alternator support bracket.

22 The joint between the cylinder head and gasket and the cylinder block/crankcase must now be broken without disturbing the wet liners; although these liners are better located and sealed than some wet-liner engines, there is still a risk of coolant and foreign matter leaking into the sump if the cylinder head is lifted carelessly. If care is not taken and the liners are moved, there is also a possibility of the bottom seals being disturbed, causing leakage after refitting the head.

Caution: If the liner bottom seals are disturbed, it will be necessary to remove the pistons and liners in order to fit new seals.

23 To break the joint, use the exhaust manifold as a leverage point, and gently rock the cylinder head free towards the front of the vehicle. When the joint is broken, lift the cylinder head away over the four studs; use assistance if possible, as it is a heavy assembly, especially if it is removed complete with the manifolds. Remove the gasket and discard it.

24 **Do not** attempt to rotate the crankshaft with the cylinder head removed, otherwise the cylinder liners will be displaced. Operations that would normally require the rotation of the crankshaft (eg, cleaning the piston crowns), must be carried out with great care to ensure that no particles of dirt or foreign matter are left behind. If the crankshaft is to be turned, the liners must first be clamped in position using a couple of suitable bolts and large flat washers **(see illustration)**.

25 If the engine is to be left for any time with the head off, it might be worth attaching warning notices to ensure that no attempt is

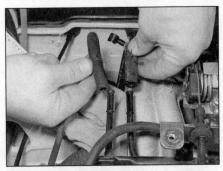

6.17 Disconnecting the fuel hoses from the fuel rail

made to turn the engine if the liners are not clamped.

26 If the cylinder head is to be dismantled, then refer to the relevant Sections in Part E of this Chapter.

Manifold separation

27 Inlet manifold removal and refitting is described in Chapter 4A.

28 Progressively slacken and remove the exhaust manifold retaining nuts; discard the old nuts if they are in poor condition. Lift the manifold away from the cylinder head, and recover the gaskets.

29 Ensure that the mating surfaces are completely clean, then refit the exhaust manifold, using new gaskets. Fit new manifold retaining nuts, and tighten to the specified torque (see Chapters 4A and 4C).

Preparation for refitting

30 Check the condition of the cylinder head bolts and nuts, paying particular attention to their threads, whenever they are removed. Wash and wipe dry them, then check each for any sign of visible wear or damage, renewing them as necessary. **Note:** *There is no requirement to renew the bolts/nuts from Skoda.*

31 The mating faces of the cylinder head, liners and cylinder block/crankcase must be perfectly clean before refitting the head. Refer to paragraph 24 before turning the engine to clean the piston crowns – the engine must not be turned if the cylinder liners have not been clamped.

32 Use a hard plastic or wood scraper to remove all traces of gasket and carbon; also clean the piston crowns. Take particular care, as the soft aluminium alloy is easily damaged. Also, make sure that the carbon is not allowed to enter the oil and water passages – this is particularly important for the lubrication system, as carbon could block the oil supply to any of the engine's components. Using adhesive tape and paper, seal the water, oil and bolt holes in the cylinder block/crankcase. To prevent carbon entering the gap between the pistons and bores, smear a little grease in the gap. After cleaning each piston, use a small brush to remove all traces of grease and carbon from

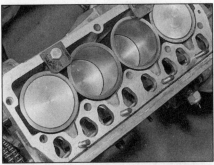

6.24 If the crankshaft is to be rotated with the head removed, the liners must be clamped in position

the gap, then wipe away the remainder with a clean rag. Clean all the pistons in the same way.

33 Check the mating surfaces of the cylinder block/crankcase and the cylinder head for nicks, deep scratches and other damage. If slight, they may be removed carefully with a file, but if excessive, machining may be the only alternative to renewal.

34 If warpage is suspected of the cylinder head gasket surface, use a straight-edge to check it for distortion. Refer to Part E of this Chapter if necessary.

Refitting

Note: *Only unwrap the new cylinder head gasket immediately before fitting it to the cylinder block.*

35 Wipe clean the mating surfaces of the cylinder head and cylinder block/crankcase and position the new gasket on the cylinder block/crankcase surface so that its part number is uppermost. Ensure that the holes in the gasket align with the oilways on the left- and right-hand ends of the cylinder block.

36 Locate the cylinder head on the studs, and carefully lower it into position.

37 Lightly oil under the heads and on the threads of each bolt and nut. Insert the bolts in their correct locations (except those for the rocker gear) and screw on the nuts, hand-tightening them at this stage. Three lengths of bolt are fitted – make sure they are in the correct location **(see illustration 6.40)**. Bolts 1, 2, 3, 6 and 7 are 168 mm long, bolts 4, 5, 8 and 9, 185 mm, and bolt 10, 132 mm long.

38 Remove the pushrods from the cardboard template, and insert them into their original positions in the cylinder head, ensuring that each pushrod is correctly located in its hydraulic tappet.

39 Refit the rocker gear as described in Section 5, but tighten the cylinder head bolts finger-tight only. **Note:** *It is not necessary to make the basic adjustment of the hydraulic tappets if only the cylinder head gasket is renewed.*

40 Working progressively and in sequence, use first a torque wrench, then an ordinary socket extension bar, to tighten the cylinder

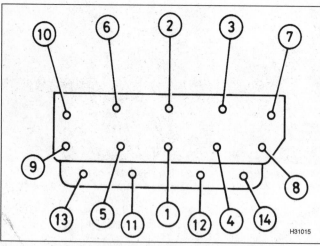

6.40 Cylinder head tightening sequence

6.41 Tighten all bolts to the Stage 1 setting with a torque wrench

head bolts in the stages given in the Specifications Section of this Chapter **(see illustration)**.

41 First tighten bolts 1 to 10 to the Stage 1 torque setting, using a torque wrench **(see illustration)**.

42 Now angle-tighten these bolts, in the same sequence, through the specified Stage 2 angle, using a socket and extension bar. It is recommended that an angle-measuring gauge is used during this stage of the tightening, to ensure accuracy **(see illustration)**. If a gauge is not available, use white paint to make alignment marks between the bolt head and cylinder head prior to tightening; the marks can then be used to check that the bolt has been rotated through

the correct angle during tightening. Repeat the exercise for the Stage 3 setting.

43 Once the ten cylinder head bolts have been correctly tightened, apply a drop of engine oil to the threads and underside of the heads of the cylinder head nuts. Refit the nuts and washers onto the studs situated along the front edge of the cylinder head, not forgetting the bracket for the alternator support bracket. Tighten the nuts to their specified torque setting in order (numbers 11 to 14) **(see illustration)**.

44 On models with air conditioning, refit the auxiliary drivebelt with reference to Chapter 1A.

45 Reconnect the solenoid valve ventilation hose, and the hose to the coolant expansion tank.

46 Reconnect the fuel supply hose and the ignition wiring.

47 Refit the dipstick tube and inlet manifold support brackets.

48 Reconnect the vacuum hose to the brake servo unit.

49 Reconnect the coolant hoses to the thermostat housing.

50 Reconnect the crankcase ventilation hoses to the rocker cover.

51 Refit the wiring loom to the conduit and secure with the clips.

52 Reconnect the wiring disconnected on removal.

53 Refit the exhaust front pipe together with the catalytic converter as described in Chapter 4C.

54 Refit the air cleaner, air inlet components and warm-air duct.

55 Refit the spark plugs (Chapter 1A) and reconnect the battery negative lead.

56 Refill the cooling system with coolant as described in Chapter 1A.

7 Timing cover, chain and sprockets – removal, inspection and refitting

6.42 Use an angle gauge for the Stage 2 and 3 tightening

6.43 Tighten the cylinder head nuts to the specified torque

7.5 Remove the retaining bolt and washer, and slide off the crankshaft pulley

7.6 Undo the timing cover retaining bolts and remove the cover

Removal

1 Position No 1 cylinder at TDC as described in Section 3.

2 Remove the alternator as described in Chapter 5A.

3 Remove the oil pick-up/strainer and withdraw the oil pump gears as described in Section 8.

4 To prevent crankshaft rotation while the pulley bolt is unscrewed, select top gear and have an assistant apply the brakes hard. If the engine has been removed from the vehicle, lock the flywheel using the arrangement shown in Section 11.

5 Slacken and remove the pulley retaining bolt and washer, then slide the pulley off the crankshaft **(see illustration)**.

6 Slacken and remove all the timing chain cover retaining bolts and screws **(see illustration)**.

HAYNES HiNT

The camshaft sprocket can be retained with a holding tool fabricated from two lengths of steel strip (one long, the other short) and three nuts and bolts. One nut and bolt form the pivot of the forked tool, with the remaining two nuts and bolts at the tips of the 'forks' to engage with the sprocket spokes.

Manoeuvre the cover downwards and away from the engine. Remove the gasket and discard it.

7 On early models, using a flat-bladed screwdriver, bend back the tab of the camshaft bolt tab washer. **Note:** *There is no tab fitted on later models, and the retaining bolt is circular, requiring an Allen key to unscrew it.* To prevent camshaft rotation while the bolt is slackened, select top gear and have an assistant apply the brakes hard **(see Tool Tip)**.

8 Unscrew the camshaft bolt and on early models remove it along with the tab washer and dished washer. Discard the tab washer; a new one must be used on refitting. Withdraw the oil pump drivegear from the camshaft end, noting which way around it is fitted **(see illustrations)**.

9 Prior to removing the timing chain and sprockets, note the position of the sprocket timing marks, and crankshaft and camshaft keyways.

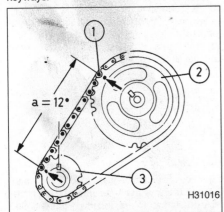

7.18 Crankshaft and camshaft Woodruff key and sprocket timing mark positions with No 1 cylinder at TDC

1 Timing chain	*3 Crankshaft*
2 Camshaft	*sprocket*
sprocket	*a = 12 chain rollers*

7.8a Remove the camshaft bolt, along with its tab washer and dished washer . . .

10 Simultaneously withdraw the timing chain and sprockets from the crankshaft and camshaft, and manoeuvre the assembly away from the engine.

11 Remove the Woodruff key from the crankshaft keyway, noting which way around it is fitted. If the camshaft Woodruff key is a loose fit in the camshaft, remove it and store it with the sprocket for safe-keeping.

Inspection

12 Examine the teeth on both the crankshaft and camshaft sprockets for signs of wear or damage such as chipped, hooked or missing teeth. If there is any sign of wear or damage on either sprocket, both sprockets and the chain should be renewed as a set.

13 Inspect the links of the timing chain for signs of wear on the rollers. The extent of wear on the chain can be judged by checking the amount by which the chain can be bent sideways: a new chain will have very little sideways movement.

14 If there is an excessive amount of side play in the timing chain, the chain must be renewed. Note that it is a sensible precaution to renew the chain, regardless of its apparent condition, at about 30 000 miles or at a lesser mileage if the engine is undergoing a major overhaul.

15 Although not strictly necessary, it is always worth renewing the chain and sprockets as a matched set, since it is false economy to run a new chain on worn sprockets and *vice-versa*.

16 Inspect all other components for signs of wear or damage, and renew as necessary.

7.19 Locate the timing chain and sprocket assembly on the crankshaft and camshaft ends

7.8b . . . and withdraw the drivegear

7.17 Refit the Woodruff key so that its tapered end is innermost

Refitting

17 Refit the Woodruff key to the crankshaft keyway so that its tapered end is innermost **(see illustration)**. Also refit the Woodruff key to the camshaft keyway if it was removed.

18 Engage the camshaft and crankshaft sprockets with the timing chain. The dot on the camshaft sprocket must be aligned with the twelfth timing chain roller along from the roller which aligns with the dot on the crankshaft sprocket, counting the roller above the crankshaft sprocket dot as number 1 **(see illustration)**.

19 Offer up the chain and sprocket assembly, and simultaneously slide on the sprockets, ensuring that the timing dot on each sprocket is facing outwards **(see illustration)**.

20 With the sprockets in position, recheck the position of the timing dots **(see illustration)**.

21 Locate the oil pump drivegear on the

7.20 Recheck that the timing dots (arrowed) are still positioned as described in text

7.21a Tab washer locating peg correctly engaged with the drivegear

7.21b Bend tab washer up against one of camshaft bolt flats to secure it in position

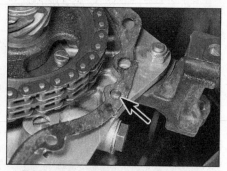

7.23 Locate a new gasket over pegs (arrowed) on block mating surface

7.25 Refit the timing cover and trim off the ends of the gasket which protrude beyond the sump mating face

7.27 Ensure that the thrustwasher locating tabs are aligned with the bearing cap cut-outs

7.28 Tighten the crankshaft pulley retaining bolt to the specified torque

camshaft end, noting that its flange must face inwards, then on early models refit the dished washer so that its concave face is outermost. Fit a new tab washer, engaging its locating peg with the slot in the drivegear, and refit the camshaft bolt. On later models, apply locking fluid to the threads of the retaining bolt before inserting it. Tighten the bolt to the specified torque whilst using the method employed on removal to prevent rotation. On early models, secure the bolt by bending up the tab washer against one of the flats of the bolt head **(see illustrations)**.

22 Remove all traces of oil and gasket from the mating surfaces of the timing chain cover and block. Inspect the crankshaft oil seal in the cover for signs of damage or deterioration, and renew it if necessary, as described in Section 10.

23 Fit a new gasket over the locating pegs in the cylinder block, using a smear of grease to hold it in place **(see illustration)**.
24 Carefully manoeuvre the timing chain cover into position, and locate the cover on the pegs. Apply thread-locking fluid to the cover retaining bolts and screws, then refit them and tighten them to the specified torque.
25 Using a sharp knife, carefully trim of the ends of the gasket which protrude beyond the cylinder block sump mating face **(see illustration)**.
26 Align the crankshaft pulley slot with the Woodruff key and carefully slide the pulley onto the crankshaft, taking great care not to damage the oil seal lip. Refit the retaining bolt and washer, and tighten it by hand only.
27 Check that the inner and outer thrustwasher locating tabs are aligned with

the cut-outs on the right-hand main bearing cap, and that the thrustwashers are correctly seated in their recesses **(see illustration)**.
28 Tighten the crankshaft pulley bolt to the specified torque whilst preventing rotation using the method employed on removal **(see illustration)**.
29 Note that if the thrustwashers are not properly seated, the crankshaft will lock up as the bolt is tightened, and the thrustwashers will be damaged. Check that the crankshaft rotates freely before proceeding further.
30 Refit the oil pump gears and the oil pick-up/strainer as described in Section 8, then refit the sump as described in Section 9.
31 Refit the alternator as described in Chapter 5A.

8 Oil pump –
removal, inspection and refitting

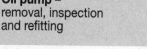

Removal

1 Remove the sump as described in Section 9.
2 Undo the four bolts securing the oil pump pick-up/strainer to the underside of the timing cover, and the single bolt securing it to the centre main bearing cap. Carefully lower the pick-up/strainer away from the timing cover, noting that the oil pump gears will drop out as soon as the cover is removed **(see illustrations)**. Remove the gasket (where fitted) and discard it.

8.2a Undo the oil pump pick-up/strainer retaining bolts ...

8.2b ... then carefully lower it away from the engine ...

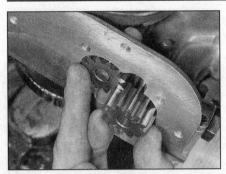

8.2c . . . and withdraw the oil pump gears

Inspection

3 Inspect the oil pump gears and the pump body for signs of wear ridges or obvious damage such as chipped teeth.

4 If the necessary measuring equipment is available, the extent of wear on the pump shafts and body can be determined by direct measurement.

5 If there is any obvious sign of wear, or if the tolerances given in the Specifications are exceeded, both the pump gears and the timing chain cover (which incorporates the oil pump body) must be renewed as a complete set **(see illustration)**. Refer to Section 7 for information on timing chain cover removal and refitting.

6 Temporarily insert the gears into the pump body, and use a straight-edge and feeler blades to measure the gear-to-cover clearance (endfloat) **(see illustration)**. Skoda states that there must be a maximum of 0.13 mm clearance between the gears and cover. If there is approximately 0.13 mm clearance present, then the pick-up/strainer should be refitted without a gasket. If there is very little or no measurable clearance, then a gasket must be positioned behind the cover on refitting to provide the necessary clearance. If the clearance exceeds 0.13 mm, then the pump body and/or gears are worn, and the oil pump assembly must be renewed.

7 Extract the split pin from the pick-up/strainer assembly, and withdraw the oil pressure relief valve spring and ball **(see illustrations)**. Inspect the ball and spring for signs of wear or damage, and renew as necessary. If a new ball is to be fitted, insert the ball into position in the pick-up/strainer then, using a hammer and

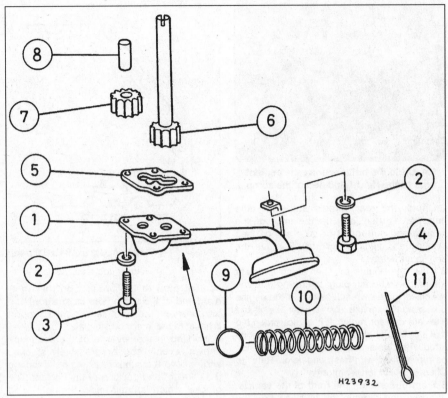

8.5 Exploded view of the oil pump components

1 *Oil pump pick-up/strainer*	6 *Oil pump drivegear*
2 *Spring washer*	7 *Oil pump driven gear*
3 *Bolt – pick-up/strainer to timing cover*	8 *Oil pump driven gear shaft*
4 *Bolt – pick-up/strainer to bearing cap*	9 *Oil pressure relief valve ball*
5 *Gasket (where fitted)*	10 *Oil pressure relief valve spring*
	11 *Split pin*

suitable soft-metal drift, tap the ball firmly into its seat; this will help the ball to seat properly and ensure correct operation of the valve. On refitting, secure the ball and spring in position with a new split pin.

Refitting

8 Where necessary, stick a new gasket onto the pick-up/strainer pipe mating surface, using a dab of grease to hold it in position.

9 Generously lubricate the oil pump gears and shafts, then insert the gears into the pump body. Holding them in position, offer up the pick-up/strainer and insert its five

retaining bolts. Tighten the pick-up/strainer pipe retaining bolts to the specified torque.

10 Refit the sump as described in Section 9.

9 Sump – removal and refitting

Removal

1 Disconnect the battery negative lead (refer to *Disconnecting the battery* in the *Reference* Chapter at the end of this manual).

8.6 Checking oil pump gear-to-cover clearance (endfloat)

8.7a Extract the split pin (arrowed) . . .

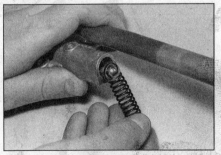

8.7b . . . and withdraw the pressure relief valve ball and spring from the pick-up/strainer

9.4 Undo the bolt securing the coolant pipe to the right-hand end of the sump

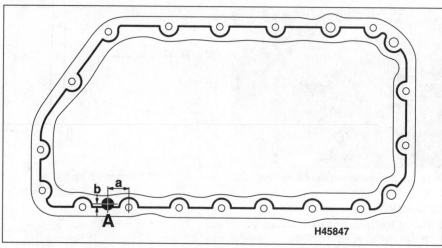

9.9 Apply a 2.0 to 3.0 bead of sealant to the sump flange

A = Apply additional sealant at the point shown (a = 15 mm, b = 4 mm)

2 Chock the rear wheels and apply the handbrake, then jack up the front of the vehicle and support it on axle stands (see *Jacking and vehicle support*). Remove the engine undertray.

3 Drain the engine oil, then clean and refit the engine oil drain plug, tightening it to the specified torque wrench setting. If the engine is nearing the service interval when the oil and filter are due for renewal, it is recommended that the filter is also removed and a new one fitted. After reassembly, the engine can then be replenished with fresh engine oil. Refer to Chapter 1A for further information.

4 From underneath the front of the vehicle, unscrew and remove the bolt securing the

coolant pipe to the bracket on the right-hand end of the sump **(see illustration)** and also unscrew the bolts securing the support bracket to the intermediate plate.

5 Working in the **reverse** of the sequence shown, evenly and progressively slacken and remove the sump retaining bolts, noting the correct fitted position of the coolant pipe bracket which is fitted under the right-hand sump bolt and the support bracket fitted on the left-hand side.

6 Break the joint by striking the sump with the palm of the hand, then lower the sump away from the engine and withdraw it. **Note:** *A gasket is only fitted to the 1.0 litre engine (not covered by this Manual).*

7 While the sump is removed, take the opportunity to clean the oil pump pick-up/strainer pipe mesh using a suitable solvent. Inspect the strainer mesh for signs of clogging or splitting and renew if necessary, referring to Section 8 for further information.

Refitting

8 Thoroughly clean all traces of sealant and oil

from the mating surfaces of the cylinder block/crankcase and sump, then use a clean rag to wipe out the sump and the engine's interior.

9 Apply a 2.0 to 3.0 mm diameter bead of sealant to the sump mating flange **(see illustration)** making sure that the bead is around the inner edges of the bolt holes. The bead must not exceed 3.0 mm diameter, and additional sealant must be applied to the point where the timing cover meets the cylinder block. **Note:** *The sump must be refitted within 5 minutes of applying the sealant, so have an assistant ready to hold the coolant pipe bracket to one side.*

10 Offer up the sump to the cylinder block/crankcase. Refit the sump retaining bolts, not forgetting the coolant pipe bracket and support bracket, and progressively tighten them to the specified torque in sequence **(see illustrations)**.

11 Refit and tighten the coolant pipe retaining bolt and support bracket bolts, then lower the vehicle to the ground and reconnect the battery negative lead.

12 Refill the engine with oil as described in Chapter 1A.

9.10a Refitting the sump to the engine

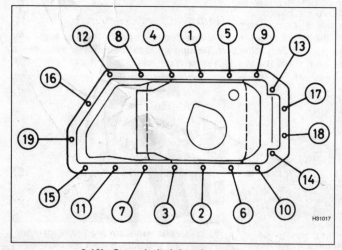

9.10b Sump bolt tightening sequence

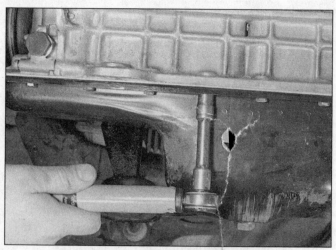

9.10c Tightening the sump retaining bolts

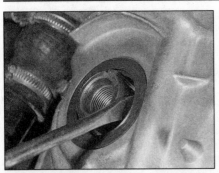

10.2 Use a large flat-bladed screwdriver to prise out the crankshaft right-hand oil seal

10.5 Tap the new seal into position using a suitable tubular drift which bears only on the seal's hard outer edge

10.8 Using a self-tapping screw to remove the crankshaft left-hand oil seal

10 Crankshaft oil seals – renewal

Right-hand oil seal

1 Remove the crankshaft pulley as described in Section 7.
2 Carefully lever the old seal out of the timing chain cover using a suitable flat-bladed screwdriver, taking great care not to damage the cover or crankshaft (see illustration).
3 Alternatively, punch or drill two small holes opposite each other in the seal, then screw a self-tapping screw into each and pull on the screws with pliers to extract the seal.
4 Clean the seal housing, and polish off any burrs or raised edges on the crankshaft which may have caused the seal to fail in the first place.
5 Lubricate the lips of the new seal with clean engine oil, and press it into position until its outer edge is flush with the timing chain cover surface. If necessary, the seal can be tapped into position using a suitable tubular drift, such as a socket, which bears only on the hard outer edge of the seal (see illustration). Note that the sealing lips must face inwards.
6 Clean off any traces of oil, then refit the crankshaft pulley as described in Section 7. Note that, should the crankshaft lock up as described, the sump will have to be removed to check the thrustwasher location.

Left-hand oil seal

7 Remove the flywheel as described in Section 11.
8 Carefully punch or drill two small holes opposite each other in the seal. Screw a self-tapping screw into each hole, and pull on the screws with pliers to extract the seal (see illustration).
9 Clean the seal housing, and polish off any burrs or raised edges on the crankshaft which may have caused the seal to fail in the first place.
10 Lubricate the lips of the new seal and the crankshaft shoulder with clean engine oil, then offer the seal to the cylinder block/crankcase, ensuring its sealing lip is facing inwards.
11 Ease the sealing lip of the seal over the

crankshaft shoulder by hand only, and press the seal evenly into its housing until its outer flange seats evenly on the housing shoulder. If necessary, a soft-faced mallet can be used to tap the seal gently into place.
12 Clean off any traces of oil, then refit the flywheel as described in Section 11.

11 Flywheel – removal, inspection and refitting

Removal

1 Remove the transmission as described in Chapter 7A, then remove the clutch assembly as described in Chapter 6.
2 Prevent the flywheel from turning by locking the ring gear teeth as shown (see Tool Tip), or by bolting a strap between the flywheel and the cylinder block/crankcase.
3 Slacken and remove the flywheel retaining bolts; discard the bolts, as they must be renewed whenever they are disturbed.
4 Mark the relative positions of the flywheel centre and the crankshaft (see illustration). It is only possible to refit the flywheel in one position as the bolt holes are asymmetrical

To prevent flywheel rotation as the retaining bolts are loosened or tightened, a locking tool can be made from a suitably thick piece of sheet metal, with a tooth shape to engage the flywheel teeth, and a bolt hole for attachment via one of the transmission housing bolts.

(this is not the case with 1.0 litre engines not covered in this Manual).
5 Remove the flywheel. Do not drop it, as it is very heavy.

Inspection

6 If the clutch mating surface of the flywheel is deeply scored, cracked or otherwise damaged, the flywheel must be renewed, unless it is possible to have it surface-ground. Seek the advice of a Skoda dealer or engine reconditioning specialist.
7 If the ring gear is badly worn or has missing teeth, it must be renewed, but this job is best left to a Skoda dealer or engine reconditioning specialist. The temperature to which the new ring gear must be heated for installation (180° to 200°C) is critical and, if not done accurately, the hardness of the teeth will be destroyed.
8 If it is felt necessary, use the correct-size tap to clean the threads in the crankshaft of any old thread-locking fluid.

Refitting

9 Clean the mating surfaces of the flywheel and crankshaft, then refit the flywheel to the crankshaft.
10 If the new flywheel retaining bolts are not supplied with their threads already pre-coated, apply a suitable thread-locking compound to the threads of each bolt. Fit the bolts, tightening them by hand only at this stage.
11 Lock the flywheel using the method employed on dismantling, and tighten the retaining bolts to the specified torque and angle settings.

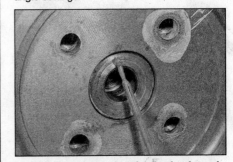

11.4 Prior to removing the flywheel, mark its correct fitted relationship with the crankshaft

12 Refit the clutch as described in Chapter 6, then remove the locking tool and refit the transmission as described in Chapter 7A.

12 Engine/transmission mounting rubbers
– inspection and renewal

Inspection

1 If improved access is required, jack up the front of the vehicle, and support it securely on axle stands (see *Jacking and vehicle support*). Remove the securing screws and remove the engine undershield(s).

2 Check the mounting rubbers to see if they are cracked, hardened or separated from the metal at any point; renew the mounting if any such damage or deterioration is evident.

3 Check that all the mounting fasteners are securely tightened; use a torque wrench to check if possible.

4 Using a large screwdriver or a crowbar, check for wear in the mounting by carefully levering against it to check for free play. Where this is not possible, enlist the aid of an assistant to move the engine/transmission back-and-forth, or from side-to-side, whilst you observe the mounting. While some free play is to be expected, even from new components, excessive wear should be obvious. If excessive free play is found, check first that the fasteners are correctly secured, then renew any worn components as described in the following paragraphs.

Renewal

Right-hand mounting

Note: *New mounting securing bolts/nut will be required on refitting.*

5 Attach a hoist and lifting tackle to the engine lifting brackets on the cylinder head, and raise the hoist to just take the weight of the engine. Alternatively the engine can be supported on a trolley jack under the engine. Use a block of wood between the sump and the head of the jack, to prevent any damage to the sump.

6 Unbolt the coolant reservoir and move it to one side, leaving the coolant hoses connected.

7 Unscrew the bolts securing the mounting to the bracket on the engine, and the bolts securing the mounting to the body, then lift the mounting from the engine compartment.

8 Unscrew the centre nut and separate the bracket from the mounting.

9 Refitting is a reversal of removal, but tighten the *new* bolts and nut to the specified torque.

Left-hand mounting

Note: *New mounting bolts will be required on refitting.*

10 Remove the engine undertray, then support the transmission with a trolley jack and block of wood.

11 Remove the battery, as described in Chapter 5A, then disconnect the main starter motor feed cable from the positive battery terminal box.

12 Release any relevant wiring or hoses from the clips on the battery tray, then unscrew the four securing bolts and remove the battery tray.

13 Where applicable, to improve access to the engine-transmission mounting, remove the air cleaner assembly as described in Chapter 4A.

14 Unscrew the bolts securing the mounting to the transmission, and the bolts securing the mounting to the body, then lift the mounting from the engine compartment.

15 Refitting is a reversal of removal, but tighten the *new* bolts to the specified torque.

Rear mounting

Note: *New mounting bolts will be required on refitting.*

16 Apply the handbrake, then jack up the front of the vehicle and support securely on axle stands (see *Jacking and vehicle support*).

17 Remove the engine undertray, then support the transmission with a trolley jack and block of wood.

18 Working under the vehicle, loosen the nut and bolt securing the rear mounting link to the transmission bracket.

19 Unscrew and remove the two bolts securing the mounting assembly to the transmission.

20 Unscrew the single bolt securing the mounting link to the subframe, then withdraw the assembly from under the vehicle.

21 Unscrew the nut and bolt and separate the link from the bracket.

22 Refitting is a reversal of removal, but use new mounting bolts (except the link-to-bracket bolt), and tighten all fixings to the specified torque.

Chapter 2 Part C:
1.4 litre DOHC petrol engine in-car repair procedures

Contents

	Section number			Section number
Auxiliary drivebelt – removal and refitting	4		Engine/transmission mountings – inspection and renewal	20
Camshaft carrier – removal and refitting	9		Flywheel/driveplate – removal, inspection and refitting	19
Camshaft oil seals – renewal	12		General information	1
Camshafts – removal, inspection and refitting	10		Oil pressure relief valve – removal, inspection and refitting	16
Compression test – description and interpretation	2		Oil pressure warning light switch – removal and refitting	17
Crankshaft oil seals – renewal	18		Oil pump – removal, inspection and refitting	15
Crankshaft pulley – removal and refitting	5		Rockers and hydraulic tappets – removal, inspection and refitting	11
Cylinder head – dismantling and overhaul	See Chapter 2E		Sump – removal and refitting	14
Cylinder head – removal, inspection and refitting	13		Timing belt covers – removal and refitting	6
Engine assembly and valve timing marks – general information and usage	3		Timing belt tensioner and sprockets – removal, inspection and refitting	8
Engine oil and filter – renewal	See Chapter 1A		Timing belt(s) – removal and refitting	7
Engine oil level – check	See Weekly checks			

Degrees of difficulty

| Easy, suitable for novice with little experience | 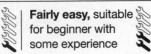 | Fairly easy, suitable for beginner with some experience | | Fairly difficult, suitable for competent DIY mechanic | | Difficult, suitable for experienced DIY mechanic | | Very difficult, suitable for expert DIY or professional | |

Specifications

General

Type	Four-cylinder in-line, belt-driven double overhead camshaft (DOHC), four stroke, 16-valve, liquid-cooled
Engine codes*:	
1390 cc 55 kW	AUA and BBY
1390 cc 74 kW	AUB and BBZ
Bore	76.5 mm
Stroke	75.6 mm
Compression ratio	10.5 : 1
Compression pressures:	
Minimum compression pressure	Approximately 7.0 bars
Maximum difference between cylinders	Approximately 3.0 bars
Firing order	1 – 3 – 4 – 2
No 1 cylinder location	Crankshaft pulley end
Direction of crankshaft rotation	Clockwise (when viewed from right-hand side of vehicle)

* Note: *See 'Vehicle identification' at the end of this manual for the location of engine code markings.*

Camshafts

Camshaft endfloat (maximum)	0.15 mm
Camshaft bearing running clearance	No figure specified
Camshaft run-out	No figure specified

Lubrication system

Oil pump type	Gear type, driven directly from front of crankshaft
Oil pressure (oil temperature 80°C):	
At idle	1.0 bar
At 2000 rpm	2.0 bar

Torque wrench settings

	Nm	lbf ft
Alternator	20	15
Ancillary (alternator, etc) bracket mounting bolts	50	37
Auxiliary drivebelt tensioner securing bolt:		
M8 bolt:		
Stage 1	20	15
Stage 2	Angle-tighten a further 90°	
M10 bolt	45	33
Big-end bearing caps bolts*:		
Stage 1	30	22
Stage 2	Angle-tighten a further 90°	
Camshaft carrier bolts*:		
Stage 1	10	7
Stage 2	Angle-tighten a further 90°	
Camshaft left-hand endplate bolts	10	7
Camshaft sprocket bolts*:		
Stage 1	20	15
Stage 2	Angle-tighten a further 90°	
Clutch pressure plate mounting bolts*:		
Stage 1	60	44
Stage 2	Angle-tighten a further 90°	
Coolant pump bolts	20	15
Crankcase breather (oil separator) bolts	10	7
Crankshaft oil seal housing bolts	12	9
Crankshaft pulley/sprocket bolt*:		
Stage 1	90	66
Stage 2	Angle-tighten a further 90°	
Cylinder head bolts*:		
Stage 1	30	22
Stage 2	Angle-tighten a further 90°	
Stage 3	Angle-tighten a further 90°	
Engine/transmission left-hand mounting to transmission:		
Stage 1	40	30
Stage 2	Angle-tighten a further 90°	
Engine/transmission left-hand mounting to body:		
Stage 1	50	37
Stage 2	Angle-tighten a further 90°	
Engine/transmission rear mounting bracket to transmission:		
Stage 1	30	22
Stage 2	Angle-tighten a further 90°	
Engine/transmission rear mounting link to subframe:		
Stage 1	40	30
Stage 2	Angle-tighten a further 90°	
Engine/transmission right-hand mounting to engine:		
Stage 1	20	15
Stage 2	Angle-tighten a further 90°	
Engine/transmission right-hand mounting to body:		
Stage 1	30	22
Stage 2	Angle-tighten a further 90°	
Engine-to-automatic transmission bolts:		
M12 bolts	80	59
M10 cylinder block-to-transmission bolts	60	44
M10 sump-to-transmission bolts	25	18
Engine-to-manual transmission bolts	80	59
Engine-to-manual transmission cover plate bolts	10	7
Exhaust manifold nuts	25	18
Exhaust pipe-to-manifold nuts	40	30
Flywheel/driveplate bolts (new)*:		
Stage 1	60	44
Stage 2	Angle-tighten a further 90°	
Knock sensor	20	15
Oil cooler securing nut	25	18
Oil level/temperature sensor-to-sump bolts	10	7
Oil pick-up pipe securing bolts	10	7
Oil pressure warning light switch	25	18
Oil pump securing bolts*	12	9

Torque wrench settings (continued)

	Nm	lbf ft
Sump:		
Sump-to-cylinder block bolts:		
Metal sump	15	11
Aluminium sump	13	10
Sump-to-transmission bolts	45	33
Sump drain plug	30	22
Timing belt idler pulley bolt	50	37
Timing belt outer cover bolts:		
Small bolts	10	7
Large bolts	20	15
Timing belt rear cover bolts:		
Small bolts	10	7
Large bolt (coolant pump bolts)	20	15
Timing belt tensioner:		
Main timing belt tensioner bolt	20	15
Secondary timing belt tensioner bolt	20	15

* Note: *Use new bolts*

---

1 General information

Using this Chapter

This Part of Chapter 2 describes those repair procedures that can reasonably be carried out on the engine while it remains in the vehicle. If the engine has been removed from the vehicle and is being dismantled as described in Part E, any preliminary dismantling procedures can be ignored.

Note that while it may be possible physically to overhaul items such as the piston/connecting rod assemblies while the engine is in the vehicle, such tasks are not usually carried out as separate operations, and usually require the execution of several additional procedures (not to mention the cleaning of components and of oilways); for this reason, all such tasks are classed as major overhaul procedures, and are described in Part E of this Chapter.

Caution: The crankshaft must not be removed on these engines. If the crankshaft or main bearing surfaces are worn or damaged, the complete crankshaft/cylinder block assembly must be renewed.

Part E describes the removal of the engine/transmission from the vehicle and the full overhaul procedures that can then be carried out.

Engine description

The engine is a water-cooled, double overhead camshaft, in-line four-cylinder unit, with an aluminium-alloy cylinder block and cylinder head. It is mounted transversely at the front of the car, with the transmission bolted to the left-hand side of the engine.

The crankshaft is of five-bearing type, and thrustwashers are fitted to the centre main bearing to control crankshaft endfloat. The crankshaft and main bearings are matched to the alloy cylinder block, and it is not possible to reassemble the crankshaft and cylinder block once the components have been

separated. If the crankshaft or bearings are worn, the complete cylinder block/crankshaft assembly must be renewed.

The inlet camshaft is driven by a toothed belt from the crankshaft sprocket, and the exhaust camshaft is driven from the inlet camshaft by a second toothed belt. The camshafts are located in a camshaft carrier, which is bolted to the top of the cylinder head.

The valves are closed by coil springs, and run in guides pressed into the cylinder head; the camshafts actuate the valves by roller rockers and hydraulic tappets. There are four valves per cylinder; two inlet valves and two exhaust valves.

The oil pump is driven directly from the end of the crankshaft. Oil is drawn from the sump through a strainer, and then forced through an externally-mounted, renewable filter. From there, it is distributed to the cylinder head, where it lubricates the camshaft journals and hydraulic tappets, and also to the crankcase, where it lubricates the main bearings, connecting rod big-ends, gudgeon pins and cylinder bores. A coolant-fed oil cooler is fitted to certain engines.

On all engines, engine coolant is circulated by a pump, driven by the main timing belt. For details of the cooling system, refer to Chapter 3.

Repairs with engine in car

The following operations can be performed without removing the engine:

a) *Compression pressure – testing.*
b) *Camshaft carrier – removal and refitting.*
c) *Crankshaft pulley – removal and refitting.*
d) *Timing belt covers – removal and refitting.*
e) *Timing belt(s) – removal, refitting and adjustment.*
f) *Timing belt tensioner and sprockets – removal and refitting.*
g) *Camshaft oil seal(s) – renewal.*
h) *Camshafts and hydraulic tappets – removal, inspection and refitting.*
i) *Cylinder head – removal and refitting*.*
j) *Sump – removal and refitting.*
k) *Oil pump – removal, overhaul and refitting.*

l) *Crankshaft oil seals – renewal.*
m) *Engine/transmission mountings – inspection and renewal.*
n) *Flywheel – removal, inspection and refitting.*

* *Cylinder head dismantling procedures are detailed in Chapter 2E, with details of camshaft and hydraulic tappet removal.*

Note: *It is possible to remove the pistons and connecting rods (after removing the cylinder head and sump) without removing the engine. However, this is not recommended. Work of this nature is more easily and thoroughly completed with the engine on the bench, as described in Chapter 2E.*

2 Compression test – description and interpretation

1 When engine performance is down, or if misfiring occurs which cannot be attributed to the ignition or fuel systems, a compression test can provide diagnostic clues as to the engine's condition. If the test is performed regularly, it can give warning of trouble before any other symptoms become apparent.

2 The engine must be fully warmed-up to normal operating temperature, the battery must be fully-charged and the spark plugs must be removed. The aid of an assistant will be required.

3 Disable the ignition system by disconnecting the wiring plug from the DIS ignition module (engine codes AUA and AUB) or ignition coils (engine codes BBY and BBZ).

4 Fit a compression tester to the No 1 cylinder spark plug hole. The type of tester that screws into the plug thread is preferred.

5 Have the assistant hold the throttle wide open and crank the engine for several seconds on the starter motor. **Note:** *The throttle will not operate until the ignition is switched on.* After one or two revolutions, the compression pressure should build-up to a maximum figure and then stabilise. Record the highest reading obtained.

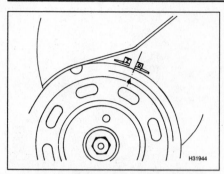

3.4a Crankshaft pulley timing mark aligned with TDC mark on timing belt cover

3.4b Timing mark scribed on inner flange of pulley aligned with TDC mark on timing belt cover

3.5 Crankshaft sprocket tooth with chamfered edge aligns with cast arrow on oil pump

6 Repeat the test on the remaining cylinders, recording the pressure in each.

7 All cylinders should produce very similar pressures. Any difference greater than that specified indicates the existence of a fault. Note that the compression should build-up quickly in a healthy engine. Low compression on the first stroke, followed by gradually increasing pressure on successive strokes, indicates worn piston rings. A low compression reading on the first stroke, which does not build-up during successive strokes, indicates leaking valves or a blown head gasket (a cracked head could also be the cause). Deposits on the undersides of the valve heads can also cause low compression.

8 If the pressure in any cylinder is reduced to the specified minimum or less, carry out the following test to isolate the cause. Introduce

a teaspoonful of clean oil into that cylinder through its spark plug hole and repeat the test.

9 If the addition of oil temporarily improves the compression pressure, this indicates that bore or piston wear is responsible for the pressure loss. No improvement suggests that leaking or burnt valves, or a blown head gasket, may be to blame.

10 A low reading from two adjacent cylinders is almost certainly due to the head gasket having blown between them and the presence of coolant in the engine oil will confirm this.

11 If one cylinder is about 20 percent lower than the others and the engine has a slightly rough idle, a worn camshaft lobe could be the cause.

12 On completion of the test, refit the spark plugs and reconnect the ignition wiring.

3 Engine assembly and valve timing marks – general information and usage

General information

1 TDC is the highest point in the cylinder that each piston reaches as it travels up and down when the crankshaft turns. Each piston reaches TDC at the end of the compression stroke and again at the end of the exhaust stroke, but TDC generally refers to piston position on the compression stroke. No 1 piston is at the timing belt end of the engine.

2 Positioning No 1 piston at TDC is an essential part of many procedures, such as timing belt removal and camshaft removal.

3 The design of the engines covered in this Chapter is such that piston-to-valve contact may occur if the camshaft or crankshaft is turned with the timing belt removed. For this reason, it is important to ensure that the camshaft and crankshaft do not move in relation to each other once the timing belt has been removed from the engine.

4 The crankshaft pulley has a marking which, when aligned with a corresponding reference marking on the timing belt cover, indicates that No 1 piston (and hence also No 4 piston) is at TDC. Note that on some models, the crankshaft pulley timing mark is located on the outer flange of the pulley. In order to make alignment of the timing marks easier, it is advisable to remove the pulley (see Section 5) and, using a set-square, scribe a corresponding mark on the inner flange of the pulley **(see illustrations)**.

5 Note that there is also a timing mark which can be used with the crankshaft sprocket – this is useful if the crankshaft pulley and timing belt have been removed. When No 1 piston is at TDC, the crankshaft sprocket tooth with the chamfered inner edge aligns with a cast arrow on the oil pump **(see illustration)**.

6 The camshaft sprockets are equipped with TDC positioning holes. When the positioning holes are aligned with the corresponding holes in the camshaft carrier, No 1 piston is at TDC on the compression stroke **(see illustration)**.

7 Additionally, on some models, the flywheel/driveplate has a TDC marking, which can be

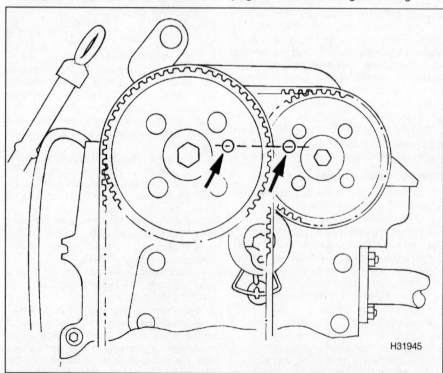

3.6 Camshaft sprocket positioning holes (arrowed) aligned with holes in camshaft carrier (No 1 piston at TDC)

observed by unscrewing a protective plastic cover from the transmission bellhousing. The mark takes the form of a notch in the edge of the flywheel on manual transmission models, or an O marking on automatic transmission models. Note that it is not possible to use these marks on all models due to the limited access available to view the marks.

Setting No 1 cylinder to TDC

Note: *Suitable locking pins will be required to lock the camshaft sprockets in position during this procedure. On some engines, it may be necessary to use a small engineer's mirror to view the timing marks from under the wheel arch.*

8 Before starting work, make sure that the ignition is switched off (ideally, the battery negative lead should be disconnected).

9 Remove the air cleaner assembly as described in Chapter 4A.

10 If desired, to make the engine easier to turn, remove all of the spark plugs as described in Chapter 1A.

11 Apply the handbrake, then jack up the front of the vehicle and support on axle stands (see *Jacking and vehicle support*).

12 Remove the right-hand front roadwheel, then remove the securing screws and/or clips, and remove the appropriate engine undershields to enable access to the crankshaft pulley.

13 Remove the upper timing belt cover as described in Section 6.

14 Turn the engine clockwise, using a spanner on the crankshaft pulley bolt, until the TDC mark on the crankshaft pulley or flywheel/driveplate is aligned with the corresponding mark on the timing belt cover or transmission casing, and the locking pin holes in the camshaft sprockets are aligned with the corresponding holes in the camshaft carrier.

15 If necessary, to give sufficient clearance for the camshaft locking tool to be engaged with the camshaft sprockets, unbolt the air cleaner support bracket from the engine mounting. Similarly, if necessary, unbolt the power steering fluid reservoir and move it to one side, leaving the fluid hoses connected.

16 A suitable tool will now be required to lock the camshaft sprockets in the TDC position. A special Skoda tool is available for this purpose, but a suitable tool can be improvised using two M8 bolts and nuts, and a short length of steel bar. With the camshaft sprocket positioned as described in paragraph 14, measure the distance between the locking pin hole centres, and drill two corresponding 8 mm holes in the length of steel bar. Slide the M8 bolts through the holes in the bar, and secure them using the nuts.

17 Slide the tool into position in the holes in the camshaft sprockets, ensuring that the pins (or bolts) engage with the holes in the camshaft carrier **(see illustration)**. The engine is now locked in position, with No 1 piston at TDC on the compression stroke.

3.17 Tool used to lock camshaft sprockets at TDC (viewed with engine removed, and timing belt removed from engine)

4 Auxiliary drivebelt – removal and refitting

General information

1 Depending on the vehicle specification, the auxiliary drivebelt, which is driven from a pulley mounted on the crankshaft, will provide drive for the alternator, power steering pump and, on models with air conditioning, the refrigerant compressor.

2 The ribbed auxiliary belt is fitted with an automatic tensioning device.

Removal

3 For improved access, apply the handbrake, then jack up the front of the vehicle and support it on axle stands (see *Jacking and vehicle support*). Remove the right-hand front roadwheel, then remove the access panel from the inner wheel arch. Also remove the engine top cover and where necessary disconnect the ventilation hose.

4 Use a spanner to turn the tensioner central bolt clockwise to release the tension on the drivebelt **(see illustration)**.

5 Note how the drivebelt is routed, then remove it from the crankshaft pulley, alternator pulley, power steering pump pulley, and air conditioning compressor pulley (where applicable).

Refitting

6 Locate the new drivebelt on the pulleys, then release the tensioner. Check that the belt is located correctly in the multi-grooves in the pulleys.

5.6 Counterhold the crankshaft pulley

4.4 Removing the auxiliary drivebelt

7 Refit the access panel, roadwheel, and top cover, and lower the vehicle to the ground.

5 Crankshaft pulley – removal and refitting

Removal

1 Disconnect the battery negative lead (refer to *Disconnecting the battery* in the *Reference* Chapter at the end of this manual).

2 For improved access, jack up the front of the vehicle, and support securely on axle stands (see *Jacking and vehicle support*). Remove the right-hand front roadwheel. Also remove the engine top cover and where necessary disconnect the ventilation hose.

3 Remove the securing screws and/or release the clips, and withdraw the relevant engine undershield(s) to enable access to the crankshaft pulley.

4 If necessary (for any later work to be carried out), turn the crankshaft using a socket or spanner on the crankshaft pulley bolt, until the relevant timing marks align (see Section 3).

5 Remove the auxiliary drivebelt, as described in Section 4.

6 To prevent the crankshaft from turning as the pulley bolt is slackened, a tool similar to that shown can be used. Engage the tool with two of the slots in the pulley **(see illustration)**.

7 Counterhold the pulley, and slacken the pulley bolt (take care – the bolt is very tight) using a socket and a suitable extension.

8 Unscrew the bolt, and remove the pulley **(see illustration)**.

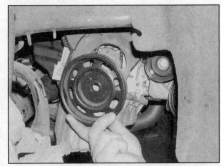

5.8 Removing the crankshaft pulley

6.2 Removing the upper outer timing belt cover

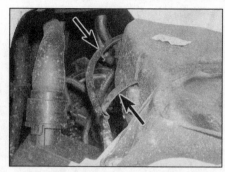

6.5a Release the two securing clips (arrowed) . . .

6.5b . . . then unscrew the two lower securing bolts (arrowed) . . .

6.5c . . . and the single bolt securing the cover to the engine mounting bracket . . .

6.8 Removing the idler pulley/bracket assembly (viewed with engine removed)

6.5d . . . and withdraw the lower timing belt cover

9 Refit the crankshaft pulley securing bolt, with a spacer washer positioned under its head, to retain the crankshaft sprocket.

Refitting

10 Unscrew the crankshaft pulley/sprocket bolt used to retain the sprocket, and remove the spacer washer, then refit the pulley to the sprocket. Ensure that the locating pin on the sprocket engages with the corresponding hole in the pulley.
11 Oil the threads of the new crankshaft pulley bolt. Prevent the crankshaft from turning as during removal, then fit the new pulley securing bolt, and tighten it to the specified torque, in the two stages given in the Specifications.
12 Refit the auxiliary drivebelt as described in Section 4.
13 Refit the engine undershield(s) and top cover.

14 Refit the roadwheel, lower the vehicle to the ground, and reconnect the battery negative lead.

---

6 Timing belt covers –
removal and refitting

Upper outer cover

1 Remove the air cleaner assembly as described in Chapter 4A. Also remove the engine top cover and, where necessary, disconnect the ventilation hose.
2 Release the two securing clips, and lift the cover from the engine (see illustration).
3 Refitting is a reversal of removal.

Lower outer cover

4 Remove the crankshaft pulley, as described in Section 5.

5 Release the two cover securing clips, located at the rear of the engine, then unscrew the two lower securing bolts, and the single bolt securing the cover to the engine mounting bracket. Withdraw the cover downwards from the engine (see illustrations).
6 Refitting is a reversal of removal, but refit the crankshaft pulley with reference to Section 5.

Rear timing belt cover

Note: *As the rear timing belt cover securing bolts also secure the coolant pump, it is advisable to drain the cooling system (see Chapter 1A) before starting this procedure, and to renew the coolant pump seal/gasket (see Chapter 3) before refitting the cover. Refill the cooling system with reference to Chapter 1A.*
7 Remove the timing belt as described in Section 7.
8 Unbolt the timing belt idler pulley/bracket assembly (see illustration).
9 Unscrew the rear timing belt cover securing bolt located next to the right-hand engine lifting eye (see illustration).
10 Unscrew the two securing bolts, and remove the rear timing belt cover. Note that the bolts also secure the coolant pump (see illustration).
11 Refitting is a reversal of removal, but tighten the timing belt idler pulley/bracket bolt to the specified torque, and refit the timing belt as described in Section 7.

6.9 Unscrew the rear timing belt cover securing bolt located next to the right-hand engine lifting eye

6.10 Removing the rear timing belt cover (viewed with engine removed)

7 Timing belt(s) – removal and refitting

Removal

1 These engines have two timing belts; the main timing belt drives the inlet camshaft from the crankshaft, and the secondary timing belt drives the exhaust camshaft from the inlet camshaft.

Main timing belt

2 Disconnect the battery negative lead (refer to *Disconnecting the battery* in the *Reference* Chapter at the end of this manual).

3 Remove the air cleaner assembly as described in Chapter 4A. Also remove the engine top cover and, where necessary, disconnect the ventilation hose.

4 Release the two securing clips and remove the upper and lower timing belt covers as described in Section 6.

5 Refit the crankshaft pulley securing bolt, with a spacer washer positioned under its head, to retain the crankshaft sprocket.

6 Turn the crankshaft to position No 1 piston at TDC on the compression stroke, and lock the camshaft sprockets in position, as described in Section 3.

7 Unscrew the securing screw, and move the power steering fluid reservoir clear of the working area, leaving the fluid hoses connected. Where necessary, unclip the charcoal canister hose from the reservoir.

8 Where applicable, on models with air conditioning, unscrew the securing bolt, and remove the auxiliary drivebelt idler pulley.

9 Attach a hoist and lifting tackle to the right-hand (timing belt end) engine lifting bracket, and raise the hoist to just take the weight of the engine.

10 Remove the complete engine right-hand mounting assembly, as described in Section 20. Also, unbolt the mounting bracket from the cylinder block.

11 Unscrew the four securing bolts, and remove the right-hand engine mounting bracket from the engine.

12 If either of the timing belts are to be refitted, mark their running directions to ensure correct refitting.

13 Engage a suitable Allen key with the hole in the main timing belt tensioner plate, then slacken the tensioner bolt, lever the tensioner anti-clockwise using the Allen key (to release the tension on the belt), and retighten the tensioner bolt **(see illustration)**.

14 Temporarily remove the camshaft sprocket locking tool, then slide the main timing belt from the sprockets, noting its routing **(see illustration)**. Refit the camshaft sprocket locking tool once the timing belt has been removed.

15 Turn the crankshaft a quarter-turn (90°) anti-clockwise to position Nos 1 and 4 pistons slightly down their bores from the TDC

7.13 Slacken the tensioner bolt, lever the tensioner anti-clockwise with an Allen key, then retighten the tensioner bolt

7.17a Slacken the secondary timing belt tensioner bolt, and lever the tensioner clockwise using an Allen key . . .

position. This will eliminate any risk of piston-to-valve contact if the crankshaft or camshaft is turned whilst the timing belt is removed.

Secondary timing belt

16 Once the main timing belt has been removed, to remove the secondary timing belt, proceed as follows.

17 Engage a suitable Allen key with the hole in the secondary timing belt tensioner plate, then slacken the tensioner bolt, and lever the tensioner clockwise using the Allen key (to release the tension on the belt). Unscrew the securing bolt, and remove the secondary timing belt tensioner **(see illustrations)**.

18 Temporarily remove the camshaft sprocket locking tool, and slide the secondary timing belt from the sprockets **(see illustration)**. Refit the sprocket locking tool once the belt has been removed.

7.18 Removing the secondary timing belt

7.14 Removing the main timing belt

7.17b . . . then unscrew the securing bolt and remove the tensioner

Refitting

Secondary timing belt

19 Check that the camshaft sprockets are still locked in position by the locking pins, then turn the crankshaft a quarter-turn (90°) clockwise to reposition Nos 1 and 4 pistons at TDC. Ensure that the crankshaft sprocket tooth with the chamfered inner edge is aligned with the corresponding mark on the oil pump housing **(see illustration)**.

20 Temporarily remove the camshaft sprocket locking tool, and fit the secondary timing belt around the camshaft sprockets. Make sure that the belt is as tight as possible on its top run between the sprockets (but note that there will be some slack in the belt). If the original belt is being refitted, observe the running direction markings. Refit the camshaft sprocket locking tool once the belt has been fitted to the sprockets.

7.19 Crankshaft sprocket tooth with chamfered edge aligned with cast arrow on oil pump

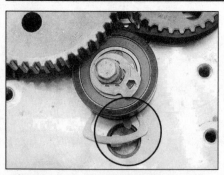

7.22 The secondary timing belt tensioner pointer should be positioned on the far right of the tensioner backplate

21 Check that the secondary timing belt tensioner pointer is positioned on the far right of the tensioner backplate.

22 Lift the lower run of the secondary timing belt using the tensioner, and fit the tensioner securing bolt (if necessary turn the tensioner with an Allen key until the bolt hole in the tensioner aligns with the bolt hole in the cylinder head). Make sure that the lug on the tensioner backplate engages with the core plug hole in the cylinder head (see illustration).

23 Use the Allen key to turn the tensioner anti-clockwise until the tensioner pointer aligns with the lug on the tensioner backplate, with the lug positioned against the left-hand stop in the core plug hole (see illustration). Tighten the tensioner bolt to the specified torque.

Main timing belt

24 Where applicable, ensure that the secondary drivebelt has been refitted and tensioned, then again temporarily remove the camshaft sprocket locking tool, and fit the main timing belt around the sprockets. If the original belt is being refitted, observe the running direction markings. Work in an anti-clockwise direction, starting at the coolant pump sprocket, followed by the tensioner roller, crankshaft sprocket, idler pulley, inlet camshaft sprocket and the second idler pulley. Once the belt has been refitted, refit the camshaft sprocket locking tool.

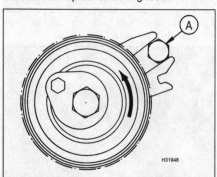

8.3 Turn the tensioner anti-clockwise to the position shown before fitting. Note that the cut-out engages with the bolt (A) when fitting

7.23 Turn the tensioner anti-clockwise until the tensioner pointer aligns with the lug on the tensioner backplate

25 Ensure that the tensioner bolt is slack, then engage an Allen key with the hole in the tensioner plate, and turn the plate clockwise until the tension indicator pointer is aligned with the centre of the cut-out in the backplate. Tighten the tensioner securing bolt to the specified torque.

26 Remove the camshaft sprocket locking tool.

27 Using a spanner or socket on the crankshaft pulley bolt, turn the engine through two complete turns in the normal direction of rotation, until the crankshaft sprocket tooth with the chamfered inner edge is aligned with the corresponding mark on the oil pump housing (refer to illustration 3.5). Check that the locking tool can again be fitted to lock the camshaft sprockets in position – if not, one or both of the timing belts may have been incorrectly fitted.

28 With the crankshaft timing marks aligned, and the camshaft sprockets locked in position, check the tension of the timing belts. The secondary and main belt tension indicators should be positioned as described in paragraphs 23 and 25 respectively – if not, repeat the appropriate tensioning procedure, then recheck the tension.

29 When the belt tension is correct, refit the right-hand engine mounting bracket, and tighten the securing bolts to the specified torque.

30 Disconnect the hoist and lifting tackle from the engine lifting bracket.

31 Where applicable, refit the auxiliary drivebelt idler pulley.

8.8a Removing the smaller ...

32 Refit the lower outer timing belt cover, with reference to Section 6 if necessary.

33 Refit the crankshaft pulley as described in Section 5.

34 Refit the upper outer timing belt cover.

35 Refit the air cleaner assembly, and reconnect the battery negative lead.

8 Timing belt tensioner and sprockets – removal, inspection and refitting

Tensioner

Main timing belt

1 Remove the main timing belt as described in Section 7.

2 Unscrew the main timing belt tensioner bolt, and remove the tensioner from the engine.

3 Engage an Allen key with the hole in the tensioner plate, and turn the tensioner anti-clockwise to the position shown (see illustration).

4 Refit the tensioner to the engine, ensuring that the cut-out in the tensioner backplate engages with the bolt on the cylinder block (refer to illustration 8.3). Refit the tensioner securing bolt, and tighten by hand.

5 Refit and tension the main timing belt as described in Section 7.

Secondary timing belt

6 Removal and refitting of the tensioner is described as part of the timing belt removal procedure in Section 7.

Main timing belt idler pulleys

7 Remove the timing belt as described in Section 7.

8 Unscrew the securing bolt and remove the relevant idler pulley. Note that the smaller pulley (the idler pulley nearest the inlet manifold side of the engine) can be removed complete with its mounting bracket (unbolt the mounting bracket bolt, leaving the pulley attached to the bracket) (see illustrations).

9 Refit the relevant idler pulley and tighten the securing bolt to the specified torque. Note that if the smaller idler pulley has been removed complete with its bracket, ensure that the bracket locates over the rear timing belt cover bolt on refitting.

8.8b ... and larger timing belt idler pulleys

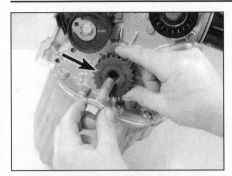

8.13 Refitting the crankshaft sprocket. Pulley locating pin (arrowed) must be outermost

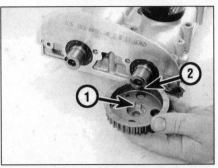

8.18 Refit the sprocket, ensuring that the lug (1) on the sprocket engages with the notch (2) in the end of the camshaft

8.19 Tighten the sprocket securing bolt using a suitable tool to hold the sprocket stationary

10 Refit and tension the main timing belt as described in Section 7.

Crankshaft sprocket

11 Remove the main timing belt as described in Section 7.

12 Unscrew the crankshaft pulley, and the washer used to retain the sprocket, and withdraw the sprocket from the crankshaft.

13 Commence refitting by positioning the sprocket on the end of the crankshaft, noting that the pulley locating pin must be outermost **(see illustration)**. Temporarily refit the pulley securing bolt and washer to retain the sprocket.

14 Refit the main timing belt as described in Section 7.

Camshaft sprockets

15 Remove the main and secondary timing belts as described in Section 7. Ensure that the crankshaft has been turned a quarter-turn (90°) anti-clockwise to position Nos 1 and 4 pistons slightly down their bores from the TDC position. This will eliminate any risk of piston-to-valve contact if the crankshaft or camshaft is turned whilst the timing belt is removed.

16 The relevant camshaft sprocket bolt must now be slackened. The camshaft must be prevented from turning as the sprocket bolt is unscrewed – **do not** rely solely on the sprocket locking tool for this. To hold the sprocket, make up a tool, and use it to hold the sprocket stationary by means of the holes in the sprocket **(refer to illustration 8.19)**.

17 Unscrew the camshaft sprocket bolt, and withdraw the sprocket from the end of the camshaft, noting which way round it is fitted.

18 Commence refitting by offering the sprocket up to the camshaft, ensuring that lug on the sprocket engages with the notch in the end of the camshaft. If both camshaft sprockets have been removed, note that the double sprocket (for the main and secondary timing belts) should be fitted to the inlet camshaft, and note that the exhaust camshaft sprocket must be fitted first **(see illustration)**.

19 Fit a new sprocket securing bolt, then use the tool to hold the sprocket stationary, as during removal, and tighten the bolt to the specified torque, in the two stages given in the Specifications **(see illustration)**.

20 Refit the secondary and main timing belts as described in Section 7.

Coolant pump sprocket

21 The coolant pump sprocket is integral with the coolant pump. Refer to Chapter 3 for details of coolant pump removal.

9 Camshaft carrier – removal and refitting

Removal

1 Disconnect the battery negative lead (refer to *Disconnecting the battery* in the *Reference* Chapter at the end of this manual).

2 Remove the main and secondary timing belts, as described in Section 7.

3 On engine codes AUA and AUB, disconnect

9.3a Use a hooked length of wire to pull the connectors from the spark plugs (AUA and AUB engines)

9.3c . . . then remove the DIS module and HT leads (AUA and AUB engines)

the HT leads from the spark plugs. Use a hooked length of stout wire to pull the connectors from the spark plugs. Release the securing lug, and disconnect the wiring plug from the DIS module, then unscrew the securing bolts, and remove the DIS module and HT leads as an assembly **(see illustrations)**.

4 On engine codes BBY and BBZ, disconnect the wiring and remove the ignition coils from the spark plugs (see Chapter 5B), then remove the cable guide.

5 Disconnect the inlet camshaft position sensor wiring connector **(see illustration)**.

6 Unscrew the bolt securing the exhaust gas recirculation solenoid valve to the end of the camshaft carrier **(see illustration)**. Move the valve to one side.

7 Disconnect the wiring plug from the oil pressure warning light switch, located at the

9.3b Unscrew the DIS module securing bolts . . .

9.5 Disconnect the wiring connector from the inlet camshaft position sensor

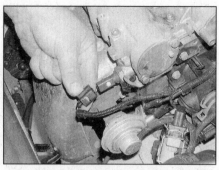

9.6 Unscrew the bolt securing the exhaust gas recirculation solenoid valve to the end of the camshaft carrier

9.7a Disconnect the oil pressure warning light switch wiring plug . . .

9.7b . . . then release the wiring from the clip on the end of the camshaft carrier

front left-hand corner of the camshaft carrier. Release the wiring harness from the clip on the end of the camshaft carrier, and move the wiring to one side **(see illustrations)**.

8 Remove the rear timing belt cover securing bolt, located next to the right-hand engine lifting eye **(see illustration)**.

9 Working progressively from the centre out, in a diagonal sequence, slacken and remove the camshaft carrier securing bolts **(see illustration)**.

10 Carefully lift the camshaft carrier from the cylinder head. The camshafts can be removed from the carrier, as described in Section 10.

Refitting

11 Commence refitting by thoroughly cleaning all traces of old sealant, and all traces of oil and grease, from the mating faces of the cylinder head and camshaft carrier. Ensure that no debris enters the cylinder head or camshaft carrier.

12 Ensure that the crankshaft is still positioned a quarter-turn (90°) anti-clockwise from the TDC position, and that the camshafts are locked in position with the locking tool, as described in Section 3.

13 Check that the valve rockers are correctly located on the valves, and securely clipped into position on the hydraulic tappets.

14 Apply a thin, even coat of sealant (Skoda AMV 188 003, or equivalent) to the cylinder head mating face of the camshaft carrier **(see illustration)**. Do not apply the sealant too thickly, as excess sealant may enter and block the oilways, causing engine damage.

15 Carefully lower the camshaft carrier onto the cylinder head, until the camshafts rest on the rockers. Note that the camshaft carrier locates on dowels in the cylinder head; if desired, to make fitting easier, two guide studs can be made up as follows:

a) Cut the heads off two M6 bolts, then cut

slots in the top of each bolt to enable the bolt to be unscrewed using a flat-bladed screwdriver.

b) Screw one bolt into each of the camshaft carrier bolt locations at opposite corners of the cylinder head.

c) Lower the camshaft carrier over the bolts to guide it into position on the cylinder head.

16 Fit new camshaft carrier securing bolts, and tighten them progressively, working from the centre out, in a diagonal sequence (ie, tighten all bolts through one turn, then tighten all bolts through a further turn, and so on). Ensure that the camshaft carrier sits squarely on the cylinder head as the bolts are tightened, and make sure that the carrier engages with the cylinder head dowels. Where applicable, once the camshaft carrier contacts the surface of the cylinder head, unscrew the two guide studs, and fit the two remaining new camshaft carrier securing bolts in their place.

17 Tighten the camshaft carrier securing bolts to the specified torque, in the two stages given in the Specifications **(see illustration)**.

18 Leave the camshaft carrier sealant to dry for approximately 30 minutes before carrying out any further work on the cylinder head or camshaft carrier.

19 Once the sealant has been allowed to dry, refit the rear timing belt cover bolt.

20 Reconnect the oil pressure warning light switch wiring plug, and clip the wiring into position on the end of the camshaft carrier.

21 Refit the exhaust gas recirculation solenoid valve bracket to the camshaft carrier, and tighten the securing bolt. Make sure that the lug on the camshaft carrier endplate engages with the corresponding hole in the solenoid valve bracket.

22 Reconnect the camshaft position sensor wiring connector.

23 On engine codes AUA and AUB, refit the DIS module and tighten the securing bolts, then reconnect the DIS module wiring connector, and the spark plug HT leads.

24 On engine codes BBY and BBZ, refit the cable guide and reconnect the ignition coils to the spark plugs.

25 Refit the secondary and main timing belts, as described in Section 7.

26 Reconnect the battery negative lead.

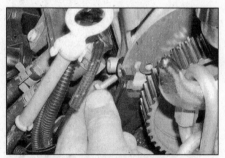

9.8 Remove the rear timing belt cover securing bolt located next to the right-hand engine lifting eye

9.9 Removing the camshaft carrier securing bolts

9.14 Apply a thin, even coat of sealant to the cylinder head mating face of the camshaft carrier

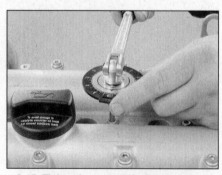

9.17 Tightening a camshaft carrier bolt through the specified Stage 2 angle

10 Camshafts – removal, inspection and refitting

Removal

1 Remove the camshaft carrier as described in Section 9.

2 Remove the camshaft sprockets, with reference to Section 8 if necessary.

3 If the inlet camshaft is to be removed, unscrew the securing bolt, and remove the inlet camshaft position sensor **(see illustration)**.

4 Remove the relevant camshaft carrier endplate **(see illustration)**. Note that on engine codes AUA and AUB the inlet camshaft endplate is secured by the DIS module bolts, which have already been removed, and the exhaust camshaft endplate is secured by three bolts, one of which also secures the exhaust gas recirculation solenoid valve.

5 Carefully withdraw the relevant camshaft from the endplate end of the camshaft carrier, taking care not to damage the bearing surfaces of the camshaft and housing as the camshaft is withdrawn **(see illustration)**.

Inspection

6 Visually inspect the camshafts for evidence of wear on the surfaces of the lobes and journals. Normally their surfaces should be smooth and have a dull shine; look for scoring, erosion or pitting and areas that appear highly polished, indicating excessive wear. Accelerated wear will occur once the hardened exterior of the camshaft has been damaged, so always renew worn items. **Note:** *If these symptoms are visible on the tips of the camshaft lobes, check the corresponding rocker, as it will probably be worn as well.*

7 If the machined surfaces of the camshaft appear discoloured or blued, it is likely that it has been overheated at some point, probably due to inadequate lubrication. This may have distorted the shaft, so check the run-out as follows: place the camshaft between two V-blocks and using a DTI gauge, measure the run-out at the centre journal. No maximum run-out figure is quoted by the manufacturers, but it should be obvious if the camshaft is excessively distorted.

8 To measure camshaft endfloat, temporarily refit the relevant camshaft to the camshaft carrier, and refit the camshaft sealing plate to the rear of the camshaft carrier. Anchor a DTI gauge to the timing belt end of the camshaft carrier and align the gauge probe with the camshaft axis. Push the camshaft to one end of the camshaft carrier as far as it will travel, then rest the DTI gauge probe on the end of the camshaft, and zero the gauge display. Push the camshaft as far as it will go to the other end of the camshaft carrier, and record the gauge reading. Verify the reading by pushing the camshaft back to its original position and checking that the gauge indicates zero again.

9 Check that the camshaft endfloat

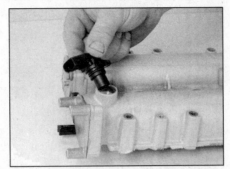

10.3 Remove the inlet camshaft position sensor

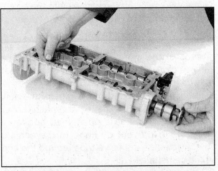

10.5 Withdraw the camshaft from the endplate end of the camshaft carrier

measurement is within the limit listed in the Specifications. Wear outside of this limit may be cured by renewing the relevant camshaft carrier endplate, although wear is unlikely to be confined to any one component, so renewal of the camshafts and camshaft carrier must be considered.

Refitting

10 Refitting is a reversal of removal, bearing in mind the following points:

a) *Before refitting the camshaft, renew the camshaft right-hand oil seal, with reference to Section 12.*

b) *Lubricate the bearing surfaces in the camshaft carrier, and the camshaft lobes before refitting the camshaft(s).*

c) *Renew the sealing O-ring on each camshaft carrier endplate **(see illustration)**.*

d) *Refit the camshaft sprocket(s) with*

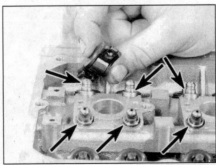

11.3 Removing a rocker (hydraulic tappets arrowed)

10.4 Remove the camshaft carrier endplate

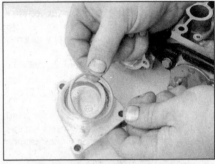

10.10 Renew the camshaft carrier endplate O-ring

reference to Section 8, noting that if both sprockets have been removed, the exhaust camshaft sprocket must be fitted first.

e) *Refit the camshaft carrier as described in Section 9.*

11 Rockers and hydraulic tappets – removal, inspection and refitting

Removal

1 Remove the camshaft carrier, as described in Section 9.

2 As the components are removed, keep them in strict order, so that they can be refitted in their original locations.

3 Unclip the rockers from the hydraulic tappets, and lift them from the cylinder head **(see illustration)**.

4 Carefully lift the hydraulic tappets from their bores in the cylinder head. It is advisable to store the tappets (in order) upright in an oil bath whilst they are removed from the engine.

Inspection

5 Check the tappet bores in the cylinder head for signs of scoring or damage. If significant scoring or damage is found, it may be necessary to renew the cylinder head and the complete set of tappets.

6 Inspect the hydraulic tappets for obvious signs of wear or damage, and renew if necessary. Check that the oil holes in the tappets are free from obstructions.

11.9 Oil the tappets before fitting

7 Check the valve, tappet, and camshaft contact faces of the rockers for wear or damage, and also check the rockers for any signs of cracking. Renew any worn or damaged rockers.

8 Inspect the camshaft lobes, as described in Section 10.

Refitting

9 Oil the tappet bores in the cylinder head, and the hydraulic tappets themselves, then carefully slide the tappets into their original bores (see illustration).

10 Oil the rocker contact faces of the tappets, and the tops of the valve stems, then refit the rockers to their original locations, ensuring that the rockers are securely clipped onto the tappets.

11 Check the endfloat of each camshaft, as described in Section 10, then refit the camshaft carrier as described in Section 9.

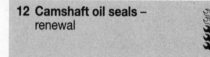

12 Camshaft oil seals – renewal

Right-hand oil seals

1 Remove the main and secondary timing belts as described in Section 7.

2 Remove the relevant camshaft sprocket as described in Section 8.

3 Drill two small holes into the existing oil seal, diagonally opposite each other. Take great care to avoid drilling through into the seal housing or camshaft sealing surface.

13.5 Home-made engine lifting bracket screwed into the hole located next to the coolant pump

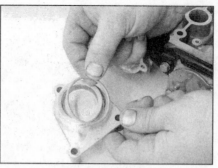

12.12 Locate the new O-ring in the groove in the endplate

Thread two self-tapping screws into the holes, and using a pair of pliers, pull on the heads of the screws to extract the oil seal.

4 Clean out the seal housing and the sealing surface of the camshaft by wiping it with a lint-free cloth. Remove any swarf or burrs that may cause the seal to leak.

5 Lubricate the lip and outer edge of the new oil seal with clean engine oil, and push it over the camshaft until it is positioned above its housing. To prevent damage to the sealing lips, wrap some adhesive tape around the end of the camshaft.

6 Using a hammer and a socket of suitable diameter, drive the seal squarely into its housing. Note: *Select a socket that bears only on the hard outer surface of the seal, not the inner lip which can easily be damaged.*

7 Refit the relevant camshaft sprocket with reference to Section 8.

8 Refit and tension the secondary and main timing belts as described in Section 7.

Left-hand oil seals

9 The camshaft left-hand oil seals take the form of O-rings located in the grooves in the camshaft carrier endplates.

10 Unscrew the securing bolts, and remove the relevant camshaft endplate, noting that on engine codes AUA and AUB the DIS ignition module securing bolts secure the exhaust camshaft endplate.

11 Prise the old O-ring from the groove in the endplate.

12 Lightly oil the new O-ring, and carefully locate it in the groove in the endplate (see illustration).

13.6 Disconnect the radiator hoses from the coolant housing at the transmission end of the cylinder head

13 Refit the endplate (and the DIS module, where applicable), and tighten the securing bolts to the specified torque.

13 Cylinder head – removal, inspection and refitting

Note: *The cylinder head must be removed with the engine cold.*

Removal

1 Disconnect the battery negative lead (refer to *Disconnecting the battery* in the *Reference* Chapter at the end of this manual).

2 Drain the cooling system as described in Chapter 1A.

3 Remove the main and secondary timing belts as described in Section 7.

4 As the engine is currently supported using a hoist attached to the engine lifting brackets bolted to the cylinder head, it is now necessary to attach a suitable bracket to the cylinder block, so that the engine can still be supported as the cylinder head is removed.

5 A suitable bracket can be bolted to the cylinder block using spacers, and a long bolt screwed into the hole located next to the coolant pump (see illustration). Ideally, attach a second set of lifting tackle to the hoist, adjust the lifting tackle to support the engine using the bracket attached to the cylinder block, then disconnect the lifting tackle attached to the bracket on the cylinder head. Alternatively, temporarily support the engine under the sump using a jack and a block of wood, then transfer the lifting tackle from the bracket on the cylinder head to the bracket bolted to cylinder block.

6 Release the hose clips, and disconnect the two radiator hoses from the coolant housing at the transmission end of the cylinder head (see illustration). Similarly, release the hose clips and disconnect the remaining three small coolant hoses from the rear of the coolant housing.

7 Remove the air cleaner assembly, complete with the air trunking, as described in Chapter 4A.

8 Unscrew the bolt securing the oil level dipstick tube bracket to the cylinder head, then lift the dipstick tube, and turn it to one side, to clear the working area (see illustration).

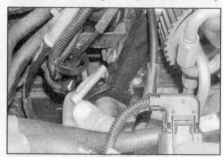

13.8 Unscrew the bolt securing the oil level dipstick tube bracket to the cylinder head

13.9 Disconnect the EGR pipe from the throttle body and recover the gasket

13.11 Lift the inlet manifold back from the engine

13.12 Unbolt the wiring connector bracket from the right-hand rear corner of the cylinder head

Release the wiring harnesses from the clip on the dipstick tube bracket. Note that the dipstick tube bracket bolt also secures the inlet manifold.

9 Unscrew the two securing bolts and disconnect the exhaust gas recirculation (EGR) pipe from the throttle body. Recover the gasket **(see illustration)**.

10 Unscrew the bolt securing the EGR pipe bracket to the coolant housing.

11 Unscrew the six securing bolts (three upper and three lower) and lift the inlet manifold back from the engine **(see illustration)**. Ensure that the inlet manifold is adequately supported in the engine compartment, and take care not to strain any wires, cables or hoses. Recover the O-rings if they are loose.

12 Unbolt the wiring connector bracket from the right-hand rear corner of the cylinder head **(see illustration)**.

13 Disconnect the wiring plug from the coolant temperature sensor, located in the coolant housing at the transmission end of the cylinder head, then unclip the wiring harnesses from the coolant housing, and move them to one side **(see illustrations)**.

14 Disconnect the vacuum hose from the exhaust gas recirculation (EGR) valve **(see illustration)**.

15 Unclip the wiring from the bracket attached to the exhaust heat shield, then unscrew the securing bolts (two upper bolts and one lower bolt), and remove the heat shield **(see illustrations)**.

16 Disconnect the exhaust front section from the manifold with reference to Chapter 4C. If desired, the exhaust manifold can be removed as follows:

a) *Unscrew the union nut securing the EGR pipe to the exhaust manifold, and remove the EGR pipe.*

b) *Unscrew the exhaust manifold securing nuts, then lift off the manifold and recover the gasket.*

17 Remove the camshaft carrier, with reference to Section 9.

18 Pull out the metal clip securing the plastic coolant pipe to the coolant housing at the left-hand rear corner of the cylinder head **(see illustration)**.

19 Progressively slacken the cylinder head bolts in order, then unscrew and remove the bolts **(see illustration)**.

20 With all the bolts removed, lift the cylinder head from the block. If the cylinder head is stuck, tap it with a soft-faced mallet to break the joint. **Do not** insert a lever into the gasket joint. As the cylinder head is lifted off, release the coolant pump pipe from the thermostat housing on the cylinder head.

21 Lift the cylinder head gasket from the block.

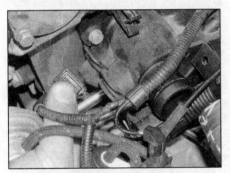

13.13a Disconnect the coolant temperature sensor wiring plug . . .

13.13b . . . then unclip the wiring harnesses and move them to one side

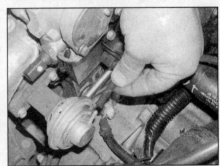

13.14 Disconnect the vacuum hose from the EGR valve

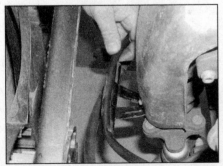

13.15a Unclip the wiring from the bracket on the exhaust heat shield . . .

13.15b . . . then remove the heat shield

13.18 Pull out the metal clip securing the coolant pipe to the coolant housing (engine removed for clarity)

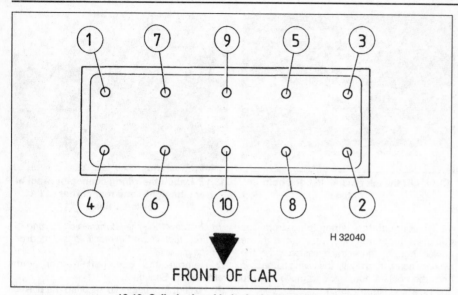

FRONT OF CAR

H 32040

13.19 Cylinder head bolt slackening sequence

Inspection

22 Dismantling and inspection of the cylinder head is covered in Part E of this Chapter. Additionally, check the condition of the coolant pump pipe-to-thermostat housing O-ring, and renew if necessary.

Refitting

23 The mating faces of the cylinder head and block must be perfectly clean before refitting the head. Use a scraper to remove all traces of gasket and carbon, also clean the tops of the pistons. Take particular care with the aluminium

13.28a Ensure that the dowels (arrowed) are in place in the cylinder block

13.28b Ensure that the part number and OBEN/TOP markings on the cylinder head gasket are uppermost

surfaces, as the soft metal is easily damaged. Make sure that debris is not allowed to enter the oil and water passages – this is particularly important for the oil circuit, as carbon could block the oil supply to the camshaft and crankshaft bearings. Using adhesive tape and paper, seal the water, oil and bolt holes in the cylinder block. To prevent carbon entering the gap between the pistons and bores, smear a little grease in the gap. After cleaning a piston, rotate the crankshaft to that the piston moves down the bore, then wipe out the grease and carbon with a cloth rag. Clean the other piston crowns in the same way.

24 Check the head and block for nicks, deep scratches and other damage. If slight, they may be removed carefully with a file. More serious damage may be repaired by machining, but this is a specialist job.

25 If warpage of the cylinder head is

suspected, use a straight-edge to check it for distortion, as described in Part E of this Chapter.

26 Ensure that the cylinder head bolt holes in the crankcase are clean and free of oil. Syringe or soak up any oil left in the bolt holes. This is most important in order that the correct bolt tightening torque can be applied, and to prevent the possibility of the block being cracked by hydraulic pressure when the bolts are tightened.

27 Ensure that the crankshaft has been turned to position Nos 1 and 4 pistons slightly down their bores from the TDC position (see Section 7). This will eliminate any risk of piston-to-valve contact as the cylinder head is refitted. Also ensure that the camshaft sprockets are locked in the TDC position using the locking tool, as described in Section 3.

28 Ensure that the cylinder head locating dowels are in place in the cylinder block, then fit a new cylinder head gasket over the dowels, ensuring that the part number is uppermost. Where applicable, the OBEN/TOP marking should also be uppermost **(see illustrations)**. Note that Skoda recommend that the gasket is only removed from its packaging immediately prior to fitting.

29 Lower the cylinder head into position on the gasket, ensuring that it engages correctly over the dowels. As the cylinder head is lowered into position, ensure that the coolant pump pipe engages with the thermostat housing (use a new O-ring if necessary).

30 Fit the new cylinder head bolts, and screw them in as far as possible by hand.

31 Working progressively, in sequence, tighten all the cylinder head bolts to the specified Stage 1 torque **(see illustration)**.

32 Again working progressively, in sequence, tighten all the cylinder head bolts through the specified Stage 2 angle.

33 Finally, tighten all the cylinder head bolts, in sequence, to the specified Stage 3 torque.

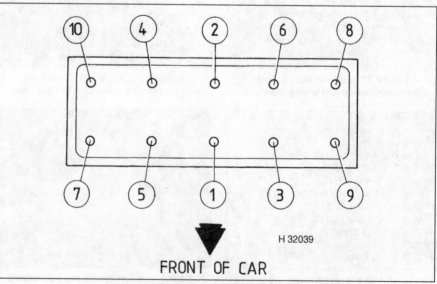

FRONT OF CAR

H 32039

13.31 Cylinder head bolt tightening sequence

34 Reconnect the lifting tackle to the right-hand engine lifting bracket on the cylinder head, then adjust the lifting tackle to support the engine. Once the engine is adequately supported using the cylinder head bracket, disconnect the lifting tackle from the bracket bolted to the cylinder block, and unbolt the improvised engine lifting bracket from the cylinder block. Alternatively, remove the trolley jack and block of wood from under the sump.

35 Refit the clip securing the plastic coolant pipe to the coolant housing.

36 Refit the camshaft carrier as described in Section 9.

37 Further refitting is a reversal of removal, bearing in mind the following points:

a) *Refit the exhaust manifold and reconnect the EGR pipe, and/or reconnect the exhaust front section to the manifold, as described in Section 4C.*

b) *Refit the inlet manifold using new O-rings.*

c) *Reconnect the EGR pipe to the throttle body using a new gasket.*

d) *Refit the secondary and main timing belts as described in Section 7.*

e) *Ensure that all wires, pipes and hoses are correctly reconnected and routed, as noted before removal.*

f) *Tighten all fixings to the specified torque, where applicable.*

g) *On completion, refill the cooling system as described in Chapter 1A.*

14 Sump – removal and refitting

Removal

1 Disconnect the battery negative lead (refer to *Disconnecting the battery* in the *Reference* Chapter at the end of this manual).

2 Chock the rear wheels and apply the handbrake, then jack up the front of the vehicle and support it on axle stands (see *Jacking and vehicle support*). Remove the engine undertray.

3 Drain the engine oil, then clean and refit the engine oil drain plug, tightening it to the specified torque wrench setting. If the engine is nearing the service interval when the oil and filter are due for renewal, it is recommended that the filter is also removed and a new one fitted. After reassembly, the engine can then be replenished with fresh engine oil. Refer to Chapter 1A for further information.

4 Remove the exhaust front pipe with reference to Chapter 4C.

5 Disconnect the wiring from the oil level/temperature sender.

6 Unscrew the two bolts securing the sump rear flange to the transmission.

7 Progressively unscrew and remove the sump retaining bolts.

8 Break the joint by striking the sump with the palm of the hand, then lower the sump away from the engine and withdraw it.

9 While the sump is removed, take the opportunity to clean the oil pump pick-up/strainer pipe mesh using a suitable solvent. Inspect the strainer mesh for signs of clogging or splitting and renew if necessary, referring to Section 15 for further information.

Refitting

10 Thoroughly clean all traces of sealant and oil from the mating surfaces of the cylinder block/crankcase and sump, then use a clean rag to wipe out the sump and the engine's interior.

11 Apply a 2.0 to 3.0 mm diameter bead of sealant to the sump mating flange, making sure that the bead is around the inner edges of the bolt holes. The bead must not exceed 3.0 mm diameter. **Note:** *The sump must be refitted within 5 minutes of applying the sealant.*

12 When refitting the sump, to guide the sump into position on the cylinder block mating face, two guide studs can be improvised by cutting the heads off two M6 bolts, and cutting slots in the ends of the bolts so that they can later by unscrewed using a flat-bladed screwdriver. Screw the guide studs into two diagonally opposite sump securing bolt holes.

13 Offer the sump into position, then refit the sump bolts and tighten them to the specified torque. Once the sump is held securely in position, unscrew the guide studs, and refit the remaining two sump securing bolts.

14 Insert the two rear flange bolts and tighten them to the specified torque.

15 Reconnect the wiring to the oil level/temperature sender.

16 Refit the exhaust front pipe with reference to Chapter 4C.

17 Refit the engine undertray and lower the vehicle to the ground.

18 Reconnect the battery negative lead.

19 Refill the engine with oil as described in Chapter 1A.

15 Oil pump – removal, inspection and refitting

Removal

1 Remove the main timing belt as described in Section 7.

15.6 Removing the oil pick-up pipe

15.2 Crankshaft sprocket TDC timing mark (A)

2 Turn the crankshaft a quarter-turn (90°) clockwise to reposition Nos 1 and 4 pistons at TDC. Ensure that the crankshaft sprocket tooth with the chamfered inner edge is aligned with the corresponding mark on the oil pump housing **(see illustration)**.

3 Turn the crankshaft to move the crankshaft sprocket three teeth anti-clockwise away from the TDC position. The third tooth to the right of the tooth with the ground-down outer edge must align with the corresponding mark on the oil pump housing. This procedure positions the crankshaft correctly to enable oil pump refitting.

4 Remove the timing belt tensioner as described in Section 8.

5 Remove the sump as described in Section 14.

6 Unscrew the securing bolts and remove the oil pick-up pipe from the oil pump and cylinder block **(see illustration)**. Recover the gasket. **Note:** *As of 06/04 a plastic pipe is fitted without support brackets to manual transmission models.*

7 Remove the crankshaft sprocket, noting which way round it is fitted.

8 Unscrew the securing bolts, noting their locations to ensure correct refitting, and remove the oil pump **(see illustration)**. Recover the gasket.

15.8 Removing the oil pump

15.10 Lifting off the oil pump rear cover

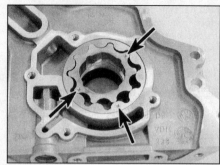
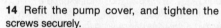

15.11 Note that the rotors fit with the punched dots (arrowed) facing the oil pump cover

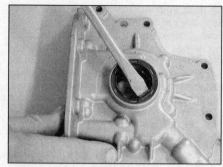

15.15 Prise the crankshaft oil seal from the oil pump

Inspection

9 No spare parts are available for the oil pump, and if worn or faulty the complete pump must be renewed.

10 To inspect the oil pump rotors, remove the securing screws, and lift off the oil pump rear cover **(see illustration)**.

11 Note that the rotors fit with the punched dots on the edges of the rotors facing the oil pump cover **(see illustration)**.

12 Lift out the rotors, and inspect them for wear and damage. If there are any signs of wear or damage, the complete oil pump assembly must be renewed.

13 Lubricate the contact faces of the rotors with clean engine oil, then refit the rotors to the pump, ensuring that the punched dots on the edges of the rotors face the pump cover.

14 Refit the pump cover, and tighten the screws securely.

15 Using a flat-bladed screwdriver, prise the crankshaft oil seal from the oil pump, and discard it **(see illustration)**.

16 Thoroughly clean the oil seal seat in the oil pump.

17 Press or drive a new oil seal into position in the oil pump, using a socket or tube of suitable diameter **(see illustration)**. Ensure that the seal seats squarely in the oil pump. Ensure that the socket or tube bears only on the hard outer ring of the seal, and take care not to damage the seal lips. Press or drive the seal into position until it is seated on the shoulder in the housing. Make sure that the closed end of the seal is facing outwards.

Refitting

18 Commence refitting by cleaning all traces of old gasket and sealant from the mating faces of the cylinder block and oil pump.

19 Wind a length of tape around the end of the crankshaft to protect the oil seal lips as the oil pump is slid into position.

20 Fit a new oil pump gasket over the dowels in the cylinder block **(see illustration)**.

21 Turn the inner oil pump rotor to align one of the drive cut-outs in the edge of the inner rotor with the line on the oil pump rear cover **(see illustration)**.

22 Lightly oil the four tips of the oil pump drive cam on the end of the crankshaft.

23 Coat the lips of the crankshaft oil seal with a thin film of clean engine oil.

24 Slide the oil pump into position over the end of the crankshaft until it engages with the dowels, taking care not to damage the oil seal, and ensuring that the inner rotor engages with the drive cam on the crankshaft **(see illustration)**.

25 Fit new oil pump securing bolts to the locations noted before removal, and tighten them to the specified torque **(see illustration)**.

26 Remove the tape from the end of the crankshaft, then refit the crankshaft sprocket, noting that the pulley locating pin must be outermost. Temporarily refit the securing bolt and washer to retain the sprocket.

27 Refit the oil pick-up pipe, using a new

15.17 Driving a new oil seal into the oil pump using a socket

15.20 Fit a new gasket over the dowels in the cylinder block

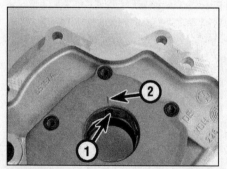

15.21 Align one of the drive cut-outs (1) in the edge of the rotor with the line (2) on the oil pump rear cover

15.24 Slide the oil pump over the end of the crankshaft. Note the tape used to protect the oil seal

15.25 Fit the new oil pump securing bolts to the locations (arrowed) noted before removal

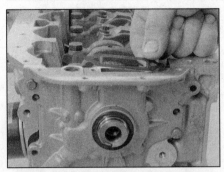

15.27 Fit a new oil pick-up pipe gasket

gasket, and tighten the securing bolts to the specified torque **(see illustration)**.

28 Refit the sump as described in Section 14.

29 Refit the timing belt tensioner as described in Section 8.

30 Refit the main timing belt as described in Section 7.

16 Oil pressure relief valve – removal, inspection and refitting

The oil pressure relief valve is an integral part of the oil pump. The valve piston and spring are located to the side of the oil pump rotors and can be inspected once the oil pump has been removed from the engine and the rear cover has been removed (see Section 15). If any sign of wear or damage is found the oil pump assembly will have to be renewed; the relief valve piston and spring are not available separately.

17 Oil pressure warning light switch – removal and refitting

Removal

1 The oil pressure warning light switch is fitted to the left-hand end of the cylinder head. To gain access to the switch, remove the air cleaner as described in Chapter 4A.

2 Disconnect the wiring connector and wipe clean the area around the switch **(see illustration)**.

3 Unscrew the switch from the cylinder head and remove it along with its sealing washer. If the switch is to be left removed from the engine for any length of time, plug the hole in the cylinder head.

Refitting

4 Examine the sealing washer for signs of damage or deterioration and if necessary renew.

5 Refit the switch, complete with washer, and tighten it to the specified torque.

6 Securely reconnect the wiring connector then refit the air cleaner. Check and, if necessary, top-up the engine oil as described in *Weekly checks*.

18 Crankshaft oil seals – renewal

Right-hand oil seal

1 Remove the main timing belt as described in Section 7, and the crankshaft sprocket with reference to Section 8.

2 To remove the seal without removing the oil pump, drill two small holes diagonally opposite each other, insert self-tapping screws, and pull on the heads of the screws with pliers.

3 Alternatively, the oil seal can be removed with the oil pump (see Section 15).

4 Thoroughly clean the oil seal seating in the oil pump.

5 Wind a length of tape around the end of the crankshaft to protect the oil seal lips as the seal is fitted.

6 Fit a new oil seal to the oil pump, pressing or driving it into position using a socket or tube of suitable diameter. Ensure that the socket or tube bears only on the hard outer ring of the seal, and take care not to damage the seal lips. Press or drive the seal into position until it is seated on the shoulder in the oil pump. Make sure that the closed end of the seal is facing outwards.

7 Refit the crankshaft sprocket with reference to Section 8, and the main timing belt as described in Section 7.

Left-hand oil seal

8 The crankshaft left-hand oil seal is integral with the housing, and must be renewed as an assembly, complete with the crankshaft speed/position sensor wheel. The sensor wheel is attached to the oil seal/housing assembly, and is a press-fit on the crankshaft flange. Skoda special tool T10017 is required to fit this assembly and, in the workshop, we found that there is no means of accurately aligning the sensor wheel on the crankshaft without the tool (there is no locating key, and there are no alignment marks). If the sensor wheel is not precisely aligned on the crankshaft, the crankshaft speed/position sensor will send incorrect TDC signals to the engine management ECU, and the engine will not run correctly (the engine may not run at all). As the appropriate special tool is only available to Skoda dealers, there is no alternative but to have the new assembly fitted by a Skoda dealer.

19 Flywheel/driveplate – removal, inspection and refitting

Flywheel

Removal

1 Remove the manual transmission and clutch as described in Chapter 7A and Chapter 6.

2 Lock the flywheel in position using a home-

17.2 Disconnecting the oil pressure switch wiring connector

made locking tool, fabricated from a piece of scrap metal **(see illustration)**. Bolt it to one of the transmission bellhousing mounting holes. Mark the position of the flywheel with respect to the crankshaft using a dab of paint.

3 Slacken and withdraw the flywheel mounting bolts, then lift off the flywheel.

Caution: Get an assistant to help, as the flywheel is extremely heavy.

Inspection

4 If the flywheel's clutch mating surface is deeply scored, cracked or otherwise damaged, the flywheel must be renewed. However, it may be possible to have it surface-ground; seek the advice of a Skoda dealer or engine reconditioning specialist.

5 If the ring gear is badly worn or has missing teeth, the flywheel must be renewed.

Refitting

6 Clean the mating surfaces of the flywheel and crankshaft. Remove any remaining locking compound from the threads of the crankshaft holes, using the correct-size tap, if available.

> **HAYNES HINT** *If a suitable tap is not available, cut two slots down the threads of one of the old flywheel bolts with a hacksaw, and use the bolt to remove the locking compound from the threads.*

7 If the new flywheel retaining bolts are not supplied with their threads pre-coated, apply a suitable thread-locking compound to the threads of each bolt **(see illustration)**.

19.2 Flywheel locked in position with a home-made tool

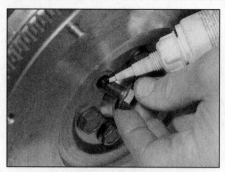

19.7 Apply locking fluid to the new flywheel bolts, if necessary

19.9 Tighten the flywheel bolts to the specified torque

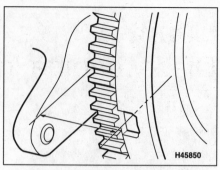

19.14 The distance (a) between the cylinder block and driveplate should be between 19.7 and 21.3 mm

8 Offer up the flywheel to the crankshaft, using the alignment marks made during removal, and fit the new retaining bolts.

9 Lock the flywheel using the method employed on dismantling, and tighten the retaining bolts to the specified torque and angle **(see illustration)**.

10 Refit the clutch as described in Chapter 6. Remove the locking tool, and refit the transmission as described in Chapter 7A.

Driveplate

Removal

11 Remove the automatic transmission as described in Chapter 7B.

12 Lock the driveplate in position by bolting

a piece of scrap metal between the driveplate and one of the transmission bellhousing mounting holes. Mark the position of the driveplate with respect to the crankshaft using a dab of paint.

13 Slacken and withdraw the driveplate mounting bolts, then lift off the driveplate. Recover the packing plate and the shim (where applicable).

Refitting

14 Refitting is a reversal of removal, using the alignment marks made during removal, but initially tighten the new mounting bolts to 30 Nm only and check the distance between the cylinder block and (inner) face of the driveplate **(see illustration)**. Make the check

at three points and calculate the average distance which should be between 19.7 and 21.3 mm. If the distance measured is outside the limits, fit a different shim and check again. With the distance correct, fully tighten the mounting bolts to their specified torque and angle.

15 Remove the locking tool, and refit the transmission as described in Chapter 7B.

20 Engine/transmission mountings – inspection and renewal

Refer to Section 12 of Part B of this Chapter

Chapter 2 Part D:
Diesel engine in-car repair procedures

Contents

Section number

Balancer shaft unit (engine code AMF) – removal and refitting 21
Camshaft and hydraulic tappets – removal, inspection and refitting 10
Camshaft cover – removal and refitting 4
Camshaft oil seals – renewal 12
Compression and leakdown tests – description and interpretation. . 2
Crankshaft oil seals – renewal 17
Crankshaft pulley – removal and refitting. 5
Cylinder head – removal, inspection and refitting 13
Engine assembly and valve timing marks – general information and
    usage 3
Engine oil cooler – removal and refitting 19
Engine/transmission mountings – inspection and renewal 18

Section number

Flywheel – removal, inspection and refitting 16
General information 1
Hydraulic tappets – testing. 11
Oil pressure warning light switch – removal and refitting. 20
Oil pump, drive chain and sprockets – removal, inspection and
    refitting 15
Pump injector rocker shaft assembly – removal and refitting 9
Sump – removal and refitting 14
Timing belt – removal, inspection and refitting. 7
Timing belt covers – removal and refitting 6
Timing belt tensioner and sprockets – removal and refitting 8

Degrees of difficulty

Easy, suitable for novice with little experience	**Fairly easy,** suitable for beginner with some experience	**Fairly difficult,** suitable for competent DIY mechanic	**Difficult,** suitable for experienced DIY mechanic	**Very difficult,** suitable for expert DIY or professional

Specifications

General

Type	Three- or four-cylinder in-line, belt-driven single overhead camshaft (SOHC), four stroke, liquid-cooled
Manufacturer's engine codes*:	
1422 cc, 3-cylinder, turbo.	AMF
1896 cc, 4-cylinder, non-turbo.	ASY
1896 cc, 4-cylinder, turbo.	ASZ and ATD
Maximum power output:	
Engine code AMF	55kW at 4000 rpm
Engine code ASY	47 kW at 4000 rpm
Engine code ATD	74 kW at 4000 rpm
Engine code ASZ	96 kW at 4000 rpm
Maximum torque output:	
Engine code AMF	195 Nm at 2200 rpm
Engine code ASY	125 Nm at 1600 to 2800 rpm
Engine code ATD	240 Nm at 1800 to 2400 rpm
Engine code ASZ	310 Nm at 1900 rpm
Bore.	79.5 mm
Stroke.	95.5 mm
Compression ratio:	
Engine codes AMF and ASY	19.5 : 1
Engine codes ASZ and ATD	19.0 : 1
Compression pressures:	
Minimum compression pressure	Approximately 19.0 bar
Maximum difference between cylinders.	Approximately 5.0 bar
Firing order:	
Engine code AMF	1 – 2 – 3
Engine codes ASY, ASZ and ATD	1 – 3 – 4 – 2
No 1 cylinder location.	Timing belt end

* **Note:** *See 'Vehicle identification' at the end of this manual for the location of engine code markings.*

Camshaft

Camshaft endfloat (maximum)	0.15 mm
Camshaft bearing running clearance (maximum).	0.11 mm
Camshaft run-out (maximum).	0.01 mm

Lubrication system

Oil pump type.	Gear type, chain-driven from crankshaft
Oil pressure (oil temperature 80°C, at 2000 rpm)	2.0 bar

Torque wrench settings

	Nm	lbf ft
Ancillary (alternator, etc) bracket mounting bolts.................	45	33
Auxiliary drivebelt tensioner securing bolt	25	18
Balancer shaft assembly to crankcase (engine code AMF)	20	15
Balancer shaft drive chain tensioner housing (engine code AMF):		
Stage 1..	8	6
Stage 2..	Angle-tighten a further 90°	
Balancer shaft weight/sprocket (engine code AMF):		
Stage 1..	100	74
Stage 2..	Angle-tighten a further 90°	
Big-end bearing caps bolts*:		
Stage 1..	30	22
Stage 2..	Angle-tighten a further 90°	
Camshaft bearing cap nuts:		
Engine code ASY	20	15
Camshaft bearing cap bolts*:		
Engine codes AMF, ASZ and ATD:		
Stage 1..	8	6
Stage 2..	Angle-tighten a further 90°	
Camshaft cover nuts/bolts..............................	10	7
Camshaft sprocket centre bolt:		
Engine code ASY	45	33
Camshaft sprocket hub centre bolt:		
Engine codes AMF, ASZ and ATD	100	74
Camshaft sprocket outer bolts:		
Engine codes AMF, ASZ and ATD:		
Stage 1..	20	15
Stage 2..	Angle-tighten a further 45°	
Coolant pump bolts	15	11
Crankshaft oil seal housing bolts (front and rear).................	15	11
Crankshaft pulley-to-sprocket bolts:		
Stage 1..	10	7
Stage 2..	Angle-tighten a further 90°	
Crankshaft speed/position sensor wheel-to-crankshaft bolts*:		
Stage 1..	10	7
Stage 2..	Angle-tighten a further 90°	
Crankshaft sprocket bolt*:		
Stage 1..	120	89
Stage 2..	Angle-tighten a further 90°	
Cylinder head bolts*:		
Engine codes AMF, ASZ and ATD:		
Stage 1..	40	30
Stage 2..	60	44
Stage 3..	Angle-tighten a further 90°	
Stage 4..	Angle-tighten a further 90°	
Engine code ASY:		
Stage 1..	35	26
Stage 2..	60	44
Stage 3..	Angle-tighten a further 90°	
Stage 4..	Angle-tighten a further 90°	
Engine mountings:		
Right-hand mounting:		
To engine:		
Stage 1.......................................	30	22
Stage 2.......................................	Angle-tighten a further 90°	
To body:		
Stage 1.......................................	20	15
Stage 2.......................................	Angle-tighten a further 90°	
Centre nut:		
Stage 1.......................................	40	30
Stage 2.......................................	Angle-tighten a further 90°	
Left-hand mounting:		
To transmission:		
Stage 1.......................................	40	30
Stage 2.......................................	Angle-tighten a further 90°	
To body:		
Stage 1.......................................	50	37
Stage 2.......................................	Angle-tighten a further 90°	

Torque wrench settings (continued)

	Nm	lbf ft
Engine mountings (continued):		
Rear torque arm:		
To subframe:		
Stage 1	40	30
Stage 2	Angle-tighten a further 90°	
To transmission:		
Stage 1	30	22
Stage 2	Angle-tighten a further 90°	
Exhaust manifold nuts	25	18
Exhaust pipe-to-manifold/turbocharger nuts	25	18
Flywheel:		
Stage 1	60	44
Stage 2	Angle-tighten a further 90°	
Fuel injector pipe union nuts	25	18
Glow plugs	15	11
Guide pulley sprocket bolt (engine code AMF)	20	15
Injection pump sprocket bolts:		
Type 1*:		
Stage 1	20	15
Stage 2	Angle-tighten a further 90°	
Type 2	25	18
Injector rocker shafts*:		
Engine codes AMF, ASZ and ATD:		
Stage 1	20	15
Stage 2	Angle-tighten a further 90°	
Main bearing cap bolts*:		
Stage 1	65	48
Stage 2	Angle-tighten a further 90°	
Oil cooler retaining cap	25	18
Oil drain plug	30	22
Oil filter housing-to-cylinder block bolts*:		
Stage 1	15	11
Stage 2	Angle-tighten a further 90°	
Oil filter cap	25	18
Oil level/temperature sensor-to-sump bolts	10	7
Oil pick-up pipe securing bolts	15	11
Oil pressure relief valve plug	40	30
Oil pressure warning light switch	20	15
Oil pump chain tensioner bolt	15	11
Oil pump securing bolts	15	11
Oil pump sprocket securing bolt/nut:		
Engine code AMF:		
Stage 1	20	15
Stage 2	Angle-tighten a further 90°	
Engine codes ASY, ASZ and ATD	25	18
Piston oil spray jet bolt	25	18
Pump injector rocker shaft:		
Stage 1	20	15
Stage 2	Angle-tighten a further 45°	
Sump:		
Sump-to-cylinder block bolts	15	11
Sump-to-transmission bolts	45	33
Timing belt large idler pulley (engine code ASY):		
Stage 1	40	30
Stage 2	Angle-tighten a further 90°	
Timing belt outer cover bolts	10	7
Timing belt rear cover bolts:		
Cover-to-cylinder head bolt	10	7
Cover-to-injection pump bolts (engine code ASY)	30	22
Timing belt small idler pulley nut/bolt	20	15
Timing belt tensioner roller securing nut:		
Engine code ASY	25	18
Engine codes AMF, ASZ and ATD:		
Stage 1	20	15
Stage 2	Angle-tighten a further 45°	
Timing belt upper idler roller bolt	20	15
Turbocharger oil return pipe-to-cylinder block banjo bolt	40	30
Turbocharger oil supply pipe-to-oil filter housing:		
Banjo bolt	25	18
Union nut	22	16

* **Note:** *Use new bolts*

1 General information

Using this Chapter

This Part of Chapter 2 describes those repair procedures that can reasonably be carried out on the engine while it remains in the vehicle. If the engine has been removed from the vehicle and is being dismantled as described in Part E, any preliminary dismantling procedures can be ignored.

Note that while it may be possible physically to overhaul items such as the piston/connecting rod assemblies while the engine is in the vehicle, such tasks are not usually carried out as separate operations, and usually require the execution of several additional procedures (not to mention the cleaning of components and of oilways); for this reason, all such tasks are classed as major overhaul procedures, and are described in Part E of this Chapter.

Part E describes the removal of the engine/transmission from the vehicle and the full overhaul procedures that can then be carried out.

Engine description

The engines are water-cooled, single overhead camshaft, in-line three- or four-cylinder units, with cast-iron cylinder blocks and aluminium-alloy cylinder heads. All are mounted transversely at the front of the vehicle, with the transmission bolted to the left-hand end of the engine.

On the 3-cylinder engine, the crankshaft is of four-bearing type, and thrustwashers are fitted to the main bearing No 3 to control crankshaft endfloat. On 4-cylinder engines, the crankshaft is of five-bearing type, and thrustwashers are fitted to the centre main bearing.

The camshaft is driven by a toothed timing belt from the crankshaft. On engine code ASY the timing belt also drives the fuel injection pump. The camshaft is mounted at the top of the cylinder head, and is secured by bearing caps.

The valves are closed by coil springs, and run in guides pressed into the cylinder head. The camshaft actuates the valves directly, via hydraulic tappets. On the 3-cylinder engine code AMF there are six valves, one inlet and one exhaust valve per cylinder. On the 4-cylinder engine codes ASY, ASZ and ATD there are eight valves, one inlet and one exhaust valve per cylinder.

A chain-driven balancer shaft assembly is bolted to the bottom of the crankcase on the 3-cylinder engine code AMF. The balancer shaft counteracts vibrations within the engine to provide smooth running throughout the engine speed range.

On the 3-cylinder engine, an oil pump is located on the bottom of the balancer shaft assembly and is driven by chain from a sprocket on the crankshaft. The balancer shaft assembly and the oil pump are enclosed in a plastic cover which incorporates an oil strainer. On all 4-cylinder engines, the oil pump is chain-driven from the front of the crankshaft.

From the sump, the oil is forced through an externally-mounted, renewable filter. From there, it is distributed to the cylinder head, where it lubricates the camshaft journals and hydraulic tappets, and also to the crankcase, where it lubricates the main bearings, connecting rod big-ends, gudgeon pins and cylinder bores. A coolant-fed oil cooler is fitted to the oil filter housing on all engines. Oil jets are fitted to the base of each cylinder – these spray oil onto the underside of the pistons, to improve cooling.

All engines are fitted with a brake servo vacuum pump driven by the camshaft on the transmission end of the cylinder head. On engine codes AMF, ASZ and ATD the pump is of tandem design, incorporating a vacuum pump and a fuel pump, driven by the camshaft.

On all engines, engine coolant is circulated by a pump, driven by the timing belt. For details of the cooling system, refer to Chapter 3.

Operations with engine in car

The following operations can be performed without removing the engine:

a) Compression pressure – testing.
b) Camshaft cover – removal and refitting.
c) Crankshaft pulley – removal and refitting.

d) Timing belt covers – removal and refitting.
e) Timing belt – removal, refitting and adjustment.
f) Timing belt tensioner and sprockets – removal and refitting.
g) Camshaft oil seals – renewal.
h) Camshaft and hydraulic tappets – removal, inspection and refitting.
i) Cylinder head – removal and refitting.
j) Cylinder head and pistons – decarbonising.
k) Sump – removal and refitting.
l) Oil pump (except engine code AMF) – removal, overhaul and refitting.
m) Crankshaft oil seals – renewal.
n) Engine/transmission mountings – inspection and renewal.
o) Flywheel – removal, inspection and refitting.

Note: *It is possible to remove the pistons and connecting rods (after removing the cylinder head and sump) without removing the engine. However, this is not recommended. Work of this nature is more easily and thoroughly completed with the engine on the bench, as described in Chapter 2E.*

2 Compression and leakdown tests – description and interpretation

Compression test

Note: *A compression tester suitable for use with diesel engines will be required for this test.*

1 When engine performance is down, or if misfiring occurs which cannot be attributed to the ignition or fuel systems, a compression test can provide diagnostic clues as to the engine's condition. If the test is performed regularly, it can give warning of trouble before any other symptoms become apparent.

2 The engine must be fully warmed-up to normal operating temperature, the battery must be fully-charged and you will require the aid of an assistant.

3 On non-turbo models, remove the inlet manifold upper section as described in Chapter 4B.

4 On engine code ASY, the stop solenoid and fuel metering control wiring must be disconnected, to prevent the engine from running or fuel from being discharged **(see illustrations)**. **Note:** *As a result of the wiring being disconnected, faults will be stored in the ECU memory. These must be erased after the compression test.*

5 On engine codes AMF, ASZ and ATD, disconnect the injector solenoids by disconnecting the connector at the end of the cylinder head **(see illustration)**. **Note:** *As a result of the wiring being disconnected, faults will be stored in the ECU memory. These must be erased after the compression test.*

6 Remove the glow plugs as described in Chapter 5C, then fit a compression tester to

2.4a Fuel cut-off solenoid wiring connector is secured by a nut (arrowed)

2.4b Wiring plug for fuel quantity adjuster is behind oil filter housing

2.5 Disconnect the injector solenoids wiring plug connector (arrowed)

the No 1 cylinder glow plug hole. The type of tester which screws into the plug thread is preferred.

7 Have your assistant, crank the engine for several seconds on the starter motor. After one or two revolutions, the compression pressure should build-up to a maximum figure and then stabilise. Record the highest reading obtained.

8 Repeat the test on the remaining cylinders, recording the pressure in each.

9 The cause of poor compression is less easy to establish on a diesel engine than on a petrol engine. The effect of introducing oil into the cylinders (wet testing) is not conclusive, because there is a risk that the oil will sit in the recess on the piston crown, instead of passing to the rings. However, the following can be used as a rough guide to diagnosis.

10 All cylinders should produce very similar pressures. Any difference greater than that specified indicates the existence of a fault. Note that the compression should build-up quickly in a healthy engine. Low compression on the first stroke, followed by gradually increasing pressure on successive strokes, indicates worn piston rings. A low compression reading on the first stroke, which does not build-up during successive strokes, indicates leaking valves or a blown head gasket (a cracked head could also be the cause).

11 A low reading from two adjacent cylinders is almost certainly due to the head gasket having blown between them and the presence of coolant in the engine oil will confirm this.

12 On completion, remove the compression tester, and refit the glow plugs, with reference to Chapter 5C.

13 Reconnect the wiring, and (where applicable) refit the inlet manifold upper section as described in Chapter 4B.

Leakdown test

14 A leakdown test measures the rate at which compressed air fed into the cylinder is lost. It is an alternative to a compression test, and in many ways it is better, since the escaping air provides easy identification of where pressure loss is occurring (piston rings, valves or head gasket).

15 The equipment required for leakdown testing is unlikely to be available to the home

mechanic. If poor compression is suspected, have the test performed by a suitably-equipped garage.

3 Engine assembly and valve timing marks – general information and usage

General information

1 TDC is the highest point in the cylinder that each piston reaches as it travels up-and-down when the crankshaft turns. Each piston reaches TDC at the end of the compression stroke and again at the end of the exhaust stroke, but TDC generally refers to piston position on the compression stroke. No 1 piston is at the timing belt end of the engine.

2 Positioning No 1 piston at TDC is an essential part of many procedures, such as timing belt removal and camshaft removal.

3 The design of the engines covered in this Chapter is such that piston-to-valve contact may occur if the camshaft or crankshaft is turned with the timing belt removed. For this reason, it is important to ensure that the camshaft and crankshaft do not move in relation to each other once the timing belt has been removed from the engine.

Setting TDC on No 1 cylinder

Engine code AMF

4 Remove the upper outer timing belt cover as described in Section 6 **(see illustrations)**.

5 Remove the glow plugs, as described in

3.4a Release the clips . . .

3.6 TDC locking pin inserted through the camshaft sprocket into the cylinder head

Chapter 5C, to allow the engine to turn more easily.

6 Turn the engine until the TDC hole in the sprocket is approximately at the 8 o'clock position and aligned with the TDC timing hole in the cylinder head; at this point a special Skoda locking pin may be inserted **(see illustration)**. An improvised tool may be fabricated out of 6.0 mm diameter metal rod, but due to the exact measurements and machining involved, it is strongly recommended that the tool is either borrowed or hired from a Skoda dealer, or purchased from a reputable tool manufacturer.

7 The engine is now set to TDC on No 1 cylinder.

Engine code ASY

Note: *Suitable tools will be required to lock the camshaft and the fuel injection pump sprocket in position during this procedure – see text.*

8 Remove the camshaft cover as described in Section 4.

9 Remove the upper outer timing belt cover as described in Section 6.

10 Remove the glow plugs, as described in Chapter 5C, to allow the engine to turn more easily.

11 Where fitted, remove the hexagon-keyed inspection plug from the transmission bellhousing, if necessary using a large nut to unscrew it **(see illustrations)**. Access to the inspection plug is greatly improved if the air cleaner is removed first, as described in Chapter 4B.

12 Rotate the crankshaft clockwise, using a socket or spanner on the crankshaft sprocket

3.4b . . . and remove the upper outer timing belt cover

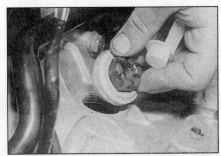

3.11a Using a large nut to unscrew the inspection plug from the transmission bellhousing

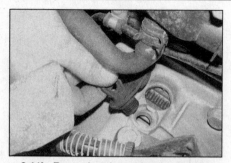

3.11b Removing the rubber bung from the bellhousing – seen with air cleaner removed

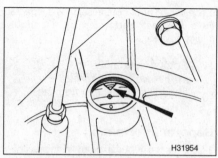

3.11c Timing mark on the edge of the flywheel (arrowed) lined up with the pointer on the bellhousing (manual transmission)

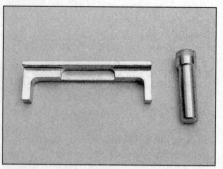

3.13 Camshaft and fuel injection sprocket locking tools

bolt, until the timing mark machined onto the edge of the flywheel/driveplate lines up with the pointer on the transmission casing **and** the timing hole in the fuel injection sprocket lines up with the hole in the support bracket.

13 To lock the engine in the TDC position, the camshaft (not the sprocket) and fuel injection pump sprocket must be locked in position, using special locking tools. Improvised tools may be fabricated but, due to the exact measurements and machining involved, it is strongly recommended that a kit of locking tools is either borrowed or hired from a Skoda dealer, or purchased from a reputable tool manufacturer **(see illustration)**.

14 Engage the edge of the locking bar (Skoda tool 3418) with the slot in the end of the camshaft **(see illustrations)**.

15 With the locking bar still inserted, turn the camshaft slightly (by turning the crankshaft clockwise, as before), so that the locking bar

rocks to one side, allowing one end of the bar to contact the cylinder head surface. At the other side of the locking bar, measure the gap between the end of the bar and the cylinder head using a feeler blade.

16 Turn the camshaft back slightly, then pull out the feeler blade. The idea now is to level the locking bar by inserting two feeler blades, each with a thickness equal to *half* the originally measured gap, on either side of the camshaft between each end of the locking bar and the cylinder head. This centres the camshaft, and sets the valve timing in its reference condition **(see illustration)**.

17 Insert the locking pin (Skoda tool 3359) through the fuel injection pump sprocket timing hole, so that it passes through the timing hole in the injection pump hub, and into the support bracket behind the hub. This locks the fuel injection pump in the TDC reference position **(see illustration)**.

18 The engine is now set to TDC on No 1 cylinder.

Engine codes ASZ and ATD

Note: *Skoda tool (T10050) is required to lock the crankshaft sprocket in the TDC position.*

19 Remove the auxiliary drivebelt(s) as described in Chapter 1B. Also, remove the auxiliary drivebelt tensioning unit.

20 Remove the crankshaft pulley/vibration damper as described in Section 5.

21 Remove the timing belt covers as described in Section 6.

22 Remove the glow plugs, as described in Chapter 5C, to allow the engine to turn more easily.

23 Using a spanner or socket on the crankshaft sprocket bolt, turn the crankshaft in the normal direction of rotation (clockwise) until the alignment mark on the face of the sprocket is almost vertical **(see illustrations)**.

24 The arrow (marked 4Z) on the rear section

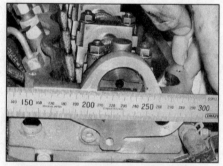

3.14a Using a straight-edge to assess alignment of the camshaft slot with the head

3.14b Engage the locking bar with the slot in the camshaft

3.16 Camshaft centred and locked using the locking bar and feeler blades

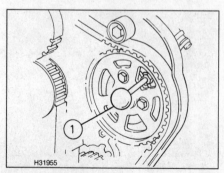

3.17 Injection pump sprocket locked using the locking pin (1)

3.23a Position the crankshaft so that the mark on the sprocket is almost vertical (arrowed) . . .

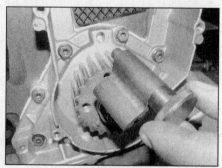

3.23b . . . then insert the Skoda tool T10050 . . .

of the upper timing belt upper cover aligns between the two lugs on the rear of the camshaft hub sender wheel **(see illustration)**.
25 While in this position it should be possible to insert Skoda tool T10050 to lock the crankshaft, and a 6 mm diameter rod to lock the camshaft sprocket **(see illustration)**.
Note: *The mark on the crankshaft sprocket and the mark on the Skoda tool T10050 must align, whilst at the same time the shaft of tool T10050 must engage in the drilling in the crankshaft oil seal housing.*
26 The engine is now set to TDC on No 1 cylinder.

4 Camshaft cover – removal and refitting

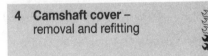

Removal

Engine code AMF

1 Remove the engine top cover by prising it from the location pillars and disconnecting the vacuum pipes. Also, remove the foam base **(see illustrations)**.
2 Remove the inlet air ducting from the rear of the cylinder head.
3 Release the clip and disconnect the crankcase ventilation hose from the camshaft cover.
4 Unclip the fuel lines from the front of the camshaft cover.
5 Remove the upper timing belt cover as described in Section 6.

3.23c . . . and align the marks (arrowed) on the tool and sprocket

6 Progressively unscrew and remove the camshaft cover retaining bolts and lift the cover away. If it sticks, do not attempt to lever it off – instead free it by working around the cover and tapping it lightly with a soft-faced mallet.
7 Recover the camshaft cover gasket. Inspect the gasket carefully, and renew it if damage or deterioration is evident.
8 Clean the mating surfaces of the cylinder head and camshaft cover thoroughly, removing all traces of oil and old gasket – take care to avoid damaging the surfaces as you do this.

Engine code ASY

9 Remove the engine top cover. Removal details vary according to model – on later models, the cover is a press-fit, however, on earlier models the cover retaining nuts are concealed under circular covers, which are prised out of the main cover. Where plastic screws or turn-fasteners are used, these can

3.24 Align the arrow on the rear of the timing belt cover (arrowed) between the lugs on the rear of the camshaft hub sender wheel

3.25 Insert a 6 mm drill bit (arrowed) through the camshaft hub into the cylinder head to lock the camshaft

be removed using a wide-bladed screwdriver. Remove the nuts or screws, and lift the cover from the engine, releasing any wiring or hoses attached **(see illustrations)**.

4.1a Lift the top cover from the location pillars . . .

4.1b . . . and remove the foam base

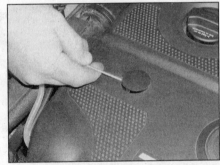

4.9a Prise out the covers . . .

4.9b . . . remove the nuts beneath . . .

4.9c . . . on this engine, the dipstick has to be removed . . .

4.9d . . . before the cover can be lifted off

4.10 Disconnecting the pressure-regulating valve breather hose

4.11a Unscrew the retaining bolts . . .

4.11b . . . and lift off the camshaft cover

4.13a Engine top cover rear mounting – engine code ATD

4.13b One of the cover locating pegs (arrowed) and also breather pipe (arrowed)

4.15 The camshaft cover gasket locates in a groove in the cover

10 Disconnect the breather hose from the air inlet duct **(see illustration)**. If wished, the breather valve can be removed from the top of the camshaft cover by carefully pulling upwards, but its removal is not essential.

11 Unscrew the securing nuts/bolts, and lift the camshaft cover from the cylinder head **(see illustrations)**. On most models, the bolts at the rear are very awkward to reach – a selection of Allen keys/bits and a knuckle joint may well be needed. Note that the gasket is vulcanised to the cover; if it is damaged, the complete cover will require renewal.

12 If necessary, unclip and remove the oil baffle.

Engine codes ASZ and ATD

13 Remove the oil filler cap then prise off and withdraw the engine top cover from the rear support. Where applicable, disconnect the

breather hose from the camshaft cover **(see illustrations)**.

14 Unscrew the camshaft cover retaining bolts and lift the cover away. If it sticks, do not attempt to lever it off – instead free it by working around the cover and tapping it lightly with a soft-faced mallet.

15 Recover the camshaft cover gasket **(see illustration)**. Inspect the gasket carefully, and renew it if damage or deterioration is evident.

16 Clean the mating surfaces of the cylinder head and camshaft cover thoroughly, removing all traces of oil and old gasket – take care to avoid damaging the surfaces as you do this.

Refitting

17 Refit the camshaft cover by following the removal procedure in reverse, noting the following points:

a) *On engine code ASY, before refitting the camshaft cover, apply a small amount of*

sealant at the front and rear of the cylinder head, to the two points where the camshaft bearing caps contact the cylinder head **(see illustration)**. Ensure that the gasket is correctly seated on the cylinder head, and take care to avoid displacing it as the camshaft cover is lowered into position.

b) *On engine codes ASZ and ATD, apply suitable sealant to the points where the camshaft bearing cap contacts the cylinder head **(see illustration)**.*

c) *Tighten the camshaft cover retaining nuts/bolts progressively to the specified torque.* **Note:** *On engine codes ASZ and ATD, tighten the retaining bolts in sequence **(see illustration)**.*

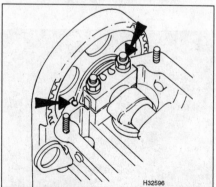

4.17a Apply sealant to the rear and front (arrowed) bearing cap joints

4.17b Apply sealant to the points (arrowed) on the cylinder head

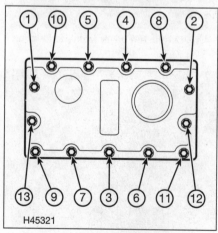

4.17c Camshaft cover tightening sequence

5 Crankshaft pulley – removal and refitting

Removal

1 Disconnect the battery negative lead (refer to *Disconnecting the battery* in the *Reference* Chapter at the end of this manual).

2 For improved access, raise the front right-hand side of the vehicle, and support securely on axle stands (see *Jacking and vehicle support*). Remove the roadwheel.

3 Remove the securing screws and withdraw the engine undershield(s) and/or wheel arch liner panels. On turbo models, unscrew the nut at the rear, and the washer-type fasteners further forward, then release the air hose clip and manipulate out the plastic air duct for the intercooler **(see illustration)**.

4 Remove the auxiliary drivebelt, as described in Chapter 1B.

5 Where applicable, prise the cover from the centre of the pulley to expose the securing bolts **(see illustration)**.

6 Slacken the bolts securing the crankshaft pulley to the sprocket **(see illustration)**. If necessary, the pulley can be prevented from turning by counterholding with a spanner or socket on the crankshaft sprocket bolt.

7 Unscrew the bolts securing the pulley to the sprocket, and remove the pulley **(see illustration)**.

Refitting

8 Refit the pulley over the locating peg on the crankshaft sprocket, then refit the pulley securing bolts.

9 Prevent the crankshaft from turning as during removal, then fit the pulley securing bolts, and tighten to the specified torque.

10 Refit and tension the auxiliary drivebelt as described in Chapter 1B.

11 Refit the engine undershield(s), wheel arch liners and the intercooler air duct, as applicable.

12 Refit the roadwheel, lower the vehicle to the ground, and reconnect the battery negative lead.

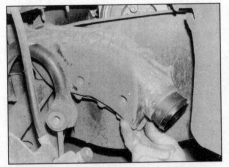

5.3 Removing the intercooler air duct for access to the crankshaft pulley

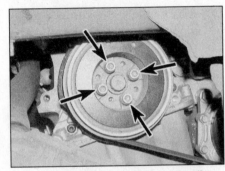

5.6 Showing the four crankshaft pulley bolts (arrowed)

6 Timing belt covers – removal and refitting

Upper outer cover

1 Where applicable, release the retaining clips and remove the air intake hose from across the top of the timing belt cover **(see illustration)**.

2 Release the uppermost part of the timing belt outer cover by prising open the metal spring clips, then withdraw the cover away from the engine **(see illustrations)**.

3 Refitting is a reversal of removal, noting that the lower edge of the upper cover engages with the centre cover.

Centre outer cover

4 Remove the auxiliary drivebelt as described in Chapter 1B.

5.5 Prising out the crankshaft pulley centre cap

5.7 Removing the crankshaft pulley

5 Remove the crankshaft pulley as described in Section 5. It is assumed that, if the centre cover is being removed, the lower cover will be also – if not, simply remove the components described in Section 5 for access to the crankshaft pulley, and leave the pulley in position.

6 With the upper cover removed (paragraphs 1 to 3), unscrew and remove the retaining bolts from the centre cover. Withdraw the centre cover from the engine (noting how it fits over the lower cover, where applicable) **(see illustration)**.

7 Refitting is a reversal of removal.

Lower outer cover

8 Remove the upper and centre covers as described previously.

9 If not already done, remove the crankshaft pulley as described in Section 5.

10 Unscrew the remaining bolt(s) securing the lower cover, and lift it out.

6.1 Removing the air intake hose from across the top of the timing belt cover

6.2a Release the retaining clips (one arrowed) . . .

6.2b . . . and withdraw the upper cover

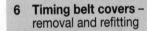

6.6 Removing the centre outer cover – engine code AMF

11 Refitting is a reversal of removal; locate the centre cover in place before fitting the top two bolts.

Rear cover

12 Remove the upper, centre and lower covers as described previously.
13 Remove the timing belt, tensioner and sprockets as described in Sections 7 and 8.
14 Slacken and withdraw the retaining bolts and lift the timing belt inner cover from the studs on the end of the engine, and remove it from the engine compartment.
15 Refitting is a reversal of removal.

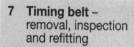

Removal

1 The primary function of the toothed timing belt is to drive the camshaft, but it also drives the coolant pump. On engine code ASY it drives the fuel injection pump, too. Should the belt slip or break in service, the valve timing will be disturbed and piston-to-valve contact may occur, resulting in serious engine damage. For this reason, it is important that the timing belt is tensioned correctly, and inspected regularly for signs of wear or deterioration.
2 Disconnect the battery negative lead (refer to *Disconnecting the battery* in the *Reference* Chapter at the end of this manual).
3 On turbo models, remove the right-hand headlight as described in Chapter 12, Section 7, and the inlet manifold-to-intercooler air trunking as described in Chapter 4C.
4 Apply the handbrake, then jack up the front of the vehicle and support securely on axle stands (see *Jacking and vehicle support*). Remove the right-hand front roadwheel.
5 Remove the securing screws and withdraw the engine undershield(s), and the right-hand wheel arch liner.
6 Using a hoist, support the weight of the engine/transmission, then remove the right-hand engine mounting and bracket, and the engine rear mounting/link as described in Chapter 2A **(see illustrations)**.
7 Remove the auxiliary drivebelt as described in Chapter 1B. On engine code AMF, also unbolt the auxiliary drivebelt tensioner **(see illustrations)**.
8 Disconnect the fuel supply and return hoses from the fuel filter **(see illustration)**, referring to Chapter 1B if necessary. Label the hoses if necessary, to ensure correct refitting.
9 If required, to further improve working room, remove the windscreen washer bottle

7.6a Use a trolley jack to support the weight of the engine/transmission

7.6b Removing the right-hand engine mounting

7.7a Unscrew the bolts . . .

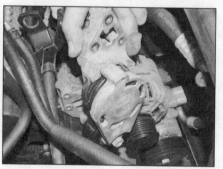

7.7b . . . and remove the auxiliary drivebelt tensioner – engine code AMF

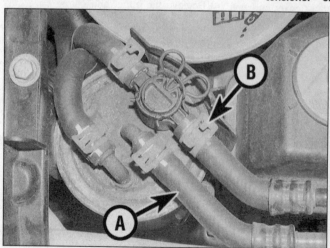

7.8 Fuel supply (A) and return (B) hoses at the fuel filter

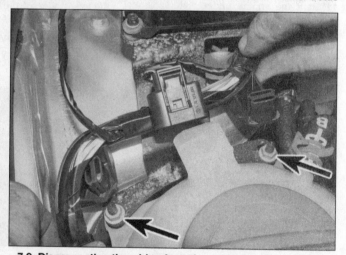

7.9 Disconnecting the wiring from the coolant expansion tank. Note the tank mounting nuts

7.10 Lower inner cover on engine code AMF

7.11a Removing the charge air pipe from the bottom right of the engine

7.11b Removing the inlet pipe from the engine compartment

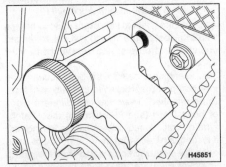

7.12a Skoda tool T10050 for locking the crankshaft sprocket in its TDC position – engine code AMF

7.12b Using the special locking tool to retain the crankshaft sprocket in its TDC position

7.13 Mark the running direction of the timing belt if it is to be re-used

(Chapter 12) and the coolant expansion reservoir (see illustration), and place them to one side without disconnecting their hoses.

10 Remove the timing belt outer covers, as described in Section 6. This procedure includes removing the crankshaft pulley as described in Section 5. Where applicable, unbolt the lower inner cover (see illustration).

Engine code AMF

11 Remove the charge air pipe and hose located at the bottom right of the engine, also the inlet pipe from the right-hand side of the engine compartment (see illustrations).

12 Turn the crankshaft to position No 1 piston at TDC on its firing stroke (see Section 3) and lock the camshaft sprocket by inserting a tight-fitting bolt through the TDC hole into the cylinder head. Skoda technicians also use a tool (T10050) to lock the crankshaft sprocket in its TDC position (see illustrations).

13 If the original timing belt is to be refitted, mark the running direction of the belt, to ensure correct refitting (see illustration).

Caution: If the belt appears to be in good condition and can be re-used, it is essential that it is refitted the same way around, otherwise accelerated wear will result, leading to premature failure.

14 Slacken the timing belt tensioner nut, and allow the tensioner to relieve the tension on the timing belt (see illustration).

15 Unscrew the nut and remove the timing belt guide pulley (see illustration).

16 Slide the belt from the sprockets, taking care not to twist or kink the belt excessively if it is to be re-used (see illustration).

Engine code ASY

17 Remove the camshaft cover as described in Section 4.

18 Remove the brake servo vacuum pump as described in Chapter 9.

19 Turn the crankshaft to position No 1 piston at TDC on the firing stroke (see Section 3), and lock the camshaft and the fuel injection pump sprocket in position, as described in Section 3.

20 If the original timing belt is to be refitted, mark the running direction of the belt, to ensure correct refitting.

Caution: If the belt appears to be in good condition and can be re-used, it is essential that it is refitted the same way around, otherwise accelerated wear will result, leading to premature failure.

21 Slacken the timing belt tensioner nut, and allow the tensioner to rotate anti-clockwise, relieving the tension on the timing belt.

22 Slide the belt from the sprockets, taking care not to twist or kink the belt excessively if it is to be re-used.

7.14 Loosening the timing belt tensioner nut

7.15 Timing belt guide pulley

7.16 Removing the timing belt from the sprockets

7.24a Turn the tensioner arm anti-clockwise until it contacts the stop (A) . . .

7.24b . . . then insert the locking tool through the slot to lock the tensioner . . .

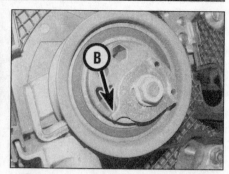

7.24c . . . and turn the tensioner arm clockwise until it contacts the stop (B) – engine codes ASZ and ATD manufactured up to the end of April 2001

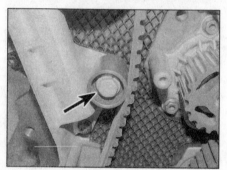

7.25 Undo the retaining bolt (arrowed) and remove the idler roller – engine codes ASZ and ATD

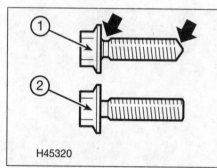

7.30 Different types of injection pump sprocket retaining bolts on engine code ASY – Type 1 bolt is a stretch bolt and must always be renewed

Engine codes ASZ and ATD

Note: There are two types of tensioner fitted; on engines manufactured up to the end of April 2001, Skoda technicians use special tool T10008 to lock the timing belt tensioner in its released position. It is possible to manufacture a home-made alternative – see below.

23 Set the engine to TDC on No 1 cylinder as described in Section 3.

24 Relieve the tension on the timing belt by first slackening the tensioner mounting nut slightly. On engines manufactured up to the end of April 2001, turn the tensioner anti-clockwise with an Allen key inserted in the hub, then lock the plunger by inserting a locking plate (Skoda tool No T10008). If this special tool is not available, an alternative can be manufactured by copying the design **(see illustrations)**. Now unscrew the mounting

7.31 Hold the camshaft sprocket stationary while loosening the three bolts

bolts and remove the plunger assembly. On later models, turn the tensioner fully anti-clockwise by hand.

25 Undo the bolt and remove the idler roller **(see illustration)**.

26 Examine the timing belt for manufacturer's markings that indicate the direction of rotation. If none are present, make your own using typist's correction fluid or a dab of paint – do not cut or score the belt in any way.

Caution: If the belt appears to be in good condition and can be re-used, it is essential that it is refitted the same way around, otherwise accelerated wear will result, leading to premature failure.

27 Slide the belt off the sprockets, taking care to avoid twisting or kinking it excessively if it is to be re-used.

Inspection

28 Examine the belt for evidence of contamination by coolant or lubricant. If this is the case, find the source of the contamination before progressing any further. Check the belt for signs of wear or damage, particularly around the leading edges of the belt teeth. Renew the belt if its condition is in doubt; the cost of belt renewal is negligible compared with potential cost of the engine repairs, should the belt fail in service. The belt must be renewed if it has covered the mileage given in Chapter 1B, however, if it has covered less, it is prudent to renew it regardless of condition, as a precautionary measure.

29 If the timing belt is not going to be refitted

for some time, it is a wise precaution to hang a warning label on the steering wheel, to remind yourself (and others) not to attempt to start the engine.

30 On engine code ASY, the bolts securing the injection pump sprocket to the hub may have to be renewed. There are two different types of bolts fitted **(see illustration)** the stretch-type of bolt (1), requires angle-tightening and it is for this reason that they cannot be re-used once loosened. Skoda state that the pump sprocket **must** be reset each time the timing belt is removed – it is not acceptable to simply refit the belt to the sprocket without carrying out the resetting procedure. Where applicable, obtain three new bolts before commencing the refitting procedure.

Refitting

Engine code AMF

31 If still fitted, remove the TDC pin from the camshaft sprocket, then hold the sprocket stationary with a suitable tool and loosen the three bolts securing it to the camshaft, so that it is free to turn within the three elongated slots **(see illustration)**. Turn the sprocket anti-clockwise so that the bolts are near the ends of the slots, then refit the TDC pin.

32 Fit the timing belt around the crankshaft sprocket, tensioner pulley, camshaft sprocket and coolant pump. Make sure that the tensioner pulley arm is correctly located in the rear timing cover hole. Check that the camshaft sprocket retaining bolts are positioned mid-way in their slots. If not, remove the timing belt and turn the sprocket slightly clockwise so that the belt can be located on the next tooth.

33 Refit the guide pulley and tighten the nut.

34 Using an Allen key in the hole provided, turn the tensioner anti-clockwise until the pointer is positioned in the middle of the cut-out of the baseplate. Hold the tensioner in this position, then tighten the retaining nut to the specified torque and angle **(see illustrations)**.

35 Tighten the bolts of the camshaft sprocket to their specified torque and angle while holding the sprocket stationary with a suitable tool inserted in two of the holes. The TDC

7.34a Turn the tensioner anti-clockwise until the pointer is positioned in the middle of the cut-out of the baseplate, then tighten the nut

7.34b The pointer must be in the middle of the cut-out

pin can remain in position, but the holding tool must take most of the torque pressure. Remove the tool after fully tightening the bolts.

36 With the TDC pins removed, turn the engine two complete turns clockwise, then re-insert the TDC pins to confirm the valve timing. **Do not** turn the engine anti-clockwise at any time to insert the pins.

37 The remaining procedure is a reversal of removal.

Engine code ASY

38 Ensure that the crankshaft and camshaft are still set to TDC on No 1 cylinder, as described in Section 3.

39 Refer to Section 8, and slacken the camshaft sprocket bolt by half-a-turn. Do not use the timing locking bar to hold the camshaft stationary; it must be removed before loosening the sprocket bolt. Release the sprocket from the camshaft taper mounting by carefully tapping it with a soft metal drift inserted through the hole provided in the timing belt rear cover **(see illustration)**.

Refit the timing locking bar (see Section 3) once the sprocket has been released.

40 Unscrew the three bolts securing the fuel injection pump sprocket to the hub on the injection pump **(see illustration)**, and screw the three bolts into position – **do not** tighten the bolts at this stage. Position the injection pump sprocket so that the securing bolts are central in the elongated holes.

⚠️ **Warning: Do not loosen the injection pump sprocket central nut, otherwise the basic setting of the injection pump will be lost, and it will require resetting by a Skoda dealer.**

41 Fit the timing belt around the crankshaft sprocket, idler pulley, coolant pump sprocket, injection pump sprocket, camshaft sprocket, and tensioner. Where applicable, ensure that the running direction markings made on the belt during removal are observed. Make

sure that the belt teeth seat correctly on the sprockets. The upper belt run must be located beneath the small upper idler pulley (it may be necessary to adjust the position of the camshaft sprocket slightly to achieve this), and the belt run between the tensioner and crankshaft sprocket should be located to the right of the lower small idler pulley (when viewed from the timing belt end of the engine) **(see illustration)**.

42 Check that the fuel injection pump sprocket is still positioned centrally in the elongated holes.

43 Ensure that any slack in the belt is in the section which passes over the tensioner.

44 Check that the tensioner is seated correctly, with the lug on the backplate positioned in the slot in the rear timing belt cover.

45 Engage a suitable tool, such as a pair of angled circlip pliers, with the two holes in the belt tensioner hub, then turn the tensioner clockwise until the notch on the hub is aligned with the raised tab on the backplate **(see illustration)**. **Note:** *If the tensioner is turned too far clockwise, it must be completely slackened off before retensioning.* With the tensioner marks aligned, tighten the tensioner nut to the specified torque.

7.39 Releasing the camshaft sprocket from the taper using a soft metal drift – engine code ASY

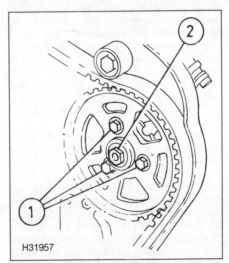

7.40 Unscrew the three bolts (1) securing the fuel injection pump to the injection pump hub

DO NOT unscrew the central nut (2)

7.41 The timing belt must locate under the upper idler pulley – engine code ASY

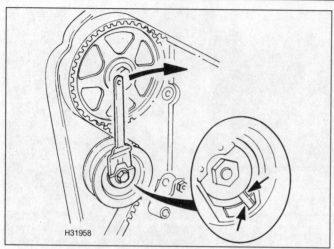

7.45 Turn the tensioner clockwise until the notch on the hub is aligned with the raised tab on the backplate – engine code ASY

7.61 Position the camshaft sprocket so that the securing bolts are in the centre part of the elongated holes – engine codes ASZ and ATD

46 Check that the crankshaft is still set to TDC on No 1 cylinder, as described in Section 3.
47 Refer to Section 8, and tighten the camshaft sprocket bolt to the specified torque. Do not use the timing locking bar to hold the camshaft stationary; it must be removed before tightening the sprocket bolt. Refit the timing locking bar (see Section 3) once the sprocket bolt has been tightened.
48 Tighten the fuel injection pump sprocket bolts to the specified torque. On models with stretch type bolts, tighten the bolts to Stage 1

7.64 Refit the idler roller – engine codes ASZ and ATD

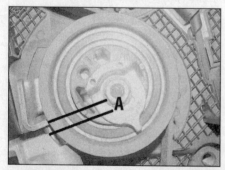

7.66 The gap between the top edge of the tensioner housing and the tensioner back plate arm (A) must be 4 mm – engine codes ASZ and ATD manufactured up to May 2001

torque setting, whilst holding the sprocket stationary. Skoda recommend that the bolts are tightened to the final Stage 2 setting only after checking the dynamic timing of the injection pump (see Chapter 4B, Section 6) – however, this requires the use of special Skoda equipment. If the dynamic timing will be checked later, tighten the bolts securely, but not to the full Stage 2 angle (the engine *can* be run with the bolts tightened to the Stage 1 setting only).
49 Remove the timing locking bar from the camshaft, and remove the timing pin from the fuel injection pump sprocket.
50 Turn the engine through two complete turns in the normal direction of rotation, until the timing locking bar and timing pin can be re-inserted to set the engine at TDC on No 1 cylinder (see Section 3).
51 Check that the timing belt tensioner notch and raised tab are aligned as previously described. If the tensioner marks align, proceed to paragraph 53.
52 If the timing belt tensioner marks are not aligned, repeat the tensioning procedure, then repeat the checking procedure in paragraphs 44 and 45.
53 Refit the centre and lower outer timing belt covers, with reference to Section 6.
54 Refit the crankshaft pulley, with reference to Section 5.
55 Refit the right-hand engine mounting assembly, as described in Chapter 2A, then disconnect the hoist and lifting tackle from the engine.
56 If not already done, remove the tools used to lock the camshaft and fuel injection pump sprocket in position with No 1 piston at TDC.
57 Further refitting is a reversal of the removal procedure. On completion, Skoda recommend that the dynamic injection timing is checked using their dedicated test equipment. Once the dynamic timing has been checked, the fuel injection pump sprocket bolts can be tightened fully to their Stage 2 torque setting (where applicable), and the upper outer timing

belt cover can be refitted.
58 Refit the splash guard under the engine compartment, then lower the vehicle to the ground. Also refit the engine top cover.
59 Reconnect the battery negative (earth) lead (see Chapter 5A).

All engine codes ASZ and ATD

60 Ensure that the crankshaft and camshaft are still set to TDC on No 1 cylinder, as described in Section 3.
61 Refer to Section 5 and slacken the camshaft sprocket bolts by half a turn so that the sprocket is free to turn. Position the camshaft sprocket so that the securing bolts are in the centre part of the elongated holes **(see illustration)**.
62 Loop the timing belt loosely under the crankshaft sprocket. **Note:** *Observe any direction of rotation markings on the belt.*
63 Engage the timing belt teeth with the camshaft sprocket, then manoeuvre it into position around the tensioning roller, crankshaft sprocket, and finally around the coolant pump sprocket. Make sure that the belt teeth seat correctly on the sprockets. **Note:** *Slight adjustment to the position of the camshaft sprocket may be necessary to achieve this.* Avoid bending the belt back on itself or twisting it excessively as you do this.
64 Refit the idler roller and tighten the bolt to the specified torque **(see illustration)**.
65 Ensure that any slack in the belt is in the section of belt that passes over the tensioner roller.

Engine codes ASZ and ATD manufactured up to May 2001

66 Using a suitable tool (eg, circlip pliers) engaged with the two holes in the tensioner hub, turn the tensioner pulley anti-clockwise until the locking plate (T10008) is no longer under tension and can be removed. Turn the tensioner in a clockwise direction until gap of 4 mm exists between the tensioner backplate arm and the top edge of the tensioner housing **(see illustration)**.

67 With the tensioner held in this position, tighten the locknut to the specified torque and angle. Note that the dimension of 4 mm will decrease slightly as the locknut is tightened, so this should be taken into account when setting the gap.

68 Tighten the camshaft sprocket bolts to the specified torque and angle, remove the sprocket locking pin and the crankshaft locking tool.

Engine codes ASZ and ATD manufactured from May 2001

69 Check that the arm on the tensioner rear plate is correctly located in the hole of the rear timing cover.

70 Loosen the tensioner mounting nut slightly, then use circlip pliers to turn the tensioner clockwise until the pointer is located in the middle of the base plate gap. Hold the tensioner in this position and tighten the mounting nut to the specified torque and angle. Note that the pointer will turn a maximum of 5.0 mm to the right when the nut is tightened, however, this must not be corrected since the timing belt settles during the running-in period.

71 Tighten the camshaft sprocket bolts to the specified torque and angle, remove the sprocket locking pin and the crankshaft locking tool.

All engine codes ASZ and ATD

72 Using a spanner or wrench and socket on the crankshaft pulley centre bolt, rotate the crankshaft through two complete revolutions. Reset the engine to TDC on No 1 cylinder, with reference to Section 3 and check that the setting tools can be inserted. If not, repeat the refitting procedure.

73 Further refitting is a reversal of the removal procedure. When refitting the lower timing belt cover and the auxiliary drivebelt drive pulley, note that the offset of the pulley mounting holes allows only one fitting position – tighten the bolts to the specified torque.

8 Timing belt tensioner and sprockets – removal and refitting

Timing belt tensioner

1 Remove the timing belt as described in Section 7.

Engine codes AMF and ASY and ASZ and ATD from May 2001

2 Unscrew the timing belt tensioner nut, and remove the tensioner from the engine **(see illustration)**.

Engine codes ASZ and ATD up to May 2001

3 Undo the retaining nut fully, and remove the tensioner pulley.

4 To remove the tensioner plunger and housing assembly, remove the right-hand cover, and the tensioner housing retaining bolts.

8.2 Timing belt tensioner nut – engine code ASY

All models

5 Refitting is a reversal of removal, with reference to Section 7 when refitting the timing belt. Except on early engine codes ASZ and ATD, make sure that the tensioner pulley arm is correctly located in the rear timing cover hole **(see illustration)**.

Idler pulleys

Note: *On engine code ASY, if the lower front idler pulley is removed, a new securing bolt will be required on refitting.*

6 Remove the timing belt as described in Section 7.

7 Unscrew the relevant idler pulley securing bolt/nut, then withdraw the pulley.

8 Refit the pulley and tighten the securing bolt (where applicable, use a new bolt when refitting the lower right-hand pulley) or nut to the specified torque.

9 Refit and tension the timing belt as described in Section 7.

Crankshaft sprocket

Note: *A new crankshaft sprocket securing bolt must be used on refitting.*

10 Remove the timing belt as described in Section 7.

11 The sprocket securing bolt must now be slackened, and the crankshaft must be prevented from turning as the sprocket bolt is unscrewed. To hold the sprocket, make up a suitable tool, and screw it to the sprocket using two bolts screwed into two of the crankshaft pulley bolt holes **(see illustration)**.

12 Hold the sprocket using the tool, then

8.11 Using a home-made tool to hold the crankshaft sprocket while the bolt is loosened

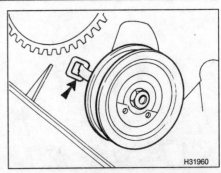

8.5 Ensure that the lug on the tensioner backplate engages with the cut-out in the rear timing belt cover

slacken the sprocket securing bolt. Take care, as the bolt is very tight. **Do not** allow the crankshaft to turn as the bolt is slackened.

13 Unscrew the bolt, and slide the sprocket from the end of the crankshaft, noting which way round the sprocket's raised boss is fitted.

14 Commence refitting by positioning the sprocket on the end of the crankshaft, with the raised boss fitted as noted on removal.

15 Fit a new sprocket securing bolt, then counterhold the sprocket using the method employed on removal, and tighten the bolt to the specified torque and angle given in the Specifications **(see illustration)**. **Do not** oil or grease the bolt threads.

16 Refit the timing belt as described in Section 7.

Camshaft sprocket

17 Remove the timing belt as described in Section 7.

18 The camshaft sprocket bolt(s) must now be slackened. Do not use the timing locking bar to hold the camshaft stationary; it must be removed before loosening the sprocket bolt. In order to eliminate any possibility of accidental piston-to-valve contact, turn the crankshaft 90° anti-clockwise so that all the pistons are halfway up the cylinder bore.

Engine code AMF, ASZ and ATD

19 Unscrew and remove the three retaining bolts and remove the camshaft sprocket from the camshaft hub.

Engine code ASY

20 With the sprocket bolt loosened, release

8.15 Fitting a new crankshaft sprocket securing bolt

8.21 Removing the camshaft sprocket

8.26 Using a fabricated tool to counterhold the camshaft hub

31 Remove the timing belt as described in Section 7.

32 Unscrew and remove the three bolts securing the fuel injection pump sprocket to the hub on the injection pump. There are two different types of bolt fitted as described in Section 7; the stretch-type requires angle-tightening and it is for this reason that they cannot be re-used once loosened. Where applicable, obtain three new bolts before commencing the refitting procedure.

⚠️ *Warning: Do not loosen the injection pump sprocket central nut, otherwise the basic setting of the injection pump will be lost, and it will require resetting by a Skoda dealer.*

33 Temporarily remove the tool used to lock the fuel injection pump sprocket and hub in the TDC position, then slide the sprocket from the hub, noting which way round it is fitted. Refit the locking tool to the pump hub once the sprocket has been removed.

34 To refit the sprocket, again temporarily remove the locking tool from the hub, then refit the sprocket, ensuring that it is fitted the correct way round, as noted before removal.

35 If necessary turn the sprocket until the locking tool can be inserted through the sprocket and hub to engage with the pump support bracket.

36 Fit the new sprocket securing bolts, then turn the sprocket to that the bolts are positioned centrally in the elongated holes. Tighten the sprocket bolts by hand only at this stage.

37 Refit and tension the timing belt as described in Section 7.

Coolant pump sprocket

38 The coolant pump sprocket is integral with the coolant pump. Refer to Chapter 3 for details of coolant pump removal.

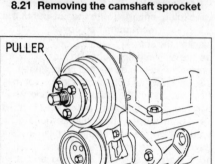

8.27 Attach a three-legged puller to the hub, and evenly tighten the puller until the hub is free of the camshaft taper

the sprocket from the camshaft taper mounting by carefully tapping it with a soft metal drift inserted through the hole provided in the timing belt rear cover. Refit the timing locking bar (see Section 3) once the sprocket has been released.

21 Unscrew and remove the sprocket bolt, then withdraw the sprocket from the end of the camshaft, noting which way round it is fitted **(see illustration)**.

All models

22 Refit the sprocket, ensuring that it is fitted the correct way round, as noted before removal.

23 Refit the sprocket bolt(s), and tighten by hand only at this stage.

24 Refit and tension the timing belt as described in Section 7.

Camshaft hub

Engine codes AMF, ASZ and ATD

Note: *Skoda technicians use special tool T10051 to counterhold the hub, however it is possible to fabricate a suitable alternative – see below.*

25 Remove the camshaft sprocket as described in this Section.

26 Engage special tool T10051 with the three locating holes in the face of the hub to prevent the hub from turning. If this tool is not available, fabricate a suitable alternative. Whilst holding the tool, undo the central hub retaining bolt about two turns **(see illustration)**.

27 Leaving the central hub retaining bolt in place, attach Skoda tool T10052 (or a similar

8.28 The built in key in the hub taper must align with the keyway in the camshaft taper (arrowed)

three-legged puller) to the hub, and evenly tighten the puller until the hub is free of the camshaft taper **(see illustration)**.

28 Ensure that the camshaft taper and the hub centre is clean and dry, locate the hub on the taper, noting that the built-in key in the hub taper must align with the keyway in the camshaft taper **(see illustration)**.

29 Hold the hub in this position with tool T10051 (or similar home-made tool), and tighten the central bolt to the specified torque.

30 The remainder of refitting is a reversal of removal.

Fuel injection pump sprocket

Engine code ASY

Note: *New fuel injection pump sprocket securing bolts will be required on refitting.*

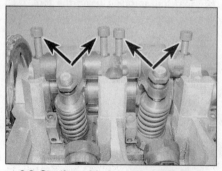

9.2 Starting with the outer bolts first, carefully and evenly slacken the rocker shaft retaining bolts (arrowed)

9 Pump injector rocker shaft assembly – removal and refitting

Note: *The injector rocker shafts are only fitted to engine codes AMF, ASZ and ATD.*

Removal

1 Remove the camshaft cover as described in Section 4. In order to ensure that the rocker arms are refitted to their original locations, use a marker pen or paint and number the arms, with No 1 nearest the timing belt end of the engine. Note that if the arms are not fitted to their original locations, the injector basic clearance setting procedure must be carried out as described in Chapter 4B, Section 4.

2 Starting with the outer bolts first, carefully and evenly unscrew the rocker shaft retaining bolts. Discard the rocker shaft bolts, new ones must be fitted **(see illustration)**.

Refitting

3 Carefully check the rocker shaft, rocker

arms and camshaft bearing cap seating surface for any signs of excessive wear or damage.

4 Ensure that the shaft seating surface is clean and position the rocker shaft assembly in the camshaft bearing caps, making sure that, if reusing the original rocker arms, they are in their original locations.

5 Insert the new rocker shaft retaining bolts, and starting from the inner bolts, progressively tighten the bolts to the Stage 1 torque setting.

6 Again, starting with the inner retaining bolts, tighten the bolts to the Stage 2 angle as listed in this Chapter's Specifications.

7 Refit the camshaft cover as described in Section 4.

10 Camshaft and hydraulic tappets – removal, inspection and refitting

Note: *A new camshaft oil seal will be required on refitting.*

Removal

1 Turn the crankshaft to position No 1 piston at TDC on the firing stroke, and lock the camshaft and the fuel injection pump sprocket in position, as described in Section 3.

2 Remove the timing belt as described in Section 7.

3 Remove the camshaft sprocket and, where applicable, the hub, as described in Section 8.

4 Remove the brake vacuum/tandem pump as described in Chapter 9.

5 On engine codes AMF, ASZ and ATD, remove the injector rocker shaft assembly as described in Section 9.

6 Check the camshaft bearing caps for identification markings **(see illustration)**. The bearing caps are normally stamped with their respective cylinder numbers. If no marks are present, make suitable marks using a scriber or punch, with No 1 at the timing belt end of the engine. Note on which side of the bearing caps the marks are made to ensure that they are refitted the correct way round.

7 On engine codes AMF, ASZ and ATD, the camshaft rotates in shell bearings. As the camshaft bearing caps are removed, recover the shell bearing halves from the camshaft. Number the back of the bearings with a felt pen to ensure that, if re-used, the bearings are fitted to their original locations. **Note:** *Fitted into the cylinder head, under each camshaft bearing cap, is a washer for each cylinder head bolt.*

8 On the 3-cylinder engine (code AMF), unscrew the securing nuts, and remove Nos 2 and 3 bearing caps. Working progressively in a diagonal sequence, slacken the nuts securing Nos 1 and 4 bearing caps. Note that as the nuts are slackened, the valve springs will push the camshaft up.

9 On the 4-cylinder engines (codes ASY, ASZ and ATD), unscrew the securing bolts, and remove Nos 1, 3 and 5 bearing caps. Working

10.6 Check the camshaft bearing caps (arrowed) for markings

progressively, in a diagonal sequence, slacken the bolts securing Nos 2 and 4 bearing caps. Note that as the bolts are slackened, the valve springs will push the camshaft up.

10 Once the nuts/bolts have been fully slackened, lift off the bearing caps.

11 Carefully lift the camshaft from the cylinder head, keeping it level and supported at both ends as it is removed so that the journals and lobes are not damaged. Remove the oil seal from the end of the camshaft and discard it – a new one will be required for refitting **(see illustration)**.

12 Lift the hydraulic tappets from their bores in the cylinder head, and store them with the valve contact surfaces facing downwards, to prevent the oil from draining out. It is recommended that the tappets are kept immersed in oil for the period they are removed from the cylinder head. Make a note of the position of each tappet, as they must be refitted in their original locations on reassembly – accelerated wear leading to early failure will result if the tappets are interchanged.

13 On engine codes AMF, ASZ and ATD, recover the lower shell bearing halves from the cylinder head; number the back of the shells with a felt pen to ensure that, if re-used, the bearings are fitted to their original locations.

Inspection

14 With the camshaft removed, examine the bearing caps and the bearing locations in the cylinder head for signs of obvious wear or pitting. If evident, a new cylinder head will probably be required. Also check that the oil supply holes in the cylinder head are free from obstructions.

15 Visually inspect the camshaft for evidence of wear on the surfaces of the lobes and journals. Normally their surfaces should be smooth and have a dull shine; look for scoring, erosion or pitting and areas that appear highly polished, indicating excessive wear. Accelerated wear will occur once the hardened exterior of the camshaft has been damaged, so always renew worn items. **Note:** *If these symptoms are visible on the tips of the camshaft lobes, check the corresponding tappet, as it will probably be worn as well.*

16 If the machined surfaces of the camshaft appear discoloured or blued, it is likely that it has been overheated at some point, probably

10.11 Remove the camshaft oil seal

due to inadequate lubrication. This may have distorted the shaft, so check the run-out as follows: place the camshaft between two V-blocks and using a DTI gauge, measure the run-out at the centre. If it exceeds the figure quoted in the Specifications at the start of this Chapter, renew the camshaft.

17 To measure the camshaft endfloat, temporarily refit the camshaft to the cylinder head, then fit Nos 1 and 4 (3-cylinder) or 1 and 5 (4-cylinder) bearing caps and tighten the retaining nuts to the specified torque setting. Anchor a DTI gauge to the timing belt end of the cylinder head **(see illustration)**. Push the camshaft to one end of the cylinder head as far as it will travel, then rest the DTI gauge probe on the end face of the camshaft, and zero the gauge. Push the camshaft as far as it will go to the other end of the cylinder head, and record the gauge reading. Verify the reading by pushing the camshaft back to its original position and checking that the gauge indicates zero again. **Note:** *The hydraulic tappets must not be fitted whilst this measurement is being taken.*

18 Check that the camshaft endfloat measurement is within the limit listed in the Specifications. If the measurement is outside the specified limit, wear is unlikely to be confined to any one component, so renewal of the camshaft, cylinder head and bearing caps must be considered.

19 The camshaft bearing running clearance should now be measured. This will be difficult to achieve without a range of micrometers or internal/external expanding calipers, measure the outside diameters of the camshaft bearing surfaces and the internal diameters formed by

10.17 Checking camshaft endfloat using a DTI gauge

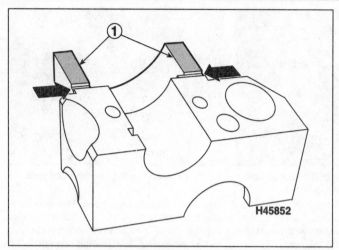

10.27 Apply sealant to the shaded surface (1) on the outer bearing caps, making sure that the lubrication grooves (arrowed) remain clear

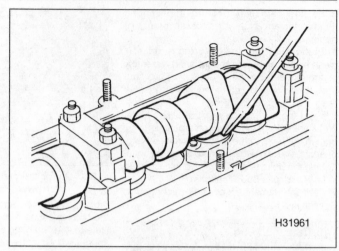

11.8 Press down on the tappet using a wooden or plastic instrument

the bearing caps (and shell bearings where applicable) and the bearing locations in the cylinder head. The difference between these two measurements is the running clearance.

20 Compare the camshaft running clearance measurements with the figure given in the Specifications; if any are outside the specified tolerance, the camshaft, cylinder head and bearing caps (and shell bearings where applicable) should be renewed.

21 Inspect the hydraulic tappets for obvious signs of wear or damage, and renew if necessary. Check that the oil holes in the tappets are free from obstructions.

Refitting

22 Smear some clean engine oil onto the sides of the hydraulic tappets, and offer them into position in their original bores in the cylinder head. Push them down until they contact the valves, then lubricate the camshaft lobe contact surfaces.

23 Lubricate the camshaft and cylinder head bearing journals (and shell bearings where applicable) with clean engine oil.

24 Carefully lower the camshaft into position in the cylinder head making sure that the cam lobes for No 1 cylinder are pointing upwards.

25 Refit a new camshaft oil seal on the end of the camshaft. Make sure that the closed end of the seal faces the camshaft sprocket end of the camshaft, and take care not to damage the seal lip. Locate the seal against the seat in the cylinder head.

26 Oil the upper surfaces of the camshaft bearing journals (and shell bearings where applicable), then fit Nos 2 and 3 (3-cylinder) or 2 and 4 (4-cylinder) bearing caps. Ensure that they are fitted the right way round and in the correct locations, then progressively tighten the retaining nuts/bolts in a diagonal sequence to the specified torque. Note that as they are tightened, the camshaft will be forced down against the pressure of the valve springs.

27 Apply sealant to the outer shoulders of bearing caps 1 and 4 (3-cylinder) or 1 and 5

(4-cylinder), making sure that the lubrication slots remain clear (see illustration).

28 Fit bearing caps 1 and 4 (3-cylinder) or 1, 3 and 5 (4-cylinder) over the camshaft and progressively tighten the nuts/bolts to the specified torque.

29 Refit the camshaft sprocket and, where applicable the hub, as described in Section 8.

30 Refit and tension the timing belt as described in Section 7.

31 Refit the brake vacuum/tandem pump as described in Chapter 9.

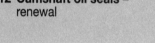

11 Hydraulic tappets –
testing

⚠️ **Warning: After fitting hydraulic tappets, wait a minimum of 30 minutes (or preferably, leave overnight) before starting the engine, to allow the tappets time to settle, otherwise the valve heads will strike the pistons.**

1 The hydraulic tappets are self-adjusting, and require no attention whilst in service.

2 If the hydraulic tappets become excessively noisy, their operation can be checked as described below.

3 Start the engine, and run it until it reaches normal operating temperature, increase the engine speed to approximately 2500 rpm for 2 minutes.

4 If any hydraulic tappets are heard to be noisy, carry out the following checks.

5 Remove the camshaft cover as described in Section 4.

6 Using a socket or spanner on the crankshaft sprocket bolt, turn the crankshaft until the tip of the camshaft lobe above the tappet to be checked is pointing vertically upwards.

7 Using feeler blades, check the clearance between the top of the tappet, and the cam lobe. If the play is in excess of 0.2 mm, renew the relevant tappet. If the play is less than 0.2 mm, or there is no play, proceed as follows.

8 Press down on the tappet using a wooden or plastic instrument (see illustration). If free play in excess of 1.0 mm is present before the tappet contacts the valve stem, renew the relevant tappet.

9 On completion, refit the camshaft cover as described in Section 4.

12 Camshaft oil seals –
renewal

Right-hand oil seal

1 Remove the timing belt as described in Section 7.

2 Remove the camshaft sprocket and, where applicable, the hub, as described in Section 8.

3 Drill two small holes into the existing oil seal, diagonally opposite each other. Take great care to avoid drilling through into the seal housing or camshaft sealing surface. Thread two self-tapping screws into the holes and, using a pair of pliers, pull on the heads of the screws to extract the oil seal.

4 Clean out the seal housing and the sealing surface of the camshaft by wiping it with a lint-free cloth. Remove any swarf or burrs that may cause the seal to leak.

5 Do not lubricate the lip and outer edge of the new oil seal, push it over the camshaft until it is positioned in place above its housing. To prevent damage to the sealing lips, wrap some adhesive tape around the end of the camshaft.

6 Using a hammer and a socket of suitable diameter, drive the seal squarely into its housing. Note: *Select a socket that bears only on the hard outer surface of the seal, not the inner lip which can easily be damaged.*

7 Refit the camshaft sprocket and, where applicable, the hub, as described in Section 8.

8 Refit and tension the timing belt as described in Section 7.

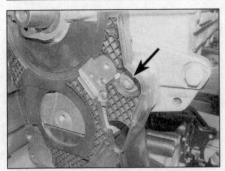

13.6a Where applicable, undo the bolt (arrowed) from the inner cover . . .

Left-hand oil seal

9 The left-hand camshaft oil seal is formed by the brake vacuum/tandem pump seal. Refer to Chapter 9 for details of brake vacuum pump removal and refitting.

13 Cylinder head –
removal, inspection and refitting

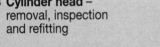

Note: *The cylinder head must be removed with the engine cold. New cylinder head bolts and a new cylinder head gasket will be required on refitting, and suitable studs will be required to guide the cylinder head into position – see text.*

Removal

1 Disconnect the battery negative lead (refer to *Disconnecting the battery* in the *Reference* Chapter at the end of this manual) and remove the engine top cover.
2 Drain the cooling system and engine oil as described in Chapter 1B.
3 Remove the camshaft cover as described in Section 4.
4 Remove the timing belt as described in Section 7.
5 Remove the camshaft sprocket and, where applicable, the hub, and timing belt tensioner as described in Section 8.
6 Where applicable, unscrew the bolt(s) securing the rear timing belt cover to the cylinder head **(see illustrations)**.
7 Using two suitable nuts locked together, unscrew the timing belt tensioner mounting stud from the cylinder head **(see illustration)**.
8 If the engine is currently supported using a hoist and lifting tackle attached to the engine lifting brackets on the cylinder head, it is now necessary to attach a suitable bracket to the cylinder block, so that the engine can still be supported as the cylinder head is removed. Alternatively, the engine can be supported using a trolley jack and a block of wood positioned under the engine sump.

Engine code ASY

9 Slacken the clip and disconnect the radiator top hose from the front of the coolant housing on the left-hand side of the cylinder head.
10 Disconnect the heater hose from the rear of the housing, and the smaller oil cooler hose

13.6b . . . and the one (arrowed) on the side of the cover

from the bottom of the housing. Move the hoses to one side.
11 Slacken the clip, and disconnect the coolant purge hose from the rear left-hand side of the cylinder head.
12 Disconnect the exhaust front section from the exhaust manifold, as described in Chapter 4C.
13 Disconnect the wiring from the following components, noting the routing of the wiring:
a) *Fuel injection pump fuel cut-off solenoid (on top of injection pump – loosen securing nut).*
b) *Fuel injection pump start-of-injection valve* **(see illustration)**.
c) *Coolant temperature sensor/temperature gauge sender (left-hand end of cylinder head).*
d) *Fuel injector needle lift sensor (behind oil filter housing).*
e) *Main glow plug feed wiring.*

13.13 Disconnect the injection system wiring plug (arrowed) behind the oil filter housing

13.16b EGR valve and vacuum hose (arrowed) – turbo models

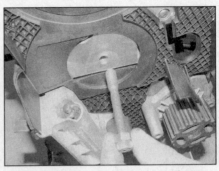

13.7 Using two nuts locked together to unscrew the tensioner mounting stud

14 Disconnect the main fuel leak-off hose from the fuel injectors.
15 Slacken the union nuts, whilst counterholding the unions with a second spanner, and remove the fuel injector pipes as an assembly.
16 Disconnect the vacuum hoses from the brake vacuum pump and EGR valve **(see illustrations)**.
17 On models fitted with an inlet manifold flap vacuum damper (see Chapter 4B), either remove the damper reservoir from the bracket on the cylinder head, or remove the reservoir with its bracket.
18 Make a final check to ensure that all relevant pipes, hoses and wires have been disconnected and moved clear of the working area to enable removal of the cylinder head.
19 Progressively slacken the cylinder head bolts, by one turn at a time, in order **(see illustration)**. Remove the cylinder head bolts.

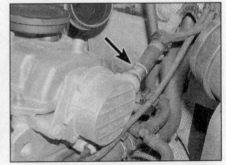

13.16a Disconnect the vacuum hose (arrowed) from the brake vacuum pump

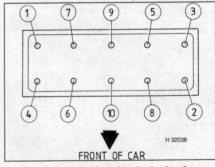

13.19 Cylinder head bolt slackening sequence

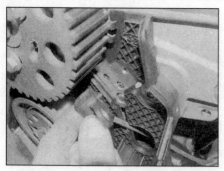

13.23 Unscrew the bolt and remove the camshaft position sensor

20 With all the bolts removed, lift the cylinder head from the block, together with the manifolds. If the cylinder head is stuck, tap it with a soft-faced mallet to break the joint. **Do not** insert a lever into the gasket joint.

21 Lift the cylinder head gasket from the block. Do not discard the gasket at this stage, as it will be required when determining the thickness of the new gasket required.

22 If desired, the manifolds can be removed from the cylinder head with reference to Chapter 4B (inlet manifold) or 4C (exhaust manifold).

Engine codes AMF, ASZ and ATD

Note: *It is necessary to unplug the central connector for the unit injectors – this may cause a fault code to be logged by the engine management ECU. This code can only be erased by a Skoda dealer or suitably-equipped specialist.*

23 Remove the bolt securing the camshaft

13.27 Undo the four tandem pump retaining bolts (arrowed)

13.32 Disconnect the vacuum pipes (arrowed)

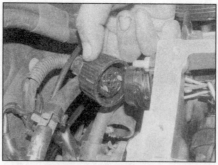

13.25 Disconnect the central connector for the injectors

position sensor to the cylinder head. There is no need to disconnect the wiring at this stage **(see illustration)**.

24 Disconnect the charge air pipe from the inlet manifold to the intercooler and place to one side.

25 Disconnect the central connector for the unit injectors **(see illustration)**.

26 Undo the two bolts securing the coolant junction to the end of the cylinder head **(see illustration)**. There is no need to disconnect the pipes or wiring plugs at this stage.

27 Unscrew the four retaining bolts and pull the tandem pump away from the cylinder head without disconnecting the fuel or vacuum hoses **(see illustration)**.

28 Disconnect and remove the hose connecting the upper coolant pipe to the pipe at the end of the cylinder head **(see illustration)**.

29 Remove the turbocharger as described in Chapter 4C.

13.28 Disconnect the coolant hose from the end of the cylinder head

13.36 The thickness of the cylinder head gasket can be identified by notches or holes

13.26 Undo the two bolts (arrowed) and remove the coolant outlet from the end of the cylinder head

30 Slacken and remove the bolt securing the upper metal coolant pipe to the cylinder head.

31 Disconnect the wiring connectors from the glow plugs – if necessary, refer to Chapter 5C.

32 Disconnect the vacuum pipes from the EGR valve and the manifold flap actuator **(see illustration)**.

33 Using a multi-splined tool, undo the cylinder head bolts, working from the outside-in, evenly and gradually. Check that nothing remains connected, and lift the cylinder head from the engine block. Seek assistance if possible, as it is a heavy assembly, especially as it is being removed complete with the manifolds.

34 Remove the gasket from the top of the block, noting the locating dowels. If the dowels are a loose fit, remove them and store them with the head for safe-keeping. Do not discard the gasket yet – it will be needed for identification purposes.

Inspection

35 Dismantling and inspection of the cylinder head is covered in Chapter 2E.

Cylinder head gasket selection

Note: *A dial test indicator (DTI) will be required for this operation.*

36 Examine the old cylinder head gasket for manufacturer's identification markings **(see illustration)**. These will be in the form of holes or notches, and a part number on the edge of the gasket. Unless new pistons have been fitted, the new cylinder head gasket must be of the same type as the old one. In this case, purchase a new gasket, and proceed to paragraph 43.

37 If new piston assemblies have been fitted as part of an engine overhaul, or if a new short engine is to be fitted, the projection of the piston crowns above the cylinder head mating face of the cylinder block at TDC must be measured. This measurement is used to determine the thickness of the new cylinder head gasket required.

38 Anchor a dial test indicator (DTI) to the top face (cylinder head gasket mating face) of the cylinder block, and zero the gauge on the gasket mating face.

39 Rest the gauge probe on No 1 piston

crown, and turn the crankshaft slowly by hand until the piston reaches TDC. Measure and record the maximum piston projection at TDC **(see illustration)**.

40 Repeat the measurement for the remaining pistons, and record the results.

41 If the measurements differ from piston-to-piston, take the highest figure, and use this to determine the thickness of the head gasket required as follows.

Piston projection	Gasket identification (number of holes/notches)
0.91 to 1.00 mm	1
1.01 to 1.10 mm	2
1.11 to 1.20 mm	3

42 Purchase a new gasket according to the results of the measurements.

Refitting

Note: If a Skoda exchange cylinder head, complete with camshaft, is to be fitted, the manufacturers recommend the following:

a) Lubricate the contact surfaces between the tappets and the cam lobes before fitting the camshaft cover.

b) Do not remove the plastic protectors from the open valves until immediately before fitting the cylinder head.

c) Additionally, if a new cylinder head is fitted, Skoda recommend that the coolant is renewed.

43 The mating faces of the cylinder head and block must be perfectly clean before refitting the head. Use a scraper to remove all traces of gasket and carbon, also clean the tops of the pistons. Take particular care with the aluminium surfaces, as the soft metal is easily damaged.

44 Make sure that debris is not allowed to enter the oil and water passages – this is particularly important for the oil circuit, as carbon could block the oil supply to the camshaft and crankshaft bearings. Using adhesive tape and paper, seal the water, oil and bolt holes in the cylinder block.

45 To prevent carbon entering the gap between the pistons and bores, smear a little grease in the gap. After cleaning a piston, rotate the crankshaft to that the piston moves down the bore, then wipe out the grease and carbon with a cloth rag. Clean the other piston crowns in the same way.

13.39 Measuring the piston projection at TDC using a dial gauge

46 Check the head and block for nicks, deep scratches and other damage. If slight, they may be removed carefully with a file. More serious damage may be repaired by machining, but this is a specialist job.

47 If warpage of the cylinder head is suspected, use a straight-edge to check it for distortion, as described in Chapter 2E.

48 Ensure that the cylinder head bolt holes in the crankcase are clean and free of oil. Syringe or soak up any oil left in the bolt holes. This is most important in order that the correct bolt tightening torque can be applied, and to prevent the possibility of the block being cracked by hydraulic pressure when the bolts are tightened.

49 Turn the crankshaft anti-clockwise until all the pistons at an equal height, approximately halfway down their bores from the TDC position (see Section 3). This will eliminate any risk of piston-to-valve contact as the cylinder head is refitted.

50 Where applicable, refit the manifolds with reference to Chapters 4B and/or 4C.

51 To guide the cylinder head into position, screw two long studs (or old cylinder head bolts with the heads cut off, and slots cut in the ends to enable the bolts to be unscrewed) into the cylinder block **(see illustration)**.

52 Ensure that the cylinder head locating dowels are in place in the cylinder block, then fit the new cylinder head gasket over the dowels, ensuring that the part number is uppermost. Where applicable, the OBEN/TOP marking should also be uppermost. Note that Skoda recommend that the gasket is only removed from its packaging immediately prior to fitting.

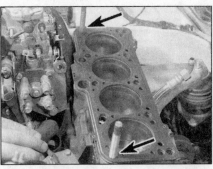

13.51 Two of the old head bolts (arrowed) can be used as cylinder head alignment guides

53 Lower the cylinder head into position on the gasket, ensuring that it engages correctly over the guide studs and dowels.

54 Fit the new cylinder head bolts to the eight remaining bolt locations, and screw them in as far as possible by hand.

55 Unscrew the two guide studs from the exhaust side of the cylinder block, then screw in the two remaining new cylinder head bolts as far as possible by hand.

56 Working progressively, in sequence, tighten all the cylinder head bolts to the specified Stage 1 torque **(see illustrations)**.

57 Again working progressively, in sequence, tighten all the cylinder head bolts to the specified Stage 2 torque.

58 Tighten all the cylinder head bolts, in sequence, through the specified Stage 3 angle **(see illustration)**.

59 Finally, tighten all the cylinder head bolts, in sequence, through the specified Stage 4 angle.

60 After finally tightening the cylinder head bolts, turn the camshaft so that the cam lobes for No 1 cylinder are pointing upwards.

61 Where applicable, reconnect the lifting tackle to the engine lifting brackets on the cylinder head, then adjust the lifting tackle to support the engine. Once the engine is adequately supported using the cylinder head brackets, disconnect the lifting tackle from the bracket bolted to the cylinder block, and unbolt the improvised engine lifting bracket from the cylinder block. Alternatively, remove the trolley jack and block of wood from under the sump.

62 The remainder of the refitting procedure is

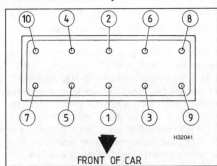

13.56a Cylinder head bolt tightening sequence

13.56b Using a torque wrench to tighten the cylinder head bolts

13.58 Angle-tighten the cylinder head bolts

14.4 Disconnect the wiring connector from the oil level/temperature sender

a reversal of the removal procedure, bearing in mind the following points.

a) *Refit the camshaft cover with reference to Section 4.*

b) *On turbo models, use new sealing rings when reconnecting the turbocharger oil return pipe to the cylinder block.*

c) *Reconnect the exhaust front section to the exhaust manifold or turbocharger, as applicable, with reference to Chapter 4C.*

d) *Refit the timing belt tensioner with reference to Section 8.*

e) *Refit the camshaft sprocket as described in Section 8, and refit the timing belt as described in Section 7.*

f) *On non-turbo engines, refit the upper section of the inlet manifold as described in Chapter 4B.*

g) *Refill the cooling system and engine oil as described in Chapter 1B.*

14 Sump –
removal and refitting

Note: *On the 3-cylinder engine code AMF, the transmission must be removed first in order to remove the sump. This is for access to the sump retaining bolts at the flywheel end of the crankcase.*

Removal

1 Apply the handbrake, then jack up the front of the vehicle and support securely on axle stands (see *Jacking and vehicle support*).

2 Remove the securing screws and withdraw the engine undershield(s).

3 Drain the engine oil as described in Chapter 1B.

4 Where fitted, disconnect the wiring connector from the oil level/temperature sender on the sump **(see illustration)**.

5 On the 3-cylinder engine code AMF, the transmission must first be removed from the engine. Refer to Chapter 7A for the procedure. For additional working room, the exhaust front pipe may also be removed as described in Chapter 4C. Also on this engine, unscrew the bolts and remove the dipstick tube from the sump, then recover the O-ring seal **(see illustrations)**.

6 Unscrew and remove the bolts securing the sump to the cylinder block, then withdraw the sump **(see illustration)**. On engine codes ASY, ASZ and ATD, access to the flywheel-end retaining bolts is limited, requiring the

use of universal joint socket bar. If necessary, release the sump by tapping with a soft-faced mallet.

Refitting

7 Commence refitting by thoroughly cleaning the mating faces of the sump and cylinder block/crankcase. Ensure that all traces of old sealant are removed.

8 Ensure that the mating face of the sump is free from all traces of old sealant, oil and grease, then apply a 2.0 to 3.0 mm thick bead of silicone sealant (D 176404 A2 or equivalent) to the sump. Note that the sealant must run around the inside of the bolt holes in the sump. The sump must be fitted within 5 minutes of applying the sealant.

9 Offer the sump up to the cylinder block, then refit the retaining bolts, and *lightly* tighten them by hand, working progressively in a diagonal sequence **(see illustration)**. On engine codes ASY, ASZ and ATD, if the sump is being refitted with the engine on the bench, use a steel rule to align the rear face of the sump with that of the engine cylinder block. Fully tighten the bolts, again working in a diagonal sequence.

10 On the 3-cylinder engine code AMF, refit the transmission with reference to Chapter 7A. Where removed, refit the exhaust front pipe.

11 Reconnect the wiring to the oil level/temperature sender on the sump.

12 Refit the engine undershield(s) and lower the vehicle to the ground.

13 Allow at least 30 minutes from the time of refitting the sump for the sealant to dry, then refill the engine with oil, with reference to Chapter 1B.

15 Oil pump, drive chain and sprockets – removal, inspection and refitting

Oil pump, drive chain and sprockets – engine code AMF

Note: *The oil pump on engine code AMF is driven by the balancer shaft drive chain; refer to Section 21 for more information. When removing the oil pump, the balancer shaft drive chain must first be removed, then realigned on refitting.*

Removal

1 Remove the timing belt as described in Section 7.

2 Remove the crankshaft sprocket as described in Section 8.

3 Remove the sump as described in Section 14.

4 Unscrew the retaining bolts and remove the oil seal housing from the front/right-hand side of the cylinder block. If it is stuck, release it by tapping with a soft-faced mallet. If the oil seal is to be re-used, wrap some tape around the end of the crankshaft to protect the oil seal lips.

5 Unscrew the mounting bolts and remove the plastic cover/strainer from the bottom of the crankcase. Recover the O-ring.

14.5a Unscrew the bolts . . .

14.5b . . . and remove the dipstick and O-ring seal

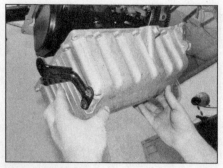

14.6 Removing the sump – engine code AMF

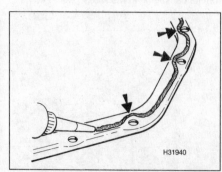

14.9 Apply the sealant around the inside of the bolt holes

6 Apply inward pressure on the drive chain, then lock the chain tensioner by fitting and tightening a bolt through the tensioner into the tensioner body.

7 Unscrew the bolt and remove the sprocket from the guide pulley. Place the sprocket to one side.

8 Unbolt and remove the drive chain tensioner assembly. Discard the bolts and obtain new ones.

9 If the chain is to be re-used, mark it with paint to indicate its fitted position and rotational direction.

10 Remove the chain from the sprockets.

11 To remove the sprocket from the balancer shaft, refer to Section 21. If necessary, the oil pump sprocket may be removed at this stage by holding it stationary and loosening the retaining bolt. Discard the bolt and obtain a new one.

12 Unscrew the mounting bolts and remove the oil pump from the bottom of the balancer shaft assembly **(see illustration)**. Recover the two location dowels.

Inspection

13 Clean the pump and sprockets, and inspect them for signs of damage or wear. Renew them as necessary.

Refitting

14 Check that the two location dowels are in position, then refit the oil pump, insert the mounting bolts and tighten them to the specified torque.

15 Refit the sprocket to the oil pump and tighten the new bolt to the specified torque and angle. If removed, refit the sprocket to the balancer shaft with reference to Section 21.

16 Refit the chain tensioner assembly and tighten the new mounting bolts to the specified torque and angle.

17 With the engine set at TDC, the mark on the crankshaft sprocket will be pointing upwards. The chain has two coloured links which are also notched; position one of these links on the crankshaft sprocket mark, then feed the chain clockwise over the tensioner pad, around the oil pump sprocket and over the balancer shaft sprocket, making sure that the remaining coloured/notched link is aligned with the mark on the sprocket **(see illustration)**.

18 Locate the guide pulley sprocket in the chain, then refit the bolt and tighten it to the specified torque.

19 Unlock the tensioner by unscrewing the retaining bolt, then recheck that the coloured/notched links are still aligned with the marks on the sprockets.

20 Clean all traces of old sealant from the crankshaft oil seal housing and the cylinder block, then coat the cylinder block mating faces of the oil seal housing with a 2.0 to 3.0 mm thick bead of sealant (Skoda D 176 404 A2, or equivalent) **(see illustration)**. Note that the seal housing must be refitted within 5 minutes of applying the sealant.

Caution: DO NOT put excessive amounts

15.12 Oil pump mounting bolts

of sealant onto the housing as it may get into the sump and block the oil pick-up pipe.

21 Refit the oil seal housing, taking care not to damage the seal and tighten the bolts progressively to the specified torque. If a new seal is to be fitted, refer to Section 17; if the oil seal is to be refitted, protect it with tin foil or plastic sheeting **(see illustration)**.

22 Refit the sump as described in Section 14.

23 Refit the crankshaft sprocket as described in Section 8.

24 Refit the timing belt as described in Section 7.

Oil pump –
engine codes ASY, ASZ and ATD

Removal

25 Remove the sump as described in Section 14.

26 Unbolt and remove the oil baffle from the crankcase, noting that on some models the baffle is retained by the oil pump rear/left-hand mounting bolt.

27 Unscrew the mounting bolts, and release the oil pump from the dowels in the crankcase **(see illustration overleaf)**. Unhook the oil pump drive sprocket from the chain and withdraw the oil pump and oil pick-up pipe from the engine. Note that the tensioner will attempt to tighten the chain, and it may be necessary to use a screwdriver to hold it in its released position before releasing the oil pump sprocket from the chain.

28 If desired, unscrew the flange bolts and remove the pick-up pipe from the oil pump.

15.20 Applying sealant to the crankshaft oil seal housing

15.17 The coloured links on the balance shaft chain must be positioned as shown

Recover the O-ring seal. Unscrew the bolts and remove the cover from the oil pump. **Note:** *If the oil pick-up pipe is removed from the oil pump, a new O-ring will be required on refitting.*

Inspection

29 Clean the pump thoroughly, and inspect the gear teeth/rotors for signs of damage or wear. If evident, renew the oil pump.

30 To remove the sprocket from the oil pump, unscrew the retaining bolt and slide off the sprocket (note that the sprocket can only be fitted in one position).

Refitting

31 Prime the pump with oil by pouring oil into the pick-up pipe aperture while turning the driveshaft.

32 Refit the cover to the oil pump and tighten the bolts securely. Where removed, refit the pick-up pipe to the oil pump, using a new O-ring seal, and tighten the securing bolts.

33 Use a screwdriver to press the tensioner against its spring to provide sufficient slack in the chain to refit the oil pump. Engage the oil pump sprocket with the drive chain, then locate the oil pump on the dowels. Refit and tighten the three mounting bolts to the specified torque.

34 Refit the oil baffle, and tighten the securing bolts.

35 Refit the sump as described in Section 14.

Drive chain and sprockets –
engine codes ASY, ASZ and ATD

Note: *Skoda sealant (D 176404 A2 or equivalent) will be required to seal the*

15.21 Using tin foil to protect the crankshaft oil seal when fitting the housing

crankshaft oil seal housing on refitting, and it is advisable to fit a new crankshaft oil seal.

Removal

36 Remove the sump as described in Section 14.

37 Unbolt and remove the oil baffle from the crankcase, noting that on some models the baffle is retained by the oil pump rear/left-hand mounting bolt.

38 To remove the oil pump sprocket, unscrew the securing bolt, then pull the sprocket from the pump shaft, and unhook it from the drive chain.

39 To remove the chain, remove the timing belt as described in Section 7, then unbolt the crankshaft oil seal housing from the cylinder block. Unbolt the chain tensioner from the cylinder block, then unhook the chain from the sprocket on the end of the crankshaft.

40 The oil pump drive sprocket is a press-fit on the crankshaft, and cannot easily be removed. Consult a Skoda dealer for advice if the sprocket is worn or damaged.

Inspection

41 Examine the chain for wear and damage. Wear is usually indicated by excessive lateral play between the links, and excessive noise in operation. It is wise to renew the chain in any case if the engine is to be overhauled. Note that the rollers on a very badly worn chain may be slightly grooved. If there is any doubt as to the condition of the chain, renew it.

42 Examine the teeth on the sprockets for wear. Each tooth forms an inverted V. If worn, the side of each tooth under tension will be slightly concave in shape when compared with the other side of the tooth (ie, the teeth will have a hooked appearance). If the teeth appear worn, the sprocket should be renewed (consult a Skoda dealer for advice if the crankshaft sprocket is worn or damaged).

Refitting

43 Refit the chain tensioner to the cylinder block, and tighten the securing bolt to the specified torque. Make sure that the tensioner spring is correctly positioned to pretension the tensioner arm.

44 Engage the oil pump sprocket with the chain, then engage the chain with the crankshaft sprocket. Use a screwdriver to press the tensioner against its spring to provide sufficient slack in the chain, then engage the sprocket with the oil pump. Note that the sprocket will only fit in one position.

45 Refit the oil pump sprocket bolt, and tighten to the specified torque.

46 Fit a new crankshaft oil seal to the housing, and refit the housing as described in Section 17.

47 Refit the oil baffle to the crankcase, and tighten the securing bolts.

48 Refit the sump as described in Section 14.

16 Flywheel – removal, inspection and refitting

Removal

1 Remove the manual transmission and clutch as described in Chapter 7A and Chapter 6.

2 Lock the flywheel in position using a home-made locking tool, fabricated from a piece of scrap metal **(see illustration)**. Bolt it to one of the transmission bellhousing mounting holes.

3 Remove the flywheel. Do not drop it, as it is very heavy. **Note:** *The bolt holes are offset, so it is only possible to fit the flywheel in one position.*

Inspection

4 If the flywheel's clutch mating surface is deeply scored, cracked or otherwise damaged, the flywheel must be renewed. However, it may be possible to have it surface-ground; seek the advice of a Skoda dealer or engine reconditioning specialist.

5 If the ring gear is badly worn or has missing teeth, the flywheel must be renewed.

Refitting

6 Clean the mating surfaces of the flywheel and crankshaft. Remove any remaining locking compound from the threads of the crankshaft holes, using the correct-size tap, if available.

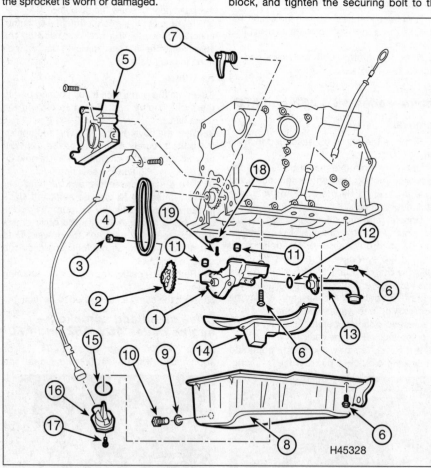

15.27 Sump and oil pump components – engine codes ASY, ASZ and ATD

1 Oil pump	*5* Crankshaft oil seal housing	*9* Seal	*15* Seal
2 Oil pump sprocket	*6* Bolt	*10* Sump drain plug	*16* Oil level/ temperature sender
3 Bolt	*7* Drive chain tensioner	*11* Dowels	*17* Bolt
4 Oil pump drive chain	*8* Sump	*12* O-ring	*18* Oil spray jet
		13 Oil pick-up pipe	*19* Bolt
		14 Oil baffle	

16.2 Flywheel locked in position with a home-made tool

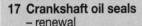 **HAYNES HiNT** *If a suitable tap is not available, cut two slots down the threads of one of the old flywheel bolts with a hacksaw, and use the bolt to remove the locking compound from the threads.*

7 If the new flywheel retaining bolts are not supplied with their threads precoated, apply a suitable thread-locking compound to the threads of each bolt **(see illustration)**.

8 Offer up the flywheel to the crankshaft, and fit the new retaining bolts.

9 Lock the flywheel using the method employed on dismantling, and tighten the retaining bolts to the specified torque and angle **(see illustration)**.

10 Refit the clutch as described in Chapter 6. Remove the locking tool, and refit the transmission as described in Chapter 7A.

17 Crankshaft oil seals – renewal

Note 1: *On engine codes ASY, ASZ and ATD, the oil seals are a PTFE (Teflon) type and are fitted dry, without using any grease or oil. These have a wider sealing lip and have been introduced instead of the coil spring type oil seal.*

Note 2: *If the oil seal housing is removed, suitable sealant (Skoda D 176 404 A2, or equivalent) will be required to seal the housing on refitting.*

Right-hand oil seal

1 Remove the timing belt as described in Section 7, and the crankshaft sprocket with reference to Section 8.

2 To remove the seal without removing the housing, drill two small holes diagonally opposite each other, insert self-tapping screws, and pull on the heads of the screws with pliers **(see illustrations)**.

3 Alternatively, to remove the oil seal complete with its housing, proceed as follows.

a) *Remove the sump as described in Section 14. This is necessary to ensure a satisfactory seal between the sump and oil seal housing on refitting.*

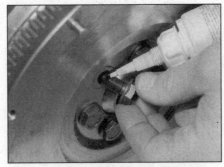
16.7 Apply locking fluid to the new flywheel bolts, if necessary

b) *Unbolt and remove the oil seal housing.*

c) *Working on the bench, lever the oil seal from the housing using a suitable screwdriver. Take care not to damage the seal seating in the housing (see illustration).*

4 Thoroughly clean the oil seal seating in the housing.

5 Wind a length of tape around the end of the crankshaft to protect the oil seal lips as the seal (and housing, where applicable) is fitted. Alternatively, use a suitable plastic cap **(see illustration)**.

6 Fit a new oil seal to the housing, pressing or driving it into position using a socket or tube of suitable diameter. Ensure that the socket or tube bears only on the hard outer ring of the seal, and take care not to damage the seal lips. Press or drive the seal into position until it is seated on the shoulder in the housing. Make sure that the closed end of the seal is facing outwards.

17.2a Drill two small holes diagonally opposite each other . . .

17.5 Using a plastic cap to protect the oil seal during fitting

16.9 Tighten the flywheel bolts to the specified torque

7 If the oil seal housing has been removed, proceed as follows, otherwise proceed to paragraph 11.

8 Clean all traces of old sealant from the crankshaft oil seal housing and the cylinder block, then coat the cylinder block mating faces of the oil seal housing with a 2.0 to 3.0 mm thick bead of sealant (Skoda D 176 404 A2, or equivalent). Note that the seal housing must be refitted within 5 minutes of applying the sealant. *Caution: DO NOT put excessive amounts of sealant onto the housing as it may get into the sump and block the oil pick-up pipe.*

9 Refit the oil seal housing, and tighten the bolts progressively to the specified torque **(see illustration)**.

10 Refit the sump as described in Section 14.

11 Refit the crankshaft sprocket with reference to Section 8, and the timing belt as described in Section 7.

17.2b . . . and use pliers to pull out the oil seal

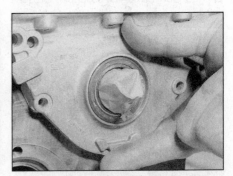
17.9 Slide the oil seal housing over the end of the crankshaft

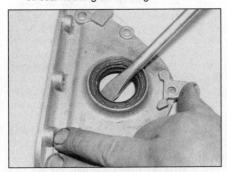
17.3 Prising the oil seal from the crankshaft oil seal housing

17.17 Locate the crankshaft oil seal fitting tool over the end of the crankshaft

17.19a Fit the oil seal/housing assembly over the end of the crankshaft . . .

17.19b . . . then tighten the securing bolts to the specified torque

Left-hand oil seal

12 Remove the flywheel as described in Section 16.

13 Remove the sump as described in Section 14. This is necessary to ensure a satisfactory seal between the sump and oil seal housing on refitting.

14 Unbolt and remove the oil seal housing, complete with the oil seal.

15 The new oil seal will be supplied ready-fitted to a new oil seal housing.

16 Thoroughly clean the oil seal housing mating face on the cylinder block.

17 New oil seal/housing assemblies are supplied with a fitting tool to prevent damage to the oil seal as it is being fitted. Locate the tool over the end of the crankshaft **(see illustration)**.

18 If the original oil seal housing was fitted using sealant, apply a thin bead of suitable sealant (Skoda D 176 404 A2, or equivalent) to the cylinder block mating face of the oil seal housing. Note that the seal housing must be refitted within 5 minutes of applying the sealant.

Caution: DO NOT put excessive amounts of sealant onto the housing as it may get into the sump and block the oil pick-up pipe.

19 Carefully fit the oil seal/housing assembly over the end of the crankshaft, then refit the securing bolts and tighten the bolts progressively, in a diagonal sequence, to the specified torque **(see illustrations)**.

20 Remove the oil seal protector tool from the end of the crankshaft.

21 Refit the sump as described in Section 14.

22 Refit the flywheel as described in Section 16.

18 Engine/transmission mountings – inspection and renewal

Inspection

1 If improved access is required, jack up the front of the vehicle, and support it securely on axle stands (see *Jacking and vehicle support*). Remove the securing screws and remove the engine undershield(s).

2 Check the mounting rubbers to see if they are cracked, hardened or separated from the metal at any point; renew the mounting if any such damage or deterioration is evident.

3 Check that all the mountings are securely tightened; use a torque wrench to check if possible.

4 Using a large screwdriver or a crowbar, check for wear in the mounting by carefully levering against it to check for free play. Where this is not possible, enlist the aid of an assistant to move the engine/transmission back-and-forth, or from side-to-side, whilst you observe the mounting. While some free play is to be expected, even from new components, excessive wear should be obvious. If excessive free play is found, check first that the fasteners are correctly secured, then renew any worn components as described in the following paragraphs.

Renewal

Right-hand mounting

Note: *New mounting securing bolts will be required on refitting.*

5 Attach a hoist and lifting tackle to the engine lifting brackets on the cylinder head, and raise the hoist to just take the weight of the engine. Alternatively the engine can be supported on a trolley jack under the engine. Use a block of wood between the sump and the head of the jack, to prevent any damage to the sump.

6 Where necessary, unbolt the coolant reservoir and move it to one side, leaving the coolant hoses connected.

7 Where applicable, move any wiring harnesses, pipes or hoses to one side to enable removal of the engine mounting.

8 Unscrew the mounting centre nut securing the bracket to the flexible mounting.

9 Unscrew the three bolts securing the mounting bracket to the engine and remove the bracket.

10 Unbolt and remove the flexible mounting from the body.

11 Refitting is a reversal of removal, bearing in mind the following points.
a) Use new securing bolts.
b) Tighten all fixings to the specified torque.

Left-hand mounting

Note: *New mounting bolts will be required on*

refitting (there is no need to renew the smaller mounting-to-body bolts).

12 Remove the engine top cover which also incorporates the air filter.

13 Attach a hoist and lifting tackle to the engine lifting brackets on the cylinder head, and raise the hoist to just take the weight of the engine and transmission. Alternatively the engine can be supported on a trolley jack under the transmission. Use a block of wood between the transmission and the head of the jack, to prevent any damage to the transmission.

14 Remove the battery, as described in Chapter 5A, then disconnect the main starter motor feed cable from the positive battery terminal box.

15 Release any relevant wiring or hoses from the clips on the battery tray, then unscrew the four securing bolts and remove the battery tray.

16 Unscrew the bolts securing the mounting to the transmission, and the remaining bolts securing the mounting to the body, then lift the mounting from the engine compartment.

17 Refitting is a reversal of removal, bearing in mind the following points:
a) Use new mounting bolts.
b) Tighten all fixings to the specified torque.

Rear mounting (torque arm)

Note: *New mounting bolts will be required on refitting.*

18 Apply the handbrake, then jack up the front of the vehicle and support securely on axle stands (see *Jacking and vehicle support*). Remove the engine undershield(s) for access to the rear mounting (torque arm).

19 Support the rear of the transmission beneath the final drive housing. To do this, use a trolley jack and block of wood, or alternatively wedge a block of wood between the transmission and the subframe.

20 Working under the vehicle, unscrew and remove the bolt securing the mounting to the subframe.

21 Unscrew the two bolts securing the mounting to the transmission, then withdraw the mounting from under the vehicle.

22 Refitting is a reversal of removal, but use new mounting securing bolts, and tighten all fixings to the specified torque.

19 Engine oil cooler – removal and refitting

Note: *New sealing rings will be required on refitting.*

Removal

1 The oil cooler is mounted under the oil filter housing on the front of the cylinder block **(see illustration)**. **Note:** *The manufacturers recommend the oil cooler is renewed if considerable quantities of metal swarf have been found in the engine oil during servicing.*
2 Position a container beneath the oil filter/cooler to catch escaping oil and coolant.
3 Clamp the oil cooler coolant hoses to minimise coolant spillage, then remove the clips, and disconnect the hoses from the oil cooler. Be prepared for coolant spillage.
4 Unscrew the oil cooler retaining cap from the bottom of the oil filter housing, then slide off the oil cooler. Recover the O-rings from the top and bottom of the oil cooler.

Refitting

5 Refitting is a reversal of removal, bearing in mind the following points:
a) Use new oil cooler O-rings.
b) Where applicable, press up the oil cooler retaining cap against the anti-twist lock before tightening it to the specified torque. Make sure the coolant hoses are positioned correctly clear of surrounding components.
c) On completion, check and if necessary top-up the oil and coolant levels.

20 Oil pressure warning light switch – removal and refitting

Removal

1 The oil pressure warning light switch is fitted to the right-hand side of the oil filter housing. Remove the engine top cover(s) to gain access to the switch (see Section 4).
2 Disconnect the wiring connector and wipe clean the area around the switch.
3 Unscrew the switch from the filter housing and remove it, along with its sealing washer. If the switch is to be left removed from the engine for any length of time, plug the oil filter housing aperture.

Refitting

4 Examine the sealing washer for signs of damage or deterioration and if necessary renew.
5 Refit the switch, complete with washer, and tighten it to the specified torque.
6 Securely reconnect the wiring connector then check and, if necessary, top-up the engine oil as described in *Weekly checks*. On completion, refit the engine top cover(s).

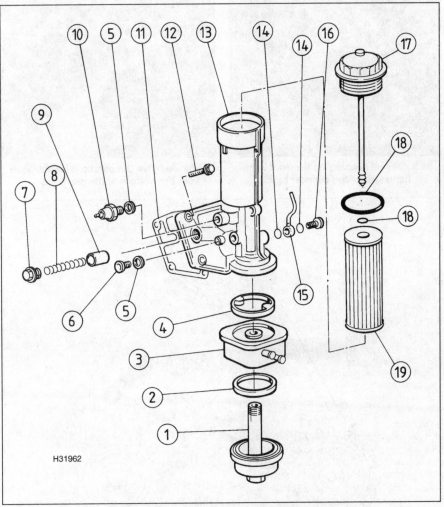

19.1 Oil filter and oil cooler mounting details

1 Oil cooler retaining cap
2 O-ring
3 Oil cooler
4 O-ring
5 Washer
6 Sealing plug
7 Sealing plug
8 Oil pressure relief valve spring (early models only)
9 Oil pressure relief valve piston (early models only)
10 Oil pressure warning light switch
11 Gasket
12 Mounting bolt
13 Oil filter housing
14 Seal
15 Oil supply pipe to turbo
16 Banjo bolt – turbo (or sealing plug – non-turbo models)
17 Oil filter cover
18 O-ring
19 Oil filter

21 Balancer shaft unit (AMF engine) – removal and refitting

Removal

1 Models fitted with the 1.4 litre 3-cylinder engine code AMF are equipped with a balancer unit bolted to the bottom of the crankcase/block. The unit consists of a single counter-rotating balancer shaft driven by the crankshaft **(see illustration overleaf)**.
2 Remove the timing belt as described in Section 7.

3 Remove the crankshaft sprocket as described in Section 8.
4 Remove the sump as described in Section 14.
5 Unscrew the retaining bolts and remove the oil seal housing from the front/right-hand side of the cylinder block **(see illustration)**. If it is stuck, release it by tapping with a soft-faced mallet. If the oil seal is to be re-used, wrap some tape around the end of the crankshaft to protect the oil seal lips.
6 Unscrew the mounting bolts and remove the plastic cover/strainer from the bottom of the crankcase. Recover the O-ring **(see illustrations)**.

21.5 Oil seal housing on the front/right-hand side of the cylinder block

21.6a Remove the plastic cover/strainer from the bottom of the crankcase . . .

21.6b . . . and recover the O-ring seal

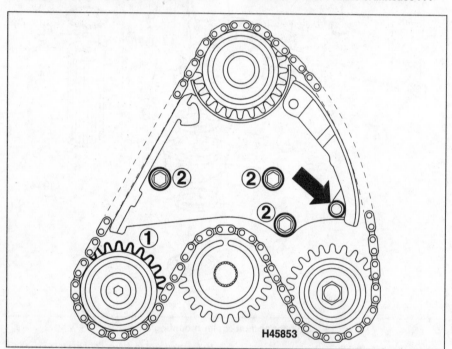

21.7 Tensioner locking bolt (arrowed)

1 Guide sprocket

7 Apply inward pressure on the drive chain, then lock the chain tensioner by fitting and tightening a bolt through the tensioner into the tensioner body **(see illustration)**.

8 Unscrew the bolt and remove the guide sprocket **(see illustration)**. Place the sprocket to one side.

2 Tensioner assembly mounting bolts

9 Unbolt and remove the drive chain tensioner assembly **(see illustration)**. Discard the bolts and obtain new ones.

10 If the chain is to be re-used, mark it with paint to indicate its fitted position and rotational direction.

11 Remove the chain from the sprockets.

12 Lock the balancer shaft by positioning a lever or long spanner between the eccentric weight at the flywheel end, and the crankcase. Loosen only the bolt securing the balancer weight at the timing end.

13 Unbolt the balancer shaft assembly from the crankcase **(see illustration)**. Recover the O-ring seal and the location dowel. Discard the seal and obtain a new one.

14 Fully unscrew the bolt and remove the balancer weight and sprocket from the balancer shaft. Mark the sprocket and weight to ensure correct refitting. Discard the bolt and obtain a new one.

15 Withdraw the balancer shaft from the housing.

Refitting

16 Thoroughly clean all the components and wipe dry. Lubricate the bearing surfaces of the balancer shaft and housing with fresh engine oil.

17 Insert the balancer shaft into the housing, then refit the sprocket and weight, noting that they can only be fitted in one position. Hand-tighten the new retaining bolt at this stage.

18 Make sure the location dowel is in place, then fit a new O-ring seal and offer the assembly to the crankcase. Insert the mounting bolts finger-tight, then check that the timing end of the assembly is correctly aligned with the cylinder block – no movement is possible near the location dowel, however some movement will be possible within the bolt holes by swivelling the assembly. With the assembly located correctly, fully tighten the mounting bolts to their specified torque.

21.8 Guide sprocket

21.9 Drive chain tensioner mounting bolts

21.13 Balance shaft assembly

19 Lock the balancer shaft as for removal, and tighten the new weight/sprocket bolt to the specified torque and angle.

20 Refit the drive chain tensioner housing and tighten the new mounting bolts to the specified torque and angle.

21 With the engine set at TDC, the mark on the crankshaft sprocket will be pointing upwards. The chain has two coloured links which are also notched; position one of these links on the crankshaft sprocket mark, then feed the chain clockwise over the tensioner pad, around the oil pump sprocket and over the balancer shaft sprocket, making sure that the remaining coloured/notched link is aligned with the mark on the sprocket **(see illustration)**.

22 Locate the guide pulley sprocket in the chain, then refit the bolt and tighten it to the specified torque.

23 Unlock the tensioner by unscrewing the retaining bolt, then recheck that the coloured/notched links are still aligned with the marks on the sprockets.

24 Clean all traces of old sealant from the crankshaft oil seal housing and the cylinder block, then coat the cylinder block mating faces of the oil seal housing with a 2.0 to 3.0 mm thick bead of sealant (Skoda D 176 404 A2, or equivalent). Note that the seal housing must be refitted within 5 minutes of applying the sealant. *Caution: DO NOT put excessive amounts of sealant onto the housing as it may get into the sump and block the oil pick-up pipe.*

25 Refit the oil seal housing, taking care not to damage the seal and tighten the bolts progressively to the specified torque. If a new seal is to be fitted, refer to Section 17.

26 Refit the sump as described in Section 14.

21.21 Coloured alignment links (arrowed

27 Refit the crankshaft sprocket as described in Section 8.

28 Refit the timing belt as described in Section 7.

Chapter 2 Part E:
Engine removal and overhaul procedures

Contents

Section number

Camshaft and hydraulic tappets (1.4 litre OHV engine) – removal and refitting 9
Crankshaft – checking endfloat and inspection.................... 14
Crankshaft – refitting and main bearing clearance check 18
Crankshaft – removal 11
Cylinder block/crankcase – cleaning and inspection............. 12
Cylinder head – dismantling.. 6
Cylinder head – reassembly.. 8
Cylinder head and valves – cleaning and inspection 7
Engine – initial start-up after overhaul and reassembly 20
Engine and transmission – removal and refitting 4

Section number

Engine overhaul – general information................................. 2
Engine overhaul – preliminary information 5
Engine overhaul – reassembly sequence............................ 16
Engine/transmission removal – preparation and precautions 3
General information 1
Main and big-end bearings – inspection 15
Piston rings – refitting.. 17
Piston/connecting rod assemblies – cleaning and inspection...... 13
Piston/connecting rod assemblies – refitting and big-end bearing clearance check 19
Piston/connecting rod assemblies – removal........................ 10

Degrees of difficulty

Easy, suitable for novice with little experience	Fairly easy, suitable for beginner with some experience	Fairly difficult, suitable for competent DIY mechanic	Difficult, suitable for experienced DIY mechanic	Very difficult, suitable for expert DIY or professional

Specifications

Cylinder head

Minimum permissible dimension between top of valve stem and top surface of cylinder head:

Petrol engines:	
1.2 litre engines:	
Engine code AWY	N/A
Engine codes AZQ and BME	7.6 mm
1.4 litre DOHC engines:	
Inlet valves	7.6 mm
Exhaust valves	7.6 mm
Diesel engines:	
1.4 litre engines	N/A
1.9 litre engines:	
Engine code ASY:	
Inlet valves	35.8 mm
Exhaust valves	36.1 mm
Engine codes ASZ and ATD:	
Inlet valves	43.4 mm
Exhaust valves	43.2 mm

Maximum permissible dimension between top of valve stem and valve spring seat surface:

1.4 litre OHV petrol engines:	
Inlet valves	42.7 mm
Exhaust valves	42.8 mm

Minimum cylinder head height:

Petrol engines:	
1.2 litre engines	N/A
1.4 OHV engines	N/A
1.4 litre DOHC engines	108.25 mm
Diesel engines	No reworking permitted

Maximum cylinder head gasket face distortion:

Petrol engines	0.05 mm
Diesel engines	0.10 mm

Pistons/connecting rods

See Note in Section 2 about all 1.2 litre engines

Connecting rod side-play on crankshaft journal:

	New	Wear limit
Petrol engines:		
1.4 litre OHV engines	N/A	N/A
1.4 litre DOHC engines	0.10 to 0.35 mm	0.40 mm
Diesel engines	N/A	0.37 mm

Piston rings

See Note in Section 2 about all 1.2 litre engines

End gaps:	New	Wear limit
Petrol engines:		
1.4 litre OHV engines:		
Top compression ring	0.40 to 0.72 mm	1.0 mm
Lower compression ring	0.30 to 0.62 mm	1.0 mm
Oil scraper ring	0.40 to 1.40 mm	N/A
1.4 litre DOHC engines:		
Top compression ring	0.20 to 0.50 mm	1.0 mm
Lower compression ring	0.40 to 0.70 mm	1.0 mm
Oil scraper ring	0.40 to 1.40 mm	N/A
Diesel engines:		
1.4 litre engines:		
Top compression ring	0.25 to 0.40 mm	1.0 mm
Lower compression ring	0.20 to 0.40 mm	1.0 mm
Oil scraper ring	0.25 to 0.50 mm	1.0 mm
1.9 litre engines:		
Compression rings	0.20 to 0.40 mm	1.0 mm
Oil scraper ring	0.25 to 0.50 mm	1.0 mm
Ring-to-groove clearance:		
Petrol engines:		
1.4 litre OHV engines:		
Compression rings	0.04 to 0.08 mm	0.15 mm
Oil scraper ring	N/A	N/A
1.4 litre DOHC engines:		
Compression rings	0.04 to 0.08 mm	0.15 mm
Oil scraper ring	N/A	N/A
Diesel engines:		
1st compression ring	0.06 to 0.09 mm	0.25 mm
2nd compression ring	0.05 to 0.08 mm	0.25 mm
Oil scraper ring	0.03 to 0.06 mm	0.15 mm

Piston and cylinder bore diameters

See Note in Section 2 about all 1.2 litre engines

	Piston	Cylinder bore
Petrol engines:		
1.4 litre OHV engines	N/A	N/A
1.4 litre DOHC engines:		
Standard	76.470 mm	76.510 mm
1st oversize	76.720 mm	76.760 mm
2nd oversize	76.970 mm	77.010 mm
Diesel engines:		
Standard	79.470 mm	79.510 mm
1st oversize	79.720 mm	79.760 mm
2nd oversize	79.970 mm	80.010 mm

Crankshaft

See Note in Section 2 about all 1.2 litre engines and 1.4 litre DOHC engines

Petrol engines:
  1.4 litre OHV engines:
    Endfloat:
      New . . . . 0.03 to 0.13 mm
      Wear limit . . . . 0.26 mm
Diesel engines:
  Main journal diameter:
    Basic dimension . . . . 54.00 mm (Nominal)
  Big-end journal diameter:
    Basic dimension . . . . 47.80 mm (Nominal)
  Endfloat:
    New . . . . 0.07 to 0.17 mm
    Wear limit . . . . 0.37 mm

Bearing running clearances:	New	Wear limit
Petrol engines:		
1.4 OHV petrol engines	N/A	N/A
Diesel engines:		
Main bearings	0.07 to 0.17 mm	0.37 mm
Big-end bearings	0.08 mm	0.37 mm

Cylinder liners (1.4 litre OHV petrol engine)

Cylinder liner diameter:
Standard – class A . . . . 75.500 mm nominal
Standard – class B . . . . 75.510 mm nominal
Standard – class C . . . . 75.520 mm nominal
Tolerance on nominal diameter . . . . + 0.009 mm / - 0 mm
Cylinder liner protrusion above cylinder block surface:
Standard . . . . 0.07 to 0.12 mm
Maximum difference between any two liners . . . . 0.04 mm

Valves

	Inlet valves	Exhaust valves
Valve stem diameter:		
Petrol engines:		
1.2 litre engines:		
Engine code AWY.	5.98 mm	5.96 mm
Engine codes AZQ and BME	5.973 mm	5.953 mm
1.4 litre OHV engines.	7.0 mm	7.0 mm
1.4 litre DOHC engines.	5.973 mm	5.953 mm
Diesel engines:		
1.4 litre engines.	6.980 mm	6.956 mm
1.9 litre engines:		
Engine code ASY	6.963 mm	6.943 mm
Engine codes ASZ and ATD	6.980 mm	6.956 mm
Valve head diameter:		
Petrol engines:		
1.2 litre engines:		
Engine code AWY.	34.5 mm	28.0 mm
Engine codes AZQ and BME	29.5 mm	26.0 mm
1.4 litre OHV engines	34.0 mm	30.0 mm
1.4 litre DOHC engines.	29.5 mm	26.0 mm
Diesel engines	35.95 mm	31.45 mm
Valve length:		
Petrol engines:		
1.2 litre engines:		
Engine code AWY.	99.25 mm	99.25 mm
Engine codes AZQ and BME	100.9 mm	100.57 mm
1.4 litre OHV engines	101.0 mm	101.0 mm
1.4 litre DOHC engines.	100.9 mm	100.5 mm
Diesel engines:		
1.4 litre engines.	89.95 mm	89.95 mm
1.9 litre engines:		
Engine code ASY	96.55 mm	96.35 mm
Engine codes ASZ and ATD	89.95 mm	89.95 mm
Valve seat angle (all engines)	45°	45°

Camshaft (1.4 litre OHV petrol engines)

Camshaft endfloat . . . . 0.020 to 0.066 mm
Camshaft journal diameter:
Pulley end. . . . . 38.950 to 38.975 mm
Middle. . . . . 38.450 to 38.475 mm
Flywheel end. . . . . 29.959 to 29.980 mm
Camshaft bearing internal diameter:
Pulley end. . . . . 39.000 to 39.025 mm
Middle. . . . . 38.500 to 38.525 mm
Flywheel end. . . . . 30.000 to 30.021 mm
Camshaft bearing running clearance . . . . 0.025 to 0.075 mm
Camshaft endfloat . . . . 0.020 to 0.066 mm
Hydraulic tappet outer diameter:
Standard. . . . . 20.980 to 21.000 mm
Oversize . . . . 21.193 to 21.200 mm
Hydraulic tappet bore internal diameter:
Standard. . . . . 21.000 to 21.021 mm
Oversize . . . . 21.200 to 21.221 mm

Torque wrench settings

Refer to Chapter 2A, 2B, 2C or 2D as applicable.

1 General information

Included in this Part of Chapter 2 are details of removing the engine from the car and general overhaul procedures for the cylinder head, cylinder block and all other engine internal components.

The information given ranges from advice concerning preparation for an overhaul and the purchase of new parts, to detailed step-by-step procedures covering removal, inspection, renovation and refitting of engine internal components.

After Section 6, all instructions are based on the assumption that the engine has been removed from the car. For information concerning in-car engine repair, as well as the removal and refitting of those external components necessary for full overhaul, refer to the relevant in-car repair procedure section (Chapters 2A, 2B, 2C and 2D) and to Section 6 of this Chapter. Ignore any preliminary dismantling operations described in the relevant in-car repair sections that are no longer relevant once the engine has been removed from the car.

Apart from torque wrench settings, which are given at the beginning of the relevant in-car repair procedure in Chapters 2A, 2B, 2C or 2D, all specifications relating to engine overhaul are given at the beginning of this part of Chapter 2.

2 Engine overhaul – general information

Note: *On all 1.2 litre petrol engines and 1.4 litre DOHC petrol engines the crankshaft must not be removed. Loosening the main bearing cap bolts will cause deformation of the cylinder block. If the crankshaft or main bearing surfaces are worn or damaged, the complete crankshaft/ cylinder block assembly must be renewed. Furthermore, the pistons and connecting rods must not be removed on 1.2 litre engines, although they can be removed on the 1.4 litre DOHC petrol engine.*

1 It is not always easy to determine when, or if, an engine should be completely overhauled, as a number of factors must be considered.
2 High mileage is not necessarily an indication that an overhaul is needed, while low mileage does not preclude the need for an overhaul. Frequency of servicing is probably the most important consideration. An engine which has had regular and frequent oil and filter changes, as well as other required maintenance, should give many thousands of miles of reliable service. Conversely, a neglected engine may require an overhaul very early in its life.
3 Excessive oil consumption is an indication that piston rings, valve seals and/or valve guides are in need of attention. Make sure that

oil leaks are not responsible before deciding that the rings and/or guides are worn. Perform a compression (or leakdown) test, as described in Part A, B, C or D of this Chapter (as applicable), to determine the likely cause of the problem.
4 Check the oil pressure with a gauge fitted in place of the oil pressure switch, and compare it with that specified (see Specifications in Chapters 2A, 2B, 2C and 2D). If it is extremely low, the main and big-end bearings, and/or the oil pump, are probably worn.
5 Loss of power, rough running, knocking or metallic engine noises, excessive valve gear noise, and high fuel consumption may also point to the need for an overhaul, especially if they are all present at the same time. If a complete service does not remedy the situation, major mechanical work is the only solution.
6 An engine overhaul involves restoring all internal parts to the specification of a new engine. During an overhaul, the pistons and the piston rings are renewed. New main and big-end bearings are generally fitted (where possible); if necessary, the crankshaft may be renewed to restore the journals. The valves are also serviced as well, since they are usually in less-than-perfect condition at this point. While the engine is being overhauled, other components, such as the starter and alternator, can be overhauled as well. The end result should be an as-new engine that will give many trouble-free miles. **Note:** *Critical cooling system components such as the hoses, thermostat and coolant pump should be renewed when an engine is overhauled. The radiator should be checked carefully, to ensure that it is not clogged or leaking. Also, it is a good idea to renew the oil pump whenever the engine is overhauled.*
7 Before beginning the engine overhaul, read through the entire procedure, to familiarise yourself with the scope and requirements of the job. Overhauling an engine is not difficult if you follow carefully all of the instructions, have the necessary tools and equipment, and pay close attention to all specifications. It can, however, be time-consuming. Plan on the car being off the road for a minimum of two weeks, especially if parts must be taken to an engineering works for repair or reconditioning. Check on the availability of parts and make sure that any necessary special tools and equipment are obtained in advance. Most work can be done with typical hand tools, although a number of precision measuring tools are required for inspecting parts to determine if they must be renewed. Often an engineering works will handle the inspection of parts and offer advice concerning reconditioning and renewal. **Note:** *Always wait until the engine has been completely dismantled, and until all components (especially the cylinder block and the crankshaft) have been inspected, before deciding what service and repair operations must be performed by an engineering works. The condition of these components will be*

the major factor to consider when determining whether to overhaul the original engine, or to buy a reconditioned unit. Do not, therefore, purchase parts or have overhaul work done on other components until they have been thoroughly inspected. As a general rule, time is the primary cost of an overhaul, so it does not pay to fit worn or sub-standard parts.
8 As a final note, to ensure maximum life and minimum trouble from a reconditioned engine, everything must be assembled with care, in a spotlessly-clean environment.

3 Engine/transmission removal – preparation and precautions

If you have decided that the engine must be removed for overhaul or major repair work, several preliminary steps should be taken.

Locating a suitable place to work is extremely important. Adequate work space, along with storage space for the vehicle, will be needed. If a workshop or garage is not available, at the very least a solid, level, clean work surface is required.

If possible, clear some shelving close to the work area and use it to store the engine components and ancillaries as they are removed and dismantled. In this manner, the components stand a better chance of staying clean and undamaged during the overhaul. Laying out components in groups, together with their fixings bolts, screws, etc, will save time and avoid confusion when the engine is refitted.

Clean the engine compartment and engine before beginning the removal procedure; this will help visibility and help to keep tools clean.

The help of an assistant is essential; there are certain instances when one person cannot safely perform all of the operations required to remove the engine from the vehicle. Safety is of primary importance, considering the potential hazards involved in this kind of operation. A second person should always be in attendance to offer help in an emergency. If this is the first time you have removed an engine, advice and aid from someone more experienced would also be beneficial.

Plan the operation ahead of time. Before starting work, obtain (or arrange for the hire of) all of the tools and equipment you will need. Access to the following items will allow the task of removing and refitting the engine to be completed safely and with relative ease: a hoist and lifting tackle – rated in excess of the weight of the engine, complete sets of spanners and sockets as described at the rear of this manual, wooden blocks, and plenty of rags and cleaning solvent for mopping-up spilled oil, coolant and fuel. A selection of different-sized plastic storage bins will also prove useful for keeping dismantled components grouped together. If any of the equipment must be hired, make sure that you arrange for it in advance, and perform all of the operations possible without it beforehand; this may save you time and money.

Plan on the vehicle being out of use for quite a while, especially if you intend to carry out an engine overhaul. Read through the whole of this Section and work out a strategy based on your own experience, and the tools, time and workspace available to you. Some of the overhaul processes may have to be carried out by a Skoda dealer or an engineering works – these establishments often have busy schedules, so it would be prudent to consult them before removing or dismantling the engine, to get an idea of the amount of time required to carry out the work.

When removing the engine from the vehicle, be methodical about the disconnection of external components. Labelling cables and hoses as they are removed will greatly assist the refitting process.

Always be extremely careful when lifting the engine from the engine compartment. Serious injury can result from careless actions. If help is required, it is better to wait until it is available rather than risk personal injury and/or damage to components by continuing alone. By planning ahead and taking your time, a job of this nature, although major, can be accomplished successfully and without incident.

4 Engine and transmission – removal and refitting

Note: *At the time of writing, no information was available for the diesel engine code ASZ fitted to vRS models.*

Removal

1 All petrol engines are removed from the front of the car, after first moving the lock carrier assembly to one side, or removed completely on models without air conditioning.
2 All diesel engines, with the exception of engine code ASY, are removed together with the transmission from the front of the car. On engine code ASY, the engine is removed together with the transmission by lowering downwards from the engine compartment.
3 Disconnect the battery negative lead (refer to *Disconnecting the battery* in the *Reference* Chapter at the end of this manual).
4 Remove the engine top cover, then remove the air cleaner and air ducting with reference to Chapter 4A or 4B.
5 Remove the battery as described in Chapter 5A, then remove the battery tray **(see illustrations)**.
6 Drain the cooling system as described in Chapter 1A or 1B.
7 Apply the handbrake, then jack up the front of the vehicle and support securely on axle stands (see *Jacking and vehicle support*) and remove the engine lower cover. Note that on diesel engine code ASY, the vehicle must be

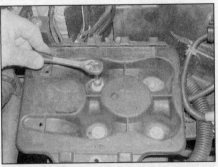

4.5a Unscrew the four securing bolts . . .

raised to give sufficient clearance to allow removal of the engine/transmission assembly from underneath the vehicle.
8 Disconnect all coolant hoses from the engine making a note of their position **(see illustration)**.
9 Disconnect the wiring from the engine and transmission, noting its location and routing to aid refitting. Note that some of the wiring can remain attached to the engine.
10 On manual transmission models, disconnect the gearchange mechanism from the transmission (Chapter 7A), then unbolt the clutch slave cylinder and position it to one side.
11 On automatic transmission models, disconnect the selector cable from the transmission (Chapter 7B), then unbolt the bracket for the pressure line of the power steering.
12 On petrol models, depressurise the fuel system as described in Chapter 4A. Place a wad of clean cloth around the fuel supply and return hose connections on the right-hand side of the engine compartment, then depress the connector locking tabs, and disconnect the fuel line connectors. Be prepared for fuel spillage, and take adequate fire precautions.
13 On diesel models, disconnect the fuel hoses from the injection pump (engine code ASY) or fuel filter (engine codes AMF, ASZ and ATD). Be prepared for fuel spillage, and plug the open ends of the hoses and connections to prevent dirt entry and further fuel loss.
14 Disconnect the following vacuum hoses:
 a) *Charcoal canister solenoid valve (petrol models only).*
 b) *EGR valve.*
 c) *Brake servo hose on the inlet manifold.*

4.8 Disconnecting the radiator top hose from the thermostat housing

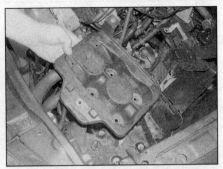

4.5b . . . and remove the battery tray

Except diesel engine code ASY

15 On models without air conditioning, carry out the following:
 a) *Remove the front bumper and bracket with reference to Chapter 11.*
 b) *Disconnect and detach the bonnet lock cable from the lock carrier.*
 c) *Disconnect the headlight wiring. To prevent damage to it, we also recommend removal of the right-hand headlight completely.*
 d) *Unbolt the lock carrier and radiator and remove from the front of the car.*
16 On models with air conditioning, carry out the following:
 a) *Remove the auxiliary drivebelt as described in Chapter 1A or 1B.*
 b) *Disconnect the wiring from the air conditioning compressor, then unbolt it and tie it to the lock carrier. Do not disconnect the refrigerant lines.*
 c) *Remove the front bumper and bracket with reference to Chapter 11.*
 d) *Disconnect and detach the bonnet lock cable from the lock carrier.*
 e) *Disconnect the headlight wiring. To prevent damage to it, we also recommend removal of the right-hand headlight completely.*
 f) *Unbolt the lock carrier and swivel it out from the front of the car, leaving the air conditioning lines still attached. Support the assembly on axle stands or blocks of wood.*

Diesel engine code ASY

17 Remove the auxiliary drivebelt as described in Chapter 1B.
18 Remove the alternator as described in Chapter 5A.
19 On models with air conditioning, disconnect the wiring from the air conditioning compressor, then unbolt it and tie it to the lock carrier, leaving sufficient room for the engine to be lowered. **Do not** disconnect the refrigerant lines.

All models

20 Remove the rear engine mounting/link with reference to the relevant part of Chapter 2.
21 Remove the right-hand driveshaft as described in Chapter 8, and disconnect the left-hand driveshaft from the transmission.

22 Remove the exhaust front section as described in Chapter 4C.
23 Connect a hoist and lifting tackle to the engine lifting brackets on the cylinder head, and raise the hoist to just take the weight of the engine.
24 Remove the right-hand and left-hand engine/transmission mountings, with reference to the relevant part of Chapter 2.
25 On all models except diesel engine code ASY, carefully lift the engine/transmission assembly from the engine compartment until it can be withdrawn from the front of the car **(see illustration)**. On diesel engine code ASY, carefully lower the engine and transmission assembly to the ground taking care not to damage the surrounding bodywork or components. If necessary, detach the transmission with reference to Chapter 7A or 7B.

Refitting

26 Refitting is a reversal of removal, bearing in mind the following points:
 a) *Ensure that any brackets noted before removal are in place on the engine-to-transmission bolts.*
 b) *Tighten all fixings to the specified torque, where given.*
 c) *Refit the engine mountings with reference to Chapter 2A, 2B, 2C or 2D.*
 d) *Reconnect the driveshafts to the transmission with reference to Chapter 8.*
 e) *Check that all wiring, hoses and pipes are correctly reconnected and routed as noted before removal.*
 f) *Ensure that the fuel lines are correctly reconnected. The lines are colour-coded, white for supply, and blue for return.*
 g) *On completion, refill the cooling system as described in Chapter 1A or 1B. On models with automatic transmission, check and if necessary top-up the automatic transmission fluid level as described in Chapter 1A.*
 h) *Have the engine management system checked for fault codes by a Skoda dealer.*

5	Engine overhaul – preliminary information

1 It is much easier to dismantle and work on the engine if it is mounted on a portable engine stand. These stands can often be hired from a tool hire shop. Before the engine is mounted on a stand, the flywheel should be removed, so that the stand bolts can be tightened into the end of the cylinder block/crankcase. **Note:** *Do not measure cylinder bore dimensions with the engine mounted on this type of stand.*
2 If a stand is not available, it is possible to dismantle the engine with it blocked up on a sturdy workbench, or on the floor. Be very careful not to tip or drop the engine when working without a stand.

4.25 Removing the engine/transmission assembly – diesel engine code AMF

3 If you intend to obtain a reconditioned engine, all ancillaries must be removed first, to be transferred to the new engine (just as they will if you are doing a complete engine overhaul yourself). These components include the following (it may be necessary to transfer additional components, such as the oil level dipstick/tube assembly, oil filter housing, etc, depending on which components are supplied with the reconditioned engine):

Petrol engines

 a) *Alternator (including mounting brackets) and starter motor (Chapter 5A).*
 b) *The ignition system components including all sensors and spark plugs (Chapters 1A and 5B).*
 c) *The fuel injection system components (Chapter 4A).*
 d) *All electrical switches, actuators and sensors, and the engine wiring harness (Chapters 3, 4A and 5B).*
 e) *Inlet and exhaust manifolds (Chapter 4C).*
 f) *Engine mountings (Chaptesr 2A, 2B or 2C).*
 g) *Clutch components (Chapter 6).*
 h) *Oil separator (where applicable).*

Diesel engines

 a) *Alternator (including mounting brackets) and starter motor (Chapter 5A).*
 b) *The glow plug/preheating system components (Chapter 5C).*
 c) *All fuel system components, including the fuel injection pump (engine code ASY), fuel injectors, all sensors and actuators (Chapter 4B).*
 d) *The brake vacuum/tandem pump (Chapter 9).*
 e) *All electrical switches, actuators and sensors, and the engine wiring harness (Chapters 3, 4B and 5C).*
 f) *Inlet and exhaust manifolds, and turbocharger (except engine code ASY) (Chapters 4B and 4C).*
 g) *Engine mountings (Chapter 2B).*
 h) *Clutch components (Chapter 6).*

All engines

Note: *When removing the external components from the engine, pay close attention to details that may be helpful or important during refitting. Note the fitted position of gaskets,*

seals, spacers, pins, washers, bolts, and other small components.

4 If you are obtaining a short engine (the engine cylinder block/crankcase, crankshaft, pistons and connecting rods, all fully assembled), then the cylinder head, sump, oil pump, timing belt(s) and chain (as applicable – together with tensioner(s) and covers), auxiliary drivebelt (together with its tensioner), coolant pump, thermostat housing, coolant outlet elbows, oil filter housing and where applicable oil cooler will also have to be removed.
5 If you are planning a full overhaul, the engine can be dismantled in the order given below:
 a) *Inlet and exhaust manifolds (see the relevant parts of Chapter 4).*
 b) *Timing chain/belt(s), sprockets and tensioner(s) (see Chapter 2A, 2B, 2C or 2D).*
 c) *Cylinder head (see Chapter 2A, 2B, 2C or 2D).*
 d) *Flywheel/driveplate (see Chapter 2A, 2B, 2C or 2D).*
 e) *Sump (see Chapter 2A, 2B, 2C or 2D).*
 f) *Oil pump (see Chapter 2A, 2B, 2C or 2D).*
 g) *Camshaft on 1.4 litre OHV petrol engine.*
 h) *Piston/connecting rod assemblies (see Section 10).*
 i) *Crankshaft (see Section 11).*

6	Cylinder head – dismantling	

Note: *A valve spring compressor tool will be required for this operation.*

Petrol engines

1 With the cylinder head removed as described in the relevant part of Chapter 2, proceed as follows.
2 Remove the inlet and exhaust manifolds as described in Chapter 4A, 4B or 4C.
3 On all engines except the 1.4 litre OHV petrol engine, remove the camshaft and hydraulic tappets/roller rocker fingers as described in Chapter 2A or 2C.
4 If desired, unbolt the coolant housing from the rear of the cylinder head, and recover the seal.
5 Where applicable, remove the camshaft position sensor, with reference to Chapter 4A, Section 4.
6 Where applicable, unscrew the securing nut, and recover the washer, and remove the timing belt tensioner pulley from the stud on the cylinder head.
7 Unbolt any remaining auxiliary brackets and/or engine lifting brackets from the cylinder head as necessary, noting their locations to aid refitting. Where applicable, unscrew the securing bolt and remove the secondary timing belt tensioner from the timing belt end of the cylinder head.
8 Turn the cylinder head over, and rest it on one side.
9 Using a valve spring compressor, compress each valve spring in turn, until the split collets

6.9a Compressing a valve spring with a compressor tool

6.9b Removing the spring cap . . .

6.9c . . . and valve spring

6.10a Using a removal tool . . .

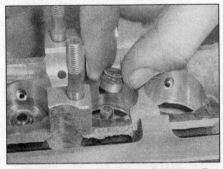

6.10b . . . to remove the valve stem oil seals

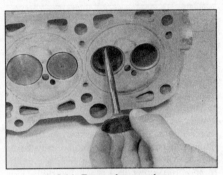

6.11 Removing a valve

can be removed. Release the compressor, and lift off the spring cap and spring. If, when the valve spring compressor is screwed down, the spring cap refuses to free and expose the split collets, gently tap the top of the tool, directly over the spring cap, with a light hammer. This will free the retainer (see illustrations).

10 Using a pair of pliers, or a removal tool, carefully extract the valve stem oil seal from the top of the valve guide (see illustrations).

11 Withdraw the valve from the gasket side of the cylinder head (see illustration).

12 It is essential that each valve is stored together with its collets, cap, spring and spring seat. The valves should be kept in their correct sequences, unless they are so badly worn that they are to be renewed.

> **HAYNES HINT** If they are going to be kept and used again, place each valve assembly in a labelled polythene bag or similar small container. Label each bag, noting that No 1 valve is nearest to the timing belt/chain end of the cylinder head.

Diesel engines

13 With the cylinder head removed as described in Chapter 2D, proceed as follows.

14 Remove the inlet and exhaust manifolds (and turbocharger, where applicable) as described in Chapters 4B and 4C.

15 Remove the camshaft and hydraulic tappets, as described in Chapter 2D.

16 Remove the glow plugs, with reference to Chapter 5C.

17 Remove the fuel injectors, with reference to Chapter 4B.

18 Unscrew the nut and remove the timing belt tensioner pulley from the stud on the timing belt end of the cylinder head.

19 Unbolt any remaining auxiliary brackets and/or engine lifting brackets from the cylinder head as necessary, noting their locations to aid refitting.

20 Proceed as described in paragraphs 8 to 12.

7 Cylinder head and valves – cleaning and inspection

1 Thorough cleaning of the cylinder head and valve components, followed by a detailed inspection, will enable you to decide how much valve service work must be carried out during engine overhaul. **Note:** *If the engine has been severely overheated, it is best to assume that the cylinder head is warped – check carefully for signs of this.*

Cleaning

2 Using a suitable degreasing agent, remove all traces of oil deposits from the cylinder head, paying particular attention to the camshaft bearing surfaces, hydraulic tappet bores, valve guides and oilways. Scrape off any traces of old gasket from the mating surfaces, taking care not to score or gouge them. If using emery paper, do not use a grade of less than 100. Turn the head over and, using a blunt blade, scrape any carbon deposits from

the combustion chambers and ports. Finally, wash the entire head casting with a suitable solvent to remove the remaining debris.

3 Clean the valve heads and stems using a fine wire brush (or a power-operated wire brush). If the valve is covered with heavy carbon deposits, scrape off the majority of the deposits with a blunt blade first, then use the wire brush.

4 Thoroughly clean the remainder of the components using solvent and allow them to dry completely. Discard the oil seals, as new ones must be fitted when the cylinder head is reassembled.

Inspection

Cylinder head

Note: *If the valve seats are to be recut, ensure that the maximum permissible reworking dimension is not exceeded (the maximum dimension will only allow minimal reworking to produce a perfect seal between valve and seat). If the maximum dimension is exceeded, the function of the hydraulic tappets cannot be guaranteed, and the cylinder head must be renewed. Refer to paragraph 6 for details of how to calculate the maximum permissible reworking dimension.*

5 Examine the head casting closely to identify any damage or cracks that may have developed. Cracks can often be identified from evidence of coolant or oil leakage. Pay particular attention to the areas around the valve seats and spark plug/fuel injector holes. If cracking is discovered in this area, Skoda state that, on diesel engines, the cylinder

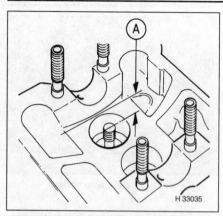

7.6 Measure the distance (A) between the top face of the valve stem and the top surface of the cylinder head

head may be re-used, provided the cracks are no larger than 0.5 mm wide. More serious damage will mean the renewal of the cylinder head casting.

6 Moderately pitted and scorched valve seats can be repaired by lapping the valves in during reassembly, as described later in this Chapter. Badly worn or damaged valve seats may be restored by recutting, however the maximum permissible reworking dimension **must** not be exceeded, which will only allow minimal reworking (see note at beginning of paragraph 5). To calculate the maximum permissible reworking dimension, proceed as follows **(see illustration)**:

a) If a new valve is to be fitted, use the new valve for the following calculation.

7.7 Measuring the distortion of the cylinder head gasket surface

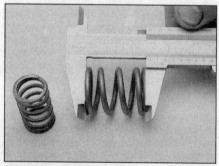

7.13 Measure the free length of each valve spring

b) Insert the valve into its guide in the cylinder head, and push the valve firmly on to its seat.

c) Measure the distance between the top face of the valve stem, and either the top surface of the cylinder head or spring seat surface (as applicable). Record the measurement obtained.

d) Consult the Specifications, and compare the measured distance with that given in the Specifications.

7 Measure any distortion of the gasket surfaces using a straight-edge and a set of feeler blades. Take one measurement longitudinally on the manifold mating surface(s). Take several measurements across the head gasket surface, to assess the level of distortion in all planes **(see illustration)**. Compare the measurements with the figures in the Specifications.

8 On petrol engines, if the head is distorted beyond the specified limit, it may be possible to have it machined by an engineering works, provided that the minimum permissible cylinder head height is maintained.

9 On diesel engines, if the head is distorted beyond the specified limit, the head must be renewed.

Valves and associated components

Note: *On all engines, the valve heads cannot be recut, although they may be lapped in.*

10 Examine each valve closely for signs of wear. Inspect the valve stems for wear ridges, scoring or variations in diameter; measure their diameters at several points along their lengths with a micrometer, and compare with

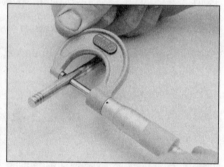

7.10 Measure the diameter of the valve stems using a micrometer

7.14 Checking the squareness of a valve spring

the figures given in the Specifications **(see illustration)**.

11 The valve heads should not be cracked, badly pitted or charred. Note that light pitting of the valve head can be rectified by lapping-in the valves during reassembly, as described in Section 8.

12 Check that the valve stem end face is free from excessive pitting or indentation; this could be caused by defective hydraulic tappets.

13 Using vernier calipers, measure the free length of each of the valve springs. As a manufacturer's figure is not quoted, the only way to check the length of the springs is by comparison with a new component. Note that valve springs are usually renewed during a major engine overhaul **(see illustration)**.

14 Stand each spring on its end on a flat surface, against an engineer's square **(see illustration)**. Check the squareness of the spring visually, and renew it if it appears distorted.

15 Renew the valve stem oil seals regardless of their apparent condition.

8 Cylinder head – reassembly
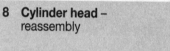

Note: *A valve spring compressor tool will be required for this operation.*

1 To achieve a gas-tight seal between the valves and their seats, it will be necessary to lap-in (or grind-in) the valves. To complete this process you will need a quantity of fine/coarse grinding paste and a grinding tool – this can either be of the rubber sucker type, or the automatic type which is driven by a rotary power tool.

2 Smear a small quantity of *fine* grinding paste on the sealing face of the valve head. Turn the cylinder head over so that the combustion chambers are facing upwards and insert the valve into the correct guide. Attach the grinding tool to the valve head and using a backward/forward rotary action, grind the valve head into its seat. Periodically lift the valve and rotate it to redistribute the grinding paste **(see illustration)**.

3 Continue this process until the contact

8.2 Grinding-in a valve

between valve and seat produces an unbroken, matt grey ring of uniform width, on both faces. Repeat the operation on the remaining valves.

4 If the valves and seats are so badly pitted that coarse grinding paste must be used, bear in that there is a maximum permissible reworking dimension for the valves and seats. Refer to the Specifications at the beginning of this Chapter for the limits, and note that if exceeded due to excessive lapping-in, the hydraulic tappets may not operate correctly, and the cylinder head must be renewed.

5 Assuming the repair is feasible, work as described previously, but use coarse grinding paste initially, to achieve a dull finish on the valve face and seat. Wash off the coarse paste with solvent and repeat the process using fine grinding paste to obtain the correct finish.

6 When all the valves have been ground in, remove all traces of grinding paste from the cylinder head and valves using solvent, and allow the head and valves to dry completely.

7 Turn the cylinder head on its side.

8 Working on one valve at a time, lubricate the valve stem with clean engine oil, and insert the valve into its guide. Fit one of the protective plastic sleeves supplied with the new valve stem oil seals over the end of the valve stem – this will protect the oil seal as it is being fitted (see illustrations).

9 Dip a new valve stem seal in clean engine oil, and carefully push it over the valve stem and onto the top of the valve guide – take care not to damage the stem seal as it is fitted. Use a suitable long-reach socket or a suitable valve stem seal fitting tool to press the seal firmly into position (see illustration). Remove the protective sleeve from the valve stem.

10 Locate the valve spring over the valve stem, ensuring that the lower end of the spring seats correctly on the cylinder head (see illustration).

11 Fit the upper spring seat over the top of the spring then, using a valve spring compressor, compress the spring until the upper seat is pushed beyond the collet grooves in the valve stem. Refit the split collets. Gradually release the spring compressor, checking that the collets remain correctly seated as the spring extends. When correctly seated, the upper spring seat should force the collets securely

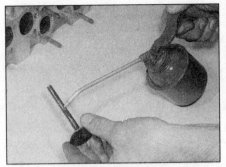
8.8a Lubricate the valve stem with clean engine oil

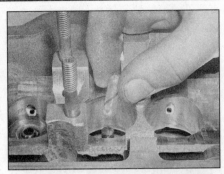
8.8b Fitting a protective sleeve over the valve stem before fitting the stem seal

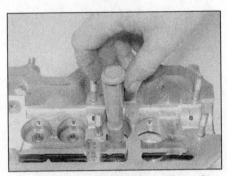
8.9 Using a special installer to fit a valve stem oil seal

8.10 Fitting a valve spring

into the grooves in the end of the valve stem (see illustrations).

HAYNES HINT Use a little dab of grease to hold the collets in position on the valve stem while the spring compressor is released.

12 Repeat this process for the remaining sets of valve components, ensuring that all components are refitted to their original locations. To settle the components after installation, strike the end of each valve stem with a mallet, using a block of wood to protect the stem from damage. Check before progressing any further that the split collets remain firmly seated in the grooves in the end of the valve stem.

Petrol engines

13 Refit the brackets previously removed,

and also where applicable refit the secondary timing belt tensioner.

14 Where applicable, refit the timing belt tensioner pulley on the stud, and loosely refit the securing nut and washer.

15 Where applicable, refit the camshaft position sensor, with reference to Chapter 4A.

16 If removed, refit the coolant housing to the cylinder head, together with a new seal, and tighten the mounting bolts.

17 On all engines except the 1.4 litre OHV petrol engine, refit the camshaft and hydraulic tappets/roller rocker fingers with reference to Chapter 2A or 2C.

18 Refit the inlet and exhaust manifolds with reference to Chapter 4A and 4C.

Diesel engines

19 Refit the brackets previously removed, then refit the timing belt tensioner pulley on the stud, and loosely refit the securing nut and washer.

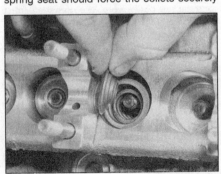
8.11a Fitting the upper spring seat

8.11b Use grease to hold the split collets in the groove

8.11c Compressing a valve spring using a compressor tool – 1.4 litre DOHC engine

9.3 Store the hydraulic tappets in a partitioned container to ensure correct refitting

20 Refit the fuel injectors, with reference to Chapter 4B.

21 Refit the glow plugs, with reference to Chapter 5C.

22 Refit the camshaft and hydraulic tappets, with reference to Chapter 2D.

23 Refit the inlet and exhaust manifolds (and turbocharger, where applicable) with reference to Chapters 4B and 4C.

9 Camshaft and hydraulic tappets (1.4 litre OHV engine) – removal and refitting

Removal

1 Remove the rocker gear as described in Chapter 2B.

2 Lift out each pushrod in turn, and store it in its correct fitted order by pushing it through a clearly-marked cardboard template. This will help ensure

9.7a Undo the thrustplate retaining screws . . .

9.7c . . . and withdraw the camshaft

9.5 Checking camshaft endfloat

that the pushrods are refitted in their original positions on reassembly. Note that the inlet valve pushrods are made of aluminium – those for the exhaust valves are made of cast iron.

3 Using a piece of bent wire in the centre holes, withdraw each hydraulic tappet in turn from the cylinder block, and either label them or place them in a small partitioned container **(see illustration)**. This will help ensure that, if the tappets are to be re-used, they are refitted in their original positions; this is essential to minimise the amount of wear between the tappets and cam lobes.

4 Remove the timing chain and sprockets as described in Chapter 2B.

5 Prior to removing the camshaft, check the endfloat as follows. Temporarily refit the distributor/oil pump drivegear, dished washer, tab washer and sprocket bolt to the end of the camshaft, and tighten the bolt to the specified torque. Set up a dial gauge on the end of

9.7b . . . remove the thrustplate . . .

9.14 Measuring a camshaft bearing journal

the camshaft, and measure the endfloat whilst moving the camshaft to and fro **(see illustration)**.

6 If the endfloat exceeds the specified limit, renew the camshaft thrustplate on refitting.

7 Remove the temporarily-installed components, then slacken and remove the three screws securing the camshaft thrustplate to the cylinder block. Remove the plate and withdraw the camshaft from the block **(see illustrations)**.

Inspection

8 Inspect the hydraulic tappets for wear ridges and pitting of their camshaft lobe contact surfaces.

9 Insert each tappet into its respective bore in the cylinder block, and check that it is free to move smoothly up-and-down, but that there is no excessive side-to-side movement of the follower.

10 If the necessary measuring equipment is available, the amount of wear on the hydraulic tappets and their bores in the cylinder block can be checked by direct measurement.

11 If any of the hydraulic tappets are badly marked or excessively-worn (compare with the figures quoted in the Specifications), it will be necessary to renew the affected ones.

12 If the amount of side-to-side movement of any tappet in its bore seems excessive, or if any of the bores in the cylinder block have worn beyond their specified limits, it will be necessary to have the bores in the cylinder block reamed and to install oversize tappets. This task should be entrusted to a Skoda dealer, who will be able to obtain a set of oversize tappets, and will have the necessary tools to ream out the bores.

13 Examine the camshaft lobes and bearing journals for signs of wear such as pitting or scoring, along with the camshaft bearings which are in the cylinder block.

14 If the necessary measuring equipment is available, measure the diameter of the camshaft journals **(see illustration)** and the internal diameter of each bearing in the cylinder block, and compare the results to the figures given in the Specifications. The bearing running clearance can be calculated by subtracting the camshaft journal outer diameter from the bearing internal diameter.

15 If the camshaft lobes or the bearing journals are badly worn, the camshaft must be renewed. If the camshaft bearings are excessively-worn (compare with the figures quoted in the Specifications), then the advice of a Skoda dealer or engine repair specialist must be sought. It may be possible to have the cylinder block bored out and camshaft bearing shells installed. If this is not possible, the block will have to be renewed.

16 Inspect the camshaft thrustplate for signs of scuffing, and renew if worn.

Refitting

17 Liberally oil the camshaft lobes and bearing journals, then slide the camshaft into position in the cylinder block.

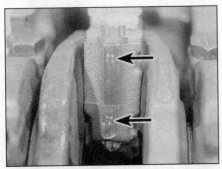

10.2 Mark the big-end caps and connecting rods with their cylinder numbers (arrowed)

10.16a Unscrew the big-end bearing cap bolts . . .

10.16b . . . and remove the cap

18 Fit the camshaft thrustplate over the camshaft end, and securely tighten its three retaining screws. Check the camshaft endfloat as described in paragraph 6.

19 Refit the timing chain and sprockets as described in Chapter 2B.

20 Liberally oil the outer surfaces of the hydraulic tappets, and insert them into their respective bores in the cylinder block. If the original tappets are being re-used, ensure they are refitted in their original locations to minimise wear.

21 Remove the pushrods from the cardboard template, and insert them into their original positions in the cylinder head, ensuring that each pushrod is correctly located in its hydraulic tappet.

22 Refit the rocker gear as described in Chapter 2B, then carry out the basic adjustment of the valve clearances as described in Chapter 2B, Section 5.

10 Piston/connecting rod assemblies – removal

Caution: The pistons and connecting rods must not be removed on 1.2 litre petrol engines.

1.4 litre OHV petrol engines

1 Remove the cylinder head, sump and oil pump gears as described in Chapter 2B. Ensure that the cylinder liners are securely clamped in position.

2 Prior to removing the connecting rods, note the two numbers which are stamped on one side of each assembly, next to the connecting rod/big-end cap mating surface; one on the big-end cap and one on the connecting rod **(see illustration)**. These numbers indicate the cylinder number of each respective connecting rod assembly, No 1 cylinder being at the right-hand end (nearest the timing chain).

3 If any of the numbers are no longer visible, or the number stamped on the assembly does not correspond to the cylinder to which it is fitted, use a hammer and centre-punch, or paint, to mark each connecting rod and big-end bearing cap with its respective cylinder number on the flat, machined surface provided.

4 With the connecting rods still installed on

the crankshaft, use a feeler blade to check the amount of endfloat between the caps and crankshaft webs. If the measured endfloat greatly exceeds the specified tolerance, then the affected connecting rods will require renewal.

5 Rotate the crankshaft until Nos 2 and 3 cylinder pistons are at the bottom of their stroke.

6 Unscrew and remove the big-end bearing cap nuts/bolts, and withdraw the cap, complete with bearing shell, from the connecting rod.

7 If only the bearing shells are being attended to, push the connecting rod up and off the crankpin, ensuring that the connecting rod big-ends do not mark the cylinder bore walls, then remove the upper bearing shell.

8 Keep the cap, nuts/bolts and (if they are to be refitted) the bearing shells together in their correct sequence.

9 With Nos 2 and 3 cylinder big-ends disconnected, repeat the procedure (exercising great care to prevent damage to any of the components) to remove Nos 1 and 4 cylinder bearing caps.

10 Remove the ridge of carbon from the top of each bore. Push each piston/connecting rod assembly up, and remove it from the top of the bore, taking great care to ensure the connecting rod big-ends do not mark the cylinder bore walls. Immediately refit the bearing cap, shells and nuts to each piston/connecting rod assembly, so that they are all kept together as a matched set.

1.4 litre DOHC petrol engines and all diesel engines

11 Remove the cylinder head, sump, oil baffle and oil pump pick-up pipe, as applicable, with reference to Chapters 2A, 2C or 2D. On the 3-cylinder diesel engine code AMF, also remove the balancer shaft assembly.

12 Inspect the tops of the cylinder bores for ridges at the point where the pistons reach top dead centre. These must be removed otherwise, the pistons may be damaged when they are pushed out of their bores. Use a scraper or ridge reamer to remove the ridges. Such a ridge indicates excessive wear of the cylinder bore.

13 Check the connecting rods and big-end caps for identification markings. Both connecting rods and caps should be marked

with the cylinder number on one side of each assembly. Note that No 1 cylinder is at the timing belt end of the engine. If no marks are present, using a hammer and centre-punch, paint or similar, mark each connecting rod and big-end bearing cap with its respective cylinder number – note on which side of the connecting rods and caps the marks are made **(see illustration 10.2)**.

14 Similarly, check the piston crowns for direction markings. An arrow on each piston crown should point towards the timing belt end of the engine. On some engines, this mark may be obscured by carbon build-up, in which case the piston crown should be cleaned to check for a mark. In some cases, the direction arrow may have worn off, in which case a suitable mark should be made on the piston crown using a scriber – do not deeply score the piston crown, but ensure that the mark is easily visible.

15 Turn the crankshaft to bring No 1 piston to bottom dead centre (on 4-cylinder engines, No 4 piston will also be at BDC).

16 Unscrew the bolts or nuts, as applicable, from No 1 piston big-end bearing cap. Lift off the cap, and recover the bottom half bearing shell. If the bearing shells are to be re-used, tape the cap and bearing shell together. Note that if the bearing shells are to be re-used, they must be fitted to the original connecting rod and cap **(see illustrations)**.

17 Where the bearing caps are secured with nuts, wrap the threaded ends of the bolts with insulating tape to prevent them scratching the crankpins and bores when the pistons are removed **(see illustration)**.

18 Using a hammer handle, push the piston

10.17 Wrap the threaded ends of the bolts with tape

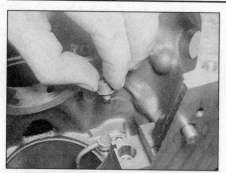

10.22a Remove the securing bolts . . .

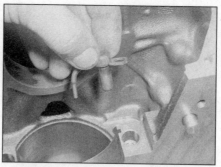

10.22b . . . and withdraw the piston cooling oil spray jets

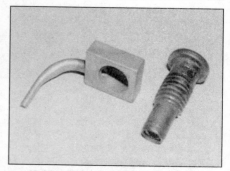

10.22c Piston cooling spray jet and retainer

up through the bore, and remove it from the top of the cylinder block. Where applicable, take care not to damage the piston cooling oil spray jets in the cylinder block as the piston/connecting rod assembly is removed. Recover the upper bearing shell, and tape it to the connecting rod for safe-keeping.

19 Loosely refit the big-end cap to the connecting rod, and secure with the bolts or nuts, as applicable – this will help to keep the components in their correct order.

20 On 4-cylinder engines, remove No 4 piston assembly in the same way.

21 Turn the crankshaft as necessary to bring No 2 piston to bottom dead centre, and remove them in the same way (on 4-cylinder engines, No 3 piston will also be at BDC).

22 Where applicable, remove the securing bolts, and withdraw the piston cooling oil spray jets from the bottom of the cylinder block **(see illustrations)**.

11 Crankshaft – removal

Caution: On 1.2 litre petrol engines and 1.4 litre DOHC petrol engines, the crankshaft must not be removed. Loosening the main bearing cap bolts will cause deformation of the cylinder block. On these engines, if the crankshaft or main bearing surfaces are worn or damaged, the complete crankshaft/cylinder block assembly must be renewed. The following procedure applies to 1.4 litre OHV petrol engine, and all diesel engines.

11.5 Slacken and remove the main bearing cap bolts

Note: *If no work is to be done on the pistons and connecting rods, there is no need to remove the cylinder head and push the pistons out of the cylinder bores. The pistons should just be pushed far enough up the bores so that they are positioned clear of the crankshaft journals.*

1 Proceed as follows according to engine type:
a) *On 1.4 litre OHV petrol engines, remove the timing chain and sprockets, sump, oil pump and pick-up pipe, the flywheel and the crankshaft left-hand oil seal housing as described in Chapter 2B.*
b) *On diesel engines, remove the timing belt and crankshaft sprocket, sump and oil baffle plate, oil pump and pick-up pipe, flywheel, and the crankshaft oil seal housings, as described in Chapter 2D.*

2 Remove the pistons and connecting rods, or disconnect them from the crankshaft, as described in Section 10.

3 Check the crankshaft endfloat as described in Section 14, then proceed as follows.

4 The main bearing caps should be numbered 1 to 5 (4-cylinder) or 4 (3-cylinder) from the timing belt end of the engine, but note on the 1.4 litre OHV petrol engine, the three main bearing caps are incorporated into the single 'ladder-type' cap. If the bearing caps are not marked, mark them accordingly using a centre-punch. Note the orientation of the markings to ensure correct refitting.

5 Slacken and remove the main bearing cap bolts, and lift off each cap. If the caps appear to be stuck, tap them with a soft-faced mallet to free them from the cylinder block **(see**

11.6 Lifting the crankshaft from the cylinder block

illustration). Recover the lower bearing shells, and tape them to their caps for safe-keeping.

6 Lift the crankshaft from the cylinder block **(see illustration)**. Take care, as the crankshaft is heavy. On engines with a crankshaft speed/position sensor fitted, lay the crankshaft on wooden blocks – **do not** rest the crankshaft on the sensor wheel.

7 Recover the upper bearing shells from the cylinder block, and tape them to their respective caps for safe-keeping. Similarly, recover the upper crankshaft endfloat control thrustwasher halves from either side of No 3 main bearing, noting their orientation.

8 On engines with a crankshaft speed/position sensor wheel fitted, unscrew the securing bolts, and remove the sensor wheel, noting which way round it is fitted.

12 Cylinder block/crankcase – cleaning and inspection

Cleaning

1 Remove all external components and electrical switches/sensors from the block, including mounting brackets, the coolant pump, the camshaft (1.4 litre OHV petrol engine), the oil filter/cooler housing, etc. For complete cleaning, the core plugs should ideally be removed. Drill a small hole in the plugs, then insert a self-tapping screw into the hole. Extract the plugs by pulling on the screw with a pair of grips, or by using a slide hammer.

2 Scrape all traces of gasket and sealant from the cylinder block/crankcase, taking care not to damage the sealing surfaces.

3 Remove all oil gallery plugs (where fitted). The plugs are usually very tight – they may have to be drilled out, and the holes retapped. Use new plugs when the engine is reassembled.

4 If the casting is extremely dirty, it should be steam-cleaned. After this, clean all oil holes and galleries one more time. Flush all internal passages with warm water until the water runs clear. Dry thoroughly, and apply a light film of oil to all mating surfaces and cylinder bores, to prevent rusting. If you have access to compressed air, use it to speed up the drying process, and to blow out all the oil holes and galleries.

 Warning: Wear eye protection when using compressed air.

5 If the castings are not very dirty, you can do an adequate cleaning job with hot, soapy water and a stiff brush. Take plenty of time, and do a thorough job. Regardless of the cleaning method used, be sure to clean all oil holes and galleries very thoroughly, and to dry all components well. Protect the cylinder bores as described above, to prevent rusting.

6 Where applicable, check the piston cooling oil spray jets for damage, and renew if necessary. Check the oil spray hole and the oil passages for blockage.

7 All threaded holes must be clean, to ensure accurate torque readings during reassembly. To clean the threads, run the correct-size tap into each of the holes to remove rust, corrosion, thread sealant or sludge, and to restore damaged threads **(see illustration)**. If possible, use compressed air to clear the holes free of debris produced by this operation. **Note:** *Take extra care to exclude all cleaning liquid from blind tapped holes, as the casting may be cracked by hydraulic action if a bolt is threaded into a hole containing liquid.*

 HAYNES HINT *A good alternative is to inject aerosol-applied water dispersant lubricant into each hole, using the long spout usually supplied.* **Warning: Wear eye protection when cleaning out these holes in this way.**

8 After coating the mating surfaces of the new core plugs with suitable sealant, fit them to the cylinder block. Make sure that they are driven in straight and seated correctly, or leakage could result.

 HAYNES HINT *A large socket with an outside diameter which will just fit into the core plug can be used to drive the core plug into position.*

9 Apply suitable sealant to the new oil gallery plugs, and insert them into the holes in the block. Tighten them securely.

10 If the engine is not going to be reassembled immediately, cover it with a large plastic bag to keep it clean; protect all mating surfaces and the cylinder bores, to prevent rusting.

Inspection

1.4 litre OHV petrol engines

11 Visually check the castings for cracks and corrosion. Look for stripped threads in the threaded holes. If there has been any history of internal water leakage, it may be worthwhile having an engine overhaul specialist check the cylinder block/crankcase with special equipment. If defects are found have them repaired, if possible, or renew the assembly.

12 Remove the liners as described in paragraph 28, and check the bore of each liner for scuffing and scoring. The liners are grouped into three size classes to allow for manufacturing tolerances; the size group is stamped on the side of the each liner.

13 Measure the diameter of each cylinder liner just below the wear ridge at the top of the bore, halfway down the bore, and just up from the base of the bore. Take measurements both parallel to the crankshaft axis and at right-angles to it.

14 Compare the results with the Specifications for the relevant class of liner given at the beginning of this Chapter; if any measurement exceeds the tolerances specified, the liner must be renewed.

15 To measure the piston-to-bore clearance, measure the bore and piston skirt as described in Section 13, and subtract the skirt diameter from the bore measurement.

16 Alternatively, insert each piston into the original bore, select a feeler blade, and slip it into the bore along with the piston. The piston must be aligned exactly in its normal attitude, and the feeler blade must be between the piston and bore on one of the thrust faces, just up from the bottom of the bore.

17 If the clearance is excessive, a new piston will be required. If the piston binds at the lower end of the bore and is loose towards the top, the bore is tapered. If tight spots are encountered as the piston/feeler gauge blade is rotated in the bore, the bore is out-of-round.

18 Repeat this procedure for the remaining pistons and cylinder liners.

19 If the cylinder liner walls are badly scuffed or scored, or if they are excessively-worn, out-of-round or tapered, obtain new cylinder liners; new pistons will also be required.

20 Skoda state that all the pistons and liners installed in the engine must be of the same size class. The liner size class is stamped on the outer surface of the liner, and the piston size class is stamped on the piston crown.

21 If the bores are in reasonably good condition and not worn to the specified limits, and if the piston-to-bore clearances can be maintained properly, then it may only be necessary to renew the piston rings.

22 If this is the case, the bores should be honed to allow the new rings to bed in correctly and provide the best possible seal.

23 Honing involves using an abrasive tool to produce a fine, cross-hatch pattern on the inner surface of the bore. This has the effect of seating the piston rings, resulting in a good seal between the piston and cylinder. There are two types of honing tool available to the home mechanic, both are driven by a rotary power tool, such as a drill. The bottle brush hone is a stiff, cylindrical brush with abrasive stones bonded to its bristles. The more conventional

12.7 To clean the cylinder block threads, run a correct-size tap into the holes

surfacing hone has abrasive stones mounted on spring-loaded legs. For the inexperienced home mechanic, satisfactory results will be achieved more easily using the bottle brush hone. **Note:** *If you are unwilling to tackle cylinder bore honing, an engineering workshop will be able to carry out the job for you at a reasonable cost.*

24 Carry out the honing as follows; you will need one of the honing tools described above, a power drill/air wrench, a supply of clean rags, some honing oil and a pair of safety glasses.

25 Fit the honing tool in the drill chuck. Lubricate the cylinder bores with honing oil and insert the honing tool into the first bore, compressing the stones to allow it to fit. Turn on the drill and as the tool rotates, move it up-and-down in the bore at a rate that produces a fine cross-hatch pattern on the surface. The lines of the pattern should ideally cross at about 50 to 60°, although some piston ring manufacturers may quote a different angle; check the literature supplied with the new rings **(see illustration)**.

 Warning: Wear safety glasses to protect your eyes from debris flying off the honing tool.

26 Use plenty of oil during the honing process. Do not remove any more material than is necessary to produce the required finish. When removing the hone tool from the bore, do not pull it out whilst it is still rotating; maintain the up/down movement until the chuck has stopped, then withdraw the tool whilst rotating the chuck by hand, in the normal direction of rotation.

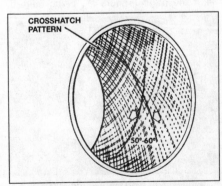

12.25 Cylinder bore honing pattern

12.33 Fit a sealing washer of the required thickness to the base of the liner . . .

12.34 . . . and install the liner in the block

27 Wipe out the oil and swarf with a rag and proceed to the next bore. When all four bores have been honed, thoroughly clean the whole cylinder block in hot soapy water to remove all traces of honing oil and debris. The block is clean when a clean rag, moistened with new engine oil does not pick up any grey residue when wiped along the bore.

28 To remove the liners, invert the cylinder block/crankcase and support it on blocks of wood, then use a hard wood drift to tap out each liner from the crankshaft side.

29 When all the liners are released, tip the cylinder block/crankcase on its side, and remove each liner from the cylinder head side.

30 Remove the sealing washer from the base of the liner, and measure its thickness. The washer is available in various sizes, and is used to adjust the cylinder liner protrusion (see paragraph 35); obtain a new washer of the relevant thickness for each liner to use on refitting.

31 If the liners are to be re-used, mark each one by sticking masking tape on its right-hand (timing chain) face and writing the cylinder number on the tape.

32 To install the liners, thoroughly clean the liner mating surfaces in the cylinder block/crankcase, and use fine abrasive paper to polish away any burrs or sharp edges which might damage the liner sealing washer.

33 Clean the liners and wipe dry, then fit a new sealing washer of the required thickness to the base of each liner **(see illustration)**. Apply a thin coat of engine oil to the bore.

34 If the original liners are being refitted,

use the marks made on removal to ensure that each is refitted the same way round into its original bore. Insert each liner into the cylinder block/crankcase, taking great care not to displace the washer, and press it home as far as possible by hand **(see illustration)**. Using a hammer and a block of wood, tap each liner lightly but fully onto its locating shoulder.

35 With all four liners installed, using a dial gauge or a straight-edge and feeler blade, check that the protrusion of each liner above the upper surface of the cylinder block is within the limits given in the Specifications, and that the maximum difference between any two liners is not exceeded **(see illustration)**.

36 If this is not the case, it will be necessary to remove the appropriate liner and to obtain another sealing washer of the required thickness. Washers are available in three thicknesses: 0.10 mm, 0.12 mm and 0.14 mm.

37 Fit the necessary washer to the liner, then install the liner and recheck the protrusion.

38 Repeat as necessary until all liner protrusions are within the specified limits and the maximum difference between any two is not exceeded, then securely clamp the liners in position **(see illustration)**.

All petrol engines except 1.4 litre OHV and diesel engines

39 Visually check the castings for cracks and corrosion. Look for stripped threads in the threaded holes. If there has been any history of internal coolant leakage, it may be worthwhile having an engine overhaul specialist check the cylinder block/crankcase

for cracks with special equipment. If defects are found, have them repaired, if possible, or renew the assembly.

40 Check each cylinder bore for scuffing and scoring.

41 If in any doubt as the condition of the cylinder block have the block/bores inspected and measured by an engine reconditioning specialist. They will be able to advise on whether the block is serviceable, whether a rebore is necessary, and supply the appropriate pistons and rings.

42 If the bores are in reasonably good condition and not excessively worn, then it may only be necessary to renew the piston rings.

43 If this is the case, the bores should be honed, to allow the new rings to bed-in correctly and provide the best possible seal. Consult an engine reconditioning specialist.

44 On diesel engines, if the oil filter/cooler housing was removed, it can be refitted at this stage if wished. Use a new gasket, and before fully tightening the bolts, align the housing faces with those of the engine block.

45 The cylinder block/crankcase should now be completely clean and dry, with all components checked for wear or damage, and repaired or overhauled as necessary.

46 Apply a light coating of engine oil to the mating surfaces and cylinder bores to prevent rust forming.

47 Refit as many ancillary components as possible, for safe-keeping. If reassembly is not to start immediately, cover the block with a large plastic bag to keep it clean, and protect the machined surfaces as described above to prevent rusting.

13 Piston/connecting rod assemblies – cleaning and inspection

Cleaning

1 Before the inspection process can begin, the piston/connecting rod assemblies must be cleaned, and the original piston rings removed from the pistons.

2 The rings should have smooth, polished working surfaces, with no dull or carbon-coated sections (showing that the ring is not sealing correctly against the bore wall, so allowing combustion gases to blow-by) and no traces of wear on their top and bottom surfaces. The end gaps should be clear of carbon, but not polished (indicating a too-small end gap), and all the rings (including the elements of the oil control ring) should be free to rotate in their grooves, but without excessive up-and-down movement. If the rings appear to be in good condition, they are probably fit for further use; check the end gaps (in an unworn part of the bore) as described in Section 17.

3 If any of the rings appears to be worn or damaged, or has an end gap significantly

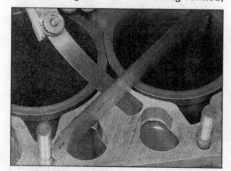

12.35 Using a straight-edge and feeler blade to check liner protrusion

12.38 Once liner protrusions are within specified limits, clamp all the liners in position

13.4 Old feeler blades can be used to prevent piston rings from dropping into empty grooves

13.9 Using a micrometer to measure the diameter of a piston

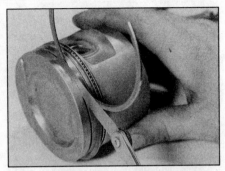

13.18 Measuring the piston ring-to-groove clearance using a feeler blade

different from the specified value, the usual course of action is to renew all of them as a set. **Note:** *While it is usual to renew piston rings when an engine is overhauled, they may be re-used if in acceptable condition. If re-using the rings, make sure that each ring is marked during removal to ensure that it is refitted correctly.*

4 Carefully expand the old rings over the top of the pistons. The use of two or three old feeler blades will be helpful in preventing the rings dropping into empty grooves **(see illustration)**. Be careful not to scratch the piston with the ends of the ring. The rings are brittle, and will snap if they are spread too far. They are also very sharp – protect your hands and fingers. Note that the third ring incorporates an expander. Keep each set of rings with its piston if the old rings are to be re-used. Note which way up each ring is fitted to ensure correct refitting.

5 Scrape away all traces of carbon from the top of the piston. A hand-held wire brush (or a piece of fine emery cloth) can be used, once the majority of the deposits have been scraped away.

6 Remove the carbon from the ring grooves in the piston, using an old ring. Break the ring in half to do this (be careful not to cut your fingers – piston rings are sharp). Be careful to remove only the carbon deposits – do not remove any metal, and do not nick or scratch the sides of the ring grooves.

7 Once the deposits have been removed, clean the piston/connecting rod assembly with paraffin or a suitable solvent, and dry thoroughly. Make sure that the oil return holes in the ring grooves are clear.

Inspection

8 If the pistons and cylinder bores are not damaged or worn excessively, and if the cylinder block does not need to be rebored, the original pistons can be refitted.

9 Using a micrometer, measure the diameter of all four pistons at a point 10 mm from the bottom of the skirt, at right-angles to the gudgeon pin axis **(see illustration)**. Compare the measurements with those listed in the Specifications. Note that the piston size grades are stamped on the piston crowns.

10 If the piston diameter is incorrect for its

particular size, then it must be renewed. **Note:** *If the cylinder block was rebored during a previous overhaul (or if new liners have been fitted on 1.4 litre OHV petrol engines), oversize pistons may already have been fitted.* Record all of the measurements and use them to check the piston clearances against the cylinder bore measurements made in Section 12.

11 Normal piston wear shows up as even vertical wear on the piston thrust surfaces, and slight looseness of the top ring in its groove. New piston rings should always be used when the engine is reassembled.

12 Carefully inspect each piston for cracks around the skirt, around the gudgeon pin holes, and at the piston ring 'lands' (between the ring grooves).

13 Look for scoring and scuffing on the piston skirt, holes in the piston crown, and burned areas at the edge of the crown. If the skirt is scored or scuffed, the engine may have been suffering from overheating, and/or abnormal combustion which caused excessively high operating temperatures. The cooling and lubrication systems should be checked thoroughly.

14 Scorch marks on the sides of the pistons show that blow-by has occurred.

15 A hole in the piston crown, or burned areas at the edge of the piston crown, indicates that abnormal combustion (pre-ignition, knocking, or detonation) has been occurring.

16 If any of the above problems exist, the causes must be investigated and corrected, or the damage will occur again. The causes may include incorrect ignition/injection pump timing, inlet air leaks or incorrect air/fuel

mixture (petrol engines), or a faulty fuel injector (diesel engines).

17 Corrosion of the piston, in the form of pitting, indicates that coolant has been leaking into the combustion chamber and/or the crankcase. Again, the cause must be corrected, or the problem may persist in the rebuilt engine.

18 Locate a new piston ring in the appropriate groove and measure the ring-to-groove clearance using a feeler blade **(see illustration)**. Note that the rings are of different widths, so use the correct ring for the groove. Compare the measurements with those listed; if the clearances are outside of the tolerance band, then the piston must be renewed. Confirm this by checking the width of the piston ring with a micrometer.

19 New pistons can be purchased from a Skoda dealer.

20 Examine each connecting rod carefully for signs of damage, such as cracks around the big-end and small-end bearings. Check that the rod is not bent or distorted. Damage is highly unlikely, unless the engine has been seized or badly overheated. Detailed checking of the connecting rod assembly can only be carried out by a Skoda dealer or engine repair specialist with the necessary equipment.

21 The gudgeon pins are of the floating type, secured in position by two circlips. The pistons and connecting rods can be separated as follows:

22 Using a small flat-bladed screwdriver, prise out the circlips, and push out the gudgeon pin **(see illustrations)**. Hand pressure should be sufficient to remove the pin. Identify the piston and rod to ensure correct reassembly.

13.22a Use a small flat-bladed screwdriver to prise out the circlip . . .

13.22b . . . then push out the gudgeon pin and separate the piston and connecting rod

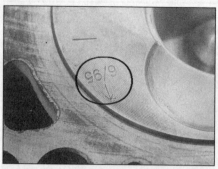

13.25a The piston crown is marked with an arrow which must point towards the timing belt end of the engine

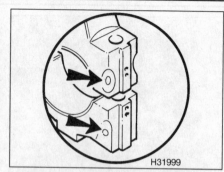

13.25b The recesses (arrowed) in the connecting rod and bearing cap must face towards the timing belt end of the engine

Discard the circlips – new ones *must* be used on refitting. If the gudgeon pin proves difficult to remove, heat the piston to 60°C with hot water – the resulting expansion will then allow the two components to be separated.

23 Examine the gudgeon pin and connecting rod small-end bearing for signs of wear or damage. It should be possible to push the gudgeon pin through the connecting rod bush by hand, without noticeable play. Wear can be cured by renewing both the pin and bush. Bush renewal, however, is a specialist job – press facilities are required, and the new bush must be reamed accurately.

24 Examine all components, and obtain any new parts from your Skoda dealer. If new pistons are purchased, they will be supplied complete with gudgeon pins and circlips. Circlips can also be purchased individually.

25 The orientation of the piston with respect to the connecting rod must be correct when the two are reassembled. The piston crown is marked with an arrow (which may be obscured by carbon deposits). On 1.4 litre OHV petrol engines, the arrow points towards the oil filter/camshaft side of the engine, and the oilway in the connecting rod faces the opposite side of the engine. On all other engines, the arrow must point towards the timing belt end of the engine when the piston is installed. The connecting rod and its bearing cap both have recesses machined into them on one side, close to their mating surfaces – these recesses must both face the same way as the arrow on the piston crown when correctly installed. Reassemble the two

components to satisfy this requirement **(see illustrations)**.

26 Apply a smear of clean engine oil to the gudgeon pin. Slide it into the piston and through the connecting rod small-end. Check that the piston pivots freely on the rod, then secure the gudgeon pin in position with two new circlips. Ensure that each circlip is correctly located in its groove in the piston.

27 Repeat the cleaning and inspection process for the remaining pistons and connecting rods.

14 Crankshaft – checking endfloat and inspection

Checking endfloat

1 If the crankshaft endfloat is to be checked, this must be done when the crankshaft is still installed in the cylinder block/crankcase, but is free to move (see Section 11).

2 Check the endfloat using a dial gauge in contact with the end of the crankshaft. Push the crankshaft fully one way, and then zero the gauge. Push the crankshaft fully the other way, and check the endfloat. The result can be compared with the specified amount, and will give an indication as to whether new thrustwasher halves are required **(see illustration)**. Note that all thrustwashers must be of the same thickness.

3 If a dial gauge is not available, feeler blades can be used. First push the crankshaft fully

towards the flywheel end of the engine, then use feeler blades to measure the gap between the web of No 3 crankpin and the thrustwasher halves **(see illustration)**.

Inspection

4 Clean the crankshaft using paraffin or a suitable solvent, and dry it, preferably with compressed air if available. Be sure to clean the oil holes with a pipe cleaner or similar probe, to ensure that they are not obstructed.

⚠️ **Warning: Wear eye protection when using compressed air.**

5 Check the main and big-end bearing journals for uneven wear, scoring, pitting and cracking.

6 Big-end bearing wear is accompanied by distinct metallic knocking when the engine is running (particularly noticeable when the engine is pulling from low speed) and some loss of oil pressure.

7 Main bearing wear is accompanied by severe engine vibration and rumble – getting progressively worse as engine speed increases – and again by loss of oil pressure.

8 Check the bearing journal for roughness by running a finger lightly over the bearing surface. Any roughness (which will be accompanied by obvious bearing wear) indicates that the crankshaft requires regrinding (where possible) or renewal.

9 If the crankshaft has been reground, check for burrs around the crankshaft oil holes (the holes are usually chamfered, so burrs should not be a problem unless regrinding has been carried out carelessly). Remove any burrs with a fine file or scraper, and thoroughly clean the oil holes as described previously.

10 Using a micrometer, measure the diameter of the main and big-end bearing journals, and compare the results with the Specifications, where given **(see illustration)**. By measuring the diameter at a number of points around each journal's circumference, you will be able to determine whether or not the journal is out-of-round. Take the measurement at each end of the journal, near the webs, to determine if the journal is tapered.

11 Check the oil seal contact surfaces at each end of the crankshaft for wear and damage. If the seal has worn a deep groove in the

14.2 Measuring crankshaft endfloat using a dial gauge

14.3 Measuring crankshaft endfloat using feeler blades

14.10 Use a micrometer to measure the diameter of each crankshaft bearing journal

surface of the crankshaft, consult an engine overhaul specialist; repair may be possible, but otherwise a new crankshaft will be required.

12 If the crankshaft journals have not already been reground, it may be possible to have the crankshaft reconditioned, and to fit oversize shells (see Section 18). If no oversize shells are available and the crankshaft has worn beyond the specified limits, it will have to be renewed. Consult your Skoda dealer or engine specialist for further information on parts availability.

15 Main and big-end bearings – inspection

Inspection

1 Even though the main and big-end bearings should be renewed during the engine overhaul, the old bearings should be retained for close examination, as they may reveal valuable information about the condition of the engine **(see illustration).**

2 Bearing failure can occur due to lack of lubrication, the presence of dirt or other foreign particles, overloading the engine, or corrosion. Regardless of the cause of bearing failure, the cause must be corrected before the engine is reassembled, to prevent it from happening again.

3 When examining the bearing shells, remove them from the cylinder block/crankcase, the main bearing caps, the connecting rods and the connecting rod big-end bearing caps. Lay them out on a clean surface in the same general position as their location in the engine. This will enable you to match any bearing problems with the corresponding crankshaft journal. *Do not* touch any shell's internal bearing surface with your fingers while checking it, or the delicate surface may be scratched.

4 Dirt and other foreign matter gets into the engine in a variety of ways. It may be left in the engine during assembly, or it may pass through filters or the crankcase ventilation system. It may get into the oil, and from there into the bearings. Metal chips from machining operations and normal engine wear are often present. Abrasives are sometimes left in engine components after reconditioning, especially when parts are not thoroughly cleaned using the proper cleaning methods. Whatever the source, these foreign objects often end up embedded in the soft bearing material, and are easily recognised. Large particles will not embed in the bearing, but will score or gouge the bearing and journal. The best prevention for this cause of bearing failure is to clean all parts thoroughly, and keep everything spotlessly-clean during engine assembly. Frequent and regular engine oil and filter changes are also recommended.

5 Lack of lubrication (or lubrication breakdown) has a number of interrelated causes. Excessive heat (which thins the oil), overloading (which squeezes the oil from the bearing face) and oil leakage (from excessive bearing clearances, worn oil pump or high engine speeds) all contribute to lubrication breakdown. Blocked oil passages, which usually are the result of misaligned oil holes in a bearing shell, will also oil-starve a bearing, and destroy it. When lack of lubrication is the cause of bearing failure, the bearing material is wiped or extruded from the steel backing of the bearing. Temperatures may increase to the point where the steel backing turns blue from overheating.

6 Driving habits can have a definite effect on bearing life. Full-throttle, low-speed operation (labouring the engine) puts very high loads on bearings, tending to squeeze out the oil film. These loads cause the bearings to flex, which produces fine cracks in the bearing face (fatigue failure). Eventually, the bearing material will loosen in pieces, and tear away from the steel backing.

7 Short-distance driving leads to corrosion of bearings, because insufficient engine heat is produced to drive off the condensed water and corrosive gases. These products collect in the engine oil, forming acid and sludge. As the oil is carried to the engine bearings, the acid attacks and corrodes the bearing material.

8 Incorrect bearing installation during engine assembly will lead to bearing failure as well. Tight-fitting bearings leave insufficient bearing running clearance, and will result in oil starvation. Dirt or foreign particles trapped behind a bearing shell result in high spots on the bearing, which lead to failure.

9 *Do not* touch any shell's internal bearing surface with your fingers during reassembly as there is a risk of scratching the delicate surface, or of depositing particles of dirt on it.

10 As mentioned at the beginning of this Section, the bearing shells should be renewed as a matter of course during engine overhaul. To do otherwise is false economy.

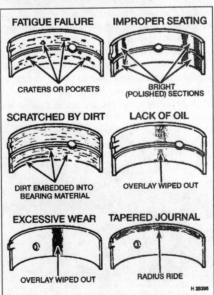

15.1 Typical bearing failures

Bearings selection

11 Main and big-end bearings for the engines described in this Chapter are available in standard sizes and a range of undersizes to suit reground crankshafts.

12 The running clearances will need to be checked when the crankshaft is refitted with its new bearings (see Sections 18 and 19).

16 Engine overhaul – reassembly sequence

1 Before reassembly begins, ensure that all new parts have been obtained, and that all necessary tools are available. Read through the entire procedure to familiarise yourself with the work involved, and to ensure that all items necessary for reassembly of the engine are at hand. In addition to all normal tools and materials, thread-locking compound will be needed. A suitable tube of liquid sealant will also be required for the joint faces that are fitted without gaskets.

2 In order to save time and avoid problems, engine reassembly can be carried out in the following order, referring to Part A, B, C or D of this Chapter. Where applicable, use new gaskets and seals when refitting the various components.

a) *Crankshaft (Section 18).*
b) *Piston/connecting rod assemblies (Section 19).*
c) *Camshaft on 1.4 litre OHV petrol engine.*
d) *Oil pump.*
e) *Sump.*
f) *Flywheel/driveplate.*
g) *Cylinder head.*
h) *Timing chain/belt(s), tensioner and sprockets.*
i) *Inlet and exhaust manifolds.*
j) *Engine external components.*

3 At this stage, all engine components should be absolutely clean and dry, with all faults repaired. The components should be laid out (or in individual containers) on a completely clean work surface.

17 Piston rings – refitting

1 Before fitting new piston rings, the ring end gaps must be checked as follows.

2 Lay out the piston/connecting rod assemblies and the new piston ring sets, so that the ring sets will be matched with the same piston and cylinder during the end gap measurement and subsequent engine reassembly.

3 Insert the top ring into the first cylinder, and push it down the bore using the top of the piston. This will ensure that the ring remains square with the cylinder walls. Position the ring approximately 15.0 mm the bottom of the cylinder bore, at the lower limit of ring travel. Note that the top and second compression rings are different.

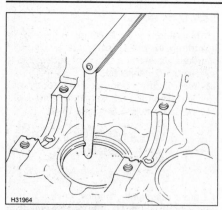

17.4 Checking a piston ring end gap using a feeler blade

4 Measure the end gap using feeler blades, and compare the measurements with the figures given in the Specifications **(see illustration)**.

5 If the gap is too small (unlikely if genuine Skoda parts are used), it must be enlarged, or the ring ends may contact each other during engine operation, causing serious damage. Ideally, new piston rings providing the correct end gap should be fitted. As a last resort, the end gap can be increased by filing the ring ends very carefully with a fine file. Mount the file in a vice equipped with soft jaws, slip the ring over the file with the ends contacting the file face, and slowly move the ring to remove material from the ends. Take care, as piston rings are sharp, and are easily broken.

6 With new piston rings, it is unlikely that the end gap will be too large. If the gaps are too large, check that you have the correct rings for your engine and for the particular cylinder bore size.

7 Repeat the checking procedure for each ring in the first cylinder, and then for the rings in the remaining cylinders. Remember to keep rings, pistons and cylinders matched up.

8 Once the ring end gaps have been checked and if necessary corrected, the rings can be fitted to the pistons.

9 Fit the piston rings using the same technique as for removal. Fit the bottom (oil control) ring first, and work up. Note that a two- or three-

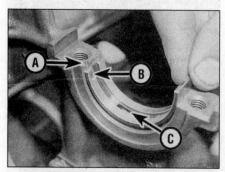

18.4 Bearing shell correctly refitted

A   *Recess in cylinder block*
B   *Lug on bearing shell*
C   *Oil hole*

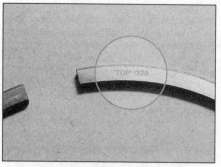

17.9 Piston ring TOP marking

section oil control ring may be fitted; where a two-section ring is fitted, first insert the wire expander, then fit the ring. Ensure that the rings are fitted the correct way up – the top surface of the rings is normally marked TOP **(see illustration)**. Offset the piston ring gaps by 120° from each other. **Note:** *Always follow any instructions supplied with the new piston ring sets – different manufacturers may specify different procedures. Do not mix up the top and second compression rings, as they have different cross-sections.*

18 Crankshaft –
refitting and main bearing
clearance check

Main bearing clearance check

1 The running clearance check can be carried out using the original bearing shells. However, it is preferable to use a new set, since the results obtained will be more conclusive. If new shells are being fitted, ensure that all traces of the protective grease are cleaned off using paraffin.

2 If still fitted, carefully lift the crankshaft out of the cylinder block, and wipe off the surfaces of the bearing shells in the crankcase and bearing cap(s).

3 Clean the backs of the bearing shells, and the bearing locations in both the cylinder block/crankcase and the main bearing cap(s).

4 With the cylinder block positioned on a clean work surface, with the crankcase uppermost, press the bearing shells into their

18.8 Lubricate the upper bearing shells

locations, ensuring that the tab on each shell engages in the notch in the cylinder block or bearing cap, and that the oil holes in the cylinder block and bearing shell are aligned **(see illustration)**. Take care not to touch any shell's bearing surface with your fingers. If the original bearing shells are being used for the check, ensure that they are refitted in their original locations.

5 Fit the crankshaft endfloat control thrust-washer halves either side of the No 3 main bearing location. Use a small quantity of grease to hold them in place. Ensure that the thrustwashers are seated correctly in the machined recesses, with the oil grooves facing outwards.

6 The running clearance can be checked, although this will be difficult to achieve without a range of internal micrometers or internal/external expanding calipers. Refit the main bearing cap(s) to the cylinder block/crankcase, with bearing shells in place. With the original cap retaining bolts tightened to the specified torque, measure the internal diameter of each assembled pair of bearing shells. If the diameter of each corresponding crankshaft journal is measured and then subtracted from the bearing internal diameter, the result will be the main bearing running clearance.

Final crankshaft refitting

7 Where applicable, refit the speed/position sensor wheel to the crankshaft, and tighten the securing bolts to the specified torque. Make sure that the sensor wheel is correctly orientated as noted before removal.

8 Liberally coat the bearing shells in the crankcase with clean engine oil of the appropriate grade **(see illustration)**. Make sure that the bearing shells are still correctly seated in their locations.

9 Lower the crankshaft into position so that No 1 cylinder crankpin is at BDC, ready for fitting No 1 piston. Ensure that the crankshaft endfloat control thrustwasher halves, either side of the No 3 main bearing location, remain in position. Where applicable, take care not to damage the crankshaft speed/position sensor wheel as the crankshaft is lowered into position.

10 Lubricate the lower bearing shells in the main bearing caps with clean engine oil. Make sure that the crankshaft endfloat control thrust-

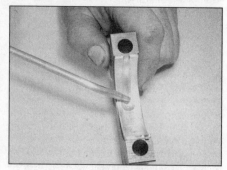

18.10a Lubricate the lower bearing shells . . .

washer halves are still correctly seated either side of No 3 bearing cap **(see illustrations)**.

11 Fit the main bearing cap(s) in the correct location and orientation – where applicable, No 1 bearing cap must be at the timing end of the engine and the bearing shell tab locating recesses in the crankcase and bearing caps must be adjacent to each other **(see illustration)**. Insert the bearing cap bolts (using new bolts where necessary – see Torque wrench settings in the Specifications), and hand-tighten them only.

12 Working from the centre bearing cap outwards, tighten the bearing cap bolts to their specified torque. On diesel engines where two Stages are given for the torque, tighten all bolts to the Stage 1 torque, then go round again, and tighten all bolts through the Stage 2 angle **(see illustrations)**.

13 Check that the crankshaft rotates freely by turning it by hand. If resistance is felt, recheck the bearing running clearances, as described previously.

14 Check the crankshaft endfloat as described at the beginning of Section 14. If the thrust surfaces of the crankshaft have been checked and new thrustwashers have been fitted, then the endfloat should be within specification.

15 Refit the pistons and connecting rods or reconnect them to the crankshaft as described in Section 19.

16 Proceed as follows according to engine type:

a) *On 1.4 litre OHV petrol engines, refit the crankshaft left-hand oil seal housing, flywheel, oil pump and pick-up pipe, sump and timing chain and sprockets as described in Chapter 2B.*

b) *On diesel engines, refit the crankshaft oil seal housings, flywheel, oil pump and pick-up pipe, sump and oil baffle plate, crankshaft sprocket and timing belt as described in Chapter 2D.*

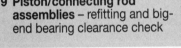

19 Piston/connecting rod assemblies – refitting and big-end bearing clearance check

Note: *A piston ring compressor tool will be required for this operation.*

Big-end bearing clearance check

1 The running clearance check can be carried out using the original bearing shells. However, it is preferable to use a new set, since the results obtained will be more conclusive.

2 Clean the backs of the bearing shells, and the bearing locations in both the connecting rods and the big-end bearing caps.

3 Press the bearing shells into their locations, ensuring that the tab on each shell engages in the notch in the connecting rod or cap. Take care not to touch any shell's bearing surface with your fingers. If the original bearing shells are being used for the check, ensure that they are refitted in their original locations.

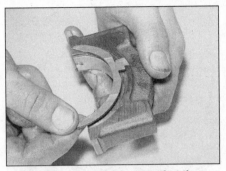

18.10b . . . and make sure that the thrustwashers are correctly seated

18.12a Tighten the main bearing cap bolts to the specified torque . . .

19.9a Lubricate the pistons . . .

4 The running clearance can be checked, although this will be difficult to achieve without a range of internal micrometers or internal/external expanding calipers. Refit the big-end bearing cap to the connecting rod, using the marks made or noted on removal to ensure that they are fitted the correct way around, with the bearing shells in place. With the original cap retaining bolts or nuts (as applicable) correctly tightened, use an internal micrometer or vernier caliper to measure the internal diameter of each assembled pair of bearing shells. If the diameter of each corresponding crankshaft journal is measured, and then subtracted from the bearing internal diameter, the result will be the big-end bearing running clearance.

Piston/connecting rods refitting

5 Note that the following procedure assumes that the crankshaft main bearing caps are in place.

18.11 Fitting No 1 main bearing cap

18.12b . . . then through the specified angle

6 Where applicable, refit the piston cooling oil spray jets to the bottom of the cylinder block, and tighten the securing bolts to the specified torque.

7 On engines where the big-end bearing caps are secured by nuts, renew the bolts/studs in the connecting rods. Tap the old bolts/studs out of the connecting rods using a soft-faced mallet, and tap the new bolts/studs into position. On engines where the caps are secured by bolts, renew the bolts.

8 Ensure that the bearing shells are correctly fitted, as described at the beginning of this Section. If new shells are being fitted, ensure that all traces of the protective grease are cleaned off using paraffin. Wipe dry the shells and connecting rods with a lint-free cloth.

9 Lubricate the cylinder bores/liners, the pistons, piston rings and upper bearing shells with clean engine oil **(see illustrations)**. Lay out each piston/connecting rod assembly

19.9b . . . and big-end upper bearing shells with clean engine oil

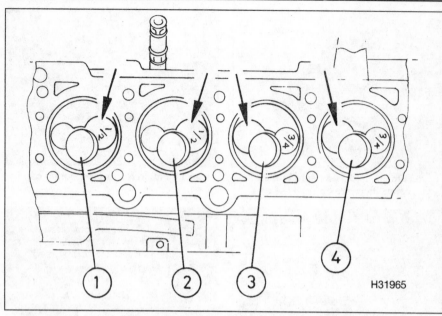

19.12 Piston orientation and coding on diesel engines –
3-cylinder engine use 1 to 3

16 Fit the big-end bearing cap, tightening its new retaining nuts or bolts (as applicable) finger-tight at first. On diesel engines, the connecting rod and its bearing cap both have recesses machined into them on one side, close to their mating surfaces – these recesses must both face the same way as the arrow on the piston crown (ie, towards the timing belt end of the engine) when correctly installed. Reassemble the two components to satisfy this requirement.

17 Tighten the retaining bolts or nuts to the specified torque and angle as given in the Specifications (see illustrations).

18 Refit the remaining piston/connecting rod assemblies in the same way.

19 Rotate the crankshaft by hand. Check that it turns freely; some stiffness is to be expected if new parts have been fitted, but there should be no binding or tight spots.

20 On diesel engines, if new pistons have been fitted, or if a new short engine has been fitted, the projection of the piston crowns above the cylinder head mating face of the cylinder block at TDC must be measured. This measurement is used to determine the thickness of the new cylinder head gasket required. This procedure is described as part of the Cylinder head – removal, inspection and refitting procedure in Chapter 2D.

21 Proceed as follows according to engine type:

a) On the 1.4 litre OHV petrol engine, refit the oil pump gears, sump and cylinder head as described in Chapter 2B.

b) On the 3-cylinder diesel engine code AMF, refit the balancer shaft assembly as described in Chapter 2D.

c) On the 1.4 litre DOHC petrol engine and all diesel engines, refit the oil pump pick-up pipe and oil baffle, the sump and the cylinder head as described in Chapters 2C or 2D.

in order on a clean work surface. Where the bearing caps are secured with nuts, pad the threaded ends of the bolts with insulating tape to prevent them scratching the crankpins and bores when the pistons are refitted.

10 Start with piston/connecting rod assembly No 1. Make sure that the piston rings are still spaced as described in Section 17, then clamp them in position with a piston ring compressor tool.

11 Insert the piston/connecting rod assembly into the top of No 1 cylinder/liner. Lower the big-end in first, guiding it to protect the cylinder bores. Where oil jets are located at the bottoms of the bores, take particular care not to damage them when guiding the connecting rods onto the crankpins.

12 Ensure that the orientation of the piston in its cylinder/liner is correct – refer to Section 13 for details. On diesel engines, the piston crowns are specially shaped to improve the engine's combustion characteristics. Because of this, pistons 1 and 2 are different to pistons 3 and 4. When correctly fitted, the larger inlet valve chambers on pistons 1 and 2 must face the flywheel end of the engine, and the larger

inlet valve chambers on the remaining pistons must face the timing belt end of the engine. Note that on the 3-cylinder engine code AMF, the pattern follows that of cylinders 1, 2 and 3. New pistons have number markings on their crowns to indicate their type – 1/2 denotes piston 1 or 2, 3/4 indicates piston 3 or 4 (see illustration).

13 Using a block of wood or hammer handle against the piston crown, tap the assembly into the cylinder/liner until the piston crown is flush with the top of the cylinder (see illustration).

14 Ensure that the bearing shell is still correctly installed in the connecting rod, then liberally lubricate the crankpin and both bearing shells with clean engine oil.

15 Taking care not to mark the cylinder/liner bores, tap the piston/connecting rod assembly down the bore and onto the crankpin. On engines where the big-end caps are secured by nuts, remove the insulating tape from the threaded ends of the connecting rod bolts. Oil the bolt threads, and on engines where the big-end caps are secured by bolts, oil the undersides of the bolt heads.

20 Engine –
initial start-up after overhaul and reassembly

1 Refit the remainder of the engine components in the order listed in Section 5 of this Chapter. Refit the engine to the vehicle as

19.13 Using a hammer handle to tap the piston into its bore

19.17a Tighten the big-end bearing cap bolts/nuts to the specified torque . . .

19.17b . . . then through the specified angle

described in Section 4 of this Chapter. Double-check the engine oil and coolant levels, and make a final check that everything has been reconnected. Make sure that there are no tools or rags left in the engine compartment.

2 Reconnect the battery negative lead (refer to *Disconnecting the battery* in the *Reference* Chapter at the end of this manual).

Petrol models

3 Remove the spark plugs, referring to Chapter 1A for details.

4 The engine must be immobilised such that it can be turned over using the starter motor, without starting – refer to Section 2 of Chapters 2A, 2B and 2C. Also, disable the fuel pump by unplugging the fuel pump power relay from the relay board with reference to Chapter 12.

Caution: To prevent damage to the catalytic converter, it is important to disable the fuel system.

5 Turn the engine using the starter motor until the oil pressure warning lamp goes out. If the lamp fails to extinguish after several seconds of cranking, check the engine oil level and oil filter security. Assuming these are correct, check the security of the oil pressure switch

wiring – do not progress any further until you are satisfied that oil is being pumped around the engine at sufficient pressure.

6 Refit the spark plugs, and reconnect the ignition and fuel pump wiring.

Diesel models

7 On engine code ASY, the stop solenoid and fuel metering control wiring must be disconnected, to prevent the engine from running or fuel from being discharged. On engine codes AMF, ASZ and ATD, disconnect the injector solenoids by disconnecting the connector at the end of the cylinder head. **Note:** *As a result of the wiring being disconnected, faults will be stored in the ECU memory. These must be erased after the compression test.*

8 Turn the engine using the starter motor until the oil pressure warning lamp goes out.

9 If the lamp fails to extinguish after several seconds of cranking, check the engine oil level and oil filter security. Assuming these are correct, check the security of the oil pressure switch cabling – do not progress any further until you are satisfied that oil is being pumped around the engine at sufficient pressure.

10 Reconnect the wiring as applicable.

All models

11 Start the engine, but be aware that as fuel system components have been disturbed, the cranking time may be a little longer than usual.

12 While the engine is idling, check for fuel, water and oil leaks. Don't be alarmed if there are some odd smells and the occasional plume of smoke as components heat up and burn off oil deposits.

13 Assuming all is well, keep the engine idling until hot water is felt circulating through the top hose.

14 After a few minutes, stop the engine then recheck the oil and coolant levels, and top-up as necessary.

15 There is no need to retighten the cylinder head bolts once the engine has been run following reassembly.

16 If new cylinder liners, pistons, rings or crankshaft bearings have been fitted, the engine must be treated as new, and run-in for the first 600 miles (1000 km). *Do not operate the engine at full-throttle, or allow it to labour at low engine speeds in any gear.* It is recommended that the engine oil and filter are changed at the end of this period.

Chapter 3
Cooling, heating and air conditioning systems

Contents

Section number

Antifreeze mixture . . . . See Chapter 1A or 1B
Auxiliary drivebelt checking and renewal . . . . . . See Chapter 1A or 1B
Coolant level check . . . . See *Weekly checks*
Coolant pump – removal and refitting 7
Cooling system electrical switches and sensors – testing, removal and refitting 6
Cooling system hoses – disconnection and renewal 2
Electric cooling fan – testing, removal and refitting 5

Section number

General information and precautions 1
Heating/air conditioning system – general information and precautions 8
Heating/air conditioning system components – removal and refitting 9
Heating/ventilation system vents – removal and refitting 10
Radiator – removal, inspection and refitting 3
Thermostat – removal, testing and refitting 4

Degrees of difficulty

Easy, suitable for novice with little experience	**Fairly easy,** suitable for beginner with some experience	**Fairly difficult,** suitable for competent DIY mechanic	**Difficult,** suitable for experienced DIY mechanic	**Very difficult,** suitable for expert DIY or professional

Specifications

Cooling system pressure cap

Opening pressure . . . .   1.4 to 1.6 bar

Thermostat

Petrol engines

1.2 litre engines	N/A
1.4 litre OHV engines:	
Begins to open	88°C
Fully open	103°C
1.4 litre DOHC engines:	
Begins to open	84°C
Fully open	98°C

Diesel engines

1.4 litre engines:	
Begins to open	85°C
Fully open	105°C
1.9 litre engines	N/A

Cooling fan

Fan speeds:	
1st speed cut-in	91 to 97°C
1st speed cut-out	91 to 84°C
2nd speed cut-in	99 to 105°C
2nd speed cut-out	98 to 91°C

Coolant temperature sensor

Resistances:

1.2 litre petrol engines:

At 30°C	1500 to 2000 ohms
At 80°C	275 to 375 ohms

1.4 litre OHV petrol engines:

At 20°C	2340 to 2680 ohms
At 80°C	290 to 330 ohms

1.4 litre DOHC petrol engines:

At 30°C	1500 to 2000 ohms
At 80°C	275 to 375 ohms

1.4 litre diesel engines:

At 30°C	1500 to 2000 ohms
At 80°C	275 to 375 ohm

1.9 litre diesel engines:

At 30°C	1500 to 2000 ohms
At 80°C	275 to 375 ohms

Torque wrench settings

	Nm	lbf ft
Air conditioning condenser	5	4
Coolant pump:		
1.2 litre petrol engines	24	18
1.4 litre OHV petrol engines	20	15
1.4 litre DOHC petrol engines.	20	15
Diesel engines	15	11
Coolant pump pulley:		
1.2 litre petrol engines	22	16
1.4 litre OHV petrol engines	10	7
Distribution housing (diesel engines)	10	7
Radiator	5	4
Radiator cooling fan shroud bolts	10	7
Radiator cooling fan thermoswitch	35	26
Thermostat cover (diesel engines)	15	11
Thermostat/distribution housing:		
1.2 litre petrol engines	8	6
1.4 litre OHV petrol engines	20	15
1.4 litre DOHC petrol engines.	10	7
Timing belt guide pulley:		
1.4 litre DOHC petrol engines.	50	37
1.9 litre diesel (engine code ASY only):		
Stage 1	40	30
Stage 2	Angle-tighten a further 90°	

1 General information and precautions

The cooling system comprises a centrifugal pump, crossflow radiator, electric cooling fan, thermostat and a heater matrix, as well as the interconnecting hoses. The system functions as follows. Cold coolant from the radiator passes through the bottom hose to the coolant pump where it is pumped around the cylinder block and head passages. After cooling the cylinder bores, combustion surfaces and valve seats, the coolant reaches the top of the engine and passes through the top hose to the radiator. The coolant also passes through the heater matrix where it heats incoming air to the inside of the car.

When the engine is cold the coolant circulation is restricted to the cylinder block, cylinder head, expansion tank, and heater by a thermostat positioned in the radiator circuit. On petrol engines the thermostat is located in the coolant distribution housing on the left-hand end of the cylinder head, however, on diesel engines it is located in the coolant return on the front of the cylinder block. When the coolant reaches a predetermined temperature, the wax-filled thermostat opens and the coolant passes through to the radiator. As the coolant circulates through the radiator it is cooled by the inrush of air when the car is in forward motion. Airflow is supplemented by the action of the electric cooling fan(s) when necessary. Upon leaving the radiator, the coolant has cooled and the cycle is repeated.

A thermostatic switch controls the electric cooling fan(s) mounted on the rear of the radiator. At a preset coolant temperature, the switch actuates the fan(s).

Precautions

⚠ *Warning: Do not attempt to remove the expansion tank filler cap or disturb any part of the cooling system while the engine is hot, as there is a high risk of scalding. If the expansion tank filler cap must be removed before the engine and radiator have fully cooled (even though this is not recommended) the pressure in the cooling system must first be relieved. Cover the cap with a thick layer of cloth, to avoid scalding, and slowly unscrew the filler cap until a hissing sound can be heard. When the hissing has stopped, indicating that the pressure has reduced, slowly unscrew the filler cap until it can be removed; if more hissing sounds are heard, wait until they have stopped before unscrewing the cap completely. At all times keep well away from the filler cap opening.*

• *Do not allow antifreeze to come into contact with skin or painted surfaces of the vehicle. Rinse off spills immediately with plenty of water. Never leave antifreeze lying around in an open container or in a puddle in the driveway or on the garage floor. Children and pets are attracted by its sweet smell. Antifreeze can be fatal if ingested.*

• *If the engine is hot, the electric cooling fan may start rotating even if the engine is not running, so be careful to keep hands, hair and loose clothing well clear when working in the engine compartment.*

2.4 Pull out the retaining clip

3.3 Disconnecting the thermoswitch wiring

3.4 Disconnecting the top hose from the radiator

• *Refer to Section 8 for additional precautions to be observed when working on models with air conditioning.*

2 Cooling system hoses – disconnection and renewal

Note: *Refer to the warnings given in Section 1 of this Chapter before proceeding.*

1 If the checks described in the relevant part of Chapter 1 reveal a faulty hose, it must be renewed as follows.

2 First drain the cooling system as described in Chapter 1A or 1B. If the coolant is not due for renewal, it may be re-used if it is collected in a clean container.

3 To disconnect a hose, release its retaining clips, and then move them along the hose, clear of the relevant inlet/outlet union. Carefully work the hose free.

4 In order to disconnect the radiator inlet and outlet hoses, apply pressure to hold the hose on to the relevant union, pull out the spring clip and pull the hose from the union **(see illustration)**. Note that the radiator inlet and outlet unions are fragile; do not use excessive force when attempting to remove the hoses. If a hose proves to be difficult to remove, try to release it by rotating the hose ends before attempting to free it.

 If all else fails, cut the hose with a sharp knife, then slit it so that it can be peeled off in two pieces. Although this may prove expensive if the hose is otherwise undamaged, it is preferable to buying a new radiator.

5 When fitting a hose, first slide the clips onto the hose, then work the hose into position. If clamp type clips were originally fitted, it is a good idea to use screw-type clips when refitting the hose. If the hose is stiff, use a little soapy water as a lubricant, or soften the hose by soaking it in hot water.

6 Work the hose into position, checking that it is correctly routed, then slide each clip along the hose until it passes over the flared end of the relevant union, before securing it in position with the retaining clip.

7 Prior to refitting a radiator inlet or outlet hose, renew the connection O-ring regardless of condition. The connections are a push-fit over the radiator unions.

8 Refill the cooling system as described in Chapter 1A or 1B.

9 Check thoroughly for leaks as soon as possible after disturbing any part of the cooling system.

3 Radiator – removal, inspection and refitting

Removal

1 Disconnect the battery negative lead. **Note:** *Before disconnecting the battery, refer to 'Disconnecting the battery' in the Reference section at the rear of this manual.*

2 Drain the cooling system as described in the relevant part of Chapter 1.

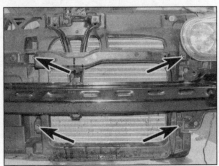

3.9a Undo the radiator mounting screws (arrowed)

3 Disconnect the wiring from the cooling fan thermoswitch and the cooling fan on the left-hand side of the radiator **(see illustration)**.

4 Disconnect the upper and lower hoses from the left-hand side of the radiator. To do so, pull out the spring clip, then ease the hoses from the stubs **(see illustration)**.

Models without air conditioning

5 Remove the front bumper and bracket with reference to Chapter 11.

6 Disconnect and detach the bonnet lock cable from the lock carrier.

7 Disconnect the headlight wiring. To prevent damage to it, we also recommend removal of the right-hand headlight completely.

8 Unbolt the lock carrier and radiator and remove from the front of the car.

9 Unbolt the radiator from the lock carrier, then unbolt the cooling fan and shroud from the radiator **(see illustrations)**.

3.9b Radiator mounting rubbers

3.9c Undo the cooling fan screws (arrowed)

3.9d Remove the radiator shroud screws (arrowed)

3.15 Lowering the radiator from the air conditioning condenser

Models with air conditioning

10 Disconnect the wiring from the air conditioning compressor, then unbolt it and tie it to the lock carrier. **Do not** disconnect the refrigerant lines.

11 Remove the front bumper and bracket with reference to Chapter 11.

12 Disconnect and detach the bonnet lock cable from the lock carrier.

13 Disconnect the headlight wiring. To prevent damage to it, we also recommend removal of the right-hand headlight completely.

14 Unbolt the lock carrier and swivel it out from the front of the car, leaving the air conditioning lines still attached. Support the assembly on axle stands or blocks of wood.

15 Unbolt the condenser from the radiator, and the radiator from the lock carrier, then lower the radiator to the floor and tie the condenser to the inner body with cable ties **(see illustration)**.

4.5 Removing the coolant distribution housing from the cylinder block

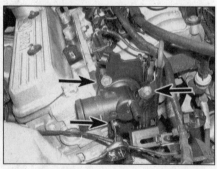

4.11a Slacken and remove the retaining bolts . . .

3.21 Radiator rubber mounting

Inspection

16 If the radiator has been removed due to suspected blockage, reverse flush it as described in the relevant part of Chapter 1.

17 Clean dirt and debris from the radiator fins, using an air line (in which case, wear eye protection) or a soft brush. Be careful, as the fins are sharp and easily damaged.

18 If necessary, a radiator specialist can perform a 'flow test' on the radiator, to establish whether an internal blockage exists.

19 A leaking radiator must be referred to a specialist for permanent repair. Do not attempt to weld or solder a leaking radiator, as damage may result.

20 If the radiator is to be sent for repair or renewed, remove the cooling fan and thermoswitch.

Refitting

21 Refitting is a reversal of removal, but

4.10 Release the retaining clips and disconnect the coolant hoses from the thermostat housing

4.11b . . . and remove the thermostat housing cover

check the condition of the mounting rubbers and renew if necessary **(see illustration)**. On completion, refill the cooling system using the correct type of antifreeze as described in the relevant part of Chapter 1.

4 Thermostat – removal, testing and refitting

1.2 litre petrol engines

Removal

1 The thermostat is integral with the coolant distribution housing bolted to the left-hand end of the cylinder block. If it is faulty, the complete housing must be renewed.

2 Drain the cooling system as described in Chapter 1A.

3 To provide working room, remove the battery, air cleaner and ducting as described in Chapter 5A and 4A.

4 Loosen the clips and disconnect the hoses from the distribution housing.

5 Unscrew the mounting bolts and withdraw the housing from the distribution housing and intermediate coolant pipe on the rear of the engine **(see illustration)**. Recover the O-ring.

Testing

6 As the thermostat is integral with the distribution housing, it is not possible to test it by heating in water in the conventional way. Symptoms of a faulty thermostat will be overheating if it sticks in the closed position, or slow warm-up if it sticks in the open position.

Refitting

7 Refitting is a reversal of removal, but refill the cooling system with the correct type and quantity of coolant as described in Chapter 1A.

1.4 litre OHV petrol engines

Removal

8 The thermostat is located beneath a cover in a housing on the rear, left-hand end of the cylinder head.

9 Drain the cooling system as described in Chapter 1A.

10 Release the retaining clips and disconnect the coolant hoses from the thermostat cover **(see illustration)**.

11 Unscrew the retaining bolts and remove the thermostat housing cover and sealing ring/ gasket from the engine **(see illustrations)**. Discard the sealing ring/gasket; a new one must be used on refitting.

12 The thermostat is clipped into the thermostat housing cover. Note the fitted location, then unclip the retaining clip from the cover, and remove the spring and thermostat plunger **(see illustrations)**.

Testing

13 Note that the thermostat must be installed in the cover before testing can commence.

4.12a Free the retaining clip from the housing cover . . .

4.12b . . . then remove the spring . . .

4.12c . . . and thermostat plunger

14 A rough test of the thermostat may be made by suspending it with a piece of string in a container full of water. Heat the water to bring it to the boil – the thermostat must open by the time the water boils. If not, renew it.

15 If a thermometer is available, the precise opening temperature of the thermostat may be determined, and compared with the figures given in the Specifications. The opening temperature is also marked on the thermostat.

16 A thermostat which fails to close as the water cools must also be renewed.

Refitting

17 Refitting is a reversal of removal, but fit a new sealing ring/gasket, and refill the cooling system with the correct type and quantity of coolant as described in Chapter 1A.

1.4 litre DOHC petrol engines

Removal

18 The thermostat is located beneath a cover in a housing on the left-hand end of the cylinder head.

19 Drain the cooling system as described in Chapter 1A.

20 Release the retaining clip and disconnect the coolant radiator bottom hose from the thermostat cover (see illustration).

21 Unscrew the retaining bolts and remove the thermostat housing cover and sealing ring from the engine. Discard the sealing ring; a new one must be used on refitting (see illustration).

22 Remove the thermostat from the housing (see illustration). Note that the thermostat

is only available together with its spring housing.

Testing

23 Refer to paragraphs 14 to 16.

Refitting

24 Refitting is a reversal of removal, but fit a new sealing ring, and refill the cooling system with the correct type and quantity of coolant as described in Chapter 1A.

Diesel engines

Removal

25 The thermostat is located beneath a cover on the front of the engine, in the coolant return from the bottom of the radiator.

26 Drain the cooling system as described in Chapter 1A.

27 Release the retaining clip and disconnect the coolant hose from the thermostat cover.

28 Unscrew the retaining bolts and remove

the thermostat housing cover and sealing ring from the engine (see illustrations). Discard the sealing ring; a new one must be used on refitting.

29 To remove the thermostat from the cover, twist the thermostat 90° anti-clockwise, and pull it from the cover.

Refitting

30 Refitting is a reversal of removal, bearing in mind the following points.

 a) *Refit the thermostat using a new O-ring.*
 b) *Insert the thermostat into the cover and twist 90° clockwise.*
 c) *The thermostat should be fitted with the brace almost vertical.*
 d) *Ensure that any brackets are in place on the thermostat cover bolts as noted before removal.*
 e) *Refill the cooling system with the correct type and quantity of coolant as described in Chapter 1B.*

4.20 Disconnect the hose

4.21 Remove and discard the seal

4.22 Remove the thermostat

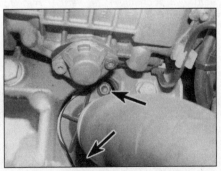

4.28a Thermostat cover screws . . .

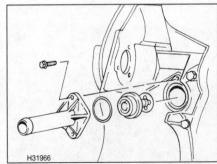

4.28b . . . and thermostat – diesel engines

5.9 Removing the cooling fan and shroud from the radiator

5 Electric cooling fan – testing, removal and refitting

Testing

1 Vehicles may be fitted with one or two cooling fans, depending on model. The cooling fan is supplied with current through the ignition switch, cooling fan control unit (where applicable), the relay(s) and fuses/fusible link (see Chapter 12). The circuit is completed by the cooling fan thermostatic switch, which is mounted in the left-hand end of the radiator. The cooling fan has two speed settings; the thermostatic switch actually contains two switches, one for the stage 1 fan speed setting and another for the stage 2 fan speed setting. Testing of the cooling fan circuit is as follows, noting that the following check should be carried out on both the stage 1 speed circuit and speed 2 circuit (see wiring diagrams at the end of Chapter 12).

2 If a fan does not appear to work, first check the fuses/fusible links. If they are good, run the engine until normal operating temperature is reached, then allow it to idle. If the fan does not cut in within a few minutes, switch off the ignition and disconnect the wiring plug from the cooling fan switch. Bridge the relevant two contacts in the wiring plug using a length of spare wire, and switch on the ignition. If the fan now operates, the switch is probably faulty and should be renewed.

3 If the switch appears to work, the motor can be checked by disconnecting the motor wiring

6.6 Unscrew the thermoswitch

connector and connecting a 12 volt supply directly to the motor terminals. If the motor is faulty, it must be renewed, as no spares are available.

4 If the fan still fails to operate, check the cooling fan circuit wiring (Chapter 12). Check each wire for continuity and ensure that all connections are clean and free of corrosion.

5 On models with a cooling fan control unit, if no fault can be found with the fuses/fusible links, wiring, fan switch, or fan motor, then it is likely that the cooling fan control unit is faulty. Testing of the unit should be entrusted to a Skoda dealer or specialist; if the unit is faulty it must be renewed.

Removal

6 Disconnect the battery negative lead. **Note:** *Before disconnecting the battery, refer to 'Disconnecting the battery' in the Reference section at the rear of this manual.*

7 Remove the engine top cover.

8 Disconnect the wiring plug from the cooling fan motor, and slide the connector from the retaining bracket.

9 Unscrew the bolts and remove the cooling fan and shroud from the radiator **(see illustration)**. Take care not to damage the radiator fins.

10 Undo the three Torx screws securing the fan to the radiator shroud, and withdraw the fan.

Refitting

11 Refitting is a reversal of removal.

6 Cooling system electrical switches and sensors – testing, removal and refitting

Cooling fan thermostatic switch

Testing

1 Testing of the switch is described in Section 5, as part of the electric cooling fan test procedure.

Removal

2 The thermoswitch is located in the left-hand side of the radiator. The engine and radiator must be cold before removing the switch.

3 Disconnect the battery negative lead. **Note:** *Before disconnecting the battery, refer to 'Disconnecting the battery' in the Reference section at the rear of this manual.* Where necessary, remove the engine top cover.

4 Either drain the radiator to below the level of the switch (as described in Chapter 1A or 1B), or have ready a suitable plug which can be used to plug the switch aperture in the radiator whilst the switch is removed. If a plug is used, take great care not to damage the radiator, and do not use anything which will allow foreign matter to enter the radiator.

5 Disconnect the wiring plug from the thermoswitch.

6 Carefully unscrew the thermoswitch from the radiator **(see illustration)**.

Refitting

7 Refitting is a reversal of removal, but apply a smear of suitable grease to the threads of the switch and tighten it to the specified torque. On completion, refill the cooling system with the correct type and quantity of coolant as described in Chapter 1A or 1B, or to-up as described in *Weekly checks*.

8 Start the engine and run it until it reaches normal operating temperature, then continue to run the engine and check that the cooling fan cuts in and functions correctly.

Coolant temperature sensor

Testing

9 The coolant temperature sensor is located on the coolant distribution housing on the left-hand end of the cylinder head. On petrol engines it is on the top or front of the housing, and on diesel engines it is on the rear of the housing.

10 The sensor contains a thermistor, which consists of an electronic component whose electrical resistance decreases at a predetermined rate as its temperature rises. When the coolant is cold, the sensor resistance is high, current flow through the gauge is reduced, and the gauge needle points towards the 'cold' end of the scale. Typical resistances are given in the Specifications, however, the sensor can also be checked by a Skoda dealer or specialist using diagnostic equipment. If the sensor is faulty, it must be renewed.

Removal and refitting

11 Remove the engine top cover.

12 Disconnect the wiring plug from the sensor, located on the thermostat housing at the left-hand end of the cylinder head. Partially drain the cooling system to below the level of the sensor (as described in Chapter 1A or 1B).

13 Carefully withdraw the retaining clip and pull the sensor from the housing. Recover the O-ring.

14 Refitting is a reversal of removal, bearing in mind the following points.

  a) Refit the sensor with a new O-ring.

  b) Refill the cooling system as described in Chapter 1A or 1B, or top-up as described in 'Weekly checks'.

7 Coolant pump – removal and refitting

Note: *New coolant pumps may be of a modified design, which do not require gaskets. Use a suitable sealer.*

1.2 litre petrol engines

Removal

1 Drain the cooling system as described in Chapter 1A.

2 Before removing the auxiliary drivebelt, loosen only the coolant pump pulley mounting bolts.

7.4 Removing the coolant pump pulley – engine code BME

7.5 Removing the coolant pump – engine code BME

7.18 Withdraw the coolant pump – 1.4 litre DOHC engines

3 Remove the auxiliary drivebelt as described in Chapter 1A.

4 Fully unscrew the bolts and remove the pulley from the coolant pump (see illustration).

5 Unscrew the coolant pump retaining bolts, and withdraw the pump and gasket (if fitted) from the engine block. Identify the front retaining bolt, as it has sealant on its threads. If faulty, the pump must be renewed (see illustration).

Refitting

6 Refitting is a reversal of removal, bearing in mind the following points.

a) *Refit the pump using a new gasket (refer to note above).*
b) *Apply suitable sealant to the threads of the front retaining bolt.*
c) *Refill the cooling system as described in Chapter 1A.*

1.4 litre OHV petrol engines

Removal

7 Drain the cooling system as described in Chapter 1A.

8 Remove the right-hand engine mounting as described in Chapter 2B. This procedure involves supporting the engine with a hoist. Note that the coolant pump body forms the base bracket for the engine mounting.

9 Before removing the auxiliary drivebelt, loosen only the coolant pump pulley mounting bolts.

10 Remove the auxiliary drivebelt as described in Chapter 1A.

11 Unbolt the metal coolant pipe from the cylinder block.

12 Release the clip and disconnect the short hose connecting the pump to the metal coolant pipe.

13 Fully unscrew the bolts and remove the pulley from the coolant pump.

14 Unscrew the mounting bolts/nuts and withdraw the pump and gasket from the engine block.

Refitting

15 Refitting is a reversal of removal, bearing in mind the following points.

a) *Refit the pump using a new gasket.*
b) *Refill the cooling system as described in Chapter 1A.*

1.4 litre DOHC petrol engines

Removal

16 Remove the main timing belt as described in Chapter 2C. If the belt is to be re-used, note the direction of rotation.

17 Remove the timing belt idler roller, and rear timing belt cover.

18 Unscrew the coolant pump retaining bolts, and withdraw the pump from the engine block. Note the gasket is integral with the pump and must not be removed. If faulty, the pump must be renewed (see illustration).

Refitting

19 Refitting is a reversal of removal, bearing in mind the following points.

a) *Clean the surface of the engine block before refitting the pump.*
b) *Refill the cooling system as described in Chapter 1A.*

Diesel engines

Removal

20 Drain the cooling system as described in Chapter 1B.

21 Remove the timing belt as described in Chapter 2D, noting the following points.

a) *The lower part of the timing belt guard need not be removed.*
b) *The timing belt should be left in position on the crankshaft sprocket.*

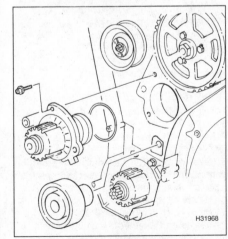

7.23a Coolant pump – diesel engines

c) *Cover the timing belt with a cloth to protect it from coolant.*

22 On the 1.9 litre engine code ASY only, unscrew the timing belt idler pulley, and push the pulley downwards approximately 30 mm.

23 Unscrew the coolant pump retaining bolts, and remove the pump and O-ring seal from the engine block. If the pump is faulty, it must be renewed (see illustrations).

Refitting

24 Refitting is a reversal of removal, bearing in mind the following points.

a) *Fit the coolant pump with a new O-ring, lubricated with a little coolant.*
b) *Install the pump with the cast lug facing down.*
c) *Refill the cooling system as described in Chapter 1B.*

8 Heating/air conditioning system – general information and precautions

Heating system

1 The heating/ventilation system consists of a four-speed blower motor (housed in the passenger compartment), face-level vents in the centre and at each end of the facia, and air ducts to the front and rear footwells.

2 The control unit is located in the facia, and the controls operate flap valves to deflect and mix the air flowing through the various parts of the heating/ventilation system. The flap valves are contained in the air distribution housing, which acts as a central distribution

7.23b Coolant pump – diesel engine code AMF

TOOL TIP

Many car accessory shops sell one-shot air conditioning recharge aerosols. These generally contain refrigerant, compressor oil, leak sealer and system conditioner. Some also have a dye to help pinpoint leaks.

⚠️ *Warning: These products must only be used as directed by the manufacturer, and do not remove the need for regular maintenance.*

unit, passing air to the various ducts and vents.

3 Cold air enters the system through the grille at the rear of the engine compartment. On some models (depending on specification) a pollen filter is fitted in the heater assembly to filter out dust, soot, pollen and spores from the air entering the vehicle.

4 The airflow, which can be boosted by the blower, then flows through the various ducts, according to the settings of the controls. Stale air is expelled through ducts below the rear window. If warm air is required, the cold air is passed through the heater matrix, which is heated by the engine coolant.

5 If necessary, the outside air supply can be closed off, allowing the air inside the vehicle to be recirculated. This can be useful to prevent unpleasant odours entering from outside the vehicle, but should only be used briefly, as the recirculated air inside the vehicle will soon deteriorate.

Air conditioning system

6 Air conditioning is fitted as standard to most UK models. It enables the temperature of incoming air to be lowered, and dehumidifies the air, which makes for rapid demisting and increased comfort.

7 The cooling side of the system works in the same way as a domestic refrigerator. Refrigerant gas is drawn into a belt-driven compressor and passes into a condenser mounted in front of the radiator, where it loses heat and becomes liquid. The liquid passes through an expansion valve to an evaporator, where it changes from liquid under high pressure to gas under low pressure. This change is accompanied by a drop in temperature, which cools the evaporator. The refrigerant returns to the compressor and the cycle begins again.

8 Air blown through the evaporator passes to the air distribution unit, where it is mixed with hot air blown through the heater matrix to achieve the desired temperature in the passenger compartment.

9 The heating side of the system works in the same way as on models without air conditioning.

10 The operation of the system is controlled electronically by coolant temperature switches, and pressure switches which are screwed into the compressor high-pressure line. Any problems with the system should be referred to a Skoda dealer or an air conditioning specialist **(see Tool Tip)**.

Precautions

• **When an air conditioning system is fitted, it is necessary to observe special precautions whenever dealing with any part of the system, its associated components and any items which require disconnection of the system. If for any reason the system must be disconnected, entrust this task to your Skoda dealer or an air conditioning specialist.**

⚠️ *Warning: The refrigeration circuit contains a refrigerant and it is therefore dangerous to disconnect any part of the system without specialised knowledge and equipment. The refrigerant is potentially dangerous and should only be handled by qualified persons. If it is splashed onto the skin it can cause frostbite. It is not itself poisonous, but in the presence of a naked flame (including a cigarette) it forms a poisonous gas. Uncontrolled discharging of the refrigerant is dangerous and potentially damaging to the environment, and is illegal in most countries.*

• **Do not operate the air conditioning system if it is known to be short of refrigerant, as this may damage the compressor.**

---

9 Heating/air conditioning system components – removal and refitting

System control unit

Removal

1 Switch off the ignition and all electrical consumers.

2 Remove the centre part of the facia with reference to Chapter 11.

3 Carefully prise off the trim panel from the control unit. To ensure correct refitting, use tape to secure the control knobs.

4 Disconnect the wiring.

5 Depress the clips and disconnect the flexible control wires from the control unit.

6 If necessary, the wires can be disconnected from the unit by depressing the plastic lugs with a screwdriver.

Refitting

7 Refitting is a reversal of removal.

System assembly

Removal

8 Disconnect the battery negative lead (refer to *Disconnecting the battery* in the *Reference* Chapter at the end of this manual).

9 On models with air conditoning, have the refrigerant evacuated from the system by a Skoda dealer or air conditioning specialist.

10 Remove the pollen filter element as described in Chapter 1A and 1B.

11 Unscrew the expansion tank cap (engine cold) to release any pressure present in the cooling system, then securely refit the cap.

12 Remove the engine cover. Clamp both heater hoses as close to the bulkhead as possible to minimise coolant loss. Alternatively, drain the cooling system as described in the relevant part of Chapter 1A or 1B. To ensure correct refitting, mark the hoses for position, as they differ according to model. Basically, on models with temperature-control, the outlet nearest the centre of the car is the return hose to the water pump and the outer hose is the supply hose from the cylinder head. On models without temperature-control the hose positions are reversed.

13 Release the clips and disconnect both hoses from the heater matrix outlets. To prevent spillage of coolant when the heater is removed, use low air pressure to blow out the remaining coolant then plug the outlets.

14 Remove the centre console and facia assembly as described in Chapter 11.

15 Unbolt and remove the holder for the front passenger airbag **(see illustration)**.

16 Remove the air vents from the top of the heater, and the air ducting from the side. Also, remove the rear footwell duct from the bottom of the heater **(see illustrations)**.

17 The support bracket must now be removed to facilitate removal of the heater assembly. On RHD models, the left-hand bracket must be removed, and on LHD models, the right-hand bracket must be removed. Unclip the wiring loom and remove the bracket **(see illustration)**.

18 Disconnect the wiring and remove the

9.15 Removing the front passenger airbag holder

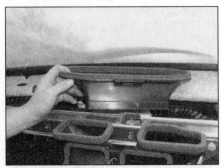

9.16a Removing the top air vent . . .

9.16b . . . and bottom air vent from the heater assembly

9.17 Removing the support bracket

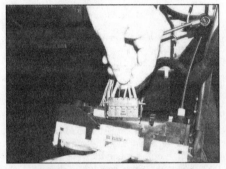

9.18 Disconnect the wiring from the control unit

9.19 Removing the driver's footwell vent

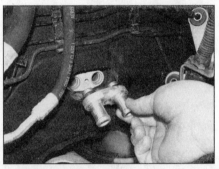

9.22 Removing the heater matrix adaptor

heater/air conditioning control unit **(see illustration)**. Also, disconnect the wiring from the heater blower motor.

19 Remove the driver's footwell vent **(see illustration)**.

20 Where fitted, slide the convenience control

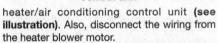

9.23 Unbolt the refrigerant lines from the evaporator expansion valve

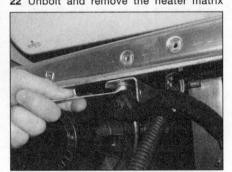
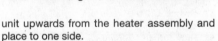

9.24 Unscrew the mounting bolts . . .

9.25 . . . then withdraw the heater/air conditioning assembly from inside the car

9.26 Check the condition of the foam gasket between the heater assembly and bulkhead

unit upwards from the heater assembly and place to one side.

21 Where fitted, disconnect the wiring and earth cable for the auxiliary heating. Cut free any cable ties securing wiring to the heater assembly.

22 Unbolt and remove the heater matrix

adapter from the bulkhead in the engine compartment **(see illustration)**.

23 On models with air conditioning, unbolt the refrigerant lines from the evaporator expansion valve on the bulkhead in the engine compartment, and recover the O-ring seals **(see illustration)**.

24 Unscrew and remove the mounting bolts **(see illustration)**.

25 Place cloth rags in the passenger footwell, then carefully withdraw the heater/air conditioning assembly and remove from the car **(see illustration)**. Be prepared for some coolant spillage.

Refitting

26 Refitting is reversal of removal, noting the following points:

a) Check the condition of the foam gasket which fits between the heater assembly and the bulkhead, and renew if necessary **(see illustration)**.

b) Make sure that all wiring is correctly reconnected and routed.

c) Make sure that the air ducts are securely clipped into position.

d) On completion, check the coolant level and top-up if necessary as described in 'Weekly checks'.

Heater matrix

Removal

27 It is possible to remove the heater matrix from the bottom of the heater assembly with the assembly *in situ*, however, this sub-section describes the procedure with the assembly removed as described earlier.

9.28 Removing the heater matrix and cover from the bottom of the heater assembly

28 With the assembly on the bench, use a screwdriver to prise off the spring clips, then remove the heater matrix and cover from the bottom of the unit **(see illustration)**.

Refitting

29 Refitting is a reversal of removal.

Heater blower motor

Removal

30 Switch off the ignition and all electrical consumers.
31 Remove the glovebox as described in Chapter 11, Section 27.
32 Disconnect the small wire from the terminal near the centre of the blower motor housing. Also, disconnect the large plug from the connector and release the wiring loom from the cable ties on the housing.

9.33 Removing the heater blower motor

33 Undo the screws and withdraw the motor assembly from the housing **(see illustration)**.
34 Using a screwdriver, depress the pegs and push the wiring plug connection out of the catch.
35 Depress the catches and remove the blower motor and fan wheel from the housing.

Refitting

36 Refitting is a reversal of removal.

Blower motor series resistor

Removal

37 Switch off the ignition and all electrical consumers.
38 Remove the glovebox as described in Chapter 11, Section 27.
39 Disconnect the wiring, then turn the series

resistor 45° anti-clockwise to remove it from the housing.

Refitting

40 Refitting is a reversal of removal, but check the operation of the blower motor in all 4 speeds before refitting the glovebox.

Air conditioning compressor

 Warning: Do not attempt to open the refrigerant circuit. Refer to the precautions given in Section 8.

41 For removal of the engine or radiator, the compressor may be unbolted from the engine and tied to the lock carrier, after disconnecting the wiring. **Do not** disconnect the refrigerant lines.

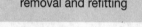

10 Heating/ventilation system vents –
removal and refitting

Side vents

1 To remove a vent, carefully prise it from the housing using a small flat-bladed screwdriver. Take care not to damage the surrounding trim.
2 To refit, carefully push the vent into position until the locating clips engage.

Central facia vents

3 Proceed as described previously for the side vents, but note that each vent must be prised progressively from both sides to release it from the housing.

Chapter 4 Part A:
Petrol engine fuel systems

Contents

Section number

Air cleaner and inlet system – removal and refitting.............. 2
Air cleaner filter element – renewal.................See Chapter 1A
Cruise control system – general information 11
Fuel filter – renewal.. 5
Fuel injection system – depressurisation...................... 8
Fuel injection system – testing and adjustment............... 10

Section number

Fuel pump and gauge sender unit – removal and refitting......... 6
Fuel system components – removal and refitting 4
Fuel tank – removal and refitting 7
General information and precautions......................... 1
Inlet air temperature control system – general information 3
Inlet manifold – removal and refitting........................ 9

Degrees of difficulty

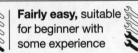

Easy, suitable for novice with little experience	**Fairly easy,** suitable for beginner with some experience	**Fairly difficult,** suitable for competent DIY mechanic	**Difficult,** suitable for experienced DIY mechanic	**Very difficult,** suitable for expert DIY or professional

Specifications

Engine codes

1.2 litre:	
SOHC..	AWY
DOHC..	AZQ, BME
1.4 litre OHV:	
44 kW...	AZE and AZF
50 kW...	AME, AQW and ATZ
1.4 litre DOHC:	
55 kW...	AUA and BBY
74 kW...	AUB and BBZ

System type

1.2 litre engines:	
Engine code AWY..	Siemens Simos 3PD
Engine code AZQ..	Siemens Simos 3PE
Engine code BME..	Siemens Simos 3PG
1.4 litre OHV engines:	
Engine codes AME, AZE and AZF	Siemens Simos 3PB
Engine codes AQW and ATZ	Siemens Simos 3PA
1.4 litre DOHC engines:	
Engine codes AUA and AUB	Magneti Marelli 4LV
Engine codes BBY and BBZ	Magneti Marelli 4MV

Recommended fuel

Minimum octane rating:	
All models...	95 RON unleaded
	(91 RON unleaded may be used, but with reduced performance)

Fuel system data

Fuel pump type	Electric, immersed in fuel tank
Fuel pump delivery rate	600 cc/30 secs (battery voltage of 12.5 V)
Regulated fuel pressure	2.5 bar
Engine idle speed (non-adjustable, electronically controlled):	
1.2 litre engines:	
Engine code AWY	610 to 830 rpm
Engine codes AZQ and BME	580 to 800 rpm
1.4 litre engines:	
OHV engines	730 to 870 rpm
Engine code AUA:	
Manual gearbox	650 to 850 rpm
Automatic transmission	580 to 780 rpm
Engine code BBY:	
Manual gearbox	660 to 860 rpm
Automatic transmission	580 to 780 rpm
Engine code AUB	740 to 940 rpm
Engine code BBZ	580 to 780 rpm
Idle CO content (non-adjustable, electronically controlled)	0.5 % max
Injector electrical resistance (typical)	12 to 17 ohms

Torque wrench settings

	Nm	lbf ft
Camshaft position sensor	8	6
Fuel rail mounting bolts:		
1.2 litre engines:		
Engine code AWY	8	6
Engine codes AZQ and BME	10	7
1.4 litre engines:		
OHV engines	20	15
DOHC engines	10	7
Fuel tank	25	18
Inlet air temperature/pressure sensor	2	1.5
Inlet manifold:		
1.2 litre engines:		
Engine code AWY:		
To inlet manifold	20	15
Lower mounting	15	11
Engine codes AZQ and BME	20	15
1.4 litre engines:		
OHV engines	25	18
DOHC engines	20	15
Knock sensor(s)	20	15
Oxygen sensor(s)	50	37
Throttle valve control unit:		
1.2 litre engines	8	6
1.4 litre engines	10	7

1 General information and precautions

General information

The systems described in this Chapter are all self-contained engine management systems, which control both the fuel injection and ignition. This Chapter deals with the fuel system components only – see Chapter 4C for information on the exhaust and emission control systems, and to Chapter 5B for details of the ignition system.

The fuel injection system comprises a fuel tank, an electric fuel pump/level sender unit, a fuel filter, fuel supply and return lines, a throttle valve control unit, a fuel rail, four electronic fuel injectors, and an Electronic Control Unit (ECU) together with its associated sensors, actuators and wiring. All the fuel systems used operate in the same manner, but there are some detail differences. The electronic power control system (EPC) is completely electronic, and no accelerator cable is fitted. The position of the accelerator pedal is signalled from the pedal control unit by two variable resistors, and the throttle valve is then activated by an electric motor in the throttle valve control unit on the inlet manifold. With the engine stopped, the position of the throttle valve is directly comparable to the position of the accelerator pedal, however, when the engine is running the engine control unit opens and closes the throttle valve independently according to the prevailing conditions. This may mean, for example, that the throttle valve may be fully open even though the accelerator pedal is only half open. The engine electronic control unit (ECU) determines the best position for the throttle valve in the interests of exhaust gas emission and fuel consumption. In the event of a fault in the system, the EPC warning light will illuminate on the instrument panel and the fault will be stored in the fault memory. The system then switches to its emergency settings and the engine speed is increased to allow the driver to take the vehicle to a Skoda dealer, however, the accelerator pedal position senders are no longer operational.

The fuel pump is immersed in the fuel inside the tank, and delivers a constant supply of fuel through a cartridge filter to the fuel rail. On the 1.2 litre engine code AWY the fuel rail incorporates a pressure regulator, and a return line is taken from the regulator to the fuel tank at the rear of the vehicle, however, on all other models, the pressure regulator is integral with the fuel filter located next to the fuel tank, and the return line is taken from the filter to the fuel tank. The fuel pressure regulator maintains a constant fuel pressure to the fuel injectors, and returns excess fuel to the tank through the return line. This constant flow system also helps to reduce fuel temperature, and prevents vaporisation.

The fuel injectors are opened and closed by the Electronic Control Unit (ECU), which calculates the injection timing and duration according to engine speed, crankshaft/camshaft position, throttle position and rate of opening, inlet manifold depression, inlet air temperature, coolant temperature and exhaust gas oxygen content information, received from sensors mounted on and around the engine.

Inlet air is drawn into the engine through the air cleaner, which contains a renewable paper filter element. On 1.2 litre engines and 1.4 litre DOHC engines, the air cleaner is integral with the engine top cover, however, on 1.4 litre OHV engines, it is located at the left-hand rear corner of the engine compartment. On all engines, the inlet air temperature is regulated by a valve mounted in the air cleaner inlet trunking, which blends air at ambient temperature with hot air, drawn from over the exhaust manifold.

The temperature and pressure of the air entering the engine is measured by a sensor located on the inlet manifold. This information is used by the ECU to fine-tune the fuelling requirements for different operating conditions.

Idle speed is determined by the ECU, and manual adjustment of the engine idle speed is not necessary or possible.

The exhaust gas oxygen content is constantly monitored by the ECU through one or two oxygen sensors (also known as lambda sensors). On engines with one sensor, it is fitted before the catalytic converter, and on engines with two sensors, one is fitted before the catalytic converter, and the other after – this improves sensor response time and accuracy, and the ECU compares the signals from each sensor to confirm that the converter is working correctly. The ECU uses the information from the sensor(s) to modify the injection timing and duration to maintain the optimum air/fuel ratio – a result of this is that manual adjustment of the idle exhaust CO content is not necessary or possible. 1.2 litre engine models are fitted with a single catalytic converter incorporated into the exhaust manifold. 1.4 litre OHV engine models are fitted with a single catalytic converter in the exhaust front pipe. 1.4 litre DOHC engine models are fitted with two catalytic converters, one in the exhaust manifold and the other in the exhaust front pipe.

1.2 litre engine code AWY is fitted with either one or two oxygen (lambda) sensors depending on territory, whereas 1.2 litre engine codes AZQ and BME are fitted with two oxygen sensors – the upstream one is located in the exhaust manifold and, where fitted, the downstream one is located in the exhaust front pipe. 1.4 litre OHV engine codes AME and AZE have a single oxygen sensor located at the top of the exhaust front pipe,

and engine codes AQW, ATZ and AZF have two sensors, one located at the top of the front pipe and the other located behind the catalytic converter at the rear of the front pipe. All 1.4 litre DOHC engines have two sensors. Refer to Chapter 4C for more information.

On all engines, the ECU controls the operation of the activated charcoal filter evaporative loss system – refer to Chapter 4C for further details.

It should be noted that fault diagnosis of all the engine management systems described in this Chapter is only possible with dedicated electronic test equipment. Problems with the systems operation should therefore be referred to a Skoda dealer for assessment. Once the fault has been identified, the removal/refitting sequences detailed in the following Sections will then allow the appropriate component(s) to be renewed as required.

Precautions

 Warning: Petrol is extremely flammable – great care must be taken when working on any part of the fuel system.

• *Do not smoke, or allow any naked flames or uncovered light bulbs near the work area. Note that gas-powered domestic appliances with pilot flames, such as heaters boilers and tumble-dryers, also present a fire hazard – bear this in mind if you are working in an area where such appliances are present. Always keep a suitable fire extinguisher close to the work area, and familiarise yourself with its operation before starting work. Wear eye protection when working on fuel systems, and wash off any fuel spilt on bare skin immediately with soap and water. Note that fuel vapour is just as dangerous as liquid fuel – possibly more so; a vessel that has been emptied of liquid fuel will still contain vapour, and can be potentially explosive.*

• *Many of the operations described in this Chapter involve the disconnection of fuel lines, which may cause an amount of fuel spillage. Before commencing work, refer to the above 'Warning' and the information in 'Safety first!' at the beginning of this manual.*

• *Residual fuel pressure always remains in the fuel system, long after the engine has been switched off. This pressure must be relieved in a controlled manner before work can commence on any component in the fuel system – refer to Section 8 for details.*

• *When working with fuel system components, pay particular attention to cleanliness – dirt entering the fuel system may cause blockages, which will lead to poor running.*

• *In the interests of personal safety and equipment protection, many of the procedures in this Chapter suggest that the negative lead be removed from the battery terminal. This firstly eliminates the possibility of accidental short-circuits being caused as the vehicle is being*

worked upon, and secondly prevents damage to electronic components (eg, sensors, actuators, ECUs) which are particularly sensitive to the power surges caused by disconnection or reconnection of the wiring harness whilst they are still 'live'. Refer to 'Disconnecting the battery' at the rear of this manual.

2 Air cleaner and inlet system – removal and refitting

Removal

1.2 litre engine

1 The air filter is incorporated in the engine top cover. To remove the top cover on engine code AWY, detach the air guide from the lock carrier then lift the cover slightly and disconnect the small vacuum hose from the clips. Disconnect the two remaining hoses and withdraw the top cover and air cleaner from the engine.

2 To remove the top cover on engine codes AZQ and BME, disconnect the crankcase ventilation hose by squeezing together the sides of the hose elbow. Disconnect the remaining hose, and withdraw the top cover and air cleaner from the engine.

1.4 litre OHV engine

3 Remove the engine top cover.

4 The air cleaner is located at the left-hand rear corner of the engine compartment, behind the battery.

5 Disconnect the air inlet hose from the air cleaner cover by releasing the spring clip with a pair of grips.

6 Undo the screw and remove the hot air control flap duct from the air cleaner base.

7 Undo the retaining screw and remove the air cleaner assembly from its mounting rubbers.

8 To remove the intake pipe and hose from the throttle valve control unit, first disconnect the crankcase ventilation hose, then unscrew the mounting bolts and withdraw.

1.4 litre DOHC engine

9 The air filter is incorporated in the engine top cover.

10 Lift the cover and disconnect the hot-air hose from the control flap housing.

Refitting

11 Refitting is a reversal of removal, but check that the adapter ring is correctly located and ensure that all hoses are securely fitted.

3 Inlet air temperature control system – general information

1 The inlet air temperature control system consists of a temperature-controlled flap valve, mounted on the air cleaner housing, and a hose to the warm-air collector plate over the exhaust manifold.

4.5 Disconnecting the wiring from the throttle valve control unit

2 The temperature sensor in the flap valve housing senses the temperature of the inlet air, and opens the valve when a preset lower limit is reached. As the flap valve opens, warm air drawn from around the exhaust manifold blends with the inlet air.

3 As the temperature of the inlet air rises, the sensor closes the flap progressively, until the warm-air supply from the exhaust manifold is completely closed off, and only air at ambient temperature is admitted to the air cleaner.

4 With the warm-air hose removed from the temperature control flap valve housing, a hairdryer may be used to test the action of the sensor.

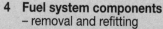

4 Fuel system components – removal and refitting

Note: *Observe the precautions in Section 1*

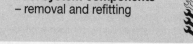

4.11a Fuel injector wiring and fuel rail – engine code BME

4.15a Unscrew the mounting bolts . . .

4.6 Throttle valve control unit mounting screws

before working on any component in the fuel system. Information on the engine management system sensors which are more directly related to the ignition system will be found in Chapter 5B. After fitting any of the components in this Section, have the engine management ECU's fault memory interrogated and any resident faults erased by a Skoda dealer or suitably-equipped specialist.

Throttle valve control unit

Caution: If the throttle valve control unit is renewed, it will be necessary to program the new unit to the vehicle before it can be used – this must be carried out by a Skoda dealer.

Removal

1 Remove the engine top cover and, on 1.4 litre OHV engines, remove the air intake pipe from the top of the throttle valve control unit as described in Section 2.

4.11b Fuel injector wiring and fuel rail – engine code AZF

4.15b . . . and lift the fuel rail with injectors from the inlet manifold . . .

2 On 1.2 litre engine code AWY, disconnect the hose for the evaporative loss charcoal canister, and the hose for the crankcase ventilation hose from the intermediate plate located between the throttle valve control unit and inlet manifold. On 1.2 litre engine codes AZQ and BME, unbolt the EGR valve pipe from the intermediate plate.

3 On 1.4 litre OHV engines, disconnect the hose on the control unit from the evaporative loss charcoal canister.

4 On 1.4 litre DOHC engines manufactured before 08/2003, unbolt the crankcase ventilation pipe from the intermediate plate located between the throttle valve control unit and inlet manifold.

5 Disconnect the wiring plug from the throttle valve control unit **(see illustration)**.

6 Progressively unscrew the mounting screws and lift the throttle valve control unit from the top of the inlet manifold **(see illustration)**. Recover the O-ring or gasket (as applicable) and discard it, as a new one will be required on refitting.

7 Where applicable, remove the intermediate plate from the inlet manifold and recover the O-ring. Discard the O-ring as a new one will be required on refitting.

8 Clean the contact faces of the control unit, inlet manifold and intermediate plate as applicable.

Refitting

9 Refitting is a reversal of removal, but use new O-rings/gaskets and progressively tighten the mounting screws to the specified torque.

Fuel injectors and fuel rail

Note: *If a faulty injector is suspected, before removing the injectors, it is worth trying the effect of one of the proprietary injector-cleaning treatments. These can be added to the petrol in the tank, and are intended to clean the injectors as you drive.*

Removal

10 Remove the engine top cover as described in Section 2.

11 Unplug the injector harness connectors, labelling them to aid correct refitting later **(see illustrations)**. Release the wiring harness clips from the top of the fuel rail, and lay the harness to one side.

12 Refer to Section 8 and depressurise the fuel system.

13 On 1.2 litre engine code AWY only, disconnect the vacuum hose from the fuel pressure regulator on the fuel rail.

14 Squeeze the catch on the quick-release fitting(s), and disconnect the fuel supply hose (and return where applicable) from the bulkhead. Alternatively, release the spring clip(s) securing the hose(s) to the fuel rail.

15 Unscrew and remove the fuel rail mounting bolts, then carefully lift the rail away from the inlet manifold, together with the injectors. Recover the injector lower O-ring seals as they emerge from the manifold **(see illustrations)**.

16 The injectors can be removed individually

from the fuel rail by extracting the relevant metal clip and easing the injector out of the rail. Recover the injector upper O-ring seals **(see illustrations)**.

17 Check the electrical resistance of the injectors using a multimeter, and compare it with the Specifications.

Refitting

18 Refit the injectors and fuel rail by following the removal procedure in reverse, noting the following points:

a) *Renew the injector O-ring seals if they appear worn or damaged. Apply a little engine oil to the seals to assist their refitting* **(see illustration)**.

b) *Ensure that the injector retaining clips are securely seated.*

c) *Check that all electrical connections are remade correctly.*

d) *On 1.2 litre engine codes AZQ and BME, and all 1.4 litre models, purge air from the fuel rail by loosening the vent valve and temporarily switching on the ignition in order to operate the fuel pump. Tighten the vent valve when the fuel is free of air bubbles.*

e) *On completion, check for fuel leaks before bringing the vehicle back into service.*

Fuel pressure regulator (1.2 litre engine code AWY only)

Note: *Observe the precautions in Section 1 before working on any component in the fuel system.*

Removal

19 Refer to Section 8 and depressurise the fuel system.

20 Remove the engine top cover.

21 Disconnect the vacuum hose from the fuel pressure regulator.

22 Release the spring clip and temporarily disconnect the fuel supply hose from the end of the fuel rail. This will allow the majority of fuel in the regulator to drain out. Be prepared for an amount of fuel loss – position a small container and some old rags underneath the fuel regulator housing. Reconnect the hose once the fuel has drained. **Note:** *The supply hose is marked with a black or white arrow.*

22 Extract the retaining spring clip from the

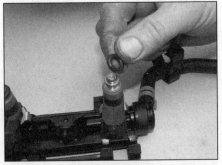

4.15c . . . then recover the injector lower O-ring seals

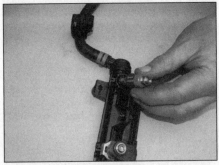

4.16b . . . withdraw the injector from the fuel rail . . .

top of the regulator housing and lift out the regulator body, recovering the O-ring seals.

Refitting

23 Refit the fuel pressure regulator by following the removal procedure in reverse, noting the following points:

a) *Renew the O-ring seals if they appear worn or damaged.*

b) *Ensure that the regulator retaining clip is securely seated.*

c) *Refit the regulator vacuum hose securely.*

Engine speed sensor

Removal

24 On all 1.2 litre engines, and 1.4 litre DOHC engines, the engine speed sensor is mounted at the left-hand rear of the cylinder block, next to the transmission bellhousing, and access is very difficult. Where necessary, prise out the rubber bung for access to the sensor. On the

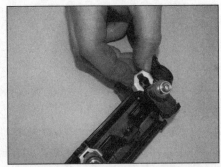

4.16a Extract the metal clip . . .

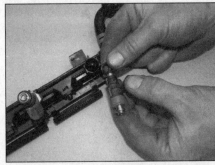

4.16c . . . and recover the injector upper O-ring seal

1.4 litre OHV engines, the sensor is mounted at the left-hand end of the engine, in the transmission bellhousing.

25 Trace the wiring back from the sensor, and unplug the harness connector.

26 Unscrew the retaining bolt and withdraw the sensor from the cylinder block/transmission **(see illustrations)**.

Refitting

27 Refitting is a reversal of removal.

Inlet air temperature/ pressure sensor

Removal

28 The combined inlet air temperature and pressure sensor is located on the inlet manifold. On the 1.2 litre engine code AWY, it is located on the left-hand rear (as seen from the driver's seat), and on engine codes AZQ and BME, it is on the right-hand end of the

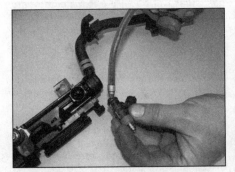

4.18 Apply a little engine oil to the O-ring seals to assist their refitting

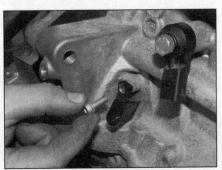

4.26a Unscrew the bolt . . .

4.26b . . . and remove the engine speed sensor – 1.2 litre engine

4.32 The knock sensor is located on the rear of the cylinder block

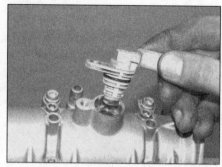

4.40 Removing the camshaft position sensor

Removal

37 On 1.2 litre engines the camshaft position sensor is located on the left-hand end of the cylinder head, and on 1.4 litre OHV engines, it is located centrally on the front of the cylinder block.

38 Remove the engine top cover.

39 Disconnect the wiring from the sensor.

40 Unscrew the mounting bolt, and remove the sensor **(see illustration)**.

Refitting

41 Refitting is a reversal of removal.

Coolant temperature sensor

42 Refer to Chapter 3, Section 6.

Oxygen (lambda) sensor(s)

Removal

43 On 1.2 litre engines, one oxygen sensor is located on the exhaust manifold and, where fitted, a second sensor is located downstream of the catalytic converter at the top of the exhaust downpipe **(see illustrations)**. Access to the upstream sensor is from above, and to the downstream sensor from below.

44 On 1.4 litre OHV engines, one oxygen sensor is located upstream of the catalytic converter at the top of the exhaust front pipe and, where fitted, a second sensor is located downstream of the catalytic converter at the rear of the front exhaust pipe. The upstream sensor is accessible from above after removing the engine top cover and the exhaust hot air cowl. The downstream sensor, where fitted, is accessible after raising the front of the car and supporting on axle stands.

45 On 1.4 litre DOHC engines, one oxygen sensor is located upstream of the catalytic converter in the exhaust manifold, and a second sensor is located downstream of the catalytic converter in the exhaust front pipe. The upstream sensor is accessible after removing the engine top cover and the exhaust hot air cowl, however, it is difficult to access as it is hidden between the manifold and the cylinder head. Access to the downstream sensor is possible after raising the front of the car and supporting on axle stands.

⚠ *Warning: Working on the sensor(s) is only advisable with the engine (and therefore the exhaust system) completely cold. The catalytic converter in particular will be very hot for some time after the engine has been switched off.*

46 Working from the sensor, trace the wiring harness from the oxygen sensor back to the connector, and disconnect it. Typically, the wiring plug is coloured black for the upstream sensor, and brown for the downstream sensor. Unclip the sensor wiring from any retaining clips, noting how it is routed.

47 Slacken and withdraw the sensor, taking care to avoid damaging the sensor probe as it is removed. **Note:** *As a flying lead remains connected to the sensor after it has been disconnected, if the correct-size spanner is not available, a slotted socket will be required to remove the sensor* **(see illustrations)**.

manifold. On the 1.4 litre OHV engines it is located on the rear of the inlet manifold, below the position of the throttle valve control unit. On 1.4 litre DOHC engines it is located on the rear, right-hand end of the inlet manifold.

29 Remove the engine top cover and disconnect the wiring from the sensor.

30 Undo the two mounting screws and remove the sensor from the inlet manifold. Recover the O-ring seal(s). **Note:** *There are two O-ring seals and a guide plate on 1.4 litre DOHC engines – note how the guide plate is fitted.*

Refitting

31 Refitting is a reversal of removal, but renew the O-ring(s) and guide plate if necessary.

Knock sensor

Removal

32 The knock sensor is located on the rear of the cylinder block and is difficult to access **(see illustration)**.

4.43a Oxygen (lambda) sensor on the exhaust manifold

4.47a Using a slotted socket to loosen the oxygen (lambda) sensor

33 Remove the engine top cover to gain access from above. Alternatively, firmly apply the handbrake then jack up the front of the vehicle and support it on axle stands (see *Jacking and vehicle support*), then remove the engine undertray.

34 Disconnect the wiring connector from the sensor or trace the wiring back from the sensor and disconnect its wiring connector.

35 Unscrew the mounting bolt and remove the sensor from the cylinder block.

Refitting

36 Refitting is the reverse of removal. Ensure the mating surfaces of the sensor and cylinder block are clean and dry and ensure the mounting bolt is tightened to the specified torque to ensure correct operation.

Camshaft position sensor

Note: *No camshaft position sensor is fitted to 1.4 litre DOHC engines.*

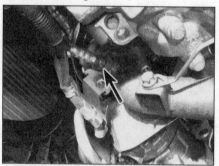

4.43b Oxygen (lambda) sensor on the exhaust downpipe

4.47b Removing the oxygen (lambda) sensor from the exhaust manifold

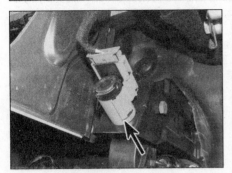

4.50 Clutch pedal switch

4.55 The ECU is located on the left-hand side of the engine compartment bulkhead

4.58 Disconnecting the wiring and removing the ECU

Refitting

48 Apply a little high-temperature anti-seize grease to the sensor threads – avoid contaminating the probe tip.
49 Refit the sensor, tightening it to the correct torque. Restore the harness connection.

Clutch pedal switch

Removal

50 Fitted to all engines, the clutch switch is mounted on the clutch pedal bracket, and sends a signal to the ECU **(see illustration)**. The purpose of the switch is to avoid engine over-revving and load change jolts when the clutch is released. The switch also deactivates the cruise control system (where fitted) when the pedal is pressed.
51 To remove the switch, first remove the facia lower trim panel on the driver's side, as described in Chapter 11.
52 Locate the switch wiring plug in front of the clutch pedal, and disconnect it.
53 Release the switch retaining lugs, and withdraw it from the pedal.

Refitting

54 When refitting the switch, first extend the switch plunger to its fullest extent, then hold the clutch pedal depressed when offering it into position. Once the switch has been clipped into place, release the pedal – this sets the switch adjustment. Further refitting is a reversal of removal.

Electronic control unit (ECU)

Caution: Always wait at least 30 seconds after switching off the ignition before disconnecting the wiring from the ECU. When the wiring is disconnected, all the learned values are erased, although any contents of the fault memory are retained. After reconnecting the wiring, the basic settings must be reinstated by a Skoda dealer using a special test instrument. Note also that if the ECU is renewed, the identification of the new ECU must be transferred to the immobiliser control unit by a Skoda dealer.

Removal

55 The ECU is located on the left-hand side of the engine compartment bulkhead **(see**

illustration). First disconnect the battery negative lead (refer to *Disconnecting the battery* in the *Reference* Chapter at the end of this manual).
56 Where necessary, remove the air cleaner assembly as described in Section 2.
57 Pull away the upper and lower retaining clips and, at the same time, slide the ECU outwards to release it.
58 Disconnect the wiring plug by releasing the catches **(see illustration)**.

Refitting

59 Refitting is a reversal of removal. Press the unit to the left, once in position, to secure it. Bear in mind the comments made in the Caution above – the ECU will not work correctly until it has been electronically coded.

---

5 Fuel filter – renewal

Note: *Observe the precautions in Section 1 before working on any component in the fuel system.*
1 Depressurise the fuel system as described in Section 8. Remember, however, that this procedure merely relieves the fuel pressure, reducing the risk of fuel spraying when the connections are disturbed – fuel will still be spilt during filter renewal, so take precautions accordingly.
2 The fuel filter is located in front of the fuel tank, on the right-hand underside of the car.
3 Jack up the right-hand rear of the car, and support it on an axle stand (see *Jacking and vehicle support*). When positioning the axle stand, ensure that it will not inhibit access to the filter.
4 To further improve access, unhook the handbrake cable from the adjacent wire clip.
5 Disconnect the fuel hoses at either end of the filter, noting their locations for refitting. On the 1.2 litre engine code AWY, there is a single hose at each end of the filter, however, on all other models, at the tank end of the filter there are two hoses, a feed hose coloured black and a return hose coloured blue, and at the engine/fuel rail end of the filter there is just one hose coloured black. The connections are of quick-release type, disconnected by squeezing the

catch on each. It may be necessary to release the hoses from the clips on the underside of the car, to allow greater movement.
6 The filter is held in position by a large-diameter worm-drive clip. Before removing the filter, look for an arrow marking, which points in the direction of fuel flow – in this case, towards the front of the car. The new filter must be fitted the same way round.
7 Loosen the worm-drive clip, and slide the filter out of position. Try to keep it as level as possible, to reduce fuel spillage. Dispose of the old filter carefully – even if the fuel inside is tipped out, the filter element will still be soaked in fuel, and will be highly flammable.
8 Offer the new filter into position, ensuring that the direction-of-flow arrow is pointing towards the front of the car. Tighten the worm-drive clip securely, but without risking crushing the filter body.
9 Connect the fuel hoses to each end of the filter, in the same positions as noted on removal. Push the hoses fully onto the filter stubs and, if necessary, clip them back to the underside of the car. Hook the handbrake cable back in place, if it was disturbed.
10 Lower the car to the ground, then start the engine and check for signs of fuel leakage at both ends of the filter.

---

6 Fuel pump and gauge sender unit – removal and refitting

Note: *Observe the precautions in Section 1 before working on any component in the fuel system.*

⚠ **Warning: Avoid direct skin contact with fuel – wear protective clothing and gloves when handling fuel system components. Ensure that the work area is well-ventilated to prevent the build-up of fuel vapour.**

General information

1 The fuel pump and gauge sender unit are combined in one assembly, which is mounted in the top of the fuel tank. Access is through a hatch provided in the load space floor.
Caution: Removal of the sender unit involves exposing the contents of the fuel tank to the atmosphere.

6.5 Lift the access hatch . . .

6.6 . . . unplug the wiring harness . . .

6.7 . . . and disconnect the fuel hoses

Removal

2 Depressurise the fuel system as described in Section 8.

3 Ensure that the vehicle is parked on a level surface, then disconnect the battery negative lead (refer to *Disconnecting the battery* in the *Reference* Chapter at the end of this manual).

4 Fold the rear seat cushion forwards, and lift the carpet section from the load space floor.

5 Slacken and withdraw the access hatch screws, and lift the hatch away from the floorpan **(see illustration)**.

6 Unplug the wiring harness connector from the pump/sender unit **(see illustration)**.

7 Pad the area around the supply and return fuel hoses with rags to absorb any spilt fuel, then squeeze the catch to release the hose clips and disconnect them from the ports at the sender unit (alternatively, use a screwdriver to depress the catch) **(see illustration)**. Observe the supply and return arrow markings on the

ports – label the fuel hoses accordingly to ensure correct refitting later. The supply pipe is black, and may have white markings, while the return pipe is blue, or has blue markings.

8 Note the position of the alignment marks, then unscrew the plastic securing ring and remove it. Use a pair of water pump pliers or a suitable tool to grip and rotate the plastic securing ring, if necessary **(see illustrations)**.

9 Lift out the pump/sender unit, holding it above the level of the fuel in the tank until the excess fuel has drained out. Recover the flange seal **(see illustrations)**.

10 Remove the pump/sender unit from the car, and lay it on an absorbent card or rag. Inspect the float at the end of the sender unit swinging arm for punctures and fuel ingress – renew the unit if it appears damaged.

11 The fuel pick-up incorporated in the assembly is spring-loaded to ensure that it always draws fuel from the lowest part of the

tank. Check that the pick-up is free to move under spring tension with respect to the sender unit body.

12 Inspect the rubber seal from the fuel tank aperture for signs of fatigue – renew it if necessary.

13 Inspect the sender unit wiper and track; clean off any dirt and debris that may have accumulated, and look for breaks in the track.

14 If required, the sender unit can be separated from the assembly, as follows. Disconnect the two small wires (note their positions), then remove the four screws and slide the unit downwards to remove **(see illustration)**.

15 The unit top plate can be removed by releasing the plastic tags at either side; recover the large spring which fits onto a peg on the plate underside.

Refitting

16 Refit the pump/sender unit by following the removal procedure in reverse, noting the following points:

a) *Take care not to bend the float arm as the unit is refitted.*

b) *Smear the outside of tank aperture rubber seal with clean fuel or lubricating spray, to ease fitting. Unless a new seal is required, the seal should be left on the pump unit before fitting. When the unit is almost fully in place, slide the seal down and locate it on the rim of the tank aperture, then slide the unit fully home.*

c) *The arrow markings on the sender unit body and the access aperture must be aligned.*

6.8a Note the alignment marks . . .

6.8b . . . then unscrew the plastic securing ring

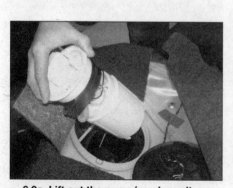

6.9a Lift out the pump/sender unit . . .

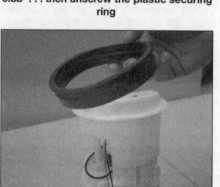

6.9b . . . and recover the flange seal

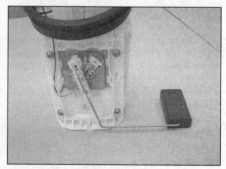

6.14 Sender unit retaining screws

d) *Reconnect the fuel hoses to the correct ports – observe the direction-of-flow arrow markings, and refer to paragraph 7. The return port is marked R, while the supply port is marked V; on some models, there may be arrow markings indicating fuel flow. Ensure that the fuel hose fittings click fully into place.*
e) *On completion, check that all associated pipes are securely clipped to the tank.*
f) *Before refitting the access hatch and rear seat, run the engine and check for fuel leaks.*

7 Fuel tank – removal and refitting

Note: *Observe the precautions in Section 1 before working on any component in the fuel system.*

Removal

1 Before the tank can be removed, it must be drained of as much fuel as possible. As no drain plug is provided, it is preferable to carry out this operation with the tank almost empty.
2 Open the fuel filler flap, and unscrew the fuel filler cap – leave the cap loosely in place.
3 Disconnect the battery negative lead (refer to *Disconnecting the battery* in the *Reference* Chapter at the end of this manual). Using a hand pump or syphon, remove any remaining fuel from the bottom of the tank.
4 Loosen the right-hand rear wheel bolts, then jack up the rear of the car and remove the right-hand rear wheel.
5 Remove the right-hand rear wheel arch liner as described in Chapter 11, Section 23.
6 Gain access to the top of the fuel pump/sender unit as described in Section 6, and disconnect the wiring harness from the top of the pump/sender unit at the multiway connector.
7 Unscrew the fuel filler flap unit retaining screw where fitted (on the side opposite the flap hinge), and ease the flap unit out of position. Recover the rubber seal which fits around the filler neck.
8 Undo the screw securing the filler tube.
9 Fold the rear seat cushion forwards and lift the carpet section from the load space floor.
10 Slacken and withdraw the access hatch screws, and lift the hatch away from the floorpan.
11 Unplug the wiring harness connector from the pump/sender unit.
12 Remove the activated charcoal (evaporative) filter from its location behind the filler tube as described in Chapter 4C.
13 The fuel tank is protected from below by one or more plastic covers. Undo the fasteners and remove the covers.
14 Referring to Chapter 4C if necessary, unbolt the exhaust rear silencer mounting, and carefully lower the rear section of the exhaust system. Given that the rear axle assembly has

to be removed (or at least lowered) to allow the tank to be removed, it is preferable to remove the rear section of the exhaust system completely.
15 Refer to Chapter 10 and remove the rear axle assembly. Alternatively, it is possible to just lower the axle out of position, rather than completely removing it.
16 Depressurise the fuel system as described in Section 8.
17 Remove the fuel filter as described in Section 5, or alternatively disconnect the single outlet hose from the engine side of the filter.
18 Disconnect the activated charcoal (evaporative) filter just in front of the right-hand side of the fuel tank.
19 Unscrew and remove the retaining bolts and detach the tensioning strap from the tank.
20 Position a trolley jack under the centre of the tank. Insert a block of wood between the jack head and the tank to prevent damage to the tank surface. Raise the jack to support the weight of the tank.
21 Unscrew and remove the tank mounting bolts.
22 Lower the tank from the underside of the vehicle. If necessary, detach the various pipes and hoses from the tank, and remove the fuel pump and gauge sender unit with reference to Section 6.
23 If the tank is contaminated with sediment or water, swill the tank out with clean fuel. The tank is injection-moulded from a synthetic material and, if damaged, should be renewed. However, in certain cases it may be possible to have small leaks or minor damage repaired. Seek the advice of a suitable specialist before attempting to repair the fuel tank.

Refitting

24 Refitting is the reverse of the removal procedure, noting the following points:
a) *When lifting the tank back into position, take care to ensure none of the hoses get trapped between the tank and vehicle body.*
b) *Ensure that all pipes and hoses are correctly routed, are not kinked, and are securely held in position with their retaining clips.*
c) *Tighten the tank strap retaining bolts to the specified torque.*
d) *On completion, refill the tank with fuel, and check for signs of leakage prior to taking the vehicle out on the road.*

8 Fuel injection system – depressurisation

Note: *Observe the precautions in Section 1 before working on any component in the fuel system.*

⚠ **Warning: The following procedure will merely relieve the pressure in the fuel system – remember**

that fuel will still be present in the system components and take precautions accordingly before disconnecting any of them.

1 The fuel system referred to in this Section is defined as the tank-mounted fuel pump, the fuel filter, the fuel injectors, and the metal pipes and flexible hoses of the fuel lines between these components. All these contain fuel, which will be under pressure while the engine is running and/or while the ignition is switched on. The pressure will remain for some time after the ignition has been switched off, and must be relieved before any of these components are disturbed for servicing work. Ideally, the engine should be allowed to cool completely before work commences.
2 Place a suitable container beneath the relevant connection/union to be disconnected, then wrap clean cloth around it. Where a union connection is fitted, loosen it slightly before wrapping the cloth around.
3 Slowly open the connection to avoid a sudden release of pressure. Once the pressure has been released, disconnect the fuel line. Insert plugs to minimise fuel loss and prevent the entry of dirt into the fuel system.

9 Inlet manifold – removal and refitting

Note: *Observe the precautions in Section 1 before working on any component in the fuel system.*

Removal

1 A one-piece inlet manifold is fitted to the rear of the cylinder head on all models. First, disconnect the battery negative lead (refer to *Disconnecting the battery* in the *Reference* Chapter at the end of this manual).
2 Remove the engine top cover. Where applicable, unclip the hose from the top of the inlet manifold **(see illustration)**.
3 With reference to Section 4, remove the throttle valve control unit from the inlet manifold.
4 Disconnect the vacuum hose for the brake vacuum servo noting how it is routed.
5 To allow the manifold to be removed completely, and to improve access to the

9.2 Hose retaining clips on the top of the inlet manifold

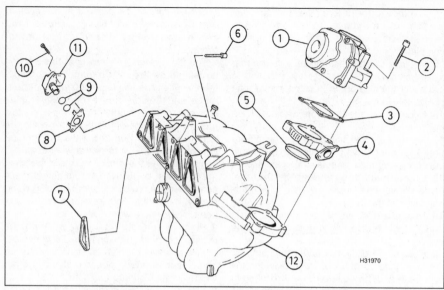

9.6 Inlet manifold – 1.4 litre DOHC engine up to 08/2003

1 Throttle valve control	5 Seal	9 O-rings
unit	6 Inlet manifold	10 Screw
2 Bolt	bolt	11 Inlet air temperature/
3 Gasket	7 Manifold seal	pressure sensor
4 EGR pipe flange	8 Guide plate	12 Inlet manifold

**9.8 Removing the inlet manifold –
1.2 litre engine**

manifold mounting bolts, remove the fuel rail and injectors as described in Section 4. However, if the manifold is being removed as part of another procedure (such as cylinder head or engine removal), the fuel rail can be left in place.

6 Disconnect the wiring plug from the inlet air temperature/pressure sensor, referring if necessary to Section 4 for more details **(see illustration)**. Alternatively, remove it completely.

7 On the 1.2 litre engine code AWY, unscrew the two lower mounting bolts and recover the mounting rubbers and sleeves.

8 Progressively loosen the bolts (or nuts on 1.4 litre OHV engines) and withdraw the manifold from the cylinder head. Recover the O-ring seals on 1.2 litre engines and 1.4 litre DOHC engines. Recover the gasket on 1.4 litre OHV engines – all should be renewed when refitting the manifold **(see illustration)**.

Refitting

9 Refitting is a reversal of removal. Use a new gasket or seals, as applicable, and tighten the retaining bolts/nuts to the specified torque.

10 Fuel injection system
– testing and adjustment

1 If a fault appears in the fuel injection system, first ensure that all the system wiring connectors are securely connected and free

of corrosion. Then ensure that the fault is not due to poor maintenance; ie, check that the air cleaner filter element is clean, the spark plugs are in good condition and correctly gapped, the cylinder compression pressures are correct, the ignition system wiring is in good condition and securely connected, and the engine breather hoses are clear and undamaged, referring to Chapter 1A, Chapter 2A, 2B or 2C and Chapter 5B.

2 If these checks fail to reveal the cause of the problem, the vehicle should be taken to a suitably-equipped Skoda dealer for testing. A diagnostic connector is incorporated in the engine management system wiring harness, into which dedicated electronic test equipment can be plugged (the connector is located behind a trim panel above the front ashtray – unclip and remove the panel for access). The test equipment is capable of 'interrogating' the engine management system ECU electronically and accessing its internal fault log (reading fault codes).

3 Fault codes can only be extracted from the ECU using a dedicated fault code reader. A Skoda dealer will obviously have such a reader, but they are also available from other suppliers. It is unlikely to be cost-effective for the private owner to purchase a fault code reader, but a well-equipped local garage or auto-electrical specialist will have one.

4 Using this equipment, faults can be pinpointed quickly and simply, even if their occurrence is intermittent. Testing all the system components individually in an

attempt to locate the fault by elimination is a time-consuming operation that is unlikely to be fruitful (particularly if the fault occurs dynamically), and carries a high risk of damage to the ECU's internal components.

5 Experienced home mechanics equipped with an accurate tachometer and a carefully-calibrated exhaust gas analyser may be able to check the exhaust gas CO content and the engine idle speed; if these are found to be out of specification, then the vehicle must be taken to a suitably-equipped Skoda dealer for assessment. Neither the air/fuel mixture (exhaust gas CO content) nor the engine idle speed are manually adjustable.

11 Cruise control system
– general information

1 Certain models may be equipped with a cruise control system, in which the driver can set a chosen speed, which the system will then try to maintain regardless of gradients, etc.

2 Once the desired speed has been set, the system is entirely under the control of the engine management ECU, which regulates the speed via the throttle valve control unit.

3 The system refers to signals from the engine speed sensor (see Section 4) and roadspeed sensor (on the transmission).

4 The system is deactivated if the clutch or brake pedals are pressed, signalled by the clutch pedal switch (Section 4) or the brake stop-light switch (Chapter 9).

5 The cruise control switch is part of the steering column combination switch assembly, which can be removed as described in Chapter 12, Section 4.

6 Any problems with the system which are not caused by wiring faults or failure of the components mentioned in this Section should be referred to a Skoda dealer. In the event of a problem occurring, it is advisable to first take the car to a suitably-equipped dealer for electronic fault diagnosis, using a fault code reader – refer to Section 10.

Chapter 4 Part B:
Diesel engine fuel system

Contents

Section number

Air cleaner assembly – removal and refitting 2
Diesel engine management system – component removal and
   refitting 3
Fuel cooler – removal and refitting 13
Fuel cut-off solenoid valve (engine code ASY only) – removal and
   refitting 7
Fuel filter renewal . . . . See Chapter 1B
Fuel gauge sender unit – removal and refitting 9
Fuel injection pump timing (engine code ASY only) – checking and
   adjustment 6

Section number

Fuel tank – removal and refitting 10
General information and precautions 1
Injection pump (engine code ASY only) – removal and refitting 5
Injectors – general information, removal and refitting 4
Inlet manifold – removal and refitting 8
Inlet manifold changeover flap and valve – removal and refitting . . . 12
Intercooler – removal and refitting . . . . See Chapter 4C
Tandem fuel pump – removal and refitting 11
Turbocharger – removal and refitting . . . . See Chapter 4C

Degrees of difficulty

Easy, suitable for novice with little experience	**Fairly easy,** suitable for beginner with some experience	**Fairly difficult,** suitable for competent DIY mechanic	**Difficult,** suitable for experienced DIY mechanic	**Very difficult,** suitable for expert DIY or professional

Specifications

General

Engine code by type*:
   Electronic direct injection, non-turbocharged . . . . ASY
   Electronic direct injection, unit injectors, turbocharged . . . . AMF, ASZ and ATD
Firing order:
   Engine code AMF 1-2-3
   Engine codes ASY, ASZ and ATD 1-3-4-2
Maximum engine speed . . . . N/A (ECU controlled)
Engine idle speed:
   Engine code AMF . . . . 800 to 970 rpm
   Engine code ASY . . . . 860 to 950 rpm
   Engine codes ASZ and ATD . . . . 800 to 950 rpm
Engine fast idle speed . . . . N/A (ECU controlled)
* **Note:** *See 'Vehicle identification' for the location of the code marking on the engine.*

Fuel injectors
Resistance . . . . 0.5 ohms

Tandem pump
Fuel pressure at 1500 rpm . . . . 3.5 bar

Turbocharger
Type . . . . Garrett or KKK

Torque wrench settings

	Nm	lbf ft
Accelerator pedal sender	10	7
EGR pipe flange bolts	25	18
EGR valve	10	7
EGR valve (non-turbo) clamp bolt	10	7
Fuel cooler	15	11
Fuel cut-off solenoid valve	40	30
Fuel filter bracket	25	18
Fuel pump return pipe cap nut	25	18
Fuel tank	25	18
Injection pump head fuel union stubs	45	33
Injection pump-to-support bracket bolts	25	18
Injector clamp bolt:		
Engine code ASY	20	15
Engine codes AMF, ASZ and ATD*:		
Stage 1	12	9
Stage 2	Angle-tighten a further 270°	
Injector pipe union nut	25	18
Injection pump sprocket (see Chapter 2D):		
Type 1*:		
Stage 1	20	15
Stage 2	Angle-tighten a further 90°	
Type 2	25	18
Inlet manifold flap housing to manifold	10	7
Inlet manifold to cylinder head:		
Engine code ASY	20	15
Engine codes AMF, ASZ and ATD	25	18
Pump injector rocker shaft bolts*:		
Stage 1	20	15
Stage 2	Angle-tighten a further 90°	
Tandem pump bolts:		
Upper	20	15
Lower	10	7
Turbocharger oil return pipe to cylinder block		
Engine code AMF	30	22
Engine codes ASZ and ATD	40	30
Turbocharger to catalytic converter	25	18
Turbocharger to exhaust manifold*	25	18

Use new fasteners

1 General information and precautions

General information

Two different fuel injection systems are fitted to the range of engines covered by this manual. Whilst both are direct injection systems, the difference lies in how the fuel is delivered to the injectors. Both systems consist of a fuel tank, an engine-bay mounted fuel filter with an integral water separator, fuel supply and return lines, and three or four fuel injectors.

On engine code ASY, the fuel is pressurised by an injection pump, and commencement of injection is controlled by the engine management ECU and a solenoid valve on the injection pump. The pump is driven at half crankshaft speed by the camshaft timing belt. Fuel is drawn from the fuel tank and through the filter by the injection pump, which then distributes the fuel under very high pressure to the injectors through separate delivery pipes. This engine is not fitted with a turbocharger.

On engine codes AMF, ASZ and ATD, the fuel is delivered by a camshaft driven 'tandem pump' at low pressure, through a gallery in the cylinder head to the injectors (known as 'Unit injectors'). A 'roller rocker' assembly, mounted above the camshaft bearing caps, uses an extra set of camshaft lobes to compress the top of each injector once per firing cycle. This arrangement creates far higher injection pressures. The precise timing of the pre-injection and main injection is controlled by the engine management ECU and a solenoid on each injector. The resultant effect of this system is improved engine torque and power output, greater combustion efficiency, and lower exhaust emissions. All three engines are fitted with a turbocharger, and a fuel cooler is fitted on the underbody between the fuel tank and the engine compartment. All turbo engines are fitted with a valve block located in the rear left-hand corner of the engine compartment; this unit includes the inlet manifold changeover valve, EGR valve and charge pressure control solenoid valve (see illustrations).

1.3a Fuel cooler on the underbody, fitted to turbo models

1.3b Valve block located in the rear left-hand corner of the engine compartment

The direct-injection fuelling system is controlled electronically by a diesel engine management system, comprising an Electronic Control Unit (ECU) and its associated sensors, actuators and wiring. The system is completely electronic, and no accelerator cable is fitted. The throttle position sensor at the accelerator pedal is linked to the engine management ECU, which adjusts the quantity of fuel injected, thus controlling the engine speed. Various sensors are used to enable the ECU to set the exact quantity of fuel to inject, and the pump timing (commencement of injection).

On engine code ASY, basic injection timing is set mechanically by the position of the pump on its mounting bracket. Dynamic timing and injection duration are controlled by the ECU and are dependant on engine speed, throttle position and rate of opening, inlet air flow, inlet air temperature, coolant temperature, fuel temperature, ambient pressure (altitude) and manifold depression information, received from sensors mounted on and around the engine. Closed loop control of the injection timing is achieved by means of an injector needle lift sensor. Note that injector No 3 is fitted with the needle lift sensor. Two-stage injectors are used, which improve the engine's combustion characteristics, leading to quieter running and better exhaust emissions.

In addition, the ECU manages the operation of the Exhaust Gas Recirculation (EGR) emission control system (Chapter 4C), the turbocharger boost pressure control system (Chapter 4C) and the glow plug control system (Chapter 5C).

On non-turbo models, an electrically-operated flap valve is fitted to the inlet manifold to increase the vacuum when the engine speed is less than 2200 rpm; this is necessary to operate the EGR system efficiently.

On turbo models, an electrically-operated flap valve is fitted to the inlet manifold in order to operate the EGR system efficiently. It is also closed by the ECU for 3 seconds as the engine is switched off, to minimise the air intake as the engine shuts down. This minimises the vibration felt as the pistons come up against the volume of highly compressed air present in the combustion chambers. On engine codes ASZ and ATD, a vacuum reservoir mounted on the front of the engine provides the vacuum supply to a vacuum capsule which operates the flap **(see illustrations)**.

It should be noted that fault diagnosis of the diesel engine management system is only possible with dedicated electronic test equipment. Problems with the system's operation should therefore be referred to a Skoda dealer or suitably-equipped specialist for assessment. Once the fault has been identified, the removal/refitting sequences detailed in the following Sections will then allow the appropriate component(s) to be renewed as required. *Note: Throughout this Chapter, vehicles are frequently referred to*

1.8a Vacuum reservoir for inlet manifold flap valve

by their engine code, rather than by engine capacity – refer to Chapter 2D for engine code listings.

Precautions

Many of the operations described in this Chapter involve the disconnection of fuel lines, which may cause an amount of fuel spillage. Before commencing work, refer to the warnings below and the information in *Safety first!* at the beginning of this manual.

> ⚠️ *Warning: When working on any part of the fuel system, avoid direct contact skin contact with diesel fuel – wear protective clothing and gloves when handling fuel system components. Ensure that the work area is well ventilated to prevent the build-up of diesel fuel vapour.*

• *Fuel injectors operate at extremely high pressures and the jet of fuel produced at the nozzle is capable of piercing skin, with potentially fatal results. When working with pressurised injectors, take care to avoid exposing any part of the body to the fuel spray. It is recommended that a diesel fuel systems specialist should carry out any pressure testing of the fuel system components.*

• *Do not allow diesel fuel to come into contact with coolant hoses – wipe off accidental spillage immediately. Hoses that have been contaminated with fuel for an extended period should be renewed.*

• *Diesel fuel systems are particularly sensitive to contamination from dirt, air and water. Pay particular attention to*

1.8b Vacuum capsule on inlet manifold below EGR valve

cleanliness when working on any part of the fuel system, to prevent the ingress of dirt. Thoroughly clean the area around fuel unions before disconnecting them. Only use lint-free cloths and clean fuel for component cleaning.

• *Store dismantled components in sealed containers to prevent contamination.*

2 Air cleaner assembly – removal and refitting

Removal

1 Loosen the clips (or release the spring clips) and disconnect the air ducting from the air cleaner assembly or air mass meter (as applicable) **(see illustration)**.

2 On non-turbo models, disconnect the wiring plug from the inlet air temperature sensor at the rear of the air cleaner lid.

3 On turbo models, disconnect the wiring plug from the air mass meter. Also disconnect the vacuum hose below the air mass meter wiring connector **(see illustrations)**.

4 Unclip any hoses, wiring, etc, which may be clipped to the air cleaner, noting their routing for refitting.

5 Remove the two screws securing the air cleaner lid, and unhook it from the front clips, complete with the air mass meter on turbo models **(see illustration)**. Lift out the air filter element.

6 The lower half of the air cleaner is secured by two screws. Remove the screws and

2.1 Using a pair of pliers to release the spring clip from the air inlet duct

2.3a Disconnect the air mass meter wiring plug . . .

2.3b ... and the vacuum hose below it

2.5 Removing the air cleaner lid

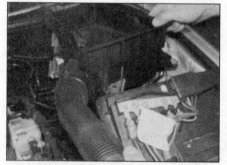

2.6 Removing the air cleaner and inlet duct

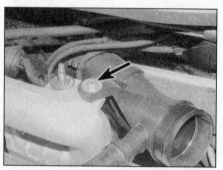

2.7 Air inlet duct securing bolt (arrowed) – depending on model

lift out the air cleaner forward, releasing the air inlet spout from its location **(see illustration)**.

7 If required, the rest of the air inlet ducting can be removed by releasing the retaining clips; however, some sections of the inlet duct are bolted in place **(see illustration)**. For details of removing the intercooler-related ducting on turbo models, refer to Chapter 4C.

Refitting

8 Refit the air cleaner by following the removal procedure in reverse.

---

3 Diesel engine management system – component removal and refitting

Note: *Observe the precautions in Section 1 before working on any component in the fuel system. After fitting any of the components*

3.4 Coolant temperature sensor wiring connector (arrowed)

in this Section, have the engine management ECU's fault memory interrogated and any resident faults erased by a Skoda dealer or suitably-equipped specialist.

Accelerator pedal position sensor

1 The position sensor is integral with the accelerator pedal. The pedal assembly can be removed once access has been gained by removing the driver's lower facia panel – Chapter 11. Disconnect the sensor wiring plug and unscrew the nuts securing the pedal to its mounting bracket.

Coolant temperature sensor

Removal

2 Refer to Chapter 1B and drain approximately one quarter of the coolant from the engine. Alternatively, be prepared for coolant spillage as the sensor is removed.

3 Where necessary for access, remove the engine top cover(s). Removal details vary according to model, but the cover retaining nuts are concealed under circular covers, which are prised out of the main cover. Remove the nuts, and lift the cover from the engine, releasing any wiring or hoses attached.

4 The sensor is at the top coolant outlet elbow, at the front of the cylinder head. Unplug the wiring from it at the connector **(see illustration)**.

5 Remove the securing clip, then extract the sensor from its housing and recover the O-ring seal.

Refitting

6 Refit the coolant temperature sensor by reversing the removal procedure, using a new O-ring seal. Refer to Chapter 1B or *Weekly checks* and top-up the cooling system.

Fuel temperature sensor

Note: *On non-turbo models (engine code ASY), the fuel temperature sensor is incorporated in the fuel quantity adjuster, which is fitted to the top of the injection pump. The sensor cannot be renewed separately.*

Removal

7 On turbo engine codes AMF, ASZ and ATD, a fuel temperature sensor is located at the left-hand front end of the cylinder head. On some models, an additional sensor may be located in the fuel tank return line, next to the fuel filter in the right-hand corner of the engine compartment.

8 To remove the sensor located in the cylinder head, place cloth rags beneath it then disconnect the wiring and unbolt it. Be prepared for some loss of fuel.

9 To remove the sensor located in the fuel return line, disconnect the wiring then place cloth rags beneath it and disconnect the hoses.

Refitting

10 Refitting is a reversal of removal.

Inlet air temperature sensor

Removal – non-turbo models

11 The sensor is mounted on the side of the air cleaner top cover.

12 Disconnect the sensor wiring plug, then remove the securing clip and extract the sensor. Recover the O-ring seal.

Removal – turbo models

13 All models have an air temperature sensor built into the air mass meter. This sensor is an integral part of the air mass meter, and cannot be renewed separately. An additional air temperature/pressure sensor is fitted, either on top of the intercooler, or on the air hose from the intercooler to the inlet manifold, and this can be renewed as described below.

14 Trace the air hose back from the inlet manifold to the point where it passes through the inner wing. If the sensor is mounted on the hose, disconnect the wiring plug, then remove the two retaining screws and withdraw the sensor. Recover the O-ring seal.

15 If the sensor is mounted on the intercooler, remove the right-hand headlight as described in Chapter 12, Section 7. The sensor can then be removed in the same way as the pipe-mounted type.

Refitting

16 Refit the inlet air temperature sensor by reversing the removal procedure, using a new O-ring seal.

Engine speed sensor

Note: *This procedure only applies to engine codes AMF, ASZ and ATD.*

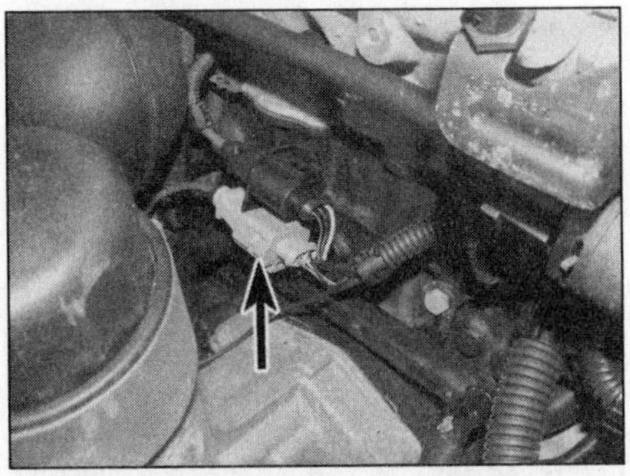

3.19a Wiring connector (arrowed) for speed sensor

Removal

17 The engine speed sensor is mounted on the front cylinder block, adjacent to the mating surface of the block and transmission bellhousing.

18 Where necessary for access, remove the engine top cover.

19 Trace the wiring back from the sensor, and disconnect it at the plug behind the oil filter housing **(see illustrations)**.

20 Remove the retaining screw and withdraw the sensor from the cylinder block.

Refitting

21 Refit the sensor by reversing the removal procedure.

Air mass meter

Note: *This procedure only applies to engine codes AMF, ASZ and ATD.*

Removal

22 With reference to Section 2, slacken the clips and disconnect the air ducting from the air mass meter, at the rear of the air cleaner housing.

23 Disconnect the wiring from the air mass meter, and the vacuum hose beneath the wiring connector (see Section 2).

24 Remove the retaining screws and extract the meter from the air cleaner housing. Recover the O-ring seal.

Caution: Handle the air mass meter carefully – its internal components are easily damaged.

Refitting

25 Refitting is a reversal of removal. Renew the O-ring seal if it appears damaged.

Absolute pressure (altitude) sensor

26 The absolute pressure sensor is an integral part of the ECU, and hence cannot be renewed separately.

Inlet manifold flap housing

Note: *This procedure only applies to engine code ASY. See Section 12 for details of the flap housing on engine codes ASZ and ATD.*

Removal

27 On turbo engine codes ASZ and ATD, the flap housing is integral with the EGR valve (see Chapter 4C). On the non-turbo engine code ASY, the flap housing is separate and attached to the left-hand end of the inlet manifold, with a separate EGR valve attached to the right-hand end of the manifold.

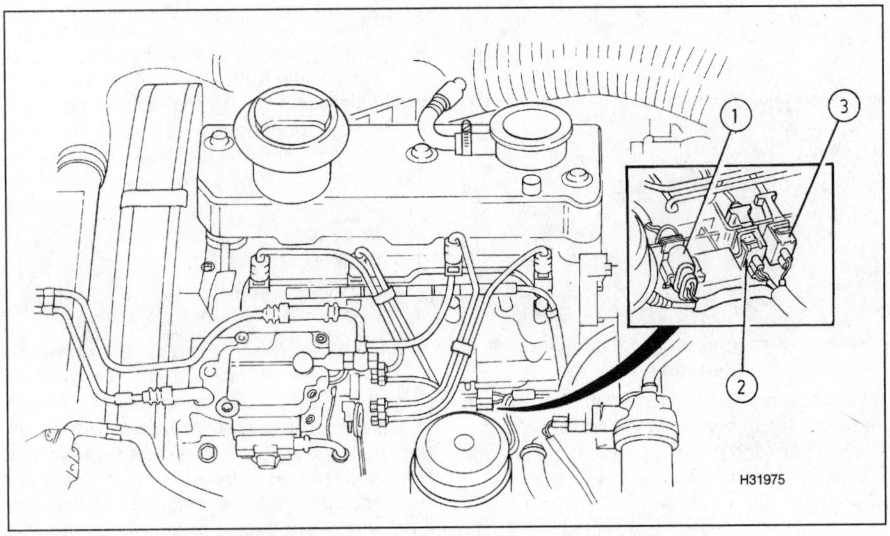

3.19b Wiring connectors behind oil filter housing

1 Fuel temperature sensor, quantity adjuster, shut-off valve and commencement of injection valve
2 Engine speed sensor
3 Needle lift sensor

28 Remove the engine top cover, then loosen the clip (or release the spring clip) and disconnect the air trunking from the turbocharger at the flap housing.

29 Disconnect the flap control motor wiring plug from the front of the housing.

30 Unscrew the four housing retaining bolts, and withdraw the housing from the inlet manifold. Recover the O-ring seal.

Refitting

31 Refitting is a reversal of removal. Renew the O-ring seal if it appears damaged.

Clutch and brake pedal switches

Removal

32 The clutch and brake pedal switches are clipped to mounting brackets directly above their respective pedals.

33 The brake pedal switch operates as a safety device, in the event of a problem with the accelerator position sensor. If the brake pedal switch is depressed while the accelerator pedal is held at a constant position, the engine speed will drop to idle. Thus, a faulty or incorrectly-adjusted brake pedal switch may result in a running problem.

34 The clutch pedal switch operation causes the injection pump to momentarily reduce its output while the clutch is disengaged, to permit smoother gearchanging.

35 To remove either switch, refer to Chapter 11 and remove the trim panels from under the steering column area of the facia, to gain access to the pedal cluster.

36 The switches can be removed by unclipping them from their mountings and disconnecting the wiring plugs.

Refitting

37 Refitting is a reversal of removal. On completion, it may be necessary to have the switches reprogrammed by a Skoda dealer.

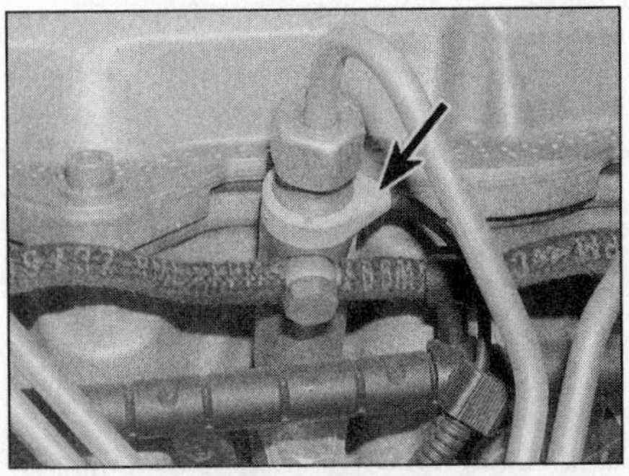

3.38 View of No 3 injector – needle lift sensor arrowed

Needle lift sender

Note: *This procedure only applies to engine code ASY.*

38 The needle lift sender is integral with No 3 injector **(see illustration)**. Refer to Section 4 for the removal and refitting procedure.

Camshaft position sensor

Note: *This procedure only applies to engine codes AMF, ASZ and ATD.*

Removal

39 On turbo engine codes AMF, ASZ and ATD, the camshaft position sensor is located behind the timing belt inner cover, on the right-hand end of the cylinder head.

40 Remove the upper timing cover as described in Chapter 2D.

41 Prise the rubber grommet from the timing belt inner cover.

4.6 View of injector pipe union nuts at injection pump

42 Trace the wiring from the camshaft position sensor to the connector and disconnect.

43 Unscrew the mounting bolt and withdraw the sensor from the engine.

Refitting

44 Refitting is a reversal of removal.

Electronic control unit (ECU)

Caution: Always wait at least 30 seconds after switching off the ignition before disconnecting the wiring from the ECU. When the wiring is disconnected, all the learned values are erased, however any contents of the fault memory are retained. After reconnecting the wiring, the basic settings must be reinstated by a Skoda dealer using a special test instrument. Note also that if the ECU is renewed, the identification of the new ECU must be transferred to the immobiliser control unit by a Skoda dealer.

Removal

45 The ECU is located on the left-hand side of the engine compartment bulkhead. First disconnect the battery negative lead (refer to *Disconnecting the battery* in the *Reference* Chapter at the end of this manual).

46 Remove the air cleaner assembly as described in Section 2.

47 Pull away the upper and lower retaining clips and, at the same time, slide the ECU outwards to release it.

48 Disconnect the wiring plug by releasing the catches.

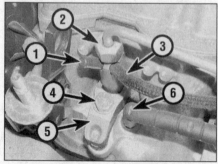

4.9 View of No 1 injector

1 End cap	*5 Retaining plate*
2 Union nut	*6 Glow plug wiring*
3 Leak-off pipe	*connector*
4 Retaining bolt	

Refitting

49 Refitting is a reversal of removal. Press the unit to the left, once in position, to secure it. Bear in mind the comments made in the Caution above – the ECU will not work correctly until it has been electronically coded.

4 Injectors – general information, removal and refitting

⚠️ *Warning: Exercise extreme caution when working on the fuel injectors. Never expose the hands or any part of the body to injector spray, as the high working pressure can cause the fuel to penetrate the skin, with possibly fatal results. You are strongly advised to have any work which involves testing the injectors under pressure carried out by a dealer or fuel injection specialist. Refer to the precautions given in Section 1 of this Chapter before proceeding.*

General information

1 Injectors do deteriorate with prolonged use, and it is reasonable to expect them to need reconditioning or renewal after 60 000 miles or so. Accurate testing, overhaul and calibration of the injectors must be left to a specialist.

2 On engine code ASY, a defective injector which is causing knocking or smoking can be located without dismantling as follows. Run the engine at a fast idle. Slacken each injector union in turn, placing rag around the union to catch spilt fuel and being careful not to expose the skin to any spray. When the union on the defective injector is slackened, the knocking or smoking will stop. **Note:** *This test is not possible on engines fitted with unit injectors (engine codes AMF, ASZ and ATD).*

Removal

Note: *Take care not to allow dirt into the injectors or fuel pipes during this procedure. Do not drop the injectors or allow the needles at their tips to become damaged. The injectors are precision-made to fine limits, and must not be handled roughly.*

4.12 Undo the adjustment screw until the rocker arm lies against the plunger pin of the injector

Engine code ASY

3 Remove the engine top cover.

4 Cover the alternator with a clean cloth or plastic bag, to protect it from any fuel being spilt onto it.

5 Carefully clean around the injectors and pipe union nuts, and disconnect the return pipes from each injector.

6 Wipe clean the pipe unions, then slacken the union nuts securing the injector pipes to each injector and the union nuts securing the pipes to the rear of the injection pump (the pipes are removed as one assembly); as each pump union nut is slackened, retain the adapter with a suitable open-ended spanner to prevent it being unscrewed from the pump **(see illustration)**.

7 With the union nuts undone, remove the injector pipes from the engine. Cover the injectors and pipe unions to prevent the entry of dirt into the system.

 HAYNES HiNT *Cut the fingertips from an old rubber glove and secure them over the open unions with elastic bands to prevent dirt ingress.*

8 Disconnect the wiring for the needle lift sender from injector No 3.

9 Unscrew and remove the retaining bolts, and recover the washers and retaining plates **(see illustration)**. Note the fitted position of all components, for use when refitting. Withdraw the injectors from the cylinder head, and recover the heat shield washers – new washers must be obtained for refitting.

Engine code AMF

10 With reference to Chapter 2D, remove the upper timing belt cover and camshaft cover.

11 On 3-cylinder engines, a single rocker arm shaft is fitted. Using a spanner or socket, turn the crankshaft pulley until the crankshaft is positioned at TDC (No 1 cylinder) as described in Chapter 2D. Adjust the position of the crankshaft so that the injector operating arms are all pointing upwards evenly, ie, the injector plunger springs are under the least amount of tension.

12 Working on each of the injectors in turn, slacken the locknut of the adjustment screw on the end of the rocker arm, and undo the adjustment screw until the rocker arm lies against the plunger pin of the injector **(see illustration)**.

13 Starting at the outside and working in, progressively slacken and remove the rocker shaft retaining bolts. Lift the rocker shaft from the camshaft bearing caps. Check the contact face of each adjustment screw, and renew any that show signs of wear.

14 Position the engine so that the exhaust lobe of No 1 cylinder (nearest camshaft sprocket) is pointing upwards. In this position, all three injector clamping pads can be removed.

4.15 Remove the clamping block securing bolt (arrowed)

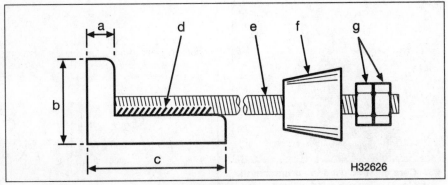

4.17a Unit injector removal tool

a 5 mm
b 15 mm
c 25 mm

d Weld/braze the rod to the angle-iron
e Threaded rod

f Cylindrical weight
g Locknut

15 Working on the first injector, undo the clamping block securing bolt and remove the block from the side of the injector (see illustration).
16 Using a small screwdriver, carefully prise the wiring connector from the injector.
17 Skoda technicians use a slide hammer (tool No T10055) to pull the injector from the cylinder head. This is a slide hammer which engages in the side of the injector. If this tool is not available, it is possible to fabricate an equivalent using a short section of angle-iron, a length of threaded rod, a cylindrical weight, and two locknuts. Weld/braze the rod to the angle-iron, slide the weight over the rod, and lock the two nuts together at the end of the rod to provide the stop for the weight (see illustration). Seat the slide hammer/tool in the slot on the side on the injector, and pull the injector out using a few gently taps. Recover circlip, the heat shield and O-rings and discard. New ones must be used for refitting (see illustration). Note: Skoda recommend that each injector is identified to ensure refitting in its original location.
18 Remove the remaining injectors using the procedure described in paragraphs 15 to 17.
19 If required, the injector wiring loom/rail can be removed from the cylinder head by undoing the two retaining nuts/bolts. To prevent the wiring connectors fouling the cylinder head casting as the assembly is withdrawn, insert the connectors into the storage slots in the plastic wiring rail. Carefully push the assembly to the rear, and out of the casting (see illustrations).

Engine codes ASZ and ATD

20 With reference to Chapter 2D, remove the upper timing belt cover and camshaft cover.
21 On 4-cylinder engines, two rocker arm shafts are fitted, each one operating a pair of injectors. Using a spanner or socket, turn the crankshaft pulley until the rocker arms for injectors 1 and 2 are both pointing upwards, ie, the injector plunger springs are under the least amount of tension.
22 Working on each of the two injectors in turn, slacken the locknut of the adjustment screw on the end of the rocker arm, and undo the adjustment screw until the rocker arm lies against the plunger pin of the injector.

4.17b Seat the slide hammer/tool in the slot on the side on the injector, and pull the injector out

23 Starting at the outside and working in, progressively slacken and remove the rocker shaft retaining bolts. Lift off the rocker shaft. Check the contact face of each adjustment screw, and renew any that show signs of wear.
24 Turn the engine one complete turn and remove the injector rocker shaft for cylinders 3 and 4, using the procedure described in paragraphs 22 and 23.
25 Position the engine so that the exhaust lobe of No 2 cylinder is pointing upwards in-line with the rear edge of the rocker shaft lower bearing support (see illustration). In this position, all four injector clamping pads can be removed.

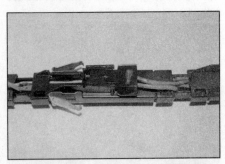

4.19b The injector connectors will slide into the loom/rail to prevent them from being damaged as the assembly is withdrawn/inserted into the cylinder head

4.19a Undo the two nuts at the back of the head and slide the injector loom/rail out

26 Follow the procedure described in paragraphs 15 to 19.

Refitting

Engine code ASY

27 Insert the injector into position, using a new heat shield washer. Make sure that the

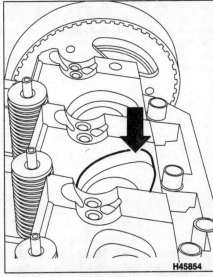

4.25 Set No 2 cylinder exhaust lobe as shown for access to all four injector clamping pads

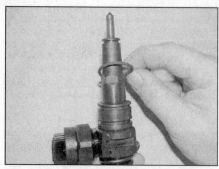

4.33 Care must be used to ensure that the injector O-rings are fitted without being twisted

injector with the needle lift sender is located in No 3 position (No 1 is at the timing belt end of the engine).

28 Fit the retaining plate then refit the bolt and tighten it to the specified torque.

29 Refit the remaining injectors using the procedure described in paragraphs 27 and 28, then reconnect the wiring for the needle lift sender on injector No 3.

30 Refit the injector pipes and tighten the union nuts to the specified torque setting. Position any clips attached to the pipes as noted before removal.

31 Reconnect the return pipes to the injectors. Remove the alternator protection.

32 Refit the engine top cover, then start the engine and check that it runs correctly.

Engine codes AMF, ASZ and ATD

33 Prior to refitting the injectors, the three O-rings, heat insulation washer and clip must be renewed. Due to the high injection pressures, it is essential that the O-rings are fitted without being twisted. Skoda recommend the use of three special assembly sleeves to install the O-rings squarely. It may be prudent to entrust O-ring renewal to a Skoda dealer or suitably-equipped injection specialist, rather than risk subsequent leaks **(see illustration)**.

34 After renewing the O-rings, fit the heat shield and secure it in place with the circlip **(see illustration)**.

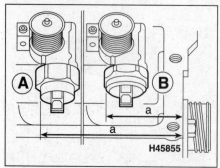

4.37a Measure the distance (a) from the rear of the cylinder head to the rounded section of the injector (see text)

A Injector with early nut
B Injector with late nut

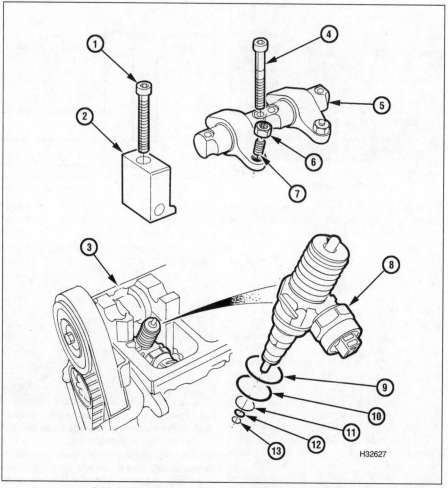

4.34 Unit injector – engine codes AMF, ASZ and ATD

1 Bolt	4 Bolt	7 Adjuster	10 O-ring
2 Clamping	5 Rocker	8 Unit	11 O-ring
block	arm	injector	12 Heat shield
3 Cylinder head	6 Nut	9 O-ring	13 Circlip

35 Smear clean engine oil onto the O-rings, and push the injector evenly down into the cylinder head onto its stop. Make sure that the injectors are refitted in their previously-noted locations.

36 Fit the clamping block alongside the injector, but only hand-tighten the new retaining bolt at this stage.

37 It is essential that the injectors are fitted at right-angles to the clamping block. In order to achieve this, measure the distance from the left-hand end face of the cylinder head to the rounded section of the solenoid valve nut, but note that there are two different types of nut fitted **(see illustrations)**. The dimensions (a) are as follows:

4.37b Use a set square against the edge of the injector . . .

4.37c . . . and measure the distance to the rear of the cylinder head

Engine code AMF

Old solenoid valve nut
Cylinder 1 = 244.2 ± 0.8 mm
Cylinder 2 = 156.2 ± 0.8 mm
Cylinder 3 = 64.8 ± 0.8 mm
New solenoid valve nut
Cylinder 1 = 245.0 ± 0.8 mm
Cylinder 2 = 157.0 ± 0.8 mm
Cylinder 3 = 65.6 ± 0.8 mm

Engine codes ASZ and ATD

Old solenoid valve nut
Cylinder 1 = 332.2 ± 0.8 mm
Cylinder 2 = 244.2 ± 0.8 mm
Cylinder 3 = 152.8 ± 0.8 mm
Cylinder 4 = 64.8 ± 0.8 mm
New solenoid valve nut
Cylinder 1 = 333.0 ± 0.8 mm
Cylinder 2 = 245.0 ± 0.8 mm
Cylinder 3 = 153.6 ± 0.8 mm
Cylinder 4 = 65.6 ± 0.8 mm

38 Once the injectors are aligned correctly, tighten the clamping bolt to the specified Stage one torque setting followed by the Stage two angle tightening setting. **Note:** *If an injector has been renewed, it is essential that the adjustment screw, locknut of the corresponding rocker and ball-pin are renewed at the same time. The ball-pins simply pull out of the injector spring cap. There is an O-ring in each spring cap to stop the ball-pins from falling out.*

39 If removed, refit the injector wiring loom/rail to the cylinder head and tighten the two retaining nuts/bolts. Reconnect the wiring to each injector.

40 Smear some grease (Skoda G000 100) onto the contact face of each rocker arm adjustment screw, and refit the rocker shaft assembly to the camshaft bearing caps, tightening the retaining bolts as follows. Starting from the inside out, hand-tighten the bolts. Again, from the inside out, tighten the bolts to the Stage one torque setting. Finally, from the inside out, tighten the bolts to the Stage two angle tightening setting.

41 The following procedure is only necessary if an injector has been renewed. Attach a DTI (Dial Test Indicator) gauge to the cylinder head upper surface, and position the DTI probe against the top of the adjustment screw **(see illustration)**. Turn the crankshaft until

5.2 Fuel return union at rear of injection pump

the rocker arm roller is on the highest point of its corresponding camshaft lobe, and the adjustment screw is at its lowest. Once this position has been established, remove the DTI gauge, screw the adjustment screw in until firm resistance is felt, and the injector spring cannot be compressed further. Turn the adjustment screw **anti-clockwise** 225°, and tighten the locknut to the specified torque.

42 Refit the camshaft cover and upper timing belt cover, as described in Chapter 2D.

43 Start the engine and check that it runs correctly.

5 Injection pump (engine code ASY only) – removal and refitting

Note: *An injection pump is only fitted to engine code ASY. After refitting, the injection pump timing (commencement of injection) must be dynamically checked and if necessary adjusted by a Skoda dealer, as dedicated electronic test equipment is needed to interface with the ECU.*

Removal

1 Remove the engine top cover.
2 Wipe around the pipe unions at the pump and the injectors **(see illustration)**.
3 Using a pair of spanners, slacken the rigid fuel pipe unions at the rear of the injection pump and at the injectors, then lift the fuel pipe assembly away from the engine.
Caution: Be prepared for some fuel leakage during this operation by placing cloth rags beneath the unions. Take care to avoid stressing the rigid fuel pipes as they are removed.
4 Cover the open pipes and ports to prevent the ingress of dirt and excess fuel leakage **(see Haynes Hint 1)**.
5 Slacken the fuel supply and return banjo bolts at the injection pump ports, again taking precautions to minimise fuel spillage. Cover the open pipes and ports to prevent the ingress of dirt and excess fuel leakage **(see Haynes Hint 2)**.

Hint 1: Cut the fingertips from an old pair of rubber gloves and secure them over the fuel ports with elastic bands.

4.41 Attach a DTI (Dial Test Indicator) gauge to the cylinder head upper surface, and position the DTI probe against the top of the adjustment screw

6 With reference to Chapter 2D, remove the upper timing belt cover and camshaft cover.
7 Remove the brake servo vacuum pump as described in Chapter 9.
8 Set the engine to TDC compression on cylinder No 1 as described in Chapter 2D. Check that the TDC mark on the flywheel is aligned with the pointer on the transmission timing hole. Also make sure that the camshaft is positioned at exact TDC with the timing bar located in the end of the camshaft.
9 Attach a hoist to the engine lifting eyes and take its weight.
10 Remove the right-hand engine mounting assembly from the engine and body as described in Chapter 2D.
11 Unbolt the right-hand engine mounting bracket from the cylinder block. Note that it is not possible to remove the bottom bolt until the bracket has been completely removed.
12 Remove the timing belt and injection pump sprocket as described in Chapter 2D.
13 Disconnect the wiring connector located behind the oil filter housing.
14 Unscrew and remove the bolt that secures the injection pump to the rear (left-hand) mounting bracket **(see illustration)**.
Caution: Do not slacken the pump distributor head bolts, as this could cause serious internal damage to the injection pump.
15 Unscrew and remove the three bolts

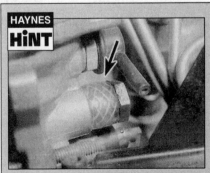

Hint 2: Fit a short length of hose over the banjo bolt (arrowed) so that the drillings are covered, then thread the bolt back into its injection pump port.

that secure the injection pump to the front (right-hand) mounting bracket. Support the pump body as the last fixing is removed. Check that nothing remains connected to the injection pump, then lift it away from the engine.

Refitting

16 Offer the injection pump to the engine, then insert the front and rear mounting bolts and tighten to the specified torque.
17 Reconnect the wiring behind the oil filter housing.
18 Refit the injection pump sprocket and timing belt as described in Chapter 2D.
19 Refit the right-hand engine mounting and bracket with reference to Chapter 2D, and tighten the bolts to the specified torque.
20 Prime the injection pump by fitting a small funnel to the fuel return pipe union and filling the cavity with clean diesel. Pad the area around the union with clean dry rags to absorb any spillage.
21 Reconnect the fuel injector delivery pipes to the injectors and injection pump head, then tighten the unions to the correct torque using a pair of spanners.
22 Reconnect the fuel supply and return pipes using new sealing washers, then tighten the banjo bolts to the specified torque. **Note:** *The inside diameter of the banjo bolt for the fuel return pipe is smaller than that of the fuel supply line, and is marked* **OUT**.
23 The commencement of injection must now be dynamically checked and if necessary adjusted by a Skoda dealer.
24 Refit the engine top cover.

6 Fuel injection pump timing (engine code ASY only) – checking and adjustment

The fuel injection pump timing can only be tested and adjusted using dedicated test equipment. Refer to a Skoda dealer for advice.

7 Fuel cut-off solenoid valve (engine code ASY only) – removal and refitting

General information

1 The fuel cut-off solenoid valve (or 'stop solenoid') provides an electro-mechanical

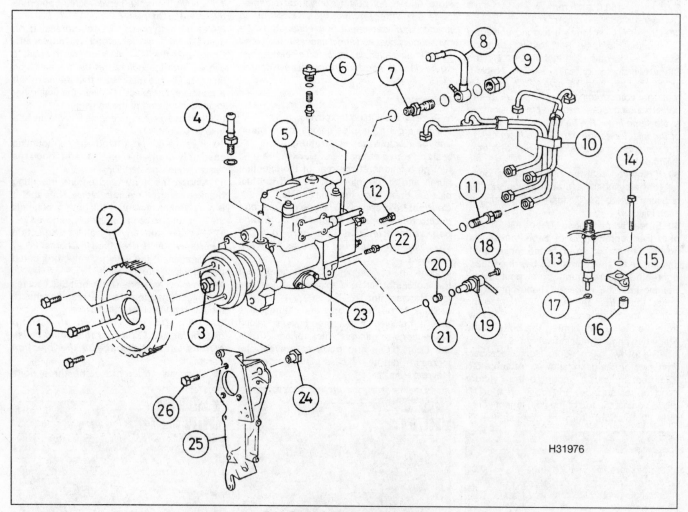

5.14 Fuel injection pump details

1 Sprocket bolts
2 Injection pump sprocket
3 Hub nut (do not loosen)
4 Fuel supply connection
5 Injection pump
6 Fuel shut-off solenoid valve
7 Fuel return connection
8 Fuel return pipe
9 Union nut
10 Injector pipe assembly
11 Injector pipe connection
12 Injection pump bracket bolt
13 No 3 injector (with needle lift sensor)
14 Injector retaining bolt
15 Retainer plate
16 Mounting sleeve
17 Heat shield
18 Mounting bolt
19 Commencement of injection valve
20 Strainer
21 O-ring
22 Injection pump bracket bolt
23 Timing control cover
24 Sleeve nut
25 Mounting bracket
26 Mounting bolt

H31976

means of switching off the engine. When the 'ignition' switch is turned off, the current supply to the solenoid is interrupted – this causes the valve plunger to drop, closing off the main fuel supply passage in the pump, and stopping the engine.

2 In the unlikely event of the cut-off solenoid failing in the open position, it will not be possible to switch off the engine. Should this happen, apply the footbrake and handbrake firmly, engage top gear, and slowly let out the clutch until the engine stalls. If the cut-off solenoid fails in the closed position, the engine will not start.

3 Note that the solenoid is linked to the anti-theft immobiliser system, preventing the engine from being started until the immobiliser is correctly deactivated by the driver.

Removal

4 The fuel cut-off valve is located at the upper, rear of the injection pump.

5 Unscrew the securing nut and disconnect the wiring from the top of the valve **(see illustration)**.

6 Unscrew and withdraw the valve body from the injection pump. Recover the seal and the plunger.

Refitting

7 Refitting is a reversal of removal, using a new seal.

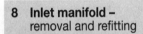

8 Inlet manifold – removal and refitting

Engine code AMF

Removal

1 Remove the engine top cover.
2 Remove the air inlet ducting from the air cleaner to the turbocharger with reference to Section 2.
3 Remove the flap housing and EGR valve from the inlet manifold as described in Section 3. Note that the engine rear lifting eye is bolted to the valve housing.
4 Unscrew and remove the mounting nuts and withdraw the inlet manifold from the rear of the cylinder head. Remove the gaskets and discard them as new ones must be used on refitting.

Refitting

5 Refitting is a reversal of removal. Ensure that the mating surfaces are clean. Use new gaskets and tighten the manifold bolts to the specified torque.

Engine code ASY

Removal

6 Remove the engine top cover.
7 Remove the air inlet ducting from the air cleaner to the inlet manifold flap housing with reference to Section 2.
8 Referring to Section 3, remove the inlet

7.5 Fuel cut-off solenoid wiring connector is secured by a nut (arrowed)

manifold flap housing from the inlet manifold. If preferred, however, the manifold can be removed with the flap housing – in this case, all services must be disconnected from the housing as described in Section 3, but the housing retaining bolts can be left in place.
9 Disconnect the wiring plug from the EGR vacuum unit solenoid valve, and unclip the wiring from the manifold. Alternatively, remove the solenoid valve completely as described in Chapter 4C.
10 Unscrew and remove the six retaining bolts, and remove the manifold from the cylinder head. Remove the gasket and discard it as a new one must be used on refitting.

Refitting

11 Refitting is a reversal of removal. Ensure that the mating surfaces are clean. Use a new gasket and tighten the manifold bolts to the specified torque.

Engine codes ASZ and ATD

Removal

12 Remove the engine top cover.
13 Remove the air inlet ducting from the air cleaner to the turbocharger with reference to Section 2.
14 Remove the flap housing and EGR valve from the inlet manifold as described in Section 3. Note that the engine rear lifting eye is bolted to the valve housing.
15 Unscrew the nuts and withdraw the inlet manifold from the studs on the cylinder head. Remove the gasket and discard it as a new one must be used on refitting.

11.2a Fuel tandem pump

Refitting

16 Refitting is a reversal of removal, using new manifold, EGR pipe and manifold flap assembly gaskets.

9 Fuel gauge sender unit – removal and refitting

Note: *Observe the precautions in Section 1 before working on any component in the fuel system.*

 Warning: Avoid direct skin contact with fuel – wear protective clothing and gloves when handling fuel system components. Ensure that the work area is well-ventilated to prevent the build-up of fuel vapour.

1 The fuel gauge sender unit is mounted on the top of the fuel tank. Access is through a hatch provided in the load space floor. The unit protrudes into the fuel tank, and its removal involves exposing the contents of the tank to the atmosphere.
2 Refer to the procedures in Chapter 4A for removal and refitting. On petrol models, the gauge sender unit is combined with the fuel pump, so ignore references to the fuel pump.

10 Fuel tank – removal and refitting

Note: *Observe the precautions in Section 1 before working on any component in the fuel system.*

1 Refer to the procedures in Chapter 4A. There is no activated charcoal breather pipe to disconnect at the front of the tank – instead, the fuel supply pipe (coloured black) should be disconnected, and, on engine code ASY only, the return pipe (coloured blue).

11 Tandem fuel pump – removal and refitting

Note: *Only engine codes AMF, ASZ and ATD are fitted with a tandem fuel pump. Note that disconnecting the central connector for the unit injectors may cause a fault code to be logged by the engine management ECU. This code can only be erased by a Skoda dealer or suitably-equipped specialist.*

Removal

1 Remove the engine top cover.
2 Disconnect the brake servo vacuum pipe from the tandem fuel pump **(see illustrations)**.
3 Position a container beneath the fuel filter in the front right-hand corner of the engine compartment, then disconnect the supply (white) and return (blue) hoses from the filter. Drain the fuel into the container.

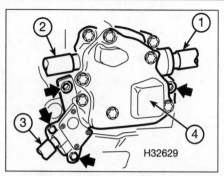

11.2b Fuel tandem pump securing bolts (arrowed)

1 Brake servo hose
2 Fuel supply hose
3 Fuel return hose
4 Tandem pump

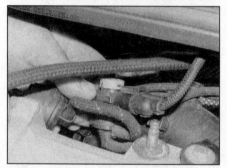

12.4 Unclip the inlet manifold flap solenoid valve . . .

4 Disconnect the supply (white) hose from the tandem fuel pump.

5 Unscrew the four mounting bolts and withdraw the pump from the cylinder head. Pull the pump upwards and disconnect the return (blue) hose, then remove the pump. Note how the drive pinion locates in the end of the camshaft. Be prepared for fuel spillage. There are no serviceable parts within the tandem pump. If the pump is faulty, it must be renewed.

Refitting

6 Reconnect the fuel return hose to the pump and refit the pump to the cylinder head, using new rubber seals, and ensuring that the pump pinion engages correctly with the drive slot in the camshaft **(see illustration)**.

7 Insert the pump retaining bolts, and tighten them to the specified torque.

8 Reconnect the fuel supply hose and brake servo hose to the pump.

9 Reconnect the supply (white) hose to the fuel filter.

10 Connect a hand vacuum pump to the fuel filter return hose (marked blue). Operate the vacuum pump until fuel comes out of the

11.6 Ensure that the tandem pump pinion engages correctly with the drive slot in the camshaft

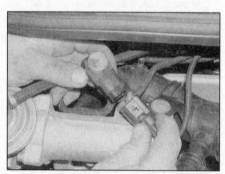

12.5 . . . and disconnect the wiring plug

return hose. This primes the tandem pump. Reconnect the return hose to the fuel filter.

11 Refit the engine top cover.

12 Have the engine management ECU's fault memory interrogated and any resident faults erased by a Skoda dealer or suitably-equipped specialist.

12 Inlet manifold changeover flap and valve – removal and refitting

Note: *Engine codes ASZ and ATD only.*

Changeover flap housing and vacuum control element

Removal and refitting

1 As diesel engines have a very high compression ratio, when the engine is turned off, the pistons still compress a large quantity of air for a few revolutions and cause the engine unit to shudder. The inlet manifold changeover flap is built into the EGR valve, and the flap is operated by a vacuum element. When the ignition switch is turned to the 'off' position, the engine management ECU-

controlled valve actuates the flap, which shuts off the air supply to the cylinders. This allows the pistons to compress very little air, and the engine runs softly to a halt. The flap must open again approximately 3 seconds after switching off the ignition switch. The EGR (Exhaust Gas Recirculation) valve is also incorporated into the flap housing.

2 Removal and refitting of the flap housing is identical to that for the EGR valve in Chapter 4C. Once removed, the flap control element can be removed by disconnecting the arm from the flap and unbolting the mounting bracket.

Changeover valve

Removal

3 The changeover valve controls the supply of vacuum to the changeover flap. The electrical supply to the valve is controlled by the engine management ECU. When the ignition key is turned to the 'off' position, the ECU signals the valve, which allows vacuum to pull the flap shut. Approximately three seconds later, the power supply to the valve is cut, the vacuum to the actuator collapses, and the flap opens.

4 The valve is located on the top of the air filter housing. Note the fitted positions and disconnect the vacuum pipes from the valve **(see illustration)**.

5 Disconnect the wiring plug from the valve **(see illustration)**.

6 Undo the retaining screw and remove the valve.

Refitting

7 Refitting is a reversal of removal.

13 Fuel cooler – removal and refitting

Removal

1 A fuel cooler is fitted in the return line to the fuel tank on models with engine codes AMF, ASZ and ATD. It is attached to the underbody. First, chock the front wheels, then jack up the rear of the vehicle and support it on axle stands (*see Jacking and vehicle support*).

2 Unbolt the cover from the fuel cooler.

3 Place cloth rags around the cooler to soak up spilt fuel, then disconnect the supply and return lines from it.

4 Unscrew the mounting nuts and remove the fuel cooler from under the car.

Refitting

5 Refitting is a reversal of removal, but tighten the mounting nuts to the specified torque.

Chapter 4 Part C:
Emission control and exhaust systems

Contents

Section number

Catalytic converter – general information and precautions 10
Crankcase emission system – general information 3
Evaporative loss emission control system – information and
   component renewal 2
Exhaust Gas Recirculation (EGR) system – component removal 4
Exhaust manifold – removal and refitting 8

Section number

Exhaust system – component renewal 9
General information 1
Intercooler – general information, removal and refitting 7
Turbocharger – general information, precautions, removal and
   refitting 5
Turbocharger boost pressure solenoid valve – removal and refitting 6

Degrees of difficulty

Easy, suitable for
novice with little
experience

Fairly easy, suitable
for beginner with
some experience

Fairly difficult,
suitable for competent
DIY mechanic

Difficult, suitable
for experienced DIY
mechanic

Very difficult,
suitable for expert
DIY or professional

Specifications

Engine codes

Petrol engines

1.2 litre:
  SOHC . . . . AWY
  DOHC . . . . AZQ, BME
1.4 litre OHV:
  44 kW . . . . AZE and AZF
  50 kW . . . . AME, AQW and ATZ
1.4 litre DOHC:
  55 kW . . . . AUA and BBY
  74 kW . . . . AUB and BBZ

Diesel engines

1.4 litre . . . . AMF
1.9 litre non-turbo . . . . ASY
1.9 litre turbo . . . . ASZ and ATD

Petrol engines

Catalytic converter

One catalytic converter fitted to engine codes . . . . AME, AQW, ATZ, AWY, AZE, AZF, AZQ and BME
Two catalytic converters fitted to engine codes . . . . AUA, AUB, BBY and BBZ

Oxygen (lambda) sensor

One or two oxygen sensors fitted to engine codes . . . . AME, AQW, ATZ, AWY, AZE, AZF, AZQ and BME
Two oxygen sensors fitted to engine codes . . . . AUA, AUB, BBY and BBZ

EGR system

Fitted to engine codes . . . . AUA, AUB, AZQ, BBY, BBZ and BME

Charcoal canister (evaporative emission control)

Fitted to all engine codes

Diesel engines

Catalytic converter

One catalytic converter fitted to all engine codes

EGR system

Fitted to all engine codes

Turbocharger

Fitted to engine codes . . . . AMF, ASZ, and ATD

Intercooler

Fitted to engine codes . . . . AMF, ASZ, and ATD

Torque wrench settings

	Nm	lbf ft
Petrol engines		
EGR adapter to cylinder head	20	15
EGR connecting pipe to intermediate plate or inlet manifold	10	7
EGR valve...	20	15
Exhaust clamp nuts	25	18
Exhaust manifold nuts*...................................	25	18
Exhaust manifold support bracket to engine:		
Engine codes AUA, AUB, BBY and BBZ	40	30
Exhaust mounting bracket bolts	25	18
Oxygen sensor...	50	37
Diesel engines		
EGR connecting pipe-to-exhaust manifold (engine code ASY).......	25	18
EGR pipe nuts/bolts......................................	25	18
EGR valve/flap housing-to-inlet manifold:		
Engine codes AMF, ASZ and ATD	10	7
EGR valve-to-inlet manifold (engine code ASY).................	25	18
Exhaust clamp nuts	40	30
Exhaust manifold nuts*...................................	25	18
Exhaust manifold/turbocharger-to-downpipe nuts*..............	25	18
Intercooler mounting bolts	8	6
Turbocharger oil feed union adapter	30	22
Turbocharger oil feed union nut	22	16
Turbocharger oil return pipe flange bolts	15	11
Turbocharger oil return union bolt	30	22
Turbocharger vacuum union bolt (engine code AMF)	15	11
Turbocharger-to-manifold bolts (engine code AMF)*.............	30	22

Use new nuts/bolts

1 General information

Petrol engine systems

All petrol models are designed to use unleaded petrol, and are controlled by engine management systems that are programmed to give the best compromise between driveability, fuel consumption and exhaust emission production. In addition, a number of systems are fitted that help to minimise other harmful emissions. A crankcase emission control system is fitted, which reduces the release of pollutants from the engine's lubrication system, and one or two catalytic converters are fitted to reduce exhaust gas pollutant. An evaporative loss emission control system is fitted which reduces the release of gaseous hydrocarbons from the fuel tank.

Crankcase emission control

To reduce the emission of unburned hydrocarbons from the crankcase into the atmosphere, the engine is sealed and the blow-by gases and oil vapour are drawn from inside the crankcase, through a wire-mesh oil separator, into the inlet tract to be burned by the engine during normal combustion.

Under conditions of high manifold depression, the gases will be sucked positively out of the crankcase. Under conditions of low manifold depression, the gases are forced out of the crankcase by the (relatively) higher crankcase pressure. If the engine is worn, the raised crankcase pressure (due to increased blow-by) will cause some of the flow to return under all manifold conditions. 1.2 litre engines and 1.4 litre engine codes BBY and BBZ, are fitted with a PCV valve which supplies fresh air to the crankcase under certain conditions.

Exhaust emission control

To minimise the amount of pollutants which escape into the atmosphere, all petrol models are fitted with one or two catalytic converters in the exhaust system. The fuelling system is of the closed-loop type, in which one or two oxygen (lambda) sensors in the exhaust system provide the engine management system ECU with constant feedback, enabling the ECU to adjust the air/fuel mixture to optimise combustion.

1.2 litre models have one catalytic converter built into the exhaust manifold. 1.4 litre OHV models have one catalytic converter located in the rear of the exhaust front pipe. 1.4 litre DOHC models have two catalytic converters, one located in the exhaust manifold and the other in the rear of the exhaust front pipe.

1.2 litre and 1.4 litre OHV engine models have either one or two oxygen sensors fitted according to the emission standard and country. 1.4 litre DOHC engine models have two oxygen sensors fitted. Models fitted with two oxygen sensors have one before and one after the catalytic converter(s) – this enables more efficient monitoring of the exhaust gas, allowing a faster response time. The overall efficiency of the converter itself can also be checked. Details of the oxygen sensor removal and refitting are given in Chapter 4A.

The oxygen sensor has a built-in heating element, controlled by the ECU through the oxygen sensor relay, to quickly bring the sensor's tip to its optimum operating temperature. The sensor's tip is sensitive to oxygen, and sends a voltage signal to the ECU that varies according on the amount of oxygen in the exhaust gas. If the inlet air/fuel mixture is too rich, the exhaust gases are low in oxygen so the sensor sends a low-voltage signal, the voltage rising as the mixture weakens and the amount of oxygen rises in the exhaust gases. Peak conversion efficiency of all major pollutants occurs if the inlet air/fuel mixture is maintained at the chemically-correct ratio for the complete combustion of petrol of 14.7 parts (by weight) of air to 1 part of fuel (the stoichiometric ratio). The sensor output voltage alters in a large step at this point, the ECU using the signal change as a reference point and correcting the inlet air/fuel mixture accordingly by altering the fuel injector pulse width.

An Exhaust Gas Recirculation (EGR) system is also fitted to some models (see Specifications). This reduces the level of nitrogen oxides produced during combustion by introducing a proportion of the inert exhaust gas back into the inlet manifold, under certain engine operating conditions, through a plunger valve. The system is controlled electronically by the engine management ECU.

Evaporative emission control

To minimise the escape of unburned hydrocarbons into the atmosphere, an evaporative loss emission control system is fitted to all petrol models. The fuel tank filler cap is sealed and a charcoal canister is mounted underneath the right-hand rear wheel arch to collect the petrol vapours released from the fuel contained in the fuel tank. It stores them until they can be drawn from the canister (under the control of the fuel injection/ignition system ECU) through the purge valve(s) into the inlet tract, where they are then burned by the engine during normal combustion.

To ensure that the engine runs correctly when it is cold and/or idling and to protect the catalytic converter from the effects of an over-rich mixture, the purge control valve(s) are not opened by the ECU until the engine has warmed-up, and the engine is under load; the valve solenoid is then modulated on and off to allow the stored vapour to pass into the inlet tract.

Exhaust systems

The exhaust system comprises the exhaust manifold, front pipe, intermediate pipe and silencer, and tailpipe and silencer. When new, the intermediate and tailpipe sections are one, however, service replacement sections are available separately.

The system is supported by various metal brackets attached to the underbody, with rubber vibration dampers fitted to suppress noise.

Diesel engine systems

All diesel-engined models have a crankcase emission control system and, in addition, are fitted with a catalytic converter. All diesel engines are also fitted with an Exhaust Gas Recirculation (EGR) system to reduce exhaust emissions.

Crankcase emission control

To reduce the emission of unburned hydrocarbons from the crankcase into the atmosphere, the engine is sealed and the blow-by gases and oil vapour are taken from inside the crankcase, through a wire mesh oil separator, into the inlet tract to be burned by the engine during normal combustion.

The gases are forced out of the crankcase by the relatively higher crankcase pressure. All diesel engines have a pressure-regulating valve on the camshaft cover, to control the flow of gases from the crankcase.

Exhaust emission control

An oxidation catalyst (catalytic converter) is fitted in the exhaust system of all diesel-engined models. This has the effect of removing a large proportion of the gaseous hydrocarbons, carbon monoxide and particulates present in the exhaust gas.

An Exhaust Gas Recirculation (EGR) system is fitted to all diesel-engined models. This reduces the level of nitrogen oxides produced during combustion by introducing a proportion of the exhaust gas back into the inlet manifold, under certain engine operating conditions, through a plunger valve. The system is controlled electronically by the diesel engine management ECU.

Exhaust systems

The exhaust system comprises the exhaust manifold, front pipe with catalytic converter, intermediate pipe (and silencer according to model), and tailpipe and silencer. On turbo models, the turbocharger is either bolted to, or integral with, the exhaust manifold, and is driven by the exhaust gases.

The system is supported by various metal brackets attached to the underbody, with rubber vibration dampers fitted to suppress noise.

2 Evaporative loss emission control system – information and component renewal

Note: This system is only fitted to petrol engine models.

1 The evaporative loss emission control system consists of the purge valve, the activated charcoal filter canister and connecting vacuum hoses.

2 The purge (or solenoid) valve is located in the right-hand rear corner of the engine compartment, and the canister is located near the fuel tank behind the right-hand rear wheel arch liner.

3 To remove the purge valve, check that the ignition is switched off, then disconnect the wiring plug and the two hoses.

4 To remove the canister, chock the front wheels, then jack up the rear of the vehicle and support it on axle stands (*see Jacking and vehicle support*). Remove the right-hand rear roadwheel and the wheel arch liner. Disconnect the hose leading to the solenoid valve from the top of the adapter, then disconnect the hose from the fuel tank from the side of the adapter. Unscrew the mounting bolt and lower the canister from the body.

5 Refitting is a reversal of removal.

3 Crankcase emission system – general information

1 The crankcase emission control system

4.4 EGR valve connecting tube on the inlet manifold

consists of hoses connecting the crankcase to the air cleaner or inlet manifold.

2 On some petrol engines, an oil separator unit is fitted to the rear of the engine.

3 On diesel engines, a pressure-regulating valve is fitted to the camshaft cover.

4 The system requires no attention other than to check at regular intervals that the hoses, valve and oil separator (as applicable) are free of blockages and in good condition.

4 Exhaust Gas Recirculation (EGR) system – component removal

Petrol engines

EGR valve

1 The EGR system consists of a combined EGR valve and potentiometer (solenoid) valve, together with a series of connecting vacuum hoses. The EGR valve is mounted on an adapter located on the front, left-hand end of the cylinder head. It is connected by a metal pipe to a flange joint on the intermediate plate at the throttle valve control unit on engine codes AUA, and pre-09/2003 engine code BBY, or directly to the inlet manifold on 09/2003-on engine code BBY, and engine codes AZQ, BBZ and BME. A vacuum hose is connected between the EGR valve and the air filter.

2 To remove the EGR valve/potentiometer, first remove the engine top cover.

3 Disconnect the wiring plug and vacuum hose.

4 Unbolt the connecting tube from the throttle valve control unit or inlet manifold as applicable (see illustration). Remove and discard the gasket, as a new one must be used on refitting. Also, unscrew the tube support bolt.

5 Unscrew the mounting nuts (engine codes AZQ and BME) or bolts (engine codes AUA, AUB, BBY and BBZ) securing the EGR valve to the adapter flange on the cylinder head and recover the gasket(s). The nuts/bolts also secure the connecting tube to the valve (see illustrations). Remove and discard the gaskets, as new ones must be used on refitting.

4.5a Unscrew the nuts and remove the connecting pipe . . .

4.5b . . . and gasket . . .

4.5c . . . and remove the EGR valve from the adapter – engine code BME

6 If necessary, unbolt the adapter from the cylinder head and discard the gasket.

7 Refitting is a reversal of removal. Use new gaskets, and tighten the mounting nuts/bolts to the specified torque.

Diesel engines

8 The EGR system consists of the EGR (mechanical) valve, the modulator (solenoid) valve and a series of connecting vacuum hoses. On the non-turbo engine code ASY, the EGR valve is mounted on a flange joint at the inlet manifold and is connected to a second flange joint at the exhaust manifold by a short metal pipe. On turbo engine codes AMF, ASZ and ATD, the EGR valve is part of the inlet manifold flap housing, and is joined to the exhaust manifold by a flanged pipe.

9 On engine code ASY, and engine codes ATD and ASZ up to 11/2001, the solenoid valve is mounted on the bulkhead at the right-hand rear of the engine compartment. On later engine codes ATD and ASZ, and all engine code AMF, it is combined into one valve block which includes the flap changeover valve and turbo charge pressure control valve; the valve block can only replaced as one unit.

EGR valve (engine code ASY)

10 Remove the engine top cover.

11 Disconnect the vacuum hose from the port on the EGR valve.

12 Loosen the clamp bolt which secures the valve to the short connecting pipe.

13 Unscrew and remove the two EGR valve mounting bolts **(see illustration)**.

14 Separate the valve from the lower section of the inlet manifold, and recover the gasket. Ease the valve upwards out of the clamp and connecting pipe, and remove it.

15 The connecting pipe can also be removed if required. Unscrew the pipe flange nuts, and separate the pipe from the exhaust manifold. Recover the gasket.

16 Refitting is a reversal of removal. Use new gaskets as required, and tighten the nuts and bolts to the specified torques.

EGR valve (engine codes AMF, ASZ and ATD)

17 The EGR valve is part of the inlet manifold flap housing, and cannot be removed separately.

18 If required, the pipe from the housing to the exhaust manifold can be removed, after unscrewing the flange nuts and bolts. Recover the gasket from each end of the pipe **(see illustration)**.

19 Refitting the pipe is a reversal of removal. Use new gaskets, and tighten the flange nuts and bolts to the specified torque.

EGR solenoid valve/valve block

20 Disconnect the wiring plug.

21 Identify their locations, then disconnect the vacuum hoses.

22 Remove the retaining screw, and withdraw the valve from the bulkhead.

23 Refitting is a reversal of removal. Ensure that the hoses and wiring plug are reconnected securely and correctly.

H31986

4.13 EGR valve details – non-turbo diesel engine code ASY

1 *Inlet manifold lower section*	5 *Clamp*
2 *Gasket*	6 *Clamp bolt*
3 *EGR valve*	7 *Connecting pipe*
4 *EGR valve mounting bolts/nuts*	8 *Exhaust manifold*

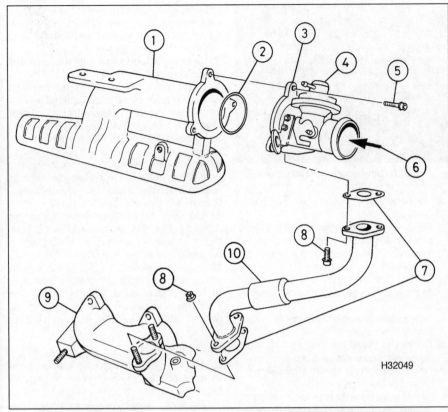

4.18 EGR pipe mounting details – turbo diesel engine codes AMF, ATD and ASZ

1 Inlet manifold	4 EGR valve	7 Gasket
2 O-ring	5 Mounting bolt	8 Flange nut/bolt
3 Inlet manifold flap housing	6 From intercooler	9 Exhaust manifold
		10 EGR pipe

5 Turbocharger – general information, precautions, removal and refitting

General information

The turbocharger is only fitted to diesel engine codes AMF, ASZ and ATD. On engine code AMF, it is bolted to the bottom of the exhaust manifold, but on engine codes ASZ and ATD, it is integral with the manifold.

The turbocharger increases engine efficiency by raising the pressure in the inlet manifold above atmospheric pressure. Instead of the air simply being sucked into the cylinders, it is forced in. Additional fuel is supplied by the injection pump, in proportion to the increased amount of air.

Energy for the operation of the turbocharger comes from the exhaust gas. The gas flows through a specially-shaped housing (the turbine housing) and in so doing spins the turbine wheel. The turbine wheel is attached to a shaft, at the end of which is another vaned wheel, known as the compressor wheel. The compressor wheel spins in its own housing, and compresses the inducted air on the way to the inlet manifold.

Between the turbocharger and the inlet manifold, the compressed air passes through an intercooler. The purpose of the intercooler is to remove from the inducted air some of the heat gained by being compressed. Because cooler air is denser, removal of this heat further increases engine efficiency.

Boost pressure (the pressure in the inlet manifold) is limited by a wastegate, which diverts the exhaust gas away from the turbine wheel in response to a pressure-sensitive actuator.

The turbo shaft is pressure-lubricated by an oil feed pipe from the engine oil filter mounting. The shaft 'floats' on a cushion of oil. Oil is returned to the sump through a return pipe that connects to the sump.

Some engines have a so-called 'adjustable' turbocharger, which further boosts the engine's power output compared with a normal turbo installation. At low engine speeds, vanes are used to restrict the exhaust gas supply pathway before the gases hit the turbine wheel – this has the effect of increasing the gas flow through the restriction, and the wheel reaches optimum speed faster (reducing turbo 'lag'). At higher engine speeds, the vanes open up the supply pathway, which lowers the exhaust back-pressure and reduces fuel consumption.

Precautions

The turbocharger operates at extremely high speeds and temperatures. Certain precautions must be observed to avoid premature failure of the turbo, or injury to the operator.

• *Do not operate the turbo with any parts exposed. Foreign objects falling onto the rotating vanes could cause excessive damage and (if ejected) personal injury.*

• *Cover the turbocharger air inlet ducts to prevent debris entering, and clean using lint-free cloths only.*

• *Do not race the engine immediately after start-up, especially if it is cold. Give the oil a few seconds to circulate.*

• *Always allow the engine to return to idle speed before switching it off – do not blip the throttle and switch off, as this will leave the turbo spinning without lubrication.*

• *Allow the engine to idle for several minutes before switching off after a high-speed run.*

• *Observe the recommended intervals for oil and filter changing, and use a reputable oil of the specified quality. Neglect of oil changing, or use of inferior oil, can cause carbon formation on the turbo shaft and subsequent failure. Thoroughly clean the area around all oil pipe unions before disconnecting them, to prevent the ingress of dirt. Store dismantled components in a sealed container to prevent contamination.*

Engine code AMF

Removal

1 Apply the handbrake, then jack up the front of the vehicle and support it on axle stands (see *Jacking and vehicle support*). Remove the engine compartment undershield.

2 Remove the engine top cover.

3 Loosen the clips and remove the charge air pipe leading from the intercooler to the flap/EGR housing on the inlet manifold. Also disconnect the charge air pipe from the air cleaner to the rear tube.

4 Loosen the clip and disconnect the hose from the turbocharger inlet **(see illustration)**, then unbolt and remove the rear tube.

5 Unscrew the nuts and remove the connecting tube leading from the exhaust

5.4 Turbocharger inlet hose

5.5 Connecting tube from the exhaust manifold to the flap/EGR valve housing

manifold to the flap/EGR valve housing. Recover the gaskets **(see illustration)**.

6 Unscrew the union nuts connecting the oil feed pipe to the turbocharger and engine **(see illustration)**, then unscrew the nut from the support bracket. Remove the oil feed pipe.

7 Unscrew the two bolts securing the turbocharger to the bottom of the exhaust manifold. Do not remove the mounting nut at this stage.

8 Remove the right-hand driveshaft as described in Chapter 8. Also, unbolt the driveshaft heat shield from the cylinder block.

9 Release the clip and disconnect the outlet air hose from the bottom of the turbocharger.

10 Identify then disconnect the wastegate and valve block vacuum hoses from the turbocharger.

11 Working beneath the vehicle, unscrew the union nut connecting the oil return line from the turbocharger to the cylinder block **(see illustration)**. Unscrew the bolts and detach the return line flange from the turbocharger. Recover the gasket.

12 Refer to Section 9 and remove the exhaust front pipe and catalytic converter. Recover the gasket from the studs on the turbocharger **(see illustration)**.

13 Support the turbocharger, then unscrew the remaining mounting nut from the manifold stud. Lower the turbocharger and remove from under the car. No gasket is fitted between the turbocharger and exhaust manifold.

Refitting

14 Refit the turbocharger by following the removal procedure in reverse, noting the following points:

5.11 Oil return line and turbocharger outlet hose

5.6 Turbocharger oil feed pipe

a) *Renew all gaskets, sealing washers and O-rings.*

b) *Renew the turbocharger mounting bolts and nut, and before fitting them, coat their threads and heads with anti-seize compound.*

c) *Before reconnecting the oil supply pipe, fill the turbocharger with fresh oil using an oil can.*

d) *Tighten all nuts and bolts to the specified torque, where given.*

e) *Ensure that the air hose clips are securely tightened, to prevent air leaks.*

f) *When the engine is started after refitting, allow it to idle for approximately one minute to give the oil time to circulate around the turbine shaft bearings. Check for signs of oil or coolant leakage from the relevant unions.*

Engine codes ASZ and ATD

Removal

15 Apply the handbrake, then jack up the front of the vehicle and support it on axle stands (see *Jacking and vehicle support*). Remove the engine compartment undershield.

16 Remove the engine top cover.

17 Remove the right-hand driveshaft as described in Chapter 8. Also, unbolt the driveshaft heatshield from the cylinder block.

18 Release the clips and disconnect the air hose and connecting tube leading from the bottom of the intercooler to the turbocharger outlet hose by the crankshaft pulley, then disconnect both charge air hoses from the

5.12 Exhaust front pipe-to-turbocharger gasket

turbocharger. Also disconnect the charge air pipe from the air cleaner.

19 Unscrew the union nut and detach the oil return line from the cylinder block.

20 Unbolt and remove the turbocharger lower support bracket.

21 Disconnect the vacuum hose from the wastegate control on the turbocharger.

22 Refer to Section 9 and remove the exhaust front pipe and catalytic converter from the turbocharger. Recover the gasket from the studs.

23 Unscrew the nuts and remove the connecting tube leading from the exhaust manifold to the flap/EGR valve housing. Recover the gaskets.

24 Unscrew the union nuts connecting the oil feed pipe to the turbocharger and engine, then unscrew the nut/bolt from the support bracket. Remove the oil feed pipe.

25 Progressively unscrew the nuts and bolts securing the exhaust manifold/turbocharger to the cylinder head, then withdraw the assembly and recover the gasket. Discard the gasket as a new one must be used for refitting.

Refitting

26 Refit the turbocharger by following the removal procedure in reverse, noting the following points:

a) *Renew all gaskets, sealing washers and O-rings.*

b) *Before reconnecting the oil supply pipe, fill the turbocharger with fresh oil using an oil can.*

c) *Tighten all nuts and bolts to the specified torque, where given.*

d) *Ensure that the air hose clips are securely tightened, to prevent air leaks.*

e) *When the engine is started after refitting, allow it to idle for approximately one minute to give the oil time to circulate around the turbine shaft bearings. Check for signs of oil or coolant leakage from the relevant unions.*

---

6 Turbocharger boost pressure solenoid valve – removal and refitting

Note: *This Section only applies to diesel engine codes ASZ and ATD.*

Removal

1 The boost pressure solenoid valve is mounted separately on the right-hand side of the bulkhead on models manufactured up to the end of 10/2001. On later models, the valve is incorporated into a valve block, also in the same location.

2 Disconnect the wiring plug.

3 Identify their locations, then disconnect the vacuum hoses **(see illustrations)**.

4 Remove the retaining screw and withdraw the valve from the bulkhead.

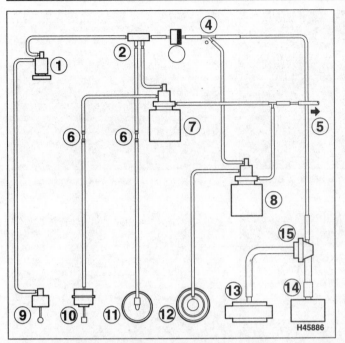

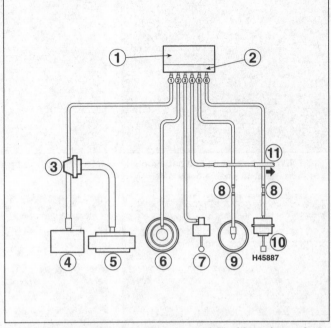

6.3a Vacuum hose connections on models with engine codes ATD and ASZ up to the end of 10/2001

1	Changeover valve for inlet manifold flap	8	EGR solenoid valve
2	Connector	9	Vacuum unit for inlet manifold flap valve
3	Non-return valve	10	Vacuum unit
4	Connector	11	Vacuum reservoir
5	To air cleaner	12	Mechanical EGR valve
6	Connectors	13	Brake vacuum servo unit
7	Turbocharger boost pressure solenoid valve	14	Tandem vacuum pump
		15	Connector

6.3b Vacuum hose connections on models with engine codes ATD and ASZ from 11/2001

1	Valve block	7	Vacuum unit for inlet manifold flap valve
2	Vacuum connector strip	8	Connectors
3	Connector	9	Vacuum reservoir
4	Tandem vacuum pump	10	Charge pressure control vacuum unit
5	Brake vacuum servo unit	11	To air cleaner
6	Mechanical EGR valve		

Refitting

5 Refitting is a reversal of removal. Ensure that the hoses and wiring plug are reconnected securely and correctly.

7 Intercooler – general information, removal and refitting

Note: *This Section only applies to diesel engine codes AMF, ASZ and ATD.*

General information

1 The intercooler is effectively an 'air radiator', used to cool the pressurised inlet air before it enters the engine. When the turbocharger compresses the inlet air, one side-effect is that the air is heated, causing the air to expand. If the inlet air can be cooled, a greater effective volume of air will be inducted, and the engine will produce more power.

2 The compressed air from the turbocharger, which would normally be fed straight into the inlet manifold, is instead ducted around the engine to the base of the intercooler. The intercooler is mounted behind the wheel arch liner beneath the right-hand front wing, in the airflow. The heated air entering the base of

the unit rises upwards, and is cooled by the airflow over the intercooler fins, much as with the radiator. When it reaches the top of the intercooler, the cooled air is then ducted into the inlet manifold.

Removal

3 To gain access to the intercooler, remove the bumper as described in Chapter 11, and the right-hand headlight as described in Chapter 12, Section 7. Also, remove the right-hand front wheel arch liner, and the intercooler air ducting (see illustration).

4 Disconnect the wiring from the inlet manifold

pressure/temperature sender located on the top of the intercooler.

5 Release the outlet hose/ducting from its supports, then use grips to release the spring clip and disconnect the hose from the top of the intercooler. **Note:** *Some models have quick-release fittings; pull out the clip to release it.*

6 Release the spring clip and disconnect the inlet hose from the bottom of the intercooler.

7 Unscrew the mounting bolts and withdraw the intercooler from the engine compartment (see illustration).

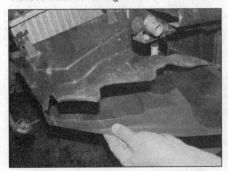

7.3 Removing the intercooler air ducting

7.7 The intercooler is located beneath the right-hand front wheel arch

8.1 Exhaust manifold and catalytic converter on engine code BME

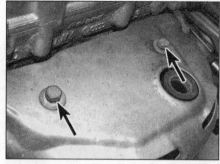

8.5a Heat shield upper mounting bolts . . .

8.5b . . . and lower mounting bolts

8.5c Removing the heat shield from the exhaust manifold

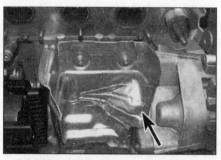

8.5d Heat shield fitted on the cylinder block on engine code BME (exhaust manifold removed)

8.9 Unscrew the retaining nuts . . .

8 Examine the intercooler for any damage, and check the air hoses for splits. The charge pressure/temperature sender may be removed from the top of the intercooler by unscrewing the two mounting bolts – recover the O-ring seal and examine it for condition.

Refitting

9 Refitting is a reversal of removal. Ensure that the hose clips are securely tightened, to prevent air leaks, and fit a new O-ring seal to the charge pressure/temperature sender.

8 Exhaust manifold – removal and refitting

Petrol engines

Removal

1 Engine codes AUA, AUB, AWY, AZQ, BBY, BBZ and BME have a catalytic converter integrated into the exhaust manifold **(see illustration)**. Engine codes AME, AQW, ATZ, AZE and AZF have a conventional exhaust manifold.
2 Remove the engine top cover.
3 Apply the handbrake, then jack up the front of the vehicle and support it on axle stands (see *Jacking and vehicle support*). Remove the engine undertray. If necessary for additional working room, remove the electric cooling fan and shroud from the rear of the radiator as described in Chapter 3.
4 Pull the warm-air hose (for the air cleaner)

from the heat shield over the manifold, and place the hose end to one side.
5 Unscrew the bolts and remove the heat shield from the manifold. Note that on some models, additional extended shields are fitted, including some bolted to the cylinder block **(see illustrations)**.
6 On models with an oxygen sensor screwed into the manifold, trace the wiring from the sensor to the connector plug. Disconnect the wiring plug, and free the wiring from any retaining clips or ties. Unscrew and remove the sensor or, alternatively, leave it in position until after the manifold has been removed.
7 Where fitted, unbolt and remove the manifold support bracket.
8 Unscrew the nuts and detach the exhaust front pipe from the bottom of the exhaust manifold. On some models, it may be necessary to completely remove the front

pipe with reference to Section 9. Discard the gasket, and obtain a new one for refitting.
9 Unscrew and remove the manifold retaining nuts, noting that some manifold studs may come out with the nuts **(see illustration)**.
10 Remove the washers, then withdraw the manifold from the cylinder head, and recover the gasket(s) from the studs **(see illustrations)**.
11 Where any studs have unscrewed, grip them in a vice and unscrew the nuts. Apply locking fluid to the threads before refitting and tightening the studs into the cylinder head again. Use two nuts tightened against each other to tighten the studs.

Refitting

12 Refitting is a reversal of the removal procedure, noting the following points:
a) *Always fit new gaskets.*
b) *If any studs were broken when removing,*

8.10a . . . remove the exhaust manifold . . .

8.10b . . . and recover the gasket

drill out the remains of the stud, and fit new studs and nuts.

c) Tighten all nuts and bolts to the specified torque where given.

Diesel engines

Note: *Removal and refitting of the exhaust manifold/turbocharger on engine codes ASZ and ATD is covered in Section 5. This subsection covers removal on engine codes AMF and ASY only.*

Removal

13 Engine code AMF has a turbocharger bolted to the underside of the exhaust manifold. On engine codes ASZ and ATD, the turbocharger is integral with the exhaust manifold and cannot be separated from it. On the non-turbo engine code ASY, the exhaust front pipe bolts directly onto the exhaust manifold.

14 Remove the engine top cover.

15 Apply the handbrake, then jack up the front of the vehicle and support it on axle stands (see *Jacking and vehicle support*). Remove the engine undertray.

16 Access to the exhaust manifold is greatly improved if the inlet manifold is removed first, as described in Part B of this Chapter.

17 On engine code AMF, remove the turbocharger as described in Section 5.

18 Referring to Section 4, remove the EGR connecting pipe from the exhaust manifold. On the non-turbo engine code ASY, if the inlet manifold has not been removed, unbolt the EGR valve from the inlet manifold, so that the connecting pipe can be removed.

19 Unscrew the retaining nuts, and separate the exhaust downpipe from the manifold or turbocharger **(see illustration)**. There should be sufficient movement in the pipe to free it from the studs – if not, loosen the bolts securing the exhaust front mounting.

20 Support the manifold, then unscrew and remove the manifold retaining nuts and recover the washers. Withdraw the exhaust manifold from the cylinder head studs and withdraw from under the vehicle. Recover the manifold gasket from the cylinder head studs, and discard them.

Refitting

21 Refitting is a reversal of the removal

9.3 Front pipe and catalytic converter on engine code BBY

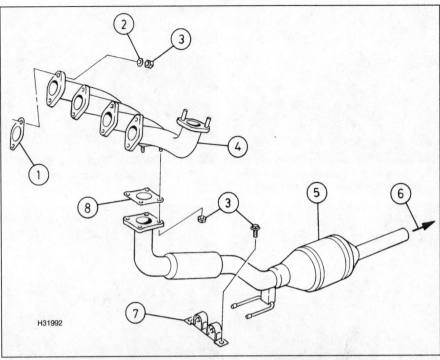

H31992

8.19 Exhaust manifold and front pipe – diesel non-turbo models

1 Manifold gasket	5 Catalytic converter
2 Washer	6 To exhaust rear section
3 Mounting nut	7 Front mounting
4 Exhaust manifold	8 Downpipe gasket

procedure, but fit new gaskets, and tighten all nut and bolts to the specified torque where given.

9 Exhaust system – component renewal

Warning: Allow ample time for the exhaust system to cool before starting work. In particular, note that the catalytic converter runs at very high temperatures. If there is any chance that the system may still be hot, wear suitable gloves.

Removal

1 The original Skoda system fitted in the factory is in two sections. The front section (including the catalytic converter or 'catalyst' on all engines except petrol engine codes AWY, AZQ and BME) can be removed separately. The original rear section cannot be removed in one piece, as it passes over the rear axle – the pipe must be cut through between the centre and rear silencers, at the point marked on the pipe. There are three markings, and the pipe must be cut on the centre mark.

2 To remove part of the system, first jack up the front or rear of the car and support it on axle stands (see *Jacking and vehicle support*). Alternatively, position the car over an inspection pit or on car ramps.

Front pipe (with catalytic converter)

Note: *Handle the flexible, braided section of the front pipe carefully, and do not bend it excessively.*

3 On petrol models, carry out the following:

a) *Before removing the front section of the exhaust, check if any oxygen sensors are fitted* **(see illustration)**. *Trace the wiring back from the sensor(s), and disconnect the wiring connector. On some models, the sensor wiring disappears behind an access panel behind the right-hand driveshaft, and it will be necessary to remove the cover fitted over the right-hand inner CV joint (or even the complete driveshaft, as described in Chapter 8) for access.*

b) *Unclip the oxygen sensor wiring from any clips or brackets, noting how it is routed for refitting.*

c) *If a new front section is being fitted, unscrew the oxygen sensor(s) from the pipe where applicable. If two sensors are fitted, note which fits where, as they must not be interchanged.*

4 Loosen the two nuts on the clamp at the rear of the front pipe, and free the clamp so that it can be moved relative to the front and rear pipes **(see illustration)**.

5 Unscrew and remove the nuts securing the front flange to the exhaust manifold or turbocharger **(see illustration)**. On some models, the shield over the right-hand driveshaft inner CV joint must be removed to improve access,

9.4 Removing the clamp securing the exhaust front pipe to the rear pipe

9.5a Exhaust front flange on manifold

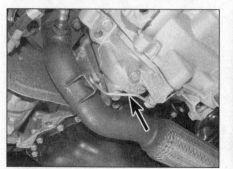

9.5b Front exhaust pipe support rod on engine code BME

9.6 Using a special tool to remove the exhaust rubber mountings

and additionally on some models, the front pipe is supported by a metal rod (see illustration). Separate the front joint, and move the front pipe down sufficiently to clear the mounting studs. Recover and discard the gasket.

6 Release the rubber mountings from the metal pegs and support the front of the pipe (see illustration).

7 Slide the clamp behind the catalyst either forwards or backwards to separate the joint. Twist the front pipe slightly from side-to-side, while pulling towards the front to release it from the rear section. When the pipe is free, lower it to the ground and remove it from under the car.

Rear pipe and silencer(s)

8 If the factory-fitted Skoda rear section is being worked on, examine the pipe for three pairs of punch marks, or three line markings. The centre marking indicates the point at which to cut the pipe, while the outer marks indicate the position for the ends of the new clamp required when refitting. Cut through the pipe using the centre mark as a guide, making the cut as square to the pipe as possible if either resulting section is to be re-used.

9 If the factory-fitted rear section has already been renewed, loosen the nuts securing the clamp between the two sections so that the clamp can be moved.

Centre silencer

10 To remove the centre silencer, loosen the nuts on the front and rear clamps.

11 Slide the clamps at either end of the silencer section to release the pipe ends, withdraw the support peg from the rubber mounting, and withdraw the silencer from under the car.

Rear silencer

12 The rear silencer is supported in front and behind by rubber mountings attached to the underside of the car. Loosen the nuts on the clamp securing the rear silencer to the centre silencer.

13 Ease the rear silencer from the clamp, withdraw the support pegs from the rubber mountings and withdraw the silencer from under the car.

Refitting

14 Each section is refitted by a reversal of the removal sequence, noting the following points:

a) *Ensure that all traces of corrosion have been removed from the flanges or pipe ends, and renew the downpipe gasket where removed.*

b) *The design of the clamps used between the exhaust sections means that they play a greater role in ensuring a gas-tight seal – fit new clamps if they are in less than perfect condition.*

c) *When fitting the clamps, use the markings on the pipes as a guide to the clamp's correct fitted position.*

d) *Inspect the mountings for signs of*

damage or deterioration, and renew as necessary.

e) *If using exhaust assembly paste, make sure this is only applied to joints downstream of the catalyst.*

f) *Prior to tightening the exhaust system mountings and clamps, ensure that all rubber mountings are correctly located and that there is adequate clearance between the exhaust system and vehicle underbody. Try to ensure that no unnecessary twisting stresses are applied to the pipes – move the pipes relative to each other at the clamps to relieve this.*

10 Catalytic converter – general information and precautions

The catalytic converter is a reliable and simple device which needs no maintenance in itself, but there are some facts of which an owner should be aware if the converter is to function properly for its full service life:

a) *DO NOT use leaded or lead-replacement petrol in a car equipped with a catalytic converter – the lead (or other additives) will coat the precious metals, reducing their converting efficiency and will eventually destroy the converter.*

b) *Always keep the ignition/fuel systems well-maintained in accordance with the manufacturer's schedule.*

c) *If the engine develops a misfire, do not drive the car at all (or at least as little as possible) until the fault is cured.*

d) *DO NOT use fuel or engine oil additives – these may contain substances harmful to the catalytic converter.*

e) *DO NOT continue to use the car if the engine burns oil to the extent of leaving a visible trail of blue smoke.*

f) *Remember that the catalytic converter operates at very high temperatures. DO NOT, therefore, park the car in dry undergrowth, over long grass or piles of dead leaves after a long run.*

g) *Remember that the catalytic converter is FRAGILE – do not strike it with tools during servicing work, and take care handling it when removing it from the car for any reason.*

h) *In some cases, a sulphurous smell (like that of rotten eggs) may be noticed from the exhaust. This is common to many catalytic converter-equipped cars, and has more to do with the sulphur content of the brand of fuel being used than the converter itself.*

i) *The catalytic converter, used on a well-maintained and well-driven car, should last for between 50 000 and 100 000 miles – if the converter is no longer effective, it must be renewed.*

Chapter 5 Part A:
Starting and charging systems

Contents

	Section number		Section number
Alternator – brush holder/regulator module renewal	6	Electrical system check	See *Weekly checks*
Alternator – removal and refitting	5	General information and precautions	1
Alternator/charging system – testing in vehicle	4	Starter motor – removal and refitting	8
Battery – removal and refitting	3	Starter motor – testing and overhaul	9
Battery – testing and charging	2	Starting system – testing	7
Battery check	See *Weekly checks*		

Degrees of difficulty

Easy, suitable for novice with little experience	**Fairly easy,** suitable for beginner with some experience	**Fairly difficult,** suitable for competent DIY mechanic	**Difficult,** suitable for experienced DIY mechanic	**Very difficult,** suitable for expert DIY or professional

Specifications

Engine codes

Petrol engines

1.2 litre:	
SOHC	AWY
DOHC	AZQ, BME
1.4 litre OHV:	
44 kW	AZE and AZF
50 kW	AME, AQW and ATZ
1.4 litre DOHC:	
55 kW	AUA and BBY
74 kW	AUB and BBZ

Diesel engines

1.4 litre	AMF
1.9 litre non-turbo	ASY
1.9 litre turbo	ASZ and ATD

General

System type	12 volt, negative earth

Starter motor

Rating:	
Petrol engines	12V, 1.1 kW
Diesel engines	12V, 2.0 kW

Battery

Ratings	36 to 72 Ah (depending on model and market)

Alternator

Rating	55, 60, 70 or 90 amp
Minimum brush length	5.0 mm

Torque wrench settings	Nm	lbf ft
Alternator mounting bolts:		
1.2 litre petrol engines	23	17
1.4 litre OHV petrol engines	30	22
1.4 litre DOHC petrol engines	20	15
Diesel engines	25	18
Battery clamping plate bolt	22	16
Battery tray	20	15
Starter motor mounting bolts	65	48

1 General information and precautions

General information

The engine electrical system consists mainly of the charging and starting systems. Because of their engine-related functions, these are covered separately from the body electrical devices such as the lights, instruments, etc (which are covered in Chapter 12). On petrol engine models refer to Part B of this Chapter for information on the ignition system, and on diesel models refer to Part C for information on the preheating system.

The electrical system is of the 12 volt negative earth type.

The battery may of the low maintenance or maintenance-free (sealed for life) type and is charged by the alternator, which is belt-driven from the crankshaft pulley.

The starter motor is of the pre-engaged type, with an integral solenoid. On starting, the solenoid moves the drive pinion into engagement with the flywheel ring gear before the starter motor is energised. Once the engine has started, a one-way clutch prevents the motor armature being driven by the engine until the pinion disengages from the flywheel.

Further details of the various systems are given in the relevant Sections of this Chapter. While some repair procedures are given, the usual course of action is to renew the component concerned. The owner whose interest extends beyond mere component renewal should obtain a copy of the *Automotive Electrical & Electronic Systems Manual*, available from the publishers of this manual.

Precautions

⚠️ *Warning: It is necessary to take extra care when working on the electrical system to avoid damage to semi-conductor devices (diodes and transistors), and to avoid the risk of personal injury. In addition to the precautions given in 'Safety first!', observe the following when working on the system:*
• *Always remove rings, watches, etc before working on the electrical system.* Even with the battery disconnected, capacitive discharge could occur if a component's live terminal is earthed through a metal object. This could cause a shock or nasty burn.
• *Do not reverse the battery connections.* Components such as the alternator, electronic control units, or any other components having semi-conductor circuitry could be irreparably damaged.
• If the engine is being started using jump leads and a slave battery, connect the batteries *positive-to-positive* and *negative-to-negative* (see *Jump starting*). This also applies when connecting a battery charger.
• Never disconnect the battery terminals,

the alternator, any electrical wiring or any test instruments when the engine is running.
• Do not allow the engine to turn the alternator when the alternator is not connected.
• Never 'test' for alternator output by 'flashing' the output lead to earth.
• Never use an ohmmeter of the type incorporating a hand-cranked generator for circuit or continuity testing.
• Always ensure that the battery negative lead is disconnected when working on the electrical system.
• Before using electric-arc welding equipment on the car, disconnect the battery, alternator and components such as the fuel injection/ ignition electronic control unit to protect them from the risk of damage.
Caution: Certain radios fitted as standard equipment by Skoda have a built-in security code to deter thieves. If the power source to the unit is cut, the anti-theft system will activate. Even if the power source is immediately reconnected, the radio will not function until the correct security code has been entered. Therefore, if you do not know the correct security code for the radio do not disconnect the battery negative terminal or remove the radio/cassette unit from the vehicle. Refer to your Skoda dealer for further information on whether the unit fitted to your car has a security code. Refer to 'Disconnecting the battery' in the Reference section at the rear of this manual.

2 Battery – testing and charging

Testing

Standard and low-maintenance battery

1 If the vehicle covers a small annual mileage, it is worthwhile checking the specific gravity of the electrolyte every three months to determine the state of charge of the battery. Remove the battery (see Section 3) then remove the cell caps/cover (as applicable) and use a hydrometer to make the check, comparing the results with the following table. Note that the specific gravity readings assume an electrolyte temperature of 15°C (60°F); for every 10°C (18°F) below 15°C (60°F) subtract 0.007. For every 10°C (18°F) above 15°C (60°F) add 0.007. If the electrolyte level of any cell is low, top it up to the MAX level mark with distilled water.

	Above 25°C	Below 25°C
Fully-charged	1.210 to 1.230	1.270 to 1.290
70% charged	1.170 to 1.190	1.230 to 1.250
Discharged	1.050 to 1.070	1.110 to 1.130

2 If the battery condition is suspect, first check the specific gravity of electrolyte in each cell. A variation of 0.040 or more between any cells indicates loss of electrolyte or deterioration of the internal plates.

3 If the specific gravity variation is 0.040 or more, the battery should be renewed. If the cell variation is satisfactory but the battery is discharged, it should be charged as described later in this Section.

Maintenance-free battery

4 In cases where a sealed for life maintenance-free battery is fitted, topping-up and testing of the electrolyte in each cell is not possible. The condition of the battery can therefore only be tested using a battery condition indicator or a voltmeter.

5 Certain models may be fitted with a maintenance-free battery with a built-in charge condition indicator. The indicator is located in the top of the battery casing, and indicates the condition of the battery from its colour. If the indicator shows green, then the battery is in good condition and charged up. If the indicator turns darker, eventually to black, then the battery requires charging, as described later in this Section. If the indicator shows clear/yellow, then the electrolyte is low and in a critical condition, and should be topped-up with distilled water. If charging the battery does not return the eye to green, the battery should be scrapped.

6 If testing the battery using a voltmeter, connect the voltmeter across the battery and note the voltage. The test is only accurate if the battery has not been subjected to any kind of charge for the previous six hours. If this is not the case, switch on the headlights for 30 seconds, then wait four to five minutes before testing the battery after switching off the headlights. All other electrical circuits must be switched off, so check that the doors and tailgate are fully shut when making the test.

7 If the voltage reading is less than 12.2 volts, then the battery is discharged, whilst a reading of 12.2 to 12.4 volts indicates a partially-discharged condition.

8 If the battery is to be charged, remove it from the vehicle and charge it as described later in this Section.

Charging

Note: *The following is intended as a guide only. Always refer to the manufacturer's recommendations (often printed on a label attached to the battery) before charging a battery.*

Standard and low maintenance battery

9 Charge the battery at a rate equivalent to 10% of the battery capacity (eg, for a 45 Ah battery charge at 4.5 A) and continue to charge the battery at this rate until no further rise in specific gravity is noted over a four-hour period.

10 Alternatively, a trickle charger charging at the rate of 1.5 amps can safely be used overnight.

11 Specially rapid boost charges which are claimed to restore the power of the battery in 1 to 2 hours are not recommended, as they can cause serious damage to the battery plates through overheating.

12 While charging the battery, note that the temperature of the electrolyte should never exceed 37.8°C (100°F).

Maintenance-free battery

13 This battery type takes considerably longer to fully recharge than the standard type, the time taken being dependent on the extent of discharge, but it can take anything up to three days.

14 A constant voltage type charger is required, to be set, when connected, to 13.9 to 14.9 volts with a charger current below 25 amps. Using this method, the battery should be useable within three hours, giving a voltage reading of 12.5 volts, but this is for a partially-discharged battery and, as mentioned, full charging can take far longer.

15 If the battery is to be charged from a fully-discharged state (condition reading less than 12.2 volts), have it recharged by your local automotive electrician, as the charge rate is higher and constant supervision during charging is necessary.

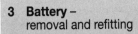

3 Battery – removal and refitting

Note: *If the vehicle has a security-coded radio, make sure that you have the code number before disconnecting the battery. If necessary, a 'code-saver' or 'memory-saver' can be used to preserve the radio code and any other relevant memory values whilst the battery is disconnected (see 'Disconnecting the battery' in the Reference Section).*

Removal

1 The battery is located in the front, left-hand corner of the engine compartment. First, open the cover and lift the fuse carrier from the top of the battery, then unclip the box section from the battery tray. On models manufactured before 06/2001, depress the catches at each end of the carrier and fold the carrier forwards. On later models, lift the right-hand end of the carrier and position it over the engine compartment front crossmember **(see illustrations)**.

2 Loosen the clamp nut and disconnect the battery negative (-) lead from the terminal **(see illustration)**.

3 Loosen the clamp nut and disconnect the positive (+) lead from the battery terminal **(see illustration)**.

4 Unscrew the bolt and remove the battery mounting clamp **(see illustration)**. The battery can then be lifted out of position.

Refitting

5 Refit the battery by following the removal procedure in reverse. Tighten the mounting clamp bolt to the correct torque. Tighten the terminal clamp nuts securely, but do not over-tighten them to the point where the clamps are distorted.

6 Where applicable, enter the code on the

3.1a Battery located in the left-hand corner of the engine compartment

3.1c ... followed by the box section

security-coded radio. Adjust the clock to the correct time, and initialise the electric windows with reference to Chapter 11.

4 Alternator/charging system – testing in vehicle

Note: *Refer to Section 1 of this Chapter before starting work.*

1 If the charge warning light fails to illuminate when the ignition is switched on, first check the alternator wiring connections for security. If the light still fails to illuminate, check the continuity of the warning light feed wire from the alternator to the bulbholder. If all is satisfactory, the alternator is at fault and should be renewed or taken to an auto-electrician for testing and repair.

3.3 Disconnecting the positive terminal

3.1b Remove the cover and fuse carrier ...

3.2 Disconnecting the negative terminal

2 Similarly, if the charge warning light comes on with the ignition, but is then slow to go out when the engine is started, this may indicate an impending alternator problem. Check all the items listed in the preceding paragraph, and refer to an auto-electrical specialist if no obvious faults are found.

3 If the charge warning light illuminates when the engine is running, stop the engine and check that the auxiliary drivebelt is intact and correctly tensioned, and that the alternator connections are secure. If all is so far satisfactory, check the alternator brushes and slip-rings as described in Section 6. If the fault persists, the alternator should be renewed, or taken to an auto-electrician for testing and repair.

4 If the alternator output is suspect even though the warning light functions correctly, the regulated voltage may be checked as follows.

3.4 Unscrew the clamp bolt

5.3 Unplug the 2-pin connector

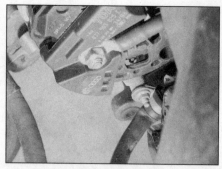

5.4 Disconnect the positive lead

5.6 Unscrew the mounting bolts

6.3 Remove the outer cover

5 Connect a voltmeter across the battery terminals, and start the engine.

6 Increase the engine speed until the voltmeter reading remains steady; the reading should be approximately 12 to 13 volts, and no more than 14 volts.

7 Switch on as many electrical accessories (eg, the headlights, heated rear window and heater blower) as possible, and check that the alternator maintains the regulated voltage at around 13 to 14 volts.

8 If the regulated voltage is not as stated,

this may be due to worn brushes, weak brush springs, a faulty voltage regulator, a faulty diode, a severed phase winding or worn or damaged slip-rings. The brushes and slip-rings may be checked as described in Section 6, but if the fault persists, the alternator should be renewed or taken to an auto-electrician.

5 Alternator – removal and refitting

Removal

1 Disconnect the battery negative lead (refer to *Disconnecting the battery* in the *Reference* Chapter at the end of this manual).

2 Remove the auxiliary drivebelt from the alternator pulley (see Chapter 1A or 1B). Mark the drivebelt for direction of rotation to ensure it is refitted correctly.

3 Pull the 2-pin push-in connector from the alternator **(see illustration)**.

4 Remove the protective cap (where fitted), unscrew and remove the nut and washers, then disconnect the battery positive cable from the alternator terminal. Where applicable, unscrew the nut and remove the cable guide **(see illustration)**.

5 On all diesel models and some petrol models, it is necessary to unbolt the air conditioning compressor and suspend it to one side. Also, on models with the heavy duty cooling system, remove the auxiliary electric cooling fan from the right-hand side of the radiator, and protect the radiator with a piece of cardboard.

6 Unscrew and remove the lower, then upper bolts, then lift the alternator away from its bracket **(see illustration)**.

Refitting

7 The alternator mounting bushes are self-centralising and should be carefully tapped back approximately 1.0 mm before refitting.

8 Refitting is a reversal of removal. Refer to Chapter 1A or 1B as applicable for details of refitting the auxiliary drivebelt. Tighten the alternator mounting bolts to the specified torque.

6 Alternator – brush holder/regulator module renewal

1 Remove the alternator, as described in Section 5.

2 Place the alternator on a clean work surface, with the pulley facing down.

3 Undo the screw and the two retaining nuts, and lift away the outer plastic cover **(see illustration)**.

4 Undo the three screws, and remove the voltage regulator **(see illustrations)**.

5 Measure the free length of the brush contacts **(see illustration)**. Check the measurement with the Specifications; renew

6.4a Undo the three screws . . .

6.4b . . . and remove the brush holder/ regulator

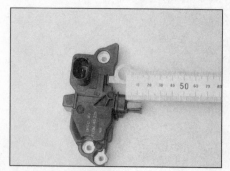

6.5 Measure the brush length

6.6 Clean and inspect the surfaces of the slip-rings

the module if the brushes are worn below the minimum limit.

6 Clean and inspect the surfaces of the slip-rings, at the end of the alternator shaft **(see illustration)**. If they are excessively worn, or damaged, the alternator must be renewed.

7 Before refitting the module, depress the brushes in their released position, and hold them there by pulling out the cap – with the module in position, press the cap to release the brushes. The remaining reassembly is a reversal of the dismantling procedure. On completion, refer to Section 5 and refit the alternator.

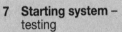
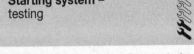

7 Starting system – testing

Note: *Refer to Section 1 of this Chapter before starting work.*

1 If the starter motor fails to operate when the ignition key is turned to the appropriate position, the following faults may be the cause:

 a) *The battery is faulty.*
 b) *The electrical connections between the switch, solenoid, battery and starter motor are somewhere failing to pass the necessary current from the battery through the starter to earth.*
 c) *The solenoid is faulty.*
 d) *The starter motor is mechanically or electrically defective.*

2 To check the battery, switch on the headlights. If they dim after a few seconds, this indicates that the battery is discharged – recharge (see Section 2) or renew the battery. If the headlights glow brightly, operate the ignition switch and observe the lights. If they dim, then this indicates that current is reaching the starter motor, therefore the fault must lie in the starter motor. If the lights continue to glow brightly (and no clicking sound can be heard from the starter motor solenoid), this indicates that there is a fault in the circuit or solenoid – see following paragraphs. If the starter motor turns slowly when operated, but the battery is in good condition, then this indicates that either the starter motor is faulty, or there is considerable resistance somewhere in the circuit.

3 If a fault in the circuit is suspected, disconnect the battery leads (including the earth connection to the body), the starter/solenoid wiring and the engine/transmission earth strap. **Note:** *Before disconnecting the battery, refer to 'Disconnecting the battery' in the Reference section at the rear of this manual.* Thoroughly clean the connections, and reconnect the leads and wiring, then use a voltmeter or test light to check that full battery voltage is available at the battery positive lead connection to the solenoid, and that the earth is sound.

4 If the battery and all connections are in good condition, check the circuit by disconnecting the wire from the solenoid blade terminal. Connect a voltmeter or test light between the

8.3 Solenoid trigger wire

wire end and a good earth (such as the battery negative terminal), and check that the wire is live when the ignition switch is turned to the start position. If it is, then the circuit is sound, if not, the circuit wiring can be checked as described in Chapter 12.

5 The solenoid contacts can be checked by connecting a voltmeter or test light between the battery positive feed connection on the starter side of the solenoid, and earth. When the ignition switch is turned to the start position, there should be a reading or lighted bulb, as applicable. If there is no reading or lighted bulb, the solenoid is faulty and should be renewed.

6 If the circuit and solenoid are proved sound, the fault must lie in the starter motor. It may be possible to have the starter motor overhauled by a specialist, but check on the availability and cost of spares before proceeding, as it may prove more economical to obtain a new or exchange motor.

8 Starter motor – removal and refitting

Removal

1 Disconnect the battery negative lead (refer to *Disconnecting the battery* in the *Reference* Chapter at the end of this manual). Remove the engine top cover.

2 Where necessary for improved access, remove the battery with reference to Section 3, then unbolt and remove the battery mounting bracket.

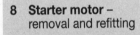
8.5a Remove the earth cable . . .

8.4 Battery positive cable on the starter solenoid terminal

3 Disconnect the trigger wiring from the solenoid **(see illustration)**.

4 Remove the cap (if fitted), then unscrew the nut and disconnect the battery positive cable from the solenoid terminal **(see illustration)**.

5 Unscrew the upper starter motor mounting bolts, noting that one of the bolts is facing inwards and the other outwards. On most models, an earth cable is located on the bolt facing outwards **(see illustrations)**.

6 In order to gain access to the underside of the vehicle, apply the handbrake, then jack up the front of the vehicle and support it on axle stands (see *Jacking and vehicle support*). Remove the engine undertray.

7 Unscrew the remaining lower mounting bolt, withdraw the starter motor and lift it from the engine.

Refitting

8 Refit the starter motor by following the removal procedure in reverse. Tighten the mounting bolts to the specified torque.

9 Starter motor – testing and overhaul

If the starter motor is thought to be defective, it should be removed from the vehicle and taken to an auto-electrician for assessment. In the majority of cases, new starter motor brushes can be fitted at a reasonable cost. However, check the cost of repairs first as it may prove more economical to purchase a new or exchange motor.

8.5b . . . then unscrew the starter top bolt

Notes

Chapter 5 Part B:
Ignition system – petrol engines

Contents

Section number

General information 1
HT coil – removal and refitting 3
Ignition switch removal and refitting. . . . . .See Chapter 10
Ignition system – testing. 2

Section number

Ignition timing – checking and adjusting 4
Knock sensor – removal and refitting. 5
Spark plug renewal. . . . . .See Chapter 1A

Degrees of difficulty

Easy, suitable for novice with little experience	Fairly easy, suitable for beginner with some experience	Fairly difficult, suitable for competent DIY mechanic	Difficult, suitable for experienced DIY mechanic	Very difficult, suitable for expert DIY or professional

Specifications

Engine codes

1.2 litre:
SOHC	AWY
DOHC	AZQ, BME

1.4 litre OHV:
44 kW	AZE and AZF
50 kW	AME, AQW and ATZ

1.4 litre DOHC:
55 kW	AUA and BBY
74 kW	AUB and BBZ

System type*

1.2 litre engines:
Engine code AWY.	Siemens Simos 3PD
Engine code AZQ	Siemens Simos 3PE
Engine code BME.	Siemens Simos 3PG

1.4 litre OHV engines:
Engine codes AME, AZE and AZF	Siemens Simos 3PB
Engine codes AQW and ATZ	Siemens Simos 3PA

1.4 litre DOHC engines:
Engine codes AUA and AUB	Magneti Marelli 4LV
Engine codes BBY and BBZ	Magneti Marelli 4MV

* **Note:** *See 'Vehicle identification' at the end of this manual for the location of code marking on the engine.*

Ignition coil

Type:
1.2 litre engines	Individual coil per cylinder (no HT leads), camshaft position sensor (in cylinder head), knock sensor
1.4 litre OHV engines	Single DIS coil in single module over spark plugs (no HT leads), camshaft position sensor (in cylinder block)

1.4 litre DOHC engines:
Engine codes AUA and AUB	Single remote DIS coil with four HT leads, camshaft position sensor (in cylinder head)
Engines codes BBY and BBZ.	Individual coil per cylinder (no HT leads), camshaft position sensor (in cylinder head), knock sensor

Primary winding resistance	N/A

Secondary resistance:
Single DIS coil (four HT lead outputs)	4000 to 6000 ohms

Spark plugs

See Chapter 1A Specifications

Torque wrench settings

	Nm	lbf ft
Ignition coil mounting bolts (single DIS coil)	10	7
Knock sensor mounting bolt	20	15
Spark plugs	30	22

1 General information

The Siemens and Magneti-Marelli ignition systems described in this Chapter, are part of the self-contained engine management systems which control both the fuel injection and ignition. This Chapter deals with the ignition system components only – refer to Chapter 4A for details of the fuel system components.

The ignition system comprises the spark plugs, High Tension (HT) leads where fitted (1.4 litre engine codes AUA and AUB), ignition coil(s), and the Electronic Control Unit (ECU) together with its associated sensors, actuators and wiring. The component layout varies from system to system but the basic operation is the same for all models.

The ECU supplies a voltage to the input stage of the ignition coil which causes the primary windings in the coil to be energised. The supply voltage is periodically interrupted by the ECU and this results in the collapse of the primary magnetic field, which then induces a much larger voltage (called the HT voltage) in the secondary coil. This voltage is directed to the spark plug in the cylinder where the piston is currently at the end of its compression stroke. The spark plug electrodes form a gap small enough for the HT voltage to arc across, and the resulting spark ignites the fuel/air mixture in the cylinder. The timing of this sequence of events is critical and is regulated solely by the ECU.

1.4 litre engine codes AME, AQW, ATZ, AUA, AUB, AZE and AZF are fitted with a single DIS (Distributorless Ignition System) ignition coil, which operates on the 'wasted spark' principle. The coil unit in fact contains two separate coils – one for cylinders 1 and 4, the other for cylinders 2 and 3. Each of the two coils produces an HT voltage at both outputs every time its primary coil voltage is interrupted – ie, cylinders 1 and 4 always 'fire' together, then 2 and 3 'fire' together. When this happens, one of the two cylinders concerned will be on its compression stroke (and will ignite the fuel/air mixture), while the other one is on the exhaust stroke. Because the spark on the exhaust stroke has no effect, it is effectively wasted, hence the term 'wasted spark'.

On 1.2 litre engines and 1.4 litre engine codes BBY and BBZ, each spark plug has its own dedicated 'plug-top' HT coil which fits directly onto the spark plug. Unlike the 'wasted spark' system, on these models a spark is only generated at each plug once every engine cycle.

The ECU calculates and controls the ignition timing primarily according to engine speed, crankshaft/camshaft position, throttle position and inlet air temperature, received from sensors mounted on and around the engine.

Other parameters that affect ignition timing are coolant temperature and engine knock, these being monitored by sensors mounted on the engine.

The knock sensor is mounted on the cylinder block in order to detect engine pre-ignition (or 'pinking'). If pre-ignition occurs, the ECU retards the ignition timing in steps until the pre-ignition ceases. The ECU then advances the ignition timing in steps until it is restored to normal, or until pre-ignition occurs again.

Idle speed control is achieved partly by the electronic throttle valve positioning module, and partly by the ignition system, which gives fine control of the idle speed by altering the ignition timing. Manual adjustment of the engine idle speed or ignition timing is not necessary or possible.

It should be noted that comprehensive fault diagnosis of all the engine management systems described in this Chapter is only possible with dedicated electronic test equipment. Problems with the system's operation that cannot be pinpointed by following the basic guidelines in Section 2 should therefore be referred to a Skoda dealer for assessment. Once the fault has been identified, the removal/refitting sequences detailed in the following Sections will then allow the appropriate components to be renewed as required.

2 Ignition system – testing

⚠️ **Warning: Extreme care must be taken when working on the system with the ignition switched on; it is possible to get a substantial electric shock from a vehicle's ignition system. Persons with cardiac pacemaker devices should keep well clear of the ignition circuits, components and test equipment. Always switch off the ignition before disconnecting or connecting any component and when using a multimeter to check resistances.**

Engine codes AUA and AUB

1 Refer to the information given in paragraphs 1 to 3. The only other likely cause of ignition trouble is the HT leads, linking the HT coil to the spark plugs. Check the leads as follows. Never disconnect more than one HT lead at a time to avoid possible confusion.

2 Pull the first lead from the plug by gripping the end fitting, not the lead, otherwise the lead connection may be fractured. Check inside the end fitting for signs of corrosion, which will look like a white crusty powder. Push the end fitting back onto the spark plug, ensuring that it is a tight fit on the plug. If not, remove the lead again and use pliers to carefully crimp the metal connector inside the end fitting until it fits securely on the end of the spark plug.

3 Using a clean rag, wipe the entire length of the lead to remove any built-up dirt and grease. Once the lead is clean, check for burns, cracks and other damage. Do not bend the lead excessively, nor pull the lead lengthwise – the conductor inside is quite fragile, and might break.

4 Disconnect the other end of the lead from the HT coil. Again, pull only on the end fitting. Check for corrosion and a tight fit in the same manner as the spark plug end.

5 If an ohmmeter is available, check for continuity between each end of the HT lead. If there is no continuity the lead is faulty and must be renewed (as a guide, the resistance of each lead should be in the region of 4 to 8 kΩ).

6 Refit the lead securely on completion of the check then check the remaining leads one at a time, in the same way. If there is any doubt about the condition of any HT leads, renew them as a complete set.

All other engines

7 If a fault appears in the engine management (fuel injection/ignition) system which is thought to be ignition related, first ensure that the fault is not due to a poor electrical connection or poor maintenance; ie, check that the air cleaner filter element is clean, the spark plugs are in good condition and correctly gapped, that the engine breather hoses are clear and undamaged, referring to Chapter 1A for further information. If the engine is running very roughly, check the compression pressures as described in Chapter 2A, 2B or 2C.

8 If these checks fail to reveal the cause of the problem the vehicle should be taken to a Skoda dealer for testing. A diagnostic connector is incorporated in the engine management circuit into which a special electronic diagnostic tester can be plugged (see Chapter 4A). The tester will locate the fault quickly and simply, alleviating the need to test all the system components individually which is a time consuming operation that carries a high risk of damaging the ECU.

9 The only ignition system checks which can be carried out by the home mechanic are those described in Chapter 1A, relating to the spark plugs. If necessary, the system wiring and wiring connectors can be checked as described in Chapter 12 ensuring that the ECU wiring connector has first been disconnected.

3 HT coil – removal and refitting

Removal

Engine codes AUA and AUB

1 The ignition coil unit is mounted on the top left-hand end of the engine **(see illustration)**.

2 Make sure the ignition is switched off, then remove the engine top cover.

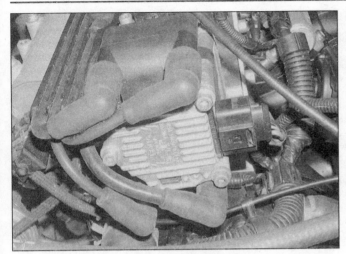

3.1 On engine codes AUA and AUB, the coil is mounted on the left-hand end of the cylinder head

3.3 Disconnect the LT wiring plug from the ignition coil

3 Unplug the main wiring plug (LT connector) from the ignition coil (see illustration).

4 The original HT leads should be marked from 1 to 4, corresponding to the cylinder/spark plug they serve (No 1 is at the timing end of the engine). Some leads are also marked from A to D, and corresponding markings are found on the ignition coil HT terminals – in this case, cylinder A corresponds to No 1, B to No 2, and so on. If there are no markings present, label the HT leads before disconnecting, and either paint a marking on the ignition coil terminals or make a sketch of the lead positions for use when reconnecting.

5 Disconnect the HT leads from the ignition coil terminals, then unscrew the three mounting bolts and remove the coil unit from the engine (see illustrations).

Engine codes AME, AQW, ATZ, AZE and AZF

6 The ignition coil module incorporating the DIS coil, is mounted over the spark plugs on the front of the engine (see illustration).

7 Make sure the ignition is switched off, then remove the engine top cover.

8 Disconnect the wiring plug from the left-hand end of the ignition coil module (see illustration).

9 Unscrew the two module mounting bolts using an Allen key, and carefully withdraw it while disconnecting the terminals from the spark plugs.

Engine codes AWY, AZQ, BBY, BBZ and BME

10 Removal of the ignition coils is covered in the spark plug renewal procedure in Chapter 1A, since the coils must be removed for access to the plugs (see illustration).

Refitting

11 Refitting is a reversal of the relevant removal procedure.

4 Ignition timing – checking and adjusting

The ignition timing is under the control of the engine management system ECU and is not manually adjustable without access to dedicated electronic test equipment. A basic setting cannot be quoted because the ignition timing is constantly being altered to control engine idle speed (see Section 1 for details).

The vehicle must be taken to a Skoda dealer if the timing requires checking or adjustment.

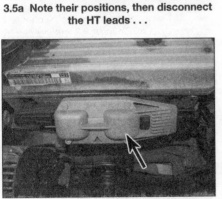

3.5a Note their positions, then disconnect the HT leads . . .

3.5b . . . unscrew the three Allen bolts, and remove the coil

3.6 Ignition coil module on engine code AZF

3.8 Disconnect the wiring plug

3.10 Ignition coils on engine code BME

5.1 The knock sensor is located on the rear of the cylinder block

5 Knock sensor – removal and refitting

Removal

1 The knock sensor is located on the rear of the cylinder block, beneath the inlet manifold **(see illustration)**.

2 Remove the engine top cover to gain access to the sensor from above. Alternatively for access from below, apply the handbrake, then jack up the front of the vehicle and support it on axle stands (see *Jacking and vehicle support*). Access to the knock sensor is very awkward, and can only be improved by removing the inlet manifold (see Chapter 4A).

3 Disconnect the wiring from the sensor or trace the wiring back from the sensor and disconnect its wiring connector.

4 Unscrew the mounting bolt and remove the sensor from the cylinder block.

Refitting

5 Refitting is the reverse of removal. Ensure the mating surfaces of the sensor and cylinder block are clean and dry and ensure the mounting bolt is tightened to the specified torque to ensure correct operation.

Chapter 5 Part C:
Preheating system – diesel engines

Contents

General description 1
Glow plugs – testing, removal and refitting 2

Section number   Section number

Degrees of difficulty

Easy, suitable for novice with little experience	**Fairly easy,** suitable for beginner with some experience	**Fairly difficult,** suitable for competent DIY mechanic	**Difficult,** suitable for experienced DIY mechanic	**Very difficult,** suitable for expert DIY or professional

Specifications

Glow plugs

Electrical resistance (typical – no value quoted by Skoda) . . . .   1.5 ohms
Current consumption (typical – no value quoted by Skoda) . . . .   8 amps (per plug)

Torque wrench setting	**Nm**	**lbf ft**
Glow plug to cylinder head	15	11

1 General information

To assist cold starting, diesel engined models are fitted with a preheating system, which comprises one glow plug per cylinder, a glow plug control unit (incorporated in the ECU), a facia-mounted warning light and the associated electrical wiring.

The glow plugs are miniature electric heating elements, encapsulated in a metal case with a probe at one end and electrical connection at the other. Each combustion chamber has a glow plug threaded into it, which is positioned directly in line with the incoming spray of fuel.

When the glow plug is energised, the fuel passing over it is heated, allowing its optimum combustion temperature to be achieved more quickly.

The duration of the preheating period is governed by the glow plug control unit (in the ECU), which monitors the temperature of the engine via the coolant temperature sensor and alters the preheating time to suit the conditions.

A facia-mounted warning light informs the driver that preheating is taking place. The light extinguishes when sufficient preheating has taken place to allow the engine to be started, but power will still be supplied to the glow plugs for a further period until the engine is started. If no attempt is made to start the engine, the power supply to the glow plugs is

switched off to prevent battery drain and glow plug burn-out. Note that if a fault occurs in the engine management system while the car is moving, the glow plug warning lamp will start flashing and the system will then switch to fail-safe mode. Should this occur, the car must be taken to a Skoda dealer for fault diagnosis.

If the warning light flashes, or comes on during normal driving, this indicates a fault with the diesel engine management system, which should be investigated by a Skoda dealer as soon as possible.

After the engine has been started, the glow plugs continue to operate for a further period of time. This helps to improve fuel combustion whilst the engine is warming-up, resulting in quieter, smoother running and reduced exhaust emissions.

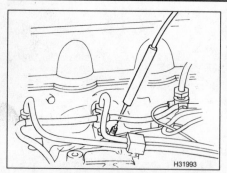

2.9 Testing the glow plugs using a multimeter

2.12a Glow plug wiring connector (arrowed) for No 1 injector – engine code ASY

2.12b Wiring loom/rail for the glow plugs – engine codes AMF, ATD and ASZ

2 Glow plugs – testing, removal and refitting

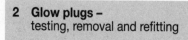

⚠️ *Warning: A correctly-functioning glow plug will become red-hot in a very short time. This fact should also be borne in mind when removing the glow plugs, if they have recently been in use.*

Testing

1 If the engine is difficult to start, one or more of the glow plugs may be faulty or the preheating system circuit may not be operating correctly. Some preliminary checks may be made as described in the following paragraphs.

2 Before testing the system, check that the battery voltage is at least 11.5 volts, using a multimeter. Switch off the ignition.

3 Remove the engine top cover.

4 Disconnect the wiring plug from the coolant temperature sender at the left-hand end of the engine (as seen from the driver's seat) with reference to Chapter 3. Disconnecting the sender in this way simulates a cold engine, which is a requirement for the glow plug system to activate.

5 Disconnect the wiring connector from the most convenient glow plug, and connect a suitable voltmeter between the wiring connector and a good earth.

6 Have an assistant switch on the ignition for approximately 20 seconds.

7 Battery voltage should be displayed – note that the voltage will drop to zero when the preheating period ends.

8 If no supply voltage can be detected at the glow plug, then either the glow plug relay (where applicable) or the supply wiring must be faulty. Also check that the glow plug fuse or fusible link (usually located on top of the battery) has not blown – if it has, this may indicate a faulty glow plug or serious wiring fault; consult a Skoda dealer for advice.

9 To locate a faulty glow plug, make sure that the ignition is switched off, then disconnect the wiring plug from the glow plug terminal. Measure the electrical resistance between the glow plug terminal and the engine earth **(see illustration)**. At the time of writing, this information is not available – as a guide, a resistance of more than a few ohms indicates that the plug is defective.

10 If a suitable ammeter is available, connect it between the glow plug and its wiring connector, and measure the steady-state current consumption (ignore the initial current surge, which will be about 50% higher). As a guide, high current consumption (or no current draw at all) indicates a faulty glow plug.

11 As a final check, remove the glow plugs and inspect them visually, as described in the next sub-Section.

Removal

Note: *Refer to the Warning at the start of this Section before proceeding.*

12 Make sure the ignition is switched off, then disconnect the wiring connectors/rail from the glow plugs, where necessary label the wiring to make refitting easier **(see illustrations)**. On some models, the glow plug wiring is clipped to the injector leak-off hoses – make sure that the clips are not lost as the wiring is pulled away.

13 Unscrew and remove the glow plugs. On engine code ASY, access to the plugs is not easy with the injector pipes in place – an extension handle and universal joint will probably be needed.

14 Inspect the glow plug stems for signs of damage. A badly burned or charred stem may be an indication of a faulty fuel injector.

Refitting

15 Refitting is a reversal of removal, but tighten the glow plug to the specified torque.

Chapter 6
Clutch

Contents

Section number

Clutch friction disc and pressure plate – removal, inspection and refitting 6
Clutch pedal – removal and refitting. 3
General information 1

Section number

Hydraulic system – bleeding 2
Master cylinder – removal, overhaul and refitting 4
Release bearing and lever – removal, inspection and refitting. 7
Slave cylinder – removal, overhaul and refitting. 5

Degrees of difficulty

Easy, suitable for novice with little experience		Fairly easy, suitable for beginner with some experience		Fairly difficult, suitable for competent DIY mechanic		Difficult, suitable for experienced DIY mechanic		Very difficult, suitable for expert DIY or professional	

Specifications

Engine codes

Petrol engines

1.2 litre:	
SOHC	AWY
DOHC	AZQ, BME
1.4 litre OHV:	
44 kW	AZE and AZF
50 kW	AME, AQW and ATZ
1.4 litre DOHC:	
55 kW	AUA and BBY
74 kW	AUB and BBZ

Diesel engines

1.4 litre	AMF
1.9 litre non-turbo.	ASY
1.9 litre turbo	ASZ and ATD

General

Type	Single dry plate, diaphragm spring
Operation	Hydraulic with master and slave cylinders
Application:	
Petrol models:	
All except 1.4 litre OHV engines	5-speed transmission 02T
1.4 litre OHV engines	5-speed transmission 002
Diesel models:	
1.4 litre engine	5-speed transmission 02T or 02R
1.9 litre engine:	
Engine code ASY	5-speed transmission 02T
Engine code ATD	5-speed transmission 02T or 02R
Engine code ASZ	5-speed transmission 02T
Friction disc diameter:	
5-speed transmission 02T	200 mm
5-speed transmission 002	190 mm
5-speed transmission 02R	228 mm

Torque wrench settings

	Nm	lbf ft
Clutch master cylinder mounting nuts*	28	21
Clutch pedal mounting bracket nuts*.	28	21
Clutch pedal pivot nut*.	25	18
Clutch pressure plate-to-flywheel bolts	20	15
Clutch slave cylinder mounting bolts	20	15
Guide tube-to-transmission bolts	9	7

* Use new bolts/nuts.

1 General information

The clutch is of single dry plate type, incorporating a diaphragm spring pressure plate, and is hydraulically-operated.

The pressure plate is bolted to the rear face of the flywheel, and the friction disc is located between the pressure plate and the flywheel friction surface. The friction disc hub is splined to the transmission input shaft and is free to slide along the splines. Friction lining material is riveted to each side of the disc, and the disc hub incorporates cushioning springs to absorb transmission shocks and ensure a smooth take-up of drive.

When the clutch pedal is depressed, the slave cylinder pushrod moves the top of the release lever towards the engine, and the lower end of the lever pivots on a ball-stud located in the transmission bellhousing. The release bearing is forced onto the pressure plate diaphragm spring fingers. As the centre of the diaphragm spring is pushed in, the outer part of the spring moves out and releases the pressure plate from the friction disc. Drive then ceases to be transmitted to the transmission.

When the clutch pedal is released, the diaphragm spring forces the pressure plate into contact with the linings on the friction disc, and at the same time pushes the disc slightly forward along the input shaft splines into engagement with the flywheel. The friction disc is now firmly sandwiched between the pressure plate and flywheel. This causes drive to be taken up.

As the linings wear on the friction disc, the pressure plate rest position moves closer to the flywheel resulting in the 'rest' position of the diaphragm spring fingers being raised. The hydraulic system requires no adjustment since the quantity of hydraulic fluid in the circuit automatically compensates for wear every time the clutch pedal is operated.

2 Hydraulic system – bleeding

 Warning: Hydraulic fluid is poisonous; thoroughly wash off spills from bare skin without delay. Seek immediate medical advice if any fluid is swallowed or gets into the eyes. Certain types of hydraulic fluid are inflammable and may ignite when brought into contact with hot components. Hydraulic fluid is also an effective paint stripper. If spillage occurs onto painted bodywork or fittings, it should be washed off immediately, using copious quantities of cold water. It is also hygroscopic (it absorbs moisture from the air) therefore old fluid should never be re-used.

1 The correct operation of any hydraulic system is only possible after removing all air from the components and circuit; this is achieved by bleeding the system.

2 During the bleeding procedure, add only clean, unused hydraulic fluid of the recommended type; never re-use fluid that has already been bled from the system. Ensure that sufficient fluid is available before starting work.

3 If there is any possibility of incorrect fluid being already in the system, the hydraulic circuit must be flushed completely with uncontaminated, correct fluid.

4 If hydraulic fluid has been lost from the system, or air has entered because of a leak, ensure that the fault is cured before continuing further.

5 The bleed screw is located on the slave cylinder located on the left-hand upper side of the transmission. As access to the bleed screw is limited it will be necessary to jack up the front of the vehicle and support it on axle stands so that the screw can be reached from below.

6 Check that all pipes and hoses are secure, unions tight and the bleed screw is closed. Clean any dirt from around the bleed screw.

7 Unscrew the master cylinder fluid reservoir cap (the clutch shares the same fluid reservoir as the braking system), and top the master cylinder reservoir up to the upper (MAX) level line. Refit the cap loosely, and remember to maintain the fluid level at least above the lower (MIN) level line throughout the procedure, or there is a risk of further air entering the system.

8 There is a number of one-man, do-it-yourself bleeding kits currently available from motor accessory shops. It is recommended that one of these kits is used whenever possible, as they greatly simplify the bleeding operation, and reduce the risk of expelled air and fluid being drawn back into the system. If such a kit is not available, the basic (two-man) method must be used, which is described in detail below.

9 If a kit is to be used, prepare the vehicle as described previously, and follow the kit manufacturer's instructions, as the procedure may vary slightly according to the type being used; generally, they are as outlined below in the relevant sub-section.

Bleeding

Basic (two-man) method

10 Collect a clean glass jar, a suitable length of plastic or rubber tubing which is a tight fit over the bleed screw, and a ring spanner to fit the screw. The help of an assistant will also be required.

11 Remove the dust cap from the bleed screw. Fit the spanner and tube to the screw, place the other end of the tube in the jar, and pour in sufficient fluid to cover the end of the tube.

12 Ensure that the fluid level is maintained at least above the lower level line in the reservoir throughout the procedure.

13 Have the assistant fully depress the clutch pedal several times to build up pressure, then maintain it on the final downstroke.

14 While pedal pressure is maintained, unscrew the bleed screw (approximately one turn) and allow the compressed fluid and air to flow into the jar. The assistant should maintain pedal pressure and should not release it until instructed to do so. When the flow stops, tighten the bleed screw again, have the assistant release the pedal slowly, and recheck the reservoir fluid level.

15 Repeat the steps given in paragraphs 13 and 14 until the fluid emerging from the bleed screw is free from air bubbles. If the master cylinder has been drained and refilled allow approximately five seconds between cycles for the master cylinder passages to refill.

16 When no more air bubbles appear, tighten the bleed screw securely, remove the tube and spanner, and refit the dust cap. Do not overtighten the bleed screw.

Using a one-way valve kit

17 As their name implies, these kits consist of a length of tubing with a one-way valve fitted, to prevent expelled air and fluid being drawn back into the system; some kits include a translucent container, which can be positioned so that the air bubbles can be more easily seen flowing from the end of the tube.

18 The kit is connected to the bleed screw, which is then opened. The user returns to the driver's seat, depresses the clutch pedal with a smooth, steady stroke, and slowly releases it; this is repeated until the expelled fluid is clear of air bubbles.

19 Note that these kits simplify work so much that it is easy to forget the fluid reservoir level; ensure that this is maintained at least above the lower level line at all times.

Using a pressure-bleeding kit

20 These kits are usually operated by the reservoir of pressurised air contained in the spare tyre. However, note that it will probably be necessary to reduce the pressure to a lower level than normal; refer to the instructions supplied with the kit.

21 By connecting a pressurised, fluid-filled container to the fluid reservoir, bleeding can be carried out simply by opening the bleed screw and allowing the fluid to flow out until no more air bubbles can be seen in the expelled fluid.

22 This method has the advantage that the large reservoir of fluid provides an additional safeguard against air being drawn into the system during bleeding.

All methods

23 When bleeding is complete, and correct pedal feel is restored, tighten the bleed screw securely and wash off any spilt fluid. Refit the dust cap to the bleed screw.

24 Check the hydraulic fluid level in the master cylinder reservoir, and top-up if necessary (see *Weekly checks*).

25 Discard any hydraulic fluid that has been bled from the system; it will not be fit for re-use.

26 Check the operation of the clutch pedal. If the clutch is still not operating correctly, air must still be present in the system, and further bleeding is required. Failure to bleed satisfactorily after a reasonable repetition of the bleeding procedure may be due to worn master cylinder/release cylinder seals.

3 Clutch pedal – removal and refitting

Removal

1 Remove the driver's side lower facia trim panel and storage compartment, with reference to Chapter 11.
2 Where fitted, remove the clutch pedal switch from the pedal bracket by turning it 90° anti-clockwise.
3 The over-centre spring must now be disconnected from the pedal and removed. On RHD models, position a screwdriver between the clutch pedal and the spring, then depress the pedal and unhook the spring. On LHD models, make up a tool from a length of metal bar, then press it into position over the spring to hold the clutch pedal over-centre spring in the compressed position – depress the pedal to unhook the spring. If necessary, this method can also be used on RHD models (**see illustrations**).
4 With the over-centre spring removed, remove the spring seat from the pedal bracket. The seat must be renewed whenever removed.
5 The master cylinder pushrod is attached to the clutch pedal by a plastic clip. Ideally, a scissor-type caliper tool should be used to compress the ends of the clip through the access holes in the pedal, however, two screwdrivers can be used instead.
6 With the pedal disconnected from the pushrod, if necessary, remove the plastic retaining clip from the pushrod using pliers.
7 Unscrew the nut from the pedal pivot bolt.
8 Pull out the pivot bolt until the pedal can be removed from the bracket assembly into the driver's footwell.
9 If necessary, remove the spacer bushes and centre sleeve from the pedal.

Refitting

10 Examine the pedal components for wear, and renew as necessary.
11 Refitting is a reversal of removal, noting the following points:
a) *Fit a new over-centre spring seat in the pedal bracket, making sure that the tab is locked in the master cylinder recess.*
b) *Use a new pedal pivot bolt nut, and tighten it to the specified torque.*
c) *Make sure that the pedal-to-master cylinder pushrod retaining clip is fitted to the master cylinder pushrod before attempting to reconnect the pushrod to the pedal.*

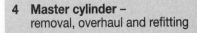

3.3a Using a screwdriver to disconnect the over-centre spring on RHD models

d) *Push the pedal onto the pushrod to engage the retaining clip. Make sure that the clip is securely engaged.*
e) *On completion, check the brake/clutch fluid level, and top-up if necessary.*

4 Master cylinder – removal, overhaul and refitting

Note: Refer to the warning at the beginning of Section 2.

Removal

1 The clutch master cylinder is located inside the car on the clutch and brake pedal mounting bracket (**see illustration**). Hydraulic fluid for the unit is supplied from the brake master cylinder reservoir.
2 On LHD models, remove the air cleaner assembly as described in Chapter 4A or 4B, then unclip the auxiliary relay carrier on the left-hand side of the engine compartment, and position it to one side.
3 Before proceeding, place cloth rags on the carpet inside the car to prevent damage from spilt hydraulic fluid.
4 Working in the engine compartment, clamp the hydraulic fluid hose leading from the brake fluid reservoir to the clutch master cylinder using a brake hose clamp.
5 Similarly, clamp the rubber section of the hydraulic hose leading from the master cylinder to the slave cylinder using a brake hose clamp, to prevent loss of hydraulic fluid.
6 Position a suitable container, or some cloth

4.1 Clutch master cylinder

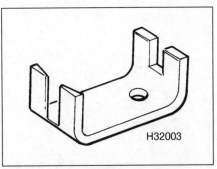

3.3b Over-centre spring retaining tool

rags, beneath the master cylinder to catch escaping hydraulic fluid.
7 Pull the hydraulic supply hose from the clutch master cylinder on the bulkhead.
8 Pull the fluid outlet hose retaining clip from the union on the master cylinder, then pull the pipe from the union. Again, be prepared for fluid spillage.
9 Remove the driver's side lower facia trim panel and storage compartment, with reference to Chapter 11.
10 Where fitted, remove the clutch pedal switch from the pedal bracket by turning it 90° anti-clockwise.
11 The pedal must now be disconnected from the master cylinder pushrod by squeezing together the tabs of the retaining clip (see Section 3), and moving the pushrod away from the pedal.
12 Twist the clutch pedal stop anti-clockwise, and remove it from the bulkhead.
13 Unscrew the three nuts securing the clutch pedal mounting bracket to the bulkhead, then remove the mounting bracket complete with pedal from the bulkhead (**see illustration**).
14 With the mounting bracket on the bench, the over-centre spring must be disconnected and removed from the pedal. On RHD models, position a screwdriver between the clutch pedal and the spring, then depress the pedal and unhook the spring. On LHD models, make up a tool from a length of metal bar, then press it into position over the spring to hold the clutch pedal over-centre spring in the compressed position – depress the pedal to unhook the spring. If necessary, this method can also be used on RHD models.

4.13 Undo the pedal bracket nuts (arrowed)

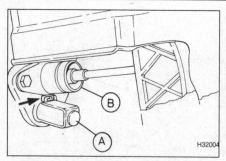

4.18 Ensure that the stop (A) is positioned with the lug (arrowed) nearest the master cylinder (B)

15 With the over-centre spring removed, remove the spring seat from the pedal bracket. The seat must be renewed whenever removed.
16 Remove the master cylinder from the bracket.

Overhaul

17 No spare parts are available from Skoda for the master cylinder. If the master cylinder is faulty or worn, the complete assembly must be renewed.

Refitting

18 Refitting is a reversal of removal, bearing in mind the following points:
a) Ensure that the pedal-to-master cylinder pushrod retaining clip is fitted to the master cylinder pushrod before attempting to reconnect the pushrod to the pedal.
d) Push the pedal onto the pushrod to engage the retaining clip. Make sure that the clip is securely engaged.
c) When refitting the pedal stop on early models, ensure that the stop is positioned with the lug nearest the master cylinder (see illustration).
d) On completion, bleed the clutch hydraulic system as described in Section 2.

5 Slave cylinder –
removal, overhaul and refitting

Note: *Refer to the warning at the beginning of Section 2 regarding the hazards of working with hydraulic fluid.*

5.9 Removing the clutch slave cylinder

Removal

1 The slave cylinder is located on the top of the transmission casing. First remove the engine top cover.
2 Remove the battery as described in Chapter 5A, then unbolt and remove the battery tray.
3 Where necessary, remove the air cleaner and air ducting with reference to Chapter 4A or 4B.
4 Unscrew the nut and remove the gearchange lever from the top of the transmission.
5 Extract the circlip and disconnect the selector cable from the relay lever.
6 Unscrew the three bolts and tie the support bracket to one side.
7 Clamp the rubber section of the hydraulic hose leading from the master cylinder to the slave cylinder using a brake hose clamp, to prevent loss of hydraulic fluid. Place a wad of clean rag beneath the fluid line connection on the slave cylinder to catch escaping fluid.
8 Pull the fluid pipe retaining clip from the union on the slave cylinder, then disconnect the pipe from the union. Release the fluid line from the bracket, and position it clear of the slave cylinder. Be prepared for fluid spillage.
9 Unscrew the two bolts securing the slave cylinder to the transmission casing, and withdraw the slave cylinder (see illustration).

Overhaul

10 No spare parts are available from Skoda for the slave cylinder. If the slave cylinder is faulty or worn, the complete assembly must be renewed.

Refitting

11 Refitting is a reversal of removal, bearing in mind the following points:
a) Apply a little molybdenum sulphide-based grease to the end of the slave cylinder plunger.
b) Tighten the slave cylinder securing bolts to the specified torque.
c) On completion, bleed the clutch hydraulic system as described in Section 2.

6 Clutch friction disc and pressure plate – removal, inspection and refitting

⚠️ **Warning: Dust created by clutch wear and deposited on the clutch components may contain asbestos, which is a health hazard. DO NOT blow it out with compressed air or inhale any of it. DO NOT use petrol or petroleum-based solvents to clean off the dust. Brake system cleaner or methylated spirit should be used to flush the dust into a suitable receptacle. After the clutch components are wiped clean with clean rags, dispose of the contaminated rags and cleaner in a sealed container.**

Removal

1 Access to the clutch is obtained by removing the transmission as described in Chapter 7A.
2 Mark the clutch pressure plate and flywheel in relation to each other (see illustration).
3 Hold the flywheel stationary, then unscrew the clutch pressure plate bolts progressively in diagonal sequence (see illustration). With the bolts unscrewed two or three turns, check that the pressure plate is not binding on the dowel pins. If necessary, use a screwdriver to release the pressure plate.
4 Remove all the bolts, then lift the clutch pressure plate and friction disc from the flywheel (see illustration).

Inspection

5 Clean the pressure plate, disc and flywheel. Do not inhale the dust, as it may contain asbestos which is dangerous to health.
6 Examine the fingers of the diaphragm

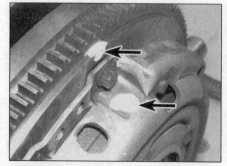

6.2 Mark the clutch pressure plate and flywheel in relation to each other

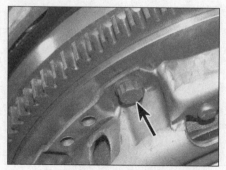

6.3 Unscrew the pressure plate bolts . . .

6.4 . . . then lift the pressure plate and friction disc away from the flywheel

6.11 Locating the friction disc on the flywheel

6.12 Locating the clutch pressure plate over the friction disc

6.13 Insert the bolts finger-tight initially

spring for wear or scoring. If the depth of wear exceeds half the thickness of the fingers, a new pressure plate assembly must be fitted.

7 Examine the pressure plate for scoring, cracking and discoloration. Light scoring is acceptable, but if excessive, a new pressure plate assembly must be fitted.

8 Examine the friction disc linings for wear and cracking, and for contamination with oil or grease. The linings are worn excessively if they are worn down to, or near, the rivets. Check the disc hub and splines for wear, by temporarily fitting it on the transmission input shaft. Renew the friction disc as necessary.

9 Examine the flywheel friction surface for scoring, cracking and discoloration (caused by overheating). If excessive, it may be possible to have the flywheel machined by an engineering works, otherwise it should be renewed.

10 Ensure that all parts are clean, and free of oil or grease, before reassembling. Apply just a small amount of high-melting-point grease to the splines of the friction disc hub. Note that new pressure plates may be coated with protective grease. It is only permissible to clean the grease away from the friction disc lining contact area. Removal of the grease from other areas will shorten the service life of the clutch.

Refitting

11 Commence reassembly by locating the friction disc on the flywheel, with the raised, torsion spring side of the hub facing outwards. If necessary, the centralising tool (see paragraph 14) may be used to hold the disc on the flywheel at this stage **(see illustration)**.

12 Locate the clutch pressure plate on the disc, and fit it onto the location dowels **(see illustration)**. If refitting the original pressure plate, make sure that the previously-made marks are aligned.

13 Insert the bolts finger-tight to hold the pressure plate in position **(see illustration)**.

14 The friction disc must now be centralised, to ensure correct alignment of the transmission input shaft with the spigot bearing in the crankshaft. To do this, a proprietary tool may be used, or alternatively, use a wooden mandrel made to fit inside the friction disc and flywheel spigot bearing. Insert the tool through the friction disc into the spigot bearing, and make sure that it is central.

15 Tighten the pressure plate bolts progressively and in diagonal sequence, until the specified torque setting is achieved, then remove the centralising tool.

16 Check the release bearing in the transmission bellhousing for smooth operation, and if necessary renew it with reference to Section 7.

17 Refit the transmission with reference to Chapter 7A.

<table><tr><td>**7**</td><td>**Release bearing and lever** – removal, inspection and refitting</td></tr></table>

Removal

1 The release bearing and lever are removed together with the guide tube, then separated on the bench. First, remove the transmission as described in Chapter 7A.

7.2 Unscrew the retaining bolts

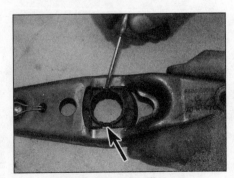

7.5a Depress the clips . . .

2 Unscrew and remove the two retaining bolts **(see illustration)**, then prise the release lever from the ball-stud on the transmission housing. To do this, press the retaining spring through the release lever.

3 Slide the guide tube, together with the release lever and bearing, over the transmission input shaft.

4 Turn the guide tube 90° to align the tabs with the slots in the release bearing, and withdraw the tube **(see illustration)**.

5 Using a screwdriver, depress the clips and remove the bearing from the release lever **(see illustrations)**.

Inspection

6 Spin the release bearing by hand, and check it for smooth running. Any tendency to seize or run rough will necessitate renewal of the bearing. If the bearing is to be re-used, wipe it clean with a dry cloth; the bearing should

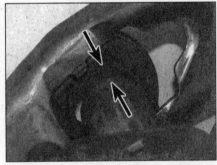

7.4 Removing the guide tube from the release bearing. Note the tab and slot (arrowed)

7.5b . . . and remove the bearing from the release lever

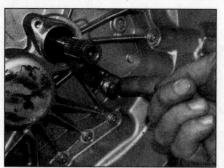

7.8 Lubricate the ball-stud with molybdenum disulphide-based grease

7.9a Hook the spring over the end of the lever . . .

7.9b . . . and press the other end into the hole

7.12 Locating the release lever and spring onto the ball-stud

not be washed in a liquid solvent, as this will remove the internal grease.

7 Clean the release lever, ball-stud and guide sleeve.

Refitting

8 Lubricate the ball-stud in the transmission bellhousing with molybdenum disulphide-based grease **(see illustration)**. Also smear a little grease on the release bearing surface which contacts the diaphragm spring fingers in the clutch cover.

9 Refit the ball-stud spring to the release lever **(see illustrations)**.

10 Locate the bearing on the lever, and press until the clips engage.

11 Locate the guide tube on the bearing, align the tabs with the slots, then insert and turn through 90°.

12 Locate the release lever on the ball-stud, and press until the retaining spring holds it in position **(see illustration)**.

13 Slide the guide tube with bearing and lever, over the input shaft, then insert the retaining bolts and tighten to the specified torque.

14 Refit the transmission as described in Chapter 7A.

Chapter 7 Part A:
Manual transmission

Contents

	Section number			Section number
Gearchange cables – checking and adjustment	2	Manual transmission overhaul – general information		4
General information	1	Reversing light switch – testing, removal and refitting		5
Manual transmission – removal and refitting	3	Roadspeed sensor/speedometer drive – removal and refitting		6

Degrees of difficulty

Easy, suitable for novice with little experience		Fairly easy, suitable for beginner with some experience		Fairly difficult, suitable for competent DIY mechanic		Difficult, suitable for experienced DIY mechanic		Very difficult, suitable for expert DIY or professional	

Specifications

Engine codes

Petrol engines

1.2 litre:	
SOHC	AWY
DOHC	AZQ, BME
1.4 litre OHV:	
44 kW	AZE and AZF
50 kW	AME, AQW and ATZ
1.4 litre DOHC:	
55 kW	AUA and BBY
74 kW	AUB and BBZ

Diesel engines

1.4 litre	AMF
1.9 litre non-turbo	ASY
1.9 litre turbo	ASZ and ATD

General

Note: *At the time of writing, no information was available for the 6-speed transmission (code 0A8) fitted to vRS models.*

Type	Transversely-mounted, front-wheel-drive layout with integral transaxle differential/final drive. Five forward speeds, one reverse.
Application:	
Petrol models:	
All except 1.4 litre OHV engines	5-speed transmission 02T
1.4 litre OHV engines	5-speed transmission 002
Diesel models:	
1.4 litre engine	5-speed transmission 02T or 02R
1.9 litre engine:	
Engine code ASY and ASZ	5-speed transmission 02T
Engine code ATD	5-speed transmission 02T or 02R

Torque wrench settings

	Nm	lbf ft
Engine mounting to transmission:		
Stage 1	40	30
Stage 2	Angle-tighten a further 90°	
Reversing light switch:		
002 transmission	15	11
02T transmission	25	18
02R transmission	20	15
Speedometer pinion:		
002 transmission	20	15
02R transmission	10	7
Speedometer sensor (02T transmission):		
Stage 1	8	6
Stage 2	Angle-tighten a further 90°	
Transmission to engine:		
M12 bolts	80	59
M10 bolts	45	33

1 General information

Note: *At the time of writing, no information was available for the 6-speed transmission (code 0A8) fitted to vRS models.*

The manual transmission is bolted directly to the left-hand end of the engine. This layout has the advantage of providing the shortest possible drive path to the front wheels, as well as locating the transmission in the airflow through the engine bay, optimising cooling. The unit is cased in aluminium alloy.

Drive from the crankshaft is transmitted by the clutch to the gearbox input shaft, which is splined to accept the clutch friction disc.

All forward gears are fitted with synchromesh. The floor-mounted gear lever is connected to the gearbox by selector and shift cables **(see illustration)**. This actuates selector forks inside the gearbox which are slotted onto the synchromesh sleeves. The sleeves, which are locked to the gearbox shafts but can slide axially by means of splined hubs, press baulk rings into contact with the respective gear/pinion. The coned surfaces between the baulk rings and the pinion/gear act as a friction clutch, that progressively matches the speed of the synchromesh sleeve (and hence the gearbox shaft) with that of the gear/pinion. This allows gearchanges to be carried out smoothly.

Drive is transmitted to the differential crownwheel, which rotates the differential case and planetary gears, thus driving the sun gears and driveshafts. The rotation of the differential planetary gears on their shaft allows the inner roadwheel to rotate at a slower speed than the outer roadwheel during cornering.

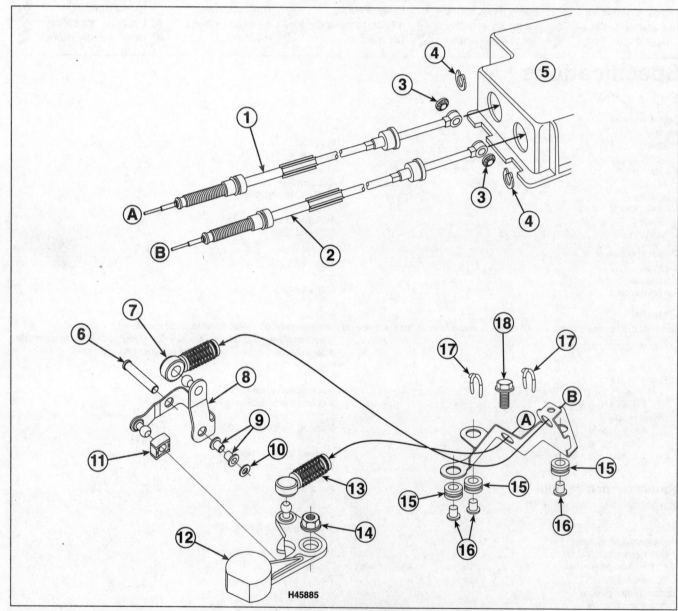

H45885

1.3 Gearchange cable components

1 Shift cable	5 Shift housing	8 Relay lever	12 Shift lever with weight	15 Grommet
2 Selector cable	6 Pivot	9 Bushes	13 Shift cable lock	16 Spacer
3 Press stud	7 Selector cable lock	10 Circlip	14 Nut	17 Circlip
4 Circlip		11 Sliding shoe		18 Bolt

2 Gearchange cables
– checking and adjustment

Note: *Skoda locking pin T10027, or a suitable alternative, will be required for this operation.*

Checking

1 The following check will enable you to decide whether adjustment is necessary. First, engage neutral so that the shift lever is in the gate of 3rd/4th.

2 Start the engine and allow it to idle, then depress the clutch pedal. Allow 3 to 6 seconds for the input shaft to stop rotating, then move the gear lever through all the gears, checking in particular that reverse gear engages smoothly.

3 If any gear is difficult to engage, have an assistant observe the *shift* lever on the top of the gearbox while you engage 1st gear and temporarily move the gear lever to the left. The *shift* lever should make a stroke of approximately 1.0 mm. If not, carry out the following adjustment.

Adjustment

4 On 1.4 litre petrol models with the 002 transmission, remove the air cleaner assembly and ducting as described in Chapter 4A.

5 With the gearchange set in the neutral position, push the two locking collars (one on each cable) forwards to compress the springs, then turn them clockwise (looking from the driver's seat) to lock them in position **(see illustration)**.

6 Press down on the *selector* shaft on the top of the transmission and, at the same time, turn the angle lever on the side of the transmission clockwise **(see illustration)**.

7 Working inside the vehicle, carefully unclip the gear lever gaiter from the centre console. Still in the neutral position, move the gear lever as far to the left as possible so that it is in the gate of the 1st/2nd gear, and insert the locking pin (or drill bit) through the hole in the base of the gear lever and into the hole in the housing **(see illustration)**.

8 Working back in the engine bay, turn the two locking collars on the cables anti-clockwise to unlock them, so that the springs will release the cables to their initial position **(see illustration)**.

9 With the cable adjustment set, the angle lever can now be turned anti-clockwise to its original position.

10 Inside the vehicle, remove the locking pin/drill bit from the gear lever, then check the operation of the selector mechanism as described in paragraphs 1 to 3. When the gear lever is at rest in neutral, it should be central in the gate of the 3rd/4th gear. The gear lever gaiter can now be refitted to the centre console.

11 Where applicable, refit the air cleaner assembly and ducting with reference to Chapter 4A.

2.5 Push the collar down and lock in position

2.7 Locking the gear lever in position with a drill bit

3 Manual transmission
– removal and refitting

Removal

1 Select a solid, level surface to park the vehicle upon. Give yourself enough space to move around it easily. Apply the handbrake and chock the rear wheels.

2 Raise the front of the vehicle and support it securely on axle stands (see *Jacking and vehicle support*). Remove the engine top cover and engine/transmission undertray. Remove the left-hand front roadwheel and wheel arch liner.

3 Position a suitable container beneath the transmission, then unscrew the drain plug and drain the transmission oil.

4 Undo the retaining nuts/screws, and remove the engine cover(s).

5 Remove the battery and battery tray

3.9a Disconnect the cables . . .

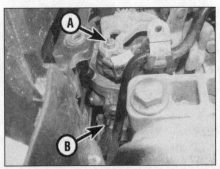

2.6 Press down on (A), then turn the angle lever (B)

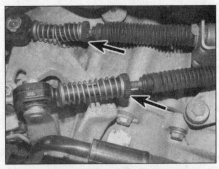

2.8 Release the two locking collars (arrowed)

with reference to Chapter 5A (also refer to *Disconnecting the battery* in the *Reference* Chapter at the end of this manual). On some models, it may also be necessary to disconnect the battery positive lead from the starter motor solenoid.

6 Except on transmission 02T, refer to the relevant part of Chapter 4 and remove the air cleaner housing and ducting.

7 On transmission 002, unscrew the bolt and remove the engine speed sender. Also, unscrew the support nut and tie the rear engine wiring harness up from the transmission.

8 Unscrew the three bolts securing the gearchange cable bracket to the top of the transmission.

9 Detach the relay/reversing lever together with the selector and shift cables from the top of the transmission, by extracting the circlip and pulling out the pivot. Recover the bushes. Alternatively, disconnect the cables and unbolt the bracket **(see illustrations)**.

3.9b . . . and unbolt the bracket

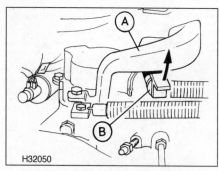

3.10 Gate selector cable (B) and balance weight (A)

3.13 Unbolt the clutch slave cylinder and bracket and tie to one side

3.18 On transmission 02R, temporarily remove the left-hand drive flange

10 Unscrew the nut and remove the gearchange lever with the balance weight **(see illustration)**. Note that the lever will only engage with the shaft in one position. Tie the cable assembly to one side.

11 Remove the starter motor as described in Chapter 5A.

12 Disconnect the wiring from the speedometer sender and reversing light switch as applicable.

13 Unbolt the clutch slave cylinder and support bracket from the transmission, and tie to one side **(see illustration)**.

Caution: Do not depress the clutch pedal with the slave cylinder removed from the transmission.

14 Loosen the exhaust clamp securing the exhaust front pipe to the intermediate section, and slide the clamp forwards. On 002 and 02T transmissions, this will allow the engine to be lowered without removing the front pipe. However, on transmission 02R it will be necessary to completely remove the front pipe as described in Chapter 4C.

15 Release the oxygen sensor wiring from the clip on the underbody, to enable lowering the exhaust without straining the wiring.

16 Unbolt the earth cable from the front of the transmission.

17 Unscrew the nut and move aside the wiring support bracket.

18 With reference to Chapter 8, unbolt the driveshafts from the gearbox drive flanges. On transmission 02R remove the shield for the right-hand steering inner joint boot. Also on transmission 02R, we found it an advantage to temporarily unbolt the left-hand drive flange from the transmission, to allow the transmission bellhousing extra clearance during removal **(see illustration)**.

19 Refer to Chapter 10 and mark the position of the bolts securing the left-hand swivel hub to the front suspension lower arm, then unscrew and remove the bolts. Unscrew the nut and disconnect the end of the anti-roll bar link from the left-hand strut.

20 Turn the steering fully to the left-hand lock, then use string or wire to tie up the driveshafts as high as possible away from the gearbox. Do not damage the surrounding bodywork. For additional working room, remove the left-hand driveshaft completely.

21 Working under the rear of the engine,

unscrew the single nut from the transmission-to-engine mounting stud. On transmission 02R, unbolt the small cover plate for the flywheel, located behind the right-hand drive flange.

22 Unbolt and remove the engine rear mounting/link from the transmission and subframe.

23 Using a suitable hoist, support the weight of the engine.

24 On transmission 02R only, remove the right-hand engine mounting top section, by first positioning the coolant expansion tank to one side, and then removing the nut and bolts securing the section to the bracket on the engine.

25 Slightly raise the hoist, and unscrew the bolts securing the left-hand engine/transmission mounting to the body. Now slightly lower the hoist and unscrew the mounting lower bolts from the transmission. Remove the mounting.

26 Unscrew and remove the upper and lower transmission-to-engine mounting bolts.

27 Position a trolley jack beneath the transmission so that it can be withdrawn from the left-hand side of the car.

28 Carefully pull the transmission directly away from the engine, taking care not to allow its weight to rest on the clutch friction disc hub. It may be necessary to push the engine forwards slightly during the separation.

 Warning: Support the transmission to ensure that it remains steady on the jack head. Keep the transmission level until the input shaft is fully withdrawn from the clutch friction disc.

29 When the transmission is clear of the locating dowels and clutch components, lower the transmission to the ground and withdraw from under the car.

Refitting

30 Refitting the transmission is a reversal of the removal procedure, but note the following points:

a) *Apply a smear of high-melting-point grease to the clutch friction disc hub splines, taking care to avoid contamination of the friction surfaces.*

b) *Check that the location dowels are correctly fitted to the cylinder block.*

c) *Tighten all bolts to the specified torque*

where given, with reference to the relevant Chapters.

d) *Refer to Section 2 and check the gearchange cable adjustment.*

e) *Refill the transmission with the correct grade and quantity of oil. Refer to 'Lubricants and fluids' and Chapter 1A or 1B, as appropriate.*

4 Manual transmission overhaul – general information

The overhaul of the manual transmission is a complex and often expensive task for the DIY home mechanic to undertake, which requires access to specialist equipment. It involves dismantling and reassembly of many small components, measuring clearances precisely and, if necessary, adjusting them by selecting shims and spacers. Internal transmission components are also often difficult to obtain and in many instances, extremely expensive. Because of this, if the transmission develops a fault or becomes noisy, the best course of action is to have the unit overhauled by a specialist repairer or to obtain an exchange reconditioned unit.

Nevertheless, it is not impossible for the more experienced mechanic to overhaul the transmission if the special tools are available and the job is carried out in a deliberate step-by-step manner, to ensure nothing is overlooked.

The tools necessary for an overhaul include internal and external circlip pliers, bearing pullers, a slide hammer, a set of pin punches, a dial test indicator and possibly a hydraulic press. In addition, a large, sturdy workbench and a vice will be required.

During dismantling of the transmission, make careful notes of how each component is fitted to make reassembly easier and accurate.

Before dismantling the transmission, it will help if you have some idea of where the problem lies. Certain problems can be closely related to specific areas in the transmission, which can make component examination and renewal easier. Refer to the *Fault finding* Section in this manual for more information.

5 Reversing light switch – testing, removal and refitting

Testing

1 Ensure that the ignition switch is turned to the 'off' position.

2 Disconnect the wiring from the reversing light switch. The switch is screwed into the front of the casing on 002 and 02T transmissions, and into the shift cover on the top of the 02R transmission.

3 Connect the probes of a continuity tester, or multimeter set to the resistance measurement function, across the terminals of the reversing light switch.

4 The switch contacts are open when any gear other than reverse is selected; the tester/meter should indicate an open circuit or infinite resistance. When reverse gear is selected, the switch contacts should close, causing the tester/meter to indicate continuity or zero resistance.

5 If the switch does not operate correctly, it should be renewed.

Removal

6 Ensure that the ignition switch is turned to the 'off' position.

7 Disconnect the wiring from the reversing light switch.

8 Unscrew and remove the switch, and on the 02T transmission recover the sealing ring.

Refitting

9 Refitting is a reversal of removal, but tighten the switch to the specified torque. On the 002 transmission, apply a little sealant to the threads of the switch. On the 02T transmission, renew the sealing ring. On the 02R transmission, apply some molybdenum disulphide grease to the peg.

6 Roadspeed sensor/ speedometer drive – removal and refitting

General information

1 All models without ABS are fitted with an electronic speedometer transducer. This device measures the rotational speed of the transmission final drive and converts the information into an electronic signal, which is then sent to the speedometer module in the instrument panel. On some models, the signal is also used as an input by the engine management system ECU.

Removal

2 Ensure that the ignition switch is turned to the 'off' position.

3 Locate the speed transducer, on the top rear of the transmission casing and disconnect the wiring.

4 On the 002 transmission, the roadspeed sensor is fitted directly on top of the drive pinion. Unscrew the transducer from the drive pinion. To remove the pinion, unscrew the retaining bolt and withdraw it from the transmission casing. Recover the O-ring seal.

5 On the 02T transmission, the roadspeed sensor is fitted on top of the final drive casing, and is retained by a single bolt. Use an Allen key to unscrew the bolt, then withdraw the sensor from the transmission casing. Recover the O-ring seal.

6 On the 02R transmission, the roadspeed sensor is fitted directly on top of the drive pinion. Hold the pinion housing with a spanner, then unscrew the transducer from the top. Unscrew the pinion housing from the transmission casing.

Refitting

7 Refitting is a reversal of removal, but renew the O-ring seal where fitted, and tighten the housing/bolts to the specified torque.

Notes

Chapter 7 Part B:
Automatic transmission

Contents

Section number

Automatic transmission – removal and refitting 2
Automatic transmission overhaul – general information 3
Electronic control unit – removal and refitting 6

Section number

General information 1
Selector cable – removal, refitting and adjustment 4
Selector lever housing – removal and refitting 5

Degrees of difficulty

Easy, suitable for novice with little experience	Fairly easy, suitable for beginner with some experience	Fairly difficult, suitable for competent DIY mechanic	Difficult, suitable for experienced DIY mechanic	Very difficult, suitable for expert DIY or professional

Specifications

General

Transmission type number 001
Application . . . . 1.4 litre DOHC petrol engine models
Description . . . . Electro-hydraulically controlled planetary gearbox providing four forward speeds and one reverse speed. Drive transmitted through hydrokinetic torque converter. Lock-up clutch on 3rd and 4th speeds, electronic control unit (ECU). Two driving modes, selected automatically by ECU. Shift points controlled by the ECU using 'Fuzzy logic'

Ratios

1st. 2.875:1
2nd 1.510:1
3rd 1.000:1
4th 0.726:1
Reverse 2.656:1
Final drive 4.050:1

Torque wrench settings

	Nm	lbf ft
Transmission bellhousing-to-engine bolts:		
Upper M12 bolts.	80	59
Rear M12 bolt.	80	59
Front lower M12 bolt	45	33
Torque converter-to-driveplate nuts.	85	63
Sump to transmission shield	45	33
Roadspeed sensor mounting bolt	6	4
Transmission speed sensor mounting bolt.	6	4

1 General information

Automatic transmission is available as an option on 1.4 litre DOHC petrol engine models only.

The type 001 automatic transmission **(see illustration)** has four forward speeds (and one reverse). The automatic gearchanges are electronically-controlled, rather than hydraulically as with previous conventional types. The advantage of electronic management is to provide a faster gearchange response. The separate transmission ECU (located behind the battery) employs 'Fuzzy logic' to determine the gear shift points. Instead of having predetermined points for up-shift and down-shift, the ECU takes into account several influencing factors before deciding to shift. These factors include engine speed, driving 'resistance' (engine load), brake pedal position, throttle position, and the rate at which the throttle pedal position is changed. This results in an almost infinite number of shift points, which the ECU can tailor to match the driving style, be that sporty or economic. A kickdown facility is also provided, to enable a faster acceleration response when required.

The transmission consists of three main assemblies, these being the torque converter, which is directly coupled to the engine; the final drive unit, which incorporates the differential unit; and the planetary gearbox, with its multi-disc clutches and brake bands. The transmission is lubricated with automatic transmission fluid (ATF), and is regarded by the manufacturers as being 'filled for life', with no requirement for the fluid to be changed at regular intervals. No provision is made for easy DIY checking of the fluid level, either – this must be carried out by a Skoda dealer, using special equipment capable of monitoring the fluid temperature (see Chapter 1A).

The torque converter incorporates an automatic lock-up feature, which eliminates converter slip in 3rd and 4th gears; this aids performance and economy. In addition to the normal alternative of manual change, two further modes are available – Sport and Economy mode. In Sport mode, upshifts are delayed longer and downshifts occur at higher engine speeds, to make full use of engine power, whereas in Economy mode, upshifts are taken sooner and downshifts are delayed as late as possible, to permit optimum economy. The decision as to which operating mode to use is determined by the ECU, based on the driving style of the driver; a moderate style will invoke the economy mode, and a faster style will invoke the sport mode.

Another feature of this transmission is the automatic selector lever lock when the ignition is on with P or N selected, and the vehicle is stationary or moving at less than 5 km/h. In order to move the selector lever, the brake pedal must first be depressed and the Shiftlock button pressed at the same time.

The kickdown function of the transmission, which acts to select a lower gear (where possible) on full-throttle acceleration, is operated by the throttle pedal position sensor (see Chapter 4A for details).

A starter inhibitor relay is fitted, to prevent starter motor operation unless the transmission is in P or N. The relay is located on the relay carrier behind the storage area on the driver's side, and is marked with the number 53.

Some models also feature a security/safety device which locks the transmission in P when the ignition key is removed (see Section 5).

The transmission is fitted with an electronic roadspeed sensor. This device measures the rotational speed of the transmission final drive, and converts the information into an electronic signal, which is then sent to the speedometer module in the instrument panel. The signal is also used as an input by the engine management system ECU.

A fault diagnosis system is integrated into the control unit, but analysis can only be undertaken with specialised equipment. If a malfunction should occur in the transmission electrical system, control will switch to one of two emergency programmes; either the transmission still switches automatically but the changes are not smooth, or the transmission does not change automatically and manual selection of 3rd and reverse gears is only possible. When the transmission enters emergency mode, it is important that any fault be identified and rectified at the earliest possible opportunity. Delay in doing so will only cause further problems. A Skoda dealer can 'interrogate' the ECU fault memory for stored fault codes, enabling him to pinpoint the fault quickly. Once the fault has been corrected and any fault codes have been cleared, normal transmission operation should be restored.

Because of the need for special test equipment, the complexity of some of the parts, and the need for scrupulous cleanliness when servicing automatic transmissions, the

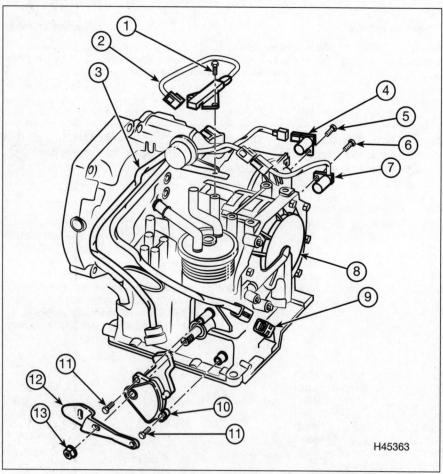

1.2 External components on the 001 automatic transmission

1	Bolt	6	Bolt	10	Multi-function
2	Series resistance	7	Transmission speed		switch
3	Wiring harness		sender	11	Bolt
4	Roadspeed	8	Transmission	12	Selector shaft lever
	sensor	9	Solenoid valve wiring	13	Nut
5	Bolt		harness		

H45363

amount of work which the owner can do is limited. Repairs to the final drive differential are also not recommended. Major repairs and overhaul operations should be left to a Skoda dealer, who will be equipped with the necessary equipment for fault diagnosis and repair. The information in this Chapter is therefore limited to a description of the removal and refitting of the transmission as a complete unit. The removal, refitting and adjustment of the selector cable is also described.

In the event of a transmission problem occurring, consult a Skoda dealer or transmission specialist before removing the transmission from the car, since the majority of fault diagnosis is carried out with the transmission *in situ*.

2 Automatic transmission – removal and refitting

Removal

1 Select a solid, level surface to park the vehicle upon. Give yourself enough space to move around it easily. Apply the handbrake and chock the rear wheels.

2 Loosen the front wheel bolts, and the left-hand driveshaft hub nut/bolt, then raise the front of the vehicle and support it securely on axle stands (see *Jacking and vehicle support*). Remove the front wheels, the left-hand front wheel arch liner and the engine undertray. Allow a suitable working clearance underneath for the eventual withdrawal of the transmission.

3 If necessary for the hoist or lifting bar being used, remove the bonnet with reference to Chapter 11.

4 Remove the engine top cover.

5 Remove the battery and battery tray with reference to Chapter 5A (also refer to *Disconnecting the battery* in the *Reference* Chapter at the end of this manual).

6 Pull out the retaining clip and detach the selector lever control cable from the support bracket on the front of the transmission.

7 Using a 13 mm open-ended spanner, lever the control cable end fitting from the gearchange lever/shaft.

8 Clamp off the automatic transmission fluid cooler hoses with brake hose type clamps. Release the retaining clips and detach the hoses from the cooler. Tape over or plug the cooler stubs to prevent entry of dust and dirt.

9 Unbolt and remove the control cable support bracket.

10 Disconnect all wiring and connectors from the transmission, noting the location to ensure correct refitting **(see illustration)**.

11 Unbolt and remove the wiring support bracket, noting that an earth cable is located beneath one of the bolts.

12 Release the plastic wiring conduit from the transmission lifting eye and from the special transmission-to-engine bolt.

13 Unscrew and remove the upper transmission-to-engine bolts.

14 Refer to Chapter 5A and remove the starter motor.

15 Remove the left-hand driveshaft as described in Chapter 8.

16 Remove the exhaust front pipe as described in Chapter 4C.

17 Unbolt the right-hand driveshaft from the transmission flange with reference to Chapter 8, then tie it to one side.

18 Unclip the blanking cap, located next to the right-hand transmission flange, and turn the engine to locate one of the torque converter-to-driveplate nuts in the opening. Unscrew and remove the nut whilst preventing the engine from turning by using a wide-bladed screwdriver engaged with the ring gear teeth on the driveplate visible through the starter aperture. Unscrew the remaining two nuts, turning the engine a third of a turn at a time to locate them.

19 Unbolt the engine rear mounting link and bracket from the transmission and subframe. Also remove the transmission oil pan guard.

20 Unbolt the cover plate from the bottom of the transmission bellhousing.

21 Working under the rear of the engine, unscrew the single nut from the transmission-to-engine mounting stud.

22 Support the engine with a hoist, or with a support bar located on the front wing inner channels. Depending on the engine, temporarily remove components as necessary to attach the hoist.

23 Remove the right-hand engine mounting completely, by first positioning the coolant expansion tank to one side, and then removing the bolts securing the mounting sections to the body and engine. There is no need to separate the two sections.

24 Position a trolley jack underneath the transmission, and raise it to just take the weight of the unit.

25 Undo and remove the two bolts securing the left-hand gearbox mounting to the triangular mounting spacer. By controlling both the engine hoist/support bar and the trolley jack, lower the transmission approximately 60 mm. Unscrew the two remaining bolts and one nut, and remove the transmission mounting spacer.

26 Unscrew and remove the lower bolts securing the transmission bellhousing to the engine, noting the bolt locations, as they are of different sizes and lengths.

27 Check that all the fixings and attachments are clear of the transmission. Enlist the aid of an assistant to help in guiding and supporting the transmission during its removal.

28 The transmission is located on two dowels, and it may be necessary to prise the transmission from them. Once the transmission is disconnected from the location dowels, swivel the unit out and lower it out of the vehicle.

 Warning: Support the transmission to ensure that it remains steady on the jack head. Ensure that the

torque converter remains in position on its shaft in the torque converter housing.

29 With the transmission removed, bolt a suitable bar and spacer across the front face of the torque converter housing, to retain the torque converter in position.

Refitting

30 Refitting is a reversal of the removal procedure, but note the following special points:

a) *When reconnecting the transmission to the engine, ensure that the location dowels are in position, and that the transmission is correctly aligned with them before pushing it fully into engagement with the engine. As the torque converter is refitted, ensure that the drive pins at the centre of the torque converter hub engage with the recesses in the automatic transmission fluid pump inner wheel.*

b) *Tighten all retaining bolts to their specified torque.*

c) *Reconnect and adjust the selector cable, as described in Section 4.*

d) *On completion, check the transmission fluid level (see Chapter 1A).*

e) *If a new transmission unit has been fitted, it may be necessary to have the transmission ECU 'matched' to the engine management ECU electronically, to ensure correct operation – seek the advice of your Skoda dealer.*

3 Automatic transmission overhaul – general information

In the event of a fault occurring, it will be necessary to establish whether the fault is electrical, mechanical or hydraulic in nature, before repair work can be contemplated.

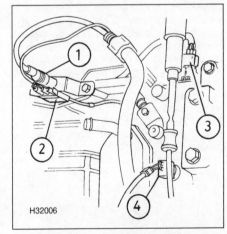

H32006

2.10 Gearbox electrical connections

1 *Solenoid valves*
2 *Roadspeed sensor*
3 *Multi-function switch*
4 *Gearbox speed sensor*

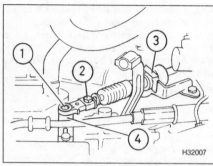

H32007

4.4 Selector cable

1 Selector cable	3 Circlip
2 Nut	4 Selector lever

Diagnosis requires detailed knowledge of the transmission's operation and construction, as well as access to specialised test equipment, and so is deemed to be beyond the scope of this manual. It is therefore essential that problems with the automatic transmission are referred to a Skoda dealer for assessment.

Note that a faulty transmission should not be removed before the vehicle has been assessed by a dealer, as fault diagnosis is carried out with the transmission *in situ*.

4 Selector cable – removal, refitting and adjustment

Removal

1 Disconnect the battery negative lead (refer to *Disconnecting the battery* in the *Reference* Chapter at the end of this manual).
2 Apply the handbrake, then jack up the front of the vehicle and support it on axle stands (see *Jacking and vehicle support*). Allow a suitable working clearance underneath the vehicle. Remove the engine undertray and engine top cover as applicable.
3 Move the selector lever to the P position.
4 Pull out the retaining clip and detach the selector lever control cable from the support bracket on the front of the transmission **(see illustration)**.
5 Using a 13 mm open-ended spanner, lever the control cable end fitting from the gearchange lever/shaft. Also release the cable from its supports.
6 Working beneath the car, unbolt the underbody crossmember from under the exhaust system.
7 Separate the exhaust downpipe from the intermediate pipe with reference to Chapter 4C.

8 Release the exhaust intermediate pipe mounting rubber, and lower the rear exhaust system as far as possible. Remove the exhaust heatshield from the underbody tunnel.
9 Undo the screws and remove the cover from the bottom of the selector lever housing.
10 Using a screwdriver, prise the selector cable end fitting from the lever, then pull out the clip and remove the selector cable from the housing. Recover the seal.
11 Withdraw the selector cable from the engine compartment.

Refitting

12 Refit the selector cable by reversing the removal procedure, noting the following points:
  a) *Lightly grease the cable end fittings before refitting the cable.*
  b) *Ensure that the cable is correctly routed, as noted on removal, and that it is securely held by its retaining clips.*
  c) *Check and if necessary renew the cable and housing cover seals.*
  d) *Take care not to bend or kink the cable.*
  e) *Carry out the cable adjustment procedure described below.*

Adjustment

13 Inside the car, check that the selector lever is still in the P position.
14 At the front of the transmission, slacken the cable adjustment locking bolt at the ball socket.
15 Check that the selector lever on the transmission is in the P position. It must not be possible to simultaneously rotate both front roadwheels in the same direction.
16 Tighten the cable adjustment locking bolt securely.
17 Verify the operation of the selector lever by shifting through all gear positions and checking that every gear can be selected smoothly and without delay.
18 Lower the car to the ground.

5 Selector lever housing – removal and refitting

Removal

1 Disconnect the battery negative lead (refer to *Disconnecting the battery* in the *Reference* Chapter at the end of this manual).
2 Apply the handbrake, then jack up the front of the vehicle and support it on axle stands (see *Jacking and vehicle support*). Remove the engine undertray.

3 Inside the car, move the selector lever to position 2, then push down the sleeve beneath the lever grip, and pull off the grip upwards **(see illustration)**.
4 Move the selector lever to the P position.
5 Remove the centre console as described in Chapter 11.
6 Remove the selector lever cover and position indicator, by pulling upwards from the housing, and at the same time disconnect the wiring at the front.
7 Disconnect the wiring for the selector lever lock solenoid.
8 Working beneath the car, unbolt the underbody crossmember from under the exhaust system.
9 Separate the exhaust downpipe from the intermediate pipe with reference to Chapter 4C.
10 Release the exhaust intermediate pipe mounting rubber, and lower the rear exhaust system as far as possible. Remove the exhaust heatshield from the underbody tunnel.
11 Undo the screws and remove the cover from the bottom of the selector lever housing.
12 Using a screwdriver, prise the selector cable end fitting from the lever, then pull out the clip and remove the selector cable from the housing. Recover the seal.
13 Support the housing from below, then unscrew the mounting nuts from inside the car. Withdraw the housing from under the car.

Refitting

14 Refitting is a reversal of removal, but check and if necessary renew the cable and housing cover seals. Finally, check and adjust the cable as described in Section 4.

6 Electronic control unit – removal and refitting

Note: *If the electronic control unit is renewed, the new unit must be initialised by a Skoda dealer.*

Removal

1 The transmission electronic control unit (ECU) is located behind the battery on the battery tray.
2 With the ignition switched off, unlock and disconnect the wiring plug from the ECU.
3 Undo the two retaining screws and withdraw the ECU from the engine compartment.

Refitting

4 Refitting is a reversal of removal.

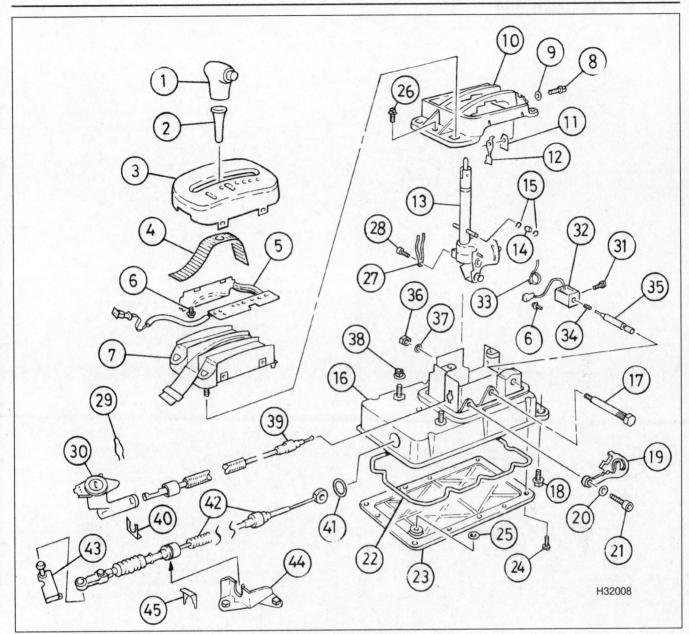

5.3 Selector lever assembly

1 Selector lever handle	9 Shim	18 Bolt	28 Bolt	38 Nut
2 Sleeve	10 Locking segment	19 Locking lever	29 Clip	39 Locking cable
3 Cover	11 Plate	20 Washer	30 Steering lock	40 Circlip
4 Cover strip	12 Locating spring with roller	21 Bolt	31 Bolt	41 Gasket
5 Lever position display	13 Selector lever	22 Gasket	32 Lock solenoid	42 Selector cable
6 Retaining clip	14 Roller	23 Cover	33 Cable tie	43 Lever
7 Frame	15 Circlip	24 Bolt	34 Spring	44 Support bracket
8 Bolt	16 Lever housing	25 O-ring	35 Locking pin	45 Circlip
	17 Pivot pin	26 Bolt	36 Nut	
		27 Contact spring	37 Washer	

H32008

Notes

Chapter 8
Driveshafts

Contents

Section number

Driveshaft – removal and refitting............................ 2
Driveshaft overhaul – general information 4

Section number

Driveshaft rubber gaiters – renewal 3
General information 1

Degrees of difficulty

Easy, suitable for novice with little experience	Fairly easy, suitable for beginner with some experience	Fairly difficult, suitable for competent DIY mechanic	Difficult, suitable for experienced DIY mechanic	Very difficult, suitable for expert DIY or professional

Specifications

Lubrication

Type of grease	G 000 603 or G 000 633 grease
Quantity of grease per joint:	
Outer joint:	
Joint diameter 90 mm..............................	80 g (all in joint)
Joint diameter 100 mm.............................	100 g (all in joint)
Inner joint:	
Tripod type CV joint:	
Joint diameter 108 mm............................	110 g
Ball-and-cage type CV joint:	
Joint diameter 90 mm.............................	80 g (40g in joint, 40g in gaiter)
Joint diameter 100 mm............................	110 g (55g in joint, 55g in gaiter)

Torque wrench settings

	Nm	lbf ft
Driveshaft shield..	35	26
Driveshaft-to-transmission flange bolts:		
M8:		
Models up to 04/03:		
Stage 1...	10	7
Stage 2...	40	30
Models from 05/03:		
Stage 1...	10	7
Stage 2...	20	15
Stage 3...	Angle-tighten a further 90°	
M10:		
Models up to 04/03:		
Stage 1...	10	7
Stage 2...	70	52
Models from 05/03:		
Stage 1...	10	7
Stage 2...	50	37
Stage 3...	Angle-tighten a further 45°	
Hub nut*:		
12-point nut*:		
Stage 1...	50	37
Stage 2...	Angle-tighten a further 45°	
Plated nut (early models)**	30	22
Lower arm-to-balljoint bolts*:		
Stage 1...	20	15
Stage 2...	Angle-tighten a further 90°	

* Use new nut/bolt

** Recommended to be replaced by 12-point nut

2.1 Home-made tool for holding the front hub while loosening the hub nut

1 General information

Drive is transmitted from the differential to the front wheels by means of two steel driveshafts of either solid or hollow construction (depending on model). Both driveshafts are splined at their outer ends, to accept the wheel hubs, and are secured to the hub by a large nut or bolt. The inner end of each driveshaft is bolted to the transmission drive flange.

Constant velocity (CV) joints are fitted to each end of the driveshafts, to ensure the smooth and efficient transmission of drive at all the angles possible as the roadwheels move up-and-down with the suspension, and as they turn from side-to-side under steering. On all models with manual transmission, both

2.3 Remove the heat shield

inner and outer constant velocity joints are of the ball-and-cage type. On all models with automatic transmission, the outer joint is of the ball-and-cage type, but the inner joint is of the tripod type.

Rubber or plastic gaiters are secured over both CV joints with steel clips. The gaiters contain the grease which lubricates the joints, and also protect the joints from the entry of dirt and debris.

2 Driveshaft – removal and refitting

Note: A new hub nut will be required on refitting. On automatic transmission models, in order to gain the necessary clearance required to withdraw the left-hand driveshaft, it may be necessary to unbolt the rear engine

transmission mounting from the subframe, and lift the engine slightly.

Removal

1 Remove the wheel trim/hub cap (as applicable) then have an assistant depress the footbrake, and partially slacken the hub/driveshaft nut with the vehicle resting on its wheels – note that the nut is very tight, and a suitable extension bar will probably be required to aid slackening. Alternatively, the hub nut may be loosened later using a home-made tool consisting of two lengths of metal bar **(see illustration)**. Also slacken the roadwheel securing bolts.

2 Apply the handbrake, then jack up the front of the vehicle and support it on axle stands (see *Jacking and vehicle support*). Remove the appropriate front roadwheel.

3 Remove the retaining screws and/or clips, and remove the undershields from beneath the engine/transmission unit to gain access to the driveshafts. Where necessary, also unbolt the heat shield from the transmission housing to improve access to the driveshaft inner joint **(see illustration)**.

4 Mark the inner driveshaft joint and drive flange in relation to each other, then, using a multi-splined tool, unscrew and remove the bolts and, where applicable, recover the retaining plates from underneath the bolts. Place a plastic bag over the joint to prevent entry of dust and dirt **(see illustrations)**.

Caution: Support the driveshaft by suspending it with wire or string – do not allow it to hang under its own weight, or the joint may be damaged.

5 Using a suitable marker pen or scriber, draw around the outline of the end of the suspension lower arm on the lower arm balljoint, marking the correct fitted position of the balljoint.

6 Unscrew the lower arm balljoint securing bolts, and remove the retaining plate/hub assembly from the top of the lower arm. **Note:** *On some models, the balljoint inner securing bolt hole is slotted; on these models the inner securing bolt can be slackened, leaving the retaining plate and bolt in position in the arm, and the balljoint disengaged from the bolt.*

7 Unscrew and remove the hub/driveshaft nut, and discard it as a new one is required for refitting **(see illustration)**. If the early *plated* nut is fitted, it is recommended that a new *12-point* nut is obtained.

8 Carefully pull the hub carrier outwards, and withdraw the driveshaft outer constant velocity joint from the hub. The joint may be a very tight fit in the hub; tap the joint out of the hub using a soft-faced mallet (refit the hub nut to the end of the driveshaft to protect the threads). If this fails to free the driveshaft from the hub, the joint will have to be pressed out using a suitable tool bolted to the hub.

9 Manoeuvre the driveshaft out from underneath the vehicle and (where fitted) recover the gasket from the end of the inner constant velocity joint. Discard the gasket – a new one should be used on refitting.

2.4a Mark the driveshaft joint and flange in relation to each other . . .

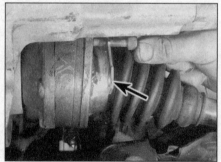

2.4b . . . then unscrew and remove the bolts and retaining plates

2.4c Place plastic bags over the joint and flange to protect them

2.7 Removing the hub/driveshaft nut

2.13 Fit a new 12-point hub/driveshaft nut

Caution: Do not allow the vehicle to rest on its wheels with one or both driveshaft(s) removed, as damage to the wheel bearings may result.

10 If moving the vehicle is unavoidable, temporarily insert the outer end of the driveshaft in the hub, and tighten the driveshaft retaining nut/bolt; in this case, the inner end of the driveshaft must be supported, for example by suspending with string from the vehicle underbody.

Refitting

11 Ensure that the transmission flange and inner joint mating surfaces are clean and dry. Where necessary, fit a new gasket to the joint by peeling off its backing foil and sticking it in position.

12 Ensure that the outer joint and hub splines are clean and dry. Coat the splines of the outer constant velocity joint, the threads on the end of the outer joint, the splines in the hub, and the contact face of the hub nut with a little grease.

13 Manoeuvre the driveshaft into position, and engage the outer joint with the hub. Fit the new hub/driveshaft nut and use it to draw the joint fully into position **(see illustration)**.

14 Align the suspension lower arm balljoint, lower arm, and retaining plate/hub assembly, then fit new lower arm balljoint securing bolts, and tighten them to the specified torque setting, using the marks made on removal to ensure that the balljoint is correctly positioned.

15 Align the driveshaft inner joint with the transmission flange, and refit the retaining bolts and (where necessary) plates. Tighten the retaining bolts to the specified torque.

16 Where applicable (see Note at the beginning of this Section), fit new rear engine/transmission mounting-to-subframe bolts, and tighten the bolts to the specified torque (see relevant part of Chapter 2).

17 Ensure that the outer joint is drawn fully into position, then refit the roadwheel and lower the vehicle to the ground.

18 Tighten the driveshaft nut to the torque (and angle where applicable) given in the Specifications.

19 Once the driveshaft nut is correctly tightened, tighten the wheel bolts to the specified torque (see relevant part of Chapter 1) and refit the wheel trim/hub cap.

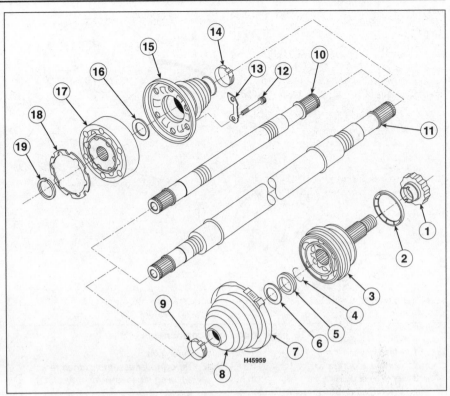

3.1a Driveshaft with inner CV joint components

1 *12-point hub/driveshaft nut*	8 *Outer joint gaiter*	13 *Retaining plate*
2 *Thrower ring*	9 *Gaiter securing clip*	14 *Gaiter securing clip*
3 *Outer CV joint*	10 *Left-hand driveshaft (solid)*	15 *Inner joint gaiter*
4 *Circlip*	11 *Right-hand driveshaft (tubular)*	16 *Dished washer*
5 *Thrust ring*	12 *Driveshaft-to-transmission flange bolts*	17 *Inner CV joint*
6 *Dished washer*		18 *Gasket*
7 *Gaiter securing clip*		19 *Circlip*

3 Driveshaft rubber gaiters – renewal

1 Remove the driveshaft from the car, as described in Section 2. Continue as described under the relevant sub-heading. Driveshafts with a tripod type inner joint can be identified by the shape of the inner CV joint; the driveshaft retaining bolt holes are in cast extensions, giving it a six-pointed star-shaped exterior, in contrast to the smooth, circular shape of the ball-and-cage joint **(see illustrations)**.

Outer CV joint gaiter

2 Secure the driveshaft in a vice equipped with soft jaws, and release the two outer joint gaiter retaining clips. If necessary, the retaining clips can be cut to release them.

3 Slide the rubber gaiter down the shaft to expose the constant velocity joint, and scoop out excess grease.

4 Using a soft-faced mallet, tap the joint off the end of the driveshaft.

5 Remove the circlip from the driveshaft

groove, and slide off the thrustwasher and dished washer, noting which way around it is fitted.

6 Slide the rubber gaiter off the driveshaft and discard it.

7 Thoroughly clean the constant velocity joint(s) using paraffin, or a suitable solvent, and dry thoroughly. Carry out a visual inspection as follows.

8 Move the inner splined driving member from side-to-side to expose each ball in turn at the top of its track. Examine the balls for cracks, flat spots or signs of surface pitting.

9 Inspect the ball tracks on the inner and outer members. If the tracks have widened, the balls will no longer be a tight fit. At the same time, check the ball cage windows for wear or cracking between the windows.

10 If on inspection any of the constant velocity joint components are found to be worn or damaged, it will be necessary to renew the complete joint assembly. If the joint is in satisfactory condition, obtain a new gaiter and retaining clips, a constant velocity joint circlip and the correct type of grease. Grease is often supplied with the joint repair kit – if not, use a good-quality molybdenum disulphide grease.

11 Tape over the splines on the end of the

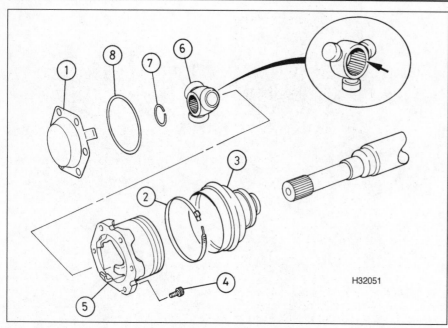

H32051

3.1b Inner tripod joint components

1 Metal cover
2 Gaiter securing clip
3 Inner joint gaiter
4 Driveshaft-to-transmission flange
   bolts

5 Inner joint
6 Tripod/roller assembly (chamfer
   arrowed faces towards driveshaft)
7 Circlip
8 Seal

driveshaft, to protect the new gaiter as it is slid into place **(see illustration)**.
12 Slide the new gaiter onto the end of the driveshaft, then remove the protective tape from the driveshaft splines.

13 Slide on the dished washer, making sure its convex side is innermost, followed by the thrustwasher **(see illustrations)**.
14 Fit a new circlip to the driveshaft, then tap the joint onto the driveshaft until the circlip engages

3.11 Tape over the driveshaft splines, then slide the new gaiter along the shaft

in its groove **(see illustrations)**. Make sure that the joint is securely retained by the circlip.
15 Pack the joint with the specified type of grease. Work the grease well into the bearing tracks whilst twisting the joint, and fill the rubber gaiter with any excess.
16 Ease the gaiter over the joint, and ensure that the gaiter lips are correctly located on both the driveshaft and constant velocity joint. Lift the outer sealing lip of the gaiter to equalise air pressure within the gaiter **(see illustration)**.
17 Fit the large metal retaining clip to the gaiter. Pull the clip as tight as possible, and locate the hooks on the clip in their slots. Remove any slack in the gaiter retaining clip by carefully compressing the raised section of the clip. In the absence of the special tool, a pair of side-cutters may be used, taking care not to cut the clip **(see illustrations)**. Secure the small retaining clip using the same procedure.

3.13a Slide on the dished washer, with its convex side innermost . . .

3.13b . . . then slide on the thrustwasher

3.14a Fit the new circlip to the driveshaft groove . . .

3.14b . . . then locate the joint on the driveshaft splines . . .

3.14c . . . and tap the joint onto the driveshaft

3.16 Seat the gaiter on the outer joint and driveshaft, then lift its inner lip to equalise the air pressure

3.17a Compress the raised section of the gaiter securing clip . . .

3.17b . . . taking great care not to cut through the clip

3.28 Check the tripod rollers and outer member for signs of wear

18 Check the constant velocity joint moves freely in all directions, then refit the driveshaft to the vehicle, as described in Section 2.

Tripod inner CV joint gaiter

19 Secure the driveshaft in a vice equipped with soft jaws, with the inner joint uppermost, and release the two inner joint gaiter retaining clips. If necessary, the retaining clips can be cut to release them. Slide the rubber gaiter down the shaft, away from the joint housing.

20 Using a screwdriver, prise up the tabs of the metal cap over the inner end of the joint. Lever off the cover.

21 Scoop out excess grease from the joint, then remove the O-ring from the groove in the joint housing.

22 Using a suitable marker pen or a scriber, make alignment marks between the end of the driveshaft, the tripod roller assembly, and the housing.

23 Slide the joint housing down the driveshaft, away from the joint.

24 Remove the circlip from the end of the driveshaft.

25 Press or drive the driveshaft from the tripod, taking great care not to damage the rollers.

26 Slide the housing and the rubber gaiter from the end of the driveshaft.

27 Thoroughly clean the joint components using paraffin, or a suitable solvent, and dry thoroughly. Carry out a visual inspection as follows.

28 Inspect the tripod rollers and the joint outer housing for signs of wear, pitting or scuffing on their mating surfaces. Check that the joint rollers rotate smoothly, with no traces of roughness **(see illustration)**.

29 If the rollers or outer housing shown signs of wear or damage, it will be necessary to renew the complete driveshaft, since the joint is not available separately. If the joint is in satisfactory condition, obtain a repair kit, consisting of a new gaiter, retaining clips, circlip, and the correct type and quantity of grease.

30 Tape over the splines on the end of the driveshaft, to protect the new gaiter as it is slid into place, then slide the new gaiter and securing clips, and the joint housing over the end of the driveshaft **(see illustrations)**. Remove the protective tape from the driveshaft splines.

31 Press or drive the tripod onto the end of the driveshaft until it contacts the stop, ensuring that the marks made on the end of the driveshaft and the tripod before dismantling are aligned. Note that the chamfered edge of the internal splines on the tripod should face towards the driveshaft. Take care not to damage the rollers as the tripod is refitted.

32 Fit the new circlip to retain the tripod on the end of the driveshaft.

33 Work half of the grease supplied with the repair kit into the inner end of the joint housing, then slide the housing over the tripod, ensuring that the marks made during dismantling are aligned, and clamp the housing in the vice.

34 Work the rest of the grease supplied with the repair kit into the outer end of the joint housing **(see illustration)**.

35 Slide the rubber gaiter up the driveshaft onto the joint housing, ensuring that the end of the gaiter seats in the groove in the joint

3.30a Tape over the driveshaft splines to protect the new gaiter . . .

3.34 Work the grease into the joint outer member

housing, and secure with the large clip as described in paragraph 17.

36 Lift the gaiter outer end to equalise the air pressure in the gaiter, then secure the outer gaiter securing clip in position using the same method used previously **(see illustration)**.

37 Check that the grease in the joint outer housing is evenly distributed around the tripod rollers.

38 Wipe any excess grease from the inner face of the joint housing, then fit the O-ring provided in the repair kit into the groove.

39 Fit the new cover supplied in the repair kit to the inner end of the joint housing, ensuring that the bolt holes in the housing and cover are aligned.

40 Secure the cover by bending the securing tabs around the edge of the outer housing flange.

41 Check the driveshaft joint moves freely in all directions, then refit the driveshaft to the

3.30b . . . then lever the gaiter carefully over the ridge on the driveshaft

3.36 Lift the gaiter outer end to equalise the air pressure

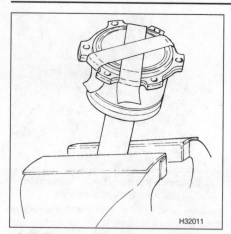

3.41 Tape over the end of the driveshaft joint

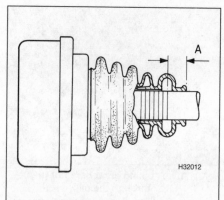

3.52 Installation position of inner joint gaiter on left-hand driveshaft

A = 17.0 mm

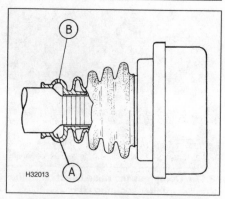

3.56 Installation position of inner joint gaiter on right-hand driveshaft

A Vent chamber   B Vent hole
   in gaiter

vehicle, as described in Section 2. To prevent the tripod joint from being pushed back down the driveshaft during refitting, temporarily stick adhesive tape over the open end of the joint outer member (see illustration). Remove the tape just before reconnecting the inner end of the driveshaft to the transmission.

Ball-and-cage inner CV joint

42 Secure the driveshaft in a vice equipped with soft jaws, then release the gaiter outer securing clip, securing the gaiter to the driveshaft. If necessary, the clip can be cut to release it.

43 Using a hammer and a small drift, carefully drive the inner end of the gaiter from the joint housing.

44 Slide the gaiter down the driveshaft to expose the constant velocity joint, and scoop out excess grease.

45 Remove the circlip from the end of the driveshaft.

46 Press or drive the driveshaft from the joint, taking great care not to damage the joint. Recover the dished washer fitted between the constant velocity joint and the gaiter.

47 Slide the gaiter from the end of the driveshaft.

48 Proceed as described previously in paragraphs 7 to 12.

49 Slide the dished washer onto the driveshaft, making sure its convex side is innermost.

50 Fit the joint to the end of the driveshaft, noting that the chamfered edge of the internal splines on the joint should face towards the driveshaft. Drive or press the joint into position until it contacts the shoulder on the driveshaft.

51 Fit a new circlip to retain the joint on the end of the driveshaft.

52 If the left-hand driveshaft is being worked on, mark the final installation position of the gaiter outboard end on the driveshaft using tape or paint – do not scratch the surface of the driveshaft (see illustration).

53 Pack the joint with the recommended quantity of grease (see Specifications), then pack the gaiter with the recommended quantity of grease.

54 Slide the gaiter up the driveshaft, and push or drive the inner end of the gaiter onto the joint housing.

55 If the left-hand driveshaft is being worked on, slide the outboard end of the gaiter into position using the mark made previously (see paragraph 52), then secure the outer gaiter securing clip in position as described in paragraph 17.

56 If the right-hand driveshaft is being worked on, slide the outboard end of the gaiter into position, and secure the outer gaiter securing clip in position as described in paragraph 17 (see illustration).

57 Check the driveshaft joint moves freely in all directions, then refit the driveshaft to the vehicle, as described in Section 2.

4 Driveshaft overhaul – general information

If any of the checks described in Chapter 1A or 1B reveal wear in any driveshaft joint, first remove the roadwheel trim or centre cap (as applicable) and check that the hub nut is tight. If the nut is loose, obtain a new nut, and tighten it to the specified torque (see Section 2). If the nut is tight, refit the centre cap/trim, and repeat the check on the other hub nut/bolt.

Road test the vehicle, and listen for a metallic clicking from the front of the vehicle as the vehicle is driven slowly in a circle on full-lock. If a clicking noise is heard, this indicates wear in the outer constant velocity joint; this means that the joint must be renewed.

If vibration consistent with roadspeed is felt through the car when accelerating, there is a possibility of wear in the inner constant velocity joints.

To check the joints for wear, remove the driveshafts, then dismantle them as described in Section 3. If any wear or free play is found, the affected joint must be renewed. Refer to a Skoda dealer for information on the availability of driveshaft components.

Chapter 9
Braking system

Contents

Section number

Anti-lock braking system (ABS) – general information and
  precautions 22
Anti-lock braking system (ABS) components – removal and
  refitting 23
Brake disc – inspection, removal and refitting 6
Brake fluid level check .... See *Weekly checks*
Brake fluid renewal .... See Chapter 1A or 1B
Brake light switch – removal and refitting 21
Brake pad and shoe check .... See Chapter 1A or 1B
Brake pedal – removal and refitting 13
Front brake caliper – removal, overhaul and refitting 5
Front brake disc shield – removal and refitting 7
Front brake pads – removal, inspection and refitting 4
General information and precautions 1
Handbrake – adjustment 17

Section number

Handbrake 'on' warning light switch – removal and refitting 20
Handbrake cables – removal and refitting 19
Handbrake lever – removal and refitting 18
Hydraulic pipes and hoses – renewal 3
Hydraulic system – bleeding 2
Master cylinder – removal, overhaul and refitting 14
Rear brake caliper – removal, overhaul and refitting 9
Rear brake drum – removal, inspection and refitting 10
Rear brake pads – removal, inspection and refitting 8
Rear brake shoes – removal, inspection and refitting 11
Rear wheel cylinder – removal, overhaul and refitting 12
Servo non-return valve – testing, removal and refitting 16
Servo unit – testing, removal and refitting 15
Servo unit mechanical vacuum pump (diesel models) – testing,
  removal and refitting 24

Degrees of difficulty

Easy, suitable for novice with little experience 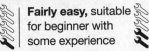 | **Fairly easy,** suitable for beginner with some experience | **Fairly difficult,** suitable for competent DIY mechanic | **Difficult,** suitable for experienced DIY mechanic | **Very difficult,** suitable for expert DIY or professional

Specifications

Engine codes

Petrol engines

1.2 litre:
SOHC .... AWY
DOHC .... AZQ, BME
1.4 litre OHV:
44 kW .... AZE and AZF
50 kW .... AME, AQW and ATZ
1.4 litre DOHC:
55 kW .... AUA and BBY
74 kW .... AUB and BBZ

Diesel engines

1.4 litre .... AMF
1.9 litre non-turbo .... ASY
1.9 litre turbo .... ASZ and ATD

Rear drum brakes

Drum diameter:
New .... 200 mm
Maximum diameter .... 201 mm (stamped on inner surface of drum)
Brake shoe friction material thickness:
New .... 5.4 mm
Minimum .... 1.5 mm

Rear disc brakes

Disc diameter . . . .   232 mm
Disc thickness:
   New . . . .   9.0 mm
   Minimum thickness. . . . .   7.0 mm
Maximum disc run-out. . . . .   0.1 mm
Brake pad thickness:
   New (including backing plate) . . . .   16.9 mm
   Minimum (including backing plate).   7.6 mm
   Minimum (friction lining only. . . . .   2.0 mm

Front brakes

Caliper types:
   Engine codes AWY and AZF without power steering. . . . .   FSII
   Engine code ASZ C54-II
   All other engine codes . . . .   FSIII
Disc diameter:
   Engine codes AWY and AZF without power steering. . . . .   239 mm
   Engine code ASZ . . . .   288 mm
   All other engine codes . . . .   256 mm
Disc thickness:
   New:
      Engine codes AWY and AZF without power steering. . . . .   18.0 mm
      Engine code ASZ . . . .   25.0 mm
      All other engine codes . . . .   22.0 mm
   Minimum permissible thickness:
      Engine codes AWY and AZF without power steering. . . . .   15.0 mm
      Engine code ASZ . . . .   22.0 mm
      All other engine codes . . . .   19.0 mm
Maximum disc run-out. . . . .   0.1 mm
Brake pad thickness:
   New (including backing plate):
      Engine codes AWY and AZF without power steering. . . . .   17.6 mm
      Engine code ASZ . . . .   18.6 mm
      All other engine codes . . . .   19.6 mm
   Minimum (including backing plate). . . . .   7.0 mm
   Minimum (friction lining only)*. . . . .   2.0 mm

* The pad wear warning light illuminates when the pads wear to 2 to 3 mm thick.

Torque wrench settings

	Nm	lbf ft
ABS control unit bracket-to-wing nuts.	20	15
ABS control unit retaining bolts .	8	6
ABS wheel sensor retaining bolts.	8	6
Brake pedal pivot shaft nut .	25	18
Front brake caliper:		
Guide pins (FSII and FSIII) .	28	21
Guide pin bolts (C54-II)* .	30	22
Mounting bracket bolts (C54-II) .	125	92
Front brake disc shield.	10	7
Handbrake lever bracket:		
Stage 1 .	20	15
Stage 2 .	Angle-tighten a further 90°	
Master cylinder mounting nuts.	20	15
Pedal bracket.	28	21
Rear brake caliper (disc brakes):		
Guide pin bolts* .	35	26
Mounting bracket bolts:		
Stage 1 .	30	22
Stage 2 .	Angle-tighten a further 30°	
Rear wheel cylinder (drum brakes).	8	6
Roadwheel bolts.	120	89
Servo unit mechanical vacuum pump (diesel models).	20	15
Servo unit mounting nuts.	28	21

* Use new bolts

1 General information and precautions

General information

The braking system is of servo-assisted, diagonal dual-circuit hydraulic type. The arrangement of the hydraulic system is such that each circuit operates one front and one rear brake from a tandem master cylinder. Under normal circumstances, both circuits operate in unison. However, if there is hydraulic failure in one circuit, full braking force will still be available at two wheels.

All models covered by this manual are equipped with disc brakes at the front. Either rear drum brakes or rear disc brakes may be fitted. ABS is fitted to most models.

The front disc brakes are actuated by single-piston sliding type calipers, which ensure that equal pressure is applied to each disc pad.

On models with rear drum brakes, the rear brakes incorporate leading and trailing shoes, which are actuated by twin-piston wheel cylinders. A self-adjust mechanism is incorporated, to compensate for brake shoe wear. The handbrake lever operates the rear shoes by two cables.

On models with rear disc brakes, the brakes are actuated by single-piston sliding calipers which incorporate mechanical handbrake mechanisms.

Precautions

• When servicing any part of the system, work carefully and methodically; also observe scrupulous cleanliness when overhauling any part of the hydraulic system. Always renew components in axle sets (where applicable) if in doubt about their condition, and use only genuine Skoda parts, or at least those of known good quality. Note the warnings given in *Safety first!* and at relevant points in this Chapter concerning the dangers of asbestos dust and hydraulic fluid.

2 Hydraulic system – bleeding

⚠ **Warning: Hydraulic fluid is poisonous; wash off immediately and thoroughly in the case of skin contact, and seek immediate medical advice if any fluid is swallowed or gets into the eyes. Certain types of hydraulic fluid are flammable, and may ignite when allowed into contact with hot components; when servicing any hydraulic system, it is safest to assume that the fluid is flammable, and to take precautions against the risk of fire as though it is petrol that is being handled. Hydraulic fluid is also an effective paint stripper, and will attack plastics; if any is spilt, it should be washed off immediately, using copious quantities of fresh water. Finally, it is hygroscopic (it absorbs moisture from the air) – old fluid may be contaminated and unfit for further use. When topping-up or renewing the fluid, always use the recommended type, and ensure that it comes from a freshly-opened sealed container.**
Note: *It is recommended that at least 0.25 litre of brake is expelled from each caliper.*

General

1 The correct operation of any hydraulic system is only possible after removing all air from the components and circuit; this is achieved by bleeding the system. Since the clutch hydraulic system also uses fluid from the brake system reservoir, it should also be bled at the same time by referring to Chapter 6, Section 2.

2 During the bleeding procedure, add only clean, unused hydraulic fluid of the recommended type; never re-use fluid that has already been bled from the system. Ensure that sufficient fluid is available before starting work.

3 If there is any possibility of incorrect fluid being already in the system, the brake components and circuit must be flushed completely with uncontaminated, correct fluid, and new seals should be fitted to the various components.

4 If hydraulic fluid has been lost from the system, or air has entered because of a leak, ensure that the fault is cured before continuing further.

5 Park the vehicle on level ground, then chock the wheels and release the handbrake.

6 Check that all pipes and hoses are secure, unions tight and bleed screws closed. Clean any dirt from around the bleed screws.

7 Unscrew the master cylinder reservoir cap, and top the reservoir up to the MAX level line; refit the cap loosely, and remember to maintain the fluid level at least above the MIN level line throughout the procedure, or there is a risk of further air entering the system.

8 There is a number of one-man, do-it-yourself brake bleeding kits currently available from motor accessory shops. It is recommended that one of these kits is used whenever possible, as they greatly simplify the bleeding

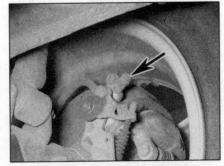

2.14 Remove the dust cap (arrowed) from the first screw in the sequence

operation, and reduce the risk of expelled air and fluid being drawn back into the system. If such a kit is not available, the basic (two-man) method must be used, which is described in detail below.

9 If a kit is to be used, prepare the vehicle as described previously, and follow the kit manufacturer's instructions, as the procedure may vary slightly according to the type being used; generally, they are as outlined below in the relevant sub-section.

10 Whichever method is used, the same sequence must be followed (paragraphs 11 and 12) to ensure the removal of all air from the system.

Bleeding sequence

11 If the system has been only partially disconnected, and suitable precautions were taken to minimise fluid loss, it should be necessary only to bleed that part of the system.

12 If the complete system is to be bled, then it should be done working in the following sequence:

Left-hand drive models
  a) *Right-hand rear brake.*
  b) *Left-hand rear brake.*
  c) *Right-hand front brake.*
  d) *Left-hand front brake.*

Right-hand drive models
  a) *Left-hand rear brake.*
  b) *Right-hand rear brake.*
  c) *Left-hand front brake.*
  d) *Right-hand front brake.*

Bleeding

Basic (two-man) method

13 Collect together a clean glass jar of reasonable size, a suitable length of plastic or rubber tubing which is a tight fit over the bleed screw, and a ring spanner to fit the screw. The help of an assistant will also be required.

14 Remove the dust cap from the first screw in the sequence **(see illustration)**. Fit the spanner and tube to the screw, place the other end of the tube in the jar, and pour in sufficient fluid to cover the end of the tube.

15 Ensure that the master cylinder reservoir fluid level is maintained at least above the MIN level line throughout the procedure.

16 Have the assistant fully depress the brake pedal several times to build-up pressure, then maintain it on the final downstroke.

17 While pedal pressure is maintained, unscrew the bleed screw (approximately one turn) and allow the compressed fluid and air to flow into the jar. The assistant should maintain pedal pressure, following it down to the floor if necessary, and should not release it until instructed to do so. When the flow stops, tighten the bleed screw again, have the assistant release the pedal slowly, and recheck the reservoir fluid level.

18 Repeat the steps given in paragraphs 16 and 17 until the fluid emerging from the bleed screw is free from air bubbles. If the master

2.22 Bleeding a brake using a one-way valve kit

cylinder has been drained and refilled, and air is being bled from the first screw in the sequence, allow approximately five seconds between cycles for the master cylinder passages to refill.

19 When no more air bubbles appear, tighten the bleed screw securely, remove the tube and spanner, and refit the dust cap. Do not overtighten the bleed screw.

20 Repeat the procedure on the remaining screws in the sequence, until all air is removed from the system and the brake pedal feels firm again.

Using a one-way valve kit

21 As their name implies, these kits consist of a length of tubing with a one-way valve fitted, to prevent expelled air and fluid being drawn back into the system; some kits include a translucent container, which can be positioned so that the air bubbles can be more easily seen flowing from the end of the tube.

22 The kit is connected to the bleed screw, which is then opened. The user returns to the driver's seat, depresses the brake pedal with a smooth, steady stroke, and slowly releases it; this is repeated until the expelled fluid is clear of air bubbles **(see illustration)**.

23 Note that these kits simplify work so much that it is easy to forget the master cylinder reservoir fluid level; ensure that this is maintained at least above the MIN level line at all times.

Using a pressure-bleeding kit

24 These kits are usually operated by the reservoir of pressurised air contained in the spare tyre. However, note that it will be

4.4a Remove the protective rubber caps . . .

probably necessary to reduce the pressure to less than 1.0 bar (14.5 psi); refer to the instructions supplied with the kit.

25 By connecting a pressurised, fluid-filled container to the master cylinder reservoir, bleeding can be carried out simply by opening each screw in turn (in the specified sequence), and allowing the fluid to flow out until no more air bubbles can be seen in the expelled fluid.

26 This method has the advantage that the large reservoir of fluid provides an additional safeguard against air being drawn into the system during bleeding.

27 Pressure-bleeding is particularly effective when bleeding 'difficult' systems, or when bleeding the complete system at the time of routine fluid renewal.

All methods

28 When bleeding is complete, and firm pedal feel is restored, wash off any spilt fluid, tighten the bleed screws securely, and refit their dust caps.

29 Check the hydraulic fluid level in the master cylinder reservoir, and top-up if necessary (see *Weekly checks*).

30 Discard any hydraulic fluid that has been bled from the system; it will not be fit for re-use.

31 Check the feel of the brake pedal. If it feels at all spongy, air must still be present in the system, and further bleeding is required. Failure to bleed satisfactorily after a reasonable repetition of the bleeding procedure may be due to worn master cylinder seals.

3 Hydraulic pipes and hoses – renewal

Note: *Refer to the note in Section 2 concerning the dangers of hydraulic fluid.*

1 If any pipe or hose is to be renewed, minimise fluid loss by first removing the master cylinder reservoir cap, then tightening it down onto a piece of polythene to obtain an airtight seal. Alternatively, flexible hoses can be sealed, if required, using a proprietary brake hose clamp; metal brake pipe unions can be plugged (if care is taken not to allow dirt into the system) or capped immediately they are disconnected. Place a wad of rag under any union that is to be disconnected, to catch any spilt fluid.

2 If a flexible hose is to be disconnected, where applicable unscrew the brake pipe union nut before removing the spring clip which secures the hose to its mounting bracket.

3 To unscrew the union nuts, it is preferable to obtain a brake pipe spanner of the correct size; these are available from most large motor accessory shops. Failing this, a close-fitting open-ended spanner will be required, though if the nuts are tight or corroded, their flats may be rounded-off if the spanner slips. In such a case, a self-locking wrench is often the only way to unscrew a stubborn union, but it follows

that the pipe and the damaged nuts must be renewed on reassembly. Always clean a union and surrounding area before disconnecting it. If disconnecting a component with more than one union, make a careful note of the connections before disturbing any of them.

4 If a brake pipe is to be renewed, it can be obtained, cut to length and with the union nuts and end flares in place, from Skoda dealers. All that is then necessary is to bend it to shape, following the line of the original, before fitting it to the car. Alternatively, most motor accessory shops can make up brake pipes from kits, but this requires very careful measurement of the original, to ensure that the new pipe is of the correct length. The safest answer is usually to take the original to the shop as a pattern.

5 On refitting, do not overtighten the union nuts. It is not necessary to exercise brute force to obtain a sound joint.

6 Ensure that the pipes and hoses are correctly routed, with no kinks, and that they are secured in the clips or brackets provided. After fitting, remove the polythene from the reservoir, and bleed the hydraulic system as described in Section 2. Wash off any spilt fluid, and check carefully for fluid leaks.

4 Front brake pads – removal, inspection and refitting

⚠️ *Warning: Renew both sets of brake pads at the same time – never renew the pads on only one wheel, as uneven braking may result. Note that the dust created by wear of the pads may contain asbestos, which is a health hazard. Never blow it out with compressed air, and do not inhale any of it. An approved filtering mask should be worn when working on the brakes. DO NOT use petrol or petroleum-based solvents to clean brake parts; use brake cleaner or methylated spirit only.*

FSII and FSIII calipers

Removal

1 Apply the handbrake, then jack up the front of the vehicle and support it on axle stands (see *Jacking and vehicle support*). Remove the front roadwheels.

2 Trace the brake pad wear sensor wiring (where fitted) back from the pads, and disconnect it from the wiring connector. Note the routing of the wiring, and free it from any relevant retaining clips.

3 Where applicable, to improve access, undo the retaining bolts and remove the air deflector shield from the caliper.

4 Remove the two protective rubber caps and, using a suitable hexagon key, loosen and remove the two caliper guide pins from the caliper **(see illustrations),** then lift the caliper together with the pads away from the hub carrier.

5 Remove the two brake pads from the caliper, noting their correct fitted locations.

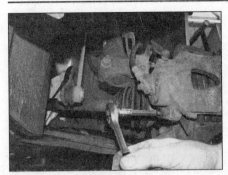

4.4b . . . then use an Allen key to unscrew . . .

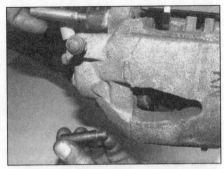

4.4c . . . and remove the two caliper guide pins

4.5a Remove the outer brake pad from the caliper cut-out . . .

The inner pad is retained in the caliper piston by a white clip, and the outer pad is retained in the caliper cut-out by a black clip. If the original pads are to be refitted, mark them so that they can be refitted in their original positions. Tie the caliper to the suspension strut or coil spring using a piece of wire. Do not allow the caliper to hang unsupported on the flexible brake hose **(see illustrations)**.

Inspection

6 First measure the thickness of the lining on each brake pad. If either pad is worn at any point to the specified minimum thickness or less, all four pads must be renewed. Also, the pads should be renewed if any are fouled with oil or grease; there is no satisfactory way of degreasing friction material, once contaminated. If any of the brake pads are worn unevenly, or are fouled with oil or grease, trace and rectify the cause before reassembly. New brake pad kits are available from Skoda dealers.

7 If the brake pads are still serviceable, carefully clean them using a clean, fine wire brush or similar, paying particular attention to the sides and back of the metal backing. Clean out the grooves in the friction material (where applicable), and pick out any large embedded particles of dirt or debris. Carefully clean the pad locations in the caliper body.

8 Prior to fitting the pads, check that the guide pins are free to slide easily in the caliper body bushes, and are a reasonably tight fit. Brush the dust and dirt from the caliper and piston, but *do not* inhale it, as it is injurious to health. Inspect the dust seal around the piston for

4.5b . . . then remove the inner brake pad from the caliper piston

damage, and the piston for evidence of fluid leaks, corrosion or damage. If attention to any of these components is necessary, refer to Section 5.

Refitting

9 If new brake pads are to be fitted, the caliper piston must be pushed back into the cylinder to make room for them. Either use a G-clamp or similar tool, or use suitable pieces of wood as levers. To avoid any dirt entering the ABS solenoid valves, connect a pipe to the bleed nipple and, as the piston is pushed back, open the nipple and allow the displaced fluid to flow through the pipe into a suitable container **(see illustration)**.

10 Fit the new pads to the caliper. The inboard pad is marked 'piston side' with a white clip which must be located in the piston. The outboard pad has a black clip which must be located in the outer cut-out of the caliper.

11 Apply a little high melting point grease to

4.5c Tie the caliper to the suspension strut or coil spring

the caliper lower mounting lug, then position the caliper and pads over the disc and onto the hub carrier, ensuring that the lower lug engages correctly **(see illustrations)**. Pass the pad warning sensor wiring (where fitted) through the caliper aperture.

12 Press the caliper into position sufficiently until it is possible to install the caliper guide pins. Tighten the guide pins to the specified torque, then refit the protective rubber caps.

13 Where applicable, reconnect the brake pad wear sensor wiring connectors, ensuring that the wiring is correctly routed. Where applicable, refit the air deflector shield to the caliper.

14 Depress the brake pedal repeatedly, until the pads are pressed into firm contact with the brake disc, and normal (non-assisted) pedal pressure is restored.

4.11b . . . then locate the caliper and pads over the disc and onto the hub carrier. Check that the caliper is correctly located on the lower mounting lug

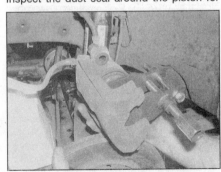

4.9 Open the bleed nipple as the piston is pushed back into the caliper

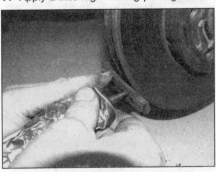

4.11a Apply a little high melting-point grease to the lower mounting lug . . .

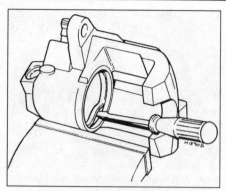

5.8 Use a small screwdriver to extract the caliper piston hydraulic seal

15 Repeat the above procedure on the remaining front brake caliper.
16 Refit the roadwheels, then lower the vehicle to the ground and tighten the roadwheel bolts to the specified torque.
17 New pads will not give full braking efficiency until they have bedded-in. Be prepared for this, and avoid hard braking as far as possible for the first hundred miles or so after pad renewal.

C54-II caliper

Removal

18 Apply the handbrake, then jack up the front of the vehicle and support it on axle stands (see *Jacking and vehicle support*). Remove the front roadwheels.
19 Slacken and remove the lower caliper guide pin bolt, using a slim open-ended spanner to prevent the guide pin itself from rotating. Discard the guide pin bolt – a new bolt must be used on refitting.
20 With the lower guide pin bolt removed, pivot the caliper upwards until it is clear of the brake pads and mounting bracket. If it is loose, recover the heat shield from the caliper piston.
21 Withdraw the two brake pads from the caliper mounting bracket.

Inspection

22 Refer to paragraphs 6, 7 and 8. Clean and examine the pad retaining springs in the mounting bracket. If they are damaged or distorted, renew them.

Refitting

23 Install the pads in the caliper mounting bracket, ensuring that the friction material of each pad is against the brake disc. Note the pad with the wear sensor wiring should be installed as the inner pad.
24 If removed, refit the heat shield to the caliper piston. **Note:** *A new heat shield is supplied with genuine replacement Skoda pads.* Pivot the caliper down into position, and pass the pad warning sensor wiring through the caliper aperture. If the threads of the new guide pin bolt are not already precoated with locking compound, apply a suitable thread-locking compound to them. Install the lower guide pin bolt, tightening it to the specified

torque setting while retaining the guide pin with an open-ended spanner.
25 Depress the brake pedal repeatedly, until the pads are pressed into firm contact with the brake disc, and normal (non-assisted) pedal pressure is restored.
26 Repeat the above procedure on the remaining front brake caliper.
27 Refit the roadwheels, then lower the vehicle to the ground and tighten the roadwheel bolts to the specified torque.
28 New pads will not give full braking efficiency until they have bedded-in. Be prepared for this, and avoid hard braking as far as possible for the first hundred miles or so after pad renewal.

5 Front brake caliper –
removal, overhaul and refitting

Note: *Before starting work, refer to the note at the beginning of Section 2 concerning the dangers of hydraulic fluid, and to the warning at the beginning of Section 4 concerning the dangers of asbestos dust.*

Removal

1 Apply the handbrake, then jack up the front of the vehicle and support it on axle stands (see *Jacking and vehicle support*). Remove the appropriate roadwheel.
2 Minimise fluid loss by first removing the master cylinder reservoir cap, and then tightening it down onto a piece of polythene, to obtain an airtight seal. Alternatively, use a brake hose clamp, a G-clamp or a similar tool to clamp the flexible hose.
3 Clean the area around the union, then loosen the brake hose union nut.
4 Remove the brake pads as described in Section 4, but on the C54-II caliper, unscrew the upper guide pin bolt.
5 Unscrew the caliper from the end of the brake hose and remove it from the vehicle.

Overhaul

6 With the caliper on the bench, wipe away all traces of dust and dirt, but *avoid inhaling the dust, as it is injurious to health.*

 HAYNES HINT *If the piston cannot be withdrawn by hand, it can be pushed out by applying compressed air to the brake hose union hole. Only low pressure should be required, such as is generated by a foot pump. As the piston is expelled, take great care not to trap your fingers between the piston and caliper.*

7 Withdraw the partially-ejected piston from the caliper body, and remove the dust seal.
8 Using a small screwdriver, extract the piston hydraulic seal, taking great care not to damage the caliper bore **(see illustration)**.

9 Thoroughly clean all components, using only methylated spirit, isopropyl alcohol or clean hydraulic fluid as a cleaning medium. Never use mineral-based solvents such as petrol or paraffin, as they will attack the hydraulic system rubber components. Dry the components immediately, using compressed air or a clean, lint-free cloth. Use compressed air to blow clear the fluid passages.
10 Check all components, and renew any that are worn or damaged. Check particularly the cylinder bore and piston; these should be renewed if they are scratched, worn or corroded in any way (note that this means the renewal of the complete caliper body assembly). Similarly check the condition of the guide pins and their bushes; both pins should be undamaged and a reasonably tight sliding fit in their bores. If there is any doubt about the condition of any component, renew it.
11 If the assembly is fit for further use, obtain the appropriate repair kit; the components are available from Skoda dealers in various combinations.
12 Renew all rubber seals, dust covers and caps disturbed on dismantling as a matter of course; these should never be re-used.
13 On reassembly, ensure that all components are clean and dry.
14 Thinly coat the piston and piston seal with brake fitting paste (Skoda no G 052 150 A2). This should be included in the Skoda caliper overhaul/repair kit.
15 Fit the new piston (fluid) seal, using only your fingers (no tools) to manipulate it into the cylinder bore groove. Fit the new dust seal to the piston, and refit the piston to the cylinder bore using a twisting motion; ensure that the piston enters squarely into the bore. Press the piston fully into the bore, then press the dust seal into the caliper body.

Refitting

16 Screw the caliper fully onto the flexible hose union.
17 Refit the brake pads as described in Section 4. On the C54-II caliper, also tighten the upper guide pin bolt.
18 Securely tighten the brake hose union nut.
19 Remove the brake hose clamp or polythene, as applicable, and bleed the hydraulic system as described in Section 2. Note that, providing the precautions described were taken to minimise brake fluid loss, it should only be necessary to bleed the relevant front brake.
20 Refit the roadwheel, then lower the vehicle to the ground and tighten the roadwheel bolts to the specified torque.

6 Brake disc –
inspection, removal and refitting

Note: *Before starting work, refer to the note at the beginning of Section 4 concerning the dangers of asbestos dust. If either disc*

6.4 Using a DTI gauge to measure disc run-out

6.8 Undo the disc retaining screw

6.13 Lift away the disc

requires renewal, BOTH should be renewed at the same time, to ensure even and consistent braking. New brake pads should also be fitted.

Front brake disc

Inspection

1 Apply the handbrake, then jack up the front of the car and support it on axle stands (see *Jacking and vehicle support*). Remove the appropriate front roadwheel.
2 Slowly rotate the brake disc so that the full area of both sides can be checked; remove the brake pads if better access is required to the inboard surface. Light scoring is normal in the area swept by the brake pads, but if heavy scoring or cracks are found, the disc must be renewed.
3 It is normal to find a lip of rust and brake dust around the perimeter of the disc; this can be scraped off if required. If, however, a lip has formed due to excessive wear of the brake pad swept area, then the disc thickness must be measured using a micrometer. Take measurements at several places around the disc, at the inside and outside of the pad swept area; if the disc has worn at any point to the specified minimum thickness or less, the disc must be renewed.
4 If the disc is thought to be warped, it can be checked for run-out. Either use a dial gauge mounted on any convenient fixed point, while the disc is slowly rotated, or use feeler blades to measure (at several points all around the disc) the clearance between the disc and a fixed point, such as the caliper mounting bracket. If the measurements obtained are at the specified maximum or beyond, the disc is excessively warped, and must be renewed; however, it is worth checking first that the hub bearing is in good condition (Chapter 1A or 1B, as appropriate). If the run-out is excessive, the disc must be renewed **(see illustration)**.
5 Check the disc for cracks, especially around the wheel bolt holes, and any other wear or damage, and renew if necessary.

Removal

6 Remove the brake pads as described in Section 4.
7 On models with the C54-II caliper, unscrew and remove the caliper upper guide pin bolt, then use a piece of wire or string to tie the caliper to the front suspension coil spring, to avoid placing any strain on the brake hose. Unscrew the two bolts securing the brake caliper mounting bracket to the hub carrier, and remove the bracket.
8 Use paint to mark the relationship of the disc to the hub, then remove the screw securing the brake disc to the hub, and remove the disc **(see illustration)**. If it is tight, apply penetrating fluid, and tap its rear face with a hide or plastic mallet, but bear in mind that the use of excessive force could damage the disc.

Refitting

9 Refitting is the reverse of the removal procedure, noting the following points:
 a) Ensure that the mating surfaces of the disc and hub are clean.
 b) Align the marks made on removal, and securely tighten the disc retaining screw.
 c) If a new disc has been fitted, use a suitable solvent to wipe any preservative coating from the disc, before refitting the caliper.
 d) On models with the C54-II brake caliper, tighten the bracket mounting bolts to the specified torque.
 e) Fit the pads as described in Section 4.
 f) Refit the roadwheel, then lower the vehicle to the ground and tighten the roadwheel bolts to the specified torque. On completion, repeatedly depress the brake pedal until normal (non-assisted) pedal pressure returns.

Rear brake disc

Inspection

10 Firmly chock the front wheels, then jack up the rear of the car and support it on axle stands. Remove the appropriate rear roadwheel.
11 Inspect the disc as described in paragraphs 2 to 5.

Removal

12 Unscrew the two bolts securing the brake caliper mounting bracket in position, then slide the caliper assembly off the disc. Using a piece of wire or string, tie the caliper to the rear suspension coil spring, to avoid placing any strain on the hydraulic brake hose.
13 Use paint to mark the relationship of the disc to the hub, then remove the screw securing the brake disc to the hub, and remove the disc **(see illustration)**. If it is tight, apply penetrating fluid, and tap its rear face gently with a hide or plastic mallet. The use of excessive force could cause the disc to be damaged.

Refitting

14 Refitting is a reversal of the removal procedure, noting the following points:
 a) Ensure that the mating surfaces of the disc and hub are clean and flat.
 b) Align (if applicable) the marks made on removal, and securely tighten the disc retaining screw.
 c) If a new disc has been fitted, use a suitable solvent to wipe any preservative coating from the disc, before refitting the caliper.
 d) Slide the caliper into position over the disc, making sure the pads pass either side of the disc. Tighten the caliper bracket mounting bolts to the specified torque. If new discs have been fitted and there is insufficient clearance between the pads to accommodate the new, thicker disc, it may be necessary to push the piston back into the caliper body as described in Section 8.
 e) Refit the roadwheel, then lower the vehicle to the ground and tighten the roadwheel bolts to the specified torque. On completion, repeatedly depress the brake pedal until normal (non-assisted) pedal pressure returns.

7 Front brake disc shield – removal and refitting

Removal

1 Remove the brake disc as described in Section 6.
2 Unscrew the securing bolts, and remove the brake disc shield.

Refitting

3 Refitting is a reversal of removal. Tighten the shield retaining bolts to the specified torque. Refit the brake disc with reference to Section 6.

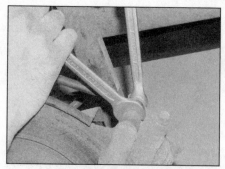

8.4 Counterhold the guide pins

8.5 Remove the caliper

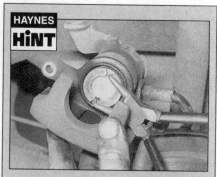

In the absence of the special tool, the piston can be screwed back into the caliper using a pair of circlip pliers.

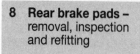

8 Rear brake pads – removal, inspection and refitting

Note: *Before starting work, refer to the note at the beginning of Section 4 concerning the dangers of asbestos dust. New caliper guide pin bolts will be required on refitting.*

Removal

1 Chock the front wheels, then jack up the rear of the vehicle and support it on axle stands (see *Jacking and vehicle support*). Remove the rear wheels.
2 Where applicable, disconnect the pad wear wiring at the plug.
3 Extract the clip securing the outer handbrake cable to the caliper, then push down the lever and disconnect the inner cable. Pull the handbrake cable from the caliper.
4 Slacken and remove the guide pin bolts, using a slim open-ended spanner to prevent the guide pins from rotating **(see illustration)**. Discard the bolts – new ones must be used on refitting.
5 Lift the caliper away from the brake pads, and tie it to the suspension strut using a suitable piece of wire **(see illustration)**. Do not allow the caliper to hang unsupported on the flexible brake hose.
6 Withdraw the two brake pads from the caliper mounting bracket and recover the location spring clips from the mounting bracket, noting their correct fitted locations.

Inspection

7 First measure the thickness of each brake

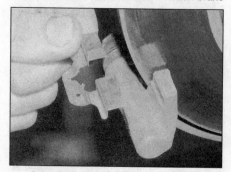

8.11 Refit the location spring clips

pad (including the backing plate). If either pad is worn at any point to the specified minimum thickness or less, **all four** pads must be renewed. Also, the pads should be renewed if any are fouled with oil or grease; there is no satisfactory way of degreasing friction material, once contaminated. If any of the brake pads are worn unevenly, or fouled with oil or grease, trace and rectify the cause before reassembly. New brake pads are available from Skoda dealers.
8 If the brake pads are still serviceable, carefully clean them using a clean, fine wire brush or similar, paying particular attention to the sides and back of the metal backing. Clean out the grooves in the friction material (where applicable), and pick out any large embedded particles of dirt or debris. Carefully clean the pad locations in the caliper mounting bracket.
9 Prior to fitting the pads, check that the guide pins are free to slide easily in the caliper bracket, and check that the rubber guide pin gaiters are undamaged. Brush the dust and dirt from the caliper and piston, but **do not** inhale it, as it is injurious to health. Inspect the dust seal around the piston for damage, and the piston for evidence of fluid leaks, corrosion or damage. If attention to any of these components is necessary, refer to Section 9.

Refitting

10 If new brake pads are to be fitted, it will be necessary to retract the piston fully, by rotating it in a clockwise direction as it is pushed into the caliper bore **(see Haynes Hint)**. To avoid any dirt entering the ABS solenoid valves, connect a pipe to the bleed nipple, and as the

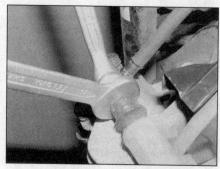

8.12 Hold the guide pin whilst tightening the retaining bolt

piston is pushed back open the nipple and allow the displaced fluid to flow through the pipe into a suitable container.
11 Fit the location spring clips to the caliper mounting bracket, ensuring that they are correctly located. Install the pads in the mounting bracket, ensuring that each pad's friction material is against the brake disc. Remove the protective foil from the outer pad backing plate **(see illustration)**.
12 Slide the caliper fully into position over the pads, then refit the new guide pin bolts, tightening them to the specified torque setting while retaining the guide pin with an open-ended spanner **(see illustration)**.
13 Depress the brake pedal repeatedly, until the pads are pressed into firm contact with the brake disc, and normal (non-assisted) pedal pressure is restored.
14 Repeat the above procedure on the remaining rear brake caliper. Where applicable, reconnect the pad wear wiring.
15 Reconnect the handbrake cables to the calipers, and adjust the handbrake as described in Section 17.
16 Refit the roadwheels, then lower the vehicle to the ground and tighten the roadwheel bolts to the specified torque setting.
17 Check the hydraulic fluid level as described in *Weekly checks*.
18 New pads will not give full braking efficiency until they have bedded-in. Be prepared for this, and avoid hard braking as far as possible for the first hundred miles or so after pad renewal.

9 Rear brake caliper – removal, overhaul and refitting

Note: *Before starting work, refer to the note at the beginning of Section 2 concerning the dangers of hydraulic fluid, and to the warning at the beginning of Section 4 concerning the dangers of asbestos dust.*

Removal

1 Chock the front wheels, then jack up the rear of the vehicle and support on axle stands (see *Jacking and vehicle support*). Remove the relevant rear wheel.

2 Minimise fluid loss by first removing the master cylinder reservoir cap, and then tightening it down onto a piece of polythene, to obtain an airtight seal. Alternatively, use a brake hose clamp, a G-clamp or a similar tool to clamp the flexible hose.

3 Clean the area around the union on the caliper, then unscrew the brake hose union bolt.

4 Remove the brake pads as described in Section 8.

5 Withdraw the caliper and remove it from the vehicle.

Overhaul

Note: *It is not possible to overhaul the brake caliper handbrake mechanism. If the mechanism is faulty, or fluid is leaking from the handbrake lever seal, the caliper assembly must be renewed.*

6 With the caliper on the bench, wipe away all traces of dust and dirt, but avoid inhaling the dust, as it is injurious to health.

7 Using a small screwdriver, carefully prise out the dust seal from the caliper, taking care not to damage the piston.

8 Remove the piston from the caliper bore by rotating it in an anti-clockwise direction. This can be achieved using a suitable pair of circlip pliers engaged in the caliper piston slots. Once the piston turns freely but does not come out any further, the piston can be withdrawn by hand.

 HAYNES HINT *If the piston cannot be withdrawn by hand, it can be pushed out by applying compressed air to the brake hose union hole. Only low pressure should be required, such as is generated by a foot pump. As the piston is expelled, take care not to trap your fingers between the piston and caliper.*

9 Using a small screwdriver, extract the piston hydraulic seal, taking care not to damage the caliper bore.

10 Withdraw the guide pins from the caliper, and remove the guide sleeve gaiters.

11 Thoroughly clean all components, using only methylated spirit, isopropyl alcohol or clean hydraulic fluid as a cleaning medium. Never use mineral-based solvents such as petrol or paraffin, as they will attack the hydraulic system rubber components. Dry the components immediately, using compressed air or a clean, lint-free cloth. Use compressed air to blow clear the fluid passages.

12 Check all components, and renew any that are worn or damaged. Check particularly the cylinder bore and piston; these should be renewed (note that this means the renewal of the complete caliper body assembly) if they are scratched, worn or corroded in any way. Similarly check the condition of the guide pins and their bores; both pins should be undamaged and a reasonably tight sliding fit in their bores. If there is any doubt about the condition of any component, renew it.

13 If the assembly is fit for further use, obtain the appropriate repair kit; the components are available from Skoda dealers in various combinations.

14 Renew all rubber seals, dust covers and caps disturbed on dismantling as a matter of course; these should never be re-used.

15 On reassembly, ensure that all components are clean and dry.

16 Smear a thin coat of brake fitting paste (Skoda part no G 052 150 A2) on the piston, seal and caliper bore. This should be included in the overhaul/repair kit. Fit the new piston (fluid) seal, using only the fingers (no tools) to manipulate into the cylinder bore groove.

17 Fit the new dust seal to the piston groove, then refit the piston assembly. Turn the piston in a clockwise direction, using the method employed on dismantling, until it is fully retracted into the caliper bore.

18 Press the dust seal into position in the caliper housing.

19 Apply the grease supplied in the repair kit, or a copper-based brake grease or anti-seize compound, to the guide pins. Fit the new gaiters to the guide pins and fit the pins to the caliper ensuring that the gaiters are correctly located in the grooves on both the pins and caliper.

20 Prior to refitting, fill the caliper with fresh hydraulic fluid by slackening the bleed screw

and pumping the fluid through the caliper until bubble-free fluid is expelled from the union hole.

Refitting

21 Refit the brake pads as described in Section 8.

22 Refit the brake hose union bolt and tighten it.

23 Remove the brake hose clamp or remove the polythene from the fluid reservoir, as applicable, and bleed the hydraulic system as described in Section 2. Note that, providing the precautions described were taken to minimise brake fluid loss, it should only be necessary to bleed the relevant rear brake.

24 Adjust the handbrake as described in Section 17.

25 Refit the roadwheel, then lower the vehicle to the ground and tighten the roadwheel bolts to the specified torque. On completion, check the hydraulic fluid level as described in *Weekly checks*.

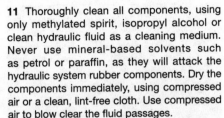

10 Rear brake drum – removal, inspection and refitting

Note: *Before starting work, refer to the warning at the beginning of Section 4 concerning the dangers of asbestos dust.*

Removal

1 Remove the wheel trim (where applicable), then loosen the rear roadwheel bolts and chock the front wheels. Jack up the rear of the vehicle, and support on axle stands positioned under the body side members (see *Jacking and vehicle support*). Remove the roadwheel.

2 Fully release the handbrake.

3 Extract the drum securing screw and remove the drum. The drum may be tight due to the brake shoes binding on the inner circumference of the drum. If this is the case, insert a screwdriver through one of the wheel bolt holes in the brake drum and hub, and lever up the wedge key in order to allow the brake shoes to retract fully. The wedge key is located beneath the front of the wheel cylinder **(see illustrations)**. The brake drum can now be withdrawn.

10.3a Rear brake drum securing screw

10.3b If the drum is tight, insert a screwdriver in through one of the wheel bolt holes . . .

10.3c . . . and lever up on the wedge key to fully retract the brake shoes (shown with drum removed for clarity)

10.3d Removing the rear brake drum

10.6 The maximum diameter of the drum is stamped on its inner surface

11.5 Note the position of the brake shoes before dismantling them

Inspection

Note: *If either drum requires renewal, BOTH should be renewed at the same time, to ensure even and consistent braking. New brake shoes should also be fitted.*

4 Brush the dust and dirt from the drum, taking care not to inhale it.

5 Examine the internal friction surface of the drum. If deeply scored, or so worn that the drum has become ridged to the width of the shoes, then both drums must be renewed.

6 Regrinding of the friction surface may be possible provided the maximum diameter given in the Specifications and on the drum itself is not exceeded **(see illustration)**.

Refitting

7 If a new brake drum is to be fitted, use a suitable solvent to remove any preservative

11.7 Release the shoe retainer spring cup by depressing it and rotate through 90°, then lift off the spring and remove the retainer pin . . .

coating that may have been applied to its interior. Prior to refitting the drum, fully retract the brake shoes by lifting up the wedge key.

8 Refit the brake drum and tighten the securing screw.

9 Adjust the brakes by operating the footbrake a number of times. A clicking noise will be heard at the drum as the automatic adjuster operates. When the clicking stops, adjustment is complete.

10 Refit the roadwheel and lower the vehicle to the ground.

11 Repeat the above procedure on the remaining rear brake assembly, then check and, if necessary, adjust the handbrake cable (see Section 17).

12 On completion, refit the roadwheels, then lower the vehicle to the ground and tighten the wheel bolts to the specified torque.

11 Rear brake shoes – removal, inspection and refitting

Note: *Refer to the warning at the start of Section 4 before starting work.*

1 Remove the brake drum (see Section 10), then carefully remove all traces of brake dust from the brake drum, backplate and shoes.

2 Measure the thickness of the friction material of each brake shoe at several points; if either shoe is worn at any point to the specified minimum thickness or less, **all four** shoes must be renewed as a set. The shoes should also be renewed if any are fouled with oil or grease; there is no way of degreasing friction material, once contaminated.

3 If any of the brake shoes are worn unevenly, or fouled with oil or grease, trace and rectify the cause before reassembly.

4 To renew the brake shoes, continue as follows. If all is well, refit the brake drum as described in Section 10.

5 Note the position of the brake shoes and springs, and mark the webs of the shoes, if necessary, to aid refitting **(see illustration)**.

6 To facilitate easy removal and refitting of the brake shoes, we found it necessary to remove the hub first (see Chapter 10), although this may not be necessary on some models.

7 Using a pair of pliers, remove the shoe retainer spring cups by depressing and turning them through 90°. With the cups removed, lift off the springs and withdraw the retainer pins **(see illustration)**.

8 Ease the shoes out one at a time from the lower pivot point, to release the tension of the return spring, then disconnect the lower return spring from both shoes **(see illustrations)**.

9 Ease the upper end of both shoes out from their wheel cylinder locations, taking care not to damage the wheel cylinder seals, and disconnect the handbrake cable from the trailing shoe. The brake shoe assembly can then be manoeuvred out of position and away from the backplate. Do not depress the brake pedal until the brakes are reassembled; wrap a strong elastic band or fit a cable tie around the wheel cylinder pistons to retain them **(see illustrations)**.

10 Make a note of the correct fitted positions of all components, then unhook the upper return spring, and disengage the wedge key spring **(see illustration)**.

11.8a Ease the shoes out from the lower pivot point . . .

11.8b . . . and detach the lower return spring

11.9a Ease the upper ends of the shoes from their wheel cylinder locations . . .

11 Unhook the upper return spring and remove the trailing shoe from the leading shoe and strut. A length of bent welding rod may be used to unhook the spring **(see illustrations)**.
12 Withdraw the wedge key, noting which way around it is fitted, then ease the strut out from the leading shoe and detach the tensioning spring. If necessary, mount the strut in a vice, and use the length of bent welding rod to remove the spring **(see illustrations)**.
13 Examine all components for signs of wear or damage, and renew as necessary.
14 Peel back the rubber protective caps, and check the wheel cylinder for fluid leaks or other damage; check that both cylinder pistons are free to move easily. Refer to Section 12, if necessary, for information on wheel cylinder overhaul.
15 Apply a little brake grease to the contact areas of the pushrod and handbrake lever.
16 Hook the tensioning spring into the leading shoe. Engage the strut with the opposite end of the spring, and pivot the strut into position into the leading shoe slot.
17 Insert the wedge key between the leading shoe and pushrod, making sure it is fitted the correct way around **(see illustration)**.
18 Fit the upper return spring to the leading shoe and engage the spring in its hole in the trailing shoe **(see illustration)**. Ensure the spring is correctly fitted then pivot the trailing shoe into position making sure both the shoe and handbrake lever are correctly engaged with the strut.
19 Fit the spring to the wedge key, and hook it onto the trailing shoe.

11.9b . . . then disconnect the handbrake cable and remove the shoe assembly from the vehicle

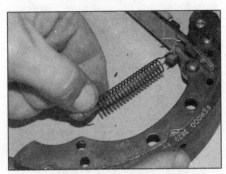

11.10 Unhook the adjuster wedge key spring and remove it

20 Prior to installation, clean the backplate, and apply a thin smear of high-temperature brake grease or anti-seize compound to the shoe contact areas **(see illustration)**, and to the wheel cylinder pistons and lower pivot

11.9c Use a cable tie or elastic band to retain the wheel cylinder pistons

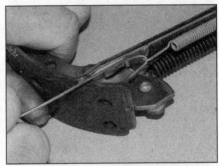

11.11a Using a length of bent welding rod to unhook the upper return spring

point. Do not allow the lubricant to foul the friction material.
21 Remove the elastic band or cable tie fitted to the wheel cylinder, and offer up the shoe assembly.

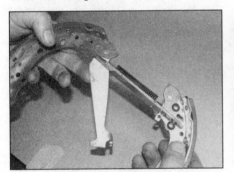

11.11b Remove the trailing shoe from the leading shoe and strut

11.12a Mount the strut in a vice, and use welding rod to unhook the tensioning spring

11.12b Remove the wedge key and unhook the spring . . .

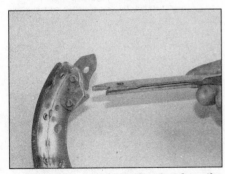

11.12c . . . then separate the strut from the leading shoe

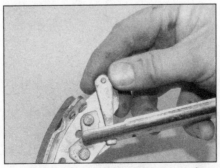

11.17 Insert the wedge key into position ensuring its peg is facing away from the shoe

11.18 Refitting the upper return spring

22 Connect the handbrake cable to the handbrake lever, and locate the top of the shoes in the wheel cylinder piston slots.
23 Fit the lower return spring to the shoes, then lever the bottom of the shoes onto the bottom anchor.
24 Tap the shoes to centralise them with the backplate, then refit the shoe retainer pins and springs, and secure them in position with the spring cups.
25 Refit the hub and brake drum as described in Section 10.
26 Repeat the above procedure on the remaining rear brake.
27 Once both sets of rear shoes have been renewed, adjust the lining-to-drum clearance by repeatedly depressing the brake pedal until normally (non-assisted) pedal pressure returns.
28 Check and, if necessary, adjust the handbrake as described in Section 17.
29 On completion, check the hydraulic fluid level as described in *Weekly checks*.

> **HAYNES HiNT** *New shoes will not give full braking efficiency until they have bedded-in. Be prepared for this, and avoid hard braking as far as possible for the first hundred miles or so after shoe renewal.*

12 Rear wheel cylinder – removal, overhaul and refitting

Note: *Before starting work, refer to the note at the beginning of Section 2 concerning the dangers of hydraulic fluid, and to the*

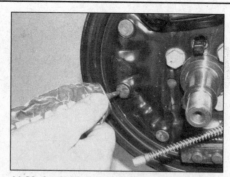

11.20 Apply high-temperature brake grease to the shoe contact areas on the backplate

warning at the beginning of Section 4 concerning the dangers of asbestos dust.

Removal

1 Remove the brake drum (see Section 10).
2 Using pliers, carefully unhook the upper brake shoe return spring, and remove it from both brake shoes. Pull the upper ends of the shoes away from the wheel cylinder to disengage them from the pistons.
3 Minimise fluid loss by first removing the master cylinder reservoir cap, and then tightening it down onto a piece of polythene, to obtain an airtight seal. Alternatively, use a brake hose clamp, a G-clamp or a similar tool to clamp the flexible hose at the nearest convenient point to the wheel cylinder.
4 Wipe away all traces of dirt around the brake pipe union at the rear of the wheel cylinder, and unscrew the union nut. Carefully ease the pipe out of the wheel cylinder, and plug or tape over its end to prevent dirt entry. Wipe off any spilt immediately.
5 Unscrew the two wheel cylinder retaining bolts from the rear of the backplate, and

remove the cylinder, taking great care not to allow surplus hydraulic fluid to contaminate the brake shoe linings.

Overhaul

6 Brush the dirt and dust from the wheel cylinder, but take care not to inhale it.
7 Pull the rubber dust seals from the ends of the cylinder body **(see illustration)**.
8 The pistons will normally be ejected by the pressure of the coil spring, but if they are not, tap the end of the cylinder body on a piece of wood, or apply low air pressure – eg, from a foot pump – to the hydraulic fluid union hole to eject the pistons from their bores.
9 Inspect the surfaces of the pistons and their bores in the cylinder body for scoring, or evidence of metal-to-metal contact. If evident, renew the complete wheel cylinder assembly.
10 If the pistons and bores are in good condition, discard the seals and obtain a repair kit, which will contain all the necessary renewable items.
11 Remove the seals from the pistons noting their correct fitted orientation. Lubricate the new piston seals with clean brake fluid, and fit them onto the pistons with their larger diameters innermost.
12 Dip the pistons in clean brake fluid, then fit the spring to the cylinder.
13 Insert the pistons into the cylinder bores using a twisting motion.
14 Fit the dust seals, and check that the pistons can move freely in their bores.

Refitting

15 Ensure that the backplate and wheel cylinder mating surfaces are clean, then spread the brake shoes and manoeuvre the wheel cylinder into position. Engage the brake pipe, and screw in the union nut two or three turns to ensure that the thread has started.
16 Insert the two wheel cylinder retaining bolts, and tighten them to the specified torque. Now fully tighten the brake pipe union nut.
17 Remove the clamp from the flexible brake hose, or the polythene from the master cylinder reservoir (as applicable).
18 Ensure that the brake shoes are correctly located in the cylinder pistons, then refit the brake shoe upper return spring, using a screwdriver to stretch the spring into position.
19 Refit the brake drum (see Section 10).
20 Bleed the brake hydraulic system as described in Section 2. Providing suitable precautions were taken to minimise loss of fluid, it should only be necessary to bleed the relevant rear brake.

13 Brake pedal – removal and refitting

Removal

1 Disconnect the battery negative lead (refer to *Disconnecting the battery* in the *Reference* Chapter at the end of this manual).

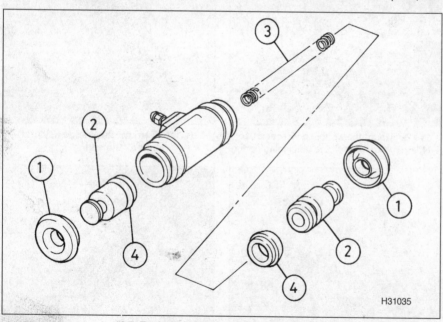

12.7 Exploded view of a rear wheel cylinder

1 Dust seal	*2 Piston*	*3 Coil spring*	*4 Fluid seal*

H31035

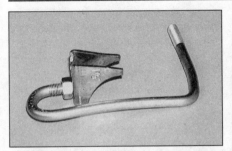

13.5a Improvised special tool constructed from a modified exhaust clamp, used to release the brake pedal from the servo pushrod

13.5b Using the tool to release the brake pedal from the servo pushrod

13.5c Rear view of the brake pedal (pedal removed) showing plastic lugs (arrowed) securing pedal to servo pushrod

2 With reference to Chapter 11, remove the driver's side lower facia trim panels, and the trim panel below the dash.

3 Where fitted, remove the convenience system central control unit from its location above the accelerator pedal with reference to Chapter 12.

4 Remove the brake light switch as described in Section 21, then disconnect the wiring from the pedal position sender.

5 It is now necessary to release the brake pedal from the ball on the vacuum servo pushrod. To do this, a Skoda special tool is available, but a suitable alternative can be improvised. Note that the plastic lugs in the pedal are very stiff, and it will not be possible to release them by hand. Using the tool, release the securing lugs, and pull the pedal from the servo pushrod **(see illustrations)**.

6 If removing the pedal bracket support, undo and remove the retaining nut **(see illustration)**.

7 Where necessary, unscrew the nuts securing the pedal support bracket to the bulkhead/servo sufficiently to allow the bracket some movement. Do not remove the nuts completely **(see illustration)**.

8 Undo the pivot shaft nut and slide the pivot shaft to the right, until the pedal is free. Remove the pedal and recover the pivot bush **(see illustration)**.

9 Carefully clean all components, and renew any that are worn or damaged.

Refitting

10 Prior to refitting, apply a smear of multi-purpose grease to the pivot shaft and pedal bearing surfaces.

11 Using a screwdriver, lever the pedal bracket away from the bulkhead **(see illustration)**.

12 Pull the servo unit pushrod down, and at the same time manoeuvre the pedal into position, ensuring that the pivot bush is correctly located.

13 Tighten the pedal bracket retaining nuts securely, and refit the bracket support retaining nut.

14 Hold the servo unit pushrod, and push the pedal back onto the pushrod ball. Make sure the pedal is securely fastened to the pushrod.

15 Insert the pedal pivot bolt and tighten the retaining nut to the specified torque.

16 Reconnect the wiring to the pedal position

sender, then refit the brake light switch as described in Section 21.

17 Where fitted, refit the convenience system central control unit.

18 Refit the facia trim panels as described in Chapter 11.

19 Reconnect the battery negative lead (refer to *Disconnecting the battery* in the *Reference* Chapter at the end of this manual).

14 Master cylinder – removal, overhaul and refitting

Note: *Before starting work, refer to the warning at the beginning of Section 2 concerning the dangers of hydraulic fluid. A new master cylinder O-ring will be required on refitting.*

Removal

1 Remove the engine top cover, then remove

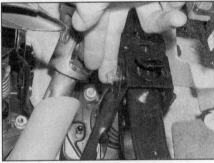

13.6 Undo the support bracket nut

13.8 Recover the pivot bush

the air inlet ducts as necessary from the rear of the engine compartment (refer to the relevant part of Chapter 4).

2 Remove the battery and battery tray as described in Chapter 5A.

3 Remove the master cylinder reservoir cap (disconnect the wiring plug from the brake fluid level sender unit), and syphon the hydraulic fluid from the reservoir. **Note:** *Do not syphon the fluid by mouth, as it is poisonous; use a syringe or an old poultry baster.*

4 Release the vacuum hose from the clip on the brake fluid reservoir.

5 Wipe clean the area around the brake pipe unions on the side of the master cylinder, and place absorbent rags beneath the pipe unions to catch any leaking fluid. Make a note of the correct fitted positions of the unions, then unscrew the union nuts and carefully withdraw the pipes. Plug or tape over the pipe ends and master cylinder orifices, to minimise the

13.7 Slacken the five securing nuts

13.11 Lever the bracket away from the bulkhead

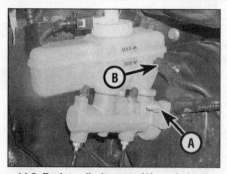

14.8 Brake cylinder nuts (A), and clutch cylinder supply hose (B)

loss of brake fluid, and to prevent the entry of dirt into the system. Wash off any spilt fluid immediately with cold water.

6 Disconnect and plug the clutch master cylinder supply hose from the brake fluid reservoir.

7 On vehicles equipped with ESP (Electronic Stability Program – see Chapter 10), disconnect the two pressure sensors from the underside of the master cylinder.

8 Unscrew and remove the two nuts and washers securing the master cylinder to the vacuum servo unit, remove the heat shield (where fitted), then withdraw the unit from the engine compartment **(see illustration)**. Remove the O-ring from the rear of the master cylinder, and discard it.

Overhaul

9 If the master cylinder is faulty, it must be renewed. Repair kits are not available from Skoda dealers, so the cylinder must be considered a sealed unit.

10 The only items which can be renewed are the mounting seals for the fluid reservoir; if these show signs of deterioration, withdraw the retaining pin, pull off the reservoir and remove the old seals. Lubricate the new seals with clean brake fluid, and press them into the master cylinder ports. Ease the fluid reservoir into position, push it fully home, and insert the retaining pin.

Refitting

11 Clean the master cylinder and servo unit mating surfaces, and fit a new O-ring to the groove on the master cylinder body.

15.11 Brake servo unit mounting nuts

12 Fit the master cylinder to the servo unit, ensuring that the servo unit pushrod enters the master cylinder bore centrally. Refit the heat shield (where applicable), and the master cylinder mounting nuts and washers, and tighten them to the specified torque.

13 Wipe clean the brake pipes and unions, then refit them to the master cylinder ports and tighten them securely.

14 On vehicles equipped with ESP, reconnect the pressure sensors on the underside of the master cylinder.

15 Reconnect the clutch master cylinder supply hose to the reservoir.

16 Secure the vacuum hose to the clip on the brake fluid reservoir.

17 Refit the battery and battery tray (Chapter 5A), air inlet ducts (Chapter 4) and engine top cover.

18 Refill the master cylinder reservoir with new fluid, and bleed the complete hydraulic system as described in Section 2. Also bleed the clutch hydraulic system.

15 Servo unit – testing, removal and refitting

Testing

1 To test the operation of the servo unit, depress the footbrake several times to exhaust the vacuum, then start the engine whilst keeping the pedal firmly depressed. As the engine starts, there should be a noticeable 'give' in the brake pedal as the vacuum builds-up. Allow the engine to run for at least two minutes, then switch it off. If the brake pedal is now depressed, it should feel normal, but further applications should result in the pedal feeling firmer, with the pedal stroke decreasing with each application.

2 If the servo does not operate as described, first inspect the servo unit non-return valve as described in Section 16. On diesel models, also check the operation of the vacuum pump as described in Section 24.

3 If the servo unit still fails to operate satisfactorily, the fault lies within the unit itself. Repairs to the unit are not possible – if faulty, the servo unit must be renewed.

Removal

Note: *A new servo unit gasket will be required on refitting.*

4 Remove the master cylinder as described in Section 14.

5 Remove the heating/air conditioning air duct from the driver's footwell.

6 Where fitted, remove the convenience system central control unit from its location above the accelerator pedal with reference to Chapter 12.

7 Where applicable remove the heat shield from the servo, then carefully ease the vacuum hose out from the sealing grommet in the front of the servo.

8 With reference to Chapter 11, remove the driver's side lower facia trim panels, and the trim panel below the dash.

9 Remove the brake light switch as described in Section 21.

10 It is now necessary to release the brake pedal from the ball on the vacuum servo pushrod. To do this, a Skoda special tool is available, but a suitable alternative can be improvised. Note that the plastic lugs in the pedal are very stiff, and it will not be possible to release them by hand. Using the tool, release the securing lugs, and pull the pedal from the servo pushrod.

11 Again working in the footwell, undo the nuts securing the servo unit to the bulkhead **(see illustration)**, then return to the engine compartment and manoeuvre the servo unit out of position, noting the gasket which is fitted to the rear of the unit.

Refitting

12 Check the servo unit vacuum hose sealing grommet for signs of damage or deterioration, and renew if necessary.

13 Fit a new gasket to the rear of the servo unit, and reposition the unit in the engine compartment.

14 From inside the vehicle, ensure that the servo unit pushrod is correctly engaged with the brake pedal, and push the pedal onto the pushrod ball. Check the pushrod ball is securely engaged, then refit the servo unit mounting nuts and tighten them to the specified torque.

15 With reference to Section 21, refit the brake light switch.

16 Refit the facia trim panels.

17 Carefully ease the vacuum hose back into position in the servo, taking great care not to displace the sealing grommet. As applicable, refit the heat shield to the servo, and reconnect the vacuum sensor wiring plug.

18 Where fitted, refit the convenience system central control unit with reference to Chapter 12.

19 Refit the heating/air conditioning air duct to the driver's footwell.

20 Refit the master cylinder as described in Section 14 of this Chapter.

21 On completion, start the engine and check the operation of the braking system.

16 Servo non-return valve – testing, removal and refitting

1 The non-return valve is located in the vacuum hose from the inlet manifold to the brake servo. If the valve is to be renewed, the complete hose/valve assembly should be renewed.

Removal

2 Ease the vacuum hose out of the servo unit, taking care not to displace the grommet.

3 Loosen the retaining clip and disconnect

the opposite end of the hose assembly from the manifold/pump hose, and remove it from the car.

Testing

4 Examine the check valve and vacuum hose for signs of damage, and renew if necessary.
5 The valve may be tested by blowing through it in both directions, air should flow through the valve in one direction only; when blown through from the servo unit end of the valve. Renew the valve if this is not the case.
6 Examine the servo unit rubber sealing grommet for signs of damage or deterioration, and renew as necessary.

Refitting

7 Ensure that the sealing grommet is correctly fitted to the servo unit.
8 Ease the hose union into position in the servo unit, taking great care not to displace or damage the grommet.
9 Connect the hose to the inlet manifold/pump hose, and ensure that the hose is secured in the retaining clips.
10 On completion, start the engine and check the operation of the braking system.

17 Handbrake – adjustment

1 To check the handbrake adjustment, first apply the footbrake firmly several times to establish correct shoe-to-drum/pad-to-disc clearance, then apply and release the handbrake three times.
2 Applying normal moderate pressure, pull the handbrake lever to the fully-applied position, counting the number of clicks emitted from the handbrake ratchet mechanism. If adjustment is correct, there should be approximately 4 clicks before the handbrake is fully applied. If there are more clicks, adjust as follows.
3 Remove the centre console as described in Chapter 11 to gain access to the handbrake lever. **Note:** *Note on some models, the handbrake adjusting nut can be accessed by simply removing the ashtray from the rear of the centre console (see illustration).*
4 Chock the front wheels, then jack up the rear of the vehicle and support it on axle

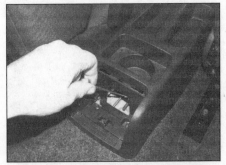

17.3 On some models, access to the handbrake adjusting nut can be gained by removing the ashtray

stands. Continue as described under the relevant sub-heading.

Rear drum brake models

5 With the handbrake set on the 1st notch of the ratchet mechanism, turn the adjustment nut until it is just difficult to turn both rear wheels. Now release the handbrake lever, and check that the wheels rotate freely; if not, back off the adjustment nut. Apply the handbrake fully, and check that the handbrake is fully applied on the 4th notch.
6 Once adjustment is correct, refit the centre console as described in Chapter 11.

Rear disc brake models

7 With the handbrake fully released, slacken the adjustment nut until both the rear caliper hand-brake levers are back against their stops.
8 Tighten the adjustment nut until both handbrake levers just move off the caliper stops. **Note:** *The nut is contoured to prevent it coming loose, and it is important that the adjustment is checked with the nut fully seated in the equaliser bar.* The gap between each caliper handbrake lever and its stop must be between 1.0 and 1.5 mm **(see illustration)**.
9 Fully apply the handbrake lever three times, then release it and check that both wheels still rotate freely. Check the adjustment by applying the handbrake fully, counting the clicks emitted from the handbrake ratchet. The handbrake must be fully applied on the 4th notch.
10 Once adjustment is correct, refit the centre console as described in Chapter 11.

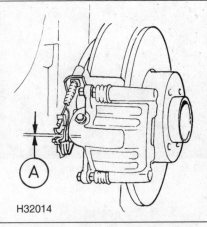

H32014

17.8 Turn the adjustment nut until a gap (A) can be seen between the caliper handbrake levers and the end stops

18 Handbrake lever – removal and refitting

Removal

1 Remove the centre console as described in Chapter 11.
2 If desired, remove the handbrake lever cover sleeve by depressing the locating tag with a screwdriver, then sliding the sleeve from the lever **(see illustration)**.
3 Disconnect the wiring plug from the handbrake 'on' warning light switch.
4 Loosen the handbrake cable adjuster nut sufficiently to allow the ends of the cables to be disengaged from the equaliser plate **(see illustration)**.
5 Unscrew the retaining nuts, and withdraw the lever **(see illustration)**.

Refitting

6 Refitting is a reversal of removal, bearing in mind the following points.
a) Before refitting the handbrake lever cover, adjust the handbrake as described in Section 17.
b) Check the operation of the handbrake 'on' warning switch before refitting the centre console.

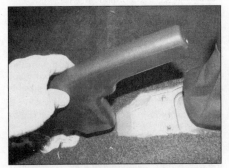

18.2 Removing the handbrake lever cover sleeve

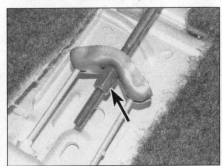

18.4 Handbrake cable adjusting nut

18.5 Handbrake lever mounting nuts

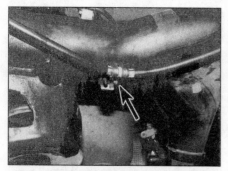

19.4a Handbrake cable fixing on the rear trailing arm

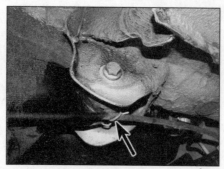

19.4b Handbrake cable clip on the front of the rear trailing arm

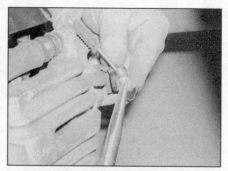

19.6 Release the inner cable from its lever and withdraw the cable from the caliper

19 Handbrake cables – removal and refitting

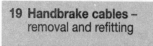

Removal

1 Remove the centre console as described in Chapter 11, to gain access to the handbrake lever. The handbrake cable consists of two sections, a right- and a left-hand section, which are linked to the handbrake lever by an equaliser plate. Each section can be removed individually.

2 Loosen the handbrake cable adjuster nut sufficiently to allow the ends of the cables to be disengaged from the equaliser plate.

3 Chock the front wheels, then jack up the rear of the car and support it on axle stands (see *Jacking and vehicle support*).

4 Work back along the length of the cable, noting its correct routing, and free it from all the relevant guides and retaining clips **(see illustrations)**.

5 On rear drum brake models, remove the brake shoes as described in Section 11, then release the cable from the backplate.

6 On rear disc brake models, disengage the inner cable from the caliper handbrake lever, then remove the outer cable retaining clip and detach the cable from the caliper **(see illustration)**.

7 Withdraw the cable from beneath the vehicle.

Refitting

8 Refitting is a reversal of removal, but adjust the handbrake as described in Section 17 before refitting the centre console.

20 Handbrake 'on' warning light switch – removal and refitting

Removal

1 Remove the centre console as described in Chapter 11.

2 Disconnect the wiring from the switch **(see illustration)**.

3 Squeeze the securing lugs, and withdraw the switch from the handbrake lever assembly **(see illustration)**.

Refitting

4 Refitting is a reversal of removal.

21 Brake light switch – removal and refitting

Removal

1 The brake light switch is located on the pedal bracket beneath the facia. Working in the driver's footwell, remove the lower facia panels with reference to Chapter 11.

2 Reach up behind the facia and disconnect the wiring connector from the switch **(see illustration)**.

3 Twist the switch anti-clockwise through 90° (models up to 07/2001) or 45° (models from 08/2001), and release it from the mounting bracket.

Refitting

4 For models up to 07/2001, first, fully extend the brake light switch plunger. Fully depress and hold down the brake pedal, then manoeuvre the switch into position. Align the shaped lug of the switch with the corresponding cut-out in the bracket **(see illustration)**. Secure the switch in position it by pushing it into the bracket and twisting it clockwise through 90°, then release the brake pedal to reset the switch.

5 For models from 08/2001, first, fully extend the brake light switch plunger. Do not depress the brake pedal, but simply insert the switch into the bracket and twist it clockwise through 45°. The switch will automatically set itself.

20.2 Handbrake 'on' warning switch

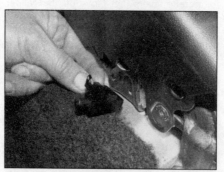

20.3 Removing the handbrake 'on' warning switch

21.2 Disconnect the brake switch wiring

21.4 Align the shaped lug with the corresponding cut-out in the bracket

6 Reconnect the wiring, and check the operation of the brake lights. The brake lights should illuminate after the brake pedal has travelled approximately 5 mm. If the switch is not functioning correctly, it is faulty and must be renewed.

7 Finally, refit the lower facia panel with reference to Chapter 11.

22 Anti-lock braking system (ABS) – general information and precautions

ABS is fitted as standard on most models covered by this manual; the system may also be referred to as including EBD (Electronic Brake Distribution), which means it adjusts the front and rear braking forces according to the weight being carried. Three types of ABS are fitted **(see illustrations)**. On models equipped with traction control (TCS), the ABS unit has a dual function, controlling both the anti-lock braking system (ABS) and the electronic differential locking (EDL) system. On models with ESP (Electronic Stability Programme), the system recognizes critical driving conditions and stabilises the vehicle by individual wheel braking and by intervention in the engine control, which occurs independently of the position of the brake and accelerator pedals.

The system comprises a hydraulic unit which contains the hydraulic solenoid valves and accumulators, the electrically-driven fluid return pump, four roadwheel sensors (one fitted for each wheel), and the electronic control module (ECM). The purpose of the system is to prevent wheels locking during heavy braking. This is achieved by automatic release of the brake on the relevant wheel, followed by re-application of the brake.

The solenoids are controlled by the ECM, which itself receives signals from the four wheel sensors, which monitor the speed of

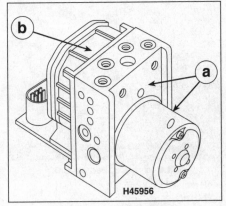

22.1a Bosch 5.7 ABS

a   Return flow pump   b   Control unit

rotation of each wheel. By comparing these speed signals, the ECM can determine the speed at which the car is travelling. It can then use this speed to determine when a wheel is decelerating at an abnormal rate, compared to the speed of the car, and therefore predicts when a wheel is about to lock. During normal operation, the system functions in the same way as a non-ABS braking system.

If the ECM senses that a wheel is about to lock, it operates the relevant solenoid valve in the hydraulic unit, which then isolates the brake caliper on the wheel which is about to lock from the master cylinder, effectively sealing-in the hydraulic pressure.

If the speed of rotation of the wheel continues to decrease at an abnormal rate, the ECM switches on the electrically-driven return pump, which pumps the hydraulic fluid back into the master cylinder, releasing pressure on the brake caliper so that the brake is released. Once the speed of rotation of the wheel returns to an acceptable rate, the pump stops and the solenoid valve opens, allowing the hydraulic master cylinder pressure to return to the caliper, which then re-applies the brake.

This cycle can be carried out at up to 10 times a second.

The action of the solenoid valves and return pump creates pulses in the hydraulic circuit. When the ABS system is functioning, these pulses can be felt through the brake pedal.

The operation of the ABS system is entirely dependent on electrical signals. To prevent the system responding to any inaccurate signals, a built-in safety circuit monitors all signals received by the ECM. If an inaccurate signal or low battery voltage is detected, the ABS system is automatically shut down, and the warning light on the instrument panel is illuminated, to inform the driver that the ABS system is not operational. Normal braking should still be available, however.

If a fault does develop in the ABS system, the car must be taken to a Skoda dealer for fault diagnosis and repair.

23 Anti-lock braking system (ABS) components – removal and refitting

Hydraulic unit

1 Removal and refitting of the hydraulic unit is best entrusted to a Skoda dealer, as a fault diagnosis check must be performed on completion using specialist equipment **(see illustration)**.

Electronic control module (ECM)

2 The ECM is mounted underneath the hydraulic unit. Although it can be separated from the hydraulic unit, due to the delicacy of the components and the need for absolute cleanliness, it is recommended that the work be entrusted to a Skoda dealer.

Front wheel sensor

Removal

3 Chock the rear wheels, then firmly apply

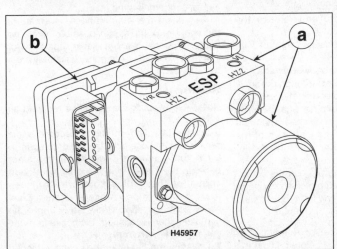

22.1b Bosch 8.0 ABS and ABS/TCS

a   Return flow pump   b   Control unit

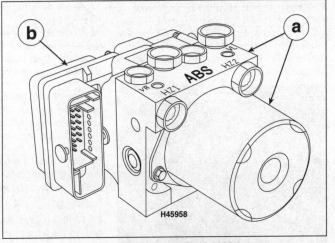

22.1c Bosch 8.0 ABS/TCS/ESP

a   Return flow pump   b   Control unit

23.1 ABS hydraulic unit located on the left-hand side of the engine compartment

the handbrake, jack up the front of the car and support on axle stands (see *Jacking and vehicle support*). Remove the appropriate front roadwheel.

4 Disconnect the electrical connector from the sensor by carefully lifting up the retaining tag, and pulling the connector from the sensor **(see illustration)**.

5 Slacken and remove the hexagon socket-head bolt securing the sensor to the hub carrier, and remove the sensor.

Refitting

6 Ensure that the sensor and hub carrier sealing faces are clean.

7 Apply a little anti-seize grease to the mounting hole inner surface, then fit the sensor to the hub carrier. Refit the retaining bolt and tighten it to the specified torque.

8 Ensure that the sensor wiring is correctly routed and retained by all the necessary clips, and reconnect the wiring connector.

9 Refit the roadwheel, then lower the car to the ground and tighten the roadwheel bolts to the specified torque.

Rear wheel sensor

Removal

10 The sensor is located to the inner face of the rear stub axle, and is secured with a single hexagon socket-head bolt.

11 Chock the front wheels, then jack up the rear of the vehicle and support it on axle stands (*see Jacking and vehicle support*). Remove the appropriate roadwheel.

12 Remove the sensor as described in paragraphs 4 and 5.

24.1 Brake vacuum pump on diesel engine code AMF

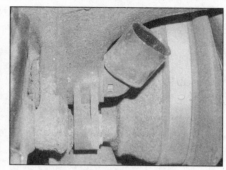

23.4 Wheel speed sensor

Refitting

13 Refit the sensor as described above in paragraphs 6 to 9.

Wheel sensor rings

14 The sensor rings are integral with and built into the inner ends of the wheel hubs. Unlike the earlier type of reluctor with teeth, the sensor rings have alternating magnetic cores within the continuous rings. Examine the rings for any damage. If renewal is necessary, the complete hub assembly must be renewed together with the bearings as described in Chapter 10.

Steering angle sender

Note: *When removing or installing the steering angle sender, use tape to ensure that the coil connector remains in its central position.*

Removal

15 The steering angle sender is located beneath the steering wheel, on the steering column, and is incorporated into the airbag wiring slip-ring (see Chapter 12). **Do not** attempt to separate the steering angle sender from the airbag slip-ring. First, turn the front wheels to their straight-ahead position.

16 Disconnect the battery negative lead (refer to *Disconnecting the battery* in the *Reference* Chapter at the end of this manual).

17 Refer to Chapter 10 and remove the steering wheel.

18 Remove the steering column shrouds with reference to Chapter 10.

19 Check that with the front wheels straight-ahead, a yellow dot is visible through the small hole in the top right-hand corner of the sender. The markings in the bottom right-hand corner of the sender must also be aligned with each other. Use tape to hold the inner hub of the sender to the outer housing while the sender is removed.

20 Disconnect the wiring plug on the under-side on the unit. Release the locking lugs, and pull the unit with the slip-ring from the column.

Refitting

21 Refitting is a reversal of removal, but remove the temporary tape before refitting the steering wheel. As a safety precaution, ensure that no-one is inside the vehicle as the wiring plug is reconnected.

Lateral acceleration/ yaw rate sender

Removal

22 The lateral acceleration sender is located beneath the left-hand front seat, just in front of the crossmember. First, disconnect the battery negative lead (refer to *Disconnecting the battery* in the *Reference* Chapter at the end of this manual).

23 Remove the driver's seat as described in Chapter 11.

24 Note that the wiring plug is located on the rear of the sender, then disconnect it.

25 Unscrew the mounting nuts and remove the sender.

Refitting

26 Refitting is a reversal of removal.

24 Servo unit mechanical vacuum pump – testing, removal and refitting

Testing

1 A vacuum pump is fitted to diesel engine models to provide vacuum for the brake servo unit **(see illustration)**. On turbo models, the pump includes a fuel lift pump for the injection system, however, on non-turbo models, only a vacuum pump is fitted. The operation of the braking system vacuum pump can be checked using a vacuum gauge.

2 Remove the engine top cover, then disconnect the vacuum hose from the pump, and connect the gauge to the pump union using a suitable length of hose.

3 Start the engine and allow it to idle, then measure the vacuum created by the pump. As a guide, after one minute, a minimum of approximately 500 mm Hg should be recorded. If the vacuum registered is significantly less than this, it is likely that the pump is faulty. However, seek the advice of a Skoda dealer before condemning the pump.

4 Reconnect the vacuum hose. Overhaul of the vacuum pump is not possible, since no major components are available separately for it. If faulty, the complete pump assembly must be renewed.

Removal

Note: *A new pump O-ring will be required on refitting.*

5 Loosen the clip, and disconnect the brake servo vacuum hose from the top of the pump.

6 On turbo models, position a container beneath the fuel filter in the front right-hand corner of the engine compartment, then disconnect the supply (white) and return (blue) hoses from the filter. Drain the fuel into the container, then disconnect the hoses from the pump **(see illustration)**.

7 Unscrew the mounting bolts and withdraw the pump from the cylinder head. Recover the gasket/ring and discard it, as a new one must be used for refitting. Note how the drive

24.6 Fuel inlet and outlet hoses fitted to the vacuum pump on the diesel engine

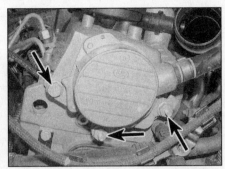

24.7 Undo the pump retaining nuts and bolt

24.9 Align the drive gear with the slot in the end of the camshaft

pinion locates in the end of the camshaft **(see illustration)**. Be prepared for fuel spillage. There are no serviceable parts within the pump. If the pump is faulty, it must be renewed.

Refitting

8 On turbo models, reconnect the fuel hoses to the pump.

9 Refit the pump to the cylinder head, using a new gasket/ring, and ensuring that the pump pinion engages correctly with the drive slot in the camshaft **(see illustration)**.

10 Insert the pump retaining bolts, and tighten them to the specified torque.

11 Reconnect the fuel and vacuum hoses as applicable, however, on turbo models connect a hand vacuum pump to the fuel filter return hose (marked blue). Operate the vacuum pump until fuel comes out of the return hose. This primes the tandem pump. Reconnect the return hose to the fuel filter.

12 Refit the engine top cover.

Chapter 10
Suspension and steering systems

Contents

Section number

Electric power steering pump – removal and refitting 22
Front anti-roll bar – removal and refitting 7
Front anti-roll bar connecting link – removal and refitting 8
Front hub and bearings – renewal 3
Front suspension and steering check . . . . .See Chapter 1A or 1B
Front suspension lower arm and bracket – removal, overhaul and refitting 5
Front suspension lower arm balljoint – removal, inspection and refitting 6
Front suspension strut – removal, overhaul and refitting 4
Front wheel bearing housing – removal and refitting 2
General information 1
Ignition switch and steering column lock – removal and refitting . . . 18
Power steering fluid level check. . . . . .See Chapter 1A or 1B
Power steering system – bleeding 21
Rear anti-roll bar – removal and refitting 12

Section number

Rear axle assembly – removal and refitting 13
Rear axle rubber mountings – renewal. 14
Rear hub assembly – removal and refitting 9
Rear stub axle – removal and refitting 10
Rear suspension shock absorber and coil spring – removal, inspection and refitting. 11
Steering column – removal, inspection and refitting 17
Steering gear assembly (EPHS) – removal, overhaul and refitting. . . 19
Steering gear rubber gaiters and track rods – renewal 20
Steering wheel – removal and refitting. 16
Track rod end – removal and refitting. 23
Vehicle level sender – removal and refitting 15
Wheel alignment and steering angles – general information 24
Wheel and tyre maintenance, and tyre pressure checks . . . . .See *Weekly checks*

Degrees of difficulty

Easy, suitable for novice with little experience	Fairly easy, suitable for beginner with some experience 🔧	Fairly difficult, suitable for competent DIY mechanic 🔧	Difficult, suitable for experienced DIY mechanic 🔧	Very difficult, suitable for expert DIY or professional

Specifications

Front suspension

Type . . . . Independent, with MacPherson struts incorporating coil springs and telescopic shock absorbers. Anti-roll bar fitted to all models

Rear suspension

Type . . . . Transverse torsion beam axle with trailing arms. Separate gas-filled telescopic shock absorbers and coil springs. Anti-roll bar fitted to all models

Steering

Type . . . . Rack-and-pinion. Power assistance standard

Wheel alignment and steering angles*

Front wheel:

Camber angle:

Standard suspension	-30' ± 30'
Sports suspension	-33' ± 30'
Heavy duty suspension	-16' ± 30'
Maximum difference between sides (all models)	30'

Castor angle:

Standard suspension	7° 40' ± 30'
Sports suspension	7° 50' ± 30'
Heavy duty suspension	7° 15' ± 30'
Maximum difference between sides (all models)	30'
Toe setting	0° ± 10'

Toe-out on turns (20° left or right):

Standard suspension	1° 30' ± 20'
Sports suspension	1° 31' ± 20'
Heavy duty suspension	1° 27' ± 20'

Rear wheel:

Camber angle	-1°27' ± 10'
Maximum difference between sides	30'

Toe setting:

Except Estate:

Standard suspension	20' ± 10'
Sports suspension	25' ± 10'
Heavy duty suspension	10' +10'/-7'

Estate:

Standard suspension	16' ± 10'
Sports suspension	22' ± 10'
Heavy duty suspension	10' +10'/-7'

Refer to a Skoda dealer for the latest recommendations.

Roadwheels

Type	Aluminium alloy

Tyres

Size	175/80R14, 195/65R15, 205/60R15, 205/55R16, 225/45R17 and 225/40ZR18
Pressures	see *Weekly checks* on page 0•18

Torque wrench settings

	Nm	lbf ft
Front suspension		
Anti-roll bar:		
Links	40	30
Mounting clamp:		
Stage 1	20	15
Stage 2	Angle-tighten a further 90°	
Engine rear mounting link:		
To transmission:		
Stage 1	30	22
Stage 2	Angle-tighten a further 90°	
To subframe:		
Stage 1	40	30
Stage 2	Angle-tighten a further 90°	
Hub nut*	See Chapter 8	
Lower arm:		
Front pivot bolt:		
Stage 1	70	52
Stage 2	Angle-tighten a further 90°	
Lower arm mounting bracket rear plate:		
Small bolts:		
Stage 1	20	15
Stage 2	Angle-tighten a further 90°	
Large bolt:		
Stage 1	70	52
Stage 2	Angle-tighten a further 90°	
Balljoint-to-lower arm bolts*:		
Stage 1	20	15
Stage 2	Angle-tighten a further 90°	

Torque wrench settings (continued)

	Nm	lbf ft
Lower arm (continued):		
Balljoint nut*:		
Stage 1	20	15
Stage 2	Angle-tighten a further 90°	
Mounting bracket to subframe:		
Stage 1	50	37
Stage 2	Angle-tighten a further 90°	
Splash plate to wheel housing	10	7
Subframe-to-underbody bolts*:		
Stage 1	50	37
Stage 2	Angle-tighten a further 90°	
Suspension strut:		
Bottom clamp bolt nut*:		
Stage 1	60	44
Stage 2	Angle-tighten a further 90°	
Piston rod nut*	60	44
Upper mounting-to-body*:		
Stage 1	15	11
Stage 2	Angle-tighten a further 90°	
Rear suspension		
Axle mounting bolts and nuts*:		
Stage 1	45	33
Stage 2	Angle-tighten a further 90°	
Hub nut (12-point)*:		
Stage 1	70	52
Stage 2	Angle-tighten a further 30°	
Shock absorber:		
Lower mounting bolt and nut*:		
Stage 1	40	30
Stage 2	Angle-tighten a further 90°	
Upper mounting bracket-to-body bolts*:		
Stage 1	30	22
Stage 2	Angle-tighten a further 90°	
Upper mounting nut to bracket*	25	18
Stub axle bolts*:		
Stage 1	30	22
Stage 2	Angle-tighten a further 90°	
Vehicle level sender:		
Sender to underbody (pop-rivet screw)	8	6
Sender link to lower arm...........................	6	4
Steering		
Power steering hose union to electric pump	30	22
Power steering hose union to steering gear:		
Supply..	35	26
Return..	30	22
Steering column:		
Upper mounting bolts to bracket	23	17
Lower mounting bolt........................	19	14
Steering column mounting bracket to cross bar	23	17
Steering column universal joint clamp bolt*:		
Stage 1	20	15
Stage 2	Angle-tighten a further 90°	
Steering gear mounting bolts*:		
Stage 1	50	37
Stage 2	Angle-tighten a further 90°	
Steering wheel bolt...............................	55	41
Track rod balljoint nut*:		
Stage 1	20	15
Stage 2	Angle-tighten a further 90°	
Track rod balljoint locknut	50	37
Track rod inner balljoint to steering rack	80	59
Roadwheels		
Roadwheel bolts...................................	120	89

Renew the nut/bolt every time it is removed

2.3 Removing the driveshaft retaining nut

1 General information

The independent front suspension is of the MacPherson strut type, incorporating coil springs and integral telescopic shock absorbers. The struts are located by transverse lower suspension arms, which use rubber inner mounting bushes, and incorporate a balljoint at the outer ends. The front wheel bearing housings, which carry the wheel bearings, brake calipers and the hub/disc assemblies, are attached to the MacPherson struts by clamp bolts, and connected to the lower arms through the balljoints. A front anti-roll bar is fitted to all models. The anti-roll bar is rubber-mounted, and is connected to both lower suspension arms by short links.

The rear suspension consists of a torsion beam axle with telescopic shock absorbers and coil springs. An anti-roll bar is incorporated into the rear axle beam.

The safety steering column incorporates an intermediate shaft at its lower end. The inter-mediate shaft is connected to both the steering column and steering gear by universal joints, although the shaft is supplied as part of the column assembly and cannot be separated. Both the inner steering column and intermediate shaft have splined sections which collapse during a major frontal impact. The outer column is also telescopic with two sections, to facilitate reach adjustment.

The steering gear is mounted onto the front subframe, and is connected by two track rods, with balljoints at their inner and outer ends, to the steering arms projecting rearwards from the wheel bearing housings. The track rod ends are threaded to the track rods in order to allow adjustment of the front wheel toe setting.

Electrically Powered Hydraulic Steering (EPHS) is fitted as standard on all UK models. The system electric pump and hydraulic fluid reservoir are located behind the front bumper, on the left-hand side.

Most UK models are fitted with an Anti-lock Brake System (ABS), and most models can also be fitted with a Traction Control System (TCS), an Electronic Differential Lock (EDL) system and an Electronic Stability Program (ESP). The ABS may also be referred to as including EBD (Electronic Brake Distribution) which means it adjusts the front and rear braking forces according to the weight being carried, and the TCS may also be referred to as ASR (Anti Slip Regulation).

The TCS system prevents the front wheels from losing traction during acceleration by reducing the engine output. The system is switched on automatically when the engine is started, and it utilises the ABS system sensors to monitor the rotational speeds of the front wheels.

The ESP system extends the ABS, TCS and EDL functions to reduce wheel spin in difficult driving conditions. It does this by using highly-sensitive sensors which monitor the speed of the vehicle, lateral movement of the vehicle, the brake pressure, and the steering angle of the front wheels. If, for example, the vehicle is tending to oversteer, the brake will be applied to the front outer wheel to correct the situation. If the vehicle is tending to understeer, the brake will be applied to the rear inside wheel. The steering angle of the front wheels is monitored by an angle sensor on the top of the steering column.

The TCS/ESP systems are switched on automatically each time the engine is started, and should be left on except when driving with snow chains, driving in snow or driving on loose surfaces, when some wheel spin may be advantageous. The ESP switch is located in the centre of the facia.

Some models are also fitted with an Electronic Differential Lock (EDL) which reduces unequal traction from the front wheels. If one front wheel spins 100 rpm or more faster than the other, the faster wheel is slowed down by applying the brake to that wheel. The system is not the same as the traditional differential lock, where the actual differential gears are locked. Because the system applies a front brake, in the event of a brake disc overheating the system will shut down until the disc has cooled. No warning light is displayed if the system shuts down. As is the case with the TCS system, the EDL system uses the ABS sensors to monitor front wheel speeds.

2 Front wheel bearing housing – removal and refitting

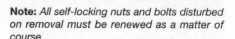

Note: *All self-locking nuts and bolts disturbed on removal must be renewed as a matter of course.*

Removal

1 Remove the wheel trim/hub cap (as applicable) and loosen the driveshaft retaining nut with the vehicle resting on its wheels. Also loosen the wheel bolts.

2 Apply the handbrake, then jack up the front of the vehicle and support it on axle stands (see *Jacking and vehicle support*). Remove the front roadwheel and also remove the engine compartment undershield.

3 Unscrew and remove the driveshaft retaining nut **(see illustration)**.

4 Unscrew the nut securing the link to the anti-roll bar, and separate the link.

5 Remove the ABS wheel sensor as described in Chapter 9.

6 Remove the brake disc as described in Chapter 9 **(see illustrations)**. This procedure includes removing the brake caliper, however **do not** disconnect the hydraulic brake hose from the caliper. Using a piece of wire or string, tie the caliper to the front suspension coil spring, to avoid placing any strain on the hydraulic brake hose.

7 Unbolt the splash plate from the wheel bearing housing.

8 Loosen the nut securing the steering track rod balljoint to the wheel bearing housing. To do this, fit a ring spanner to the nut, then, where

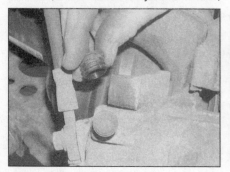

2.6a Remove the caps . . .

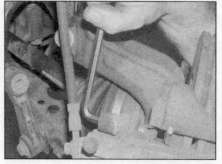

2.6b . . . then loosen the guide pins with an Allen key . . .

2.6c . . . remove the guide pins . . .

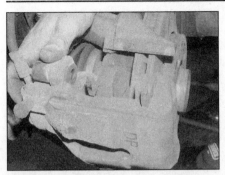

2.6d . . . withdraw the brake caliper . . .

2.6e . . . then undo the screws . . .

2.6f . . . and remove the brake disc

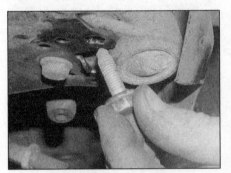

2.9a Unscrew the bolts . . .

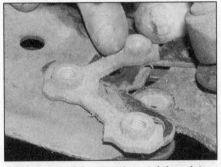

2.9b . . . and remove the retaining plate from the top of the lower arm

2.9c Pull out the wheel bearing housing and release the driveshaft from the hub

applicable, hold the balljoint pin stationary using an Allen key. With the nut removed, it may be possible to release the balljoint from the wheel bearing housing by turning the balljoint pin with an Allen key. If not, leave the nut on by a few turns to protect the threads, then use a universal balljoint separator to release the balljoint. Remove the nut completely once the taper has been released.

9 Unscrew the front suspension lower balljoint-to-lower arm retaining bolts, and remove the retaining plate from the top of the lower arm. Now use a soft-faced mallet to tap the driveshaft from the hub splines while pulling out the bottom end of the wheel bearing housing. If the driveshaft is tight on the splines, it may be necessary to use a puller bolted to the hub to remove it **(see illustrations)**.

10 Note which way round it is fitted, then unscrew the nut and remove the clamp bolt securing the wheel bearing housing to the bottom of the strut.

11 The wheel bearing housing must now be released from the strut. To do this, Skoda technicians insert a special tool into the split wheel bearing housing, and turn it through 90° to open up the clamp. A similar tool can be made out of an old screwdriver, or alternatively a suitable cold chisel can be driven into the split as a wedge. Slightly press inwards the top of the wheel bearing housing, then push it downwards from the bottom of the strut **(see illustrations)**.

12 Unscrew the nut and remove the balljoint from the bottom of the wheel bearing housing. If it is tight, use a puller.

Refitting

13 Note that all self-locking nuts and bolts disturbed on removal must be renewed as a matter of course.

14 Refit the balljoint to the wheel bearing

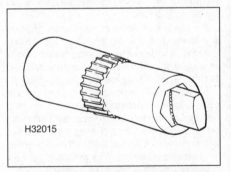

H32015

2.11a Tool used by Skoda technicians to open up the split wheel bearing housing

2.11c Withdrawing the wheel bearing housing from the bottom of the suspension strut

housing and tighten the nut to the specified torque.

15 Ensure that the driveshaft outer joint and hub splines are clean and dry, then lubricate the splines with fresh engine oil. Also lubricate

2.11b Using a cold chisel to open up the wheel bearing housing and release the suspension strut

2.11d Wheel bearing housing

3.2 Driving out the hub and bearing with a lump hammer

3.3 Using a press to remove the hub and bearing from the wheel bearing housing

the threads and contact surface of the hub nut with oil.

16 Lift the wheel bearing assembly into position, and engage the hub with the splines on the outer end of the driveshaft. Fit the new hub nut, tightening it by hand only at this stage.

17 Engage the wheel bearing housing with the bottom of the suspension strut, making sure that the hole in the side plate aligns with the holes in the split housing. Remove the tool used to open the split.

18 Insert the strut-to-wheel bearing housing clamp bolt from the front, and fit the new retaining nut. Tighten the nut to the specified torque.

19 Refit the lower arm balljoint and retaining plate, and tighten the bolts to the specified torque.

20 Refit the track rod balljoint to the wheel bearing housing, then fit a new retaining nut and tighten it to the specified torque. If necessary, hold the balljoint pin with an Allen key while tightening the nut.

21 Refit the splash plate and tighten the bolts.

22 Refit the brake disc and caliper with reference to Chapter 9.

23 Refit the ABS wheel sensor as described in Chapter 9.

24 Refit the link to the anti-roll bar and tighten the nut to the specified torque.

25 Ensure that the outer joint is drawn fully into the hub, then refit the roadwheel and engine compartment undershield. Lower the vehicle to the ground, and tighten the roadwheel bolts.

26 Tighten the driveshaft retaining nut in the stages given in the Specifications. It is

3.7a Pressing the hub and bearing into the wheel bearing housing

recommended that an angle gauge is used to ensure the correct tightening angle.

3 Front hub and bearings – renewal

Note: *The front hub is supplied complete with bearings, and it is not possible to renew the bearings separately. Note that the hub and bearing assembly must be assembled to the hub carrier in one single operation, by applying force to the bearing and **not** the hub. Skoda technicians use special tools MP 6-414 which locate only on the bearing, however, it is possible to fabricate spacers to insert between the hub flange and the bearing, making it possible to apply pressure to the hub itself. If these tools cannot be obtained of fabricated, it is recommended that the work be carried out by a Skoda dealer.*

1 Remove the wheel bearing housing as described in Section 2.

2 A press will be required to remove the hub and bearing, however, if such a tool is not available, a large bench vice and spacers (such as large sockets) will serve as an adequate substitute. As a last resort, it is possible to use a lump hammer to drive out the hub and bearing **(see illustration)**.

3 Support the wheel bearing housing securely on blocks or in a vice. Using a metal tube which bears on the inner end of the hub, press the hub and bearing out of the housing **(see illustration)**. Note that the internal circlip, retaining the bearing in the housing, will be destroyed during the removal operation.

3.7b Make sure the circlip is fully entered in its groove

4 Thoroughly clean the wheel bearing housing, removing all traces of dirt and grease, and polish away any burrs or raised edges which might hinder reassembly. Check for cracks or any other signs of wear or damage, and renew if necessary. Note that the new hub and bearing is supplied with a new circlip, which locates automatically if the special Skoda tool is used.

5 On reassembly, apply a light coating of molybdenum disulphide grease to the bearing outer race and bearing surface of the wheel bearing housing.

6 If using the special Skoda tools MP 6-414, fit it to the bearing, then draw the assembly into the hub carrier until the circlip is heard to click into position. **Note:** *The tools include grippers and spacers which cannot be fabricated locally.* Check that the hub rotates freely, and wipe off any excess oil or grease.

7 If not using the special tools, make up suitable spacers to fit firmly between the hub flange and the bearing, then press the hub with bearing fully into the wheel bearing housing. Using this method, it may be necessary to tap the circlip into its groove **(see illustrations)**.

8 Refit the wheel bearing housing as described in Section 2.

4 Front suspension strut – removal, overhaul and refitting

Note: *All self-locking nuts and bolts disturbed on removal must be renewed as a matter of course.*

Removal

1 Remove the wheel trim/hub cap (as applicable) and loosen the driveshaft retaining nut with the vehicle resting on its wheels. Also loosen the wheel bolts.

2 Apply the handbrake, then jack up the front of the vehicle and support it on axle stands (see *Jacking and vehicle support*). Remove the front roadwheel and also remove the engine compartment undershield.

3 Unscrew and remove the driveshaft retaining nut.

4 Unscrew the nuts securing the link to the anti-roll bar and strut, and remove the link.

5 Using a suitable marker pen or scriber, draw around the outline of the end of the suspension lower arm on the lower arm balljoint, marking the correct fitted position of the balljoint.

6 Unscrew the front suspension balljoint-to-lower arm retaining bolts, and remove the retaining plate from the top of the lower arm. This is necessary to provide additional room in order to lower the wheel bearing housing from the strut.

7 Disconnect the wiring from the ABS wheel sensor, and remove the wiring from the strut support.

8 Loosen the nut securing the steering track rod balljoint to the wheel bearing housing. To do this, fit a ring spanner to the nut, then, where applicable, hold the balljoint pin stationary using an Allen key. With the nut removed, it

4.12a Unscrew the upper mounting bolts . . .

4.12b . . . and lower the strut from the wheel bearing housing

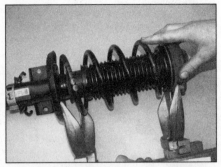

4.13 Fitting the coil spring compressor

4.14a Hold the piston rod with an Allen key while the nut is loosened . . .

4.14b . . . then remove the nut

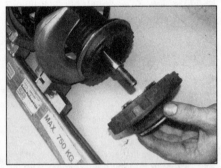

4.15a Remove the strut mounting . . .

may be possible to release the balljoint from the wheel bearing housing by turning the balljoint pin with an Allen key. If not, leave the nut on by a few turns to protect the threads, then use a universal balljoint separator to release the balljoint. Remove the nut completely once the taper has been released.

9 Pull the front hub and carrier from the driveshaft, then tie the driveshaft to one side. Support the weight of the hub carrier on a trolley jack.

10 Note which way round it is fitted, then unscrew the nut and remove the clamp bolt securing the wheel bearing housing to the bottom of the strut.

11 Release the wheel bearing housing from the strut by slightly opening the split housing with reference to Section 2, then slightly pressing inwards the top of the wheel bearing housing, and lowering it from the bottom of the strut.

12 Support the strut, then unscrew and remove the upper mounting bolts. Lower the strut from the wheel bearing housing and manoeuvre it out from underneath the wheel arch **(see illustrations)**. Discard the upper mounting bolts, as new ones must be used on refitting.

Overhaul

⚠️ *Warning: Before attempting to dismantle the suspension strut, a suitable tool to hold the coil spring in compression must be obtained. Adjustable coil spring compressors are readily available, and are recommended for this operation. Any attempt to dismantle the strut without such a tool is likely to result in damage or personal injury.*

13 Support the lower end of the strut in a vice, then fit the coil spring compressor into position, and check that it is securely located **(see illustration)**.

14 Compress the spring until the upper spring seat is free of tension, then remove the nut from the top of the piston rod. Hold the piston rod with an Allen key while the nut is unscrewed **(see illustrations)**. The need to hold the piston rod means that an ordinary deep socket cannot readily be used; in the workshop, we used a deep angled ring spanner (a short box spanner together with an open-ended spanner would also work). The nut is especially tight – don't expect to use makeshift means to loosen it safely.

15 Remove the strut mounting, followed by the bellows **(see illustrations)**. Note the fitted order and orientation of all components, for use when refitting.

16 Withdraw the bump stop from the piston rod **(see illustration)**.

17 Lift the coil spring from the strut with the compressor still in position **(see illustration)**. Mark the top of the spring for reference.

4.15b . . . and bellows

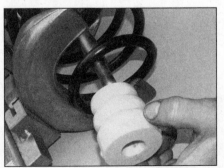

4.16 Remove the bump stop . . .

4.17 . . . and coil spring

4.20 The ends of the coil springs must locate correctly in the seatings

18 Move the shock absorber piston rod up-and-down through its complete stroke, and check that the resistance is even and smooth. If there are any signs or seizing or lack of resistance, or if fluid has been leaking excessively, the shock absorber should be renewed.

19 The coil springs are normally colour-coded, and if the springs are to be renewed (it is advisable to renew both at the same time), be sure to get the correct type with an identical colour code.

20 Reassembly is a reversal of disassembly, but make sure that the ends of the coil spring are correctly located in the seatings **(see illustration)**. On completion, secure it all with the shock absorber piston rod nut, tightened to the specified torque.

Refitting

21 Manoeuvre the strut into position under the

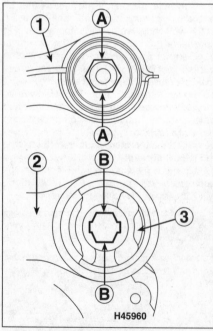

5.8 The surfaces (A) on the lower arm rear pin, must align with the surfaces (B) in the rubber mounting

1 *Lower arm*   3 *Rubber*
2 *Bracket*   *mounting*

wheel arch, then fit the upper mounting bolts and tighten them to the specified torque.

22 Engage the wheel bearing housing with the bottom of the suspension strut, making sure that the hole in the side plate aligns with the holes in the split housing. Remove the tool used to open the split.

23 Insert the new strut-to-wheel bearing housing clamp bolt from the front, and fit the new retaining nut. Tighten the nut to the specified torque.

24 Manoeuvre the driveshaft into position, and engage the outer joint with the hub. Fit the new hub nut and use it to draw the joint fully into position.

25 Align the suspension lower arm balljoint, lower arm, and retaining plate/hub assembly, then fit the new lower arm balljoint securing bolts, and tighten them to the specified torque and angle setting, using the marks made on removal to ensure that the balljoint is correctly positioned.

26 Refit the steering track rod balljoint to the wheel bearing housing and tighten the nut to the specified torque.

27 Reconnect the wiring to the ABS wheel sensor, and attach the wiring to the strut support.

28 Refit the anti-roll bar link and tighten the nuts to the specified torque.

29 Ensure that the outer joint is drawn fully into position, then refit the roadwheel and engine compartment undershield, and lower the vehicle to the ground.

30 Tighten the driveshaft nut in the Stages given in the Specifications.

31 Once the driveshaft nut is correctly tightened, tighten the wheel bolts to the specified torque and refit the wheel trim/hub cap.

5 Front suspension lower arm and bracket – removal, overhaul and refitting

Note: *All self-locking nuts and bolts disturbed on removal must be renewed as a matter of course.*

Removal

1 Apply the handbrake, then jack up the front of the vehicle and support it on axle stands

6.2a The front suspension lower balljoint on the wheel bearing housing

(see *Jacking and vehicle support*). Remove the appropriate front roadwheel and the engine compartment undershield.

2 Mark their position, then unscrew the front suspension lower balljoint-to-lower arm retaining bolts, and remove the retaining plate from the top of the lower arm. **Note:** *On early models, the camber setting is adjusted by the position of the balljoint on the lower arm.*

3 Unscrew and remove the lower arm front pivot bolt.

4 Swivel out the front of the lower arm, and withdraw it forwards to release the rear pin from the rubber mounting. Only swivel out the arm sufficiently to clear the mounting bracket, and if necessary use a slide hammer to force the rear pin from the rubber mounting.

5 If it is required to renew the rear mounting rubber, unbolt the mounting bracket from the subframe.

Overhaul

6 Thoroughly clean the lower arm and bracket, then check carefully for cracks or any other signs of wear or damage, paying particular attention to the pivot and rear mounting rubber bushes. If either bush requires renewal, the lower arm and bracket should be taken to a Skoda dealer or suitably-equipped garage. A hydraulic press and suitable spacers are required to press out the bushes and install the new ones. When fitting a new mounting bush, make sure that it is correctly aligned with the markings.

Refitting

7 Refit the mounting bracket to the subframe and tighten the bolts to the specified torque.

8 Locate the lower arm rear pin in the rubber mounting making sure that the hexagon profile aligns correctly **(see illustration)**.

9 Insert the front pivot bolt and tighten to the specified torque.

10 Refit the balljoint and retaining plate to the lower arm using new bolts, align it with the markings previously-made, then tighten the bolts to the specified torque and angle.

11 Refit the roadwheel and undershield then lower the vehicle to the ground.

6 Front suspension lower arm balljoint – removal, inspection and refitting

Note: *All self-locking nuts and bolts disturbed on removal must be renewed as a matter of course.*

Removal

Method 1

1 Remove the wheel bearing housing as described in Section 2.

2 Unscrew and remove the balljoint retaining nut, then release the balljoint from the wheel bearing housing using a universal balljoint separator **(see illustrations)**. Withdraw the balljoint.

Method 2

3 Remove the wheel trim/hub cap (as applicable) and loosen the driveshaft retaining nut with the vehicle resting on its wheels. Also loosen the wheel bolts.

4 Apply the handbrake, then jack up the front of the vehicle and support it on axle stands (see *Jacking and vehicle support*). Remove the front roadwheel and also remove the engine compartment undershield.

5 Unscrew and remove the driveshaft retaining nut.

6 Unscrew the nut securing the anti-roll bar link to the strut.

7 Using a suitable marker pen or scriber, draw around the outline of the end of the suspension lower arm on the lower arm balljoint, marking the correct fitted position of the balljoint.

8 Unscrew the front suspension balljoint-to-lower arm retaining bolts, and remove the retaining plate from the top of the lower arm.

9 Disconnect the wiring from the ABS wheel sensor, and remove the wiring from the strut support.

10 Loosen the nut securing the steering track rod balljoint to the wheel bearing housing. To do this, fit a ring spanner to the nut, then, where applicable, hold the balljoint pin stationary using an Allen key. With the nut removed, it may be possible to release the balljoint from the wheel bearing housing by turning the balljoint pin with an Allen key. If not, leave the nut on by a few turns to protect the threads, then use a universal balljoint separator to release the balljoint. Remove the nut completely once the taper has been released.

11 Pull the front hub and carrier from the driveshaft, then tie the driveshaft to one side. Retain the wheel bearing housing away from the lower arm by inserting a block of wood between the strut and the inner body panel.

12 Unscrew and remove the balljoint retaining nut, then release the balljoint from the wheel bearing housing using a universal balljoint separator. Withdraw the balljoint.

Inspection

13 With the balljoint removed, check that it moves freely, without any sign of roughness. Check also that the balljoint rubber gaiter shows no sign of deterioration, and is free from cracks and splits. Renew as necessary.

Refitting

Method 1

14 Fit the balljoint to the wheel bearing housing and fit the new retaining nut. Tighten the nut to the specified torque setting, noting that the balljoint shank can be retained with an Allen key if necessary to prevent it from rotating.

15 Refit the wheel bearing housing with reference to Section 2.

Method 2

16 Fit the balljoint to the wheel bearing housing and fit the new retaining nut. Tighten the nut

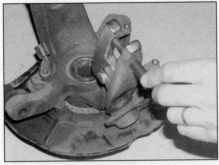

6.2b Using a universal balljoint separator tool to remove the lower balljoint

to the specified torque setting, noting that the balljoint shank can be retained with an Allen key if necessary to prevent it from rotating.

17 Remove the wooden block and move the strut inwards, at the same time inserting the driveshaft into the hub splines.

18 Refit the balljoint and retaining plate to the lower arm using new bolts, and tighten the bolts to the specified torque and angle.

19 Fit the new hub nut and use it to draw the joint fully into position.

20 Refit the steering track rod balljoint to the wheel bearing housing and secure with a new nut tightened to the specified torque.

21 Reconnect the ABS wiring and attach to the strut support.

22 Refit the anti-roll bar link to the strut and tighten the nut to the specified torque.

23 Ensure that the outer joint is drawn fully into position, then refit the roadwheel and engine compartment undershield, and lower the vehicle to the ground.

24 Tighten the driveshaft nut in the Stages given in the Specifications.

25 Once the driveshaft nut is correctly tightened, tighten the wheel bolts to the specified torque and refit the wheel trim/hub cap.

7 Front anti-roll bar – removal and refitting

Note: *All self-locking nuts and bolts disturbed on removal must be renewed as a matter of course.*

Removal

1 Apply the handbrake, then jack up the front of the vehicle and support it on axle stands (see *Jacking and vehicle support*). Remove both front roadwheels and the engine compartment undershield.

2 Unscrew the bolts securing the engine rear mounting link to the bottom of the transmission.

3 Unscrew the bolts securing the anti-roll bar clamps to the rear of the lower arm brackets. Note that the lower right-hand bolt cannot be completely removed at this stage.

4 Unscrew the nuts and disconnect the side connecting links from the anti-roll bar.

5 Unscrew the steering gear mounting bolts from the bottom of the subframe. Tie the steering gear to the underbody.

6 Mark the position of the subframe on the underbody to retain the wheel alignment. Also, mark the anti-roll bar to indicate which way round it is fitted, and the position of the rubber mounting bushes. This will aid refitting.

7 Support the subframe on a trolley jack, then unscrew the mounting bolts and lower the subframe approximately 4 cm.

8 Remove the clamp, then turn the anti-roll bar upwards and withdraw towards the rear of the car. Remove the rubber mounting bushes from the bar.

9 Carefully examine the anti-roll bar components for signs of wear, damage or deterioration, paying particular attention to the rubber mounting bushes. Renew worn components as necessary.

Refitting

10 Fit the rubber mounting bushes to the anti-roll bar, aligning them with the marks made prior to removal.

11 Manoeuvre the anti-roll bar into position, then refit the mounting clamps and insert the retaining bolts. Ensure that the bush markings are still aligned with the marks on the bars, then tighten the mounting clamp retaining bolts to the specified torque.

12 Raise the subframe and align with the previously-made marks. Insert the mounting bolts and tighten to the specified torque and angle.

13 Untie the steering gear, then secure it to the subframe with the bolts tightened to the specified torque.

14 Refit the anti-roll bar side connecting links and tighten the nuts to the specified torque.

15 Tighten the anti-roll bar mounting clamp bolts to the specified torque.

16 Refit the engine rear mounting link bolts, then push the transmission forwards as far as possible and tighten the bolts to the specified torque.

17 Refit the roadwheels and engine compartment undershield, then lower the vehicle to the ground and tighten the wheel bolts to the specified torque.

8 Front anti-roll bar connecting link – removal and refitting

Note: *All self-locking nuts and bolts disturbed on removal must be renewed as a matter of course.*

Removal

1 Apply the handbrake, then jack up the front of the vehicle and support it on axle stands (see *Jacking and vehicle support*). Remove the relevant front roadwheel.

2 Unscrew the nuts securing the anti-roll bar link to the front suspension strut and anti-roll bar and remove it.

9.3 Use a cold chisel or screwdriver to remove the rear hub dust cap

9.4 Unscrew the self-locking 12-point hub nut . . .

9.5 . . . and remove the hub and bearings from the stub axle

3 Inspect the link rubbers for signs of damage or deterioration. If evident, renew the link complete.

Refitting

4 Refitting is a reversal of removal, but delay fully tightening the link bolts until the weight of the car is on the front suspension.

9 Rear hub assembly – removal and refitting

Note: *The rear wheel bearings cannot be renewed independently of the rear hub, because the outer races are formed in the hub itself. If excessive wear is evident, the rear hub must be renewed complete. The rear hub nut must always be renewed after removal.*

Removal

1 Chock the front roadwheels, then jack up the rear of the vehicle and support on axle stands (see *Jacking and vehicle support*). Release the handbrake and remove the relevant rear roadwheel.
2 Remove the rear brake drum or disc (as applicable) with reference to Chapter 9.
3 Remove the dust cap from the centre of the hub using a screwdriver or cold chisel **(see illustration)**.
4 Unscrew and remove the self-locking 12-point hub nut. Note that it is tightened to a high torque and a socket extension bar may be required to loosen it **(see illustration)**. It is recommended that the nut is renewed whenever removed.

9.8 Using a socket to drive the hub onto the stub axle

5 Using a suitable puller if necessary, pull the hub and bearings from the stub axle **(see illustration)**. Take care not to damage the ABS sensor ring on the inside of the hub.
6 Examine the hub and bearings for wear, pitting and damage. If all the bearing surfaces and balls appear to be in good order upon inspection, the hub may be re-used.

Refitting

7 Wipe clean the stub axle, then check that the bearing races are adequately lubricated with suitable grease.
8 Locate the hub as far as possible onto the stub axle. Skoda technicians use a special drift to drive the inner race onto the stub, however, a suitable metal tube or deep socket will do the same **(see illustration)**. Make sure that the tube is only located on the inner race.
9 Screw on the new self-locking nut and tighten it to the specified torque and angle.

10.3 ABS rear wheel speed sensor

10 Check the dust cap for damage and renew it if necessary. Use a hammer to carefully tap the cap into the hub. **Note:** *A badly fitting dust cap will allow moisture to enter the bearing, reducing its service life.*
11 Refit the brake drum or disc (as applicable) with reference to Chapter 9.
12 Refit the roadwheel and lower the vehicle to the ground.

10 Rear stub axle – removal and refitting

Note: *All self-locking nuts and bolts disturbed on removal must be renewed as a matter of course.*

Removal

1 Chock the front roadwheels, then jack up the rear of the vehicle and support on axle stands (see *Jacking and vehicle support*). Release the handbrake and remove the relevant roadwheel.
2 Remove the rear hub as described in Section 9.
3 Disconnect the wiring, then unscrew the bolt and remove the ABS speed sensor from the rear axle trailing arm **(see illustration)**.
4 Unscrew the mounting bolts securing the stub axle and backplate to the rear axle trailing arm. Carefully withdraw the backplate and stub axle, taking care not to bend the brake line excessively. If necessary, remove the rear wheel cylinder or rear caliper as applicable with reference to Chapter 9.
5 Inspect the stub axle for signs of damage and renew if necessary. **Do not** attempt to straighten the stub axle.

Refitting

6 Ensure the mating surfaces of the axle, stub axle and backplate are clean and dry. Check the backplate for signs of damage.
7 Refit the stub axle together with the backplate, then insert the new bolts and progressively tighten to the specified torque.
8 If removed, refit the rear wheel cylinder or rear caliper as applicable with reference to Chapter 9.
9 Refit the speed sensor, tighten the bolt, and reconnect the wiring.
10 Refit the rear hub with reference to Section 9.
11 Refit the roadwheel and lower the vehicle to the ground.

11 Rear suspension shock absorber and coil spring – removal, inspection and refitting

Note: *All self-locking nuts and bolts disturbed on removal must be renewed as a matter of course.*

Shock absorber

Removal

1 Before removing the shock absorber, an idea of how effective it is can be gained by depressing

11.3 Position the trolley jack and block of wood beneath the trailing arm

11.5a Remove the lower mounting bolt . . .

11.5b . . . and withdraw the shock absorber from the trailing arm

the rear corner of the car. If the shock absorber is in good condition, the body should rise then settle in its normal position. If the body oscillates more than this, the shock absorber is defective. **Note:** *The rear shock absorbers can be renewed individually if necessary.*

2 Chock the front roadwheels, then jack up the rear of the vehicle and support on axle stands (see *Jacking and vehicle support*). Remove the relevant rear roadwheel.

3 Position a trolley jack and block of wood beneath the coil spring position on the trailing arm, and raise the arm so that the shock absorber is slightly compressed **(see illustration)**. Note that on some models, it may be necessary to remove the stone protection guard first.

4 On models with gas-discharge (Xenon) headlights, disconnect the tension rod for the rear sender.

5 Unscrew and remove the shock absorber lower mounting nut and bolt, and lever the bottom of the shock absorber from the trailing arm **(see illustrations)**.

6 Support the shock absorber, then unscrew the upper mounting bolts located in the rear wheel arch. Lower the shock absorber and withdraw from under the wheel arch **(see illustrations)**.

7 With the shock absorber on the bench, prise off the cover, then unscrew the nut from the top of the piston rod and remove the upper mounting bracket. The piston rod can be held stationary with a pair of grips on the raised peg on the top of the rod. Remove the rubber stop and protectors from the top of the rod.

Inspection

8 If necessary, the action of the shock absorber can be checked by mounting it upright in a vice. Fully depress the rod, then pull it up fully. The piston rod must move smoothly over its complete length.

Refitting

9 Locate the rubber stop and protectors on the piston rod followed by the upper mounting bracket. Fit the new nut and tighten to the specified torque while holding the piston rod as for removal, then refit the cover.

10 Locate the shock absorber in the rear wheel arch, then insert the upper mounting bolts and tighten to the specified torque.

11.6a Unscrew the upper mounting bolts . . .

11 Locate the bottom of the shock absorber in the trailing arm, insert the bolt from the outside, then screw on the nut. Raise the trailing arm with the jack to take the weight of the rear suspension, then tighten the lower mounting bolt to the specified torque.

12 Lower the jack, and where necessary refit the stone protection guard.

13 On models with gas-discharge (Xenon) headlights, reconnect the tension rod and adjust it so that the lever points towards the rear and not upwards when the rear suspension is flexed.

14 Refit the roadwheel and lower the vehicle to the ground.

Coil spring

Note: *It is possible to remove the rear coil spring without the use of a coil spring compressor; both methods are described in the following paragraphs.*

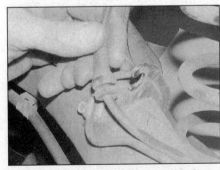

11.20 Release the handbrake cable from the bracket on the trailing arm

11.6b . . . and withdraw the rear shock absorber from under the wheel arch

15 Chock the front roadwheels, then jack up the rear of the vehicle and support on axle stands (see *Jacking and vehicle support*). Remove the relevant rear roadwheel.

16 If removing the left-hand rear coil spring, first remove the exhaust tail pipe and silencer as described in Chapter 4C.

With a spring compressor

⚠ *Warning: Adjustable coil spring compressors are readily available, and are recommended for this operation.*

17 Support the trailing arm with a trolley jack, then fit the tool to the coil spring and compress it until it can be removed from the trailing arm and underbody. With the coil spring on the bench, carefully release the tension of the tool and remove it.

Without a spring compressor

18 Position a trolley jack and block of wood beneath the coil spring position on the trailing arm, and raise the arm so that the shock absorber is slightly compressed. Note on some models, it may be necessary to remove the stone protection guard first.

19 Unscrew and remove the shock absorber lower mounting nut and bolt, and lever the bottom of the shock absorber from the trailing arm.

20 Release the handbrake cable from the bracket on the trailing arm **(see illustration)**.

21 Lower the trolley jack and remove it from under the trailing arm, then carefully lever the arm down until the coil spring can be removed. Lever against a block of wood to

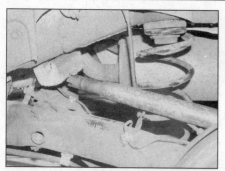

11.21a Lever down the trailing arm . . .

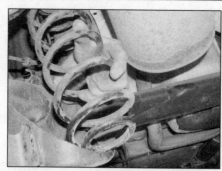

11.21b . . . then release the coil spring from its lower seat . . .

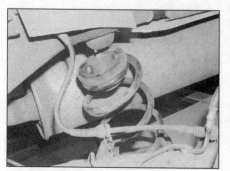

11.21c . . . and underbody seat

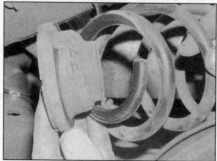

11.22 Recover the upper and lower spring seats

prevent damage to the underbody. Make sure that the vehicle is adequately supported on the axle stands **(see illustrations)**.

Inspection

22 With the coil spring removed, recover the upper and lower spring seats and check them for damage **(see illustration)**. Obtain new ones if necessary. Also clean the spring locations on the underbody and trailing arm.

Refitting

23 Refitting is a reversal of removal, but make sure that the upper spring seat is located correctly on the top of the coil spring, with the spring end abutting the shoulder on the seat. The lower seat is circular and locates only in the centre of the spring. Before tightening the shock absorber lower mounting bolt to the specified torque, raise the trailing arm to its normal running position.

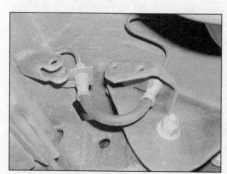

13.7 Flexible brake hose on the rear axle and underbody

12 Rear anti-roll bar – removal and refitting

The rear anti-roll bar runs along the length of the rear axle beam. It is an integral part of the axle assembly, and cannot be removed. If the anti-roll bar is damaged, which is unlikely, the complete axle assembly must be renewed.

13 Rear axle assembly – removal and refitting

Note: *All self-locking nuts and bolts disturbed on removal must be renewed as a matter of course.*

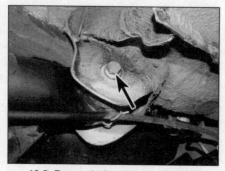

13.9 Rear axle front mounting bolt

Removal

1 Chock the front roadwheels, then jack up the rear of the vehicle and support on axle stands positioned beneath the underbody (see *Jacking and vehicle support*). Remove both rear roadwheels. Fully release the handbrake.

2 Working on each side at a time, slightly raise the trailing arm so that the shock absorber is not fully extended, then unscrew and remove the shock absorber upper mounting bolts from inside the rear wheel arch. Carefully lower the trailing arm to relieve the tension in the coil spring.

3 On models fitted with gas-discharge (Xenon) headlights, disconnect the tension rod at the rear of the vehicle level sensor. If necessary, disconnect the wiring and unbolt the sensor.

4 With both shock absorber upper mountings detached, lower the trailing arms until the coil springs and seats can be removed.

5 Remove the stone protection plates from the trailing arms where fitted, then unscrew the lower mounting bolts and remove the shock absorbers from the rear axle.

6 Release the handbrake cable from the supports/clips on the rear axle and underbody.

7 Pull out the clips and disconnect the flexible brake hoses from the supports on the rear axle and underbody bracket on both sides **(see illustration)**. **Do not** disconnect the rigid brake lines from the hoses.

8 Refer to Section 10 and remove the rear stub axles from the rear trailing arms. Release the rigid pipes from their clips and place the rear wheel cylinders or calipers (as applicable) to one side, together with the handbrake cables. Where fitted, also unbolt the rear brake load regulator.

9 Support the rear axle with a trolley jack, then unscrew and remove the rear axle front mounting bolts from the underbody brackets **(see illustration)**.

10 Manoeuvre the rear axle down from the underbody brackets and withdraw from under the vehicle. The help of an assistant is recommended.

11 Inspect the rear axle mountings for signs of damage or deterioration, and refer to Section 14 if renewal is necessary.

Refitting

12 Apply a little brake grease or soapy water to the kidney-shaped cavity in the front mounting rubbers, then manoeuvre the rear axle into the underbody brackets and insert the mounting bolts from the outside. Screw on the nuts finger-tight at this stage. **Note:** *Make sure that the bolts are inserted through the centres of the rubber mountings and are not located in one of the three off-centre cut-outs. If the bolts are not correctly centred, the rear wheel alignment will be incorrect causing excessive tyre wear.*

13 Refit the rear stub axles as described in Section 10. Secure the brake lines to their clips, and where applicable refit the rear brake load regulator.

14 Refit the flexible brake hoses to the supports and secure with the clips.

15 Refit the handbrake cables and locate them in the supports/clips.

16 Locate the shock absorbers on the trailing arms and insert the lower mounting bolts loosely.

17 On models with gas-discharge (Xenon) headlights, refit the vehicle level sensor if removed, then reconnect the wiring and tension rod.

18 Carefully locate the coil springs and seats on the rear axle with reference to Section 11.

19 Working on each side at a time, raise the trailing arm until the shock absorber upper mounting bolts can be inserted. Tighten the bolts to the specified torque.

20 Working on each side at a time, raise the trailing arm with a trolley jack until the weight of the car is taken on the coil spring. Fully tighten the front mounting bolts to the specified torque, then tighten the shock absorber mounting bolts to the specified torque.

21 Refit the stone protection plates under the trailing arms.

22 Check and if necessary adjust the handbrake as described in Chapter 9.

23 Refit the roadwheels and lower the vehicle to the ground.

14 Rear axle rubber mountings – renewal

Note: *It is recommended that the rubber mountings are renewed on both sides at the same time to ensure the correct rear wheel alignment.*

1 Most models covered by this manual are fitted with hydraulic type rubber mountings to the rear axle when new, although early 1.4 litre models may have the solid rubber type. In the event of leakage or excessive wear of the hydraulic type, both sides MUST be renewed with the solid rubber type. The following paragraphs describe renewal of the solid rubber type mountings,

however the procedure for *removing* the hydraulic type is the same.

2 Chock the front roadwheels, then jack up the rear of the vehicle and support on axle stands positioned beneath the underbody (see *Jacking and vehicle support*). Remove both rear roadwheels.

3 Release the handbrake cables from the supports/clips on the rear axle and underbody.

4 Pull out the clips and disconnect the flexible brake hoses from the supports on the rear axle and underbody brackets.

5 Unscrew and remove both rear axle front mounting bolts from the underbody brackets.

6 Working on one side at a time, pull the front end of the trailing arm down from the underbody bracket and retain it in this position by placing a block of wood between the arm and underbody.

7 Note the fitted position of the rubber mounting to aid refitting.

8 Skoda technicians use a slide hammer tool to remove the rubber mounting from the rear axle. If a similar tool is not available, use a long bolt with suitable-sized metal tubing and washers to force out the mounting.

9 The new mounting must be located correctly in the rear axle **(see illustrations)**. Using a suitable tool, pull the mounting into the rear axle until it is positioned as noted on removal.

10 Renew the mounting on the other side using the same procedure described in paragraphs 6 to 9 inclusive.

11 Apply a little brake grease or soapy water to the kidney-shaped cavity in the front mounting rubbers, then locate the rear axle in the underbody brackets. Insert the mounting bolts from the outside, hand-tight at this stage.

12 Refit the flexible brake hoses and handbrake cables, and secure with the clips.

13 Working on one side at a time, raise the trailing arm with a trolley jack until the weight of the car is taken on the coil spring, then fully tighten the front mounting bolt to the specified torque.

14 Refit the roadwheels and lower the vehicle to the ground.

15 Vehicle level sender – removal and refitting

Removal

1 On models with gas-discharge (Xenon) headlights, a vehicle level sender is bolted to the left-hand rear trailing arm. The sender monitors the level of the vehicle and this information, together with speed information from the instrument panel, is used to adjust the headlight height by means of a stepper motor.

2 To remove the sender, chock the front roadwheels then jack up the rear of the vehicle and support on axle stands (see *Jacking and vehicle support*). Disconnect the wiring, then unscrew the mounting bolts and nut, and withdraw the sender from under the vehicle.

Refitting

3 Refitting is a reversal of removal, but tighten the mounting bolts/nut to the specified torque. If necessary, have the sender adjustment checked by a Skoda dealer; this work requires the use special equipment not available to the home mechanic.

16 Steering wheel – removal and refitting

⚠️ **Warning:** *During the airbag removal and refitting procedures, avoid sitting in the front seats.*

Removal

1 Set the front wheels in the straight-ahead position, and release the steering lock by inserting the ignition key.

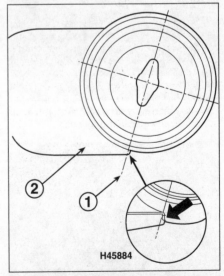

14.9b Fitting position of the rear axle rubber mounting (RS models)

The axis (1) must align with the point indicated by the arrow on the trailing arm (2)

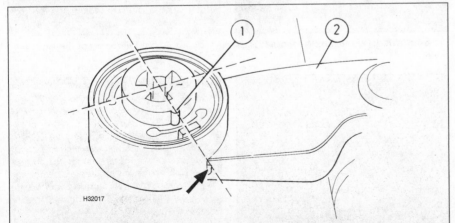

14.9a Fitting position of the rear axle rubber mounting (except RS models)

The cut-out (1) must align with the point indicated by the arrow on the trailing arm (2)

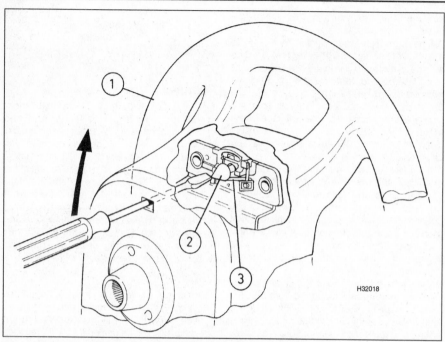

16.4a Airbag module removal

1 *Steering wheel*   2 *Locking lug*   3 *Clip*

Now turn the steering wheel through 180° and release the remaining airbag locking lug.

5 Turn the steering wheel to its central, straight-ahead position.

6 Carefully withdraw the airbag module and disconnect the wiring **(see illustrations)**.

⚠️ *Warning: Position the airbag in a safe and secure place, away from the work area, with its outer surface pointing upwards (refer to Chapter 12).*

7 Using a multi-spline socket, unscrew and remove the retaining bolt, while holding the steering wheel stationary **(see illustration)**. **Note:** *The steering wheel retaining bolt can be re-used up to 5 times, after which it must be renewed. It is recommended that the nut is marked with a centre punch to indicate the number of times it has been unscrewed.*

8 Use a centre punch or dab of paint to mark the steering wheel in relation to the column in order to aid refitting, then ease the steering wheel from the column splines by firmly rocking it side-to-side **(see illustrations)**.

Refitting

9 Note that if the combination switch has been removed from the column, it will be necessary to adjust the clearance between the steering wheel and switch before finally tightening the switch retaining clamp. The clearance must be approximately 2.5 mm. Refer to Chapter 12 for more information.

10 Locate the steering wheel on the column splines making sure that the previously-made marks are correctly aligned.

2 Disconnect the battery negative lead (refer to *Disconnecting the battery* in the *Reference* Chapter at the end of this manual), and position it away from the terminal.

3 Adjust the steering column to its lowest position by releasing the adjustment handle, then pull out the column and lower it as far as possible. Lock the column in this position by returning the adjustment handle.

4 With the spokes in the vertical position, insert a screwdriver approximately 45 mm into the hole in the upper rear of the steering wheel hub, then move it up to release the clip and free the airbag locking lug **(see illustrations)**.

16.4b Inserting a screwdriver to release the airbag module clip

16.6a Withdraw the airbag module . . .

16.6b . . . and disconnect the wiring

16.7 Removing the steering wheel retaining bolt

16.8a Mark the steering wheel in relation to the column . . .

16.8b . . . then ease the steering wheel from the splines by firmly rocking it side-to-side

17.11 Removing the plastic cover from the steering column lower universal joint

17.12a Universal joint linking the bottom of the intermediate shaft to the steering gear pinion shaft

17.12b Removing the clamp bolt

11 Apply suitable locking compound to the threads of the bolt, then screw it on and tighten to the specified torque while holding the steering wheel stationary.

12 With the steering wheel in the straight-ahead position, locate the airbag module in position and reconnect the wiring. Carefully press in the module until both locking lugs are heard to engage.

13 Reconnect the battery negative (earth) lead.

17.12c Splined pinion shaft on the steering gear

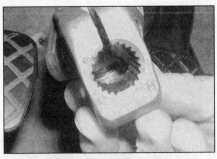

17.12d The splined universal joint, showing the flat to ensure fitting in one position only

17 Steering column –
removal, inspection and refitting

Removal

1 Disconnect the battery negative lead (refer to *Disconnecting the battery* in the *Reference* Chapter at the end of this manual), and position it away from the terminal.

2 Remove the steering wheel as described in Section 16.

3 Remove the lower facia panel/storage from beneath the steering column with reference to Chapter 11.

Models without ESP/TCS

4 Disconnect the wiring from the bottom rear of the column combination switch.

5 Use a small screwdriver to release the locking lugs, then pull the airbag slip-ring and wiring connector from the combination switch. Note that the slip-ring automatically locks itself in the central position, ready for refitting.

Models with ESP/TCS

6 Note that on models equipped with ESP (electronic stability program) and TCS (traction control system), the slip-ring is different and incorporates a steering wheel angle sensor. To remove this type, make sure that the front wheels are still pointing straight-ahead, then check that a yellow spot is visible through the hole in the top, right-hand corner of the slip-ring housing. If necessary, temporarily refit the steering wheel and move the column until the spot is visible.

7 At the rear of the slip-ring housing, release the two retaining hooks and withdraw the slip-ring and steering wheel angle sensor. Note

that the slip-ring automatically locks itself in the central position, ready for refitting.

All models

8 Remove the plastic cover from the steering lock shear bolts on top of the steering column and release the cable tie securing the wiring loom.

9 Mark the position of the combination switch on the column, then unscrew the clamp bolt and withdraw the switch.

10 Disconnect the wiring from the ignition switch and immobiliser reading coil, then unscrew the nut and disconnect the earth cable.

11 Beneath the pedal bracket, undo the plastic nuts and remove the cover for access to the steering column lower universal joint **(see illustration)**.

12 Unscrew and remove the clamp bolt and free the steering column universal joint from the steering gear pinion (the shaft is telescopic to enable it to be easily disconnected). Discard the clamp bolt as a new one should be used on refitting. Note that the pinion shaft has a cut-out to enable fitting of the clamp bolt, and the splined pinion shaft incorporates a flat, making it impossible to assemble the joint to the shaft in the wrong position **(see illustrations)**. Some models may have a clamp ring securing the universal joint to the inner column.

13 Unclip the wiring guides and release the wiring cable ties from the steering column.

14 Note that the inner and outer columns, and the intermediate shaft, are telescopic, to facilitate the reach adjustment. It is important

to keep the splined sections of the inner steering column engaged with each other while the steering column is removed. If they become detached due to the outer column sections being separated, especially on a vehicle which has completed a high mileage, it is possible that rattling noises may occur. Skoda technicians use a special plastic clip to hold the outer column sections together, although a retainer can be made out of a tapered wooden dowel, or the plastic end of a ballpoint pen can be put to good use. First, release the reach adjustment handle and position the outer column tubes so that the transportation holes are in alignment. Insert the dowel or plug to hold the sections of the column together during removal **(see illustration)**.

15 Unscrew and remove the lower mounting bolt, then support the steering column and

17.14 Insert a dowel or plug (arrowed) to hold the steering column outer sections together during removal

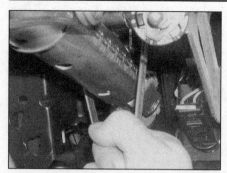

17.15a Loosen the nut . . .

17.15b . . . and remove the steering column lower mounting bolt

17.15c Unscrew the upper mounting bolts . . .

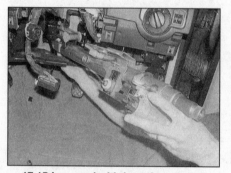

17.15d . . . and withdraw the steering column from inside the vehicle

17.15e The steering column removed from the car

unscrew the upper mounting bolts. Withdraw the steering column from inside the vehicle **(see illustrations)**.

16 If necessary, remove the ignition switch/steering column lock with reference to Section 18.

Inspection

17 The steering column is designed to collapse in the event of a front-end crash, to prevent the steering wheel injuring the driver. Before refitting the steering column, examine the column and mountings for signs of damage and deformation. Using vernier calipers, measure the distance between the upper mounting brackets **(see illustration)**. The distance must be a minimum of 37.0 mm. If it is less than this, the steering column is damaged and should be renewed.

18 Check the inner column sections for signs of free play in the column bushes. If any damage or wear is found on the steering column bushes, the column must be renewed as an assembly.

19 The intermediate shaft is permanently attached to the inner column and cannot be renewed separately **(see illustration)**. Inspect the universal joints for excessive wear. If evident, the complete steering column must be renewed.

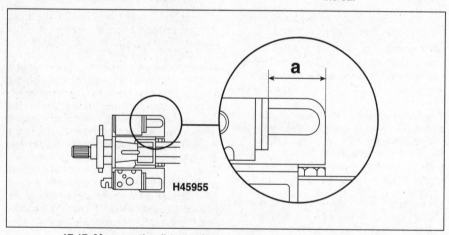

H45955

17.17 Measure the distance between the upper mounting brackets

a = 37.0 mm minimum

Refitting

20 If a new steering column is being fitted, the roller bracket must be removed from the old outer column and secured to the new one **(see illustration)**.

21 Refit the ignition switch/steering column lock with reference to Section 18.

22 Apply a little locking fluid to the threads of the mounting bolts. Offer the steering column onto its mounting bracket and insert all of the mounting bolts loosely. Tighten the lower mounting bolt to the specified torque, then tighten the upper bolts to the specified torque.

23 Remove the clip or retainer securing the telescopic tube sections, and remove the retainer/wire from the inner column.

24 Locate the universal joint onto the steering gear pinion shaft so that the cut-out is aligned with the bolt holes. Insert the new clamp bolt and tighten to the specified torque.

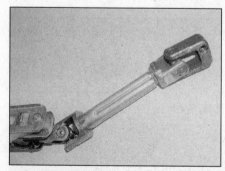

17.19 The intermediate shaft is permanently attached to the inner steering column

17.20 The roller bracket is secured to the steering column with a single shear-head bolt

25 Refit the plastic cover beneath the pedal bracket and secure with the plastic nuts.

26 Refit the earth cable and tighten the nut, then reconnect the wiring to the ignition switch and immobiliser reading coil.

27 Refit the combination switch to the top of the steering column with reference to Chapter 12, Section 4. Make sure it is aligned with the previously-made mark or adjust it before tightening the clamp bolt.

28 Refit the plastic cover over the steering lock shear bolts, and refit the cable tie.

Models without ESP/TCS

29 Refit the airbag slip-ring and wiring connector to the combination switch.

30 Reconnect the wiring to the combination switch.

Models with ESP/TCS

31 Refit the steering wheel angle sensor and slip-ring, making sure that the retaining lugs are correctly engaged.

32 Make sure that the yellow spot is visible (see paragraph 6), then refit the steering wheel angle sensor in its central position **(see illustration)**. Note: *The basic setting of the sensor must be checked by a Skoda dealer whenever it is removed or whenever the steering wheel is repositioned.*

All models

33 Temporarily locate the steering wheel on the column splines and check that the clearance between the steering wheel and the clock spring housing is approximately 2.5 mm. If not, loosen the combination switch clamp bolt and reposition it, then retighten the bolt. Remove the steering wheel.

34 Refit the upper and lower steering column shrouds and secure with the screws.

35 Refit the height and reach adjustment handle and tighten the screws.

36 Refit the lower facia panel/storage from beneath the steering column with reference to Chapter 11.

37 Refit the wiring to the guides and secure with cable ties where necessary.

38 Refit the steering wheel with reference to Section 16.

39 Reconnect the battery negative lead (refer to *Disconnecting the battery* in the *Reference* Chapter at the end of this manual).

---

18 Ignition switch and steering column lock – removal and refitting

Ignition switch

Removal

1 Disconnect the battery negative lead (refer to *Disconnecting the battery* in the *Reference* Chapter at the end of this manual).

2 Remove the steering wheel as described in Section 16.

3 Undo the screws and remove the column height and reach adjustment handle.

4 Undo the screws and remove the lower shroud from the steering column, then release the plastic clips and remove the upper shroud.

5 Remove the plastic cover from the steering lock shear bolts on top of the steering column and release the cable tie securing the wiring loom.

6 Mark the position of the combination switch on the column, then unscrew the clamp bolt and withdraw the switch.

7 Carefully pull the wiring plug from the ignition switch **(see illustration)**.

8 Remove the locking paint from the switch retaining screw heads, then loosen them slightly and pull out the switch from the steering lock housing.

Refitting

9 Insert the ignition key and turn it to the 'on' position. Also turn the switch in the same position.

10 Carefully insert the switch into the housing, then insert the screws and tighten securely. Lock the screws by applying some paint over their heads and onto the housing.

11 Reconnect the wiring plug to the ignition switch.

12 Locate the combination switch on the column, align it with the previously-made mark, and tighten the clamp bolt.

13 Refit the plastic cover on the steering lock shear bolts, and secure the wiring loom with the cable tie.

14 Refit the upper and lower shrouds, and tighten the screws.

15 Refit the height and reach adjustment handle and tighten the screws.

16 Refit the steering wheel as described in Section 16.

17 Reconnect the battery negative lead (refer to *Disconnecting the battery* in the *Reference* Chapter at the end of this manual).

Steering column lock

Removal

18 Disconnect the battery negative lead (refer to *Disconnecting the battery* in the *Reference* Chapter at the end of this manual).

19 Remove the steering wheel as described in Section 16.

20 Undo the screws and remove the column height and reach adjustment handle.

21 Undo the screws and remove the lower shroud from the steering column, then pull out and remove the upper shroud.

22 Remove the plastic cover from the steering lock shear bolts on top of the steering column and release the cable tie securing the wiring loom.

18.7 Disconnecting the ignition switch wiring plug

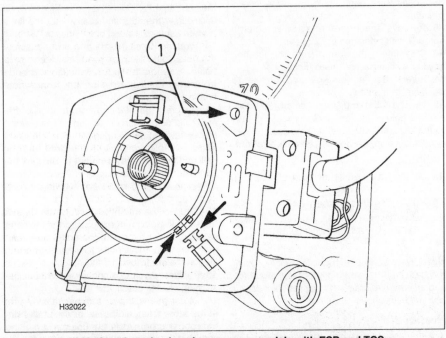

17.32 Steering wheel angle sensor on models with ESP and TCS

The yellow spot must be visible through the hole (1) with the steering angle sensor in its central position (arrowed)

18.25 The steering column lock is secured to the outer column by shear-head bolts

23 Mark the position of the combination switch on the column, then unscrew the clamp bolt and withdraw the switch.

24 Carefully pull the wiring plug from the ignition switch. Also disconnect the wiring from the ignition key immobiliser coil.

25 The lock is secured to the outer column by shear-head bolts **(see illustration)**, and the heads are broken off in the tightening procedure. To remove the old bolts, either drill them out, or use a sharp cold chisel to cut off their heads or turn them anti-clockwise. Withdraw the lock from the steering column.

26 If necessary, the lock cylinder can be removed from the steering lock housing as follows. **Note:** *The lock cylinder can be removed with the lock in situ by removing the steering wheel, shrouds and combination switch.* Insert the ignition key and turn to the 'on' position. Insert a piece of wire 1.2 mm in diameter in the drilling next to the ignition key, depress it, then withdraw the lock cylinder from the housing **(see illustration)**.

Refitting

27 If removed, refit the lock cylinder with the ignition key in the 'on' position, then remove the wire. Make sure that the immobiliser coil connection is located correctly in the guide when inserting the lock cylinder.

28 Locate the lock on the outer column and insert the new shear-head bolts. Tighten the bolts until their heads break off.

29 Reconnect the wiring plug to the ignition switch and ignition key immobiliser coil.

30 Locate the combination switch on the

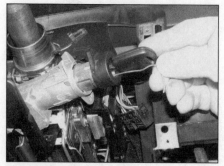

18.42 Removing the ignition switch lock cylinder from the housing

column, align it with the previously-made mark, and tighten the clamp bolt.

31 Refit the plastic cover on the steering lock shear bolts, and secure the wiring loom with the cable tie.

32 Refit the upper and lower shrouds, and tighten the screws.

33 Refit the height and reach adjustment handle and tighten the screws.

34 Refit the steering wheel as described in Section 16.

35 Reconnect the battery negative lead (refer to *Disconnecting the battery* in the *Reference* Chapter at the end of this manual).

Ignition switch lock cylinder

Removal

36 Disconnect the battery negative lead (refer to *Disconnecting the battery* in the *Reference* Chapter at the end of this manual).

37 Remove the steering wheel as described in Section 16.

38 Adjust the steering column to the lowest position.

39 Remove the upper and lower column shrouds with reference to Chapter 11.

40 Disconnect the wiring from the ignition key immobiliser sensor/reader coil.

41 Insert the ignition key and turn it to position 'ignition on'.

42 Insert a 1.5 mm diameter wire or drill fully into the hole in the lock cylinder located next to the key, then withdraw the key, lock cylinder and sensor from the housing **(see illustration)**.

Refitting

43 Refitting is a reversal of removal.

---

19 Steering gear assembly (EPHS) – removal, overhaul and refitting

Note: *New subframe mounting bolts, track rod balljoint nuts, steering gear retaining bolts, and an intermediate shaft universal joint clamp bolt will be required on refitting.*

Removal

1 Apply the handbrake, then jack up the front of the vehicle and support it on axle stands positioned on the underbody, leaving the subframe free (see *Jacking and vehicle*

18.26 Removing the ignition switch lock cylinder from its housing

support). Position the steering straight-ahead, then remove both front roadwheels. Also remove the engine compartment undershield. As a precaution against the steering wheel turning and damaging the airbag contact spring, use adhesive tape to secure it to the facia or steering column.

2 Beneath the pedal bracket, undo the plastic nuts and remove the cover for access to the steering column lower universal joint.

3 Unscrew and remove the clamp bolt and free the steering column universal joint from the steering gear pinion (the shaft is telescopic to enable it to be easily disconnected). Discard the clamp bolt as a new one should be used on refitting. Note that the pinion shaft has a cut-out to enable fitting of the clamp bolt, and the splined pinion shaft incorporates a flat making it impossible to assemble the joint to the shaft in the wrong position. Some models may have a clamp ring securing the universal joint to the inner column.

4 Remove the battery and battery tray as described in Chapter 5A.

5 Remove the air filter and air ducting from the engine compartment with reference to the relevant part of Chapter 4.

6 Release the power-assisted steering sensor wiring from the holder on the inner panel above the left-hand driveshaft.

7 On models where the front exhaust pipe runs beneath the front subframe, remove it with reference to Chapter 4C.

8 Unscrew the two bolts securing the rear engine/transmission mounting link to the underside of the transmission unit. Discard both bolts, new ones must be used on refitting, and leave the mounting attached to the subframe.

9 Unscrew the nuts and disconnect the links from the anti-roll bar on each side.

10 Working on each side at a time, unscrew the nuts from the track rod ends, then use a balljoint separator tool to release the ends from the steering arms on the front wheel bearing housings.

11 Unscrew the filler cap from the top of the hydraulic fluid reservoir on top of the electric power steering pump, then syphon all the fluid into a suitable container. Note that there will still be fluid in the system lines. Discard the removed fluid. **Note:** *Skoda specifically state that a hose clamp **must not** be fitted to the hydraulic fluid line.*

12 Support the weight of the subframe with a trolley jack, then mark the position of the bolts securing the subframe to the underbody, and unscrew them. There are four bolts on each side of the subframe.

13 Position a suitable container beneath the steering gear to catch spilt fluid.

14 Lower the subframe approximately 4 cm, at the same time guiding the pinion shaft from the rubber grommet in the floor, and making sure that the hydraulic lines are not damaged.

15 Unscrew the union nut and disconnect the supply line and return lines from the steering gear, then recover the copper sealing washers.

Tape over or plug the ends of the lines and the apertures in the steering gear to prevent entry of dust and dirt into the hydraulic system. The line ends can be wrapped in a plastic bag if preferred.

16 Unscrew the bolts and remove the power-assisted steering sensor from the steering gear pinion housing. Be prepared for some loss of fluid.

17 Unscrew the mounting bolts and withdraw the steering gear from the subframe to the rear. Note that the mounting on the passenger side of the gear incorporates a clamp and rubber mounting. Examine the mounting for wear and damage, and renew it if necessary. Discard the steering gear mounting bolts, new ones should be used on refitting.

Overhaul

18 Examine the steering gear assembly for signs of wear or damage, and check that the rack moves freely throughout the full length of its travel, with no signs of roughness or excessive free play between the steering gear pinion and rack. It is not possible to overhaul the steering gear assembly housing components, and if it is faulty the assembly must be renewed. The only components which can be renewed individually are the steering gear gaiters, the track rod end balljoints and the track rods, as described later in this Chapter.

Refitting

19 Locate the steering gear on the subframe, and insert the new mounting bolts. Make sure that the location dowel is correctly fitted. Tighten the bolts to the specified torque and Stage 2 angle.

20 Refit the power-assisted steering sensor together with a new seal to the steering gear pinion housing, and tighten the bolts.

21 Refit the hydraulic supply and return lines to the steering gear together with new copper sealing washers, and tighten to the specified torque.

22 Raise the subframe and at the same time guide the steering gear pinion shaft through the rubber grommet in the floor. Align the subframe with the previously-made marks, then insert the new mounting bolts and tighten them to the specified torque and angle.

23 Align the engine/transmission rear mounting with the transmission unit and fit the new mounting bolts. Tighten the bolts to the specified torque and angle.

24 Refit the track rod ends to the steering arms, screw on the new nuts, and tighten them to the specified torque.

25 Refit the links to the anti-roll bar and tighten the nuts to the specified torque.

26 Where applicable, refit the exhaust front pipe with reference to Chapter 4C.

27 Secure the power-assisted steering sensor to the holder on the inner panel.

28 Refit the air filter and ducting with reference to Chapter 4.

29 Refit the battery and battery tray with reference to Chapter 5A. **Note:** *On some models access to the hydraulic fluid reservoir is restricted by the battery, therefore delay refitting the battery until the hydraulic system has been bled.*

30 Working inside the car, locate the steering column universal joint on the pinion shaft, making sure that the cut-out is aligned with the bolt holes. Insert the new bolt and tighten to the specified torque.

31 Check that the rubber grommet is located correctly in the floor, then refit the plastic cover and secure with the screws.

32 Refit the engine compartment undershield and roadwheels, then lower the vehicle to the ground. On completion check and, if necessary, adjust the front wheel alignment as described in Section 24.

33 Refill and bleed the hydraulic system as described in Section 21.

34 Have the system checked for fault codes by a Skoda dealer at the earliest opportunity.

20 Steering gear rubber gaiters and track rods – renewal

Steering gear rubber gaiters

1 Remove the track rod end balljoint as described in Section 23.

2 Note the fitted position of the gaiter on the track rod, then release the retaining clips and slide the gaiter off the steering gear housing and track rod.

3 Wipe clean the track rod and the steering gear housing, then apply a film of suitable grease to the surface of the rack. To do this, turn the steering wheel as necessary to fully extend the rack from the housing, then reposition it in its central position.

4 Carefully slide the new gaiter onto the track rod, and locate it on the steering gear housing. Position the gaiter as previously noted on removal, making sure that it is not twisted, then lift the outer sealing lip of the gaiter to equalise air pressure within the gaiter.

5 Secure the gaiter in position with new retaining clips. Where crimped-type clips are used, pull the clip as tight as possible, and locate the hooks in their slots. Remove any slack in the clip by carefully compressing the raised section. In the absence of the special crimping tool, a pair of side-cutters may be used, taking care not to cut the clip.

6 Refit the track rod end balljoint as described in Section 23.

Track rods

7 Remove the relevant steering gear rubber gaiter as described earlier. If there is insufficient working room with the steering gear mounted in the car, remove it as described in Section 19 and hold it in a vice while renewing the track rod.

8 Hold the steering rack stationary with one spanner on the flats provided, then loosen the balljoint nut with another spanner. Fully unscrew the nut and remove the track rod from the rack.

9 Locate the new track rod on the end of the steering rack and screw on the nut. Hold the rack stationary with one spanner and tighten the balljoint nut to the specified torque. A crow's foot adapter may be required since the track rod prevents access with a socket, and care must be taken to apply the exact torque in this situation.

10 Refit the steering gear or rubber gaiter with reference to the earlier paragraphs or Section 19. On completion check and, if necessary, adjust the front wheel alignment as described in Section 24.

21 Power steering system – bleeding

1 Apply the handbrake, then jack up the front of the vehicle and support it on axle stands (see *Jacking and vehicle support*). Turn the front roadwheels to their straight-ahead position.

2 Unscrew the filler cap from the electric power steering hydraulic fluid reservoir and top-up the level to the MAX mark.

3 With the engine switched off, turn the steering from lock-to-lock ten times, then check and top-up the level again.

4 Screw on the filler cap loosely, then start the engine and allow it to idle for approximately 10 seconds.

5 Switch off the engine and top-up the fluid level.

6 Screw on the filler cap loosely, start the engine, and turn the steering from lock-to-lock ten times.

7 Switch off the engine and top-up the fluid level.

8 Repeat the procedure in paragraphs 6 and 7 until the fluid level no longer requires topping-up.

9 Refit and tighten the filler cap.

22 Electric power steering pump – removal and refitting

Removal

1 On models where access to the electric power steering hydraulic fluid reservoir is restricted by the battery, remove the battery and battery tray as described in Chapter 5A. For improved access, remove the front bumper as described in Chapter 11 **(see illustration)**.

2 Unscrew the filler cap from the top of the hydraulic fluid reservoir on top of the electric power steering pump, then syphon all the fluid into a suitable container. Note that there will still be fluid in the system lines. Discard the

22.1 Electric power steering pump viewed with the front bumper removed

22.8 Wiring plugs on the electric power steering pump

removed fluid. **Note:** *Skoda specifically state that a hose clamp **must not** be fitted to the hydraulic fluid line.*

3 Apply the handbrake, then jack up the front of the vehicle and support it on axle stands (see *Jacking and vehicle support*). Remove the left-hand front roadwheel. Remove the engine undertray.

4 Remove the left-hand front wheel arch liner with reference to Chapter 11, Section 23.

5 On models with a radiator fan control unit, disconnect the wiring and unscrew the mounting nuts, then remove the radiator fan control unit from the car.

6 Release the support clip and remove the supply and return hydraulic lines from the inner body.

7 Locate a suitable container beneath the electric power steering pump to catch spilled hydraulic fluid.

8 Note their location, then disconnect the three wiring plugs from the electric power steering pump **(see illustration)**. The plugs are for the Data BUS and terminal 15, earth plug and terminal 30, and power steering sensor.

9 Unscrew the union nut and disconnect the pressure line from the pump. Recover the O-ring seal, then loosen the clip and disconnect the return line from the pump reservoir. Tape over or plug the ends of the lines and the apertures in the steering gear to prevent entry of dust and dirt into the hydraulic system. The line ends can be wrapped in a plastic bag if preferred.

10 Unscrew the mounting bolts and lower

the electric power steering pump and bracket from the underbody.

11 Unscrew the nuts/bolts and remove the mounting bracket from the pump. Where applicable, unscrew the rubber mountings from the pump.

Caution: The power steering control unit and the electric motor must not be separated.

Refitting

12 Refitting is a reversal of removal, but finally bleed the system as described in Section 21. At the earliest opportunity, have a Skoda dealer perform a system self-diagnosis and erase any fault codes.

23 Track rod end – removal and refitting

Note: *A new balljoint retaining nut will be required on refitting.*

Removal

1 Apply the handbrake, then jack up the front of the vehicle and support it on axle stands (see *Jacking and vehicle support*). Remove the relevant roadwheel.

2 If the track rod end is to be re-used, mark its position in relation to the track rod to facilitate refitting.

3 Unscrew the track rod end locknut by a quarter of a turn. Do not move the locknut from this position, as it will serve as a handy reference mark on refitting.

4 Loosen and remove the nut securing the track rod end balljoint to the wheel bearing housing, and release the balljoint tapered shank using a universal balljoint separator. Note that the balljoint shank has a hexagon hole – hold the shank with an Allen key while loosening the nut **(see illustrations)**.

5 Counting the exact number of turns necessary to do so, unscrew the track rod end from the track rod **(see illustration)**.

6 Carefully clean the balljoint and the threads. Renew the balljoint if its movement is sloppy or too stiff, if excessively worn, or if damaged in any way; carefully check the stud taper and threads. If the balljoint gaiter is damaged, the complete balljoint assembly must be renewed; it is not possible to obtain the gaiter separately.

Refitting

7 Screw the track rod end onto the track rod by the number of turns noted on removal. This should bring the track rod end to within a quarter of a turn of the locknut, with the alignment marks that were made on removal (if applicable) lined up. Tighten the locknut.

8 Refit the balljoint shank to the steering arm on the wheel bearing housing, then fit a new retaining nut and tighten it to the specified torque. Hold the shank with an Allen key if necessary.

9 Refit the roadwheel, then lower the car to the ground and tighten the roadwheel bolts to the specified torque.

10 Check and, if necessary, adjust the front wheel toe setting as described in Section 24.

24 Wheel alignment and steering angles – general information

Definitions

1 A car's steering and suspension geometry is defined in three basic settings – all angles are expressed in degrees; the steering axis is defined as an imaginary line drawn through the axis of the suspension strut, extended where necessary to contact the ground.

2 **Camber** is the angle between each roadwheel and a vertical line drawn through its

23.4a Using an Allen key to hold the balljoint shank while loosening the nut

23.4b Using a balljoint separator to release the track rod balljoint from the steering arm on the wheel bearing housing

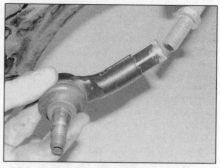

23.5 Unscrewing the track rod end from the track rod

centre and tyre contact patch, when viewed from the front or rear of the car. Positive camber is when the roadwheels are tilted outwards from the vertical at the top; negative camber is when they are tilted inwards.

3 Camber angle is only adjustable by loosening the front suspension subframe mounting bolts and moving it slightly to one side. This also alters the Castor angle. The camber angle can be checked using a camber checking gauge.

4 Castor is the angle between the steering axis and a vertical line drawn through each roadwheel's centre and tyre contact patch, when viewed from the side of the car. Positive castor is when the steering axis is tilted so that it contacts the ground ahead of the vertical; negative castor is when it contacts the ground behind the vertical. Slight castor angle adjustment is possible by loosening the front suspension subframe bolts and moving it slightly to one side. This also alters the Camber angle.

5 Castor is not easily adjustable, and is given for reference only; while it can be checked using a castor checking gauge, if the figure obtained is significantly different from that specified, the car must be taken for careful checking by a professional, as the fault can only be caused by wear or damage to the body or suspension components.

6 Toe is the difference, viewed from above, between lines drawn through the roadwheel centres and the car's centre-line. Toe-in is when the roadwheels point inwards, towards each other at the front, while toe-out is when they splay outwards from each other at the front.

7 The front wheel toe setting is adjusted by screwing the track rod(s) in/out of the outer balljoint(s) to alter the effective length of the track rod assembly.

8 Rear wheel toe setting is not adjustable, and is given for reference only. While it can be checked, if the figure obtained is significantly different from that specified, the car must be taken for careful checking by a professional, as the fault can only be caused

by wear or damage to the body or suspension components.

Checking and adjustment

Front wheel toe setting

9 Due to the special measuring equipment necessary to check the wheel alignment, and the skill required to use it properly, the checking and adjustment of these settings is best left to a Skoda dealer or similar expert. Note that most tyre-fitting centres now possess sophisticated checking equipment.

10 To check the toe setting, a tracking gauge must first be obtained. Two types of gauge are available, and can be obtained from motor accessory shops. The first type measures the distance between the front and rear inside edges of the roadwheels, as previously described, with the car stationary. The second type, known as a 'scuff plate', measures the actual position of the contact surface of the tyre, in relation to the road surface, with the car in motion. This is achieved by pushing or driving the front tyre over a plate, which then moves slightly according to the scuff of the tyre, and shows this movement on a scale. Both types have their advantages and disadvantages, but either can give satisfactory results if used correctly and carefully.

11 Make sure that the steering is in the straight-ahead position when making measurements.

12 If adjustment is necessary, apply the handbrake, then jack up the front of the vehicle and support it securely on axle stands (see *Jacking and vehicle support*). Turn the steering wheel onto full-left lock, and record the amount of exposed thread on the right-hand track rod. Now turn the steering onto full-right lock, and record the number of threads on the left-hand track rod. If there is the same amount of thread visible on both sides, then subsequent adjustment should be made equally on both sides. If there are more thread is visible on one side than the other, it will be necessary to compensate for this during adjustment.

13 First clean the track rod threads; if they are corroded, apply penetrating fluid before starting adjustment. Release the rubber gaiter outer clips, peel back the gaiters and apply a smear of grease. This will ensure that both gaiters are free and will not be twisted or strained as their respective track rods are rotated.

14 Retain the track rod with a suitable spanner, and loosen the balljoint locknut fully. Alter the length of the track rod, by screwing it into or out of the balljoint. Rotate the track rod using an open-ended spanner fitted to the track rod flats provided; shortening the track rod (screwing it onto its balljoint) will reduce toe-in/increase toe-out.

15 When the setting is correct, hold the track rod and tighten the balljoint locknut to the specified torque setting. If after adjustment, the steering wheel spokes are no longer horizontal when the wheels are in the straight-ahead position, remove the steering wheel and reposition it (see Section 16).

16 Check that the toe setting has been correctly adjusted by lowering the car to the ground and rechecking the toe setting; re-adjust if necessary. Ensure that the rubber gaiters are seated correctly and are not twisted or strained, and secure them in position with the retaining clips; where necessary, fit a new retaining clip (refer to Section 20).

Rear wheel toe setting

17 The procedure for checking the rear toe setting is the same as described for the front setting in paragraph 10. The setting is not adjustable – see paragraph 8.

Front wheel camber and castor angles

18 Checking and adjusting the front wheel camber angle should be entrusted to a Skoda dealer or other suitably-equipped specialist. Note that most tyre-fitting centres now possess sophisticated checking equipment. For reference, adjustments are made by loosening the front suspension subframe mounting bolts, and repositioning the subframe.

Chapter 11
Bodywork and fittings

Contents

Section number

Body exterior fittings – removal and refitting 23
Bonnet – removal, refitting and adjustment 8
Bonnet lock – removal and refitting 10
Bonnet release cable – removal and refitting 9
Central locking components – general. 18
Centre console – removal and refitting. 28
Door – removal, refitting and adjustment 11
Door handle and lock components – removal and refitting 13
Door inner trim panel – removal and refitting 12
Door window glass – removal and refitting 15
Electric window components – removal and refitting 19
Exterior mirrors and associated components – removal and refitting 20
Facia panel assembly – removal and refitting 29
Front bumper – removal and refitting. 6
Front seat belt tensioning mechanism – general information 25

Section number

General information 1
Interior trim – removal and refitting 27
Maintenance – bodywork and underframe. 2
Maintenance – upholstery and carpets 3
Major body damage – repair 5
Minor body damage – repair 4
Rear bumper – removal and refitting 7
Seat belt components – removal and refitting 26
Seats – removal and refitting 24
Sunroof – general information 22
Tailgate and support struts – removal and refitting 16
Tailgate lock components – removal and refitting 17
Window regulator and lock carrier – removal and refitting. 14
Windscreen, tailgate and fixed rear quarter window glass – general
   information 21

Degrees of difficulty

| **Easy,** suitable for novice with little experience | | **Fairly easy,** suitable for beginner with some experience | | **Fairly difficult,** suitable for competent DIY mechanic | | **Difficult,** suitable for experienced DIY mechanic | | **Very difficult,** suitable for expert DIY or professional | |

Specifications

Torque wrench settings	Nm	lbf ft
Bonnet hinge retaining bolts	22	16
Bonnet lock	14	10
Door hinges	72	53
Door lock retaining bolts	20	15
Door striker.	20	15
Front and rear bumpers	5	4
Front bumper crossmember.	30	22
Front seat belt height adjustment.	23	17
Front seat belt inertia reel and anchorages	35	26
Front seat mounting retaining bolts	24	18
Rear bumper crossmember.	30	22
Rear seat belt inertia reel and anchorages.	35	26
Tailgate hinge retaining bolts	15	11
Tailgate lock	22	16
Tailgate strut.	20	15

1 General information

The body shell is made of pressed-steel sections, and is available in five-door Hatchback, Estate and Saloon versions. Most components are welded together, and some use is made of structural adhesives. The front wings are bolted on.

The bonnet, door, and some other vulnerable panels are made of zinc-coated metal, and are further protected by being coated with an anti-chip primer before being sprayed.

Extensive use is made of plastic materials, mainly in the interior, but also in exterior components. The front and rear bumpers, and front grille, are injection-moulded from a synthetic material that is very strong and yet light. Plastic components such as wheel arch liners are fitted to the underside of the vehicle, to improve the body's resistance to corrosion.

2 Maintenance – bodywork and underframe

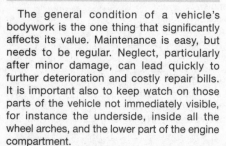

The general condition of a vehicle's bodywork is the one thing that significantly affects its value. Maintenance is easy, but needs to be regular. Neglect, particularly after minor damage, can lead quickly to further deterioration and costly repair bills. It is important also to keep watch on those parts of the vehicle not immediately visible, for instance the underside, inside all the wheel arches, and the lower part of the engine compartment.

The basic maintenance routine for the bodywork is washing – preferably with a lot of water, from a hose. This will remove all the loose solids which may have stuck to the vehicle. It is important to flush these off in such a way as to prevent grit from scratching the finish. The wheel arches and underframe need washing in the same way, to remove any accumulated mud, which will retain moisture and tend to encourage rust. Paradoxically enough, the best time to clean the underframe and wheel arches is in wet weather, when the mud is thoroughly wet and soft. In very wet weather, the underframe is usually cleaned of large accumulations automatically, and this is a good time for inspection.

Periodically, except on vehicles with a wax-based underbody protective coating, it is a good idea to have the whole of the underframe of the vehicle steam-cleaned, engine compartment included, so that a thorough inspection can be carried out to see what minor repairs and renovations are necessary. Steam-cleaning is available at many garages, and is necessary for the removal of the accumulation of oily grime, which sometimes is allowed to become thick in certain areas. If steam-cleaning facilities are not available,

there are some excellent grease solvents available which can be brush-applied; the dirt can then be simply hosed off. Note that these methods should not be used on vehicles with wax-based underbody protective coating, or the coating will be removed. Such vehicles should be inspected annually, preferably just prior to winter, when the underbody should be washed down, and any damage to the wax coating repaired. Ideally, a completely fresh coat should be applied. It would also be worth considering the use of such wax-based protection for injection into door panels, sills, box sections, etc, as an additional safeguard against rust damage, where such protection is not provided by the vehicle manufacturer.

After washing paintwork, wipe off with a chamois leather to give an unspotted clear finish. A coat of clear protective wax polish will give added protection against chemical pollutants in the air. If the paintwork sheen has dulled or oxidised, use a cleaner/polisher combination to restore the brilliance of the shine. This requires a little effort, but such dulling is usually caused because regular washing has been neglected. Care needs to be taken with metallic paintwork, as special non-abrasive cleaner/polisher is required to avoid damage to the finish. Always check that the door and ventilator opening drain holes and pipes are completely clear, so that water can be drained out. Brightwork should be treated in the same way as paintwork. Windscreens and windows can be kept clear of the smeary film which often appears, by the use of proprietary glass cleaner. Never use any form of wax or other body or chromium polish on glass.

3 Maintenance – upholstery and carpets

Mats and carpets should be brushed or vacuum-cleaned regularly, to keep them free of grit. If they are badly stained, remove them from the vehicle for scrubbing or sponging, and make quite sure they are dry before refitting. Seats and interior trim panels can be kept clean by wiping with a damp cloth. If they do become stained (which can be more apparent on light-coloured upholstery), use a little liquid detergent and a soft nail brush to scour the grime out of the grain of the material. Do not forget to keep the headlining clean in the same way as the upholstery. When using liquid cleaners inside the vehicle, do not over-wet the surfaces being cleaned. Excessive damp could get into the seams and padded interior, causing stains, offensive odours or even rot.

If the inside of the vehicle gets wet accidentally, it is worthwhile taking some trouble to dry it out properly, particularly where carpets are involved. Do not leave oil or electric heaters inside the vehicle for this purpose.

4 Minor body damage – repair

Scratches

If the scratch is very superficial, and does not penetrate to the metal of the bodywork, repair is very simple. Lightly rub the area of the scratch with a paintwork renovator, or a very fine cutting paste, to remove loose paint from the scratch, and to clear the surrounding bodywork of wax polish. Rinse the area with clean water.

Apply touch-up paint to the scratch using a fine paint brush; continue to apply fine layers of paint until the surface of the paint in the scratch is level with the surrounding paintwork. Allow the new paint at least two weeks to harden, then blend it into the surrounding paintwork by rubbing the scratch area with a paintwork renovator or a very fine cutting paste. Finally, apply wax polish.

Where the scratch has penetrated right through to the metal of the bodywork, causing the metal to rust, a different repair technique is required. Remove any loose rust from the bottom of the scratch with a penknife, then apply rust-inhibiting paint to prevent the formation of rust in the future. Using a rubber or nylon applicator, fill the scratch with bodystopper paste. If required, this paste can be mixed with cellulose thinners to provide a very thin paste which is ideal for filling narrow scratches. Before the stopper-paste in the scratch hardens, wrap a piece of smooth cotton rag around the top of a finger. Dip the finger in cellulose thinners, and quickly sweep it across the surface of the stopper-paste in the scratch; this will ensure that the surface of the stopper-paste is slightly hollowed. The scratch can now be painted over as described earlier in this Section.

Dents

When deep denting of the vehicle's bodywork has taken place, the first task is to pull the dent out, until the affected bodywork almost attains its original shape. There is little point in trying to restore the original shape completely, as the metal in the damaged area will have stretched on impact, and cannot be reshaped fully to its original contour. It is better to bring the level of the dent up to a point which is about 3 mm below the level of the surrounding bodywork. In cases where the dent is very shallow anyway, it is not worth trying to pull it out at all. If the underside of the dent is accessible, it can be hammered out gently from behind, using a mallet with a wooden or plastic head. Whilst doing this, hold a suitable block of wood firmly against the outside of the panel, to absorb the impact from the hammer blows and thus prevent a large area of the bodywork from being 'belled-out'.

Should the dent be in a section of the

bodywork which has a double skin, or some other factor making it inaccessible from behind, a different technique is called for. Drill several small holes through the metal inside the area – particularly in the deeper section. Then screw long self-tapping screws into the holes, just sufficiently for them to gain a good purchase in the metal. Now the dent can be pulled out by pulling on the protruding heads of the screws with a pair of pliers.

The next stage of the repair is the removal of the paint from the damaged area, and from an inch or so of the surrounding 'sound' bodywork. This is accomplished most easily by using a wire brush or abrasive pad on a power drill, although it can be done just as effectively by hand, using sheets of abrasive paper. To complete the preparation for filling, score the surface of the bare metal with a screwdriver or the tang of a file, or alternatively, drill small holes in the affected area. This will provide a really good 'key' for the filler paste.

To complete the repair, see the Section on filling and respraying.

Rust holes or gashes

Remove all paint from the affected area, and from an inch or so of the surrounding 'sound' bodywork, using an abrasive pad or a wire brush on a power drill. If these are not available, a few sheets of abrasive paper will do the job most effectively. With the paint removed, you will be able to judge the severity of the corrosion, and therefore decide whether to renew the whole panel (if this is possible) or to repair the affected area. New body panels are not as expensive as most people think, and it is often quicker and more satisfactory to fit a new panel than to attempt to repair large areas of corrosion.

Remove all fittings from the affected area, except those which will act as a guide to the original shape of the damaged bodywork (eg headlight shells etc). Then, using tin snips or a hacksaw blade, remove all loose metal and any other metal badly affected by corrosion. Hammer the edges of the hole inwards, in order to create a slight depression for the filler paste.

Wire-brush the affected area to remove the powdery rust from the surface of the remaining metal. Paint the affected area with rust-inhibiting paint, if the back of the rusted area is accessible, treat this also.

Before filling can take place, it will be necessary to block the hole in some way. This can be achieved by the use of aluminium or plastic mesh, or aluminium tape.

Aluminium or plastic mesh, or glass-fibre matting, is probably the best material to use for a large hole. Cut a piece to the approximate size and shape of the hole to be filled, then position it in the hole so that its edges are below the level of the surrounding bodywork. It can be retained in position by several blobs of filler paste around its periphery.

Aluminium tape should be used for small or very narrow holes. Pull a piece off the roll,

trim it to the approximate size and shape required, then pull off the backing paper (if used) and stick the tape over the hole; it can be overlapped if the thickness of one piece is insufficient. Burnish down the edges of the tape with the handle of a screwdriver or similar, to ensure that the tape is securely attached to the metal underneath.

Filling and respraying

Before using this Section, see the Sections on dent, deep scratch, rust holes and gash repairs.

Many types of bodyfiller are available, but generally speaking, those proprietary kits which contain a tin of filler paste and a tube of resin hardener are best for this type of repair. A wide, flexible plastic or nylon applicator will be found invaluable for imparting a smooth and well-contoured finish to the surface of the filler.

Mix up a little filler on a clean piece of card or board – measure the hardener carefully (follow the maker's instructions on the pack), otherwise the filler will set too rapidly or too slowly. Using the applicator, apply the filler paste to the prepared area; draw the applicator across the surface of the filler to achieve the correct contour and to level the surface. As soon as a contour that approximates to the correct one is achieved, stop working the paste – if you carry on too long, the paste will become sticky and begin to 'pick-up' on the applicator. Continue to add thin layers of filler paste at 20-minute intervals, until the level of the filler is just proud of the surrounding bodywork.

Once the filler has hardened, the excess can be removed using a metal plane or file. From then on, progressively-finer grades of abrasive paper should be used, starting with a 40-grade production paper, and finishing with a 400-grade wet-and-dry paper. Always wrap the abrasive paper around a flat rubber, cork, or wooden block – otherwise the surface of the filler will not be completely flat. During the smoothing of the filler surface, the wet-and-dry paper should be periodically rinsed in water. This will ensure that a very smooth finish is imparted to the filler at the final stage.

At this stage, the dent should be surrounded by a ring of bare metal, which in turn should be encircled by the finely 'feathered' edge of the good paintwork. Rinse the repair area with clean water, until all of the dust produced by the rubbing-down operation has gone.

Spray the whole area with a light coat of primer – this will show up any imperfections in the surface of the filler. Repair these imperfections with fresh filler paste or bodystopper, and once more smooth the surface with abrasive paper. Repeat this spray-and-repair procedure until you are satisfied that the surface of the filler, and the feathered edge of the paintwork, are perfect. Clean the repair area with clean water, and allow to dry fully.

HAYNES HiNT *If bodystopper is used, it can be mixed with cellulose thinners to form a really thin paste which is ideal for filling small holes.*

The repair area is now ready for final spraying. Paint spraying must be carried out in a warm, dry, windless and dust-free atmosphere. This condition can be created artificially if you have access to a large indoor working area, but if you are forced to work in the open, you will have to pick your day very carefully. If you are working indoors, dousing the floor in the work area with water will help to settle the dust which would otherwise be in the atmosphere. If the repair area is confined to one body panel, mask off the surrounding panels; this will help to minimise the effects of a slight mis-match in paint colours. Bodywork fittings (eg chrome strips, door handles etc) will also need to be masked off. Use genuine masking tape, and several thicknesses of newspaper, for the masking operations.

Before commencing to spray, agitate the aerosol can thoroughly, then spray a test area (an old tin, or similar) until the technique is mastered. Cover the repair area with a thick coat of primer; the thickness should be built up using several thin layers of paint, rather than one thick one. Using 400-grade wet-and-dry paper, rub down the surface of the primer until it is really smooth. While doing this, the work area should be thoroughly doused with water, and the wet-and-dry paper periodically rinsed in water. Allow to dry before spraying on more paint.

Spray on the top coat, again building up the thickness by using several thin layers of paint. Start spraying at one edge of the repair area, and then, using a side-to-side motion, work until the whole repair area and about 2 inches of the surrounding original paintwork is covered. Remove all masking material 10 to 15 minutes after spraying on the final coat of paint.

Allow the new paint at least two weeks to harden, then, using a paintwork renovator, or a very fine cutting paste, blend the edges of the paint into the existing paintwork. Finally, apply wax polish.

Plastic components

With the use of more and more plastic body components by the vehicle manufacturers (eg bumpers. spoilers, and in some cases major body panels), rectification of more serious damage to such items has become a matter of either entrusting repair work to a specialist in this field, or renewing complete components. Repair of such damage by the DIY owner is not really feasible, owing to the cost of the equipment and materials required for effecting such repairs. The basic technique involves making a groove along the line of the crack in the plastic, using a rotary burr in a power drill. The damaged part is then welded

6.3 Press the centre pins to remove the lower retaining clips

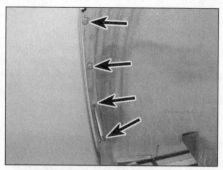

6.4a Rear mounting screws . . .

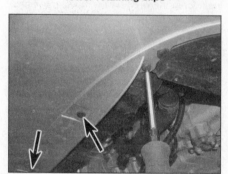

6.4b . . . and side mounting screws on the front bumper

back together, using a hot-air gun to heat up and fuse a plastic filler rod into the groove. Any excess plastic is then removed, and the area rubbed down to a smooth finish. It is important that a filler rod of the correct plastic is used, as body components can be made of a variety of different types (eg polycarbonate, ABS, polypropylene).

Damage of a less serious nature (abrasions, minor cracks etc) can be repaired by the DIY owner using a two-part epoxy filler repair material. Once mixed in equal proportions, this is used in similar fashion to the bodywork filler used on metal panels. The filler is usually cured in twenty to thirty minutes, ready for sanding and painting.

If the owner is renewing a complete component himself, or if he has repaired it with epoxy filler, he will be left with the problem of finding a suitable paint for finishing which is compatible with the type of plastic

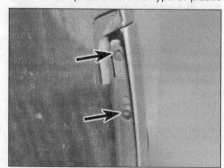

7.2 Rear bumper mounting screws in the rear wheel arch

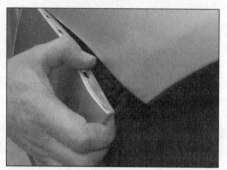

6.6 Ease the rear ends of the bumper from the guides

used. At one time, the use of a universal paint was not possible, owing to the complex range of plastics encountered in body component applications. Standard paints, generally speaking, will not bond to plastic or rubber satisfactorily. However, it is now possible to obtain a plastic body parts finishing kit which consists of a pre-primer treatment, a primer and coloured top coat. Full instructions are normally supplied with a kit, but basically, the method of use is to first apply the pre-primer to the component concerned, and allow it to dry for up to 30 minutes. Then the primer is applied, and left to dry for about an hour before finally applying the special-coloured top coat. The result is a correctly-coloured component, where the paint will flex with the plastic or rubber, a property that standard paint does not normally possess.

5 Major body damage – repair

Where serious damage has occurred, or large areas need renewal due to neglect, it means that complete new panels will need welding-in, and this is best left to professionals. If the damage is due to impact, it will also be necessary to check completely the alignment of the body shell, and this can only be carried out accurately by a Skoda dealer using special jigs. If the body is left misaligned, it is primarily dangerous, as the car will not handle properly, and secondly, uneven stresses will be imposed on the steering, suspension and

possibly transmission, causing abnormal wear, or complete failure, particularly to such items as the tyres.

6 Front bumper – removal and refitting

Removal

1 Apply the handbrake, then jack up the front of the vehicle and support it on axle stands (see *Jacking and vehicle support*).
2 On models with headlamp washers, remove the jet covers and unscrew the washer holder and hose retaining screws.
3 Remove the centre plastic retaining clips beneath the front of the bumper. To do this, press the centre pins through the clips **(see illustration)**.
4 Undo the retaining screws located on the rear ends and beneath the sides of the front bumper. There are three screws on the rear ends, and two screws beneath each side **(see illustrations)**.
5 Have an assistant support the bumper, then undo the two remaining centre top retaining screws.
6 Carefully ease the rear ends of the bumper from the guides **(see illustration)**, and withdraw from the front of the car. At the same time, disconnect the wiring from the foglights where fitted.
7 If necessary, unbolt the guides and crossmember from the front of the vehicle.

Refitting

8 Refitting is a reversal of removal.

7 Rear bumper – removal and refitting

Removal

1 Remove both rear light units as described in Chapter 12, Section 7.
2 Working in the rear wheel arches, undo the mounting screws from the ends of the rear bumper **(see illustration)**.
3 Undo the lower mounting screws beneath each end of the bumper **(see illustration)**.

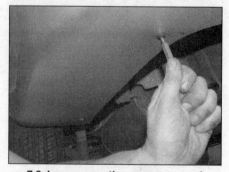

7.3 Lower mounting screw removal

7.4 Rear bumper top retaining screws

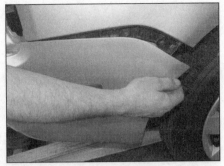

7.5a Ease the bumper from the guides . . .

7.5b . . . and remove the rear bumper

4 Have an assistant support the bumper, then undo the top retaining screws located at each end of the bumper **(see illustration)**.
5 Carefully ease the ends of the bumper from the guides, and withdraw from the rear of the car **(see illustrations)**.
6 If necessary, unbolt the guides and crossmember from the rear of the vehicle **(see illustrations)**.

Refitting

7 Refitting is a reversal of removal.

| 8 | Bonnet – removal, refitting and adjustment |

Removal

1 Open the bonnet and support with the stay, then place some cardboard or rags beneath the corners by the hinges to protect the bodywork.
2 Using a pencil or felt tip pen, mark the outline of each bonnet hinge relative to the bonnet, to use as a guide on refitting.
3 Have an assistant support the bonnet in its open position.
4 Unscrew the bonnet retaining bolts and carefully lift the bonnet clear. Store the bonnet out of the way in a safe place. If necessary, the grille and brackets can be unbolted from the bonnet.
5 Inspect the bonnet hinges for signs of wear and free play at the pivots, and if necessary renew them. Each hinge is secured to the body by two bolts; mark the position of the hinge on the body then undo the retaining bolts and remove it from the vehicle.

Refitting and adjustment

6 Where removed, refit the bonnet hinges, and align them with the previously-made marks. Tighten the bolts securely.
7 With the aid of an assistant, offer up the bonnet and loosely fit the retaining bolts. Align the hinges with the marks made on removal, then tighten the retaining bolts securely.
8 Close the bonnet, and check for alignment with the adjacent panels. If necessary, slacken the hinge bolts and re-align the bonnet. Adjust the height of the bonnet so that it is level

7.6a Rear bumper guide

with the surrounding front wings, by turning the rubber buffer at each front corner of the bonnet. Once the bonnet is correctly aligned, tighten the hinge bolts. Check that the bonnet fastens and releases satisfactorily.

| 9 | Bonnet release cable – removal and refitting |

Removal

1 Open the bonnet, then unclip the cable from the lock on the engine compartment front crossmember.
2 Working inside the vehicle, locate the release lever in the driver's footwell. Unscrew the self-tapping screws, then operate the lever and use pliers to release the cable end fitting.
3 Work along the length of the cable, noting its correct routing, and free it from the retaining clips and ties. Also, prise the rubber grommet from the bulkhead.
4 Tie a length of string (approximately 1.0 m long) to the end of the cable inside the vehicle, then withdraw the cable through into the engine compartment.
5 Once the cable is free, untie the string and leave it in position in the vehicle; the string can then be used to draw the new cable back into position.

Refitting

6 Tie the inner end of the string to the end of the cable, then use the string to draw the bonnet release cable back from the engine

7.6b Rear bumper crossmember mounting bolts

compartment. Once the cable is through, untie the string.
7 The remaining refitting procedure is a reversal of removal. Ensure the rubber grommet in the bulkhead is fitted correctly, and the cable is correctly routed and secured to all the relevant retaining clips. Before closing the bonnet, check the operation of the release lever and cable.

| 10 | Bonnet lock – removal and refitting |

Removal

1 Open the bonnet, then unclip the cable from the lock on the engine compartment front crossmember **(see illustration)**.
2 Disconnect the wiring from the alarm switch microswitch connector next to the lock.

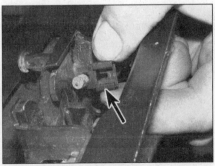

10.1 Unclip the cable end from the bonnet lock

3 Using a pencil or felt tip pen, mark the outline of the bonnet lock on the crossmember, to use as a guide on refitting.

4 Unscrew the two mounting bolts and withdraw the lock assembly **(see illustration)**.

Refitting

5 Before refitting, remove all traces of old locking compound from the lock retaining bolts and their threads in the body.

6 Refitting is a reversal of removal, ensuring the bolts are securely tightened using thread-locking compound. Check that the bonnet fastens and releases satisfactorily. If adjustment is necessary, slacken the bonnet lock retaining bolts, and adjust the position of the lock. Once the lock is operating correctly, tighten the retaining bolts.

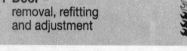
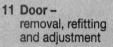

11 Door –
removal, refitting and adjustment

Note: *The hinge bolts must always be renewed if loosened.*

Removal

Front door

1 With the front door open, prise the wiring protector rubber boot from the A-pillar, then disconnect the wiring.

2 Unscrew the bolt and detach the arrestor arm from the front edge of the door **(see illustration)**.

3 Have an assistant support the front door,

10.4 Bonnet lock mounting bolts

then unscrew the nut from the top of the lower hinge, and extract the circlip from the bottom of the upper hinge **(see illustration)**.

4 Carefully lift the front door upwards from the hinges, and remove from the car. Recover the hinge pin and bolt.

5 Examine the hinges for signs of wear or damage. If renewal is necessary, mark the position of the hinge then unscrew the retaining bolts and remove the hinge from the car. If there is a requirement to remove the top hinge from the front pillar, then the facia panel must be removed as described in Section 29. Fit the new hinge, aligning it with the marks made before removal then tighten the retaining bolts to the specified torque.

Rear door

6 With the rear door open, prise the wiring protector rubber boot from the B-pillar, then disconnect the wiring.

7 Unscrew the bolt and detach the arrestor

arm from the front edge of the door **(see illustration)**.

8 Have an assistant support the rear door, then unscrew the nuts from the tops of the upper and lower hinges **(see illustration)**.

9 Carefully lift the rear door upwards from the hinges, and remove from the car.

10 Examine the hinges for signs of wear or damage. If renewal is necessary, mark the position of the hinge then unscrew the retaining bolts and remove the hinge from the car. Fit the new hinge, aligning it with the marks made before removal then tighten the retaining bolts to the specified torque.

Refitting

11 Refitting is a reversal of removal. When refitting the hinges to the A- and B-pillars, align them with the previously-made marks before tightening the bolts to the specified torque. Check the door alignment and if necessary adjust as described in the following paragraph. If the paintwork around the hinges has been damaged, paint the area with a suitable touch-in brush to prevent corrosion.

Adjustment

12 Close the door and check that the gap between the door and surrounding bodywork is equal around the complete perimeter. If necessary, slight adjustment of the door position can be made by slackening the hinge retaining bolts and repositioning the hinge/door as necessary. If there is a requirement to loosen the top hinge on the door pillar (front doors only), then the facia panel must be removed as described in Section 29. Once the door is correctly positioned, tighten the hinge bolts to their specified torque. Check that the door striker engages centrally with the lock, and if necessary, adjust the position of the striker **(see illustration)**.

12 Door inner trim panel
– removal and refitting

Removal

Front door

1 On models with electric windows, dis-

11.2 Front door arrestor arm

11.3 Front door upper hinge

11.7 Rear door arrestor arm

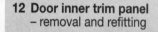

11.8 Rear door lower hinge

11.12 Front door striker

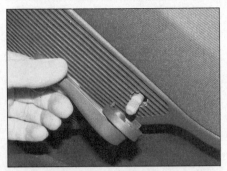

12.2 **Removing the front door window regulator handle**

12.3a **Use a small screwdriver to release the plastic clip on the oddments holder (manual window shown)**

12.3b **Removing the electric window/central locking switch panel**

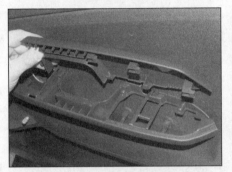

12.4 **Slide the rear cover forwards to remove it**

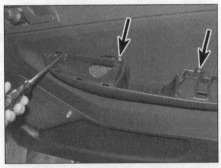

12.5 **Unscrew the centre bolts . . .**

12.6a **. . . then prise off the trim cover . . .**

connect the battery negative lead (refer to *Disconnecting the battery* in the *Reference* Chapter at the end of this manual).

2 On manual window models, with the window fully closed, note the position of the window crank, to ensure correct refitting. Slide the spacer ring to release the internal spring, then withdraw the crank handle from the splines on the regulator **(see illustration)**. Several attempts at releasing the spacer ring in different positions may be required, in order to release the internal spring.

3 The oddments holder or electric window/central locking switch panel (according to model) must now be removed from the front of the inner door pull housing. To do this, Skoda technicians use a special tool inserted from below the holder, however, a bent screwdriver or similar tool can be used instead. Insert the screwdriver/tool under the plastic clip, and lever it out while pulling the holder upwards **(see illustrations)**. Where applicable, disconnect the wiring.

4 With the oddments holder removed, slide the rear cover forwards and remove it **(see illustration)**.

5 Unscrew the three centre bolts securing the inner trim panel to the front door **(see illustration)**.

6 Prise the small trim cover from just in front of the inner door handle, then unscrew the upper bolt securing the inner trim panel **(see illustrations)**.

7 From the lower edge of the front door, undo the inner trim panel lower retaining screws **(see illustration)**.

8 Using a wide-bladed screwdriver or similar

tool, carefully prise the inner trim panel clips away from the door **(see illustration)**. The clips are tight, so position the lever as close to them as possible, otherwise they may pull out of the trim panel and remain in the door.

9 Lift the inner trim panel from the locking

12.6b **. . . unscrew the upper bolt . . .**

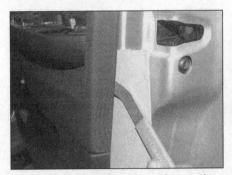

12.8 **. . . release the inner trim panel clips . . .**

knob and withdraw from the door far enough to disconnect the inner and outer cables from the inner door handle **(see illustrations)**. Where applicable, also disconnect the wiring from the courtesy light in the lower rear corner of the trim panel.

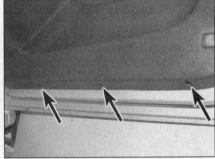

12.7 **. . . and lower retaining screws . . .**

12.9a **. . . lift the trim panel from the locking knob . . .**

12.9b ... and disconnect the cable from the inner door handle

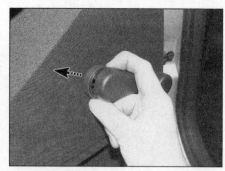

12.11 Remove the window crank ...

12.12 ... release the plastic cover ...

12.13 ... slide the rear cover forwards ...

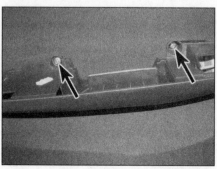

12.14 ... then unscrew the two centre bolts

Several attempts at releasing the spacer ring in different positions may be required, in order to release the internal spring.

12 The plastic cover or electric window switch panel (according to model) must now be removed from the front of the inner door pull housing. To do this, Skoda technicians use a special tool inserted from below the cover, however, a bent screwdriver or similar tool can be used instead. Insert the screwdriver/tool under the plastic clip, and lever it out while pulling the cover upwards **(see illustration)**. Where applicable, disconnect the wiring.

13 With the front cover removed, slide the rear cover forwards and remove it **(see illustration)**.

14 Unscrew the two centre bolts securing the inner trim panel to the rear door **(see illustration)**.

15 Prise the small trim cover from just in front of the inner door handle, then unscrew the upper bolt securing the inner trim panel **(see illustrations)**.

16 Using a wide-bladed screwdriver or similar tool, carefully prise the inner trim panel clips away from the door **(see illustration)**. The clips are tight, so position the lever as close to them as possible, otherwise they may pull out of the trim panel and remain in the door.

17 Lift the inner trim panel from the locking knob and withdraw from the door far enough to disconnect the inner and outer cables from the inner door handle **(see illustration)**. Where applicable, also disconnect the wiring from the courtesy light in the lower rear corner of the trim panel.

Rear door

10 On models with electric windows, disconnect the battery negative lead (refer to *Disconnecting the battery* in the *Reference* Chapter at the end of this manual).

11 On manual window models, with the window fully closed, note the position of the window crank, to ensure correct refitting. Slide the spacer ring to release the internal spring, then withdraw the crank handle from the splines on the regulator **(see illustration)**.

12.15a Prise off the small trim ...

12.15b ... then unscrew the upper bolt securing the inner trim panel

Refitting

18 Refitting is a reversal of removal, but check the operation of the door electrical equipment as applicable.

13 Door handle and lock components – removal and refitting

Removal

Interior door handle

1 The interior door handle is integral with the inner door trim panel, and cannot be removed separately.

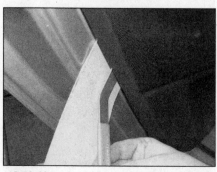

12.16 Use a wide-bladed tool to prise the inner trim panel away from the door

12.17 Disconnecting the cable from the inner door handle

13.2 Prise out the two rubber grommets . . .

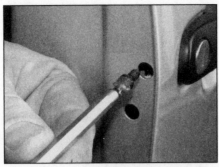

13.3 . . . unscrew the upper locking screw . . .

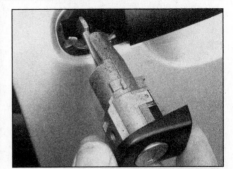

13.5 . . . pull out the lock cylinder and cap . . .

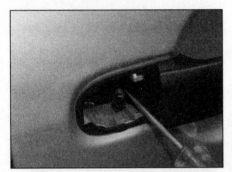

13.6a . . . disconnect the lock release cable . . .

13.6b . . . and swivel the exterior handle from the door

13.8 Prise out the rubber grommet . . .

Front door handle and lock cylinder

2 With the front door open, prise out the two rubber grommets from the holes on the door rear edge, nearest to the exterior door handle **(see illustration)**.

3 For models from 09/2000, unscrew and remove the upper locking screw **(see illustration)**.

4 Fully pull out the exterior door handle, and hold it in this position, while at the same time unscrewing the lock cylinder locking screw approximately three turns with a multi-splined key. **Do not** undo the screw further, as it may fall into the bottom of the door, requiring removal of the door lock and regulator assembly.

5 Pull out the lock cylinder and cap, and remove **(see illustration)**. If the lock cylinder is tight, use a small screwdriver to lever it out, but take care not to damage the paintwork. **Note:** *Except on early models, the passenger*

exterior door handle is fitted with a cover instead of the lock cylinder. On older vehicles, the cylinder may be corroded into the door aperture making it difficult to remove.

6 Working through the lock cylinder aperture, disconnect the lock release cable from the handle then manoeuvre the handle out from the door by swivelling it outwards **(see illustrations)**. Recover the gasket where fitted.

7 To remove the exterior door handle housing from the inside of the door, it is necessary to first remove the door lock and regulator assembly as described later, then undo the retaining screws and withdraw the housing.

Rear door handle

8 On early models, with the rear door open, pull away the weatherseal from the rear edge next to the exterior door handle. On later models, prise out the rubber grommet **(see illustration)**.

9 Fully pull out the exterior door handle, and hold it in this position, while at the same time unscrewing the lock cylinder locking screw approximately three turns with a multi-splined key **(see illustration)**. **Do not** undo the screw further, as it may fall into the bottom of the door, requiring removal of the door lock and regulator assembly.

10 Pull out the housing and cap and remove **(see illustration)**. If the housing is tight, use a small screwdriver to lever it out, but take care not to damage the paintwork.

11 Working through the aperture, disconnect the lock release cable from the handle then manoeuvre the handle out from the door by swivelling it outwards. Recover the gasket, where fitted **(see illustrations)**.

12 To remove the exterior door handle housing from the inside of the door, it is necessary to first remove the door lock and regulator assembly as described later, then

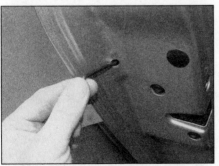

13.9 . . . then unscrew the lock cylinder locking screw about 3 turns, no more

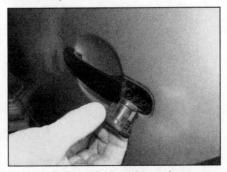

13.10 Pull out the housing and cap . . .

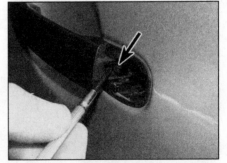

13.11a . . . disconnect the lock release cable . . .

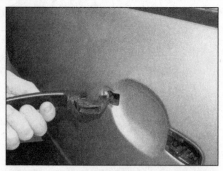

13.11b . . . and swivel the exterior handle from the door

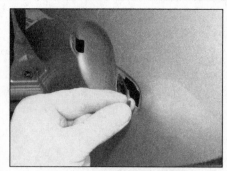

13.11c Removing the gasket

13.12a Undo the retaining screws . . .

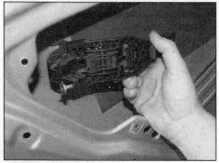

13.12b . . . and remove the exterior door handle housing

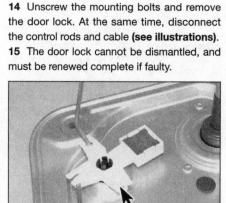

13.14a Unscrew the mounting bolts . . .

Refitting

16 Refitting is a reversal of removal.

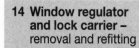

14 Window regulator and lock carrier – removal and refitting

Note: *The window regulator mechanism is part of the carrier and cannot be obtained individually.*

Removal

1 Remove the door inner trim panel as described in Section 12.
2 Remove the exterior door handle as described in Section 13, then undo the screws securing the door lock to the rear edge of the door **(see illustration)**.
3 Prise the rubber grommet(s) from the hole(s) in the carrier, for access to the window glass retaining screws or roll-pin. The front door has two holes for access to the retaining clamp screws, and the rear door has one hole for access to the single roll-pin **(see illustration)**.
4 Lower the window glass until the screws or plastic retaining roll-pin are visible in the hole **(see illustrations)**. On models with electric windows, temporarily reconnect the battery and control switch to operate the glass, then disconnect the battery again. If the electric motor is not functioning correctly, unbolt the motor from the carrier to allow the window to be lowered.
5 On the front door, unscrew the two clamp screws **(see illustration)**.

undo the retaining screws and withdraw the housing **(see illustrations)**.

Front and rear door locks

13 Remove the door window regulator and lock assembly as described in Section 14.

13.14b . . . disconnect the control rods and cable, and remove the door lock from the regulator/lock assembly

14 Unscrew the mounting bolts and remove the door lock. At the same time, disconnect the control rods and cable **(see illustrations)**.
15 The door lock cannot be dismantled, and must be renewed complete if faulty.

13.14c . . . Front door lock control rod intermediate lever

14.2 Screws securing the door lock to the rear edge of the door

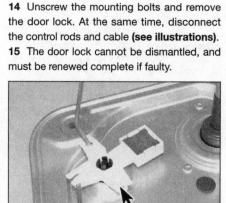

14.3 Removing the rubber grommets from the carrier (front door shown)

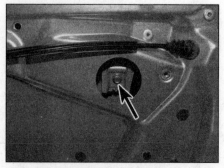

14.4a Window glass retaining clamp screw (front door)

14.4b Window glass retaining roll-pin
(rear door)

14.5 Unscrew the clamp screws
(front door)

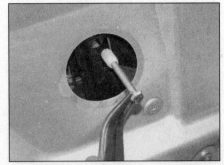

14.6 Use suitable bolts to remove the
inner and outer roll-pins (rear door)

14.7 Retain the window glass with
adhesive tape

14.8 Drill out the rivets . . .

14.9 . . . and withdraw the carrier from the
door

6 On the rear door, screw an M5 bolt approximately 70 mm long into the inner roll-pin, then use pliers to pull it out of the outer section. Similarly, screw an M8 bolt approximately 80 mm long into the outer roll-pin, and use the pliers to pull it out **(see illustration)**. This will disconnect the window glass from the regulator.

7 Lift the window glass to the top of the door and use adhesive tape to retain it in this position **(see illustration)**.

8 On models manufactured up to 11/2003 the carrier is retained to the inner door panel by screws, however, on later models it is retained by pop rivets. Undo the screws or drill out the rivets as applicable, and tap out the remains of the pop rivets which will drop down inside the door **(see illustration)**.

9 Carefully withdraw the carrier and disconnect the wiring. Also, release the wiring

harness from the cable ties. Remove the carrier from the door **(see illustration)**.

Refitting

10 To ensure correct adjustment of the door lock cable on the exterior door handle, the door lock must be set as follows. Pull out the control lever and use a screwdriver to hook the spring onto the lever **(see illustration)**. When the exterior door handle is refitted and operated, the spring will be released.

11 Before refitting the rear carrier, refit and centralise the plastic retaining roll-pins to the window glass so that the glass can be tapped down to engage the regulator **(see illustration)**. Although it is possible to refit the pins with the carrier in position, it is far easier to centralise the pins with the carrier removed. In practice, we removed the glass completely from the door to fit the pins (see Section 15).

Note that on models with electric windows, the pins must be aligned with the lug.

12 With the glass retained with the adhesive tape, refit the carrier and reconnect the wiring. At this stage retain the carrier with only two screws or pop rivets as applicable, so that the operation of the lock can be checked before fitting the remainder **(see illustration)**.

13 Remove the tape and lower the glass onto the regulator. Tighten the screws on the front door. On the rear door, gently tap the top edge of the glass until the retaining pin is heard to engage the clip on the regulator **(see illustration)**. Refit the rubber grommet(s).

14 Refit the exterior door handle with reference to Section 13, then refit and tighten the door lock mounting screws.

15 Before shutting the door for the first time, operate the lock with a screwdriver and check that it is functioning correctly.

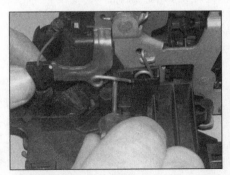

14.10 Hooking the spring onto the control
lever

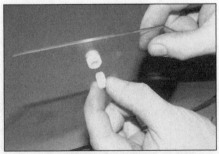

14.11 On the rear door, refit and centralise
the plastic retaining roll-pins to the
window glass

14.12 Fitting new pop rivets to retain the
carrier

14.13 On the rear door, gently tap the top edge of the glass until the retaining pin is heard to engage

16 Fit the remaining carrier screws or pop rivets as applicable.

17 Refit the door inner trim panel with reference to Section 12.

15 Door window glass –
removal and refitting

Removal

1 Remove the door inner trim panel as described in Section 12.

2 On some models it may be necessary to remove the window regulator and lock carrier first as described in Section 14, however, in our workshops, we found this unnecessary.

3 Prise the rubber grommet(s) from the hole(s) in the carrier, for access to the window glass retaining screws or roll-pin. The front door has

two holes for access to the retaining clamp screws, and the rear door has one hole for access to the single roll-pin.

4 Lower the window glass until the screws or plastic retaining roll-pin are visible in the hole. On models with electric windows, temporarily reconnect the battery and control switch to operate the glass, then disconnect the battery again. If the electric motor is not functioning correctly, unbolt the motor from the carrier to allow the window to be lowered.

5 On the front door, unscrew the two clamp screws.

6 On the rear door, screw an M5 bolt approximately 70 mm long into the inner roll-pin, then use pliers to pull it out of the outer section. Similarly, screw an M8 bolt approximately 80 mm long into the outer roll-pin, and use the pliers to pull it out. This will disconnect the window glass from the regulator.

7 To remove the front door glass, lift the window glass to the top of the door and use adhesive tape to retain it in this position. Fully lower the regulator, then tilt the glass and withdraw it from the outside of the door **(see illustration)**.

8 To remove the rear door glass, pull out and remove the rubber guide channel, and the glass inner seal, then carefully lift the glass from the inside of the door **(see illustrations)**. The glass must be positioned slightly behind the front of the quarter light guide before lifting it out.

9 To remove the rear door quarter light, first remove the rear door glass as described in

paragraph 8, then remove the outer seal, unscrew the channel retaining screw, and withdraw the quarter light from the rear door **(see illustrations)**.

Refitting

10 Refitting is a reversal of removal.

16 Tailgate and support struts
– removal and refitting

Tailgate

Note: *Removal and refitting of the rear boot lid on Saloon models is similar, but the trim panel is retained with additional screws.*

Removal

1 Disconnect the battery negative lead (refer to *Disconnecting the battery* in the *Reference* Chapter at the end of this manual).

2 With the tailgate open, release the trim panel retaining clips by carefully levering between the panel and tailgate with a wide-bladed screwdriver. Work around the outside of the panel, and when all the clips are released, remove the panel **(see illustration)**. It is likely that some of the clips will be pulled from their location in the trim panel, in which case they should be re-inserted.

3 Disconnect all wiring connectors from inside the tailgate, and disconnect the washer hose from the high-level stop-light (see Chapter 12, Section 7). Also, prise all wiring grommets from the tailgate. **Note:** *On late*

15.7 Removing the front door window glass

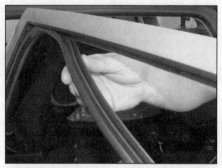

15.8a On the rear door, pull out the rubber guide channel and inner seal . . .

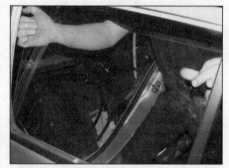

15.8b . . . then lift the glass from the inside of the door

15.9a Undo the screw . . .

15.9b . . . and withdraw the quarter light from the rear door

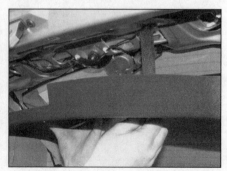

16.2 Removing the tailgate trim panel

models, a wiring multi-connector is provided near the left-hand support strut, which can be disconnected instead of removing the wiring.

4 Tie a piece of string to each end of the wiring then, noting the correct routing of the wiring harness, release the harness rubber grommets from the tailgate and withdraw the wiring. When the end of the wiring appears, untie the string and leave it in position in the tailgate; it can then be used on refitting to draw the wiring into position.

5 Using a suitable marker pen, draw around the outline of each hinge marking its correct position on the tailgate (**see illustration**).

6 With the help of an assistant to support the tailgate, remove the support struts as described below.

7 Using an Allen key, unscrew and remove the bolts securing the hinges to the tailgate. The bolts are not easy to access, and ideally a 10.0 mm angled Allen key should be used. Protect the surrounding paintwork with adhesive tape. Where necessary, recover the gaskets which are fitted between the hinge and vehicle body.

8 Inspect the hinges for signs of wear or damage and renew if necessary. The hinges are secured to the vehicle by nuts or bolts (depending on model) which can be accessed once the headlining rear cover strip has been removed.

Refitting

9 Refitting is a reversal of removal but tighten the tailgate mounting bolts to the specified torque. Check the tailgate alignment with the surrounding panels. If necessary slight adjustment can be made by slackening the retaining bolts and repositioning the tailgate on its hinges. When refitting the trim panel, insert the pull strap through the panel before tapping the retaining clips into the tailgate (**see illustration**).

Support struts

⚠️ **Warning: The support struts are filled with gas and must be disposed of safely.**

Removal

10 With the help of an assistant, support the tailgate in the open position.

11 Using a small screwdriver, lift the locking clip and pull the gas support strut off its balljoint

16.5 Tailgate hinge

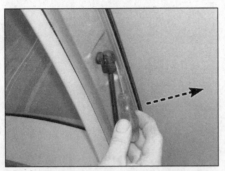

16.11a Lift the locking clips to remove the tailgate support struts

mounting on the tailgate (**see illustrations**). Repeat the procedure on the lower strut mounting and remove the strut from the vehicle body. **Note:** *If the gas strut is to be re-used, the locking clip must not be taken all the way out, or the clip will be damaged.*

Refitting

12 Refitting is a reversal of removal.

17 Tailgate lock components – removal and refitting 🔧

Removal

Note: *The following procedures are similar on Saloon models.*

Lock

1 With the tailgate open, release the trim panel

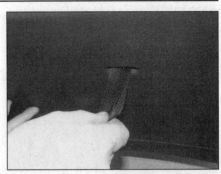

16.9 Insert the pull strap when refitting the tailgate trim panel

16.11b Tailgate support strut fixing on the body

retaining clips by carefully levering between the panel and tailgate with a wide-bladed screwdriver. Work around the outside of the panel, and when all the clips are released, remove the panel. It is likely that some of the clips will be pulled from their location in the trim panel, in which case they should be re-inserted.

2 Unscrew the mounting bolts and withdraw the lock from the tailgate, then disconnect the wiring (**see illustrations**).

Lock striker

3 With the tailgate open, pull up the weatherstrip, unclip the centre cover, and remove the trim panel from the rear valance; it is retained with clips at the top (**see illustrations**).

4 Disconnect the remote inner cable from the release lever, then loosen the locknut and

17.2a Unscrew the mounting bolts . . .

17.2b . . . withdraw the tailgate lock . . .

17.2c . . . and disconnect the wiring

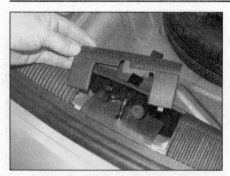

17.3a Unclip the centre cover . . .

17.3b Removing the trim panel from the rear valance . . .

17.3c . . . it is retained with clips at the top

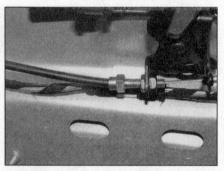

17.4 Release lever cable connection to the tailgate lock striker

17.5 Tailgate lock striker on the rear valance

remove the outer cable from the bracket **(see illustration)**.
5 Unscrew the mounting nuts and remove the lock striker from the rear valance **(see illustration)**.

Grab strap

6 Remove the trim panel as described in paragraph 1.
7 Unbolt the grab strap from the tailgate.

Grip handle

8 Remove the trim panel as described in paragraph 1.
9 Where applicable, remove the protective foil and disconnect the wiring.
10 Unscrew the mounting nuts and withdraw the grip handle from the tailgate **(see illustrations)**.

Refitting

11 Refitting is a reversal of removal. Before

refitting the trim panel, check the operation of the lock components and central locking system. If necessary, adjust the remote release cable for the tailgate striker so that the release handle on the right-hand side of the driver's seat operates correctly.

18 Central locking components – general

The operation of the central locking is integrated into the door locks and is controlled by the vehicle multi-function control unit. If a fault occurs in the system, the car should be taken to a Skoda dealer who will have the special diagnostic equipment necessary to find the fault quickly. The control unit also operates the alarm, sunroof, electric windows and exterior mirrors.

19 Electric window components – removal and refitting

Window switch

1 Refer to Chapter 12, Section 4.

Window winder motor

Removal

2 Remove the door inner trim panel as described in Section 12.
3 Disconnect the wiring from the motor.
4 Undo the mounting screws and withdraw the motor from the regulator carrier.

Refitting

5 Refitting is a reversal of removal. On completion, switch the ignition on and off, then switch it on again. Close the window and continue to press the switch for approximately 3 seconds in order to complete the basic setting and activate the automatic depth run function. Finally, switch off the ignition.

20 Exterior mirrors and associated components – removal and refitting

Removal

Exterior mirror

1 Remove the door inner trim panel as described in Section 12.

17.10a Unscrew the mounting nuts . . .

17.10b . . . and remove the grip handle from the tailgate

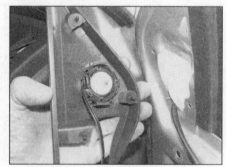

20.2 Unclip the inner trim panel and disconnect the speaker wiring

20.3 Undo the manually-operated mirror control knob mounting screw

20.4a Disconnect the mirror wiring connector . . .

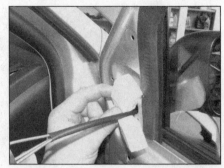

20.4b . . . and remove the packing

20.5a Undo the mounting screw . . .

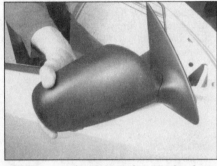

20.5b . . . and withdraw the exterior door mirror . . .

20.5c . . . while guiding the control cables through the door

2 Unclip and remove the mirror inner trim/ speaker panel, and disconnect the wiring where a speaker is fitted **(see illustration)**.

3 Where a manually-operated mirror is fitted, undo the screw securing the control knob to the door inner panel **(see illustration)**.

4 Disconnect the mirror wiring connector and remove the packing **(see illustrations)**.

5 Unscrew the mounting screw and withdraw the exterior mirror from the front door while guiding the wiring (electrically-operated mirror) or control cables (manually-operated mirror) through the hole in the door **(see illustrations)**.

Mirror glass

Note: *The mirror glass is clipped into place. Removal of the glass without the Skoda special tool (number 8-506 or 8-602/1) may result in breakage of the glass.*

6 Insert a suitable tool between the mirror glass and mirror housing. First prise out the mirror at the bottom, then at the top and carefully release the glass from the motor. Disconnect the wiring connectors from the mirror heating element where applicable. Take care when removing the glass; do not use excessive force as the glass is easily broken. If the Skoda special tool is not available, use a flat-bladed lever with tape around to prevent any damage to the mirror housing **(see illustrations)**.

Mirror housing

7 Fold the mirror assembly forwards and position the glass vertical to ease the removal of the housing.

8 Remove the small plastic plug in the bottom of the mirror assembly, then insert a screwdriver. Carefully push the screwdriver

forwards to release the securing clip, pulling the cover upwards over the mirror glass to remove.

Mirror switch

9 Refer to Chapter 12, Section 4.

Electrically-operated mirror motor

10 Remove the mirror glass as described above.

11 Undo the retaining screws and remove the motor, disconnecting its wiring connector as it becomes accessible.

Refitting

12 Refitting is a reversal of removal. When refitting the mirror glass, press firmly at the centre using a wad of cloth and taking care not to use excessive force, as the glass is easily broken **(see illustration)**.

20.6a Prise out the mirror glass . . .

20.6b . . . then carefully release it from the motor

20.12 Use a wad of cloth when refitting the mirror glass

24.2 Front seat rear mounting bolt

24.3 Front seat front mounting bolt

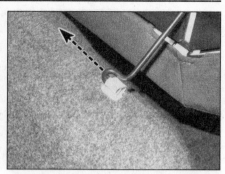

24.7 Push the hooks from the pivot brackets to remove the rear seat cushion

21 Windscreen, tailgate and fixed rear quarter window glass – general information

These areas of glass are bonded in position with a special adhesive. Renewal of such fixed glass is a difficult, messy and time-consuming task, which is beyond the scope of the home mechanic. It is difficult, unless one has plenty of practice, to obtain a secure, waterproof fit. In view of this, owners are strongly advised to have this work carried out by one of the many specialist windscreen fitters.

22 Sunroof – general information

Due to the complexity of the sunroof mechanism, considerable expertise is needed to repair, renew or adjust the sunroof components successfully. Removal of the roof first requires the headlining to be removed, which is a complex and tedious operation, and not a task to be undertaken lightly. Therefore, any problems with the sunroof should be referred to a Skoda dealer. On models with an electric sunroof, if the sunroof motor fails to operate, first check the relevant fuse. If the fault cannot be traced and rectified, the sunroof can be opened and closed manually using an Allen key to turn the motor spindle (a suitable key is supplied with the vehicle, and should be clipped onto the inside of the sunroof motor trim). To gain access to

the motor, unclip the rear of the trim cover to open. Unclip the Allen key, then insert it fully into the motor opening (against spring pressure). Rotate the key to move the sunroof to the required position.

23 Body exterior fittings – removal and refitting

Wheel arch liners and body under-panels

1 The various plastic covers fitted to the underside of the vehicle are secured in position by a mixture of screws, nuts and retaining clips and removal will be fairly obvious on inspection. Work methodically around the panel removing its retaining screws and releasing its retaining clips until the panel is free and can be removed from the underside of the vehicle. Most clips used on the vehicle are simply prised out of position. Remove the wheels to ease the removal of the wheel arch liners.
2 On refitting, renew any retaining clips that may have been broken on removal, and ensure that the panel is securely retained by all the relevant clips and screws.

Body trim strips and badges

3 The various body trim strips and badges (including the door entrance plates on vRS models) are held in position with a special adhesive tape and locating lugs. Removal requires the trim/badge to be heated, to soften the adhesive, and then carefully lifted

away from the surface. Due to the high risk of damage to the vehicle's paintwork during this operation, it is recommended that this task should be entrusted to a Skoda dealer.

24 Seats – removal and refitting

Note: *Refer to the warnings in Chapter 12 if side airbags are fitted to the vehicle. Before disconnecting the battery, refer to 'Disconnecting the battery' at the rear of this manual.*

Removal

Front seats

1 Disconnect the battery negative lead (refer to *Disconnecting the battery* in the *Reference* Chapter at the end of this manual).
2 Slide the seat fully forwards, then unscrew the rear mounting bolts securing the sliding rail to the floor, using a multi-spline key **(see illustration)**.
3 Slide the seat fully rearwards, and unscrew the front mounting bolts **(see illustration)**.
4 Tilt the seat backwards and disconnect the wiring for the seat heating, side airbag and seat belt buckle signalling.
5 Carefully remove the seat from inside the car, taking care not to damage the door opening plastic trim panels. The help of an assistant may be necessary as the seat is heavy.

Rear seat cushion

6 Pull up the front of the rear seat cushion, then lift the rear and fold the cushion forwards.
7 Push the hooks from the pivot brackets and remove the cushion from the car **(see illustration)**.

Rear seat backrest

8 Fold the rear seat cushion forwards.
9 Where an inertia reel centre seat belt is fitted in the backrest, unscrew the anchorage bolt from the floor.
10 Pull up the locking handle to release the relevant backrest section, and fold it forwards.
11 Using a screwdriver, depress the catch hook and pull the backrest pivot pin from the side bracket **(see illustration)**.
12 Slide the backrest from the pivot pin on the centre bracket and remove it from the car

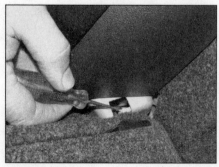

24.11 Depress the catch hook and pull the backrest pivot pin from the bracket . . .

24.12 Slide the backrest from the pivot pin

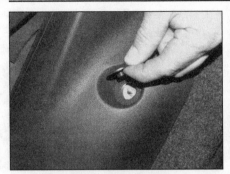

26.3a Prise out the fasteners . . .

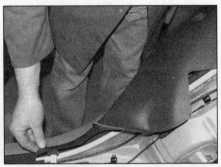

26.3b . . . and remove the door entrance sill trim and B-pillar trim

26.3c For the driver's side, unclip the knob from the tailgate release lever . . .

26.3d . . . and remove the plastic insert

26.4a Prise off the cover . . .

26.4b . . . and unscrew the upper mounting bolt from the height adjuster

(see illustration). If necessary, remove the plastic cap from the bracket.

Rear seat armrest

13 Pull up the locking handle to release the backrest section, and fold it forwards.
14 Unlock the armrest housing and remove it together with the armrest from the backrest.

Refitting

15 Refitting is a reversal of removal.

25 Front seat belt tensioning mechanism – general information

The front seat belt inertia reels are fitted with integral automatic belt tensioners (the rear seat belt inertia reels are not fitted with tensioners). The system is designed to instantaneously take up any slack in the seat belt in the case of a sudden frontal impact, therefore reducing the possibility of injury to the front seat occupants. Each front seat is fitted with its own system, the tensioner being situated behind the sill trim panel.

The seat belt tensioner is triggered by a frontal impact above a predetermined force. Lesser impacts, including impacts from behind, will not trigger the system.

When the system is triggered, the explosive gas in the tensioner mechanism retracts and locks the seat belt through a cable which acts on the inertia reel. This prevents the seat belt moving and keeps the occupant firmly in position in the seat. Once the tensioner has been triggered, the seat belt will be

permanently locked and the assembly must be renewed.

Note the following warnings before contemplating any work on the front seat belts.

⚠ **Warning: Do not expose the tensioner mechanism to temperatures in excess of 100°C (212°F).**
• *If the tensioner mechanism is dropped, it must be renewed, even it has suffered no apparent damage.*
• *Do not allow any solvents to come into contact with the tensioner mechanism.*
• *Do not attempt to open the tensioner mechanism as it contains explosive gas.*
• *Tensioners must be discharged before they are disposed of, but this task should be entrusted to a Skoda dealer.*
• *If the battery is to be disconnected, refer to 'Disconnecting the battery' at the rear of this manual.*

26 Seat belt components – removal and refitting

Removal

Front inertia reel and height adjuster

⚠ **Warning: The seat belt inertia reel incorporates a pyrotechnic automatic tensioner; do not subject the unit to temperatures in excess of 100°C (212°F), or allow any solvents or cleaning agents to contact the unit. The unit is sensitive to impact; if it is dropped or damaged it should be renewed.**

1 Disconnect the battery negative lead (refer to *Disconnecting the battery* in the *Reference* Chapter at the end of this manual).
2 Pull away the weatherseal from the B-pillar, and front/rear door entrance sills.
3 Prise out the fasteners and unclip the door entrance sill trim panels, and lower B-pillar trim panel. If removing the driver's door sill trim panel, first unclip the knob from the tailgate release lever and remove the plastic insert **(see illustrations)**.
4 Prise off the plastic cover and unscrew the upper mounting bolt securing the seat belt to the height adjuster **(see illustrations)**.
5 Carefully prise off the upper and lower trims from the B-pillar, and release the belt from the guide **(see illustrations)**.
6 Unscrew and remove the seat belt lower mounting bolt and free the seat belt from its lower anchorage **(see illustration)**.
7 Unscrew and remove the inertia reel

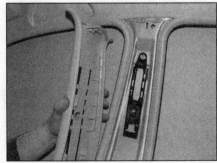

26.5a Prise off the upper . . .

26.5b ... and lower B-pillar trims ...

26.5c ... and release the belt from the guide

26.6 Front seat belt lower mounting bolt

mounting bolt and remove the seat belt assembly from the vehicle (see illustration).
8 To remove the belt height adjuster, remove the securing bolt and lift upwards from the pillar (see illustration).

Front belt stalk

9 Remove the front seat assembly as described in Section 25.
10 Where necessary, undo the screws and remove the plastic cover from the inner side of the seat.
11 Disconnect the wiring from the seat occupancy monitor and stalk buckle indicator.
12 Unscrew the stalk mounting bolt and remove the stalk from the seat (see illustration).

Rear side belt

13 Fold the rear seat cushion forwards, and remove the relevant rear seat backrest as described in Section 24.

26.7 Front seat belt inertia reel mounting bolt

14 Remove the rear carpet, then remove the fasteners, and unclip the rear luggage compartment side trim panels. When removing the left-hand side trim, disconnect the wiring for the interior light (see illustrations).

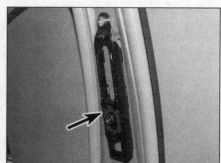

26.8 Front seat belt height adjuster

15 Unscrew the mounting bolt securing the seat belt to the floor (see illustration).
16 Unscrew the mounting bolt securing the inertia reel to the inner wheel arch, and withdraw from the car (see illustration).
17 To remove the centre stalk, unscrew the

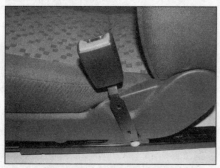

26.12 Front seat belt stalk

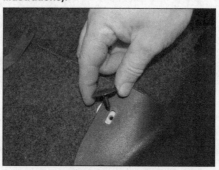

26.14a Remove the fasteners ...

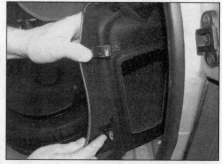

26.14b ... unclip the trim panels ...

26.14c ... and remove them from the rear luggage compartment

26.14d On the left-hand side, disconnect the wiring from the interior light

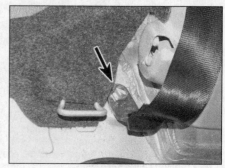

26.15 Rear seat side belt mounting bolt on the floor

26.16 Rear seat side belt inertia reel mounting bolt

26.17 Centre stalk mounting bolt

26.19a Remove the headrests . . .

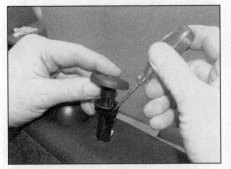

26.19b . . . then use a screwdriver to remove the guides

26.20 Prise out the plastic cover . . .

26.21 . . . then pull out the beading to remove the cover from the rear of the backrest

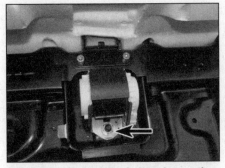

26.22 Rear seat centre belt reel mounting nut

26.23 Cable-operated safety mechanism to ensure backrest is locked before inserting seat belt buckle

27.1a Removing the headlining rear trim . . .

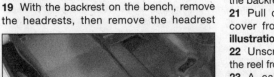

27.1b . . . and C-pillar trim

mounting bolt **(see illustration)**. Note that there are two stalks on the left-hand side; one for the side belt and the other for the centre lap belt. The right-hand side stalk also includes the anchorage for the centre belt.

Rear centre belt

18 Remove the rear seat backrest as described in Section 24.
19 With the backrest on the bench, remove the headrests, then remove the headrest guides using a small screwdriver to depress the locking tabs **(see illustrations)**.
20 Prise out the plastic cover from the top of the backrest **(see illustration)**.
21 Pull out the beading and remove the cover from the rear of the backrest **(see illustration)**.
22 Unscrew the mounting nut and remove the reel from the backrest **(see illustration)**.
23 A cable-operated safety mechanism is fitted to the backrest, to ensure that the backrest is fully locked in position before allowing the seat belt buckle to be inserted. To remove the mechanism, release the clip from the locking lever **(see illustration)**.

Refitting

24 Refitting is a reversal of the removal procedure, ensuring that all the seat belt units are located correctly and mounting bolts are tightened to their specified torque. Check all the trim panels are securely retained by all the relevant retaining clips.

27 Interior trim – removal and refitting

Interior trim panels

1 The interior trim panels are secured using either screws or various types of trim fasteners, usually studs or clips **(see illustrations)**.
2 Check that there are no other panels overlapping the one to be removed; usually there is a sequence that has to be followed,

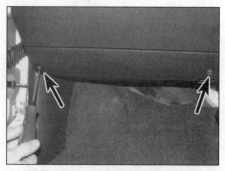

27.7a Unscrew the glovebox lower screws . . .

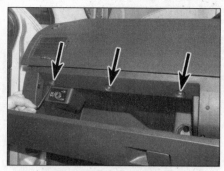

27.7b . . . and upper screws

27.8 Disconnecting the wiring from the glovebox illumination light

27.9a Disconnect the wiring from the passenger airbag on/off switch . . .

27.9b . . . then disconnect the air conditioning hose

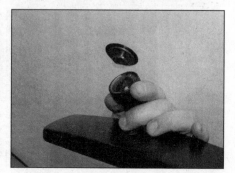

27.16 Removing the interior mirror

and this will only become obvious on close inspection.

3 Remove all obvious fasteners, such as screws. If the panel will not come free, it is held by hidden clips or fasteners. These are usually situated around the edge of the panel and can be prised up to release them; note, however that they can break quite easily so new ones should be available. The best way of releasing such clips, without the correct type of tool, is to use a large flat-bladed screwdriver. Note in many cases that the adjacent sealing strip must be prised back to release a panel.

4 When removing a panel, **never** use excessive force or the panel may be damaged; always check carefully that all fasteners or other relevant components have been removed or released before attempting to withdraw a panel.

5 Refitting is the reverse of the removal procedure; secure the fasteners by pressing them firmly into place and ensure that all disturbed components are correctly secured to prevent rattles.

Glovebox

6 Before the glovebox can be removed, the centre console front section has to be removed to gain access to one of the screws, see Section 28.

7 Unscrew the lower retaining screws, then open up the glovebox lid and unscrew the remaining screws **(see illustrations)**.

8 Slide the glovebox out of position, disconnecting the wiring connector from the glovebox illumination light (where fitted) as it becomes accessible **(see illustration)**.

9 As applicable, disconnect the wiring from the passenger airbag on/off (isolation) switch and disconnect the air conditioning hose from the glovebox **(see illustrations)**.

10 Remove the glovebox from inside the car.

11 Refitting is the reverse of removal.

Carpets

12 The passenger compartment floor carpet is in one piece and is secured at its edges by screws or clips, usually the same fasteners used to secure the various adjoining trim panels.

13 Carpet removal and refitting is reasonably straightforward but very time-consuming because all adjoining trim panels must be removed first, as must components such as the seats, the centre console and seat belt lower anchorages.

Headlining

14 The headlining is clipped to the roof and

28.1 Prise out the cover/oddments tray/ rear ashtray from the centre console . . .

can be withdrawn only once all fittings such as the grab handles, sun visors, sunroof (if fitted), and related upper trim panels have been removed and the door, tailgate and sunroof aperture sealing strips have been prised clear. To remove the sun visors and grab handles the plastic covers have to be unclipped first, to gain access to the securing screws.

15 Note that headlining removal requires considerable skill and experience if it is to be carried out without damage and is therefore best entrusted to an expert.

Interior mirror

Standard

16 Pull the mirror downwards off its retaining clip to remove **(see illustration)**. When refitting, place the mirror at 60° to 90° anti-clockwise to the mounted position; then turn clockwise until the locking clip locks into place to secure the mirror.

17 Refitting is a reversal of removal.

Facia lower trim panels

18 See Section 29.

28 Centre console – removal and refitting

Removal

1 Using a screwdriver, prise the cover/ oddments tray/ashtray from the rear of the centre console **(see illustration)**.

28.2 ... undo the rear mounting
screws ...

28.3 ... then remove the cover ...

28.4 ... and front ashtray

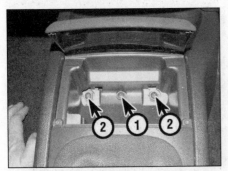

28.5a Surround (1) and console (2)
retaining screws

28.5b Unclip the surround ...

28.7 ... disconnect the 12 volt supply
wiring ...

2 Undo and remove the console rear mounting screws (see illustration).
3 Prise out the cover from beneath the handbrake lever (see illustration).
4 Prise the ashtray from the front of the centre console (see illustration). Also, prise the gear lever gaiter from the surround and pull it up onto the knob.
5 Undo the centre screw, then unclip and remove the surround from the console (see illustrations).
6 Undo and remove the console front mounting screws.
7 Remove the fastener securing the front of the centre console to the bracket on each side (see illustration).
8 Fully apply the handbrake lever, then ease the centre console rearwards until the wiring for the 12 volt supply can be disconnected.
9 Lift the console over the handbrake lever and remove from inside the car (see illustration).

Note that Velcro is used to secure the console on later models.
10 If necessary, unclip the front section from the centre console.

Refitting

11 Refitting is a reversal of removal.

29 Facia panel assembly
– removal and refitting

Note: *Refer to the warnings in Chapter 12 for airbags. Label each wiring connector as it is disconnected from its component to aid refitting. Note the exact routing of the wiring.*

Removal

1 Disconnect the battery negative lead (refer to *Disconnecting the battery* in the *Reference* Chapter at the end of this manual).

2 Remove the centre console as described in Section 28.
3 Remove the steering wheel as described in Chapter 10.
4 Remove the instrument panel as described in Chapter 12.
5 Remove the airbag contact switch (slip-ring) and combination switch from the top of the steering column as described in Chapter 12, Section 4.
6 Unclip the cover from each end of the facia panel (see illustration).
7 Remove the lighting switch as described in Chapter 12, Section 4.
8 Undo the screws and release the fusebox assembly from the end of the facia panel, and position it to one side (see illustration).
9 Disconnect the wiring from the diagnostic socket on the driver's side. Alternatively, remove the socket completely (see illustration).

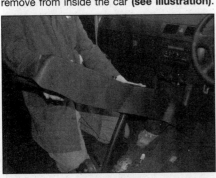

28.9 ... then lift the centre console from
inside the car

29.6 Unclip the cover from each end of the
facia panel

29.8 Undo the screws securing the
fusebox assembly to the end of the facia
panel

29.9 Removing the diagnostic socket

29.10a Undo the screws . . .

29.10b . . . and remove the trim panel . . .

29.10c . . . then disconnect the air conditioning hose and remove the lower facia panel from the driver's side

29.13 Removing a switch blank from the facia

29.14 Remove the side covers

10 Undo the screws and remove the trim panel, then disconnect the air conditioning hose and remove the lower facia panel from the driver's side **(see illustrations)**.

11 Remove the glovebox as described in Section 27.

12 Remove the radio as described in Chapter 12.

13 Remove the central push-type switches from the facia as described in Chapter 12, Section 4. Where there are blanks, prise them out **(see illustration)**

14 Where a cup holder is fitted, open it, then pull out the small upper trim, undo the screws, and remove the holder. On models without a cup holder, remove the side covers **(see illustration)**.

15 Where fitted, remove the oddments box or cover **(see illustrations)**.

16 Prise off the heater control trim panel **(see illustration)**.

17 Undo the lower screws, and push the heater controls in from the facia **(see illustration)**.

18 Undo the screws and remove the centre housing from the facia **(see illustration)**.

19 Undo the screws and remove the trim panel from over the steering column **(see illustration)**.

20 Using a screwdriver and piece of card, carefully prise out the hazard warning switch/vent panel from the facia, and disconnect the wiring from the switch **(see illustrations)**.

29.15a Undo the screws . . .

29.15b . . . and remove the oddments box

29.16 Prise off the heater control trim panel . . .

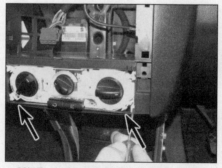

29.17 . . . then undo the heater control retaining screws

29.18 Removing the centre housing from the facia

29.19 Removing the small trim panel from over the steering column

29.20a Prise out the hazard warning switch/vent panel from the facia . . .

29.20b . . . and disconnect the wiring from the switch

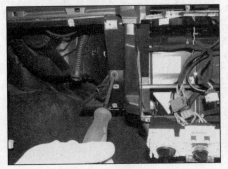

29.23a Undo the retaining screws . . .

29.23b . . . and withdraw the facia from the bulkhead

29.23c Front guides for the facia

21 Where applicable, disconnect the wiring from the passenger airbag.

22 Disconnect all wiring plugs from the rear of the facia, noting their routing for correct refitting. Also, release any wiring loom retaining straps and ties.

23 Undo the facia panel retaining screws. Check that all wiring and retaining screws have been removed, then, with the help of an assistant, withdraw the facia from the bulkhead and remove from one side of the car. The front of the facia may be tight on the front guides located just behind the windscreen **(see illustrations)**.

Refitting

24 Refitting is a reversal of the removal procedure, noting the following points:

a) *Make sure the wiring is correctly routed and connected, and secure where necessary with cable ties. Refit all the facia fasteners, and tighten them securely.*

b) *On completion, check that all the electrical components and switches function correctly. As a precaution against the airbags being activated, make sure no one is sitting in the vehicle as the battery is being reconnected.*

Notes

Chapter 12
Body electrical system

Contents

Section number

Airbag system – general information and precautions 25
Airbag system components – removal and refitting 26
Anti-theft alarm system and engine immobiliser – general
  information 24
Battery – removal and refitting . . . . See Chapter 5A
Battery check and maintenance . . . . See *Weekly checks*
Bulbs (exterior lights) – renewal 5
Bulbs (interior lights) – renewal 6
Cigarette lighter – removal and refitting 14
Clock – removal and refitting 13
Convenience system – general information 29
Electrical fault finding – general information 2
Exterior light units – removal and refitting 7
Fuses and relays – general information 3
Gas-discharge headlight system – component removal and
  refitting 28
General information and precautions 1
Headlight beam adjustment components – removal and refitting . . . 8

Section number

Headlight beam alignment – general information 9
Horn – removal and refitting 15
Instrument panel – removal and refitting 10
Instrument panel components – removal and refitting 11
Loudspeakers – removal and refitting 22
Parking aid components – general information, removal and
  refitting 27
Radio aerial – removal and refitting 23
Radio/cassette/CD player/changer – removal and refitting 21
Rear wiper motor – removal and refitting 19
Service interval indicator – general information and resetting 12
Speedometer sensor – general information 16
Switches – removal and refitting 4
Washer fluid level check . . . . See *Weekly checks*
Washer system components – removal and refitting 20
Windscreen wiper motor and linkage – removal and refitting 18
Wiper arm – removal and refitting 17
Wiper blade check and renewal . . . . See *Weekly checks*

Degrees of difficulty

| Easy, suitable for novice with little experience | 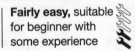 | Fairly easy, suitable for beginner with some experience | | Fairly difficult, suitable for competent DIY mechanic | | Difficult, suitable for experienced DIY mechanic | | Very difficult, suitable for expert DIY or professional | |

Specifications

System type . . . . 12 volt negative earth

Fuses . . . . See *Wiring diagrams* on page 12•21

Bulbs	Wattage	Type
Front foglight	55	H3 Halogen
Direction indicators	21	Bayonet
Door warning light	5	Festoon
Front sidelight	5	Wedge
Glovebox light	3	Wedge
Headlight:		
Halogen:		
Main beam	55	H3 Halogen
Low beam	55	H7 Halogen
Gas-discharge (Xenon):		
Main beam	55	H7 Halogen
Low beam	35	D2S (80-117 volt)
High-level stop-light	N/A	LED
Interior light	10	Festoon
Luggage compartment light	5	Festoon
Reading light	5	Festoon
Rear foglight/left-hand tail light	21/4	Bayonet
Rear number plate light	5	Wedge
Rear right-hand tail light	4	Bayonet
Reversing light	21	Bayonet
Stop-light	21	Bayonet

Torque wrench setting	Nm	lbf ft
Airbag (passenger)	10	7

1 General information and precautions

⚠️ **Warning: Before carrying out any work on the electrical system, read through the precautions given in 'Safety first!' at the beginning of this manual, and in Chapter 5A.**

The electrical system is of 12 volt negative earth type. Power for the lights and all electrical accessories is supplied by a lead-acid type battery, which is charged by the alternator.

This Chapter covers repair and service procedures for the various electrical components not associated with the engine. Information on the battery, alternator and starter motor can be found in Chapter 5A.

It should be noted that prior to working on any component in the electrical system, the ignition and all electrical consumers must be switched off. Additionally, where stated, the battery negative lead must be disconnected, however, note the information given in *Disconnecting the battery* in the *Reference* section at the end of this manual, as special procedures have to be carried out when reconnecting the battery.

Early models were only fitted with halogen headlights, however, later models may be fitted with a gas-discharge (Xenon) headlight dipped beam system. These vehicles are also equipped with automatic range control, to reduce the possibility of dazzling oncoming drivers. Note the special precautions which apply to these systems as given in Section 5.

2 Electrical fault finding – general information

Note: *Refer to the precautions given in 'Safety first!' and in Chapter 5A before starting work. The following tests relate to testing of the main electrical circuits, and should not be used to test delicate electronic circuits (such as anti-lock braking systems), particularly where an electronic control module is used.*

General

1 A typical electrical circuit consists of an electrical component, any switches, relays, motors, fuses, fusible links or circuit breakers related to that component, and the wiring and connectors which link the component to both the battery and the chassis. To help to pinpoint a problem in an electrical circuit, wiring diagrams are included at the end of this Chapter.

2 Before attempting to diagnose an electrical fault, first study the appropriate wiring diagram to obtain a complete understanding of the components included in the particular circuit concerned. The possible sources of a fault can be narrowed down by noting if other components related to the circuit are operating properly. If several components or circuits fail at one time, the problem is likely to be related to a shared fuse or earth connection.

3 Electrical problems usually stem from simple causes, such as loose or corroded connections, a faulty earth connection, a blown fuse, a melted fusible link, or a faulty relay (refer to Section 3 for details of testing relays). Visually inspect the condition of all fuses, wires and connections in a problem circuit before testing the components. Use the wiring diagrams to determine which terminal connections will need to be checked in order to pinpoint the trouble spot.

4 The basic tools required for electrical fault finding include a circuit tester or voltmeter (a 12 volt bulb with a set of test leads can also be used for certain tests); a self-powered test light (sometimes known as a continuity tester); an ohmmeter (to measure resistance); a battery and set of test leads; and a jumper wire, preferably with a circuit breaker or fuse incorporated, which can be used to bypass suspect wires or electrical components. Before attempting to locate a problem with test instruments, use the wiring diagram to determine where to make the connections.

5 To find the source of an intermittent wiring fault (usually due to a poor or dirty connection, or damaged wiring insulation), a wiggle test can be performed on the wiring. This involves wiggling the wiring by hand to see if the fault occurs as the wiring is moved. It should be possible to narrow down the source of the fault to a particular section of wiring. This method of testing can be used in conjunction with any of the tests described in the following sub-Sections.

6 Apart from problems due to poor connections, two basic types of fault can occur in an electrical circuit – open-circuit, or short-circuit.

7 Open-circuit faults are caused by a break somewhere in the circuit, which prevents current from flowing. An open-circuit fault will prevent a component from working, but will not cause the relevant circuit fuse to blow.

8 Short-circuit faults are caused by a short somewhere in the circuit, which allows the current flowing in the circuit to escape along an alternative route, usually to earth. Short-circuit faults are normally caused by a breakdown in wiring insulation, which allows a feed wire to touch either another wire, or an earthed component such as the bodyshell. A short-circuit fault will normally cause the relevant circuit fuse to blow.

Finding an open-circuit

9 To check for an open-circuit, connect one lead of a circuit tester or voltmeter to either the negative battery terminal or a known good earth.

10 Connect the other lead to a connector in the circuit being tested, preferably nearest to the battery or fuse.

11 Switch on the circuit, bearing in mind that some circuits are live only when the ignition switch is moved to a particular position.

12 If voltage is present (indicated either by the tester bulb lighting or a voltmeter reading, as applicable), this means that the section of the circuit between the relevant connector and the battery is problem-free.

13 Continue to check the remainder of the circuit in the same fashion.

14 When a point is reached at which no voltage is present, the problem must lie between that point and the previous test point with voltage. Most problems can be traced to a broken, corroded or loose connection.

Finding a short-circuit

15 To check for a short-circuit, first disconnect the load(s) from the circuit (loads are the components which draw current from a circuit, such as bulbs, motors, heating elements, etc).

16 Remove the relevant fuse from the circuit, and connect a circuit tester or voltmeter to the fuse connections.

17 Switch on the circuit, bearing in mind that some circuits are live only when the ignition switch is moved to a particular position.

18 If voltage is present (indicated either by the tester bulb lighting or a voltmeter reading, as applicable), this means that there is a short circuit.

19 If no voltage is present, but the fuse still blows with the load(s) connected, this indicates an internal fault in the load(s).

Finding an earth fault

20 The battery negative terminal is connected to earth – the metal of the engine/transmission and the car body – and most systems are wired so that they only receive a positive feed, the current returning through the metal of the car body. This means that the component mounting and the body form part of that circuit. Loose or corroded mountings can therefore cause a range of electrical faults, ranging from total failure of a circuit, to a puzzling partial fault. In particular, lights may shine dimly (especially when another circuit sharing the same earth point is in operation), motors (eg, wiper motors or the radiator cooling fan motor) may run slowly, and the operation of one circuit may have an apparently unrelated effect on another. Note that on many vehicles, earth straps are used between certain components, such as the engine/transmission and the body, usually where there is no metal-to-metal contact between components due to flexible rubber mountings, etc.

21 To check whether a component is properly earthed, disconnect the battery (refer to the warnings given in the Reference section at the rear of the manual) and connect one lead of an ohmmeter to a known good earth point. Connect the other lead to the wire or earth connection being tested. The resistance reading should be zero; if not, check the connection as follows.

22 If an earth connection is thought to be faulty, dismantle the connection and clean back to bare metal both the bodyshell and the wire terminal or the component earth connection mating surface. Be careful to remove all traces of dirt and corrosion, then use a knife to trim away any paint, so that a clean metal-to-metal joint is made. On reassembly, tighten the joint fasteners securely; if a wire terminal is being refitted, use serrated washers between the terminal and the bodyshell to ensure a clean and secure connection. When the connection is remade, prevent the onset of corrosion in the future by applying a coat of petroleum jelly or silicone-based grease or by spraying on (at regular intervals) a proprietary ignition sealer or a water dispersant lubricant.

3 Fuses and relays – general information

Fuses and fusible links

1 Fuses are designed to break a circuit when a predetermined current is reached, in order to protect the components and wiring which could be damaged by excessive current flow. Any excessive current flow will be due to a fault in the circuit, usually a short-circuit (see Section 2).

2 The main fuses are located in the fusebox on the driver's side of the facia. Open the driver's door and unclip the fusebox cover from the end of the facia to gain access to the fuses **(see illustrations)**. The fuse locations are marked onto the rear of the fusebox cover.

3 To remove a fuse, first switch off the circuit concerned (or the ignition), then pull the fuse out of its terminals **(see illustration)**.

4 The wire within the fuse should be visible; if the fuse has blown it will be broken or melted.

5 Always renew a fuse with one of the correct rating, never use a fuse with a different rating from that specified.

6 Refer to the wiring diagrams for details of the fuse ratings and the circuits protected. The fuse rating is stamped on the top of the fuse, the fuses are also colour-coded as follows.

Colour	Rating
Light brown	5A
Dark brown	7.5A
Red	10A
Blue	15A
Yellow	20A
White	25A
Green	30A

7 Never renew a fuse more than once without tracing the source of the trouble. If the new fuse blows immediately, find the cause before renewing it again; a short to earth as a result of faulty insulation is most likely. Where a fuse protects more than one circuit, try to isolate the fault by switching on each circuit in turn (where possible) until the fuse blows again.

3.2a Unclip the fusebox cover . . .

Always carry a supply of spare fuses of each relevant rating on the vehicle.

8 Additional heavy-duty fusible links are located in the fuse holder which is fitted to the top of the battery. Unclip and open the fuse holder cover to gain access to these links.

9 To renew a fusible link, first disconnect the battery negative terminal. Unscrew the retaining nuts then remove the blown link from the holder. Fit the new link to its terminals and reconnect the lead. Ensure the link and lead are correctly seated then refit the retaining nuts and tighten securely. Clip the cover back into position then reconnect the battery.

Relays

10 A relay is an electrically-operated switch, which is used for the following reasons:

a) *A relay can switch a heavy current remotely from the circuit in which the current is flowing, allowing the use of lighter-gauge wiring and switch contacts.*

b) *A relay can receive more than one control input, unlike a mechanical switch.*

c) *A relay can have a timer function – for example, the intermittent wiper relay.*

11 Most of the relays are located on the relay plate behind the driver's side facia, however, on some models additional relays are located at the rear of the engine compartment.

12 Access to the relays can be obtained after removing the driver's side lower facia panel as described in Chapter 11, then removing the two relay plate retaining screws (one at either end), and lowering the plate complete with relays. Identification details of the relays are given at the start of the wiring diagrams.

13 If a circuit or system controlled by a relay develops a fault, and the relay is suspect, operate the system. If the relay is functioning, it should be possible to hear it click as it is energised. If this is the case, the fault lies with the components or wiring of the system. If the relay is not being energised, then either the relay is not receiving a main supply or a switching voltage, or the relay itself is faulty. Testing is by the substitution of a known good unit, but be careful – while some relays are identical in appearance and in operation, others look similar but perform different functions.

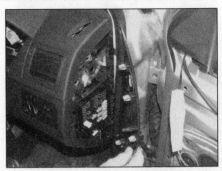

3.2b . . . for access to the fuses

14 To remove a relay, first ensure that the relevant circuit is switched off. The relay can then simply be pulled out from the socket, and pushed back into position.

15 The direction indicator/hazard flasher relay is integral with the hazard warning switch. Refer to Section 4 for the switch removal procedure.

4 Switches – removal and refitting

Ignition switch/steering lock

1 Refer to Chapter 10.

Steering column combination switch

Removal

2 Disconnect the battery negative lead (refer to *Disconnecting the battery* in the *Reference* Chapter at the end of this manual).

3 Remove the steering wheel as described in Chapter 10.

4 Remove the airbag wiring contact unit (slip-ring) as described in Section 26. Alternatively, if the switch is being removed for access, the unit may remain attached to the combination switch, and the wiring disconnected.

5 Loosen the switch clamp screw, disconnect the wiring, and pull the switch assembly from the column **(see illustrations)**.

Refitting

6 Refitting is a reversal of removal, but the

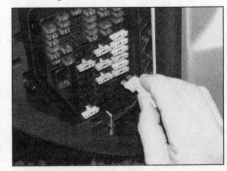

3.3 Removing a fuse from the fusebox

4.5a Loosen the switch clamp screw . . .

4.5b . . . disconnect the wiring . . .

4.5c . . . and pull the switch assembly from the column

4.6 Using feeler blades to check the clearance between the steering wheel and the coil connector with slip-ring

4.8a With the light switch in position O, press the switch centre inwards and turn it slightly to the right . . .

4.8b . . . then pull the switch from the dash . . .

switch must be accurately positioned as follows:

a) *Refit the switch to the column, but only lightly tighten the clamp screw.*

b) *If removed, refit the airbag wiring contact unit (slip-ring) with reference to Section 26.*

c) *Temporarily refit the steering wheel, and measure the clearance between the wheel and coil connector with slip-ring. The correct clearance is approximately 2.5 mm* **(see illustration).**

d) *Once the correct clearance is achieved, tighten the switch clamp screw securely.*

Lighting switch

Removal

7 Disconnect the battery negative lead (refer to *Disconnecting the battery* in the *Reference* Chapter at the end of this manual).

8 With the light switch in position O, press the

switch centre inwards and turn it slightly to the right. Hold this position and pull the switch from the dash **(see illustrations).**

9 As the switch is withdrawn from the dash, disconnect the wiring plugs **(see illustration).**

Refitting

10 Reconnect the wiring plug.

11 Insert the switch into the dash until it is heard to lock in place. Check the switch for correct operation.

Headlamp range/ illumination control

Removal

12 Remove the lighting switch as previously described, then use a screwdriver to release the catch and pull out the control unit.

Refitting

13 Refitting is a reversal of removal.

Sliding roof/interior light switch

Removal

14 Carefully prise out the lens, then undo the screws, remove the roof switch/interior light, and disconnect the wiring **(see illustrations).**

Refitting

15 Refitting is a reversal of removal.

Electric mirror switch

Removal

16 The switch is located on the interior door handle. Using a screwdriver, carefully lever out the switch together with the cover, and disconnect the wiring.

17 Unclip the switch from the cover.

Refitting

18 Refitting is a reversal of removal.

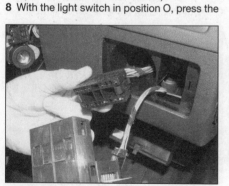

4.9 . . . and disconnect the wiring plugs

4.14a Undo the screws . . .

4.14b . . . and remove the roof switch/ interior light unit

Electric window switch

Removal

19 Disconnect the battery negative lead (refer to *Disconnecting the battery* in the *Reference* Chapter at the end of this manual).
20 To remove the switch panel, Skoda technicians use a special tool inserted from below, however, a bent screwdriver or similar tool can be used instead. Insert the screwdriver/tool under the plastic clip, and lever it out while pulling the holder upwards.
21 Disconnect the wiring.
22 Undo the screws and remove the switch assembly from the panel.

Refitting

23 Refitting is a reversal of removal.

Heated seat, heated window, ESP/TCS switches and passenger airbag indicator

Removal

24 Switch off the ignition and all electrical consumers.
25 Due to the strong retaining clips, these switches may be difficult to prise from the facia, in which case it is recommended that the radio/cassette be removed first and the relevant switch pushed out from behind **(see illustration)**. Where blanks are fitted instead of the front seat heating switches, they can be prised out easily for access to adjacent switches. Take care not to damage the surrounding trim, and use a piece of card as protection if necessary.
26 Disconnect the switch wiring plug **(see illustration)**.

Refitting

27 Reconnect the switch wiring plug, and push the switch firmly into position.

Hazard warning light switch

Removal

28 Carefully prise the centre vent unit from the facia using a screwdriver. Use a piece of card to protect the trim.
29 Disconnect the wiring from the hazard warning switch.
30 Press the switch from the centre vent unit.

Refitting

31 Refitting is a reversal of removal.

Heater blower motor and air conditioning switches

32 The switches are integral with the heater control panel, and cannot be removed separately. Refer to Chapter 3 for details of heater control panel removal and refitting.

Brake light and handbrake 'on' warning

33 Refer to Chapter 9.

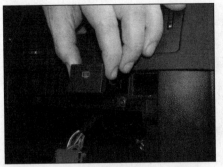

4.25 Push out the switch from behind . . .

Reversing light switch

34 Refer to Chapter 7A.

Courtesy light switches

35 The courtesy light switch is integrated into the door lock mechanism, and cannot be renewed independently. If the courtesy light switch is faulty, renew the door lock mechanism as described in Chapter 11.

Luggage area light switch

36 The luggage compartment light switch is integrated into the tailgate/boot lid lock mechanism, and cannot be renewed independently. If the luggage compartment light switch is faulty, renew the tailgate/boot lid lock mechanism as described in Chapter 11.

Glovebox light switch

Removal

37 Switch off the ignition and all electrical consumers.
38 The switch is integral with the light assembly. Note, however, that it is not possible to remove and refit the switch from inside the glovebox, as, when fitted, the wiring connector will not pass through the light mounting hole. First, remove the glovebox as described in Chapter 11, Section 27.
39 Carefully prise the light from inside the glovebox.

Refitting

40 Refitting is a reversal of removal.

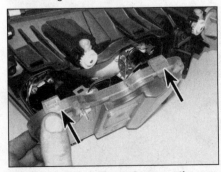

5.4 Depress the clips and remove the rear cover from the headlight . . .

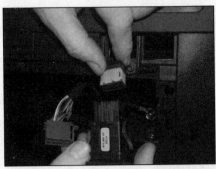

4.26 . . . and disconnect the wiring

5 Bulbs (exterior lights) – renewal

General

1 Whenever a bulb is renewed, note the following points:
a) *Switch off the ignition and all electrical consumers before commencing work.*
b) *Remember that if the light has just been in use the bulb may be extremely hot.*
c) *Always check the bulb contacts and holder, ensuring that there is clean metal-to-metal contact between the bulb and its live(s) and earth. Clean off any corrosion or dirt before fitting a new bulb.*
d) *Wherever bayonet-type bulbs are fitted ensure that the live contact(s) bear firmly against the bulb contact.*
e) *Always ensure that the new bulb is of the correct rating and that it is completely clean before fitting it.*
2 On models with standard halogen headlights, the outer bulb has two filaments, one for dipped beam and the other for main beam. On models without foglights, there is an additional inner dipped beam bulb, however, this position is taken by a foglight bulb on models with foglights.
3 On models with gas-discharge headlights, the gas-discharge dipped beam bulb is fitted in the central position of the headlight. A halogen foglight bulb is fitted on the outer position, and a halogen main beam bulb is fitted on the innermost position.

Headlight main beam

Halogen headlights

4 Working in the engine compartment, remove the cover from the rear of the headlight by depressing the two upper securing clips **(see illustration)**. Since access to the left-hand headlight is difficult, either remove the headlight completely or remove the battery (see Chapter 5A).
5 Disconnect the wire leading to the rear of the main beam bulb **(see illustration)**.
6 Unhook and release the ends of the bulb retaining clip from the light unit, then withdraw

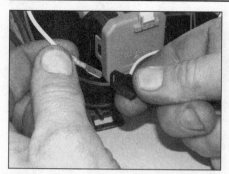

5.5 . . . then disconnect the wire . . .

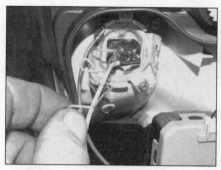

5.6a . . . unhook the retaining clip . . .

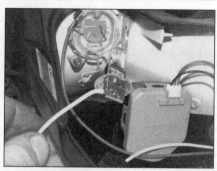

5.6b . . . and withdraw the main beam bulb together with the short length of wire

the bulb together with the short length of wire (see illustrations).

7 When handling the new bulb, use a tissue or clean cloth to avoid touching the glass with the fingers; moisture and grease from the skin can cause blackening and rapid failure of this type of bulb. If the glass is accidentally touched, wipe it clean using methylated spirit.

8 Install the new bulb, ensuring that its locating tabs are correctly located in the light cut-outs, and secure it in position with the retaining clip.

9 Reconnect the wiring and refit the headlight cover, making sure it is secure.

Gas-discharge headlights

10 For the right-hand side, remove the head-lamp assembly as described in Section 7. For the left-hand side, either remove the headlamp assembly as described in Section 7 or remove the battery as described in Chapter 5A.

11 Remove the rear cover.

12 Disconnect the wiring plug from the gas-discharge ignition/high voltage unit, then detach the unit from the gas-discharge bulb.

13 Undo the screws and remove the gas-discharge ignition/high voltage unit.

14 Disconnect the wiring plug from the rear of the main beam bulb.

15 Unhook and release the ends of the bulb retaining clip from the light unit, then withdraw the bulb.

16 When handling the new bulb, use a tissue or clean cloth to avoid touching the glass with the fingers; moisture and grease from the skin can cause blackening and rapid failure of this type of bulb. If the glass is accidentally

touched, wipe it clean using methylated spirit.

17 Install the new bulb, ensuring that its locating tabs are correctly located in the light cut-outs, and secure it in position with the retaining clip.

18 The remaining procedure is a reversal of removal.

Headlight dipped beam

Halogen headlights

19 The dipped beam bulb is located on the outer position of the headlight. First, remove the cover from the rear of the headlight. Since access to the left-hand headlight is difficult, either remove the headlight completely or remove the battery (see Chapter 5A).

20 Disconnect the wiring plug from the rear of the dipped beam bulb (see illustration).

21 Unhook and release the ends of the bulb retaining clip from the light unit, then withdraw the bulb (see illustrations).

22 When handling the new bulb, use a tissue or clean cloth to avoid touching the glass with the fingers; moisture and grease from the skin can cause blackening and rapid failure of this type of bulb. If the glass is accidentally touched, wipe it clean using methylated spirit.

23 Install the new bulb, ensuring that its locating tabs are correctly located in the light cut-outs, and secure it in position with the retaining clip.

24 Reconnect the wiring plug and refit the headlight cover, making sure it is secure.

Gas-discharge headlights

25 Remove the headlamp assembly as described in Section 7.

26 Remove the rear cover.

27 Disconnect the wiring plug from the gas-discharge ignition/high voltage unit, then detach the unit from the gas-discharge bulb.

28 Undo the screws and remove the gas-discharge ignition/high voltage unit.

29 Remove the holder and withdraw the gas-discharge bulb. **Do not** touch the glass of the gas-discharge bulb, which may be extremely hot. When handling the new bulb, use a tissue or clean cloth to avoid touching the glass with the fingers; moisture and grease from the skin can cause blackening and rapid failure of this type of bulb. If the glass is accidentally touched, wipe it clean using methylated spirit.

30 Fit the new bulb and holder, followed by the gas-discharge ignition/high voltage unit. Tighten the screws and reconnect the wiring.

31 Refit the scuttle panel.

32 Refit the headlamp assembly with reference to Section 7.

Caution: After refitting a gas-discharge headlamp, the basic setting of the Automatic Range Control system should be checked. Because of the requirement for specialised equipment, this can only be carried out by a Skoda dealer or suitably-equipped specialist.

Front foglight

33 For non-RS models manufactured up to and including MY2004, prise out the cover, then undo the two screws and withdraw the foglight.

34 For non-RS models manufactured from MY2005, prise out the cover, then undo the

5.20 Disconnect the wiring plug . . .

5.21a . . . unhook the clip . . .

5.21b . . . and withdraw the headlight dipped beam bulb

5.34a Prise out the cover . . .

5.34b . . . and undo the three screws retaining the foglight

5.41a Pull out the sidelight bulbholder . . .

5.41b . . . then pull out the push-fit bulb

5.47 Twist the bulbholder anti-clockwise to remove it . . .

5.48 . . . then depress and twist the bulb anti-clockwise

three screws and withdraw the foglight (see illustrations).

35 For RS models, remove the cover by pressing the clip to the left (right-hand light) or right (left-hand light).

36 Disconnect the wiring then unhook and release the ends of the bulb retaining clip from the light unit, and withdraw the bulb.

37 When handling the new bulb, use a tissue or clean cloth to avoid touching the glass with the fingers; moisture and grease from the skin can cause blackening and rapid failure of this type of bulb. If the glass is accidentally touched, wipe it clean using methylated spirit.

38 Install the new bulb, ensuring that its locating tabs are correctly located in the light cut-outs, and secure it in position with the retaining clip.

39 Reconnect the wiring plug and refit the foglight cover, making sure that it is secure.

Front sidelight

Halogen headlights

40 Working in the engine compartment, remove the cover from the rear of the headlight by depressing the two upper securing clips. Since access to the left-hand headlight is difficult, either remove the headlight completely or remove the battery (see Chapter 5A).

41 Carefully pull the sidelight bulbholder from the headlight unit. The bulb is a push-fit in the holder and can be removed by grasping the end of the bulb and pulling it out (see illustrations).

42 Refitting is a reversal of removal, making

sure that the headlight cover is securely refitted.

Gas-discharge headlights

43 Remove the headlamp assembly as described in Section 7.

44 Remove the rear cover.

45 Carefully pull the sidelight bulbholder from the headlight unit. The bulb is a push-fit in the holder and can be removed by grasping the end of the bulb and pulling it out.

46 Refitting is a reversal of removal, making sure that the headlight cover is securely refitted, however, note the following:

Front direction indicator

47 With the bonnet open, reach down behind the relevant headlight unit, and twist the front direction indicator bulbholder anti-clockwise to remove it (see illustration).

48 Depress and twist the bulb anti-clockwise

to remove it from the bulbholder – the bulb is a bayonet fitting (see illustration).

49 Fit the new bulb using a reversal of the removal procedure.

Direction indicator side repeater

50 Undo the two lower screws from the front wheel arch liner on the relevant side of the car.

51 Pull out the liner and reach up to the rear of the direction indicator side repeater. Depress the side clip, and push out the side repeater from the front wing (see illustrations).

52 Separate the bulbholder from the lens, and pull out the wedge-type bulb (see illustrations).

53 Fit the new bulb using a reversal of the removal procedure. Press the light fully into the front wing until the clip engages before refitting the wheel arch liner.

5.51a Pull out the wheel arch liner . . .

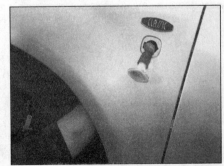

5.51b . . . and push out the side repeater light from the inside

5.52a Separate the bulbholder from the lens . . .

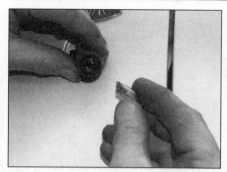

5.52b . . . and pull out the wedge-type bulb

5.54 Pull open the trim flap . . .

5.55 . . . then squeeze together the two locking clips to remove the rear light cluster

5.56 Depress and twist the relevant bulb to remove it

5.58 Removing the rear window surround trims

Rear light cluster

54 Working in the luggage compartment, pull open the relevant side panel trim flap for access to the rear of the cluster **(see illustration)**.
55 Squeeze together the two locking clips

and withdraw the rear light cluster from the light unit **(see illustration)**.
56 Depress the relevant bulb and twist anti-clockwise to remove it **(see illustration)**.
57 Fit the new bulb using a reversal of the removal procedure.

High-level stop-light

58 The high-level brake light is located at the top of the tailgate. First, remove the inner trim panel as described in Chapter 11, and the rear window surround trims **(see illustration)**.
59 On early models, the light is secured by two screws, however, on later models it is secured by plastic clips which must be squeezed together with pliers in order to remove the light **(see illustrations)**.
60 With the light unit removed, disconnect the wiring plug, and where necessary the washer tube **(see illustration)**.
61 The high-level brake light unit is not fitted with bulbs which can be renewed, but has LEDs. If an individual LED does not work, the complete light unit must be renewed.
62 Refitting is a reversal of removal. On later models, the plastic clips must be pulled through the tailgate until the securing arms

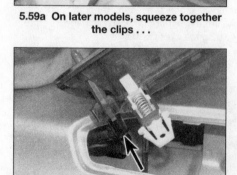

5.59a On later models, squeeze together the clips . . .

5.59b . . . and remove the high-level brake light

5.60 Washer tube connection to the high-level brake light

5.62 Using a screwdriver to pull the plastic clips through the tailgate

5.63a Undo the two screws . . .

expand. To do this, insert a small screwdriver into the hole in the clip **(see illustration)**.

Rear number plate light

63 Undo the two securing screws with a Torx key, and remove the rear number plate light **(see illustrations)**.
64 Pull the festoon-type bulb from the spring contacts and fit the new bulb **(see illustration)**. Make sure that the spring contacts are clean and sufficiently tensioned to hold the bulb firmly.
65 Refit the lens and lightly tighten the securing screws.

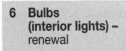

6 Bulbs (interior lights) – renewal

General

1 Whenever a bulb is renewed, note the following points:
a) *Switch off the ignition and all electrical consumers before commencing work.*
b) *Remember that if the light has just been in use the bulb may be extremely hot.*
c) *Always check the bulb contacts and holder, ensuring that there is clean metal-to-metal contact between the bulb and its live(s) and earth. Clean off any corrosion or dirt before fitting a new bulb.*
d) *Wherever bayonet-type bulbs are fitted ensure that the live contact(s) bear firmly against the bulb contact.*
e) *Always ensure that the new bulb is of the*

5.63b . . . and remove the rear number plate light

correct rating and that it is completely clean before fitting it.

Front courtesy/ reading/interior lights

2 Using a small screwdriver, carefully prise down the front edge of the lens and remove it **(see illustration)**.
3 Remove the festoon-type bulb from the spring contacts **(see illustration)**.
4 Fit the new bulb using a reversal of the removal procedure, but make sure that the spring contacts hold the bulb firmly in position, and if necessary tension them before fitting the bulb.

Rear courtesy/reading/ luggage compartment lights

5 Using a screwdriver, carefully prise the light unit from the trim. If necessary, disconnect the wiring and remove the light unit **(see illustrations)**.

5.64 Removing the festoon-type bulb

6 Remove the festoon-type bulb from the spring contacts, or pull out the wedge-type bulb as applicable **(see illustration)**.
7 Fit the new bulb using a reversal of the removal procedure, but make sure that the spring contacts hold the bulb firmly in position, and if necessary tension them before fitting the bulb.

Glovebox illumination light

8 On the project car, it was found impossible to remove and refit the illumination light with the glovebox in situ in the instrument panel, as in its fitted position, the wiring plug cannot be passed through the mounting hole in the glovebox. Therefore, the glovebox must be removed as described in Chapter 11, Section 27.
9 With the glovebox removed, depress the clip and remove the illumination light from inside **(see illustrations)**.

6.2 Remove the front courtesy/reading/ interior light lens . . .

6.3 . . . then remove the festoon-type bulb from the spring contacts

6.5a Prise the courtesy light unit from the trim . . .

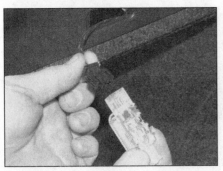

6.5b . . . disconnect the wiring . . .

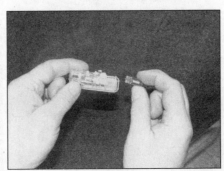

6.6 . . . and pull out the wedge-type bulb

6.9a Depress the clip . . .

6.9b ... and remove the glovebox illumination light from inside

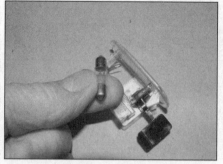

6.10 Removing the glovebox festoon-type illumination bulb

6.17 Use a length of washer tube to extract the bulb

10 Remove the festoon-type bulb from the spring contacts (see illustration).

11 Fit the new bulb using a reversal of the removal procedure, but make sure that the spring contacts hold the bulb firmly in position, and if necessary tension them before fitting the bulb.

Instrument panel illumination/warning lights

12 All warning/illumination lights in the instrument panel are non-renewable LEDs, therefore, if any are faulty, it is necessary to renew the complete instrument panel. Note, however, that a new instrument panel must be reprogrammed by a Skoda dealer using special equipment. The dealer will also transfer the mileage from the old unit onto the new one.

Cigarette lighter illumination

13 Remove the centre console as described in Chapter 11.

14 Release the clips and withdraw the cigarette lighter from the centre console.

15 Remove the festoon-type bulb from the spring contacts in the cigarette lighter housing.

16 Fit the new bulb using a reversal of the removal procedure, but make sure that the spring contacts hold the bulb firmly in position, and if necessary tension them before fitting the bulb.

Heater/ventilation control panel illumination

17 The control panel is illuminated by LEDs built into the panel. Consequently, if a fault develops, renewal of the panel is necessary. However, the centre rotary control of the panel is illuminated by a bulb. Carefully pull the control from the panel, and with a length of washer tube (or similar), pull the capless bulb from the holder (see illustration).

18 Fit the new bulb using a reversal of the removal procedure.

Switch illumination

19 The switch illumination bulbs are integral with the switches. If a bulb fails, the complete switch must be renewed.

Door warning lights

20 Open the relevant door, and carefully prise out the light unit.

21 Unplug the wiring connector.

22 Unclip the lens from the unit, and release the festoon-type bulb from the spring contacts.

23 Refitting is a reversal of removal. Make sure that the spring contacts hold the bulb firmly in position, and if necessary tension them before fitting the bulb.

7 Exterior light units – removal and refitting

Headlight

Removal

1 Remove the front bumper as described in Chapter 11.

2 Reach down behind the headlight and disconnect the wiring plugs (see illustration).

3 Unscrew the mounting bolts and withdraw the headlight forwards from the front of the car (see illustrations).

7.2 Disconnecting the headlight wiring plugs

7.3a Unscrew the front mounting bolt ...

7.3b ... rear mounting bolt ...

7.3c ... and upper mounting bolts ...

7.3d ... and withdraw the headlight from the front of the car

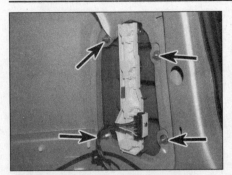

7.7a Unscrew the retaining nuts ...

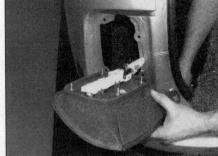

7.7b ... withdraw the rear light cluster ...

7.7c ... and disconnect the wiring

Refitting

4 Refitting is a reversal of removal, but on completion, have the headlight alignment checked at the earliest opportunity.
Caution: After refitting a gas-discharge headlamp, the basic setting of the Automatic Range Control system should be checked. Because of the requirement for specialised equipment, this can only be carried out by a Skoda dealer or suitably-equipped specialist.

Direction indicator side repeater

5 The procedure is described as part of the bulb renewal procedure in Section 5.

Rear light cluster

Removal

6 Remove the rear light bulbholder, as described in Section 5.
7 Working inside the rear luggage compartment, remove the trim as necessary, then unscrew the retaining nuts, withdraw the rear light cluster from the rear of the car, and disconnect the wiring **(see illustrations)**.

Refitting

8 Refitting is a reversal of removal, but make sure that the seal is located correctly.

High-level stop-light

9 The procedure is described as part of the bulb renewal procedure in Section 5.

Rear number plate light

10 The procedure is described as part of the rear number plate light bulb renewal procedure in Section 5.

---

8 Headlight beam adjustment components – removal and refitting

Beam adjustment control

1 The control is integral with the instrument illumination control on models *not* fitted with Xenon headlights.
2 Removal and refitting is covered in Section 4.

Range control motor (halogen)

3 Remove the headlight as described earlier in this Section, then remove the cover for access to the range control motor.
4 Disconnect the wiring from the range control motor **(see illustration)**.
5 To remove the left-hand side motor, turn the motor assembly anti-clockwise then slide the control arm down from the reflector. To remove the right-hand side motor, turn the motor assembly clockwise then slide the control arm up from the reflector **(see illustration)**.
6 Refitting is a reversal of removal.

---

9 Headlight beam alignment – general information

1 Accurate adjustment of the headlight beam is only possible using optical beam setting equipment and this work should therefore be carried out by a Skoda dealer or suitably-equipped workshop.

2 For reference, the headlights can be adjusted using the two thumbwheels at the top of each light unit **(see illustration)**. The innermost thumbwheel controls vertical adjustment and the outer thumbwheel controls horizontal adjustment. If necessary, further adjustment can be made by loosening the headlight mounting bolts.
3 On models equipped with gas-discharge headlights, the 'dipping' characteristics of the unit can be set for countries which drive on the left or right – see Section 28 for more information.

---

10 Instrument panel – removal and refitting

Note: *If the instrument panel is to be renewed, the new unit must be programmed with the current service information by a Skoda dealer.*

Removal

1 Disconnect the battery negative lead. **Note:** *Before disconnecting the battery, refer to 'Disconnecting the battery' in the Reference section at the rear of this manual.*
2 Release the steering wheel adjustment lock, pull the wheel out as far as possible, and set it in the lowest position. If preferred for additional working room, remove the steering wheel completely.
3 Unclip the small cover from over the steering column shrouds **(see illustration)**. If necessary for improved access, remove the combination switch as described in Section 4.

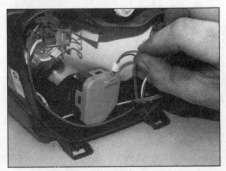

8.4 Disconnect the wiring ...

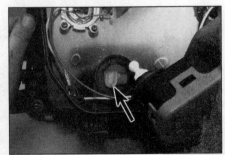

8.5 ... then turn the range control motor to remove it. Note the socket on the reflector

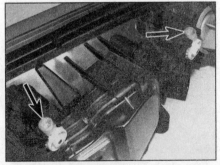

9.2 Headlight beam alignment adjustment thumbwheels on the top of the headlight

10.3 Unclip the small cover from over the steering column shrouds

10.4a Undo the retaining screws ...

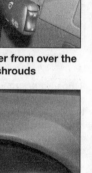

10.4b ... withdraw the instrument panel ...

10.4c ... and disconnect the wiring

4 Remove the two instrument panel retaining screws, and lift the panel out of the facia sufficiently to allow the wiring plugs on the rear of the unit to be disconnected **(see illustrations)**.

Refitting

5 Refitting is a reversal of removal, making sure that the wiring plugs are securely reconnected.

11 Instrument panel components – removal and refitting

It is not possible to dismantle the instrument panel. If any of the gauges are faulty, the complete instrument panel must be renewed.

12 Service interval indicator – general information and resetting

1 All models are equipped with a service interval indicator. After all necessary maintenance work has been completed (see the relevant part of Chapter 1), the service interval display code must be reset. This will be completed by a Skoda dealer when the service has been completed, however, it may be reset using the procedure given in Chapter 1. Note that if more than one service schedule is carried out, the relevant display intervals must be reset individually.
2 The display is reset using the trip counter reset button, as described in the relevant part of Chapter 1.

13 Clock – removal and refitting

The clock is integral with the instrument panel, and cannot be removed separately. The instrument panel is a sealed unit, and if the clock, or any other components, are faulty, the complete instrument panel must be renewed. Refer to Section 10 to remove it.

14 Cigarette lighter – removal and refitting

Removal

1 Disconnect the battery negative lead. **Note:** *Before disconnecting the battery, refer to*

15.3 Horn mounting bolt

'Disconnecting the battery' in the Reference section at the rear of this manual.
2 Remove the centre console as described in Chapter 11.
3 Remove the bulbholder as described in Section 6.
4 Push the centre element of the lighter out of the mounting.

Refitting

5 Refitting is a reversal of removal.

15 Horn – removal and refitting

Removal

1 Disconnect the battery negative lead. **Note:** *Before disconnecting the battery, refer to 'Disconnecting the battery' in the Reference section at the rear of this manual.*
2 The horns are located behind the left-hand side of the front bumper. On some models it may be possible to reach up under the front bumper, however, on most it will be necessary to remove the front bumper as described in Chapter 11.
3 Disconnect the horn wiring plug(s), then unscrew the securing nut(s) or bolt(s), and withdraw the horn(s) from the mounting bracket **(see illustration)**.

Refitting

4 Refitting is a reversal of removal.

16 Speedometer sensor – general information

All models without ABS are fitted with an electronic speedometer sensor. This device measures the rotational speed of the transmission final drive and converts the information into an electronic signal, which is then sent to the speedometer module in the instrument panel. On certain models, the signal is also used as an input by the engine management system ECU, and the trip computer.

Refer to Chapter 7A or 7B for details of the removal procedure.

17 Wiper arm – removal and refitting

Removal

1 Operate the wiper motor, then switch off so that the wiper arm(s) return to the at-rest position.
2 Stick a piece of masking tape to the glass along the edge of the wiper blade to use as an alignment aid on refitting. Note that the driver's side wiper blade inner end should be

positioned 25 mm from the bottom edge of the windscreen, and the passenger side wiper blade outer end 40 mm from the bottom edge (measured from the *bottom* of the windscreen beneath the moulding).

Front wiper arm

3 With the bonnet open, prise off the cap, then unscrew and remove the spindle nut, but do not remove it completely.

4 Lift the blade off the glass and pull the wiper arm from side-to-side until it releases from the spindle splines – if it is tight, use a puller **(see illustration)**. Remove the spindle nut. **Note:** *If both windscreen wiper arms are to be removed at the same time mark them for identification; the arms are not interchangeable.*

Rear wiper arm

5 Pull up the wiper arm spindle nut cover, then unscrew the spindle nut, but do not remove it completely **(see illustrations)**.

6 Lift the blade off the glass and pull the wiper arm from side-to-side until it releases from the spindle – if it is tight, use a puller **(see illustration)**. Remove the spindle nut.

Refitting

7 Ensure that the wiper arm and spindle splines are clean and dry, then refit the arm to the spindle, aligning the wiper blade with the tape fitted on removal. Refit the spindle nut, tightening it securely, and refit the cover.

18 Windscreen wiper motor and linkage – removal and refitting

Removal

1 Remove the wiper arms as described in Section 17.

2 Remove the rubber moulding, then remove the plenum chamber cover from in front of the windscreen. Note, however, that the retaining clips are very difficult to remove and will more than likely be destroyed during removal. Use a lever or angled long-nose pliers to extract the clips, but protect the surrounding components with card or similar. Disconnect the hoses and heater wires from the washer jets as the cover is being removed **(see illustrations)**.

17.4 Using a puller to remove the front wiper arm from the spindle

17.5b ... then unscrew the spindle nut, but do not remove it completely

3 On RHD models, unbolt and remove the engine compartment rear panel from the bulkhead **(see illustrations)**, as there is insufficient room to remove the wiper motor and linkage with the panel in position. It will be necessary to remove the engine management ECU at the same time.

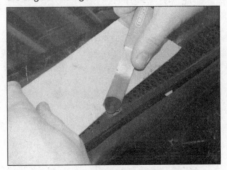
18.2a Lever out the retaining clips ...

18.3a On RHD models, unscrew the bolts ...

17.5a Pull up the spindle nut cover ...

17.6 Removing the rear wiper arm

4 Unscrew the two mounting bolts, then carefully manoeuvre the windscreen wiper motor and linkage out from the scuttle and disconnect the wiring plug **(see illustrations)**.

5 Recover the washers and spacers from the motor mounting rubbers, noting their

18.2b ... remove the plenum chamber cover and disconnect the heater wires and washer hoses

18.3b ... and remove the engine compartment rear panel from the bulkhead

18.4a Unscrew the mounting bolts ...

18.4b ... manoeuvre out the windscreen wiper motor and linkage, and disconnect the wiring

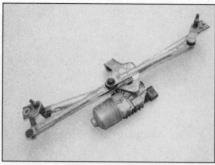

18.4c Windscreen wiper motor and linkage removed from the car

18.6a Unscrew the nut and disconnect the linkage ...

18.6b ... then undo the three screws securing the motor to the mounting plate

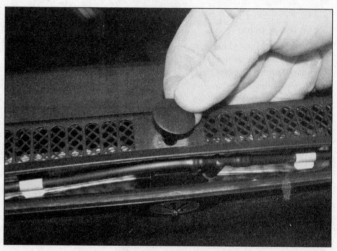

18.7 Secure the cowling with new clips

locations, then inspect the rubbers for signs of damage or deterioration, and renew if necessary.

6 To separate the motor from the linkage, proceed as follows.

a) *Make alignment marks between the motor spindle and the linkage to ensure correct alignment on refitting, and note the orientation of the linkage.*

b) *Unscrew the nut securing the linkage to the motor spindle* **(see illustration)**.

c) *Undo the three screws securing the motor to the mounting plate, then withdraw the motor* **(see illustration)**.

Refitting

7 Refitting is a reversal of removal, bearing in mind the following points.

a) *If the motor has been separated from the linkage, ensure that the marks made on the motor spindle and linkage before removal are aligned, and ensure that the linkage is orientated as noted before removal.*

b) *Ensure that the washers and spacers are fitted to the motor mounting rubbers as noted before removal.*

c) *Lubricate the plenum chamber cover mounting slots with a silicone-based*

spray lubricant to ease installation. Do not strike the cowling to seat it in position as this could result in the windscreen cracking. Secure with new clips **(see illustration)**`.

d) *Refit the wiper arms as described in Section 17.*

19 Rear wiper motor – removal and refitting

Removal

1 Remove the wiper arm as described in Section 17.

2 Open the tailgate, then remove the tailgate trim panel with reference to Chapter 11.

3 Unplug the wiring connector from the motor **(see illustration)**.

4 Where applicable, disconnect the washer fluid hose from the washer nozzle connector on the motor assembly.

5 Unscrew the three nuts securing the motor, then withdraw the assembly **(see illustration)**.

6 Remove the wiper motor shaft sealing ring from the tailgate.

19.3 Disconnecting the wiring

19.5 Removing the rear wiper motor

Refitting

7 Refitting is a reversal of removal, but ensure that the motor shaft rubber sealing ring is correctly refitted to prevent water leaks, and refit the wiper arm with reference to Section 17.

20 Washer system components – removal and refitting

Washer fluid reservoir

Removal

1 Switch off the ignition and all electrical consumers.
2 The washer fluid reservoir is located behind the left-hand side of the front bumper. First, remove the front bumper as described in Chapter 11.
3 Disconnect the wiring from the washer pump(s).
4 Disconnect and plug the washer hoses.
5 Unscrew the upper and lower mounting nuts and withdraw the fluid reservoir to the front **(see illustration)**.

Refitting

6 Refitting is a reversal of removal.

Washer fluid pumps

Removal

7 Switch off the ignition and all electrical consumers.
8 Remove the washer fluid reservoir as described previously in this Section.
9 Carefully pull the pump from its grommet in the reservoir **(see illustration)**. Disconnect the washer fluid hose(s) and the wiring plug from the pump.

Refitting

10 Refitting is a reversal of removal, but take care not to push the pump grommet into the reservoir. Use a little soapy water to ease the pump into the grommet.

Windscreen washer jets

Removal

11 The washer jets are located on the plenum chamber cover in front of the windscreen. First, remove the wiper arms as described in Section 17.
12 Remove the rubber moulding, then remove the plenum chamber cover from in front of the windscreen. Note, however, that the retaining clips are very difficult to remove and will more than likely be destroyed during removal. Use angled long-nose pliers to extract the clips, but protect the surrounding components with card or similar. Disconnect the hoses and heater wires from the washer jets as the cover is being removed.
13 Squeeze the clips and release the jets from the cover **(see illustration)**.

Refitting

14 Refitting is a reversal of removal. Note that

20.5 Washer fluid reservoir showing upper mounting nut

the jets are preset by the manufacturer and cannot be adjusted.

Tailgate washer jet

Removal

15 On Hatch models, the tailgate washer jet is located within the tailgate wiper spindle, beneath the wiper arm cover. To remove it, lift the cover, then use a pair of pliers to extract the jet from the spindle **(see illustration)**.
16 On Estate models, the tailgate washer jet is integrated into the high-level stop-light. To remove it, first remove the high-level stop-light as described in Section 5, then pull out the jet.

Refitting

17 Refitting is a reversal of removal, but check the operation of the jet. On Estate models, push in the jet so that it is pointing vertically downwards. The jet should be aimed to spray at the centre of the screen, using a pin.

Headlight washer jets

Removal

18 It is not necessary to remove the front bumper in order to remove the headlight washer jets. Lift and hold the spray nozzle holder.
19 Slightly raise the securing clip using a screwdriver, then pull out the spray nozzle holder and disconnect the hose.

Refitting

20 Refitting is a reversal of removal, but adjust the nozzle so that the to direct the spray to the centre of the headlight.

20.13 Removing the windscreen washer jets

20.9 Washer fluid pump location

Headlight washer jet lift cylinder

Removal

21 Remove the front bumper as described in Chapter 11.
22 Remove the relevant headlight as described in Section 7, and the washer jets as described in the previous sub-section.
23 Undo the two retaining screws, and withdraw the cylinder.
24 Clamp the hose, squeeze the retaining clip, and disconnect the hose.

Refitting

25 Refitting is a reversal of removal.

21 Radio/cassette/CD player/ changer – removal and refitting

Note: *This Section only applies to standard-fit audio equipment.*

Radio/cassette player

Removal

1 The radio is fitted with special side mounting spring clips, requiring the use of special removal tools, which may be supplied with the vehicle, or can be obtained from an in-car entertainment specialist **(see illustration)**. The Skoda tool number is T30005.
2 Switch off the ignition and all electrical consumers.
3 Insert the keys and push them in until they engage with the side retaining spring clips.

20.15 Pull the jet from the centre of the spindle

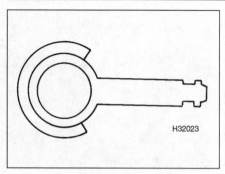

21.1 Radio removal key

Apply outward pressure, then pull out the radio/cassette player, and disconnect the wiring and aerial **(see illustrations)**.

Refitting

4 Reconnect the wiring connectors and aerial lead then push the unit into the facia until the retaining lugs snap into place.

CD player

Removal

5 The CD player is fitted with special mounting clips, requiring the use of special removal tools, which should be supplied with the vehicle, or may be obtained from an in-car entertainment specialist.
6 Switch off the ignition and all electrical consumers, then remove the radio/cassette player as described earlier in this Section.
7 Insert the tools into the slots on each side of the unit and push them until they snap into place. The CD player can then be pulled out of the facia using the tools, and the wiring disconnected.

Refitting

8 Reconnect the wiring then push the unit into the facia until the retaining lugs snap into place.

CD changer

Removal

9 The CD changer is bolted to brackets on the underside of the front passenger seat. First, remove the seat as described in Chapter 11.
10 Disconnect the wiring, then remove the side covers from the seat.

21.3a Insert the keys and pull out the radio/cassette player

11 Undo the four mounting screws and withdraw the CD changer from the seat brackets.

Refitting

12 Refitting is a reversal of removal.

22 Loudspeakers – removal and refitting

Front door-mounted treble

Removal

1 Switch off the ignition and all electrical consumers.
2 Open the door then unclip the triangular cover containing the treble loudspeaker.
3 Disconnect the wiring, then unclip the loudspeaker from the cover.

Refitting

4 Refitting is a reversal of removal.

Rear door-mounted treble

Removal

5 Switch off the ignition and all electrical consumers.
6 Remove the rear door trim panel as described in Chapter 11.
7 The loudspeaker is mounted on the inside of the door trim panel. Disconnect the wiring and unclip the loudspeaker from the panel

Refitting

8 Refitting is a reversal of removal.

Front door-mounted bass

Removal

9 Switch off the ignition and all electrical consumers.
10 Remove the front door trim panel as described in Chapter 11.
11 Disconnect the loudspeaker wiring.
12 Carefully drill out the retaining rivets, and withdraw the speaker from the front door.

Refitting

13 Refitting is a reversal of removal.

Luggage compartment bass

14 Switch off the ignition and all electrical consumers.

21.3b Disconnect the wiring and aerial

15 The rear bass loudspeakers are located beneath the rear side shelf/trims. With the tailgate open, reach under the relevant side shelf/trim and disconnect the wiring from the loudspeaker. Undo the four mounting screws and withdraw the loudspeaker.

Refitting

16 Refitting is a reversal of removal.

23 Radio aerial – removal and refitting

Removal

1 Up to MY2002 the aerial mast can be unscrewed from the base by twisting anti-clockwise. On later models, it can be folded away.
2 If the aerial base is to be removed, the rear of the headlining must be lowered for access.
3 Once the headlining has been lowered, disconnect the aerial lead at the connector, then unscrew the securing nut, and withdraw the aerial base from the roof. Hold the aerial base as the nut is being unscrewed to prevent the base from rotating and scratching the roof panel. Recover the rubber spacer.

Refitting

4 Refitting is a reversal of removal.

24 Anti-theft alarm system and engine immobiliser – general information

Note: *This information is applicable only to the anti-theft alarm system fitted by Skoda as standard equipment.*

Models in the range are fitted with an anti-theft alarm system as standard equipment. The alarm has switches on all the doors (including the tailgate), the bonnet and the ignition switch. If the tailgate, bonnet or any of the doors are opened, or the ignition switch is switched on whilst the alarm is set, the alarm horn will sound and the hazard warning lights will flash. Some models are also equipped with an internal monitoring system, which will activate the alarm system if any movement in the cabin is detected.

The alarm is set using the key in the driver's front door lock, or by the central locking remote control transmitter. The alarm system will then start to monitor its various switches approximately 30 seconds later.

The alarm is switched off if the vehicle is unlocked using the remote control transmitter, or if you switch on the ignition, however, if unlocked with the remote control, it is automatically reset if the door is not opened within 30 seconds. If the driver's door is manually unlocked with the ignition key, the key must be inserted in the ignition switch within 15 seconds to deactivate the alarm.

Most models are fitted with an immobiliser

26.4 Insert a screwdriver approximately 45 mm into the hole, and release the clip

26.6a Withdraw the airbag module . . .

26.6b . . . and disconnect the wiring

system, which is activated by the ignition switch. A module incorporated in the ignition switch reads a code contained within the ignition key. The module sends a signal to the engine management electronic control unit (ECU) which allows the engine to start if the code is correct. If an incorrect ignition key is used, the engine will not start.

If a fault is suspected with the alarm or immobiliser systems, the vehicle should be taken to a Skoda dealer for examination. They will have access to a special diagnostic tester which will quickly trace any fault present in the system.

25 Airbag system – general information and precautions

⚠️ *Warning: Before carrying out any operations on the airbag system, disconnect the battery negative terminal (refer to 'Disconnecting the battery' in the Reference section at the rear of this manual). When operations are complete, make sure no one is inside the vehicle when the battery is reconnected.*
• *Note that the airbag(s) must not be subjected to temperatures in excess of 100°C (212°F). When the airbag is removed, ensure that it is stored the with the pad upwards to prevent possible inflation.*
• *Do not allow any solvents or cleaning agents to contact the airbag assemblies. They must be cleaned using only a damp cloth.*
• *The airbags and control unit are both sensitive to impact. If either is dropped or damaged they should be renewed.*
• *Remove the airbag units prior to using arc-welding equipment on the vehicle.*

Driver's and passenger's airbags are fitted as standard equipment, and side airbags may be fitted as an option to the front seats. The airbag system comprises of the airbag unit (complete with gas generator) which is fitted to the steering wheel (driver's side), facia (passenger's side) and front seats, an impact sensor, the control unit and a warning light in the instrument panel. The front passenger airbag may be switched off when there is no one seated in the passenger seat.

The airbag system is triggered in the event of a heavy frontal or side impact above a predetermined force; depending on the point of impact. The airbag is inflated within milliseconds and forms a safety cushion between the driver and the steering wheel, the passenger and the facia, and in the case of side impact, between front seat occupants and the sides of the cabin. This prevents contact between the upper body and cabin interior, and therefore greatly reduces the risk of injury. The airbag then deflates almost immediately.

Every time the ignition is switched on, the airbag control unit performs a self-test. The self-test takes approximately 3 seconds and during this time the airbag warning light on the facia is illuminated. After the self-test has been completed the warning light should go out. If the warning light fails to come on, remains illuminated after the initial 3 second period or comes on at any time when the vehicle is being driven, there is a fault in the airbag system. The vehicle should then be taken to a Skoda dealer for examination at the earliest possible opportunity.

26 Airbag system components – removal and refitting 🔧

Note: *Refer to the warnings in Section 25 before carrying out the following operations.*
1 Disconnect the battery negative terminal, then continue as described under the relevant heading. **Note:** *Before disconnecting the*

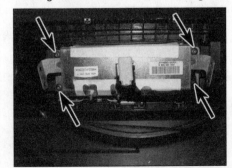

26.9 Torx screws securing the passenger's airbag

battery, refer to 'Disconnecting the battery' in the Reference section at the rear of this manual.

Driver's airbag

Removal

2 Set the front wheels in the straight-ahead position, and release the steering lock by inserting the ignition key.
3 Adjust the steering column to its lowest position by releasing the adjustment handle, then pull out the column and lower it as far as possible. Lock the column in this position by returning the adjustment handle.
4 With the spokes in the vertical position, insert a screwdriver approximately 45 mm into the hole in the upper rear of the steering wheel hub, then move it up to release the clip and free the airbag locking lug **(see illustration)**. Now turn the steering wheel through 180° and release the remaining airbag locking lug.
5 Turn the steering wheel to its central, straight-ahead position.
6 Carefully withdraw the airbag module and disconnect the wiring **(see illustrations)**. Note that the airbag module must not be knocked or dropped, and should be stored the correct way up with its active surface uppermost.

Refitting

7 On refitting, reconnect the wiring connector and locate the airbag unit in the steering wheel, making sure that the wire does not become trapped. Reconnect the battery negative lead, ensuring that no-one is inside the vehicle as the lead is connected.

Passenger's airbag

Note: *The facia panel must be renewed in the event of the passenger airbag being deployed.*

Removal

8 With reference to Chapter 11, Section 27, remove the passenger side glovebox.
9 Unscrew the four Torx screws securing the airbag support bracket to the facia crossmember **(see illustration)**.
10 Carefully withdraw the airbag unit and bracket from the facia, and disconnect the wiring connector **(see illustration)**.

26.10 Disconnect the wiring from the passenger's airbag

11 Unbolt the airbag from the bracket. Note that the airbag module must not be knocked or dropped, and should be stored with its active surface uppermost.

Refitting

12 On refitting, locate the airbag in the bracket and tighten the bolts to the specified torque.
13 Manoeuvre the airbag and bracket into position and reconnect the wiring connector. Tighten the mounting bolts.
14 Refit the passenger side glovebox with reference to Chapter 11.
15 Reconnect the battery negative lead, ensuring that no-one is inside the vehicle as the lead is connected.

Front side impact airbags

16 The side impact airbags are integral with the seats. As seat upholstery removal requires

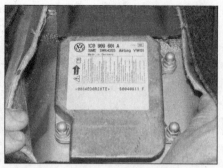

26.17 The airbag control unit is located on the tunnel under the centre of the facia

considerable skill and experience, if it is to be carried out without damage, it is best entrusted to an expert.

Airbag control unit

Removal

17 The control unit is located on the tunnel under the centre of the facia **(see illustration)**.
18 Disconnect the battery negative lead. **Note:** *Before disconnecting the battery, refer to 'Disconnecting the battery' in the Reference section at the rear of this manual.*
19 Remove the tunnel trim from the left-hand footwell as described in Chapter 11.
20 Remove the centre console as described in Chapter 11.
21 If necessary, cut the carpet in the area of the airbag control unit
22 Reach under the facia, move the retaining

clip to the open position, and disconnect the control unit wiring plug.
23 Unscrew the three mounting nuts, then withdraw the control unit.

Refitting

24 Refitting is the reverse of removal making sure the wiring connector is securely reconnected. Reconnect the battery negative lead, ensuring that no-one is inside the vehicle as the lead is connected.

Front passenger airbag switch

Removal

25 The front passenger airbag switch is located within the glovebox. First, disconnect the battery negative lead. **Note:** *Before disconnecting the battery, refer to 'Disconnecting the battery' in the Reference section at the rear of this manual.*
26 With the glovebox lid open, insert the ignition key in the airbag switch to its middle position, then carefully pull out the switch.
27 Disconnect the wiring.

Refitting

28 Refitting is a reversal of removal, but switch off the ignition before reconnecting the battery negative lead.

Airbag wiring contact unit (slip-ring)

Note: *On early models, when removing or installing the contact unit, use tape to ensure that the coil connector remains in the centre position. On later models, the contact unit has an automatic mechanism to keep it in its central position when removed.*

Removal

29 With the front wheels in their straight-ahead position, remove the steering wheel as described in Chapter 10.
30 Undo the two screws through the holes in the lower steering column shroud, and remove the upper shroud. Undo the three retaining screws for the lower shroud, release from the height adjustment lever, and withdraw the lower shroud **(see illustrations)**.
31 Disconnect the wiring plug on the underside on the unit. Release the three locking lugs with a screwdriver, and pull the

26.30a Undo the screws . . .

26.30b . . . and remove the upper steering column shroud

26.30c Undo the front screws . . .

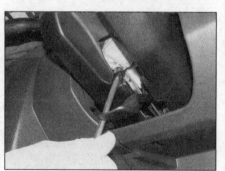

26.30d . . . and lower screw . . .

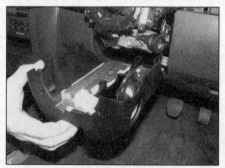

26.30e . . . and remove the lower steering column shroud

26.31a Disconnect the wiring . . .

26.31b . . . then release the three locking lugs . . .

26.31c . . . and pull the unit with the slip-ring from the column

unit with the slip-ring from the column (see illustrations).

Refitting

32 Refitting is a reversal of removal. Ensure that no-one is inside the vehicle as the wiring plug is reconnected.

27 Parking aid components – general information, removal and refitting

General information

1 The parking aid system is available as a standard fitment on certain models, and optional on other models. Four ultrasound sensors located in the rear bumper measure the distance to the closest object behind the car, and inform the driver using acoustic signals from a buzzer located under the rear luggage compartment trim. The nearer the object, the more frequent the acoustic signals.
2 The system includes a control unit and self-diagnosis program, and therefore, in the event of a fault, the vehicle should be taken to a Skoda dealer.

Control unit

Removal

3 Switch off the ignition and all electrical consumers, then remove the left-hand side trim from the luggage compartment with reference to Chapter 11, Section 27.
4 Disconnect the wiring at the plug.
5 Unscrew the two mounting nuts and withdraw the control unit.

Refitting

6 Refitting is a reversal of removal.

Range/distance sensor

Removal

7 The rear bumper must be removed as described in Chapter 11 in order to remove the sensors.
8 Squeeze together the retaining clips, then press out the sensor from the outside of the bumper.

9 Disconnect the wiring and remove the sensor.

Refitting

10 Refitting is a reversal of removal. Press the sensor firmly into position until the retaining clips engage.

Warning buzzer

Removal

11 The warning buzzer is located behind the interior light on the roof. First, remove the interior light as described in Section 6.
12 Disconnect the wiring and pull the buzzer from the Velcro on the roof.

Refitting

13 Refitting is a reversal of removal.

28 Gas-discharge headlight system – component removal and refitting

General information

1 Gas-discharge (or Xenon) headlights are available as an optional extra on all models covered by this manual. The headlight dipped beam bulbs are of special gas-discharge type, which produce light by means of an electric arc, rather than by heating a metal filament as in conventional halogen bulbs. The arc is generated by a control circuit which operates at HT voltages. The intensity of the emitted light means that the headlight beam has to be controlled dynamically to avoid dazzling other road users. An electronic control unit monitors the vehicle's pitch and overall ride height by sensors mounted on the front and rear suspension, and adjusts the beam accordingly, using the range control motors built into the headlight units.

⚠ **Warning: The discharge bulb starter circuit operates at extremely high voltages. To avoid the risk of electric shock, ensure that the battery negative cable is disconnected before working on the headlight units.**

Bulb renewal

2 Refer to Section 5.

High-voltage unit

Removal

3 The high voltage unit of the right-hand headlight is attached to the bottom of the lock carrier, whereas that of the left-hand headlight is attached to the plastic covering behind the headlight socket.
4 Remove the headlight as described in Section 7, however, for the right-hand headlight, depress the spring down and push the assembly towards the engine compartment.
5 Disconnect the wiring, then remove the cover and remove the high-voltage unit.

Refitting

6 Refitting is a reversal of removal.

Transmitter and rear controller

Note: After fitting a new transmitter, it must be reprogrammed by a Skoda dealer using specialist equipment.

Removal

7 The transmitter and rear controller is located on the left-hand rear trailing arm. First, jack up the rear of the vehicle and support it on axle stands (see Jacking and vehicle support).
8 Disconnect the wiring from the transmitter.
9 Unscrew the mounting bolt securing the unit to the trailing arm, then unscrew the nut securing the link to the rear axle crossmember. Withdraw the unit from under the vehicle.

Refitting

10 Refitting is a reversal of removal, but have the high-discharge system reprogrammed by a Skoda dealer as soon as possible.

Settings for driving on the right

11 On models equipped with gas-discharge dipped headlights, the characteristics of the units can be set for driving on the left or right of the road. Remove the headlight and rear cover with reference to Section 7, then use a screwdriver to position the lever as necessary (see illustration overleaf). **Note:** It is still necessary to mask off the headlights for main beam correction.

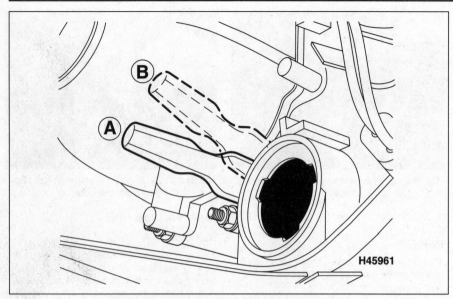

28.11 Gas-discharge dipped lighting adjustment

A For countries where traffic drives on the right
B For countries where traffic drives on the left
Note: *Illustration shows LH headlight – RH headlight is mirror image*

29 Convenience system
– general information

1 The convenience system controls the operation of the central locking, electric windows, alarm system and electric exterior mirrors. It also monitors the operation of the interior lights in the interests of battery discharge protection. The system uses CAN databus cabling which effectively reduces the amount of wiring required for operating the system, by sending different frequency signals down the same wiring rather than using several different wires. A fault memory is incorporated which allows diagnostic equipment to determine the location of faults easily.

2 The convenience system control unit is located below the driver's side of the facia panel, above the accelerator pedal position. To remove it, first remove the glovebox as described in Chapter 11, Section 27, then remove the footwell vent and disconnect the wiring. The control unit can then be withdrawn to the front and downwards. Refitting is a reversal of removal.

SKODA FABIA wiring diagrams

Diagram 1

Key to symbols

Bulb	—⊗—	Item no.	**2**
Flashing bulb	—⊗—	Single speed pump/motor	(M)
Switch	—o˞ o—		
Multiple contact switch (ganged)		Twin speed motor	(M)
		Gauge/meter	(↗)
Fuse/fusible link with rating	F28 15A	Earth point location	E4
Resistor	—▭—	Diode	—▶|—
Variable resistor		Light emitting diode (LED)	
Variable resistor		Solenoid actuator	
Wire splice, unspecified connector or soldered joint		Heating element	—⎍⎍⎍—
Connecting wires		Plug and socket connection	
Wire colour (green with yellow tracer)	Gn/Ge		

Dashed component outline denotes part of a larger item. Connectors may be shown in two ways;

Multiple connectors   Single connector

32a/1   2

32a/1   32 way connector A, pin 1
2   single connector, pin 2

Earth locations

E1   Behind battery, on strut tower
E2   Below battery, on side member
E3   Under centre console, in front of gearstick
E4   Behind battery, on strut tower
E5   At base of LH 'C' pillar

Passenger compartment fusebox   5

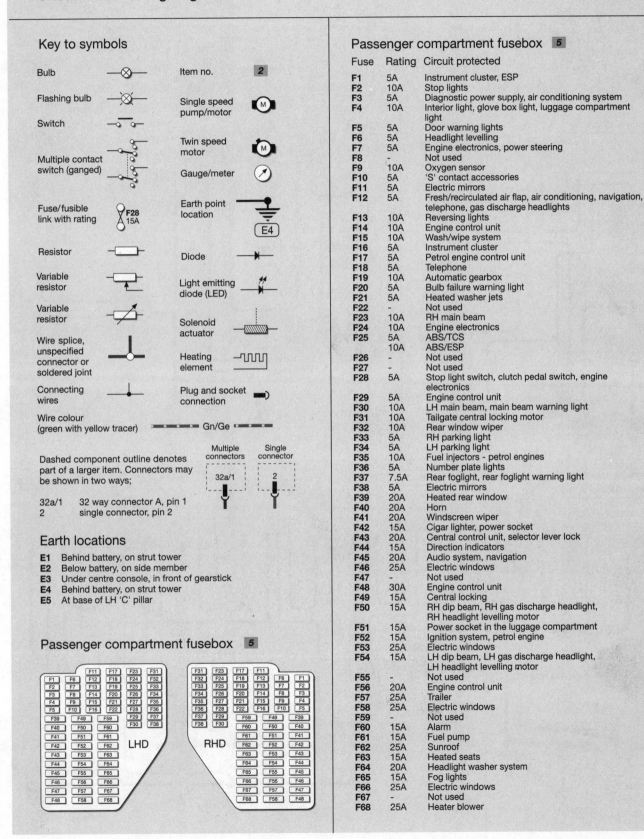

LHD   RHD

Passenger compartment fusebox   5

Fuse	Rating	Circuit protected
F1	5A	Instrument cluster, ESP
F2	10A	Stop lights
F3	5A	Diagnostic power supply, air conditioning system
F4	10A	Interior light, glove box light, luggage compartment light
F5	5A	Door warning lights
F6	5A	Headlight levelling
F7	5A	Engine electronics, power steering
F8	-	Not used
F9	10A	Oxygen sensor
F10	5A	'S' contact accessories
F11	5A	Electric mirrors
F12	5A	Fresh/recirculated air flap, air conditioning, navigation, telephone, gas discharge headlights
F13	10A	Reversing lights
F14	10A	Engine control unit
F15	10A	Wash/wipe system
F16	5A	Instrument cluster
F17	5A	Petrol engine control unit
F18	5A	Telephone
F19	10A	Automatic gearbox
F20	5A	Bulb failure warning light
F21	5A	Heated washer jets
F22	-	Not used
F23	10A	RH main beam
F24	10A	Engine electronics
F25	5A	ABS/TCS
	10A	ABS/ESP
F26	-	Not used
F27	-	Not used
F28	5A	Stop light switch, clutch pedal switch, engine electronics
F29	5A	Engine control unit
F30	10A	LH main beam, main beam warning light
F31	10A	Tailgate central locking motor
F32	10A	Rear window wiper
F33	5A	RH parking light
F34	5A	LH parking light
F35	10A	Fuel injectors - petrol engines
F36	5A	Number plate lights
F37	7.5A	Rear foglight, rear foglight warning light
F38	5A	Electric mirrors
F39	20A	Heated rear window
F40	20A	Horn
F41	20A	Windscreen wiper
F42	15A	Cigar lighter, power socket
F43	20A	Central control unit, selector lever lock
F44	15A	Direction indicators
F45	20A	Audio system, navigation
F46	25A	Electric windows
F47	-	Not used
F48	30A	Engine control unit
F49	15A	Central locking
F50	15A	RH dip beam, RH gas discharge headlight, RH headlight levelling motor
F51	15A	Power socket in the luggage compartment
F52	15A	Ignition system, petrol engine
F53	25A	Electric windows
F54	15A	LH dip beam, LH gas discharge headlight, LH headlight levelling motor
F55	-	Not used
F56	20A	Engine control unit
F57	25A	Trailer
F58	25A	Electric windows
F59	-	Not used
F60	15A	Alarm
F61	15A	Fuel pump
F62	25A	Sunroof
F63	15A	Heated seats
F64	20A	Headlight washer system
F65	15A	Fog lights
F66	25A	Electric windows
F67	-	Not used
F68	25A	Heater blower

H33372

Wire colours

Bl	Blue	**Li**	Purple
Br	Brown	**Ws**	White
Ge	Yellow	**Or**	Orange
Gr	Grey	**Ro**	Red
Gn	Green	**Sw**	Black

Key to items

1 Battery
2 Ignition switch
3 Starter motor
4 Alternator
5 Passenger compartment fusebox
6 Terminal 30 junction
7 Steering wheel clock springs
8 Horn switch
9 Horn
10 Electrical system control unit
11 Cigar lighter
12 Heater blower switch
   a = fresh air/recirc. flap switch
   b = fresh air/recirc. flap warning lamp
   c = switch illumination
   d = heater blower switch
   e = control unit
13 Heater blower motor
14 Fresh air/recirc. flap motor
15 Heater blower resistors
16 Ashtray illumination
17 Battery fuseholder
18 'X' contact relay

Diagram 2

H33373

Starting & charging

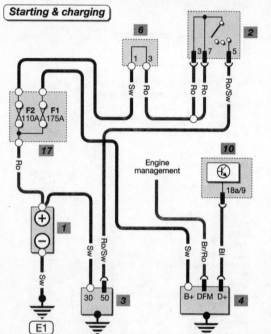

Horn

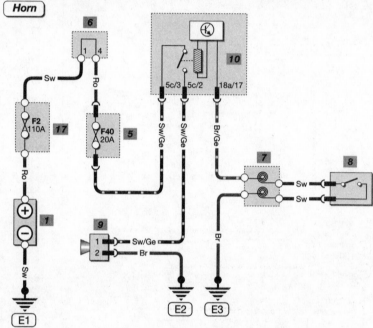

Cigar lighter & ashtray illumination

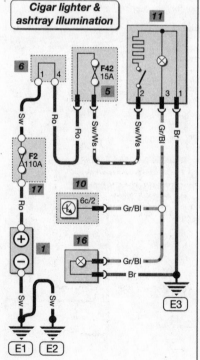

Heater blower

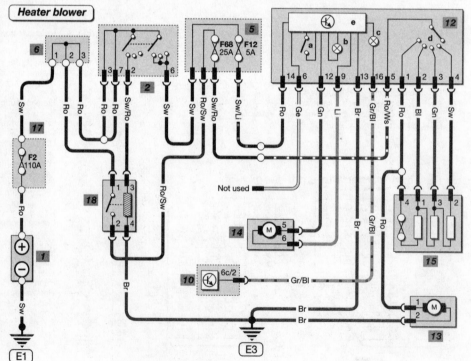

Wire colours

Bl	Blue	**Li**	Purple
Br	Brown	**Ws**	White
Ge	Yellow	**Or**	Orange
Gr	Grey	**Ro**	Red
Gn	Green	**Sw**	Black

* Estate models

Key to items

1   Battery
2   Ignition switch
5   Passenger compartment fusebox
6   Terminal 30 junction
10 Electrical system control unit
17 Battery fuseholder
20 Lighting switch
   a = side/headlight
   c = switch illumination
21 LH headlight unit
   a = side light
   b = main beam
   c = dip beam

22 RH headlight unit
   (as above)
23 LH rear light unit
   a = tail light
   b = stop light
   c = reversing light
24 RH rear light unit
   (as above)
25 Multi-function switch
   a = headlight flash
   b = main/dip switch
   c = parking light/direction
      indicator switch

26 Number plate light
27 Stop light switch
28 Reversing light switch
29 High level stop light

Diagram 3

H33374

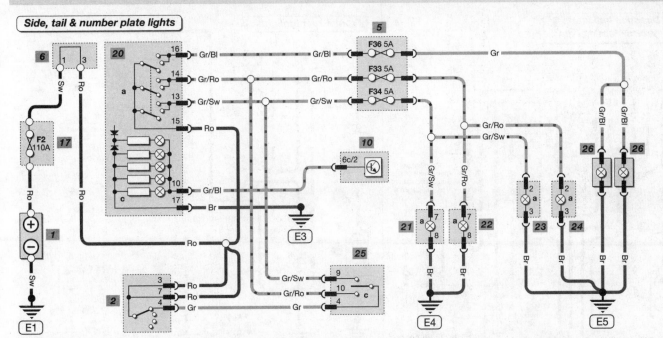

Side, tail & number plate lights

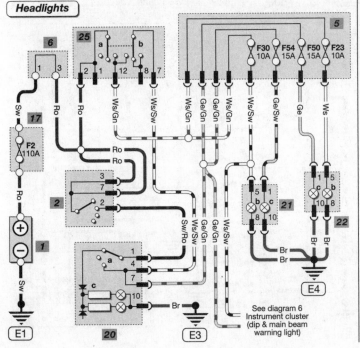

Headlights

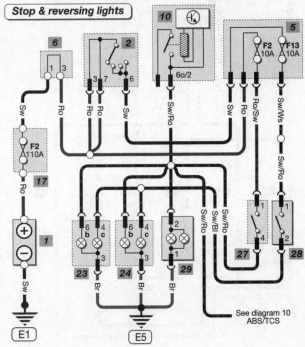

Stop & reversing lights

Wire colours

Bl	Blue	**Li**	Purple
Br	Brown	**Ws**	White
Ge	Yellow	**Or**	Orange
Gr	Grey	**Ro**	Red
Gn	Green	**Sw**	Black

Key to items

1 Battery
2 Ignition switch
5 Passenger compartment fusebox
6 Terminal 30 junction
10 Electrical system control unit
17 Battery fuseholder
18 'X' contact relief relay
20 Lighting switch
  a = side/headlight
  b = front/rear foglight
  c = switch illumination
21 LH headlight unit
  e = headlight levelling

22 RH headlight unit
  e = headlight levelling
23 LH rear light unit
  d = direction indicator
  e = rear foglight
24 RH rear light unit
  d = direction indicator
25 Multi-function switch
  b = main/dip switch
  c = parking light/direction
       indicator switch
33 LH indicator side repeater
34 RH indicator side repeater

35 Hazard warning switch
37 LH front foglight
38 RH front foglight
39 Headlight levelling/lighting rheostat
40 LH front indicator
41 RH front indicator

Diagram 4

H33375

Direction indicators & hazard warning lights

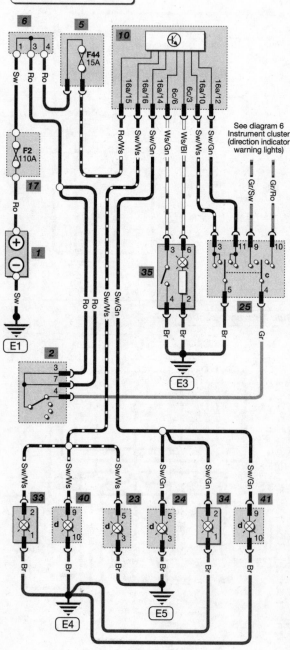

Front & rear foglights

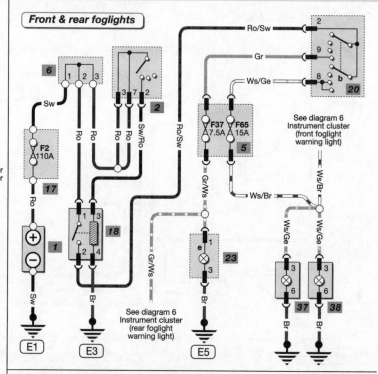

Headlight levelling

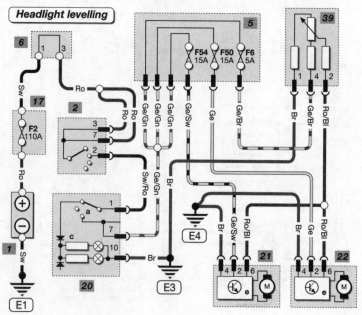

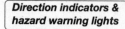

Wire colours

Bl	Blue	**Li**	Purple
Br	Brown	**Ws**	White
Ge	Yellow	**Or**	Orange
Gr	Grey	**Ro**	Red
Gn	Green	**Sw**	Black

* Models without central locking

Key to items

1 Battery
2 Ignition switch
5 Passenger compartment fusebox
6 Terminal 30 junction
10 Electrical system control unit
17 Battery fuseholder
18 'X' contact relay
43 Glovebox light/switch
44 Front interior light
  a = LH reading light
  b = interior light
  c = RH reading light

45 LH door courtesy light
46 RH door courtesy light
47 LH rear interior light
48 RH rear interior light
49 Luggage compartment light
50 Luggage compartment light switch
51 Wash/wipe switch
  a = front wash/wipe
  b = rear wash/wipe
  c = intermittent wiper rheostat
53 Front/rear washer pump

54 Front wiper motor
56 Rear wiper motor
57 LH door switch
58 RH door switch

Diagram 5

H33376

Interior lighting

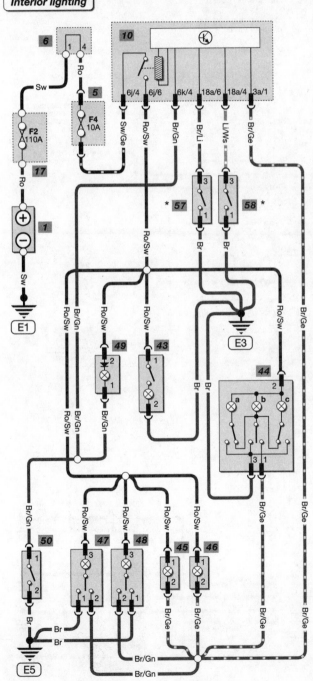

Front & rear wash/wipe

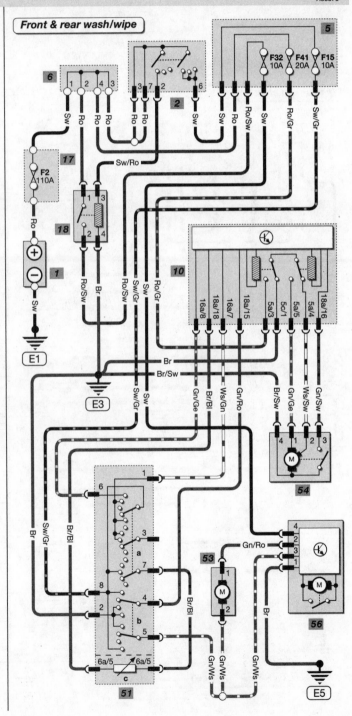

Wire colours

Bl	Blue	**Li**	Purple
Br	Brown	**Ws**	White
Ge	Yellow	**Or**	Orange
Gr	Grey	**Ro**	Red
Gn	Green	**Sw**	Black

Key to items

1 = Battery
2 = Ignition switch
5 = Passenger compartment fusebox
6 = Terminal 30 junction
10 = Electrical system control unit
17 = Battery fuseholder
59 = Handbrake switch
60 = Instrument cluster
  a = dipped beam warning light
  b = main beam warning light
  c = rear foglight warning light
  d = front foglight warning light
  e = instrument illumination
  f = digital clock
  g = alternator warning light
  h = servotronic warning light
  i = trailer warning light
  j = tailgate unlock warning light

k = TCS/ESP warning light
l = ABS warning light
m = airbag warning light
n = LH indicator warning light
o = RH indicator warning light
p = door ajar warning light
q = seatbelt warning light
r = tachometer
s = coolant temperature gauge
t = selector lever position sensor
u = immobilizer control unit
v = immobilizer warning light
w = coolant temp/low coolant warning light
x = brake system/handbrake warning light
y = low brake fluid warning light
z = pad wear warning light

a1 = buzzer
b1 = instrument cluster control unit
c1 = speedometer
d1 = odometer
e1 = oil pressure warning light
f1 = low fuel warning light
g1 = glow plug warning light
h1 = fuel gauge
61 = Immobilizer reader coil
62 = Oil pressure switch
63 = Low brake fluid switch
64 = Coolant level sender
65 = Fuel gauge sender
66 = Washer fluid level sensor
67 = Driver's seatbelt switch

Diagram 6

H33377

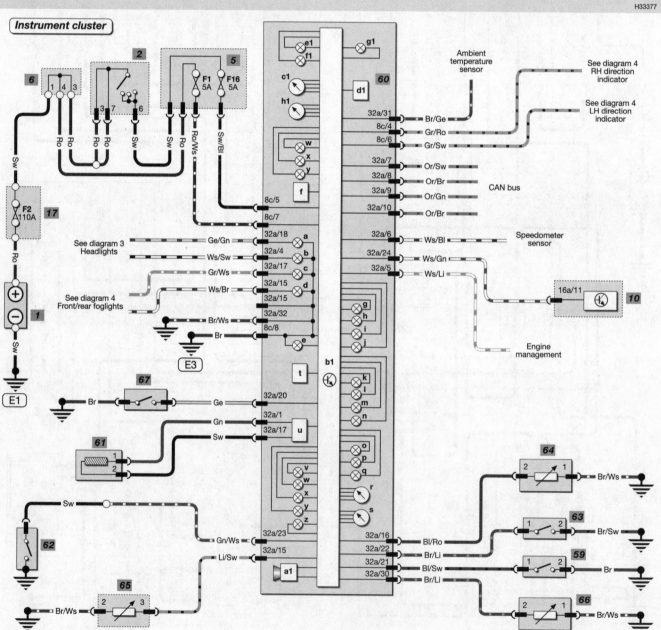

Instrument cluster

Wire colours

Bl	Blue	**Li**	Purple
Br	Brown	**Ws**	White
Ge	Yellow	**Or**	Orange
Gr	Grey	**Ro**	Red
Gn	Green	**Sw**	Black

Key to items

1   Battery
5   Passenger compartment fusebox
6   Terminal 30 junction
10 Electrical system control unit
17 Battery fuseholder
70 Driver's door control unit
71 Front passenger's door control unit
72 LH rear door control unit
73 RH rear door control unit
74 Driver's door window switch
    a = switch illumination
    b = front LH window switch
    c = front RH window switch
d = rear LH window switch
e = rear RH window switch
f = rear window isolation switch
75 Front passenger's door window switch
76 LH rear door window switch
77 RH rear door window switch

Diagram 7

H33378

Electric windows

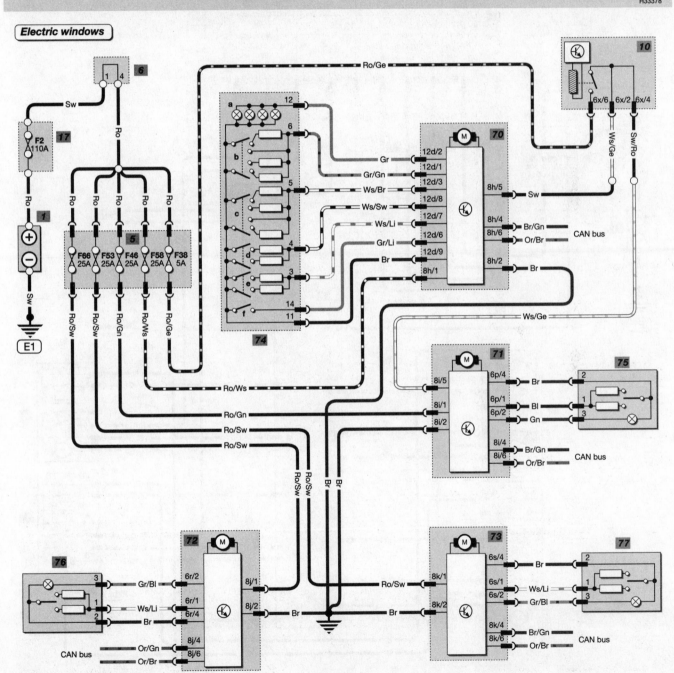

Wire colours

Bl	Blue	**Li**	Purple
Br	Brown	**Ws**	White
Ge	Yellow	**Or**	Orange
Gr	Grey	**Ro**	Red
Gn	Green	**Sw**	Black

Key to items

1 Battery
2 Ignition switch
5 Passenger compartment fusebox
6 Terminal 30 junction
10 Electrical system control unit
17 Battery fuseholder
42 Convenience system control unit
80 Driver's door lock unit
81 Front passenger's door lock unit

82 LH rear door lock unit
83 RH rear door lock unit
84 Tailgate handle release switch
85 Central locking switch (in tailgate lock)
86 Tailgate/boot locking motor

Diagram 8

H33379

Central locking

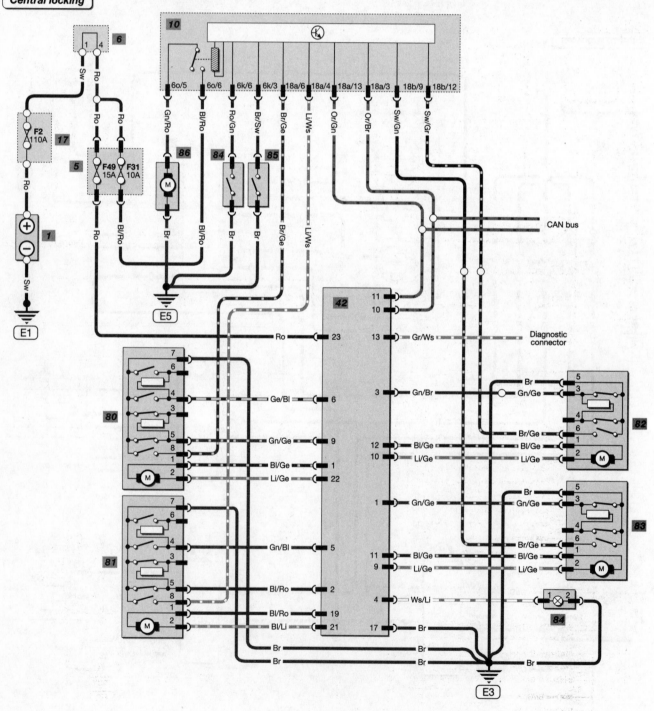

Wire colours

Bl	Blue	**Li**	Purple
Br	Brown	**Ws**	White
Ge	Yellow	**Or**	Orange
Gr	Grey	**Ro**	Red
Gn	Green	**Sw**	Black

Key to items

1 Battery
2 Ignition switch
5 Passenger compartment fusebox
6 Terminal 30 junction
10 Electrical system control unit
17 Battery fuseholder
70 Driver's door control unit
71 Front passenger's door control unit
90 Driver's mirror assembly

91 Passenger's mirror assembly
92 Mirror control switch
   a = switch illumination
   b = adjustment switch
   c = change-over switch
93 Sunroof motor
94 Sunroof control switch
95 Heated rear window switch
96 Heated rear window

Diagram 9

H33380

Electric mirrors

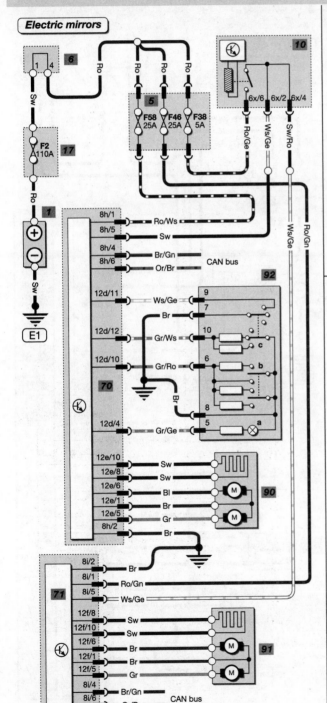

Sunroof

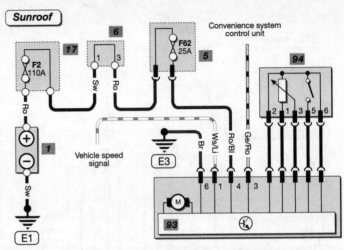

Heated rear window

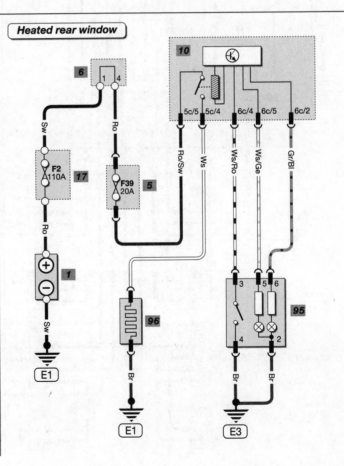

Wire colours

Bl	Blue	**Li**	Purple
Br	Brown	**Ws**	White
Ge	Yellow	**Or**	Orange
Gr	Grey	**Ro**	Red
Gn	Green	**Sw**	Black

Key to items

1 Battery
2 Ignition switch
5 Passenger compartment fusebox
6 Terminal 30 junction
10 Electrical system contol unit
17 Battery fuseholder
100 Audio unit
101 CD changer
102 LH front bass speaker
103 LH front tweeter
104 LH rear bass speaker
105 LH rear tweeter
106 RH front bass speaker

107 RH front tweeter
108 RH rear bass speaker
109 RH rear tweeter
110 ABS hydraulic unit
  a = control unit
  b = LH rear outlet valve
  c = LH rear inlet valve
  d = RH rear inlet valve
  e = RH rear outlet valve
  f = RH front inlet valve
  g = RH front outlet
  h = LH front inlet
  i = LH front outlet

  j = LH front EDL outlet
  k = RH front EDL outlet
  l = LH front EDL change over valve
  m = RH front EDL change over valve
  n = ABS solenoid valve relay
  o = return pump relay
  p = return pump
111 LH front wheel sensor
112 LH rear wheel sensor
113 RH front wheel sensor
114 RH rear wheel sensor
115 TCS switch

Diagram 10

H33381

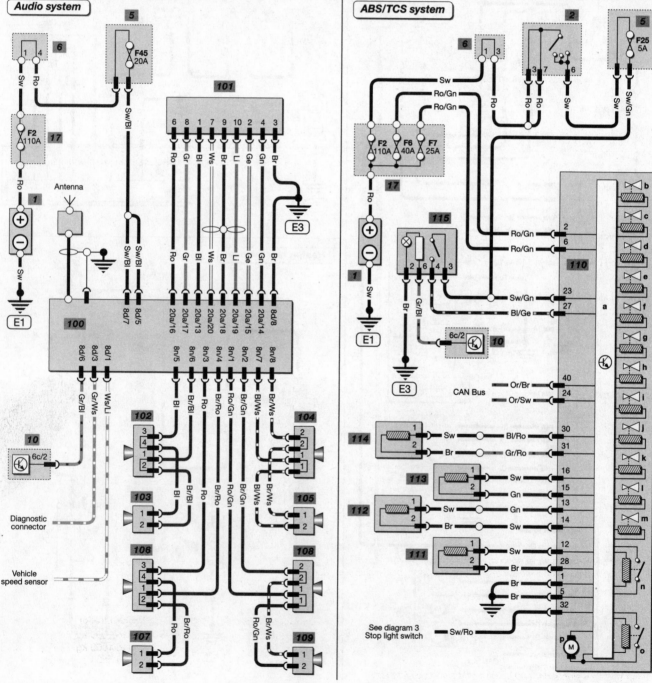

Audio system

ABS/TCS system

Dimensions and weights . . . . **REF•1**
Conversion factors. . . . . **REF•2**
Buying spare parts . . . . **REF•3**
Vehicle identification numbers . . . . **REF•3**
General repair procedures . . . . **REF•4**
Jacking and vehicle support . . . . **REF•5**

Disconnecting the battery . . . . **REF•5**
Tools and working facilities . . . . **REF•6**
MOT test checks . . . . **REF•8**
Fault finding . . . . **REF•12**
Glossary of technical terms . . . . **REF•22**
Index. . . . . **REF•30**

Dimensions and weights

Note: *All figures and dimensions are approximate and may vary according to model. Refer to manufacturer's data for exact figures.*

Overall length
Hatchback models . . . . 3970 mm
Saloon and Estate models . . . . 4232 mm

Overall width
All models:
    Excluding mirrors . . . . 1646 mm
    Including mirrors. . . . . 1890 mm

Overall height (unladen)
Hatchback models. . . . . 1451 mm
Estate models. . . . . 1452 mm
Saloon models . . . . 1449 mm

Wheelbase
All models. . . . . 2462 mm

Turning circle
All models. . . . . 10.8 m

Weights

Kerb weight*
Hatchback . . . . 1090 to 1315 kg
Estate . . . . 1185 to 1270 kg
Saloon . . . . 1185 to 1245 kg

Maximum gross vehicle weight**
Hatchback . . . . 1515 to 1720 kg
Estate . . . . 1610 to 1695 kg
Saloon . . . . 1610 to 1670 kg

* Exact kerb weights depend upon model and specification.
** Exact maximum gross vehicle weights depend upon model and specifications.

Maximum roof rack load
All models. . . . . 75 kg

Maximum towing weights*	**Unbraked trailer**	**Braked trailer**
Hatchback	450 to 500 kg	800 to 1000 kg
Estate	450 to 500 kg	750 to 1000 kg
Saloon	450	800 to 850 kg

* Exact towing weights depend upon model and specification.

Conversion factors

Length (distance)

Inches (in)	x 25.4	= Millimetres (mm)	x 0.0394	= Inches (in)
Feet (ft)	x 0.305	= Metres (m)	x 3.281	= Feet (ft)
Miles	x 1.609	= Kilometres (km)	x 0.621	= Miles

Volume (capacity)

Cubic inches (cu in; in^3)	x 16.387	= Cubic centimetres (cc; cm^3)	x 0.061	= Cubic inches (cu in; in^3)
Imperial pints (Imp pt)	x 0.568	= Litres (l)	x 1.76	= Imperial pints (Imp pt)
Imperial quarts (Imp qt)	x 1.137	= Litres (l)	x 0.88	= Imperial quarts (Imp qt)
Imperial quarts (Imp qt)	x 1.201	= US quarts (US qt)	x 0.833	= Imperial quarts (Imp qt)
US quarts (US qt)	x 0.946	= Litres (l)	x 1.057	= US quarts (US qt)
Imperial gallons (Imp gal)	x 4.546	= Litres (l)	x 0.22	= Imperial gallons (Imp gal)
Imperial gallons (Imp gal)	x 1.201	= US gallons (US gal)	x 0.833	= Imperial gallons (Imp gal)
US gallons (US gal)	x 3.785	= Litres (l)	x 0.264	= US gallons (US gal)

Mass (weight)

Ounces (oz)	x 28.35	= Grams (g)	x 0.035	= Ounces (oz)
Pounds (lb)	x 0.454	= Kilograms (kg)	x 2.205	= Pounds (lb)

Force

Ounces-force (ozf; oz)	x 0.278	= Newtons (N)	x 3.6	= Ounces-force (ozf; oz)
Pounds-force (lbf; lb)	x 4.448	= Newtons (N)	x 0.225	= Pounds-force (lbf; lb)
Newtons (N)	x 0.1	= Kilograms-force (kgf; kg)	x 9.81	= Newtons (N)

Pressure

Pounds-force per square inch (psi; lbf/in^2; lb/in^2)	x 0.070	= Kilograms-force per square centimetre (kgf/cm^2; kg/cm^2)	x 14.223	= Pounds-force per square inch (psi; lbf/in^2; lb/in^2)
Pounds-force per square inch (psi; lbf/in^2; lb/in^2)	x 0.068	= Atmospheres (atm)	x 14.696	= Pounds-force per square inch (psi; lbf/in^2; lb/in^2)
Pounds-force per square inch (psi; lbf/in^2; lb/in^2)	x 0.069	= Bars	x 14.5	= Pounds-force per square inch (psi; lbf/in^2; lb/in^2)
Pounds-force per square inch (psi; lbf/in^2; lb/in^2)	x 6.895	= Kilopascals (kPa)	x 0.145	= Pounds-force per square inch (psi; lbf/in^2; lb/in^2)
Kilopascals (kPa)	x 0.01	= Kilograms-force per square centimetre (kgf/cm^2; kg/cm^2)	x 98.1	= Kilopascals (kPa)
Millibar (mbar)	x 100	= Pascals (Pa)	x 0.01	= Millibar (mbar)
Millibar (mbar)	x 0.0145	= Pounds-force per square inch (psi; lbf/in^2; lb/in^2)	x 68.947	= Millibar (mbar)
Millibar (mbar)	x 0.75	= Millimetres of mercury (mmHg)	x 1.333	= Millibar (mbar)
Millibar (mbar)	x 0.401	= Inches of water (inH$_2$O)	x 2.491	= Millibar (mbar)
Millimetres of mercury (mmHg)	x 0.535	= Inches of water (inH$_2$O)	x 1.868	= Millimetres of mercury (mmHg)
Inches of water (inH$_2$O)	x 0.036	= Pounds-force per square inch (psi; lbf/in^2; lb/in^2)	x 27.68	= Inches of water (inH$_2$O)

Torque (moment of force)

Pounds-force inches (lbf in; lb in)	x 1.152	= Kilograms-force centimetre (kgf cm; kg cm)	x 0.868	= Pounds-force inches (lbf in; lb in)
Pounds-force inches (lbf in; lb in)	x 0.113	= Newton metres (Nm)	x 8.85	= Pounds-force inches (lbf in; lb in)
Pounds-force inches (lbf in; lb in)	x 0.083	= Pounds-force feet (lbf ft; lb ft)	x 12	= Pounds-force inches (lbf in; lb in)
Pounds-force feet (lbf ft; lb ft)	x 0.138	= Kilograms-force metres (kgf m; kg m)	x 7.233	= Pounds-force feet (lbf ft; lb ft)
Pounds-force feet (lbf ft; lb ft)	x 1.356	= Newton metres (Nm)	x 0.738	= Pounds-force feet (lbf ft; lb ft)
Newton metres (Nm)	x 0.102	= Kilograms-force metres (kgf m; kg m)	x 9.804	= Newton metres (Nm)

Power

Horsepower (hp)	x 745.7	= Watts (W)	x 0.0013	= Horsepower (hp)

Velocity (speed)

Miles per hour (miles/hr; mph)	x 1.609	= Kilometres per hour (km/hr; kph)	x 0.621	= Miles per hour (miles/hr; mph)

Fuel consumption*

Miles per gallon, Imperial (mpg)	x 0.354	= Kilometres per litre (km/l)	x 2.825	= Miles per gallon, Imperial (mpg)
Miles per gallon, US (mpg)	x 0.425	= Kilometres per litre (km/l)	x 2.352	= Miles per gallon, US (mpg)

Temperature

Degrees Fahrenheit = (°C x 1.8) + 32   Degrees Celsius (Degrees Centigrade; °C) = (°F - 32) x 0.56

It is common practice to convert from miles per gallon (mpg) to litres/100 kilometres (l/100km), where mpg x l/100 km = 282

Spare parts are available from many sources, including maker's appointed garages, accessory shops, and motor factors. To be sure of obtaining the correct parts, it will sometimes be necessary to quote the vehicle identification number. If possible, it can also be useful to take the old parts along for positive identification. Items such as starter motors and alternators may be available under a service exchange scheme – any parts returned should be clean.

Our advice regarding spare parts is as follows.

Officially appointed garages

This is the best source of parts which are peculiar to your car, and which are not otherwise generally available (eg, badges, interior trim, certain body panels, etc). It is also the only place at which you should buy parts if the vehicle is still under warranty.

Accessory shops

These are very good places to buy materials and components needed for the maintenance of your car (oil, air and fuel filters, light bulbs, drivebelts, greases, brake pads, touch-up paint, etc). Components of this nature sold by a reputable shop are usually of the same standard as those used by the car manufacturer.

Besides components, these shops also sell tools and general accessories, usually have convenient opening hours, charge lower prices, and can often be found close to home. Some accessory shops have parts counters where components needed for almost any repair job can be purchased or ordered.

Motor factors

Good factors will stock all the more important components which wear out comparatively quickly, and can sometimes supply individual components needed for the overhaul of a larger assembly (eg, brake seals and hydraulic parts, bearing shells, pistons, valves). They may also handle work such as cylinder block reboring, crankshaft regrinding, etc.

Tyre and exhaust specialists

These outlets may be independent, or members of a local or national chain. They frequently offer competitive prices when compared with a main dealer or local garage, but it will pay to obtain several quotes before making a decision. When researching prices, also ask what extras may be added – for instance fitting a new valve and balancing the wheel are both commonly charged on top of the price of a new tyre.

Other sources

Beware of parts or materials obtained from market stalls, car boot sales or similar outlets. Such items are not invariably sub-standard, but there is little chance of compensation if they do prove unsatisfactory. In the case of safety-critical components such as brake pads, there is the risk not only of financial loss, but also of an accident causing injury or death.

Second-hand components or assemblies obtained from a car breaker can be a good buy in some circumstances, but this sort of purchase is best made by the experienced DIY mechanic.

Vehicle identification numbers

Modifications are a continuing and unpublicised process in vehicle manufacture, quite apart from major model changes. Spare parts manuals and lists are compiled upon a numerical basis, the individual vehicle identification numbers being essential to correct identification of the component concerned.

When ordering spare parts, always give as much information as possible. Quote the car model, year of manufacture and registration, chassis and engine numbers as appropriate.

The *Vehicle Identification Number* (or chassis number) is located in the engine compartment, on the right-hand side suspension turret. It is also visible through the bottom left-hand corner of the windscreen (**see illustration**).

The *Vehicle Data Sticker* is located in the spare wheel well at the rear of the vehicle (**see illustration**).

The engine number is stamped into the left-hand end of the cylinder block and, in addition, a sticker is attached to the timing cover with the engine identification and a barcode (**see illustrations**).

Vehicle Identification Number (VIN) located on the left-hand front edge of the windscreen

Vehicle Data Sticker in the spare wheel well

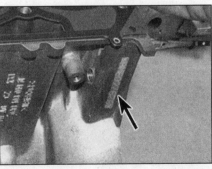

Engine number located on the left-hand end of the cylinder block

Engine code sticker located on the timing cover

Whenever servicing, repair or overhaul work is carried out on the car or its components, observe the following procedures and instructions. This will assist in carrying out the operation efficiently and to a professional standard of workmanship.

Joint mating faces and gaskets

When separating components at their mating faces, never insert screwdrivers or similar implements into the joint between the faces in order to prise them apart. This can cause severe damage which results in oil leaks, coolant leaks, etc upon reassembly. Separation is usually achieved by tapping along the joint with a soft-faced hammer in order to break the seal. However, note that this method may not be suitable where dowels are used for component location.

Where a gasket is used between the mating faces of two components, a new one must be fitted on reassembly; fit it dry unless otherwise stated in the repair procedure. Make sure that the mating faces are clean and dry, with all traces of old gasket removed. When cleaning a joint face, use a tool which is unlikely to score or damage the face, and remove any burrs or nicks with an oilstone or fine file.

Make sure that tapped holes are cleaned with a pipe cleaner, and keep them free of jointing compound, if this is being used, unless specifically instructed otherwise.

Ensure that all orifices, channels or pipes are clear, and blow through them, preferably using compressed air.

Oil seals

Oil seals can be removed by levering them out with a wide flat-bladed screwdriver or similar implement. Alternatively, a number of self-tapping screws may be screwed into the seal, and these used as a purchase for pliers or some similar device in order to pull the seal free.

Whenever an oil seal is removed from its working location, either individually or as part of an assembly, it should be renewed.

The very fine sealing lip of the seal is easily damaged, and will not seal if the surface it contacts is not completely clean and free from scratches, nicks or grooves. If the original sealing surface of the component cannot be restored, and the manufacturer has not made provision for slight relocation of the seal relative to the sealing surface, the component should be renewed.

Protect the lips of the seal from any surface which may damage them in the course of fitting. Use tape or a conical sleeve where possible. Lubricate the seal lips with oil before fitting and, on dual-lipped seals, fill the space between the lips with grease.

Unless otherwise stated, oil seals must be fitted with their sealing lips toward the lubricant to be sealed.

Use a tubular drift or block of wood of the appropriate size to install the seal and, if the seal housing is shouldered, drive the seal down to the shoulder. If the seal housing is unshouldered, the seal should be fitted with its face flush with the housing top face (unless otherwise instructed).

Screw threads and fastenings

Seized nuts, bolts and screws are quite a common occurrence where corrosion has set in, and the use of penetrating oil or releasing fluid will often overcome this problem if the offending item is soaked for a while before attempting to release it. The use of an impact driver may also provide a means of releasing such stubborn fastening devices, when used in conjunction with the appropriate screwdriver bit or socket. If none of these methods works, it may be necessary to resort to the careful application of heat, or the use of a hacksaw or nut splitter device.

Studs are usually removed by locking two nuts together on the threaded part, and then using a spanner on the lower nut to unscrew the stud. Studs or bolts which have broken off below the surface of the component in which they are mounted can sometimes be removed using a stud extractor. Always ensure that a blind tapped hole is completely free from oil, grease, water or other fluid before installing the bolt or stud. Failure to do this could cause the housing to crack due to the hydraulic action of the bolt or stud as it is screwed in.

When tightening a castellated nut to accept a split pin, tighten the nut to the specified torque, where applicable, and then tighten further to the next split pin hole. Never slacken the nut to align the split pin hole, unless stated in the repair procedure.

When checking or retightening a nut or bolt to a specified torque setting, slacken the nut or bolt by a quarter of a turn, and then retighten to the specified setting. However, this should not be attempted where angular tightening has been used.

For some screw fastenings, notably cylinder head bolts or nuts, torque wrench settings are no longer specified for the latter stages of tightening, "angle-tightening" being called up instead. Typically, a fairly low torque wrench setting will be applied to the bolts/nuts in the correct sequence, followed by one or more stages of tightening through specified angles.

Locknuts, locktabs and washers

Any fastening which will rotate against a component or housing during tightening should always have a washer between it and the relevant component or housing.

Spring or split washers should always be renewed when they are used to lock a critical component such as a big-end bearing retaining bolt or nut. Locktabs which are folded over to retain a nut or bolt should always be renewed.

Self-locking nuts can be re-used in non-critical areas, providing resistance can be felt when the locking portion passes over the bolt or stud thread. However, it should be noted that self-locking stiffnuts tend to lose their effectiveness after long periods of use, and should then be renewed as a matter of course.

Split pins must always be replaced with new ones of the correct size for the hole.

When thread-locking compound is found on the threads of a fastener which is to be re-used, it should be cleaned off with a wire brush and solvent, and fresh compound applied on reassembly.

Special tools

Some repair procedures in this manual entail the use of special tools such as a press, two or three-legged pullers, spring compressors, etc. Wherever possible, suitable readily-available alternatives to the manufacturer's special tools are described, and are shown in use. In some instances, where no alternative is possible, it has been necessary to resort to the use of a manufacturer's tool, and this has been done for reasons of safety as well as the efficient completion of the repair operation. Unless you are highly-skilled and have a thorough understanding of the procedures described, never attempt to bypass the use of any special tool when the procedure described specifies its use. Not only is there a very great risk of personal injury, but expensive damage could be caused to the components involved.

Environmental considerations

When disposing of used engine oil, brake fluid, antifreeze, etc, give due consideration to any detrimental environmental effects. Do not, for instance, pour any of the above liquids down drains into the general sewage system, or onto the ground to soak away. Many local council refuse tips provide a facility for waste oil disposal, as do some garages. If none of these facilities are available, consult your local Environmental Health Department, or the National Rivers Authority, for further advice.

With the universal tightening-up of legislation regarding the emission of environmentally-harmful substances from motor vehicles, most vehicles have tamperproof devices fitted to the main adjustment points of the fuel system. These devices are primarily designed to prevent unqualified persons from adjusting the fuel/air mixture, with the chance of a consequent increase in toxic emissions. If such devices are found during servicing or overhaul, they should, wherever possible, be renewed or refitted in accordance with the manufacturer's requirements or current legislation.

Note: It is antisocial and illegal to dump oil down the drain. To find the location of your local oil recycling bank, call this number free.

The jack supplied with the vehicle tool kit should only be used for changing the roadwheels – see *Wheel changing* at the front of this book. When carrying out any other kind of work, raise the vehicle using a hydraulic (or 'trolley') jack, and always supplement the jack with axle stands positioned under the vehicle jacking points.

When using a hydraulic jack or axle stands, always position the jack head or axle stand head under one of the relevant jacking points.

To raise the front and/or rear of the vehicle, use the jacking/support points at the front and rear ends of the door sills, indicated by the triangular depressions in the sill panel **(see illustration)**. Position a block of wood with a groove cut in it on the jack head to prevent the vehicle weight resting on the sill edge; align the sill edge with the groove in the wood so that the vehicle weight is spread evenly over the surface of the block. Supplement the jack with axle stands (also with slotted blocks of wood) positioned as close as possible to the jacking points **(see illustrations)**.

Do not jack the vehicle under any other part of the sill, sump, floor pan, or any of the steering or suspension components. With the vehicle raised, an axle stand should be positioned beneath the vehicle jack location point on the sill.

⚠ *Warning: Never work under, around, or near a raised car, unless it is adequately supported in at least two places.*

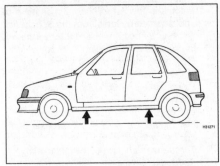

Front and rear jacking points (arrowed)

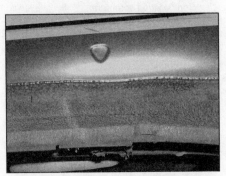

The jacking points are indicated by an arrow on the sill

Use an axle stand with a suitable block of wood

Disconnecting the battery

Caution: After reconnecting the battery, the safety function of the electric windows will not be re-instated until the windows have been reprogrammed.

Several of the systems require battery power to be available at all times (permanent live). This is either to ensure their continued operation (such as the clock), or to maintain electronic memory settings which would otherwise be erased. Whenever the battery is to be disconnected, first note the following points, to ensure there are no unforeseen consequences:

a) *Firstly, on any vehicle with central door locking, it is a wise precaution to remove the key from the ignition, and to keep it with you. This avoids the possibility of the key being locked inside the car, should the central locking engage when the battery is reconnected.*

b) *If a security-coded audio unit is fitted, and the unit and/or the battery is disconnected, the unit will not function until the correct security code has been entered. Therefore, if you do not know the correct security code for the radio/cassette unit, **do not** disconnect either of the battery terminals, or remove the radio/*

cassette unit from the vehicle. The code appears on a code card supplied with the car when new. Details for entering the code appear in the vehicle handbook. Should the code have been misplaced or forgotten, on production of proof of ownership, a Skoda dealer or in-car entertainment specialist may be able to help.

c) *The engine management system ECU is of the 'self-learning' type, meaning that, as it operates, it adapts to changes in operating conditions, and stores the optimum settings found (this is especially true for idle speed settings). When the battery is disconnected, these 'learned' settings are lost, and the ECU reverts to the base factory settings. When the engine is restarted, it may idle and run roughly until the ECU has 'relearned' the best settings. To further this 'learning' process, take the car for a road test of at least 15 minutes' duration, covering as many engine speeds and loads as possible, and concentrating on the 2000 to 4000 rpm range. On completion, let the engine idle for at least 10 minutes, turning the steering wheel occasionally*

and switching on high-current-draw equipment such as the heater fan or heated rear window. If the engine does not regain its normal performance, have the system checked for faults by a Skoda dealer.

Devices known as 'memory-savers' or 'code-savers' can be used to avoid some of the above problems. Precise details of use vary according to the device used. Typically, it is plugged into the cigarette lighter socket, and is connected by its own wiring to a spare battery; the vehicle battery is then disconnected from the electrical system, leaving the memory-saver to pass sufficient current to maintain audio unit security codes, and other memory values, and also to run permanently-live circuits such as the clock.

⚠ *Warning: Some of these devices allow a considerable amount of current to pass, which can mean that many of the vehicle's systems are still operational when the main battery is disconnected. If a memory-saver is used, ensure that the circuit concerned is actually 'dead' before carrying out any work on it.*

Introduction

A selection of good tools is a fundamental requirement for anyone contemplating the maintenance and repair of a motor vehicle. For the owner who does not possess any, their purchase will prove a considerable expense, offsetting some of the savings made by doing-it-yourself. However, provided that the tools purchased meet the relevant national safety standards and are of good quality, they will last for many years and prove an extremely worthwhile investment.

To help the average owner to decide which tools are needed to carry out the various tasks detailed in this manual, we have compiled three lists of tools under the following headings: *Maintenance and minor repair, Repair and overhaul,* and *Special.* Newcomers to practical mechanics should start off with the *Maintenance and minor repair* tool kit, and confine themselves to the simpler jobs around the vehicle. Then, as confidence and experience grow, more difficult tasks can be undertaken, with extra tools being purchased as, and when, they are needed. In this way, a *Maintenance and minor repair* tool kit can be built up into a *Repair and overhaul* tool kit over a considerable period of time, without any major cash outlays. The experienced do-it-yourselfer will have a tool kit good enough for most repair and overhaul procedures, and will add tools from the *Special* category when it is felt that the expense is justified by the amount of use to which these tools will be put.

Maintenance and minor repair tool kit

The tools given in this list should be considered as a minimum requirement if routine maintenance, servicing and minor repair operations are to be undertaken. We recommend the purchase of combination spanners (ring one end, open-ended the other); although more expensive than open-ended ones, they do give the advantages of both types of spanner.

☐ *Combination spanners:*
   Metric - 8 to 19 mm inclusive
☐ *Adjustable spanner - 35 mm jaw (approx.)*
☐ *Spark plug spanner (with rubber insert) - petrol models*
☐ *Spark plug gap adjustment tool - petrol models*
☐ *Set of feeler gauges*
☐ *Brake bleed nipple spanner*
☐ *Screwdrivers:*
   Flat blade - 100 mm long x 6 mm dia
   Cross blade - 100 mm long x 6 mm dia
   Torx - various sizes (not all vehicles)
☐ *Combination pliers*
☐ *Hacksaw (junior)*
☐ *Tyre pump*
☐ *Tyre pressure gauge*
☐ *Oil can*
☐ *Oil filter removal tool*
☐ *Fine emery cloth*
☐ *Wire brush (small)*
☐ *Funnel (medium size)*
☐ *Sump drain plug key (not all vehicles)*

Repair and overhaul tool kit

These tools are virtually essential for anyone undertaking any major repairs to a motor vehicle, and are additional to those given in the *Maintenance and minor repair* list. Included in this list is a comprehensive set of sockets. Although these are expensive, they will be found invaluable as they are so versatile - particularly if various drives are included in the set. We recommend the half-inch square-drive type, as this can be used with most proprietary torque wrenches.

The tools in this list will sometimes need to be supplemented by tools from the *Special* list:

☐ *Sockets (or box spanners) to cover range in previous list (including Torx sockets)*
☐ *Reversible ratchet drive (for use with sockets)*
☐ *Extension piece, 250 mm (for use with sockets)*
☐ *Universal joint (for use with sockets)*
☐ *Flexible handle or sliding T "breaker bar" (for use with sockets)*
☐ *Torque wrench (for use with sockets)*
☐ *Self-locking grips*
☐ *Ball pein hammer*
☐ *Soft-faced mallet (plastic or rubber)*
☐ *Screwdrivers:*
   Flat blade - long & sturdy, short (chubby), and narrow (electrician's) types
   Cross blade – long & sturdy, and short (chubby) types
☐ *Pliers:*
   Long-nosed
   Side cutters (electrician's)
   Circlip (internal and external)
☐ *Cold chisel - 25 mm*
☐ *Scriber*
☐ *Scraper*
☐ *Centre-punch*
☐ *Pin punch*
☐ *Hacksaw*
☐ *Brake hose clamp*
☐ *Brake/clutch bleeding kit*
☐ *Selection of twist drills*
☐ *Steel rule/straight-edge*
☐ *Allen keys (inc. splined/Torx type)*
☐ *Selection of files*
☐ *Wire brush*
☐ *Axle stands*
☐ *Jack (strong trolley or hydraulic type)*
☐ *Light with extension lead*
☐ *Universal electrical multi-meter*

Sockets and reversible ratchet drive

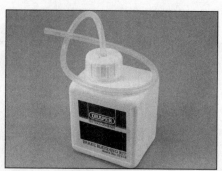
Brake bleeding kit

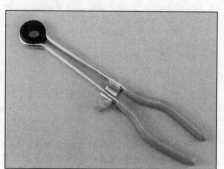
Torx key, socket and bit

Hose clamp

Angular-tightening gauge

Special tools

The tools in this list are those which are not used regularly, are expensive to buy, or which need to be used in accordance with their manufacturers' instructions. Unless relatively difficult mechanical jobs are undertaken frequently, it will not be economic to buy many of these tools. Where this is the case, you could consider clubbing together with friends (or joining a motorists' club) to make a joint purchase, or borrowing the tools against a deposit from a local garage or tool hire specialist. It is worth noting that many of the larger DIY superstores now carry a large range of special tools for hire at modest rates.

The following list contains only those tools and instruments freely available to the public, and not those special tools produced by the vehicle manufacturer specifically for its dealer network. You will find occasional references to these manufacturers' special tools in the text of this manual. Generally, an alternative method of doing the job without the vehicle manufacturers' special tool is given. However, sometimes there is no alternative to using them. Where this is the case and the relevant tool cannot be bought or borrowed, you will have to entrust the work to a dealer.

- ☐ Angular-tightening gauge
- ☐ Valve spring compressor
- ☐ Valve grinding tool
- ☐ Piston ring compressor
- ☐ Piston ring removal/installation tool
- ☐ Cylinder bore hone
- ☐ Balljoint separator
- ☐ Coil spring compressors (where applicable)
- ☐ Two/three-legged hub and bearing puller
- ☐ Impact screwdriver
- ☐ Micrometer and/or vernier calipers
- ☐ Dial gauge
- ☐ Stroboscopic timing light
- ☐ Dwell angle meter/tachometer
- ☐ Fault code reader
- ☐ Cylinder compression gauge
- ☐ Hand-operated vacuum pump and gauge
- ☐ Clutch plate alignment set
- ☐ Brake shoe steady spring cup removal tool
- ☐ Bush and bearing removal/installation set
- ☐ Stud extractors
- ☐ Tap and die set
- ☐ Lifting tackle
- ☐ Trolley jack

Buying tools

Reputable motor accessory shops and superstores often offer excellent quality tools at discount prices, so it pays to shop around.

Remember, you don't have to buy the most expensive items on the shelf, but it is always advisable to steer clear of the very cheap tools. Beware of 'bargains' offered on market stalls or at car boot sales. There are plenty of good tools around at reasonable prices, but always aim to purchase items which meet the relevant national safety standards. If in doubt, ask the proprietor or manager of the shop for advice before making a purchase.

Care and maintenance of tools

Having purchased a reasonable tool kit, it is necessary to keep the tools in a clean and serviceable condition. After use, always wipe off any dirt, grease and metal particles using a clean, dry cloth, before putting the tools away. Never leave them lying around after they have been used. A simple tool rack on the garage or workshop wall for items such as screwdrivers and pliers is a good idea. Store all normal spanners and sockets in a metal box. Any measuring instruments, gauges, meters, etc, must be carefully stored where they cannot be damaged or become rusty.

Take a little care when tools are used. Hammer heads inevitably become marked, and screwdrivers lose the keen edge on their blades from time to time. A little timely attention with emery cloth or a file will soon restore items like this to a good finish.

Working facilities

Not to be forgotten when discussing tools is the workshop itself. If anything more than routine maintenance is to be carried out, a suitable working area becomes essential.

It is appreciated that many an owner-mechanic is forced by circumstances to remove an engine or similar item without the benefit of a garage or workshop. Having done this, any repairs should always be done under the cover of a roof.

Wherever possible, any dismantling should be done on a clean, flat workbench or table at a suitable working height.

Any workbench needs a vice; one with a jaw opening of 100 mm is suitable for most jobs. As mentioned previously, some clean dry storage space is also required for tools, as well as for any lubricants, cleaning fluids, touch-up paints etc, which become necessary.

Another item which may be required, and which has a much more general usage, is an electric drill with a chuck capacity of at least 8 mm. This, together with a good range of twist drills, is virtually essential for fitting accessories.

Last, but not least, always keep a supply of old newspapers and clean, lint-free rags available, and try to keep any working area as clean as possible.

Micrometers

Dial test indicator ("dial gauge")

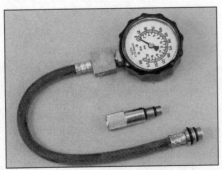

Strap wrench

Compression tester

Fault code reader

This is a guide to getting your vehicle through the MOT test. Obviously it will not be possible to examine the vehicle to the same standard as the professional MOT tester. However, working through the following checks will enable you to identify any problem areas before submitting the vehicle for the test.

Where a testable component is in borderline condition, the tester has discretion in deciding whether to pass or fail it. The basis of such discretion is whether the tester would be happy for a close relative or friend to use the vehicle with the component in that condition. If the vehicle presented is clean and evidently well cared for, the tester may be more inclined to pass a borderline component than if the vehicle is scruffy and apparently neglected.

It has only been possible to summarise the test requirements here, based on the regulations in force at the time of printing. Test standards are becoming increasingly stringent, although there are some exemptions for older vehicles.

An assistant will be needed to help carry out some of these checks.

The checks have been sub-divided into four categories, as follows:

1 Checks carried out **FROM THE DRIVER'S SEAT**

2 Checks carried out **WITH THE VEHICLE ON THE GROUND**

3 Checks carried out **WITH THE VEHICLE RAISED AND THE WHEELS FREE TO TURN**

4 Checks carried out on **YOUR VEHICLE'S EXHAUST EMISSION SYSTEM**

1 Checks carried out **FROM THE DRIVER'S SEAT**

Handbrake

☐ Test the operation of the handbrake. Excessive travel (too many clicks) indicates incorrect brake or cable adjustment.
☐ Check that the handbrake cannot be released by tapping the lever sideways. Check the security of the lever mountings.

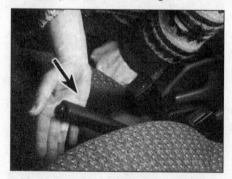

Footbrake

☐ Depress the brake pedal and check that it does not creep down to the floor, indicating a master cylinder fault. Release the pedal, wait a few seconds, then depress it again. If the pedal travels nearly to the floor before firm resistance is felt, brake adjustment or repair is necessary. If the pedal feels spongy, there is air in the hydraulic system which must be removed by bleeding.

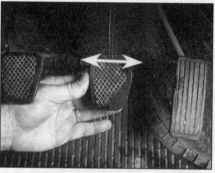

☐ Check that the brake pedal is secure and in good condition. Check also for signs of fluid leaks on the pedal, floor or carpets, which would indicate failed seals in the brake master cylinder.
☐ Check the servo unit (when applicable) by operating the brake pedal several times, then keeping the pedal depressed and starting the engine. As the engine starts, the pedal will move down slightly. If not, the vacuum hose or the servo itself may be faulty.

Steering wheel and column

☐ Examine the steering wheel for fractures or looseness of the hub, spokes or rim.
☐ Move the steering wheel from side to side and then up and down. Check that the steering wheel is not loose on the column, indicating wear or a loose retaining nut. Continue moving the steering wheel as before, but also turn it slightly from left to right.
☐ Check that the steering wheel is not loose on the column, and that there is no abnormal

movement of the steering wheel, indicating wear in the column support bearings or couplings.

Windscreen, mirrors and sunvisor

☐ The windscreen must be free of cracks or other significant damage within the driver's field of view. (Small stone chips are acceptable.) Rear view mirrors must be secure, intact, and capable of being adjusted.

☐ The driver's sunvisor must be capable of being stored in the "up" position.

Seat belts and seats

Note: *The following checks are applicable to all seat belts, front and rear.*

☐ Examine the webbing of all the belts (including rear belts if fitted) for cuts, serious fraying or deterioration. Fasten and unfasten each belt to check the buckles. If applicable, check the retracting mechanism. Check the security of all seat belt mountings accessible from inside the vehicle.

☐ Seat belts with pre-tensioners, once activated, have a "flag" or similar showing on the seat belt stalk. This, in itself, is not a reason for test failure.

☐ The front seats themselves must be securely attached and the backrests must lock in the upright position.

Doors

☐ Both front doors must be able to be opened and closed from outside and inside, and must latch securely when closed.

2 Checks carried out WITH THE VEHICLE ON THE GROUND

Vehicle identification

☐ Number plates must be in good condition, secure and legible, with letters and numbers correctly spaced – spacing at (A) should be at least twice that at (B).

☐ The VIN plate and/or homologation plate must be legible.

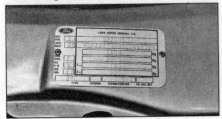

Electrical equipment

☐ Switch on the ignition and check the operation of the horn.

☐ Check the windscreen washers and wipers, examining the wiper blades; renew damaged or perished blades. Also check the operation of the stop-lights.

☐ Check the operation of the sidelights and number plate lights. The lenses and reflectors must be secure, clean and undamaged.

☐ Check the operation and alignment of the headlights. The headlight reflectors must not be tarnished and the lenses must be undamaged.

☐ Switch on the ignition and check the operation of the direction indicators (including the instrument panel tell-tale) and the hazard warning lights. Operation of the sidelights and stop-lights must not affect the indicators - if it does, the cause is usually a bad earth at the rear light cluster.

☐ Check the operation of the rear foglight(s), including the warning light on the instrument panel or in the switch.

☐ The ABS warning light must illuminate in accordance with the manufacturers' design. For most vehicles, the ABS warning light should illuminate when the ignition is switched on, and (if the system is operating properly) extinguish after a few seconds. Refer to the owner's handbook.

Footbrake

☐ Examine the master cylinder, brake pipes and servo unit for leaks, loose mountings, corrosion or other damage.

☐ The fluid reservoir must be secure and the fluid level must be between the upper (A) and lower (B) markings.

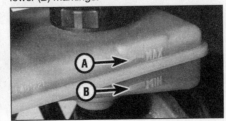

☐ Inspect both front brake flexible hoses for cracks or deterioration of the rubber. Turn the steering from lock to lock, and ensure that the hoses do not contact the wheel, tyre, or any part of the steering or suspension mechanism. With the brake pedal firmly depressed, check the hoses for bulges or leaks under pressure.

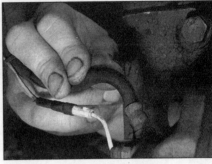

Steering and suspension

☐ Have your assistant turn the steering wheel from side to side slightly, up to the point where the steering gear just begins to transmit this movement to the roadwheels. Check for excessive free play between the steering wheel and the steering gear, indicating wear or insecurity of the steering column joints, the column-to-steering gear coupling, or the steering gear itself.

☐ Have your assistant turn the steering wheel more vigorously in each direction, so that the roadwheels just begin to turn. As this is done, examine all the steering joints, linkages, fittings and attachments. Renew any component that shows signs of wear or damage. On vehicles with power steering, check the security and condition of the steering pump, drivebelt and hoses.

☐ Check that the vehicle is standing level, and at approximately the correct ride height.

Shock absorbers

☐ Depress each corner of the vehicle in turn, then release it. The vehicle should rise and then settle in its normal position. If the vehicle continues to rise and fall, the shock absorber is defective. A shock absorber which has seized will also cause the vehicle to fail.

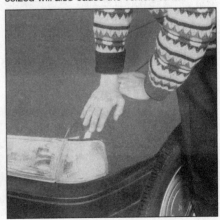

Exhaust system

☐ Start the engine. With your assistant holding a rag over the tailpipe, check the entire system for leaks. Repair or renew leaking sections.

3 Checks carried out **WITH THE VEHICLE RAISED AND THE WHEELS FREE TO TURN**

Jack up the front and rear of the vehicle, and securely support it on axle stands. Position the stands clear of the suspension assemblies. Ensure that the wheels are clear of the ground and that the steering can be turned from lock to lock.

Steering mechanism

☐ Have your assistant turn the steering from lock to lock. Check that the steering turns smoothly, and that no part of the steering mechanism, including a wheel or tyre, fouls any brake hose or pipe or any part of the body structure.

☐ Examine the steering rack rubber gaiters for damage or insecurity of the retaining clips. If power steering is fitted, check for signs of damage or leakage of the fluid hoses, pipes or connections. Also check for excessive stiffness or binding of the steering, a missing split pin or locking device, or severe corrosion of the body structure within 30 cm of any steering component attachment point.

Front and rear suspension and wheel bearings

☐ Starting at the front right-hand side, grasp the roadwheel at the 3 o'clock and 9 o'clock positions and rock gently but firmly. Check for free play or insecurity at the wheel bearings, suspension balljoints, or suspension mountings, pivots and attachments.

☐ Now grasp the wheel at the 12 o'clock and 6 o'clock positions and repeat the previous inspection. Spin the wheel, and check for roughness or tightness of the front wheel bearing.

☐ If excess free play is suspected at a component pivot point, this can be confirmed by using a large screwdriver or similar tool and levering between the mounting and the component attachment. This will confirm whether the wear is in the pivot bush, its retaining bolt, or in the mounting itself (the bolt holes can often become elongated).

☐ Carry out all the above checks at the other front wheel, and then at both rear wheels.

Springs and shock absorbers

☐ Examine the suspension struts (when applicable) for serious fluid leakage, corrosion, or damage to the casing. Also check the security of the mounting points.

☐ If coil springs are fitted, check that the spring ends locate in their seats, and that the spring is not corroded, cracked or broken.

☐ If leaf springs are fitted, check that all leaves are intact, that the axle is securely attached to each spring, and that there is no deterioration of the spring eye mountings, bushes, and shackles.

☐ The same general checks apply to vehicles fitted with other suspension types, such as torsion bars, hydraulic displacer units, etc. Ensure that all mountings and attachments are secure, that there are no signs of excessive wear, corrosion or damage, and (on hydraulic types) that there are no fluid leaks or damaged pipes.

☐ Inspect the shock absorbers for signs of serious fluid leakage. Check for wear of the mounting bushes or attachments, or damage to the body of the unit.

Driveshafts (fwd vehicles only)

☐ Rotate each front wheel in turn and inspect the constant velocity joint gaiters for splits or damage. Also check that each driveshaft is straight and undamaged.

Braking system

☐ If possible without dismantling, check brake pad wear and disc condition. Ensure that the friction lining material has not worn excessively, (A) and that the discs are not fractured, pitted, scored or badly worn (B).

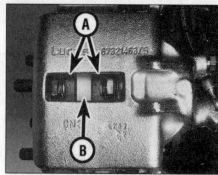

☐ Examine all the rigid brake pipes underneath the vehicle, and the flexible hose(s) at the rear. Look for corrosion, chafing or insecurity of the pipes, and for signs of bulging under pressure, chafing, splits or deterioration of the flexible hoses.

☐ Look for signs of fluid leaks at the brake calipers or on the brake backplates. Repair or renew leaking components.

☐ Slowly spin each wheel, while your assistant depresses and releases the footbrake. Ensure that each brake is operating and does not bind when the pedal is released.

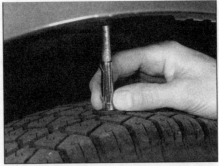

□ Examine the handbrake mechanism, checking for frayed or broken cables, excessive corrosion, or wear or insecurity of the linkage. Check that the mechanism works on each relevant wheel, and releases fully, without binding.

□ It is not possible to test brake efficiency without special equipment, but a road test can be carried out later to check that the vehicle pulls up in a straight line.

Fuel and exhaust systems

□ Inspect the fuel tank (including the filler cap), fuel pipes, hoses and unions. All components must be secure and free from leaks.

□ Examine the exhaust system over its entire length, checking for any damaged, broken or missing mountings, security of the retaining clamps and rust or corrosion.

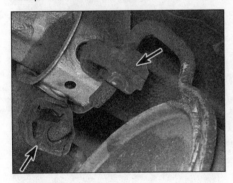

Wheels and tyres

□ Examine the sidewalls and tread area of each tyre in turn. Check for cuts, tears, lumps, bulges, separation of the tread, and exposure of the ply or cord due to wear or damage. Check that the tyre bead is correctly seated on the wheel rim, that the valve is sound and properly seated, and that the wheel is not distorted or damaged.

□ Check that the tyres are of the correct size for the vehicle, that they are of the same size and type on each axle, and that the pressures are correct.

□ Check the tyre tread depth. The legal minimum at the time of writing is 1.6 mm over at least three-quarters of the tread width. Abnormal tread wear may indicate incorrect front wheel alignment.

Body corrosion

□ Check the condition of the entire vehicle structure for signs of corrosion in load-bearing areas. (These include chassis box sections, side sills, cross-members, pillars, and all suspension, steering, braking system and seat belt mountings and anchorages.) Any corrosion which has seriously reduced the thickness of a load-bearing area is likely to cause the vehicle to fail. In this case professional repairs are likely to be needed.

□ Damage or corrosion which causes sharp or otherwise dangerous edges to be exposed will also cause the vehicle to fail.

4 Checks carried out on YOUR VEHICLE'S EXHAUST EMISSION SYSTEM

Petrol models

□ The engine should be warmed up, and running well (ignition system in good order, air filter element clean, etc).

□ Before testing, run the engine at around 2500 rpm for 20 seconds. Let the engine drop to idle, and watch for smoke from the exhaust. If the idle speed is too high, or if dense blue or black smoke emerges for more than 5 seconds, the vehicle will fail. Typically, blue smoke signifies oil burning (engine wear); black smoke means unburnt fuel (dirty air cleaner element, or other fuel system fault).

□ An exhaust gas analyser for measuring carbon monoxide (CO) and hydrocarbons (HC) is now needed. If one cannot be hired or borrowed, have a local garage perform the check.

CO emissions (mixture)

□ The MOT tester has access to the CO limits for all vehicles. The CO level is measured at idle speed, and at 'fast idle' (2500 to 3000 rpm). The following limits are given as a general guide:

At idle speed – Less than 0.5% CO
At 'fast idle' – Less than 0.3% CO
Lambda reading – 0.97 to 1.03

□ If the CO level is too high, this may point to poor maintenance, a fuel injection system problem, faulty lambda (oxygen) sensor or catalytic converter. Try an injector cleaning treatment, and check the vehicle's ECU for fault codes.

HC emissions

□ The MOT tester has access to HC limits for all vehicles. The HC level is measured at 'fast idle' (2500 to 3000 rpm). The following limits are given as a general guide:

At 'fast idle' – Less then 200 ppm

□ Excessive HC emissions are typically caused by oil being burnt (worn engine), or by a blocked crankcase ventilation system ('breather'). If the engine oil is old and thin, an oil change may help. If the engine is running badly, check the vehicle's ECU for fault codes.

Diesel models

□ The only emission test for diesel engines is measuring exhaust smoke density, using a calibrated smoke meter. The test involves accelerating the engine at least 3 times to its maximum unloaded speed.

Note: *On engines with a timing belt, it is VITAL that the belt is in good condition before the test is carried out.*

□ With the engine warmed up, it is first purged by running at around 2500 rpm for 20 seconds. A governor check is then carried out, by slowly accelerating the engine to its maximum speed. After this, the smoke meter is connected, and the engine is accelerated quickly to maximum speed three times. If the smoke density is less than the limits given below, the vehicle will pass:

Non-turbo vehicles: 2.5m-1
Turbocharged vehicles: 3.0m-1

□ If excess smoke is produced, try fitting a new air cleaner element, or using an injector cleaning treatment. If the engine is running badly, where applicable, check the vehicle's ECU for fault codes. Also check the vehicle's EGR system, where applicable. At high mileages, the injectors may require professional attention.

Engine

- [ ] Engine fails to rotate when attempting to start
- [ ] Engine rotates, but will not start
- [ ] Engine difficult to start when cold
- [ ] Engine difficult to start when hot
- [ ] Starter motor noisy or excessively-rough in engagement
- [ ] Engine starts, but stops immediately
- [ ] Engine idles erratically
- [ ] Engine misfires at idle speed
- [ ] Engine misfires throughout the driving speed range
- [ ] Engine hesitates on acceleration
- [ ] Engine stalls
- [ ] Engine lacks power
- [ ] Engine backfires
- [ ] Oil pressure warning light illuminated with engine running
- [ ] Engine runs-on after switching off
- [ ] Engine noises

Cooling system

- [ ] Overheating
- [ ] Overcooling
- [ ] External coolant leakage
- [ ] Internal coolant leakage
- [ ] Corrosion

Fuel and exhaust systems

- [ ] Excessive fuel consumption
- [ ] Fuel leakage and/or fuel odour

Clutch

- [ ] Pedal travels to floor – no pressure or very little resistance
- [ ] Clutch fails to disengage (unable to select gears).
- [ ] Clutch slips (engine speed increases, with no increase in vehicle speed).
- [ ] Judder as clutch is engaged
- [ ] Noise when depressing or releasing clutch pedal

Manual transmission

- [ ] Noisy in neutral with engine running
- [ ] Noisy in one particular gear
- [ ] Difficulty engaging gears
- [ ] Vibration
- [ ] Jumps out of gear
- [ ] Lubricant leaks

Automatic transmission

- [ ] Fluid leakage
- [ ] General gear selection problems
- [ ] Transmission fluid brown, or has burned smell
- [ ] Transmission will not downshift (kickdown) with accelerator fully depressed
- [ ] Engine will not start in any gear, or starts in gears other than Park or Neutral
- [ ] Transmission slips, shifts roughly, is noisy, or has no drive in forward or reverse gears

Braking system

- [ ] Vehicle pulls to one side under braking
- [ ] Noise (grinding or high-pitched squeal) when brakes applied
- [ ] Brakes binding
- [ ] Excessive brake pedal travel
- [ ] Brake pedal feels spongy when depressed
- [ ] Excessive brake pedal effort required to stop vehicle
- [ ] Judder felt through brake pedal or steering wheel when braking
- [ ] Rear wheels locking under normal braking

Driveshafts

- [ ] Clicking or knocking noise on turns (at slow speed on full-lock)

Suspension and steering

- [ ] Vehicle pulls to one side
- [ ] Excessive pitching and/or rolling around corners, or during braking
- [ ] Lack of power assistance
- [ ] Wandering or general instability
- [ ] Excessively-stiff steering
- [ ] Excessive play in steering
- [ ] Wheel wobble and vibration
- [ ] Tyre wear excessive

Electrical system

- [ ] Battery will not hold a charge for more than a few days
- [ ] Ignition/no-charge warning light remains illuminated with engine running
- [ ] Ignition/no-charge warning light fails to come on
- [ ] Lights inoperative
- [ ] Instrument readings inaccurate or erratic
- [ ] Horn inoperative, or unsatisfactory in operation
- [ ] Windscreen wipers inoperative, or unsatisfactory in operation
- [ ] Windscreen washers inoperative, or unsatisfactory in operation
- [ ] Electric windows inoperative, or unsatisfactory in operation
- [ ] Central locking system inoperative, or unsatisfactory in operation

Introduction

The vehicle owner who does his or her own maintenance according to the recommended service schedules should not have to use this section of the manual very often. Modern component reliability is such that, provided those items subject to wear or deterioration are inspected or renewed at the specified intervals, sudden failure is comparatively rare. Faults do not usually just happen as a result of sudden failure, but develop over a period of time. Major mechanical failures in particular are usually preceded by characteristic symptoms over hundreds or even thousands of miles. Those components that do occasionally fail without warning are often small and easily carried in the vehicle.

With any fault-finding, the first step is to decide where to begin investigations. Sometimes this is obvious, but on other occasions, a little detective work will be necessary. The owner who makes half a dozen haphazard adjustments or component renewals may be successful in curing a fault (or its symptoms). However, will be none the wiser if the fault recurs, and ultimately may have spent more time and money than was necessary. A calm and logical approach will be found to be more satisfactory in the long run.

Always take into account any warning signs or abnormalities that may have been noticed in the period preceding the fault – power loss, high or low gauge readings, unusual smells, etc – and remember that failure of components such as fuses or spark plugs may only be pointers to some underlying fault.

The pages which follow provide an easy-reference guide to the more common problems which may occur during the operation of the vehicle. These problems and their possible causes are grouped under headings denoting various components or systems, such as Engine, Cooling system, etc. The general

Chapter which deals with the problem is also shown in brackets; refer to the relevant part of that Chapter for system-specific information. Whatever the fault, certain basic principles apply. These are as follows:

Verify the fault. This is simply a matter of being sure that you know what the symptoms are before starting work. This is particularly important if you are investigating a fault for someone else, who may not have described it very accurately.

Do not overlook the obvious. For example, if the vehicle will not start, is there petrol in the tank? (Do not take anyone else's word on this particular point, and do not trust the fuel gauge either!) If an electrical fault is indicated, look for loose or broken wires before digging out the test gear.

Cure the disease, not the symptom. Substituting a flat battery with a fully-charged one will get you off the hard shoulder, but if the underlying cause is not attended to, the new battery will go the same way. Similarly, changing oil-fouled spark plugs for a new set will get you moving again, but remember that the reason for the fouling (if it was not simply an incorrect grade of plug) will have to be established and corrected.

Do not take anything for granted. Particularly, do not forget that a new component may itself be defective (especially if it's been rattling around in the boot for months). Also do not leave components out of a fault diagnosis sequence just because they are new or recently fitted. When you do finally diagnose a difficult fault, you will probably realise that all the evidence was there from the start.

Engine

Engine fails to rotate when attempting to start

- [ ] Battery terminal connections loose or corroded (*Weekly checks*).
- [ ] Battery discharged or faulty (Chapter 5A).
- [ ] Broken, loose or disconnected wiring in the starting circuit (Chapter 5A).
- [ ] Defective starter solenoid or switch (Chapter 5A).
- [ ] Defective starter motor (Chapter 5A).
- [ ] Starter pinion or flywheel ring gear teeth loose or broken (Chapters 2A, 2B, 2C, 2D and 5A).
- [ ] Engine earth strap broken or disconnected (Chapter 5A).

Engine rotates, but will not start

- [ ] Fuel tank empty.
- [ ] Battery discharged (engine rotates slowly) (Chapter 5A).
- [ ] Battery terminal connections loose or corroded (*Weekly checks*).
- [ ] Ignition components damp or damaged – petrol models (Chapters 1A and 5B).
- [ ] Broken, loose or disconnected wiring in the ignition circuit – petrol models (Chapters 1A and 5B).
- [ ] Worn, faulty or incorrectly gapped spark plugs – petrol models (Chapter 1A).
- [ ] Fuel injection system fault (Chapter 4A and 4B).
- [ ] Stop solenoid faulty – diesel models (Chapter 4B).
- [ ] Air in fuel system – diesel models (Chapter 4B).
- [ ] Major mechanical failure (eg, timing belt) (Chapter 2A, 2B, 2C or 2D).

Engine difficult to start when cold

- [ ] Battery discharged (Chapter 5A).
- [ ] Battery terminal connections loose or corroded (*Weekly checks*).
- [ ] Worn, faulty or incorrectly gapped spark plugs – petrol models (Chapter 1A).
- [ ] Fuel injection system fault (Chapter 4A and 4B).
- [ ] Other ignition system fault – petrol models (Chapters 1A and 5B).
- [ ] Preheating system fault – diesel models (Chapter 5C).
- [ ] Low cylinder compressions (Chapter 2A, 2B, 2C or 2D).

Engine difficult to start when hot

- [ ] Air filter element dirty or clogged (Chapter 1A or 1B).
- [ ] Fuel injection system fault (Chapter 4A and 4B).
- [ ] Low cylinder compressions (Chapter 2A, 2B, 2C or 2D).

Starter motor noisy or excessively rough in engagement

- [ ] Starter pinion or flywheel ring gear teeth loose or broken (Chapters 2A, 2B, 2C, 2D and 5A).
- [ ] Starter motor mounting bolts loose or missing (Chapter 5A).
- [ ] Starter motor internal components worn or damaged (Chapter 5A).

Engine starts, but stops immediately

- [ ] Loose or faulty electrical connections in the ignition circuit – petrol models (Chapters 1A and 5B).
- [ ] Vacuum leak at the throttle body or inlet manifold – petrol models (Chapter 4A).
- [ ] Blocked injector/fuel injection system fault (Chapter 4A or 4B).
- [ ] Faulty injector(s) – diesel models (Chapter 4B).
- [ ] Air in fuel system – diesel models (Chapter 4B).

Engine idles erratically

- [ ] Air filter element clogged (Chapter 1A or 1B).
- [ ] Vacuum leak at the throttle body, inlet manifold or associated hoses – petrol models (Chapter 4A).
- [ ] Worn, faulty or incorrectly gapped spark plugs – petrol models (Chapter 1A).
- [ ] Uneven or low cylinder compressions (Chapter 2A, 2B, 2C or 2D).
- [ ] Camshaft lobes worn (Chapter 2A, 2B, 2C or 2D).
- [ ] Timing belt incorrectly tensioned (Chapter 2A, 2B, 2C or 2D).
- [ ] Blocked injector/fuel injection system fault (Chapter 4A or 4B).
- [ ] Faulty injector(s) – diesel models (Chapter 4B).

Engine misfires at idle speed

- [ ] Worn, faulty or incorrectly gapped spark plugs – petrol models (Chapter 1A).
- [ ] Faulty spark plug HT leads – petrol models (Chapter 5B).
- [ ] Vacuum leak at the throttle body, inlet manifold or associated hoses (Chapter 4A or 4B).
- [ ] Blocked injector/fuel injection system fault (Chapter 4A and 4B).
- [ ] Faulty injector(s) – diesel models (Chapter 4B).
- [ ] Uneven or low cylinder compressions (Chapter 2A, 2B, 2C or 2D).
- [ ] Disconnected, leaking, or perished crankcase ventilation hoses (Chapter 4C).

Engine misfires throughout the driving speed range

- [ ] Fuel filter choked (Chapter 1A or 1B).
- [ ] Fuel pump faulty, or delivery pressure low (Chapter 4A or 4B).
- [ ] Fuel tank vent blocked, or fuel pipes restricted (Chapter 4A or 4B).
- [ ] Vacuum leak at the throttle body, inlet manifold or associated hoses – petrol models (Chapter 4A).
- [ ] Worn, faulty or incorrectly gapped spark plugs – petrol models (Chapter 1A).
- [ ] Faulty spark plug HT leads (Chapter 5B).
- [ ] Faulty injector(s) – diesel models (Chapter 4B).
- [ ] Faulty ignition coil – petrol models (Chapter 5B).
- [ ] Uneven or low cylinder compressions (Chapter 2A, 2B, 2C or 2D).
- [ ] Blocked injector/fuel injection system fault (Chapter 4A or 4B).

Engine (continued)

Engine hesitates on acceleration

☐ Worn, faulty or incorrectly gapped spark plugs – petrol models (Chapter 1A).
☐ Vacuum leak at the throttle body, inlet manifold or associated hoses – petrol models (Chapter 4A).
☐ Blocked injector/fuel injection system fault (Chapter 4A or 4B).
☐ Faulty injector(s) – diesel models (Chapter 4B).
☐ Incorrect injection pump timing – diesel models (Chapter 4B).

Engine stalls

☐ Vacuum leak at the throttle body, inlet manifold or associated hoses – petrol models (Chapter 4A).
☐ Fuel filter choked (Chapter 1A or 1B).
☐ Fuel pump faulty, or delivery pressure low – petrol models (Chapter 4A).
☐ Fuel tank vent blocked, or fuel pipes restricted (Chapter 4A or 4B).
☐ Blocked injector/fuel injection system fault (Chapter 4A or 4B).
☐ Faulty injector(s) – diesel models (Chapter 4B).
☐ Air in fuel system – diesel models (Chapter 4B).

Engine lacks power

☐ Timing belt incorrectly fitted or tensioned (Chapter 2A, 2B, 2C or 2D).
☐ Fuel filter choked (Chapter 1A or 1B).
☐ Fuel pump faulty, or delivery pressure low – petrol models (Chapter 4A).
☐ Uneven or low cylinder compressions (Chapter 2A, 2B, 2C or 2D).
☐ Worn, faulty or incorrectly gapped spark plugs – petrol models (Chapter 1A).
☐ Vacuum leak at the throttle body, inlet manifold or associated hoses – petrol models (Chapter 4A).
☐ Blocked injector/fuel injection system fault (Chapter 4A or 4B).
☐ Injection pump timing incorrect – diesel models (Chapter 4B).
☐ Brakes binding (Chapters 1A or 1B and 9).
☐ Clutch slipping (Chapter 6).

Engine backfires

☐ Timing belt incorrectly fitted or tensioned (Chapter 2A, 2B, 2C or 2D).
☐ Vacuum leak at the throttle body, inlet manifold or associated hoses – petrol models (Chapter 4A).
☐ Blocked injector/fuel injection system fault (Chapter 4A or 4B).

Oil pressure warning light illuminated with engine running

☐ Low oil level, or incorrect oil grade (Weekly checks).
☐ Faulty oil pressure warning light switch (Chapter 2A, 2B, 2C or 2D).
☐ Worn engine bearings and/or oil pump (Chapter 2A, 2B, 2C or 2D).
☐ High engine operating temperature (Chapter 3).
☐ Oil pressure relief valve defective (Chapter 2A, 2B, 2C or 2D).
☐ Oil pick-up strainer clogged (Chapter 2A, 2B, 2C or 2D).

Engine runs-on after switching off

☐ Excessive carbon build-up in engine (Chapter 2A, 2B, 2C or 2D).
☐ High engine operating temperature (Chapter 3).
☐ Fuel injection system fault (Chapter 4A or 4B).

Engine noises

Pre-ignition (pinking) or knocking during acceleration or under load

☐ Ignition timing incorrect/ignition system fault – petrol models (Chapters 1A and 5B).
☐ Incorrect grade of spark plug – petrol models (Chapter 1A).
☐ Incorrect grade of fuel (Chapter 4A).
☐ Vacuum leak at the throttle body, inlet manifold or associated hoses – petrol models (Chapter 4A).
☐ Excessive carbon build-up in engine (Chapter 2A, 2B, 2C or 2D).
☐ Blocked injector/fuel injection system fault – petrol models (Chapter 4A).

Whistling or wheezing noises

☐ Leaking inlet manifold or throttle body gasket – petrol models (Chapter 4A).
☐ Leaking exhaust manifold gasket or pipe-to-manifold joint (Chapter 4C).
☐ Leaking vacuum hose (Chapters 4A, 4B, 4C and 9).
☐ Blowing cylinder head gasket (Chapter 2A, 2B, 2C or 2D).

Tapping or rattling noises

☐ Worn valve gear or camshaft (Chapter 2A, 2B, 2C or 2D).
☐ Ancillary component fault (coolant pump, alternator, etc) (Chapters 3, 5A, etc).

Knocking or thumping noises

☐ Worn big-end bearings (regular heavy knocking, perhaps worsening under load) (Chapter 2E).
☐ Worn main bearings (rumbling and knocking, perhaps less under load) (Chapter 2E).
☐ Piston slap (most noticeable when cold) (Chapter 2E).
☐ Ancillary component fault (coolant pump, alternator, etc) (Chapters 3, 5A, etc).

Cooling system

Overheating

- [ ] Insufficient coolant in system (*Weekly checks*).
- [ ] Thermostat faulty (Chapter 3).
- [ ] Radiator core blocked, or grille restricted (Chapter 3).
- [ ] Electric cooling fan or thermoswitch faulty (Chapter 3).
- [ ] Pressure cap faulty (Chapter 3).
- [ ] Ignition system fault – petrol engines (Chapters 1A and 5B).
- [ ] Inaccurate temperature gauge sender unit (Chapter 3).
- [ ] Airlock in cooling system.

Overcooling

- [ ] Thermostat faulty (Chapter 3).
- [ ] Inaccurate temperature gauge sender unit (Chapter 3).

External coolant leakage

- [ ] Deteriorated or damaged hoses or hose clips (Chapter 1A or 1B).
- [ ] Radiator core or heater matrix leaking (Chapter 3).
- [ ] Pressure cap faulty (Chapter 3).
- [ ] Water pump seal leaking (Chapter 3).
- [ ] Boiling due to overheating (Chapter 3).
- [ ] Core plug leaking (Chapter 2E).

Internal coolant leakage

- [ ] Leaking cylinder head gasket (Chapter 2A, 2B, 2C or 2D).
- [ ] Cracked cylinder head or cylinder bore (Chapter 2E).

Corrosion

- [ ] Infrequent draining and flushing (Chapter 1A or 1B).
- [ ] Incorrect coolant mixture or inappropriate coolant type (Chapter 1A or 1B).

Fuel and exhaust systems

Excessive fuel consumption

- [ ] Air filter element dirty or clogged (Chapter 1A or 1B).
- [ ] Fuel injection system fault (Chapter 4A or 4B).
- [ ] Ignition system fault – petrol models (Chapters 1A and 5B).
- [ ] Faulty injector(s) – diesel models (Chapter 4B).
- [ ] Tyres under-inflated (*Weekly checks*).

Fuel leakage and/or fuel odour

- [ ] Damaged or corroded fuel tank, pipes or connections (Chapter 4A or 4B).
- [ ] Excessive noise or fumes from exhaust system
- [ ] Leaking exhaust system or manifold joints (Chapters 1A, 1B, or 4C).
- [ ] Leaking, corroded or damaged silencers or pipe (Chapters 1A, 1B, or 4C).
- [ ] Broken mountings causing body or suspension contact (Chapter 1A or 1B).

Clutch

Pedal travels to floor – no pressure or very little resistance

- ☐ Hydraulic fluid level low/air in hydraulic system (Chapter 6).
- ☐ Broken clutch release bearing or fork (Chapter 6).
- ☐ Broken diaphragm spring in clutch pressure plate (Chapter 6).

Clutch fails to disengage (unable to select gears)

- ☐ Clutch disc sticking on transmission input shaft splines (Chapter 6).
- ☐ Clutch disc sticking to flywheel or pressure plate (Chapter 6).
- ☐ Faulty pressure plate assembly (Chapter 6).
- ☐ Clutch release mechanism worn or incorrectly assembled (Chapter 6).

Clutch slips (engine speed increases, with no increase in vehicle speed)

- ☐ Clutch disc linings excessively worn (Chapter 6).
- ☐ Clutch disc linings contaminated with oil or grease (Chapter 6).
- ☐ Faulty pressure plate or weak diaphragm spring (Chapter 6).

Judder as clutch is engaged

- ☐ Clutch disc linings contaminated with oil or grease (Chapter 6).
- ☐ Clutch disc linings excessively worn (Chapter 6).
- ☐ Faulty or distorted pressure plate or diaphragm spring (Chapter 6).
- ☐ Worn or loose engine or transmission mountings (Chapter 2A, 2B, 2C or 2D).
- ☐ Clutch disc hub or transmission input shaft splines worn (Chapter 6).

Noise when depressing or releasing clutch pedal

- ☐ Worn clutch release bearing (Chapter 6).
- ☐ Worn or dry clutch pedal bushes (Chapter 6).
- ☐ Faulty pressure plate assembly (Chapter 6).
- ☐ Pressure plate diaphragm spring broken (Chapter 6).
- ☐ Broken clutch disc cushioning springs (Chapter 6).

Manual transmission

Noisy in neutral with engine running

- ☐ Input shaft bearings worn (noise apparent with clutch pedal released, but not when depressed) (Chapter 7A).*
- ☐ Clutch release bearing worn (noise apparent with clutch pedal depressed, possibly less when released) (Chapter 6).

Noisy in one particular gear

- ☐ Worn, damaged or chipped gear teeth (Chapter 7A).*

Difficulty engaging gears

- ☐ Clutch fault (Chapter 6).
- ☐ Worn or damaged gear linkage (Chapter 7A).
- ☐ Incorrectly adjusted gear linkage (Chapter 7A).
- ☐ Worn synchroniser units (Chapter 7A).*

Vibration

- ☐ Lack of oil (Chapter 1A or 1B).
- ☐ Worn bearings (Chapter 7A).*

Jumps out of gear

- ☐ Worn or damaged gear linkage (Chapter 7A).
- ☐ Incorrectly adjusted gear linkage (Chapter 7A).
- ☐ Worn synchroniser units (Chapter 7A).*
- ☐ Worn selector forks (Chapter 7A).*

Lubricant leaks

- ☐ Leaking differential output oil seal (Chapter 7A).
- ☐ Leaking housing joint (Chapter 7A).*
- ☐ Leaking input shaft oil seal (Chapter 7A).*

* Although the corrective action necessary to remedy the symptoms described is beyond the scope of the home mechanic, the above information should be helpful in isolating the cause of the condition. This should enable the owner can communicate clearly with a professional mechanic.

Automatic transmission

Note: *Due to the complexity of the automatic transmission, it is difficult for the home mechanic to properly diagnose and service this unit. For problems other than the following, the vehicle should be taken to a dealer service department or automatic transmission specialist. Do not be too hasty in removing the transmission if a fault is suspected, as most of the testing is carried out with the unit still fitted.*

Fluid leakage

☐ Automatic transmission fluid is usually dark in colour. Fluid leaks should not be confused with engine oil, which can easily be blown onto the transmission by airflow.

☐ To determine the source of a leak, first remove all built-up dirt and grime from the transmission housing and surrounding areas using a degreasing agent, or by steam-cleaning. Drive the vehicle at low speed, so airflow will not blow the leak far from its source. Raise and support the vehicle, and determine where the leak is coming from.

General gear selection problems

☐ Chapter 7B deals with checking and adjusting the selector cable on automatic transmissions. The following are common problems which may be caused by a poorly-adjusted cable:

a) *Engine starting in gears other than Park or Neutral.*
b) *Indicator panel indicating a gear other than the one actually being used.*
c) *Vehicle moves when in Park or Neutral.*
d) *Poor gear shift quality or erratic gearchanges.*

Transmission fluid brown, or has burned smell

☐ Transmission fluid level low (Chapter 1A or 1B). If the fluid appears to have deteriorated badly it is recommended that it is renewed.

Transmission will not downshift (kickdown) with accelerator pedal fully depressed

☐ Low transmission fluid level (Chapter 1A or 1B).
☐ Incorrect selector cable adjustment (Chapter 7B).

Engine will not start in any gear, or starts in gears other than Park or Neutral

☐ Incorrect selector cable adjustment (Chapter 7B).

Transmission slips, shifts roughly, is noisy, or has no drive in forward or reverse gears

☐ There are many probable causes for the above problems, but unless there is a very obvious reason (such as a loose or corroded wiring plug connection on or near the transmission), the car should be taken to a franchise dealer for the fault to be diagnosed. The transmission control unit incorporates a self-diagnosis facility, and any fault codes can quickly be read and interpreted by a dealer with the proper diagnostic equipment.

Braking system

Note: *Before assuming that a brake problem exists, make sure that the tyres are in good condition and correctly inflated, that the front wheel alignment is correct, and that the vehicle is not loaded with weight in an unequal manner. Apart from checking the condition of all pipe and hose connections, any faults occurring on the anti-lock braking system should be referred to a Skoda dealer for diagnosis.*

Vehicle pulls to one side under braking

☐ Worn, defective, damaged or contaminated brake pads on one side (Chapters 1A or 1B and 9).
☐ Seized or partially seized brake caliper piston (Chapters 1A or 1B and 9).
☐ A mixture of brake pad lining materials fitted between sides (Chapters 1A or 1B and 9).
☐ Brake caliper mounting bolts loose (Chapter 9).
☐ Worn or damaged steering or suspension components (Chapters 1A or 1B and 10).

Noise (grinding or high-pitched squeal) when brakes applied)

☐ Brake pad friction lining material worn down to metal backing (Chapters 1A or 1B and 9).
☐ Excessive corrosion of brake disc. This may be apparent after the vehicle has been standing for some time (Chapters 1A or 1B and 9).
☐ Foreign object (stone chipping, etc.) trapped between brake disc and shield (Chapters 1A or 1B and 9).

Brakes binding

☐ Seized brake caliper piston(s) (Chapter 9).
☐ Incorrectly adjusted handbrake mechanism (Chapter 9).
☐ Faulty master cylinder (Chapter 9).

Excessive brake pedal travel

☐ Faulty master cylinder (Chapter 9).
☐ Air in hydraulic system (Chapters 1A or 1B and 9).
☐ Faulty vacuum servo unit (Chapter 9).

Brake pedal feels spongy when depressed

☐ Air in hydraulic system (Chapters 1A or 1B and 9).
☐ Deteriorated flexible rubber brake hoses (Chapters 1A or 1B and 9).
☐ Master cylinder mounting nuts loose (Chapter 9).
☐ Faulty master cylinder (Chapter 9).

Excessive brake pedal effort required to stop vehicle

☐ Faulty vacuum servo unit (Chapter 9).
☐ Faulty brake vacuum pump – diesel models (Chapter 9).
☐ Disconnected, damaged or insecure brake servo vacuum hose (Chapter 9).
☐ Primary or secondary hydraulic circuit failure (Chapter 9).
☐ Seized brake caliper piston(s) (Chapter 9).
☐ Brake pads incorrectly fitted (Chapters 1A or 1B and 9).
☐ Incorrect grade of brake pads fitted (Chapters 1A or 1B and 9).
☐ Brake pads contaminated (Chapters 1A or 1B and 9).

Judder felt through brake pedal or steering wheel when braking

Note: *Judder felt through the brake pedal is a normal feature of models fitted with ABS.*
☐ Excessive run-out or distortion of discs (Chapters 1A or 1B and 9).
☐ Brake pads worn (Chapters 1A or 1B and 9).
☐ Brake caliper mounting bolts loose (Chapter 9).
☐ Wear in suspension or steering components or mountings (Chapters 1A or 1B and 10).

Rear wheels locking under normal braking

☐ Rear brake pads contaminated (Chapters 1A or 1B and 9).
☐ ABS system fault (Chapter 9).

Driveshafts

Clicking or knocking noise on turns (at slow speed on full-lock)

☐ Lack of constant velocity joint lubricant, possibly due to damaged gaiter (Chapter 8).
☐ Worn outer constant velocity joint (Chapter 8).
☐ Vibration when accelerating or decelerating
☐ Worn inner constant velocity joint (Chapter 8).
☐ Bent or distorted driveshaft (Chapter 8).

Suspension and steering

Note: *Before diagnosing suspension or steering faults, be sure that the trouble is not due to incorrect tyre pressures, mixtures of tyre types, or binding brakes.*

Vehicle pulls to one side

☐ Defective tyre (*Weekly checks*).
☐ Excessive wear in suspension or steering components (Chapters 1A or 1B and 10).
☐ Incorrect front wheel alignment (Chapter 10).
☐ Accident damage to steering or suspension components (Chapter 1A or 1B and 10).

Excessive pitching and/or rolling around corners, or during braking

☐ Defective shock absorbers (Chapters 1A or 1B and 10).
☐ Broken or weak spring and/or suspension component (Chapters 1A or 1B and 10).
☐ Worn or damaged anti-roll bar or mountings – where applicable (Chapter 10).

Lack of power assistance

☐ Broken or incorrectly adjusted auxiliary drivebelt (Chapter 1A or 1B).
☐ Incorrect power steering fluid level (*Weekly checks*).
☐ Restriction in power steering fluid hoses (Chapter 1A or 1B).
☐ Faulty power steering pump (Chapter 10).
☐ Faulty rack-and-pinion steering gear (Chapter 10).

Wandering or general instability

☐ Incorrect front wheel alignment (Chapter 10).
☐ Worn steering or suspension joints, bushes or components (Chapters 1A or 1B and 10).
☐ Roadwheels out of balance (Chapters 1A or 1B and 10).
☐ Faulty or damaged tyre (*Weekly checks*).
☐ Wheel bolts loose (refer to Chapter 10 for correct torque).
☐ Defective shock absorbers (Chapters 1A or 1B and 10).

Excessively stiff steering

☐ Lack of steering gear lubricant (Chapter 10).
☐ Seized track rod end balljoint or suspension balljoint Chapters 1A or 1B and 10).
☐ Broken or incorrectly adjusted auxiliary drivebelt – power steering (Chapter 1A or 1B).
☐ Incorrect front wheel alignment (Chapter 10).
☐ Steering rack or column bent or damaged (Chapter 10).

Excessive play in steering

☐ Worn steering column intermediate shaft universal joint (Chapter 10).
☐ Worn steering track rod end balljoints (Chapters 1A or 1B and 10).
☐ Worn rack-and-pinion steering gear (Chapter 10).
☐ Worn steering or suspension joints, bushes or components (Chapters 1A or 1B and 10).

Wheel wobble and vibration

☐ Front roadwheels out of balance (vibration felt mainly through the steering wheel) (Chapters 1A or 1B and 10).
☐ Rear roadwheels out of balance (vibration felt throughout the vehicle) (Chapters 1A or 1B and 10).
☐ Roadwheels damaged or distorted (Chapters 1A or 1B and 10).
☐ Faulty or damaged tyre (*Weekly checks*).
☐ Worn steering or suspension joints, bushes or components (Chapters 1A or 1B and 10).
☐ Wheel bolts loose (Chapter 10).

Tyre wear excessive

Tyres worn on inside or outside edges

☐ Tyres under-inflated (wear on both edges) (*Weekly checks*).
☐ Incorrect camber or castor angles (wear on one edge only) (Chapter 10).
☐ Worn steering or suspension joints, bushes or components (Chapters 1A or 1B and 10).
☐ Excessively hard cornering.
☐ Accident damage.

Tyre treads exhibit feathered edges

☐ Incorrect toe setting (Chapter 10).

Tyres worn in centre of tread

☐ Tyres over-inflated (*Weekly checks*).

Tyres worn on inside and outside edges

☐ Tyres under-inflated (*Weekly checks*).

Tyres worn unevenly

☐ Tyres/wheels out of balance (Chapter 1A, 1B or 10).
☐ Excessive wheel or tyre run-out (Chapter 1A, 1B or 10).
☐ Worn shock absorbers (Chapters 1A or 1B and 10).
☐ Faulty tyre (*Weekly checks*).

Electrical system

Note: *For problems associated with the starting system, refer to the faults listed under 'Engine' earlier in this Section.*

Battery will not hold a charge for more than a few days

- [ ] Battery defective internally (Chapter 5A).
- [ ] Battery terminal connections loose or corroded (*Weekly checks*).
- [ ] Auxiliary drivebelt worn or incorrectly adjusted (Chapter 1A or 1B).
- [ ] Alternator not charging at correct output (Chapter 5A).
- [ ] Alternator or voltage regulator faulty (Chapter 5A).
- [ ] Short-circuit causing continual battery drain (Chapters 5A and 12).

Ignition/no-charge warning light remains illuminated with engine running

- [ ] Auxiliary drivebelt broken, worn, or incorrectly adjusted (Chapter 1A or 1B).
- [ ] Alternator brushes worn, sticking, or dirty (Chapter 5A).
- [ ] Alternator brush springs weak or broken (Chapter 5A).
- [ ] Internal fault in alternator or voltage regulator (Chapter 5A).
- [ ] Broken, disconnected, or loose wiring in charging circuit (Chapter 5A).

Ignition/no-charge warning light fails to come on

- [ ] Warning light LED defective (Chapter 12).
- [ ] Broken, disconnected, or loose wiring in warning light circuit (Chapter 12).
- [ ] Alternator faulty (Chapter 5A).

Lights inoperative

- [ ] Bulb blown (Chapter 12).
- [ ] Corrosion of bulb or bulbholder contacts (Chapter 12).
- [ ] Blown fuse (Chapter 12).
- [ ] Faulty relay (Chapter 12).
- [ ] Broken, loose, or disconnected wiring (Chapter 12).
- [ ] Faulty switch (Chapter 12).

Instrument readings inaccurate or erratic

Fuel or temperature gauges give no reading

- [ ] Faulty gauge sender unit (Chapters 3, 4A or 4B).
- [ ] Wiring open-circuit (Chapter 12).
- [ ] Faulty gauge (Chapter 12).

Fuel or temperature gauges give continuous maximum reading

- [ ] Faulty gauge sender unit (Chapters 3, 4A or 4B).
- [ ] Wiring short-circuit (Chapter 12).
- [ ] Faulty gauge (Chapter 12).

Horn inoperative, or unsatisfactory in operation

Horn operates all the time

- [ ] Horn push either earthed or stuck down (Chapter 12).
- [ ] Horn cable-to-horn push earthed (Chapter 12).

Horn fails to operate

- [ ] Blown fuse (Chapter 12).
- [ ] Cable or cable connections loose, broken or disconnected (Chapter 12).
- [ ] Faulty horn (Chapter 12).

Horn emits intermittent or unsatisfactory sound

- [ ] Cable connections loose (Chapter 12).
- [ ] Horn mountings loose (Chapter 12).
- [ ] Faulty horn (Chapter 12).

Windscreen/tailgate wipers inoperative, or unsatisfactory in operation

Wipers fail to operate, or operate very slowly

- [ ] Wiper blades stuck to screen, or linkage seized or binding (*Weekly checks* and Chapter 12).
- [ ] Blown fuse (Chapter 12).
- [ ] Wiring loose, broken or disconnected (Chapter 12).
- [ ] Faulty relay (Chapter 12).
- [ ] Faulty wiper motor (Chapter 12).

Wiper blades sweep over too large or too small an area of the glass

- [ ] Wiper arms incorrectly positioned on spindles (Chapter 12).
- [ ] Excessive wear of wiper linkage (Chapter 12).
- [ ] Wiper motor or linkage mountings loose or insecure (Chapter 12).

Wiper blades fail to clean the glass effectively

- [ ] Wiper blade rubbers worn or perished (*Weekly checks*).
- [ ] Wiper arm tension springs broken, or arm pivots seized (Chapter 12).
- [ ] Insufficient windscreen washer additive to adequately remove road film (*Weekly checks*).

Electrical system (continued)

Windscreen/tailgate washers inoperative, or unsatisfactory in operation

One or more washer jets inoperative

- [ ] Blocked washer jet (Chapter 1A or 1B).
- [ ] Disconnected, kinked or restricted fluid hose (Chapter 12).
- [ ] Insufficient fluid in washer reservoir (Chapter 1A or 1B).

Washer pump fails to operate

- [ ] Broken or disconnected wiring or connections (Chapter 12).
- [ ] Blown fuse (Chapter 12).
- [ ] Faulty washer switch (Chapter 12).
- [ ] Faulty washer pump (Chapter 12).

Electric windows inoperative, or unsatisfactory in operation

Window glass will only move in one direction

- [ ] Faulty switch (Chapter 12).

Window glass slow to move

- [ ] Regulator seized or damaged, or in need of lubrication (Chapter 11).
- [ ] Door internal components or trim fouling regulator (Chapter 11).
- [ ] Faulty motor (Chapter 11).

Window glass fails to move

- [ ] Blown fuse (Chapter 12).
- [ ] Faulty relay (Chapter 12).
- [ ] Broken or disconnected wiring or connections (Chapter 12).
- [ ] Faulty motor (Chapter 11).

Central locking system inoperative, or unsatisfactory in operation

Complete system failure

- [ ] Blown fuse (Chapter 12).
- [ ] Faulty relay (Chapter 12).
- [ ] Broken or disconnected wiring or connections (Chapter 12).
- [ ] Faulty control module (Chapter 11).

Latch locks but will not unlock, or unlocks but will not lock

- [ ] Faulty master switch (Chapter 11).
- [ ] Broken or disconnected latch operating rods or levers (Chapter 11).
- [ ] Faulty relay (Chapter 12).
- [ ] Faulty control module (Chapter 11).

One actuator fails to operate

- [ ] Broken or disconnected wiring or connections (Chapter 12).
- [ ] Faulty actuator (Chapter 11).
- [ ] Broken, binding or disconnected latch operating rods or levers (Chapter 11).
- [ ] Fault in door lock (Chapter 11).

A

ABS (Anti-lock brake system) A system, usually electronically controlled, that senses incipient wheel lockup during braking and relieves hydraulic pressure at wheels that are about to skid.

Air bag An inflatable bag hidden in the steering wheel (driver's side) or the dash or glovebox (passenger side). In a head-on collision, the bags inflate, preventing the driver and front passenger from being thrown forward into the steering wheel or windscreen.

Air cleaner A metal or plastic housing, containing a filter element, which removes dust and dirt from the air being drawn into the engine.

Air filter element The actual filter in an air cleaner system, usually manufactured from pleated paper and requiring renewal at regular intervals.

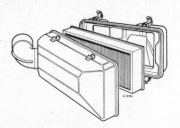

Air filter

Allen key A hexagonal wrench which fits into a recessed hexagonal hole.

Alligator clip A long-nosed spring-loaded metal clip with meshing teeth. Used to make temporary electrical connections.

Alternator A component in the electrical system which converts mechanical energy from a drivebelt into electrical energy to charge the battery and to operate the starting system, ignition system and electrical accessories.

Alternator (exploded view)

Ampere (amp) A unit of measurement for the flow of electric current. One amp is the amount of current produced by one volt acting through a resistance of one ohm.

Anaerobic sealer A substance used to prevent bolts and screws from loosening. Anaerobic means that it does not require oxygen for activation. The Loctite brand is widely used.

Antifreeze A substance (usually ethylene glycol) mixed with water, and added to a vehicle's cooling system, to prevent freezing of the coolant in winter. Antifreeze also contains chemicals to inhibit corrosion and the formation of rust and other deposits that would tend to clog the radiator and coolant passages and reduce cooling efficiency.

Anti-seize compound A coating that reduces the risk of seizing on fasteners that are subjected to high temperatures, such as exhaust manifold bolts and nuts.

Anti-seize compound

Asbestos A natural fibrous mineral with great heat resistance, commonly used in the composition of brake friction materials. Asbestos is a health hazard and the dust created by brake systems should never be inhaled or ingested.

Axle A shaft on which a wheel revolves, or which revolves with a wheel. Also, a solid beam that connects the two wheels at one end of the vehicle. An axle which also transmits power to the wheels is known as a live axle.

Axle assembly

Axleshaft A single rotating shaft, on either side of the differential, which delivers power from the final drive assembly to the drive wheels. Also called a driveshaft or a halfshaft.

B

Ball bearing An anti-friction bearing consisting of a hardened inner and outer race with hardened steel balls between two races.

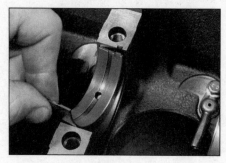

Bearing

Bearing The curved surface on a shaft or in a bore, or the part assembled into either, that permits relative motion between them with minimum wear and friction.

Big-end bearing The bearing in the end of the connecting rod that's attached to the crankshaft.

Bleed nipple A valve on a brake wheel cylinder, caliper or other hydraulic component that is opened to purge the hydraulic system of air. Also called a bleed screw.

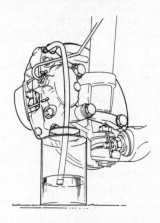

Brake bleeding

Brake bleeding Procedure for removing air from lines of a hydraulic brake system.

Brake disc The component of a disc brake that rotates with the wheels.

Brake drum The component of a drum brake that rotates with the wheels.

Brake linings The friction material which contacts the brake disc or drum to retard the vehicle's speed. The linings are bonded or riveted to the brake pads or shoes.

Brake pads The replaceable friction pads that pinch the brake disc when the brakes are applied. Brake pads consist of a friction material bonded or riveted to a rigid backing plate.

Brake shoe The crescent-shaped carrier to which the brake linings are mounted and which forces the lining against the rotating drum during braking.

Braking systems For more information on braking systems, consult the *Haynes Automotive Brake Manual*.

Breaker bar A long socket wrench handle providing greater leverage.

Bulkhead The insulated partition between the engine and the passenger compartment.

C

Caliper The non-rotating part of a disc-brake assembly that straddles the disc and carries the brake pads. The caliper also contains the hydraulic components that cause the pads to pinch the disc when the brakes are applied. A caliper is also a measuring tool that can be set to measure inside or outside dimensions of an object.

Camshaft A rotating shaft on which a series of cam lobes operate the valve mechanisms. The camshaft may be driven by gears, by sprockets and chain or by sprockets and a belt.

Canister A container in an evaporative emission control system; contains activated charcoal granules to trap vapours from the fuel system.

Canister

Carburettor A device which mixes fuel with air in the proper proportions to provide a desired power output from a spark ignition internal combustion engine.

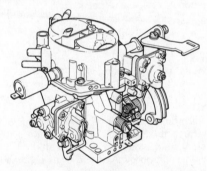

Carburettor

Castellated Resembling the parapets along the top of a castle wall. For example, a castellated balljoint stud nut.

Castellated nut

Castor In wheel alignment, the backward or forward tilt of the steering axis. Castor is positive when the steering axis is inclined rearward at the top.

Catalytic converter A silencer-like device in the exhaust system which converts certain pollutants in the exhaust gases into less harmful substances.

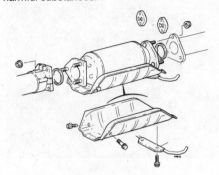

Catalytic converter

Circlip A ring-shaped clip used to prevent endwise movement of cylindrical parts and shafts. An internal circlip is installed in a groove in a housing; an external circlip fits into a groove on the outside of a cylindrical piece such as a shaft.

Clearance The amount of space between two parts. For example, between a piston and a cylinder, between a bearing and a journal, etc.

Coil spring A spiral of elastic steel found in various sizes throughout a vehicle, for example as a springing medium in the suspension and in the valve train.

Compression Reduction in volume, and increase in pressure and temperature, of a gas, caused by squeezing it into a smaller space.

Compression ratio The relationship between cylinder volume when the piston is at top dead centre and cylinder volume when the piston is at bottom dead centre.

Constant velocity (CV) joint A type of universal joint that cancels out vibrations caused by driving power being transmitted through an angle.

Core plug A disc or cup-shaped metal device inserted in a hole in a casting through which core was removed when the casting was formed. Also known as a freeze plug or expansion plug.

Crankcase The lower part of the engine block in which the crankshaft rotates.

Crankshaft The main rotating member, or shaft, running the length of the crankcase, with offset "throws" to which the connecting rods are attached.

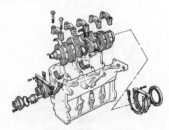

Crankshaft assembly

Crocodile clip See Alligator clip

D

Diagnostic code Code numbers obtained by accessing the diagnostic mode of an engine management computer. This code can be used to determine the area in the system where a malfunction may be located.

Disc brake A brake design incorporating a rotating disc onto which brake pads are squeezed. The resulting friction converts the energy of a moving vehicle into heat.

Double-overhead cam (DOHC) An engine that uses two overhead camshafts, usually one for the intake valves and one for the exhaust valves.

Drivebelt(s) The belt(s) used to drive accessories such as the alternator, water pump, power steering pump, air conditioning compressor, etc. off the crankshaft pulley.

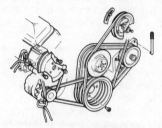

Accessory drivebelts

Driveshaft Any shaft used to transmit motion. Commonly used when referring to the axleshafts on a front wheel drive vehicle.

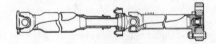

Driveshaft

Drum brake A type of brake using a drum-shaped metal cylinder attached to the inner surface of the wheel. When the brake pedal is pressed, curved brake shoes with friction linings press against the inside of the drum to slow or stop the vehicle.

Drum brake assembly

E

EGR valve A valve used to introduce exhaust gases into the intake air stream.

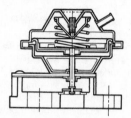

EGR valve

Electronic control unit (ECU) A computer which controls (for instance) ignition and fuel injection systems, or an anti-lock braking system. For more information refer to the *Haynes Automotive Electrical and Electronic Systems Manual.*

Electronic Fuel Injection (EFI) A computer controlled fuel system that distributes fuel through an injector located in each intake port of the engine.

Emergency brake A braking system, independent of the main hydraulic system, that can be used to slow or stop the vehicle if the primary brakes fail, or to hold the vehicle stationary even though the brake pedal isn't depressed. It usually consists of a hand lever that actuates either front or rear brakes mechanically through a series of cables and linkages. Also known as a handbrake or parking brake.

Endfloat The amount of lengthwise movement between two parts. As applied to a crankshaft, the distance that the crankshaft can move forward and back in the cylinder block.

Engine management system (EMS) A computer controlled system which manages the fuel injection and the ignition systems in an integrated fashion.

Exhaust manifold A part with several passages through which exhaust gases leave the engine combustion chambers and enter the exhaust pipe.

Exhaust manifold

F

Fan clutch A viscous (fluid) drive coupling device which permits variable engine fan speeds in relation to engine speeds.

Feeler blade A thin strip or blade of hardened steel, ground to an exact thickness, used to check or measure clearances between parts.

Feeler blade

Firing order The order in which the engine cylinders fire, or deliver their power strokes, beginning with the number one cylinder.

Flywheel A heavy spinning wheel in which energy is absorbed and stored by means of momentum. On cars, the flywheel is attached to the crankshaft to smooth out firing impulses.

Free play The amount of travel before any action takes place. The "looseness" in a linkage, or an assembly of parts, between the initial application of force and actual movement. For example, the distance the brake pedal moves before the pistons in the master cylinder are actuated.

Fuse An electrical device which protects a circuit against accidental overload. The typical fuse contains a soft piece of metal which is calibrated to melt at a predetermined current flow (expressed as amps) and break the circuit.

Fusible link A circuit protection device consisting of a conductor surrounded by heat-resistant insulation. The conductor is smaller than the wire it protects, so it acts as the weakest link in the circuit. Unlike a blown fuse, a failed fusible link must frequently be cut from the wire for replacement.

G

Gap The distance the spark must travel in jumping from the centre electrode to the side

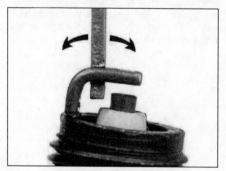

Adjusting spark plug gap

electrode in a spark plug. Also refers to the spacing between the points in a contact breaker assembly in a conventional points-type ignition, or to the distance between the reluctor or rotor and the pickup coil in an electronic ignition.

Gasket Any thin, soft material - usually cork, cardboard, asbestos or soft metal - installed between two metal surfaces to ensure a good seal. For instance, the cylinder head gasket seals the joint between the block and the cylinder head.

Gasket

Gauge An instrument panel display used to monitor engine conditions. A gauge with a movable pointer on a dial or a fixed scale is an analogue gauge. A gauge with a numerical readout is called a digital gauge.

H

Halfshaft A rotating shaft that transmits power from the final drive unit to a drive wheel, usually when referring to a live rear axle.

Harmonic balancer A device designed to reduce torsion or twisting vibration in the crankshaft. May be incorporated in the crankshaft pulley. Also known as a vibration damper.

Hone An abrasive tool for correcting small irregularities or differences in diameter in an engine cylinder, brake cylinder, etc.

Hydraulic tappet A tappet that utilises hydraulic pressure from the engine's lubrication system to maintain zero clearance (constant contact with both camshaft and valve stem). Automatically adjusts to variation in valve stem length. Hydraulic tappets also reduce valve noise.

I

Ignition timing The moment at which the spark plug fires, usually expressed in the number of crankshaft degrees before the piston reaches the top of its stroke.

Inlet manifold A tube or housing with passages through which flows the air-fuel mixture (carburettor vehicles and vehicles with throttle body injection) or air only (port fuel-injected vehicles) to the port openings in the cylinder head.

J

Jump start Starting the engine of a vehicle with a discharged or weak battery by attaching jump leads from the weak battery to a charged or helper battery.

L

Load Sensing Proportioning Valve (LSPV) A brake hydraulic system control valve that works like a proportioning valve, but also takes into consideration the amount of weight carried by the rear axle.

Locknut A nut used to lock an adjustment nut, or other threaded component, in place. For example, a locknut is employed to keep the adjusting nut on the rocker arm in position.

Lockwasher A form of washer designed to prevent an attaching nut from working loose.

M

MacPherson strut A type of front suspension system devised by Earle MacPherson at Ford of England. In its original form, a simple lateral link with the anti-roll bar creates the lower control arm. A long strut - an integral coil spring and shock absorber - is mounted between the body and the steering knuckle. Many modern so-called MacPherson strut systems use a conventional lower A-arm and don't rely on the anti-roll bar for location.

Multimeter An electrical test instrument with the capability to measure voltage, current and resistance.

N

NOx Oxides of Nitrogen. A common toxic pollutant emitted by petrol and diesel engines at higher temperatures.

O

Ohm The unit of electrical resistance. One volt applied to a resistance of one ohm will produce a current of one amp.

Ohmmeter An instrument for measuring electrical resistance.

O-ring A type of sealing ring made of a special rubber-like material; in use, the O-ring is compressed into a groove to provide the sealing action.

O-ring

Overhead cam (ohc) engine An engine with the camshaft(s) located on top of the cylinder head(s).

Overhead valve (ohv) engine An engine with the valves located in the cylinder head, but with the camshaft located in the engine block.

Oxygen sensor A device installed in the engine exhaust manifold, which senses the oxygen content in the exhaust and converts this information into an electric current. Also called a Lambda sensor.

P

Phillips screw A type of screw head having a cross instead of a slot for a corresponding type of screwdriver.

Plastigage A thin strip of plastic thread, available in different sizes, used for measuring clearances. For example, a strip of Plastigage is laid across a bearing journal. The parts are assembled and dismantled; the width of the crushed strip indicates the clearance between journal and bearing.

Plastigage

Propeller shaft The long hollow tube with universal joints at both ends that carries power from the transmission to the differential on front-engined rear wheel drive vehicles.

Proportioning valve A hydraulic control valve which limits the amount of pressure to the rear brakes during panic stops to prevent wheel lock-up.

R

Rack-and-pinion steering A steering system with a pinion gear on the end of the steering shaft that mates with a rack (think of a geared wheel opened up and laid flat). When the steering wheel is turned, the pinion turns, moving the rack to the left or right. This movement is transmitted through the track rods to the steering arms at the wheels.

Radiator A liquid-to-air heat transfer device designed to reduce the temperature of the coolant in an internal combustion engine cooling system.

Refrigerant Any substance used as a heat transfer agent in an air-conditioning system. R-12 has been the principle refrigerant for many years; recently, however, manufacturers have begun using R-134a, a non-CFC substance that is considered less harmful to the ozone in the upper atmosphere.

Rocker arm A lever arm that rocks on a shaft or pivots on a stud. In an overhead valve engine, the rocker arm converts the upward movement of the pushrod into a downward movement to open a valve.

Rotor In a distributor, the rotating device inside the cap that connects the centre electrode and the outer terminals as it turns, distributing the high voltage from the coil secondary winding to the proper spark plug. Also, that part of an alternator which rotates inside the stator. Also, the rotating assembly of a turbocharger, including the compressor wheel, shaft and turbine wheel.

Runout The amount of wobble (in-and-out movement) of a gear or wheel as it's rotated. The amount a shaft rotates "out-of-true." The out-of-round condition of a rotating part.

S

Sealant A liquid or paste used to prevent leakage at a joint. Sometimes used in conjunction with a gasket.

Sealed beam lamp An older headlight design which integrates the reflector, lens and filaments into a hermetically-sealed one-piece unit. When a filament burns out or the lens cracks, the entire unit is simply replaced.

Serpentine drivebelt A single, long, wide accessory drivebelt that's used on some newer vehicles to drive all the accessories, instead of a series of smaller, shorter belts. Serpentine drivebelts are usually tensioned by an automatic tensioner.

Serpentine drivebelt

Shim Thin spacer, commonly used to adjust the clearance or relative positions between two parts. For example, shims inserted into or under bucket tappets control valve clearances. Clearance is adjusted by changing the thickness of the shim.

Slide hammer A special puller that screws into or hooks onto a component such as a shaft or bearing; a heavy sliding handle on the shaft bottoms against the end of the shaft to knock the component free.

Sprocket A tooth or projection on the periphery of a wheel, shaped to engage with a chain or drivebelt. Commonly used to refer to the sprocket wheel itself.

Starter inhibitor switch On vehicles with an automatic transmission, a switch that prevents starting if the vehicle is not in Neutral or Park.

Strut See MacPherson strut.

T

Tappet A cylindrical component which transmits motion from the cam to the valve stem, either directly or via a pushrod and rocker arm. Also called a cam follower.

Thermostat A heat-controlled valve that regulates the flow of coolant between the cylinder block and the radiator, so maintaining optimum engine operating temperature. A thermostat is also used in some air cleaners in which the temperature is regulated.

Thrust bearing The bearing in the clutch assembly that is moved in to the release levers by clutch pedal action to disengage the clutch. Also referred to as a release bearing.

Timing belt A toothed belt which drives the camshaft. Serious engine damage may result if it breaks in service.

Timing chain A chain which drives the camshaft.

Toe-in The amount the front wheels are closer together at the front than at the rear. On rear wheel drive vehicles, a slight amount of toe-in is usually specified to keep the front wheels running parallel on the road by offsetting other forces that tend to spread the wheels apart.

Toe-out The amount the front wheels are closer together at the rear than at the front. On front wheel drive vehicles, a slight amount of toe-out is usually specified.

Tools For full information on choosing and using tools, refer to the *Haynes Automotive Tools Manual.*

Tracer A stripe of a second colour applied to a wire insulator to distinguish that wire from another one with the same colour insulator.

Tune-up A process of accurate and careful adjustments and parts replacement to obtain the best possible engine performance.

Turbocharger A centrifugal device, driven by exhaust gases, that pressurises the intake air. Normally used to increase the power output from a given engine displacement, but can also be used primarily to reduce exhaust emissions (as on VW's "Umwelt" Diesel engine).

U

Universal joint or U-joint A double-pivoted connection for transmitting power from a driving to a driven shaft through an angle. A U-joint consists of two Y-shaped yokes and a cross-shaped member called the spider.

V

Valve A device through which the flow of liquid, gas, vacuum, or loose material in bulk may be started, stopped, or regulated by a movable part that opens, shuts, or partially obstructs one or more ports or passageways. A valve is also the movable part of such a device.

Valve clearance The clearance between the valve tip (the end of the valve stem) and the rocker arm or tappet. The valve clearance is measured when the valve is closed.

Vernier caliper A precision measuring instrument that measures inside and outside dimensions. Not quite as accurate as a micrometer, but more convenient.

Viscosity The thickness of a liquid or its resistance to flow.

Volt A unit for expressing electrical "pressure" in a circuit. One volt that will produce a current of one ampere through a resistance of one ohm.

W

Welding Various processes used to join metal items by heating the areas to be joined to a molten state and fusing them together. For more information refer to the *Haynes Automotive Welding Manual.*

Wiring diagram A drawing portraying the components and wires in a vehicle's electrical system, using standardised symbols. For more information refer to the *Haynes Automotive Electrical and Electronic Systems Manual.*

Note: *References throughout this index are in the form* **"Chapter number"** • **"Page number"**. *So, for example, 2C•15 refers to page 15 of Chapter 2C.*

A

Absolute pressure (altitude) sensor – 4B•5
Accelerator pedal position sensor – 4B•4
Accessory shops – REF•3
Acknowledgements – 0•6
Aerial – 12•16
Air conditioning system – 3•8
    compressor – 3•10
    switch – 12•5
Air filter – 1A•14, 1B•13, 4A•3, 4B•3
Air mass meter – 4B•5
Air temperature control system – 4A•3
Air temperature sensor – 4A•5, 4B•4
Airbags – 0•5, 1A•13, 1B•12, 12•17
    control unit – 12•18
    indicator – 12•5
    wiring contact unit (slip-ring) – 12•18
Alarm system – 12•16
Alternator – 5A•3, 5A•4
Altitude sensor – 4B•5
Antifreeze – 0•14, 0•18, 1A•11, 1A•19, 1B•10, 1B•16
Anti-lock braking system (ABS) – 9•17
Anti-roll bar – 10•9, 10•12
Anti-theft alarm system – 12•16
Asbestos – 0•5
Automatic transmission – 7B•1 *et seq*
    fault finding – REF•17
    fluid – 0•18, 1A•17
Auxiliary drivebelt – 1A•11, 1A•16, 1B•10, 1B•13, 2C•5

B

Badges – 11•16
Balancer shaft unit – 2D•27
Battery – 0•5, 0•15, 1A•13, 1B•12, 5A•2, 5A•3, REF•5
Big-end bearings – 2E•17, 2E•19
Bleeding
    brakes – 9•3
    clutch – 6•2
    power steering system – 10•19
Blower motor – 3•10
    switch – 12•5
Body corrosion – REF•11
Body electrical system – 12•1 *et seq*
Bodywork and fittings – 11•1 *et seq*
Bonnet – 11•5
Boot light – 12•9
    switch – 12•5
Brake fluid – 0•14, 0•18, 1A•18, 1B•14
Brake pedal – 4B•5, 9•12
Braking system – 1A•11, 1A•13, 1B•10, 1B•13, 9•1 *et seq*, REF•8, REF•9, REF•10
    fault finding – REF•18
Bulbs – 12•5, 12•9
Bumpers – 11•4
Burning – 0•5
Buying spare parts – REF•3

C

Cables
    automatic transmission selector – 7B•4
    bonnet – 11•5
    gearchange – 7A•3
    handbrake – 9•16
Calipers – 9•6, 9•8
Camshaft(s) – 2A•9, 2C•11, 2D•17, 2E•10
    carrier – 2C•9
    cover – 2D•7
    hub – 2D•16
    oil seals – 2C•12, 2D•18
    position sensor – 4A•6, 4B•5
    sprockets – 2C•9, 2D•15
Carpets – 11•2, 11•20
Cassette player – 12•15
Catalytic converter – 4C•9, 4C•10
CD player – 12•16
Central locking – 11•14
Centre console – 11•20
Charging – 5A•2, 5A•3
Cigarette lighter – 12•12
    illumination – 12•10
Clock – 12•12
Clutch – 6•1 *et seq*
    fault finding – REF•16
    fluid – 0•14, 0•18, 1A•18, 1B•14
    pedal – 4B•5, 6•3
    pedal switch – 4A•7
Coil
    ignition – 5B•2
    spring – 10•11
Compression test – 2A•3, 2B•3, 2C•3, 2D•4
Compressor – 3•10
Connecting rods – 2E•11, 2E•14, 2E•19
Console – 11•20
Control unit parking aid system – 12•19
Convenience system – 12•20
Conversion factors – REF•2
Coolant – 0•14, 0•18, 1A•18, 1B•15
Coolant pump – 3•6
    sprocket – 2C•9, 2D•16
Coolant temperature sensor – 3•6, 4B•4
Cooling fan – 3•6
    thermostatic switch – 3•6
Cooling, heating and air conditioning systems – 3•1 *et seq*
    fault finding – REF•15
Courtesy light – 12•9
    switch – 12•4, 12•5
Crankcase – 2E•12
Crankcase emission control – 4C•2, 4C•3
Crankshaft – 2E•12, 2E•16, 2E•18
    oil seals – 2A•16, 2B•13, 2C•17, 2D•25
    pulley – 2A•4, 2C•5, 2D•9
    sprocket – 2C•9, 2D•15
Cruise control system – 4A•10
Crushing – 0•5
Cut-off solenoid valve – 4B•10
Cylinder block/crankcase – 2E•12
Cylinder head – 2A•12, 2B•6, 2C•12, 2D•19, 2E•6, 2E•7, 2E•8

Note: *References throughout this index are in the form* **"Chapter number"** • **"Page number"**. *So, for example, 2C•15 refers to page 15 of Chapter 2C.*

D

Dents – 11•2
Depressurisation fuel injection system – 4A•9
Diesel engine fuel system – 4B•1 *et seq*
Diesel engine in-car repair procedures – 2D•1 *et seq*
Diesel injection equipment – 0•5
Dimensions – REF•1
Direction indicator – 12•7, 12•11
Disc shield – 9•7
Disconnecting the battery – REF•5
Discs – 9•6
Door warning lights – 12•10
Doors – 11•6, 11•8, 11•10, REF•9
Drivebelt – 1A•11, 1B•10, 1A•16, 1B•13, 2C•5
Driveplate – 2C•18
Driveshafts – 1A•12, 1B•11, 8•1 *et seq*, REF•10
  fault finding – REF•18
Drivetrain – 1A•13, 1B•13
Driving on the right (gas-discharge headlight) – 12•19
Drums – 9•9

E

Earth fault – 12•2
Electric cooling fan – 3•6
Electric shock – 0•5
Electric window components – 11•14
  switch – 12•6
Electrical equipment – 0•17, 1A•13, 1B•12, REF•9
  fault finding – 12•2, REF•20, REF•21
Electronic control unit
  ABS – 9•17
  automatic transmission – 7B•4
  fuel system – 4A•7, 4B•6
Emission control and exhaust systems – 4C•1 *et seq*, REF•11
Engine fault finding – REF•13, REF•14
Engine management system – 4B•4
  self-diagnosis memory fault check – 1A•13, 1B•12
Engine oil – 0•13, 0•18, 1A•9, 1B•7
Engine removal and overhaul procedures – 2E•1 *et seq*
Engine speed sensor – 4B•4, 4A•5
Environmental considerations – REF•4
ESP/TCS switch – 12•5
Evaporative emission control – 4C•2, 4C•3
Exhaust emissions – 1A•14, 1B•13, 4C•2, 4C•3
Exhaust Gas Recirculation (EGR) system – 4C•3
Exhaust manifold – 4C•8
Exhaust system – 1A•10, 1B•9, 4C•3, 4C•9, REF•10, REF•11
  specialists – REF•3

F

Facia panel – 11•21
Fan – 3•6
  thermostatic switch – 3•6

Fault finding – REF•12 *et seq*
  automatic transmission – REF•17
  braking system – REF•18
  clutch – REF•16
  cooling system – REF•15
  driveshafts – REF•18
  electrical system – 12•2, REF•20, REF•21
  engine – REF•13, REF•14
  fuel and exhaust systems – REF•15
  manual transmission – REF•16
  suspension and steering – REF•19
Filling and respraying – 11•3
Filter
  air – 1A•14, 1B•13, 4A•3, 4B•3
  fuel – 1B•8, 1B•9, 4A•7, 1B•13
  oil – 1A•9, 1B•7
  pollen – 1A•11, 1B•11
Fire – 0•5
Fixed rear quarter window glass – 11•16
Fluid leaks – 1A•10, 1B•9
Fluids – 0•18
Flywheel – 2A•17, 2B•13, 2C•17, 2D•24, 12•6
Friction disc – 6•4
Fuel and exhaust systems fault finding – REF•15
Fuel cooler – 4B•12
Fuel cut-off solenoid valve – 4B•10
Fuel filter – 1B•8, 1B•9, 1B•13, 4A•7
Fuel gauge sender unit – 4A•7, 4B•11
Fuel injection pump – 4B•9
  sprocket – 2D•16
  timing – 4B•10
Fuel injection system – 4A•4, 4A•10, REF•11
Fuel injectors – 4A•4, 4B•6
Fuel pressure regulator – 4A•5
Fuel pump – 4A•7, 4B•11
Fuel rail – 4A•4
Fuel tank – 4A•9, 4B•11
Fuel temperature sensor – 4B•4
Fume or gas intoxication – 0•5
Fuses and fusible links – 12•3

G

Gaiters
  driveshaft – 8•3
  steering gear – 10•19
Gas-discharge headlights – 12•6, 12•19
Gashes – 11•3
Gaskets – REF•4
Gearchange cables – 7A•3
General repair procedures – REF•4
Glass
  door – 11•10
  fixed rear quarter window – 11•16
Glossary of technical terms – REF•22 *et seq*
Glovebox – 11•20
  light – 12•9
  light switch – 12•5
Glow plugs – 5C•2

Note: *References throughout this index are in the form* **"Chapter number"** • **"Page number"**. *So, for example, 2C•15 refers to page 15 of Chapter 2C.*

H

Halogen headlights – 12•5, 12•6
Handbrake – 9•15, 9•16, REF•8
Handles (door) – 11•8
Hazard warning light switch – 12•5
Headlight – 12•10, 12•19
    beam adjustment – 1A•11, 1B•11, 12•11
    dipped beam – 12•6
    main beam – 12•5
    range/illumination control – 12•4
    washer jets – 12•15
    washer system – 1A•13, 1B•12
Headlining – 11•20
Heated seat switch – 12•5
Heated window switch – 12•5
Heating system – 3•7, 3•8
    blower motor – 3•10
    blower motor switch – 12•5
    illumination – 12•10
    matrix – 3•9
    vents – 3•10
High-level stop-light – 12•8, 12•11
High-voltage unit (gas-discharge headlight) – 12•19
Hinge lubrication – 1A•13, 1B•12
Horn – 12•12
Hoses – 3•3, 9•4
    leaks – 1A•10, 1B•9
HT coil – 5B•2
Hubs – 10•6, 10•10
Hydraulic tappets – 2A•9, 2C•11, 2D•18, 2E•10
Hydraulic unit (ABS) – 9•17
Hydrofluoric acid – 0•5

I

Identification numbers – REF•3
Identifying leaks – 0•10
Idler pulleys – 2C•8, 2D•15
Ignition switch – 10•17
Ignition system – petrol engines – 5B•1 *et seq*
Immobiliser – 12•16
Indicator – 12•7, 12•11
Injection pump – 4B•9
    timing – 4B•10
Injectors – 4A•4, 4B•6
Inlet air temperature control system – 4A•3
Inlet air temperature sensor – 4A•5, 4B•4
Inlet manifold – 4A•9, 4B•11
    changeover flap and valve – 4B•12
    flap housing – 4B•5
Inlet system – 4A•3
Instrument panel – 12•11, 12•12
    lights – 12•10
Instruments – 1A•13, 1B•12
Intercooler – 4C•7
Interior light – 12•9
    switch – 12•4, 12•5

J

Jacking and vehicle support – REF•5
Joint mating faces – REF•4
Jump starting – 0•8

K

Knock sensor – 4A•6, 5B•4

L

Lambda sensor(s) – 4A•6
Lateral acceleration – 9•18
Leakdown test – 2D•5
Leaks – 0•10, 1A•10, 1B•9
Level sender – 10•13
Lighting switch – 12•4
Locknuts, locktabs and washers – REF•4
Locks
    bonnet – 11•5
    central locking – 11•14
    door – 11•8, 11•10
    lubrication – 1A•13, 1B•12
    steering column – 10•17, 10•18
    tailgate – 11•13
Loudspeakers – 12•16
Lower arm – 10•8
Lubricants and fluids – 0•18
Luggage compartment light – 12•9
    switch – 12•5

M

Main bearings – 2E•17, 2E•18
Manifold changeover flap and valve – 4B•12
    flap housing – 4B•5
Manifolds – 2B•6
    exhaust – 4C•8
    inlet – 4A•9, 4B•11
Manual transmission – 7A•1 *et seq*
    fault finding – REF•16
    oil – 0•18, 1A•11, 1B•11
Master cylinder
    brake – 9•13
    clutch – 6•3
Mirror – 11•20, REF•8
    switch – 12•4
MOT test checks – REF•8 *et seq*
Motor factors – REF•3
Mountings – 2A•17, 2B•14, 2C•18, 2D•26

N

Needle lift sender – 4B•5
Number plate light – 12•9, 12•11

Note: *References throughout this index are in the form* "**Chapter number**" • "**Page number**". *So, for example, 2C•15 refers to page 15 of Chapter 2C.*

O

Officially appointed garages – REF•3
Oil
    engine – 0•13, 0•18, 1A•9, 1B•7
    manual transmission – 0•18, 1A•11, 1B•11
Oil cooler – 2D•27
Oil filter – 1A•9, 1B•7
Oil pressure relief valve – 2C•17
Oil pressure warning light switch – 2A•15, 2C•17, 2D•27
Oil pump – 2A•15, 2B•10, 2C•15, 2D•22
Oil seals – REF•4
    camshaft – 2C•12, 2D•18
    crankshaft – 2A•1, 2B•13, 2C•17, 2D•25
Open-circuit – 12•2
Oxygen (lambda) sensor(s) – 4A•6

P

Pads – 1A•10, 1B•8, 9•4, 9•8
Parking aid components – 12•19
Parts – REF•3
Passenger airbag
    indicator – 12•5
    switch – 12•18
Pedals
    accelerator – 4B•4
    brake – 9•12
    clutch – 4A•7, 6•3
Petrol engine fuel systems – 4A•1 *et seq*
Petrol engine in-car repair procedures
    1.2 litre – 2A•1 *et seq*
    1.4 litre DOHC – 2C•1 *et seq*
    1.4 litre OHV – 2B•1 *et seq*
Pipes – 9•4
Piston rings – 2E•17
Pistons – 2E•11, 2E•14, 2E•19
Plastic components – 11•3
Poisonous or irritant substances – 0•5
Pollen filter – 1A•11, 1B•11
Power steering fluid – 0•18, 1A•17, 1B•14
Power steering pump – 10•19
Preheating system – diesel engines – 5C•1 *et seq*
Pressure plate – 6•4
Pressure sensor – 4A•5
Pump injector rocker shaft assembly – 2D•16
Puncture repair – 0•9

Q

Quarter window glass – 11•16

R

Radiator – 1A•19, 1B•15, 3•3
Radio – 12•15
    aerial – 12•16
Range control motor (halogen headlights) – 12•11

Range/distance sensor (parking aid system) – 12•19
Reading light – 12•9
Rear axle – 10•12, 10•13
Rear controller (gas-discharge headlight) – 12•19
Rear light cluster – 12•8, 12•11
Regulator
    alternator – 5A•4
    window – 11•10
Relays – 12•3
Release bearing and lever – 6•5
Respraying – 11•3
Reversing light switch – 7A•5
Road test – 1A•13, 1B•12
Roadside repairs – 0•7 *et seq*
Roadspeed sensor – 7A•5
Rockers – 2B•5, 2C•11
    cover – 2B•4
Routine maintenance – bodywork and underframe – 11•2
Routine maintenance – upholstery and carpets – 11•2
Routine maintenance and servicing – diesel models – 1B•1 *et seq*
Routine maintenance and servicing – petrol models – 1A•1 *et seq*
Rust holes or gashes – 11•3

S

Safety first! – 0•14, 0•5
Scalding – 0•5
Scratches – 11•2
Screw threads and fastenings – REF•4
Seat belts – 11•17
Seats – 11•16
Selector
    lever housing – 7B•4
    cable – 7B•4
Self-diagnosis memory fault check – 1A•13, 1B•12
Service interval display – 1A•10, 1B•8, 12•12
Servo unit – 9•14
    mechanical vacuum pump – 9•18
Shock absorbers – 10•10, REF•9, REF•10
Shoes – 1A•10, 1B•8, 9•10
Short-circuit – 12•2
Sidelight – 12•7
Silencer(s) – 4C•10
Skoda Fabia Manual – 0•6
Slave cylinder (clutch) – 6•4
Sliding roof switch – 12•4
Solenoid valve – 4B•10
Spare parts – REF•3
Spark plugs – 1A•15
Speed sensor – 4B•4, 4A•5, 7A•5
Speedometer
    drive – 7A•5
    sensor – 12•12
Springs – 10•11, REF•10
Sprockets – 2A•8, 2A•15, 2B•8, 2C•8, 2D•15, 2D•22
Starting and charging systems – 5A•1 *et seq*
Start-up after overhaul and reassembly – 2E•20
Steering – 1A•12, 1A•13, 1B•11, 1B•13, REF•9, REF•10

Note: *References throughout this index are in the form "***Chapter number***" • "***Page number***". So, for example, 2C•15 refers to page 15 of Chapter 2C.*

Steering angle sender – 9•18
Steering angles – 10•20
Steering column – 10•15, REF•8
   combination switch – 12•3
   lock – 10•17, 10•18
Steering gear – 10•18
   gaiters – 10•19
Steering wheel – 10•13, REF•8
Stop-light – 12•8, 12•11
   switch – 9•16
Struts
   suspension – 10•6
   tailgate support – 11•10
Stub axle – 10•10
Sump – 2A•14, 2B•11, 2C•15, 2D•22
Sunroof – 1A•13, 1B•12, 11•16
Support struts – 11•10
Suspension and steering systems – 1A•12, 1A•13, 1B•11, 1B•13, 10•1 *et seq,* REF•9, REF•10
   fault finding – REF•19
Switches – 12•3
   brake pedal – 4B•5
   clutch pedal – 4A•7, 4B•5
   cooling system – 3•6
   handbrake 'on' warning light – 9•16
   ignition – 10•17
   illumination – 12•10
   oil pressure warning light – 2A•15, 2C•17, 2D•27
   passenger airbag – 12•18
   reversing light – 7A•5
   stop-light – 9•16

T

Tailgate – 11•10, 11•16
   lock – 11•13
   washer jet – 12•15
   washer system – 1A•13, 1B•12
Tandem fuel pump – 4B•11

Tappets – 2A•9, 2C•11, 2D•18, 2E•10
TCS switch – 12•5
Technical terms – REF•22 *et seq*
Temperature control system – 4A•3
Temperature sensor – 3•6, 4A•5, 4B•4
Tensioner – 2A•8, 2C•8, 2D•15
Thermostat – 3•4
Throttle valve control unit – 4A•4
Timing belt(s) – 2C•7, 2D•10
   covers – 2C•6, 2D•9
Timing chain – 2A•8, 2B•8
   cover – 2A•5, 2B•8
Timing
   ignition – 5B•3
   injection pump – 4B•10
Tools and working facilities – REF•4, REF•6 *et seq*
Top Dead Centre (TDC) for No 1 piston location – 2B•3
Torque arm – 2A•18, 2D•26
Towing – 0•10
Track rod end – 10•20
Track rods – 10•19
Transmission mountings – 2A•17, 2B•14, 2C•18, 2D•26
Transmitter and rear controller (gas-discharge headlight) – 12•19
Trim panels – 11•6, 11•16, 11•19
Turbocharger – 4C•5
   boost pressure solenoid valve – 4C•6
Tyres – REF•11
   condition and pressure – 0•16
   pressures – 0•18
   specialists – REF•3

U

Underbody protection – 1A•12, 1B•11
Underbonnet check points – 0•11, 0•12, 0•13
Underframe – 11•2
Under-panels – 11•16
Upholstery – 11•2

Note: *References throughout this index are in the form* "**Chapter number**" • "**Page number**". *So, for example, 2C•15 refers to page 15 of Chapter 2C.*

V

Valve timing marks – 2A•4, 2C•4, 2D•5
Valves – 2E•7
Vehicle identification – REF•3, REF•9
Vehicle level sender – 10•13
Vehicle support – REF•5
Ventilation system
    control panel illumination – 12•10
    vents – 3•10

W

Warning buzzer parking aid system – 12•19
Warning lights – 12•10
Washer system – 1A•13, 1B•12, 12•15
    fluid – 0•15
    fluid pumps – 12•15
    fluid reservoir – 12•15
    jets – 12•15
Water pump – 3•6
Weekly checks – 0•11 *et seq*
Weights – REF•1
Wheels – REF•11
    alignment – 10•20
    bearings – 10•4, 10•6, 10•10, REF•10
    changing – 0•9
Wheel arch liners – 11•16
Wheel cylinder – 9•12
Wheel sensor – 9•17, 9•18
Window
    glass – 11•10
    regulator – 11•10
    switch – 12•6
Windscreen – 11•16, REF•8
    washer jets – 12•15
    washer system – 1A•13, 1B•12
    wiper motor and linkage – 12•13

Wiper arm – 12•12
Wiper blades – 0•17
Wiper motor – 12•14
Wiring diagrams – 12•21 *et seq*
Working facilities – REF•7

X

Xenon headlights – 12•6, 12•19

Y

Yaw rate sender – 9•18

Haynes Manuals – The Complete UK Car List

Title	Book No.
ALFA ROMEO Alfasud/Sprint (74 - 88) up to F *	0292
Alfa Romeo Alfetta (73 - 87) up to E *	0531
AUDI 80, 90 & Coupe Petrol (79 - Nov 88) up to F	0605
Audi 80, 90 & Coupe Petrol (Oct 86 - 90) D to H	1491
Audi 100 & 200 Petrol (Oct 82 - 90) up to H	0907
Audi 100 & A6 Petrol & Diesel (May 91 - May 97) H to P	3504
Audi A3 Petrol & Diesel (96 - May 03) P to 03	4253
Audi A4 Petrol & Diesel (95 - 00) M to X	3575
Audi A4 Petrol & Diesel (01 - 04) X to 54	4609
AUSTIN A35 & A40 (56 - 67) up to F *	0118
Austin/MG/Rover Maestro 1.3 & 1.6 Petrol (83 - 95) up to M	0922
Austin/MG Metro (80 - May 90) up to G	0718
Austin/Rover Montego 1.3 & 1.6 Petrol (84 - 94) A to L	1066
Austin/MG/Rover Montego 2.0 Petrol (84 - 95) A to M	1067
Mini (59 - 69) up to H *	0527
Mini (69 - 01) up to X	0646
Austin/Rover 2.0 litre Diesel Engine (86 - 93) C to L	1857
Austin Healey 100/6 & 3000 (56 - 68) up to G *	0049
BEDFORD CF Petrol (69 - 87) up to E	0163
Bedford/Vauxhall Rascal & Suzuki Supercarry (86 - Oct 94) C to M	3015
BMW 316, 320 & 320i (4-cyl) (75 - Feb 83) up to Y *	0276
BMW 320, 320i, 323i & 325i (6-cyl) (Oct 77 - Sept 87) up to E	0815
BMW 3- & 5-Series Petrol (81 - 91) up to J	1948
BMW 3-Series Petrol (Apr 91 - 99) H to V	3210
BMW 3-Series Petrol (Sept 98 - 03) S to 53	4067
BMW 520i & 525e (Oct 81 - June 88) up to E	1560
BMW 525, 528 & 528i (73 - Sept 81) up to X *	0632
BMW 5-Series 6-cyl Petrol (April 96 - Aug 03) N to 03	4151
BMW 1500, 1502, 1600, 1602, 2000 & 2002 (59 - 77) up to S *	0240
CHRYSLER PT Cruiser Petrol (00 - 03) W to 53	4058
CITROËN 2CV, Ami & Dyane (67 - 90) up to H	0196
Citroën AX Petrol & Diesel (87 - 97) D to P	3014
Citroën Berlingo & Peugeot Partner Petrol & Diesel (96 - 05) P to 55	4281
Citroën BX Petrol (83 - 94) A to L	0908
Citroën C15 Van Petrol & Diesel (89 - Oct 98) F to S	3509
Citroën C3 Petrol & Diesel (02 - 05) 51 to 05	4197
Citroen C5 Petrol & Diesel (01-08) Y to 08	4745
Citroën CX Petrol (75 - 88) up to F	0528
Citroën Saxo Petrol & Diesel (96 - 04) N to 54	3506
Citroën Visa Petrol (79 - 88) up to F	0620
Citroën Xantia Petrol & Diesel (93 - 01) K to Y	3082
Citroën XM Petrol & Diesel (89 - 00) G to X	3451
Citroën Xsara Petrol & Diesel (97 - Sept 00) R to W	3751
Citroën Xsara Picasso Petrol & Diesel (00 - 02) W to 52	3944
Citroen Xsara Picasso (03-08)	4784
Citroën ZX Diesel (91 - 98) J to S	1922
Citroën ZX Petrol (91 - 98) H to S	1881
Citroën 1.7 & 1.9 litre Diesel Engine (84 - 96) A to N	1379
FIAT 126 (73 - 87) up to E *	0305
Fiat 500 (57 - 73) up to M *	0090
Fiat Bravo & Brava Petrol (95 - 00) N to W	3572
Fiat Cinquecento (93 - 98) K to R	3501
Fiat Panda (81 - 95) up to M	0793
Fiat Punto Petrol & Diesel (94 - Oct 99) L to V	3251
Fiat Punto Petrol (Oct 99 - July 03) V to 03	4066
Fiat Punto Petrol (03-07) 03 to 07	4746
Fiat Regata Petrol (84 - 88) A to F	1167
Fiat Tipo Petrol (88 - 91) E to J	1625
Fiat Uno Petrol (83 - 95) up to M	0923
Fiat X1/9 (74 - 89) up to G *	0273
FORD Anglia (59 - 68) up to G *	0001
Ford Capri II (& III) 1.6 & 2.0 (74 - 87) up to E *	0283
Ford Capri II (& III) 2.8 & 3.0 V6 (74 - 87) up to E	1309
Ford Cortina Mk I & Corsair 1500 ('62 - '66) up to D*	0214
Ford Cortina Mk III 1300 & 1600 (70 - 76) up to P *	0070
Ford Escort Mk I 1100 & 1300 (68 - 74) up to N *	0171
Ford Escort Mk I Mexico, RS 1600 & RS 2000 (70 - 74) up to N *	0139
Ford Escort Mk II Mexico, RS 1800 & RS 2000 (75 - 80) up to W *	0735
Ford Escort (75 - Aug 80) up to V *	0280
Ford Escort Petrol (Sept 80 - Sept 90) up to H	0686
Ford Escort & Orion Petrol (Sept 90 - 00) H to X	1737
Ford Escort & Orion Diesel (Sept 90 - 00) H to X	4081
Ford Fiesta (76 - Aug 83) up to Y	0334
Ford Fiesta Petrol (Aug 83 - Feb 89) A to F	1030
Ford Fiesta Petrol (Feb 89 - Oct 95) F to N	1595
Ford Fiesta Petrol & Diesel (Oct 95 - Mar 02) N to 02	3397
Ford Fiesta Petrol & Diesel (Apr 02 - 07) 02 to 57	4170
Ford Focus Petrol & Diesel (98 - 01) S to Y	3759
Ford Focus Petrol & Diesel (Oct 01 - 05) 51 to 05	4167
Ford Galaxy Petrol & Diesel (95 - Aug 00) M to W	3984
Ford Granada Petrol (Sept 77 - Feb 85) up to B *	0481
Ford Granada & Scorpio Petrol (Mar 85 - 94) B to M	1245
Ford Ka (96 - 02) P to 52	3570
Ford Mondeo Petrol (93 - Sept 00) K to X	1923
Ford Mondeo Petrol & Diesel (Oct 00 - Jul 03) X to 03	3990
Ford Mondeo Petrol & Diesel (July 03 - 07) 03 to 56	4619
Ford Mondeo Diesel (93 - 96) L to N	3465
Ford Orion Petrol (83 - Sept 90) up to H	1009
Ford Sierra 4-cyl Petrol (82 - 93) up to K	0903
Ford Sierra V6 Petrol (82 - 91) up to J	0904
Ford Transit Petrol (Mk 2) (78 - Jan 86) up to C	0719
Ford Transit Petrol (Mk 3) (Feb 86 - 89) C to G	1468
Ford Transit Diesel (Feb 86 - 99) C to T	3019
Ford Transit Diesel (00-06)	4775
Ford 1.6 & 1.8 litre Diesel Engine (84 - 96) A to N	1172
Ford 2.1, 2.3 & 2.5 litre Diesel Engine (77 - 90) up to H	1606
FREIGHT ROVER Sherpa Petrol (74 - 87) up to E	0463
HILLMAN Avenger (70 - 82) up to Y	0037
Hillman Imp (63 - 76) up to R *	0022
HONDA Civic (Feb 84 - Oct 87) A to E	1226
Honda Civic (Nov 91 - 96) J to N	3199
Honda Civic Petrol (Mar 95 - 00) M to X	4050
Honda Civic Petrol & Diesel (01 - 05) X to 55	4611
Honda CR-V Petrol & Diesel (01-06)	4747
Honda Jazz (01 - Feb 08) 51 - 57	4735
HYUNDAI Pony (85 - 94) C to M	3398
JAGUAR E Type (61 - 72) up to L *	0140
Jaguar MkI & II, 240 & 340 (55 - 69) up to H *	0098
Jaguar XJ6, XJ & Sovereign; Daimler Sovereign (68 - Oct 86) up to D	0242
Jaguar XJ6 & Sovereign (Oct 86 - Sept 94) D to M	3261
Jaguar XJ12, XJS & Sovereign; Daimler Double Six (72 - 88) up to F	0478
JEEP Cherokee Petrol (93 - 96) K to N	1943
LADA 1200, 1300, 1500 & 1600 (74 - 91) up to J	0413
Lada Samara (87 - 91) D to J	1610
LAND ROVER 90, 110 & Defender Diesel (83 - 07) up to 56	3017
Land Rover Discovery Petrol & Diesel (89 - 98) G to S	3016
Land Rover Discovery Diesel (Nov 98 - Jul 04) S to 04	4606
Land Rover Freelander Petrol & Diesel (97 - Sept 03) R to 53	3929
Land Rover Freelander Petrol & Diesel (Oct 03 - Oct 06) 53 to 56	4623
Land Rover Series IIA & III Diesel (58 - 85) up to C	0529
Land Rover Series II, IIA & III 4-cyl Petrol (58 - 85) up to C	0314
MAZDA 323 (Mar 81 - Oct 89) up to G	1608
Mazda 323 (Oct 89 - 98) G to R	3455
Mazda 626 (May 83 - Sept 87) up to E	0929
Mazda B1600, B1800 & B2000 Pick-up Petrol (72 - 88) up to F	0267
Mazda RX-7 (79 - 85) up to C *	0460
MERCEDES-BENZ 190, 190E & 190D Petrol & Diesel (83 - 93) A to L	3450
Mercedes-Benz 200D, 240D, 240TD, 300D & 300TD 123 Series Diesel (Oct 76 - 85)	1114
Mercedes-Benz 250 & 280 (68 - 72) up to L *	0346
Mercedes-Benz 250 & 280 123 Series Petrol (Oct 76 - 84) up to B *	0677
Mercedes-Benz 124 Series Petrol & Diesel (85 - Aug 93) C to K	3253
Mercedes-Benz A-Class Petrol & Diesel (98-04) S to 54	4748
Mercedes-Benz C-Class Petrol & Diesel (93 - Aug 00) L to W	3511
Mercedes-Benz C-Class (00-06)	4780
MGA (55 - 62) *	0475
MGB (62 - 80) up to W	0111
MG Midget & Austin-Healey Sprite (58 - 80) up to W *	0265
MINI Petrol (July 01 - 05) Y to 05	4273
MITSUBISHI Shogun & L200 Pick-Ups Petrol (83 - 94) up to M	1944
MORRIS Ital 1.3 (80 - 84) up to B	0705
Morris Minor 1000 (56 - 71) up to K	0024
NISSAN Almera Petrol (95 - Feb 00) N to V	4053
Nissan Almera & Tino Petrol (Feb 00 - 07) V to 56	4612
Nissan Bluebird (May 84 - Mar 86) A to C	1223
Nissan Bluebird Petrol (Mar 86 - 90) C to H	1473
Nissan Cherry (Sept 82 - 86) up to D	1031
Nissan Micra (83 - Jan 93) up to K	0931
Nissan Micra (93 - 02) K to 52	3254
Nissan Micra Petrol (03-07) 52 to 57	4734
Nissan Primera Petrol (90 - Aug 99) H to T	1851
Nissan Stanza (82 - 86) up to D	0824
Nissan Sunny Petrol (May 82 - Oct 86) up to D	0895
Nissan Sunny Petrol (Oct 86 - Mar 91) D to H	1378
Nissan Sunny Petrol (Apr 91 - 95) H to N	3219
OPEL Ascona & Manta (B Series) (Sept 75 - 88) up to F *	0316
Opel Ascona Petrol (81 - 88)	3215
Opel Astra Petrol (Oct 91 - Feb 98)	3156
Opel Corsa Petrol (83 - Mar 93)	3160
Opel Corsa Petrol (Mar 93 - 97)	3159
Opel Kadett Petrol (Nov 79 - Oct 84) up to B	0634
Opel Kadett Petrol (Oct 84 - Oct 91)	3196
Opel Omega & Senator Petrol (Nov 86 - 94)	3157
Opel Rekord Petrol (Feb 78 - Oct 86) up to D	0543
Opel Vectra Petrol (Oct 88 - Oct 95)	3158
PEUGEOT 106 Petrol & Diesel (91 - 04) J to 53	1882
Peugeot 205 Petrol (83 - 97) A to P	0932
Peugeot 206 Petrol & Diesel (98 - 01) S to X	3757
Peugeot 206 Petrol & Diesel (02 - 06) 51 to 06	4613
Peugeot 306 Petrol & Diesel (93 - 02) K to 02	3073
Peugeot 307 Petrol & Diesel (01 - 04) Y to 54	4147
Peugeot 309 Petrol (86 - 93) C to K	1266
Peugeot 405 Petrol (88 - 97) E to P	1559
Peugeot 405 Diesel (88 - 97) E to P	3198
Peugeot 406 Petrol & Diesel (96 - Mar 99) N to T	3394
Peugeot 406 Petrol & Diesel (Mar 99 - 02) T to 52	3982

* Classic reprint

Title	Book No.
Peugeot 505 Petrol (79 - 89) up to G	0762
Peugeot 1.7/1.8 & 1.9 litre Diesel Engine (82 - 96) up to N	0950
Peugeot 2.0, 2.1, 2.3 & 2.5 litre Diesel Engines (74 - 90) up to H	1607
PORSCHE 911 (65 - 85) up to C	0264
Porsche 924 & 924 Turbo (76 - 85) up to C	0397
PROTON (89 - 97) F to P	3255
RANGE ROVER V8 Petrol (70 - Oct 92) up to K	0606
RELIANT Robin & Kitten (73 - 83) up to A *	0436
RENAULT 4 (61 - 86) up to D *	0072
Renault 5 Petrol (Feb 85 - 96) B to N	1219
Renault 9 & 11 Petrol (82 - 89) up to F	0822
Renault 18 Petrol (79 - 86) up to D	0598
Renault 19 Petrol (89 - 96) F to N	1646
Renault 19 Diesel (89 - 96) F to N	1946
Renault 21 Petrol (86 - 94) C to M	1397
Renault 25 Petrol & Diesel (84 - 92) B to K	1228
Renault Clio Petrol (91 - May 98) H to R	1853
Renault Clio Diesel (91 - June 96) H to N	3031
Renault Clio Petrol & Diesel (May 98 - May 01) R to Y	3906
Renault Clio Petrol & Diesel (June '01 - '05) Y to 55	4168
Renault Espace Petrol & Diesel (85 - 96) C to N	3197
Renault Laguna Petrol & Diesel (94 - 00) L to W	3252
Renault Laguna Petrol & Diesel (Feb 01 - Feb 05) X to 54	4283
Renault Mégane & Scénic Petrol & Diesel (96 - 99) N to T	3395
Renault Mégane & Scénic Petrol & Diesel (Apr 99 - 02) T to 52	3916
Renault Megane Petrol & Diesel (Oct 02 - 05) 52 to 55	4284
Renault Scenic Petrol & Diesel (Sept 03 - 06) 53 to 06	4297
ROVER 213 & 216 (84 - 89) A to G	1116
Rover 214 & 414 Petrol (89 - 96) G to N	1689
Rover 216 & 416 Petrol (89 - 96) G to N	1830
Rover 211, 214, 216, 218 & 220 Petrol & Diesel (Dec 95 - 99) N to V	3399
Rover 25 & MG ZR Petrol & Diesel (Oct 99 - 04) V to 54	4145
Rover 414, 416 & 420 Petrol & Diesel (May 95 - 98) M to R	3453
Rover 45 / MG ZS Petrol & Diesel (99 - 05) V to 55	4384
Rover 618, 620 & 623 Petrol (93 - 97) K to P	3257
Rover 75 / MG ZT Petrol & Diesel (99 - 06) S to 06	4292
Rover 820, 825 & 827 Petrol (86 - 95) D to N	1380
Rover 3500 (76 - 87) up to E *	0365
Rover Metro, 111 & 114 Petrol (May 90 - 98) G to S	1711
SAAB 95 & 96 (66 - 76) up to R *	0198
Saab 90, 99 & 900 (79 - Oct 93) up to L	0765
Saab 900 (Oct 93 - 98) L to R	3512
Saab 9000 (4-cyl) (85 - 98) C to S	1686
Saab 9-3 Petrol & Diesel (98 - Aug 02) R to 02	4614
Saab 9-3 Petrol & Diesel (02-07) 52 to 57	4749
Saab 9-5 4-cyl Petrol (97 - 04) R to 54	4156
SEAT Ibiza & Cordoba Petrol & Diesel (Oct 93 - Oct 99) L to V	3571
Seat Ibiza & Malaga Petrol (85 - 92) B to K	1609
SKODA Estelle (77 - 89) up to G	0604
Skoda Fabia Petrol & Diesel (00 - 06) W to 06	4376
Skoda Favorit (89 - 96) F to N	1801
Skoda Felicia Petrol & Diesel (95 - 01) M to X	3505
Skoda Octavia Petrol & Diesel (98 - Apr 04) R to 04	4285
SUBARU 1600 & 1800 (Nov 79 - 90) up to H *	0995

Title	Book No.
SUNBEAM Alpine, Rapier & H120 (67 - 74) up to N *	0051
SUZUKI SJ Series, Samurai & Vitara (4-cyl) Petrol (82 - 97) up to P	1942
Suzuki Supercarry & Bedford/Vauxhall Rascal (86 - Oct 94) C to M	3015
TALBOT Alpine, Solara, Minx & Rapier (75 - 86) up to D	0337
Talbot Horizon Petrol (78 - 86) up to D	0473
Talbot Samba (82 - 86) up to D	0823
TOYOTA Avensis Petrol (98 - Jan 03) R to 52	4264
Toyota Carina E Petrol (May 92 - 97) J to P	3256
Toyota Corolla (80 - 85) up to C	0683
Toyota Corolla (Sept 83 - Sept 87) A to E	1024
Toyota Corolla (Sept 87 - Aug 92) E to K	1683
Toyota Corolla Petrol (Aug 92 - 97) K to P	3259
Toyota Corolla Petrol (July 97 - Feb 02) P to 51	4286
Toyota Hi-Ace & Hi-Lux Petrol (69 - Oct 83) up to A	0304
Toyota RAV4 Petrol & Diesel (94-06) L to 55	4750
Toyota Yaris Petrol (99 - 05) T to 05	4265
TRIUMPH GT6 & Vitesse (62 - 74) up to N *	0112
Triumph Herald (59 - 71) up to K *	0010
Triumph Spitfire (62 - 81) up to X	0113
Triumph Stag (70 - 78) up to T *	0441
Triumph TR2, TR3, TR3A, TR4 & TR4A (52 - 67) up to F *	0028
Triumph TR5 & 6 (67 - 75) up to P *	0031
Triumph TR7 (75 - 82) up to Y *	0322
VAUXHALL Astra Petrol (80 - Oct 84) up to B	0635
Vauxhall Astra & Belmont Petrol (Oct 84 - Oct 91) B to J	1136
Vauxhall Astra Petrol (Oct 91 - Feb 98) J to R	1832
Vauxhall/Opel Astra & Zafira Petrol (Feb 98 - Apr 04) R to 04	3758
Vauxhall/Opel Astra & Zafira Diesel (Feb 98 - Apr 04) R to 04	3797
Vauxhall/Opel Astra Petrol (04 - 08)	4732
Vauxhall/Opel Astra Diesel (04 - 08)	4733
Vauxhall/Opel Calibra (90 - 98) G to S	3502
Vauxhall Carlton Petrol (Oct 78 - Oct 86) up to D	0480
Vauxhall Carlton & Senator Petrol (Nov 86 - 94) D to L	1469
Vauxhall Cavalier Petrol (81 - Oct 88) up to F	0812
Vauxhall Cavalier Petrol (Oct 88 - 95) F to N	1570
Vauxhall Chevette (75 - 84) up to B	0285
Vauxhall/Opel Corsa Diesel (Mar 93 - Oct 00) K to X	4087
Vauxhall Corsa Petrol (Mar 93 - 97) K to R	1985
Vauxhall/Opel Corsa Petrol (Apr 97 - Oct 00) P to X	3921
Vauxhall/Opel Corsa Petrol & Diesel (Oct 00 - Sept 03) X to 53	4079
Vauxhall/Opel Corsa Petrol & Diesel (Oct 03 - Aug 06) 53 to 06	4617
Vauxhall/Opel Frontera Petrol & Diesel (91 - Sept 98) J to S	3454
Vauxhall Nova Petrol (83 - 93) up to K	0909
Vauxhall/Opel Omega Petrol (94 - 99) L to T	3510
Vauxhall/Opel Vectra Petrol & Diesel (95 - Feb 99) N to S	3396
Vauxhall/Opel Vectra Petrol & Diesel (Mar 99 - May 02) T to 02	3930
Vauxhall/Opel Vectra Petrol & Diesel (June 02 - Sept 05) 02 to 55	4618
Vauxhall/Opel 1.5, 1.6 & 1.7 litre Diesel Engine (82 - 96) up to N	1222
VW 411 & 412 (68 - 75) up to P *	0091
VW Beetle 1200 (54 - 77) up to S	0036
VW Beetle 1300 & 1500 (65 - 75) up to P	0039

Title	Book No.
VW 1302 & 1302S (70 - 72) up to L *	0110
VW Beetle 1303, 1303S & GT (72 - 75) up to P	0159
VW Beetle Petrol & Diesel (Apr 99 - 07) T to 57	3798
VW Golf & Jetta Mk 1 Petrol 1.1 & 1.3 (74 - 84) up to A	0716
VW Golf, Jetta & Scirocco Mk 1 Petrol 1.5, 1.6 & 1.8 (74 - 84) up to A	0726
VW Golf & Jetta Mk 1 Diesel (78 - 84) up to A	0451
VW Golf & Jetta Mk 2 Petrol (Mar 84 - Feb 92) A to J	1081
VW Golf & Vento Petrol & Diesel (Feb 92 - Mar 98) J to R	3097
VW Golf & Bora Petrol & Diesel (April 98 - 00) R to X	3727
VW Golf & Bora 4-cyl Petrol & Diesel (01 - 03) X to 53	4169
VW Golf & Jetta Petrol & Diesel (04 - 07) 53 to 07	4610
VW LT Petrol Vans & Light Trucks (76 - 87) up to E	0637
VW Passat & Santana Petrol (Sept 81 - May 88) up to E	0814
VW Passat 4-cyl Petrol & Diesel (May 88 - 96) E to P	3498
VW Passat 4-cyl Petrol & Diesel (Dec 96 - Nov 00) P to X	3917
VW Passat Petrol & Diesel (Dec 00 - May 05) X to 05	4279
VW Polo & Derby (76 - Jan 82) up to X	0335
VW Polo (82 - Oct 90) up to H	0813
VW Polo Petrol (Nov 90 - Aug 94) H to L	3245
VW Polo Hatchback Petrol & Diesel (94 - 99) M to S	3500
VW Polo Hatchback Petrol (00 - Jan 02) V to 51	4150
VW Polo Petrol & Diesel (02 - May 05) 51 to 05	4608
VW Scirocco (82 - 90) up to H *	1224
VW Transporter 1600 (68 - 79) up to V	0082
VW Transporter 1700, 1800 & 2000 (72 - 79) up to V *	0226
VW Transporter (air-cooled) Petrol (79 - 82) up to Y *	0638
VW Transporter (water-cooled) Petrol (82 - 90) up to H	3452
VW Type 3 (63 - 73) up to M *	0084
VOLVO 120 & 130 Series (& P1800) (61 - 73) up to M *	0203
Volvo 142, 144 & 145 (66 - 74) up to N *	0129
Volvo 240 Series Petrol (74 - 93) up to K	0270
Volvo 262, 264 & 260/265 (75 - 85) up to C *	0400
Volvo 340, 343, 345 & 360 (76 - 91) up to J	0715
Volvo 440, 460 & 480 Petrol (87 - 97) D to P	1691
Volvo 740 & 760 Petrol (82 - 91) up to J	1258
Volvo 850 Petrol (92 - 96) J to P	3260
Volvo 940 petrol (90 - 98) H to R	3249
Volvo S40 & V40 Petrol (96 - Mar 04) N to 04	3569
Volvo S40 & V50 Petrol & Diesel (Mar 04 - Jun 07) 04 to 07	4731
Volvo S60 Petrol & Diesel (01-08)	4793
Volvo S70, V70 & C70 Petrol (96 - 99) P to V	3573
Volvo V70 / S80 Petrol & Diesel (98 - 05) S to 55	4263

DIY MANUAL SERIES

Title	Book No.
The Haynes Air Conditioning Manual	4192
The Haynes Car Electrical Systems Manual	4251
The Haynes Manual on Bodywork	4198
The Haynes Manual on Brakes	4178
The Haynes Manual on Carburettors	4177
The Haynes Manual on Diesel Engines	4174
The Haynes Manual on Engine Management	4199
The Haynes Manual on Fault Codes	4175
The Haynes Manual on Practical Electrical Systems	4267
The Haynes Manual on Small Engines	4250
The Haynes Manual on Welding	4176

* Classic reprint

CL24.08/09

Preserving Our Motoring Heritage

<
The Model J Duesenberg Derham Tourster. Only eight of these magnificent cars were ever built – this is the only example to be found outside the United States of America

Almost every car you've ever loved, loathed or desired is gathered under one roof at the Haynes Motor Museum. Over 300 immaculately presented cars and motorbikes represent every aspect of our motoring heritage, from elegant reminders of bygone days, such as the superb Model J Duesenberg to curiosities like the bug-eyed BMW Isetta. There are also many old friends and flames. Perhaps you remember the 1959 Ford Popular that you did your courting in? The magnificent 'Red Collection' is a spectacle of classic sports cars including AC, Alfa Romeo, Austin Healey, Ferrari, Lamborghini, Maserati, MG, Riley, Porsche and Triumph.

A Perfect Day Out

Each and every vehicle at the Haynes Motor Museum has played its part in the history and culture of Motoring. Today, they make a wonderful spectacle and a great day out for all the family. Bring the kids, bring Mum and Dad, but above all bring your camera to capture those golden memories for ever. You will also find an impressive array of motoring memorabilia, a comfortable 70 seat video cinema and one of the most extensive transport book shops in Britain. The Pit Stop Cafe serves everything from a cup of tea to wholesome, home-made meals or, if you prefer, you can enjoy the large picnic area nestled in the beautiful rural surroundings of Somerset.

>
John Haynes O.B.E., Founder and Chairman of the museum at the wheel of a Haynes Light 12.

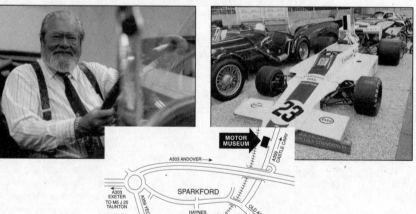

<
Graham Hill's Lola Cosworth Formula 1 car next to a 1934 Riley Sports.

The Museum is situated on the A359 Yeovil to Frome road at Sparkford, just off the A303 in Somerset. It is about 40 miles south of Bristol, and 25 minutes drive from the M5 intersection at Taunton.
Open 9.30am - 5.30pm (10.00am - 4.00pm Winter) 7 days a week, *except Christmas Day, Boxing Day and New Years Day*
Special rates available for schools, coach parties and outings Charitable Trust No. 292048